T0310920

# Revolutionizing Enterprise Interoperability through Scientific Foundations

Yannis Charalabidis
*University of the Aegean, Greece*

Fenareti Lampathaki
*National Technical University of Athens, Greece*

Ricardo Jardim-Goncalves
*Centre of Technology and Systems (CTS) – UNINOVA, Portugal*

A volume in the Advances in Business Strategy and Competitive Advantage (ABSCA) Book Series

An Imprint of IGI Global

| | |
|---|---|
| Managing Director: | Lindsay Johnston |
| Production Editor: | Jennifer Yoder |
| Development Editor: | Austin DeMarco |
| Acquisitions Editor: | Kayla Wolfe |
| Typesetter: | Deanna Jo Zombro |
| Cover Design: | Jason Mull |

Published in the United States of America by
Business Science Reference (an imprint of IGI Global)
701 E. Chocolate Avenue
Hershey PA 17033
Tel: 717-533-8845
Fax: 717-533-8661
E-mail: cust@igi-global.com
Web site: http://www.igi-global.com

Library of Congress Cataloging-in-Publication Data

Revolutionizing enterprise interoperability through scientific foundations / Yannis Charalabidis, Fenareti Lampathaki, Ricardo Jardim-Goncalves, editors.
      pages cm
 Includes bibliographical references and index.
 Summary: "This book offers information on the latest advancements and research for Enterprise Interoperability knowledge as well as core concepts, theories, and future directions"-- Provided by publisher.
 ISBN 978-1-4666-5142-5 (hardcover) -- ISBN 978-1-4666-5143-2 (ebook) -- ISBN 978-1-4666-5145-6 (print & perpetual access) 1. Internetworking (Telecommunication) 2. Enterprise application integration (Computer systems) I. Charalabidis, Yannis, 1967-

TK5105.5.R457 2014
658.4'034--dc23

This book is published in the IGI Global book series Advances in Business Strategy and Competitive Advantage (ABSCA) (ISSN: 2327-3429; eISSN: 2327-3437)

British Cataloguing in Publication Data
A Cataloguing in Publication record for this book is available from the British Library.

All work contributed to this book is new, previously-unpublished material. The views expressed in this book are those of the authors, but not necessarily of the publisher.

For electronic access to this publication, please contact: eresources@igi-global.com.

# Advances in Business Strategy and Competitive Advantage (ABSCA) Book Series

Patricia Ordóñez de Pablos
*Universidad de Oviedo, Spain*

ISSN: 2327-3429
EISSN: 2327-3437

## MISSION

Business entities are constantly seeking new ways through which to gain advantage over their competitors and strengthen their position within the business environment. With competition at an all-time high due to technological advancements allowing for competition on a global scale, firms continue to seek new ways through which to improve and strengthen their business processes, procedures, and profitability.

The **Advances in Business Strategy and Competitive Advantage (ABSCA) Book Series** is a timely series responding to the high demand for state-of-the-art research on how business strategies are created, implemented and re-designed to meet the demands of globalized competitive markets. With a focus on local and global challenges, business opportunities and the needs of society, the **ABSCA** encourages scientific discourse on doing business and managing information technologies for the creation of sustainable competitive advantage.

## COVERAGE

- Adaptive Enterprise
- Balanced Scorecard
- Business Models
- Entrepreneurship & Innovation
- Ethics and Business Strategy
- Globalization
- Outsourcing
- Small & Medium Enterprises
- Strategic Alliances
- Strategic Management
- Value Creation

IGI Global is currently accepting manuscripts for publication within this series. To submit a proposal for a volume in this series, please contact our Acquisition Editors at Acquisitions@igi-global.com or visit: http://www.igi-global.com/publish/.

# Titles in this Series

*For a list of additional titles in this series, please visit: www.igi-global.com*

*Revolutionizing Enterprise Interoperability through Scientific Foundations*
Yannis Charalabidis (University of the Aegean, Greece) Fenareti Lampathaki (National Technical University of Athens, Greece) and Ricardo Jardim-Goncalves (New University of Lisbon, Portugal)
Business Science Reference • copyright 2014 • 351pp • H/C (ISBN: 9781466651425) • US $215.00 (our price)

*Developing Business Strategies and Identifying Risk Factors in Modern Organizations*
Madjid Tavana (La Salle University, USA)
Business Science Reference • copyright 2014 • 300pp • H/C (ISBN: 9781466648609) • US $185.00 (our price)

*Information Quality and Governance for Business Intelligence*
William Yeoh (Deakin University, Australia) John R. Talburt (University of Arkansas at Little Rock, USA) and Yinle Zhou (IBM Corporation, USA)
Business Science Reference • copyright 2014 • 478pp • H/C (ISBN: 9781466648920) • US $235.00 (our price)

*International Business Strategy and Entrepreneurship An Information Technology Perspective*
Patricia Ordóñez de Pablos (Universidad de Oviedo, Spain)
Business Science Reference • copyright 2014 • 306pp • H/C (ISBN: 9781466647534) • US $185.00 (our price)

*Implementing IT Business Strategy in the Construction Industry*
Goh Bee Hua (National University of Singapore, Singapore)
Business Science Reference • copyright 2013 • 354pp • H/C (ISBN: 9781466641853) • US $185.00 (our price)

*Chaos and Complexity Theory for Management Nonlinear Dynamics*
Santo Banerjee (Politecnico di Torino, Italy)
Business Science Reference • copyright 2013 • 449pp • H/C (ISBN: 9781466625099) • US $185.00 (our price)

*Integrated Operations in the Oil and Gas Industry Sustainability and Capability Development*
Tom Rosendahl (BI Norwegian Business School, Norway) and Vidar Hepsø (Norwegian University of Science and Technology, Norway)
Business Science Reference • copyright 2013 • 457pp • H/C (ISBN: 9781466620025) • US $185.00 (our price)

*Cultural Variations and Business Performance Contemporary Globalism*
Bryan Christiansen (PryMarke, LLC, USA)
Business Science Reference • copyright 2012 • 418pp • H/C (ISBN: 9781466603066) • US $185.00 (our price)

DISSEMINATOR OF KNOWLEDGE

www.igi-global.com

701 E. Chocolate Ave., Hershey, PA 17033
Order online at www.igi-global.com or call 717-533-8845 x100
To place a standing order for titles released in this series, contact: cust@igi-global.com
Mon-Fri 8:00 am - 5:00 pm (est) or fax 24 hours a day 717-533-8661

# Table of Contents

### Section 1
### Scientific Foundations of Enterprise Interoperability

## Section 2
## Advanced Methods and Tools for Enterprise Interoperability

**Section 3**
**Perspectives and Future Research Directions for Enterprise Interoperability**

# Detailed Table of Contents

## Section 1
## Scientific Foundations of Enterprise Interoperability

**Chapter 1**

    *Keith Popplewell, Coventry University, UK*

Popplewell explores the structure devised for an Enterprise Interoperability Science Base capable of delivering benefit to a comprehensive range of stakeholders with research and industry interests. Such a science base provides an evolution path from pragmatic solution of immediate interoperability problems to the establishment of a recognizable corpus of knowledge and interests. The need for an Enterprise Interoperability Science Base, as well as its impact on its stakeholders, is debated while lessons can be learned from the development of neighbouring domains as recognizable sciences and their subsequent formalization, even though there is no common structure foreseen for their preparatory stages.

**Chapter 2**

    *Sotirios Koussouris, National Technical University of Athens, Greece*
    *Spiros Mouzakitis, National Technical University of Athens, Greece*
    *Fenareti Lampathaki, National Technical University of Athens, Greece*

Koussouris, Mouzakitis, and Lampathaki analyze the different scientific areas to which the Enterprise Interoperability landscape can be mapped. Embarking from the definition of an enterprise and the major technologies met in the business world, a set of 12 scientific areas are proposed to facilitate focused and targeted research in the domain. A series of hypotheses associated with the scientific areas as a whole and individually are elaborated. An Enterprise Interoperability Assessment Framework is also documented in order to identify the status quo of an organisation and classify it based on its performance on the different Enterprise Interoperability Scientific Areas. Three indicative cases concerning a small technological SME, providing services for the IT sector, a Large Manufacturing Industry, and a Large IT Integrator active in one country are presented as captured in the Enterprise Interoperability Assessment Framework and reveal various solution paths that could be developed in order to gradually improve the interoperability status of each organization.

## Chapter 3

*Carlos Agostinho, Centre of Technology and Systems (CTS) – UNINOVA, Portugal*

*Ricardo Jardim-Goncalves, Centre of Technology and Systems (CTS) – UNINOVA, Portugal*

*Adolfo Steiger-Garcao, Centre of Technology and Systems (CTS) – UNINOVA, Portugal*

Acknowledging that, in terms of content, any scientific field exists in an ecosystem of neighboring domains, Agostinho, Jardim-Goncalves, and Steiger-Garcao present an analysis of EI neighboring scientific domains in search for commonalities and contributions to the EISB formulation. Formalisms like logic and mathematics may be an integrant part of every science, but there are also other scientific disciplines that have common ground, such as application fields' boundaries, methodologies, techniques, or even tools. Upon a literature review on a small set of neighboring domains, their proximity to Enterprise Interoperability is investigated in three complementary steps, namely: matching to identity the high-level relationship between each neighboring domain's core features and the EISB scientific areas; learning to examine what can in fact contribute to the EISB; and extensibility to evaluate if there is evidence of interoperability-based solutions in the neighboring domains.

## Chapter 4

*Euripidis Loukis, University of Aegean, Greece*

*Yannis Charalabidis, University of Aegean, Greece*

*Vasiliki Diamantopoulou, University of Aegean, Greece*

Loukis, Charalabidis, and Diamantopoulou discuss the multi-dimensional business value in the Information Systems interoperability domain and proceed to an empirical study of the business value generated by the adoption of three main types of interoperability standards: industry-specific, proprietary, and XML-horizontal. Three hypotheses, namely (1) the adoption of IS interoperability standards increases the impact of firm's ICT infrastructure on business processes performance; (2) the adoption of IS interoperability standards increases the impact of firm's ICT infrastructure on its innovation activity; and (3) the adoption of IS interoperability standards has positive impact on firm's financial performance, are investigated in-depth and lead to significant insights on the impact of interoperability standards.

## Section 2
### Advanced Methods and Tools for Enterprise Interoperability

## Chapter 5

*Robert Woitsch, BOC Asset Management, Austria*

Woitsch introduces the Hybrid Modeling concept to observe the different layers of interoperability between different enterprises in a conceptualized way. Through hybrid modeling, different meta-models can be merged, enabling interoperability of different conceptual models at vertical and horizontal levels. Addressing process interoperability, service interoperability, rule interoperability, and ecosystem interoperability aspects, the proposed approach is supported by an underlying meta-modeling platform and validated through an indicative use case on enterprise innovation inspired by an EU-funded project.

Alexakis, Bauer, Britsch, and Kölmel demonstrate how Anything Relationship Management (xRM) can increase interoperability in many-to-many (n:n) relationships. Building upon relationship management theory, a categorization of different relationship constellations is presented and three technical xRM approaches are proposed in order to improve social network interoperability, services interoperability, and data interoperability. The deployment of xRM for creating an agile virtual enterprise environment for networks of SMEs and involving end-to-end collaboration with customers and local suppliers (co-creation) in the context of an EU-funded project is discussed.

Upon considering the challenges for a virtual enterprise in a mobile maintenance scenario, Münch, Hladik, Salmen, Altmann, Buchmann, Karagiannis, Ziegler, Pfeffer, Urbas, Lazaro, Ortiz, Lopez, Sanchez, and Haferkorn focus on the data interoperability and process interoperability facets. A detailed, fully decentralised architecture of an IT-infrastructure for virtual enterprises is designed and implemented in prototypes for three different application areas in the manufacturing domain as dictated by an EU-funded initiative. In the proposed approach, the benefits of orchestrated mobile apps and Linked Data are jointly exploited in a secure manner.

**Chapter 8**

*Alberto Armijo, TECNALIA R&I, Spain*
*Mikel Sorli, TECNALIA R&I, Spain*

Targeting at the process interoperability area, Armijo and Sorli introduce a holistic BPM method for supporting the systematic design, process modeling, collaborative execution, monitoring, and optimization and reengineering of business processes accompanied by the application of portable eco-services that integrate simulation and optimization software services, enabling a foundation for interoperability among business processes deployed within the Virtual Factory. A BPMN structural framework is incrementally applied in three Business Cases of an EU-funded project in order to build up the business model starting from the business perspective and eventually reaching the technical level.

**Chapter 9**

*Mustafa Yuksel, Software Research Development and Consultancy Ltd. (SRDC), Turkey*
*        & Middle East Technical University (METU), Turkey*
*Asuman Dogac, Software Research Development and Consultancy Ltd. (SRDC), Turkey*
*Cebrail Taskin, Argela Software and Informatics Technologies, Turkey*
*Anil Yalcinkaya, Argela Software and Informatics Technologies, Turkey*

Yuksela, Dogac, Taskin, and Yalcinkaya bring a neighbouring sciences' perspective for interoperability by discussing the problems and motivations in the health sector. Focusing on the data, process, rules, objects, and software interoperability aspects, a survey and analysis of the interoperability standards and profiles that can be used to integrate personal health records with a variety of healthcare applications and medical data resources is provided.

**Chapter 10**

*Rishi Kanth Saripalle, University of Connecticut, USA*
*Steven A. Demurjian, University of Connecticut, USA*

In their approach addressing the Knowledge Interoperability and Data Interoperability areas, Saripalle and Demurjian define ontologies leveraging Software Design Pattern (SDP) concepts to more effectively design ontologies that are structurally and semantically interoperable across multiple enterprise applications. Ontology Architectural Patterns (OAPs) as higher-level abstract reusable templates with well-defined structure and semantics are proposed in order to conceptualize modular ontology models at the domain model level, so that they are then able to capture semantics that are easier to reconcile across constituent systems for an enterprise application.

## Section 3
## Perspectives and Future Research Directions for Enterprise Interoperability

### Chapter 11

*Irene Matzakou, National Technical University of Athens, Greece*
*João Sarraipa, Universidade Nova de Lisboa, Portugal*
*Ourania Markaki, National Technical University of Athens, Greece*
*Kostas Ergazakis, National Technical University of Athens, Greece*
*Dimitris Askounis, National Technical University of Athens, Greece*

Based on the rather cutting-edge concept of the Interoperability Service Utility (ISU), enriched with a concrete methodology for ontologies' reconciliation, Matzakou, Sarraipa, Markaki, Ergazakis, and Askounis suggest an enhanced ISU that would serve as a mediator among the incompatible enterprise information systems, providing semantic harmonization of the exchanged knowledge and a fertile ground for achieving Enterprise Interoperability and Collaboration. The authors' proposition of an enhanced ISU evolves an approach inherent to the Enterprise Interoperability domain and paves the way for its further enhancement and development.

### Chapter 12

*José C. Delgado, Instituto Superior Técnico, Universidade de Lisboa, Portugal*

Delgado presents a multidimensional interoperability framework, conceived in a generic, bottom-up approach. By adding an interoperability dimension based on the concepts of compliance and conformance to an enterprise architecture framework that includes lifecycle and concreteness as its main dimensions, a universal core framework is formed. An interoperability maturity model is then proposed to express how well a given enterprise explores the potential of interoperability when interacting with another enterprise and is applied in a simple example of collaboration between several partners to achieve some common goals. Overall, Delgado conceives a systematic way to organize and structure the various aspects that interoperability entails, with orthogonality of concepts, domain independence, large-scale complexity, and extensibility as the main goals.

### Chapter 13

*H. T. Goranson, Sirius-Beta, USA*
*Beth Cardier, The University of Melbourne, Australia*

In order to allow enterprises to be as novel, agile, and productive as they could be, a radical advance is required, one based on breakthroughs in the underlying science used by enterprise engineers. Goranson and Cardier elaborate on a vision of advanced virtual enterprises and set an agenda of a research plan for a US-based programme towards increasing the scientific elements of interoperability. Such an agenda features three grand challenges: Value Feature Abstraction, Ontology Federation, and Soft Reasoning, while Category Theory, Situation Theory, and Geometric Logics provide promising pathways to investigate in this quest.

Charalabidis, Lampathaki, and Jardim-Goncalves debate the milestones and accomplishments in the fascinating quest to establish the scientific foundations of enterprise interoperability. The objectives of the Enterprise Interoperability Science Base at its various evolution phases and the key achievements made by the ENSEMBLE project are documented. The fundamentals and theoretic foundations of Enterprise Interoperability in the form of guiding principles and laws are presented and the overall picture of the actions to be implemented towards scientific rigour is provided. Finally, the perspectives opened up through such an initiative are discussed.

# Foreword

## ENTERPRISE INTEROPERABILITY: SCIENCE OR TECHNOLOGY?

Collaboration is necessary for enterprises to prosper in the current extreme dynamic and heterogeneous business environment. Enterprise integration, interoperability, and networking are the major disciplines that have studied how companies can collaborate and communicate in the most effective way. These disciplines are well-established and are supported by international conferences, initiatives, groups, task forces, and governmental projects all over the world where different domains of knowledge have been considered from different points of view and with a variety of objectives (e.g., technological or managerial). Enterprise Interoperability involves breaking down organizational barriers to improve synergy within the enterprise so that business goals are achieved in a more productive and efficient way.

The past decade of Enterprise Interoperability research and industrial implementation has seen the emergence of important new areas that involve breaking down organizational barriers to improve synergy within the enterprise and among enterprises. The ambition to achieve dynamic, efficient, and effective cooperation of enterprises within networks of companies, or in an entire industry sector, requires the improvement of existing, or the development of new, theories and technologies. Enterprise Modelling, Architecture, and semantic techniques are the pillars supporting the achievement of Enterprise Interoperability. Internet of Things and Cloud Computing now present new opportunities to realize inter enterprise and intra enterprise integration.

Since technology has evolved quite fast and become more and more accepted in the academic and industry environments, it is no longer the issue when enterprises want to work together. The Enterprise Interoperability Science Base aims at defining a practical body of knowledge in the interoperability domain. The main objective is to take advantage of the prominent technologies for structuring the knowledge in this domain. With such an approach, enterprises from the software industry can decouple research from technology and develop fundamental knowledge on complex environment integration.

This book clearly underscores the importance of developing a Science Base for studying the interoperability domain. It is a great collection of experiences, insights, and theoretical essays from both researchers and practicing people in their ambition to enhance the main issues of facilitating the collaboration between enterprises. This book describes well the strategic, conceptual, and architectural principles to adhere to, to interoperate, and to make it work.

It is my pleasure to contribute this Foreword and strongly recommend this book to all those who are open minded to achieving "interoperability" not only from a technical point of view but also following the best practices in Science, the non-sufficient but necessary condition for formally accepting and generalising the results coming from the hard work of many researchers around the world.

*Hervé Panetto*
*University of Lorraine, CNRS, France*

**Hervé Panetto** *is Professor of Enterprise Information Systems at University of Lorraine and Head of External Relationships at TELECOM Nancy, School of Engineering in Information Technology. He teaches Information Systems modelling and development, and conducts research at CRAN (Research Centre for Automatic Control), Joint Research Unit with CNRS. He is expert at AFNOR (French National standardisation body), CEN TC310, and ISO TC184/SC4 and SC5. He is the author or co-author of more than 100 papers in the field of automation engineering, enterprise modelling, and enterprise systems integration and interoperability. He is currently Chair of the IFAC Technical Committee 5.3 "Enterprise Integration and Networking."*

# Preface

## TOWARDS A SCIENCE BASE FOR ENTERPRISE INTEROPERABILITY

In a turbulent world, where technological evolution has surpassed even the most imaginary scenarios predicted a few years ago, interoperability among organizations and their systems remains an intangible and elusive challenge. Since the 1970s when its first definition appeared in Webster's Dictionary, interoperability has been considered a critical capability of organisations and their systems, promising a significant increase in their productivity and efficiency. As a result, interoperability in its legal, organizational, semantic, and technical context appears as a key enabler for organisations, processes, and systems in the public and private sector.

Enterprise Interoperability (EI) suggests that organisations can seamlessly interoperate with others, removing barriers to collaboration, fostering a new networked business culture, and transferring and applying the research results in industrial sectors. It is defined as the capacity of two or more organizations or enterprises, including all the systems within their boundaries and the external systems that they utilize or are affected by, to cooperate seamlessly over a sustained period of time to pursue common objectives. Whereas in the past it was considered that interoperability could not be addressed unless the technical, semantic, and organisational repercussions were resolved across all levels of an organization, today this vision has been extended, foreseeing that interoperability will be fully achieved only when the benefits brought by the new technology paradigms are also harvested, including those of the Future Internet, Internet of Things, Internet of Services, Cloud Computing, and Social Networks.

During the last decade, Enterprise Interoperability has been recognized as a well-established technology and applied research domain, studying the problems related with the lack of interoperability in organizations and proposing novel methods and frameworks for better performance in depth of time. Substantial progress has been made through European Union and nationally funded research in a number of areas, yet the lack of scientific foundations in the interoperability domain seem to hinder unlocking its real value and full potential to all its stakeholders, from researchers to industry and SMEs. Such a scientific orientation would document the existing knowledge and open the pathway for systematic and repeatable solutions to identified problems without the danger of repeating research or missing opportunities for application.

The creation of a science base for Enterprise Interoperability has been one of the targets of the EN-SEMBLE project – a collaborative support action implemented between 2010 and 2012 by a consortium consisting of the National Technical University of Athens, the Italian National Research Council, Coventry University, UNINOVA, and Intrasoft International. The core handful of experts from the ENSEMBLE consortium were supported by a larger team of enterprise interoperability researchers and practitioners stemming from the Future Internet Enterprise Systems research cluster (FInES) from the European

Commission, creating a team of more than 100 contributors to the task of laying the foundations of a new scientific domain: the Enterprise Interoperability Science Base (EISB).

In order to understand the potential impact of Enterprise Interoperability Science Base on systems and services, one may consider that after many years of developing software architectures and services, there is currently little concern on native interoperability design. Despite the plethora of available interoperability solutions and best practices, the actual task of making newly designed software interoperable is solely assigned to the designers and the developers of this software, as a set of abstract specifications to abide with until the final release of the product or service, without much specific support in tools or methods. Until now, the principal tools that have emerged for addressing the interoperability challenges are the various standards that seek to govern the development of information systems and their operation. However, such standards are usually linked with specific market sectors, application areas, or technology trends, and thus have a limited time span, a static nature, and quite often different interpretations amongst technology vendors and users.

The Enterprise Interoperability Science Base aims to shed light on the underlying body of knowledge in the interoperability domain. The overall objective in establishing a corresponding Science Base is to formulate and structure the knowledge gained through pragmatic research in the domain over the last decades in order to avoid repeating research and missing opportunities for application. With such an approach, enterprises from the software industry can decouple research from technology and develop fundamental knowledge on complex environment integration. Traditional industrial domains benefit from dedicated methods for assessing the interoperability of enterprise systems and applications, positioning themselves within the interoperability problem space, and finding more fit solutions targeting the exact interoperability problem identified. Software Engineering products and results can be thus made "interoperable by design" in any ecosystem rather than being embedded at the development or configuration stages.

In this quest for scientific recognition, the key challenges that Enterprise Interoperability will have to include further substantiation of value, strong engagement and support by industry, sustainable research in the domain through appropriate curricula, as well as further coordination of the efforts undertaken by many stakeholders and neighbouring disciplines.

## OBJECTIVE OF THE BOOK

This title aims at providing the latest research advancements and findings for the scientific systematization of the Enterprise Interoperability knowledge, such as core concepts, foundational principles, theories, methodologies, architectures, assessment frameworks, and future directions. It brings forward the ingredients of this new domain, proposing its needed formal and systematic tools, exploring its relation with neighboring scientific domains, and prescribing further steps for eventually achieving the thrilling goal of laying the foundations of a new science.

These research findings are organized along the following main areas of contribution:

- Presenting the scientific foundational principles of Enterprise Interoperability, by means of envisaged structure and current state of the art. This way a new set of concepts, theories, and principles is designed, with a view to long-term problem solving as opposed to short-term solution provisioning.

- Analysing the neighboring scientific domains. Since interoperability is a multi-disciplinary domain, new research challenges are also bound to touch Complexity Science, Software Engineering, Design Science, and Service Science approaches.
- Presentation of novel approaches for Enterprise Interoperability, by means of frameworks, models, methods, and tools to assist enterprises in achieving more interoperable processes, systems, and information resources.
- Envisioning future research to tackle interoperability problems and activities that need to be collectively undertaken by stakeholders with different backgrounds in a logical time frame in order to eventually lead to the general recognition of the scientific rigor of enterprise interoperability.

## TARGET AUDIENCE

The target audience of this book includes (1) researchers and practitioners in the interoperability domain, (2) university students and professors of computer and management sciences, (3) representatives of the ICT industry engaged in interoperability solutions, software design and deployment projects, and modelling methods, as well as industry in general, applying interoperability solutions, and (4) policy makers and decision drivers at local, national, or international levels.

## ORGANISATION OF THE BOOK

The book is composed of 14 chapters, structured in 3 sections. The first section is titled "Scientific Foundations of Enterprise Interoperability" and includes 4 chapters laying the foundational framework for enterprise interoperability, describing its proposed structure, giving a full-breadth view of and analyzing relations to other scientific domains. Section 2 is titled "Advanced Methods and Tools for Enterprise Interoperability," including approaches for designing and building new enterprise interoperability tools for researchers and practitioners, thus giving some initial directions for deploying new methods and tools for tackling interoperability in a systematic way. The third section on "Perspectives and Future Research Directions for Enterprise Interoperability" includes 4 chapters presenting more holistic, groundbreaking approaches for interoperable organizations and systems, leading to further research and development of the science base.

### Scientific Foundations of Enterprise Interoperability

Section 1 contains 4 chapters devoted to presenting foundational principles of enterprise interoperability and the core elements of the science base under development. Analysing its structure, the state of the art, its relation to scientific domains, and giving evidence of the overall value of interoperability for the enterprise, the authors in this section contribute to a better understanding of what is the Science Base and why it is important for industry and research.

Chapter 1, presented by Keith Popplewell representing the ENSEMBLE project team, analyses the structure of Enterprise Interoperability Science Base as defined in this project, based on analysis of its purposes, the knowledge already available from pragmatic research, and the lessons learned, both on interoperability and the theoretical structure of a science base. The resulting scientific base is now evolving from the body of knowledge used for its initial population to embrace new research results and issues.

In chapter 2, Koussouris, Mouzakitis, and Lampathaki, from the National Technical University of Athens team of the ENSEMBLE project, provide the current state of the art and the Taxonomy of Scientific Areas that comprise the Enterprise Interoperability domain. Further, the chapter presents the core elements of a framework assessing an organization's readiness to deploy interoperable solutions and services.

Chapter 3 is about presenting the relation of Enterprise Interoperability with other scientific domains. In this chapter, Agostinho, Jardim-Goncalves, and Steiger-Garcao recognize that any scientific field exists in an ecosystem of neighboring domains and present a methodology to identify EI's relationship with its neighbors, thus supporting the foundations of EI Science Base. It can be agreed that formalisms like logic and mathematics are an integrant part of every science, but others also share relationships such as application fields' boundaries, methodologies, techniques, or even tools.

Chapter 4 by Loukis, Charalabidis, and Diamantopoulou analyses the theoretical foundations of the multi-dimensional business value of interoperability among enterprise information systems and reviews the quite limited empirical literature on it. Next, it presents an empirical study of the business value generated by the adoption of three main types of information systems interoperability standards: industry-specific, proprietary, and horizontal-XML. The study is based on a large dataset from 14065 European firms (from 25 countries and 10 sectors) collected through the e-Business Watch Survey of the European Commission.

## Advanced Methods and Tools for Enterprise Interoperability

Section 2 of the book attempts to present novel approached for Enterprise Interoperability by means of innovative methods and tools for diverse industrial sectors, covering several aspects of enterprise issues, as well as organizational, semantic, and technical aspects. This way, the 6 chapters of this section act complementarily to the basic foundational principles of the Science Base, extending and giving "body" to its initial directions.

In chapter 5, Robert Woitsch from BOC Asset Management, Austria, presents Meta Modeling as a proven technology to enable interoperability by introducing conceptual models enabling computer-based processing for both machine interpretation and human-oriented information value creation. This chapter introduces (a) concept models as an instrument for interoperability, (b) the meta model approach as a flexible but stable platform, and (c) hybrid modeling as an approach to flexibly compose the conceptual integration. After discussing this theoretical background, the chapter introduces meta modeling merging patterns as different realization scenarios of hybrid modeling. Each scenario is supported differently by the underlying meta modeling platform ADOxx®.

Chapter 6, by Alexakis, Bauer, Britsch, and Kölmel, shows how Anything Relationship Management (xRM) can increase interoperability in many-to-many (n:n) relationships. Building upon relationship management theory, the authors categorize different types of relationships and link them with fitting IT solutions. They then introduce the xRM concept, present the EU research project GloNet, and propose three technical xRM approaches (collaboration spaces, integration of external services, and synchronization framework) in order to improve social network interoperability, services interoperability, and data interoperability. The chapter closes with a conclusion, an example of application, and a research outlook.

Chapter 7 by Münch et al. is a collective work of fourteen authors, stemming from the ComVantage European research project, presenting an infrastructure approach for virtual enterprises and discussing its impact with respect to the mobile maintenance domain. The approach focuses on data and process interoperability – core areas of enterprise interoperability. Regarding the interorganisational access to enterprise data, they propose a semantic abstraction layer that is completely decentralised and therefore meets the key requirement of virtuality. The execution of business processes and workflows across organisational boundaries are addressed by the unique App Orchestration Concept.

In the direction of Interoperable Process Engineering Systems, Armijo and Sorli from TECNALIA R&I in Spain, present in chapter 8 an approach covering the product life cycle. The approach is rooted on the Business Process Management (BPM) discipline and leverages process optimization through the systematic modeling and reengineering of business processes accompanied by supporting interoperable and configurable eco-services, which are conceived as sustainability-aware services designed to optimize some aspects of the product life-cycle through eco-constraints management.

Moving from production management to the health sector, chapter 9 discusses new interoperability approaches in the area of medical information and relating systems and processes. In this chapter, Yuksel, Dogac, Taskin, and Yalcinkaya provide a survey and analysis of the interoperability standards and profiles that can be used to integrate Personal Health Records with a variety of healthcare applications and medical data resources, including Electronic Health Record systems to enable access of a patient to his own medical data generated by healthcare professionals, personal medical devices to obtain the patient's instant physiological status, and clinical decision support services for patient-physician shared decision making.

Closing the section of novel methods and tools, chapter 10 by Saripalle and Demurjian discusses how to attain Semantic Enterprise Interoperability through Ontology Architectural Patterns. The authors' intent in this chapter is to enable the definition of ontologies leveraging Software Design Pattern (SDP) concepts to more effective design ontologies that are structurally and semantically interoperable. To support this, the chapter proposes Ontology Architectural Patterns (OAPs), which are higher-level abstract reusable templates with well-defined structure and semantics to conceptualize modular ontology models at the domain model level, so that they are then able to capture semantics that are easier to reconcile across constituent systems for an enterprise application.

## Perspectives and Future Research Directions for Enterprise Interoperability

The third section of the book is focusing at more generalized, forward looking, theoretical approaches towards extending the Enterprise Interoperability Science Base in the future. Going from advanced infrastructures, such as the Interoperability Service Utility, to new frameworks for assessing Enterprise Interoperability, to new formalisations for interoperability as a whole, the authors in this section underline the need for continued, focused work towards concrete objectives for science and practice.

Chapter 11, by Matzakou, Sarraipa, Markaki, Ergazakis, and Askounis, presents an extension to the notion of Interoperability Service Utility (ISU) – an advanced infrastructure introduced by the Future Internet Enterprise Systems community some years ago. The authors suggest an enhanced ISU that would serve as a mediator among the incompatible enterprise information systems, providing semantic harmonization of the exchanged knowledge and a fertile ground for achieving Enterprise Interoperability and collaboration. The authors' proposition and methodology can be useful to any stakeholder in the enterprise field, giving useful directions for any other similar implementation – thus contributing to the scientific aspects of Enterprise Interoperability.

With the goal of contributing to the establishment of the scientific foundations of interoperability, chapter 12 by José C. Delgado presents a multidimensional interoperability framework, conceived in a generic, bottom-up approach. The basic tenet is to add an interoperability dimension (based on the concepts of compliance and conformance) to an enterprise architecture framework with lifecycle and concreteness as its main dimensions, forming a universal core framework. This core is then provided with an extensibility mechanism, based on a concerns dimension, into which the specific characteristics of applications and their domains can be added to instantiate the framework, now in an application-driven fashion. The use of partial compliance and conformance reduces coupling while still allowing interoperability, which increases adaptability, changeability, and reliability, thereby contributing to a sustainable interoperability.

In chapter 13, Goranson and Cardier report on elements of a research plan developed for a US program, towards increasing the scientific elements of interoperability. A key aspect they adopt is that external operations of enterprises are integrated using lowest common denominator standards. The net result is that we are somewhat worse off now because current integration technology is a matter of conformance. So, in order to allow enterprises to be as novel, agile, and productive as they could be, a radical advance is required, one based on breakthroughs in the underlying science used by enterprise engineers.

Chapter 14 is authored by the editors of this book. In this chapter, Charalabidis, Lampathaki, and Jardim-Goncalves give the overall achievements of the ENSEMBLE project, which opened the way for the Enterprise Interoperability Science Base. Adding to the ingredients of the science base, the chapter goes beyond the interoperability structure, areas, formalisations, and neighboring sciences to discuss the overall picture and overarching enterprise interoperability laws. Furthermore, the chapter gives an outlook of the next steps needed to be taken by academia, research, industry, and policy makers to advance the state of the science base.

## CONCLUSION

Enterprise Interoperability is a promising domain of research and practice, providing enterprises with methods, systems, and services to allow them to enjoy the merits of technical, semantic, and organization interoperability. Enterprise interoperability integrates several sub-domains of information and management sciences, while also interacting with several neighboring domains – such as complex systems, networks, and service sciences.

Although delivering ideas and solutions for more than a decade, enterprise interoperability is not yet considered a rigid scientific domain, able to offer deterministic diagnosis and problem solving at the enterprise domain, by following standardized practices. Mostly relying on standards that need to be adopted—often forcing enterprises to accept the minimum "common denominator"—interoperability practitioners are in need of a more systematic approach to common problems.

This book is gathering innovative approaches, mostly stemming from the Future Internet Enterprise Systems cluster and the ENSEMBLE project, in order to give out a holistic approach for developing a Science Base for Enterprise Interoperability. This way, this title presents the various elements needed for a new scientific domain: definition of the Enterprise Interoperability areas, formal problem and solution description methods, assessment tools and metrics, systematization of empirical evidence, as well as relations with neighboring domains.

The first steps have been made towards giving birth to a new scientific domain, able to revolutionize the way enterprises organize themselves, develop and utilize information systems, structure information and knowledge, and finally prosper or reorganize. It is now the research and practice communities, from industry, academia, and policy making, that may or may not take these initial developments further towards realization and externalization. Then, enterprise interoperability science base might be the first attempt of conceiving this "science of collaboration" that covers data, systems, processes, organizations, and above all, human beings.

At least, for Enterprise Interoperability, *iacta alea est* ...

*Yannis Charalabidis*
*University of the Aegean, Greece*

*Fenareti Lampathaki*
*National Technical University of Athens, Greece*

*Ricardo Jardim-Goncalves*
*Centre of Technology and Systems (CTS) – UNINOVA, Portugal*

# Acknowledgment

This book is the result of the collective work of several scientists, industry experts, and practitioners in the fields of enterprise interoperability, information systems, management, and socio-economics. We are highly grateful to all the authors for their continued efforts towards a high quality publication. We are also very pleased to acknowledge the support of the Editorial Advisory Board and all friends and colleagues involved in overall guidance, stimulation of the community, the review process, and the book finalization.

Many thanks go to colleagues at the National Technical University of Athens, UNINOVA, Coventry University, CNR, and Intrasoft International, as the core partners of the ENSEMBLE Project ("Envisioning, Supporting, and Promoting Future Internet Enterprise Systems Research through Scientific Collaboration," Contract No: FP7-ICT-257548), as well as to the rest of the experts involved in the ENSEMBLE Scientific Experts Committee for their ideas and encouragement during the entire authoring and publication process.

This publication would have certainly been extremely difficult without the support of all experts in the Future Internet Enterprise Systems cluster, under the guidance of European Commission executives. We would like to especially thank Gerald Santucci and Cristina Martinez for their continued encouragement and critical thinking.

Special thanks also go to the publisher's team and particularly to Austin DeMarco for his professional guidance, support, and feedback—decisive in keeping this project on schedule.

May this work be an inspiration for our students, colleagues, and beloved ones on their own paths for achieving development and fulfillment.

*Yannis Charalabidis*
*University of the Aegean, Greece*

*Fenareti Lampathaki*
*National Technical University of Athens, Greece*

*Ricardo Jardim-Goncalves*
*Centre of Technology and Systems (CTS) – UNINOVA, Portugal*

*September 2013*

# Section 1
# Scientific Foundations of Enterprise Interoperability

# Chapter 1
# Enterprise Interoperability Science Base Structure

**Keith Popplewell**
*Coventry University, UK*

## ABSTRACT

*A science base for enterprise interoperability was first proposed in 2006 as a mechanism to formalize knowledge being generated by researchers and applied by industry to facilitate collaboration between enterprises through mutual interoperability of their enterprise systems. Subsequently, the community of researchers and exploiters of Enterprise Interoperability research addressed this issue as a group, culminating in a project funded by the European Commission FP7 programme. In this chapter, the authors explore the structure for an Enterprise Interoperability Science Base defined in this project, based on analysis of its purposes, the knowledge already available from pragmatic research, and the lessons learned, both on interoperability and the theoretical structure of a science base. The resulting science base is now evolving from the body of knowledge used for its initial population to embrace new research results and issues. This chapter focuses on the structure devised for an Enterprise Interoperability Science Base capable of delivering benefit to a comprehensive range of stakeholders with research and industry interests.*

## INTRODUCTION

The significance of achieving interoperability between enterprise systems operated by independent enterprises, possibly operating in states divided by differences of language and culture, and grounded in hitherto unrelated industrial sectors became apparent during the 1970s as major international collaborative industrial projects emerged. The aerospace sector, both civil and military, provides good examples of such projects, and the Airbus programme (Airbus, 2013) is often quoted as typical. Although such projects were in part politically motivated, as governments competed to demonstrate how they could be lead players in such projects, they nevertheless had to be implemented, and since they were not actually government projects, had to generate real results in a finite time, and at costs which made the project financially viable.

DOI: 10.4018/978-1-4666-5142-5.ch001

There was a clear need to be able to exchange data between the design systems used by the partners of such project consortia, as typically the partners were responsible for major components, assemblies and systems which must ultimately fly (in the case of aerospace) in quite close formation. Perhaps not so obvious, but in fact equally critical to project success was the need for logistics and operational management systems, such as material requirements planning (MRP) and the then novel enterprise requirements planning (ERP) to work in concert across the consortium. The differing environments of partners (language, culture, industrial sector, etc.) ensured that not only was it rare for partners to actually use the same software systems, but that terminologies and especially business processes conflicted. These conflicts, at all levels, must be resolved effectively for a project to proceed successfully, and it was not untypical to find that a significant portion of the project budget was devoted to achieving interoperability between these enterprise systems.

By the 1990s it was apparent that at least some interoperability problems were predictable, and susceptible to similar resolution. Rather than resolve these issues anew in each project a body of knowledge, pragmatically developed, was emerging and could be applied to reduce the cost and time to implantation for each new project. It was also emerging that there were common issues of interoperability which had not yet been resolved well in any project, and that these should be the subject of research independent of any one project, to provide benefit to future projects. In response, the IDEAS project, funded by the European Commission in 2002, made a first, and very effective, attempt to recognize the state of the art and future research issues, and to structure these into a research roadmap (Doumeingts & Chen, 2013). At or about this time the research domain acquired the title Enterprise Interoperability (EI), and as a result of the roadmap a network of excellence, INTEROP-NoE was funded by the European Commission's Framework Programme

6. This became one of a cluster of EU projects working in the domain, and entitled the Enterprise Interoperability Cluster (now re-named the Future Internet Enterprise Systems Cluster) (FInES Cluster, 2013).

The EI Cluster updated the research roadmap in 2006 (Li, Cabral, Doumeingts, & Popplewell, 2006). By this time changes in the enterprise environment in Europe led to the conclusion that EI was becoming at least as important to the commercial health of small and medium sized enterprises (SMEs), as to the large enterprises who had first encountered a need for interoperability. Indeed the growing propensity for SME collaboration to address business opportunities in close collaboration across sector boundaries made systems interoperability essential to survival. Previously SMEs tended to tied into one industrial sector or even one OEM supply chain, and were obliged to use the same systems as their customers, but now, as SMEs increasingly served multiple supply chains, frequently across industrial sectors the balance of power changed: SMEs could dictate a need for interoperability to their customers, to at least some extent. However the multi-million euro budgets employed in achieving interoperability in the major projects of the 1990s were clearly beyond the reach of small companies.

As a result a major focus of the 2006 EI Roadmap was the delivery of EI technology through service models allowing for pay-per-use of software affordable to SMEs. The roadmap identified four grand challenges:

- **Interoperability Service Utility:** Delivering software services for EI as a utility for affordable SME access.
- **Web Technologies for Enterprise Interoperability:** Harnessing the range of emerging Web capabilities to support EI.
- **Knowledge Oriented Collaboration:** Working towards the next level of EI, sharing and understanding of knowledge.

- **Science Base for Enterprise Interoperability:** Collecting and structuring EI knowledge from past research and application as a formal base accessible to researchers, end users and policy makers, and providing a rigorous scientific base for the domain.

The last of these challenges, developed by the EI Cluster, was then addressed by the ENSEMBLE (ENSEMBLE, 2012) project, funded by the EU from 2010 to 2012, and it is this that we consider in this chapter.

## BACKGROUND

### The Need for an Enterprise Interoperability Science Base

Interoperability is defined as "the ability of systems, units, or forces to provide services to and accept services from other systems, units, or forces and to use the services so exchanged to enable them to operate effectively together" (Wycisk, McKelvey, & Hulsmann, 2008), whilst an Enterprise, as defined in (Sullivan & Sheffrin, 2003) is "...an organization designed to provide goods, services, or both to consumers."

Interoperability appears as a key enabler towards unlocking the full potential of organizations, processes and systems in the public and private sector. Since its inception as "the ability of systems, units, or forces to provide services to and accept services from other systems, units, or forces and to use the services so exchanged to enable them to operate effectively together" (DODD, 1977) and through the years, interoperability tends to obtain a broader, all-inclusive scope of a repetitive, well organized, and automated at ICT level feature of organizations, as indicated in the definition of the draft EIF 2.0 (IDABC, 2008), which states "Interoperability is the ability of disparate and diverse organizations to interact towards mutually

beneficial and agreed common goals, involving the sharing of information and knowledge between the organizations via the business processes they support, by means of the exchange of data between their respective information and communication technology (ICT) systems."

Moreover, interoperability is recognized as a high-impact productivity factor both within the private and the public sector, affecting the overall quality, yield time and cost of transactions, design and manufacturing operations or digital public services. According to a recent publication in Financial Times, interoperability can dramatically decrease the costs, risks and complexity of information systems, being now the most important characteristic for organizations and their ICT infrastructures, representing a challenge to competition policies in Europe and America (Schrage, 2009). Yankee Group further advises IT departments to focus on interoperability technologies and skills as a core competency imperative, envisaging savings of more than one-third of the total cost of ownership - if they succeed in achieving business and technical interoperability. However, since projects involving integration, interoperation and interoperability have been conducted from different vantage points, are multi-faceted, complex and run a high risk of failure (Scholl & Klischewsky, 2007).

Up to now, the principal tools for targeting the previously mentioned challenges appear as the various standards that try to govern information systems development and operation (Steiger-Garcao, Jardim-Goncalves, & Farinha, 2007). Such standards are usually linked with specific market sectors, application areas or technology trends, thus having a limited time span, a static nature and quite often different interpretations by technology vendors and users (Jardim-Goncalves & Steiger-Garcao, 2002), (Figay, Steiger-Garcao, & Jardim-Goncalves, 2006).

So, interoperability has to be studied and developed as a rigorous mathematical and scientifically lawful phenomenon, following scientific practices similar to neighbouring domains – such as those of Systems/Complexity science, Information science, Services science as well as Economic and Social sciences (Jardim-Goncalves & Steiger-Garcao, 2009).

The Informal Study Group report on Value Proposition for Enterprise Interoperability (Informal Study Group on Value Proposition, 2008) advocates that "disruptive innovation at the enterprise level needs to be matched by disruptive innovation for enterprise systems of the future." Moreover, "value is delivered at the level of the system, not components or elements of such a system." This report gives a description of the properties of "openness" for enterprise systems and makes a distinction between universal interoperability and conditional interoperability. It further suggests that "the systemic view of ICT for enterprises is a central characteristic of EI, and distinguishes EI from other fields of ICT research which have a predominantly technology-driven approach." It is highly likely that the Future Internet will give rise to "new opportunities of creativity and innovation, enable new forms of participation, and further catalyze the formation of networked enterprises and communities that span the world, thereby ushering in a new generation of enterprise systems requiring a reappraisal of interoperability between those systems." In the past, it was said that EI was not achieved until the interaction could take place at the three layers of interoperability (technical, semantic and organizational); today, it is believed that EI will not be fully achieved until the benefits brought by the new technology paradigms are reaped, including the paradigms for the Future Internet.

Being an attempt to formulate a science base, the methodology for the EISB foundation should follow the scientific method, which as defined by the Merriam-Webster dictionary (Scientific Method, 2010), as "the principles and procedures for the systematic pursuit of knowledge involving the recognition and formulation of a problem, the collection of data through observation and experiment, and the formulation and testing of hypotheses." The method attempts to minimize the influence of the researchers' bias on the outcome of an experiment, i.e. personal preferences, common sense assumptions, concealing of data not supporting the hypothesis, etc. (Wolfs, 2010).

Philosopher Karl Popper (1902-1994) says that a statement is scientific only if it is open to the logical possibility of being found false (Popper, 1992). This definition means that we evaluate scientific statements by testing them and comparing them to the world about us. A statement is scientific if it is verifiable and repeatable, and non-scientific if it takes no risk of being found false, i.e., when it cannot be tested against observable facts or events (Wilson, 1999). An implication of this definition is that in natural sciences, one can never be completely sure that any scientific theory is true.

This is the positivist definition of science. However, there are other epistemological approaches, particularly in social sciences that have other scientific stances, such as using falsify conjectures due to humans' involvement. In these cases, science is about providing well-grounded arguments to support conjectures. Accepted scientific theory is, therefore, only theory that has not yet been contradicted by evidence, though the future may bring a contradiction.

Popper saw the growth of scientific knowledge as a process of conjecture and refutation. If further observation is inconsistent with the theory, then the theory is considered refuted and a new theory or conjecture must be found. To define an Enterprise Interoperability Science Base the ENSEMBLE project sought a methodology where the issues of experimental fallibility and falsification are critical since EI, particularly the relation "interoperates with," is not necessarily reflexive, symmetric or transitive. The evidence one collects by looking at interoperability is subject to endogeneity and/or confirmation bias (we see, notice and record what our a priori beliefs and models tell us is significant, and what one observer observes is far from being common knowledge). Also, due to the inter-subjectivity of the interoperable relation, it is necessary to be very careful about claiming to have derived or to tested hypotheses. Nevertheless that should not prevent EISB from developing as, according to Popper's beliefs, scientific knowledge is built upon continuous conjecture and refutation.

Within the category of modern sciences, the notion of a network, in our context collaboration and business networks, is nowadays a central issue to address science within the topics of EI. Collaborative networks are complex systems, emerging in many forms in different application domains, and consist of many facets whose proper understanding requires the contribution from multiple disciplines. One aspect of EI, namely the systems interoperability, suggests that systems can seamlessly interoperate with others across networks, through research and development in focal areas, removing barriers to interoperability, and transferring and applying the research results across industrial sectors (Research Areas, n.d.). This way, special interest for the establishment of the scientific foundations of EI have been initially identified on the research developments of distributed enterprise systems, shared data and knowledge, evolving applications, dynamics and adaptation of networked systems on a global scale. Those are all directly related with major requirements for interoperability, as: rapid evolution of technology and applications; plug and play instruments; self-monitoring capabilities; benchmarking and evaluation of degrading processing; automatic or on demand reprocessing; recompiling or fixing of components or processes. Also, to accomplish an interoperable stable state at a global scale, there is the need for human assisted supervising systems supported by embedded monitoring with learning capabilities (Li, Cabral, Doumeingts, & Popplewell, 2006).

## Relationships with Neighbouring Scientific Domains

Any scientific domain exists in an ecosystem of neighbouring scientific domains (Dodig-Crnkovic, 2002) (Agostinho, Jardim-Goncalves, & Steiger-Garcao, 2011), (Jardim-Goncalves, Grilo, Agostinho, Lampathaki, & Charalabidis, 2012), and must therefore recognize its relationship with these domains and with formal definitions of science bases already established for these domains. This relationship will include at least:

- **Boundaries between Application Fields:** Which may be fuzzy in the sense that there are some applications which could be addressed from the perspective of either domain. Formally, it may be appropriate to define membership functions to applications to recognise and resolve this overlap.
- **Shared Methodologies, Techniques and Tools:** Which may be applicable to problems in more than one domain. Recognition of such sharing provides opportunity for domains to advance by absorbing methodological and technical advances from related disciplines.
- **Conflicts in Approach:** May also exist, and present possible barriers to interdisciplinary research or application. Formal documentation of such conflict areas will reduce risk of failure in projects arising out of the application of incompatible approaches.

However there is no generally accepted definition of a "Science Base," which can describe comparable constructs in a range of scientific domains. We will therefore propose a definition of the scope, purpose and content of an EISB. This definition has guided initial research on the EISB, but the authors would be unsurprised to see future evolution of this definition. This seems both inevitable and desirable in the absence of any pre-existing definition of the term.

Although no common structure for science bases across neighbouring domains can be identified, lessons can be learned from their development as recognizable sciences, and their subsequent formalization. This can be found in details in (Charalabidis, Jardim-Gonçalves, & Popplewell, 2010), whilst the lessons are summarized as follows.

## Lessons from Social Sciences

We describe the lessons learned from the Social Sciences sub-domain Sociology as an example of matching and contribution for EISB. Sociology involves systematic methods of empirical research, analysis of data and the assessment of theories. Contrary to the natural world that can be accepted as it can be seen (e.g. a biologist can study the nucleus of a cell because it can be observed with a microscope), society is different from the natural world because it is not an object with physical existence that can be directly investigated by our senses (Gordon, 2002). Society consists of groupings of humans, and its study looks at the way these groupings behave. When a sociologist studies society, he/she looks at behaviour and the mind, which do not take physical form (Galtuno, 1967), (Hughes, 1980). Such relationship between individuals and groups in social context addresses interoperability issues, such as those related behaviour in society including the communication between individuals and groups independently of the culture, verbal and gestural languages. How these phenomena have been addressed by the sociology science, can be used as referential examples in the context of EI.

Nevertheless, the technology interoperability problem also has impact in the sociology, and in social sciences in general, as the sharing of data has been very limited. According to (Hughes, Schmidt, & Smith, 2006), the reasons for this

limited sharing are within strong privacy concerns, and lack of appropriate contextual knowledge. However, the problem of interoperability between software tools commonly used for data annotation and coding by social scientists, is critical even if the other problems identified are resolved.

Main contributions from this scientific domain to the EISB are foreseen in the relationship and behavior between individuals and groups, communication independent of the culture and languages, and related methods, models, concepts, axioms, (epi) phenomena, etc.

## Lessons from Applied Sciences

We here use the sub domain Medicine as an example of matching and contribution for EISB the applied science domain. Medicine has been contributing to the solution of some major interoperability problems concerning the human body, such as compatibility between organs in transplants. (Friedman & Peters, 2006) explains that today medicine supplies numerous scientific strategies to face incompatible live donor organ (e.g. kidney) obstacles, and achieve a perfect matching. For example, this allows finding a matching donor organ with the person seeking transplantation, identifying an organ that will be tolerated indefinitely by the body of the recipient, who can also take medications to prevent rejection. Scientific methods to solve incompatibility of organs involve pre-treating the recipient with immunoglobulin, a blood product pooled from thousands of donors. Therefore, a well-matched organ is one in which the blood types between the donor and recipient are compatible, the tissue typing is well-defined and well-matched, and the cross-match studies are negative. Application of these scientific principles has helped to make the results of live organ transplantation excellent, and to make this therapy safe.

Nevertheless, at organizational level new technologies are being introduced in hospitals at an increasing rate, and the ability to have any medical device immediately working with any other is a recognized priority for healthcare providers and industry. A compelling example is the development, propagation of, and adherence to, clinical guidelines – more generally, the emergence of "Health systems research" from "health research." Concerning patient data, today the major enabler of health care information sharing is the electronic health record (EHR) that contains all the relevant patient health care data in a shareable form, integrating functions similar to that of the bill of materials (BOM) in manufacturing (Sriram & Fenves, 2009). However, there are still severe interoperability problems in this area of medicine, where for example 60 different types of leukemia are identified, but the currently-used International Classification of Diseases (ICD) codes do not reflect the diversity of that disease.

Still in the medicine domains, an example of success is the cancer Biomedical Informatics Grid or caBIG (West, 2011), that connects several Cancer Centers, research organizations and companies. Capabilities compliant with caBIG interoperability specifications enable the collection, analysis, and exchange of a wide range of biomedical information through a well-integrated, standards-based infrastructure coupled with open-source and commercial software applications. These technologies create an integrated electronic system that enables clinical research, genomics, medical images, biospecimens, and patient outcomes data to flow easily but securely between and among authorized individuals, organizations, and institutions. With it, it is possible to identify molecularly sub-grouped patients, collect and view patients' histories individually and in the aggregate, and collaborate across organizations to test research hypotheses and evaluate new treatments.

Medicine can contribute for EISB thought bearing in mind the interoperability problems concerning the human body, and how medicine scientific methods solves such incompatibilities.

Also, the sustainability of the global system to keep it balanced and according to the normal parameters is of major relevance, including those for monitoring, control, transitory analysis and therapy.

## Lessons from Formal Scientific Domain

As examples from the area of formal scientific domain, topics can be observed in complex systems that have, as in EI, many structures and relationships. Understanding their interactions is considered a major factor in contributing to the success of interoperability solutions and the performance of the entire enterprise. Implicit in both is the view that enterprises are Complex and Adaptive Systems. Preliminary theories have been advanced in specific scientific disciplines, such as biology and ecology, to explain the importance of and the evolution of complexity in these "systems" (Nichols & Prigogine, 1989), (Axelrod, 1997). Some researchers have attempted to extrapolate these results to a "general systems theory" that could explain the importance of and the behavior of systems in all fields of science (Sugihara & May, n.d.), (Gharajedaghi, 2005). However, complexity views all systems as dynamic, "living" entities that are goal-oriented and that evolve over time. Complexity science, generally considered as a branch of systems science, has been developed to address the emergence, adaptation, evolution, and self-organization of systems (Key, Boyle, & Francis, 1999).

Contributions from this scientific domain to EISB include: systems of systems and networks, behavior and adaptability; the "system" aspects of interoperability, from software component design to organizational structure to the "ICT fabric" that provides communication, collaboration and coordination facilities; the technology trajectory of interoperability as a complex system.

# DEFINING THE STRUCTURE OF AN ENTERPRISE INTEROPERABILITY SCIENCE BASE

## Methodology

From the previous section we see that here is no view of the definition of a science base common to all, or even a related set of, scientific domains, although good examples exist, including for example that for software engineering science (Shaw & Clements, 2006). We therefore submit that the definition of a science base is to a degree dependent on the nature of the domain and the purpose for which it is designed and maintained, and indeed the definition for a particular domain will evolve as the needs of the domain evolve with its maturity.

This implies, in turn, that the definition and therefore the structure of a science base must be related to the purposes of its creation and application. In the context of a pure science, this may perhaps be primarily concerned with maintenance of scientific rigor and consistency, demonstration of experimental repeatability, documentation of domain knowledge to support re-use and reduce duplication. We might also expect such a science base to recognize the uncertainties and indeed conflicts present in current domain knowledge, and to identify the general lines of research needed to resolve such issues: this after all is the conventional scientific approach to knowledge discovery and validation.

However in the context of applied science domains, where the science is advanced so as to meet the needs of application outside the scientific community, the purposes of a science base are extended to enable efficient support of application. The requirements of a pure science base remain essential but the additional layer of application related knowledge is necessarily added. The process of defining a structure for such an applied science base therefore must begin from the perspectives of its purposes as both a repository of scientific knowledge, and as a reference for application of domain knowledge.

From these objectives we derived a high-level structure for the Enterprise Interoperability Science Base (EISB), whose components can be related to technologies which may support their eventual implementation. The approach adopted was not to go directly to a final structure but to take a crowd sourcing approach. The initial structure was presented to the Enterprise Interoperability research and application communities, hereafter referred to as the Enterprise Interoperability constituency, to interested parties from neighbouring and other scientific domains, and to as wide an audience as chose to participate. The structure and supporting documentation (Popplewell et al., 2012) was made available through an online consultation tool enabling contributors to attach comments and especially contributions, which could be associated with content, with a granularity ranging from overall comment on the document to individual paragraph or illustration. This process, whose results are summarized in the following, had a major and positive impact on the specification of EISB components, as well as on defining the context in which it might be populated and applied.

The process of structure definition was completed through definition of the tools and technologies needed to support the components. The process of population is also described in the following.

## Defining Objectives

The overall objective in creation of an EISB is to formulate and structure the knowledge gained through pragmatic research in the domain over the last decades and more. This will establish that there is indeed a coherent and specific body of scientific knowledge and understanding attributable to that research, and render it accessible to both future researchers aiming to build on existing knowledge, and to those wishing to use it in industrial applications. Without such an EISB there is danger of repeating research, and missing opportunities for application.

In particular, the EISB aims:

1. To document and catalogue domain knowledge. In this context knowledge may embrace factual knowledge, and methodologies for application.

2. To identify application areas for domain knowledge items. This will include a taxonomy of problems addressed by the Enterprise Interoperability domain, and the domain solutions to these problems.

3. To identify approaches for application, which may combine methodologies to achieve integrated solutions of complex problems. These should, if possible, characterise problems in sufficient detail to eliminate inappropriate methods and prioritise those which are applicable.

4. To identify domain related problems which are currently not resolved or addressed in the knowledge base, and which should be prioritised for research.

5. To identify related problems addressed in other sciences, directing attention to the appropriate knowledge in the addressing domain.

6. To support application of Enterprise Interoperability knowledge by clearly documenting the route from domain problems to domain solution approaches, and providing access to the solution methodologies. This may be linked to access to both the knowledge base content and to sources of expertise, consultancy or training to support application.

7. To identify, structure and document fundamental axioms and consequent theorems of interoperability, to form the foundation for establishment of Enterprise Interoperability as a new and self-standing science.

## Knowledge Sources

A Science Base for EI comprises a new set of concepts, theories and principles derived from established and emerging sciences, with a view to long-term problem-solving, as opposed to short-term solution provisioning. In order to effectively capture the work already undertaken in the domain, the state of the art as reported in (Popplewell et al., 2012) has subsequently been classified to recognize categories of knowledge (e.g. concepts, methods, tools, etc.).

(Popplewell et al., 2012) also identifies a set of 12 scientific areas related to Enterprise Interoperability. Extensive and deep "knowledge mining" performed in relation to the requirements of interoperability within these 12 scientific areas identifies a list of macro-issues that can be considered coincident with the sub-areas. Even a rapid analysis of the documents referenced there reveals a large number of initiatives and studies in each sub-area with a heavy prevalence of "local" analyses, hypotheses, experiments, while attempts at holistic views and syntheses are less popular.

The issues of EISB knowledge sources are explored fully elsewhere in this book.

## A First Proposal for an EISB Structure

Initial work based on the objectives, requirements and pre-existing knowledge discussed earlier led to the proposal of the initial structure for an EISB, destined to be the basis of further consultation within the Enterprise Interoperability constituency

We considered that the content of a science base for a science like Enterprise Interoperability may therefore consist of the following categories of knowledge:

- **Formalization of the Problem space:** A taxonomy of the spectrum of application and theoretical problems addressed by the domain, organized so as to be used to characterize real applications and to link these to elements of the solution space.

- **Formalization of the Solution space:** The converse of the problem space, as it provides a taxonomy of knowledge available for the solution of domain application problems. In turn this links to methodologies and tools in the domain knowledge base.

- **Enterprise Interoperability Knowledge Base:** The domain knowledge base contains both structuring and methodological knowledge. The former defines the structure of the domain as perceived by the Enterprise Interoperability constituency:
  - A taxonomy of topics within the domain knowledge;
  - The scientific principles which provide the foundation of knowledge in the domain, and of both future research and application;
  - Relationships between these topics, the problem space and the solution space;
  - Relationships between domain knowledge and knowledge embedded in related scientific domains.

The main components of this structure for Enterprise Interoperability are discussed hereafter. In the context of Enterprise Interoperability, structural knowledge is likely to consist of appropriate taxonomies and frameworks supporting understanding of the overall content and the relationships between Problem and Solution Spaces.

Methodological knowledge maintains understanding of how problems (both in research and application) may be addressed in the domain, and is based on both formal frameworks and processes, and on experience of domain stakeholders both individually and as a constituency. Typically this might contain, in this context, formal models, solution algorithms, simulation tools and assessment tools. However structural knowledge must

also provide understanding of how to combine methodologies to solve more complex problems, or inter-related problems.

In order to support the enterprise application of domain knowledge, the knowledge base should also embrace the knowledge of how application will impact on the enterprise. This, in the case of Enterprise Interoperability includes for example value scenarios and business models surrounding applications, based on both assessment and analysis (using the previously mentioned methodologies and tools), and on experience of real implementations.

Enterprise Interoperability is universally acknowledged to be an interdisciplinary domain, and as such interacts closely with other domains, as described in relation to neighbouring scientific domains hereafter. Understanding of the relationships with other domains, the contributions to be drawn from their respective science bases, and the necessary references to content, expertise and training, is therefore also a significant part of the Enterprise Interoperability Knowledge Base.

Figure 1 shows the summary of proposed content of the Enterprise Interoperability Science Base. The main components described previously are shown in the central area, whilst inputs to the Problem Space arise from applications requirements. Knowledge and experience of application derive from application, which provides knowledge in all three components. Another major contributor to the Knowledge Base comes from the research community. The objectives of the Science Base are summarized on the right of the figure as outputs derived from the Science Base, thus providing the rationale for its development and maintenance.

## The EISB Knowledge Base

Knowledge is distinct from both data and information: data can exist in multiple ways, independently of being usable or not. In the raw format, it does not have meaning in and of itself. However, information is data that has been given meaning by

*Figure 1. Initial view of enterprise interoperability science base structure and content*

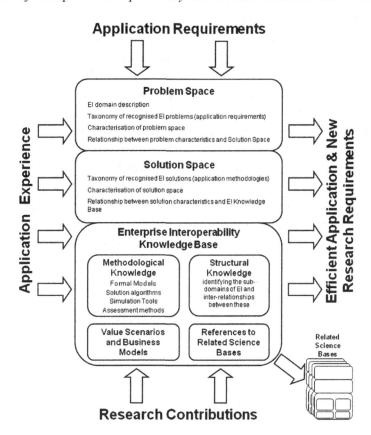

way of relational connection to a context (Breiter & Light, 2004). Nevertheless in information, this "meaning" can be useful for some, but not necessarily to all. It embodies the understanding of a relationship of some sort, possibly cause and effect, thus, people might "memorize" information (as less-aspiring students often do). Nevertheless, they would still be unable to understand it since they require a cognitive and analytical ability, i.e. knowledge (Bellinger, Castro, & Mills, 2004).

In this context, Nonaka et al. (Nonaka, Konno, & Toyama, 2001) define two kinds of knowledge:

- **Tacit:** That people carry in their minds, and which provides context for people, places, ideas, and experiences;
- **Explicit:** That has been or can be articulated, codified, and stored in certain media such as an OWL ontology.

In an ideal EI framework with semantic concerns, both should be addressed and processed to achieve more advanced stages of knowledge, such as understanding and wisdom (Bellinger, Castro, & Mills, 2004), (Syed & Shah, n.d.). The major research challenge nowadays is to gather the tacit knowledge domain stakeholders hold, in interpretable knowledge bases, thus transforming it to explicit knowledge stored in a structured organized way. To achieve this purpose, literature suggests the use of knowledge representation technologies such as dictionaries (domain, technical and natural language), glossaries, taxonomies, thesaurus and also ontologies, to build sustainable knowledge bases (Jardim-Goncalves, Sarraipa, Agostinho, & Panetto, 2009).

For the EISB formulation, explicit knowledge is proposed to be handled by a reference ontology. This establishes a common language for sharing and reusing knowledge about phenomena in a particular domain, i.e. Enterprise Interoperability in our case. An ontology is an agreed specification of how to describe all the concepts, (objects, people, processes, relationships, transactions, etc.), of a particular domain of interest. Indeed, by defining concepts and relationships used to describe and represent an area of knowledge it provides a common understanding of the same, that before may have had different views and interpretations from the different practitioners (Berners-Lee & Fischetti, 1999), (Guarino & D., 2009), (Gruber, 1995). Following very simple modelling principles, an ontology uses classes, properties and relationships to define a hierarchical view of the world (designated by taxonomy). An ontology is engineered by members of a domain which try to represent a reality as a set of agreed upon terms and logically-founded constraints on their use (Mika, 2005).

This reference ontology forms the EISB knowledge front-end, enabling terminology sharing and interoperability terms, problems, solutions and experts cross-referencing. Since normally ontology building is a long process, and involves gathering human knowledge from many experts, ENSEMBLE proposes a four-step methodology as described in Figure 2.

This methodology is based on MENTOR - Methodology for Enterprise Reference Ontology Development, by Sarraipa et al. (Sarraipa, Jardim-Goncalves, & Steiger-Garcao, 2010), which is a collaborative methodology developed for helping a group of people, or enterprises, sharing their knowledge with others from the same domains. MENTOR is also used for ontology harmonization. However those steps are omitted from ontology building, since this is the first ontology for the EISB.

*Figure 2. Methodology for EISB ontology building*

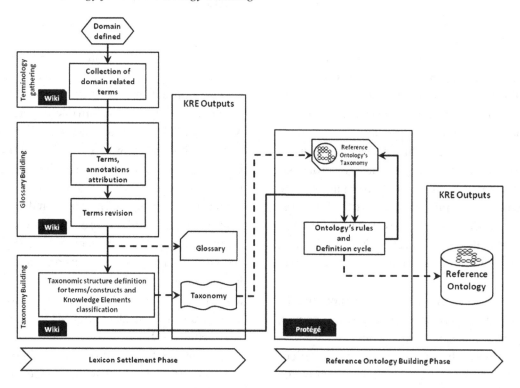

Therefore, the proposed methodology is divided on 2 phases including in total four steps, as follows:

- **Lexicon Settlement:** knowledge acquisition as a collection of terms and related definitions from all participants. This phase is divided into three steps:
  - **Terminology Gathering:** The first step is a very simple one, and represents knowledge gathering from all participants in Enterprise Interoperability constituency, in the form of a list of EI terms. This step used a Wiki as a supporting tool for the elicitation of terms and concepts.
  - **Glossary Building:** A glossary is built after a series of discussions about the terms that every participant contributed to the network on the previous step. These discussions are also supported with the Wiki tool, with all participants being able to assign definitions for the terms, moderated by an administrator deciding which are valid and compose the glossary.
  - **Glossary Building:** The final step of this phase is composed of a cycle where the Enterprise Interoperability knowledge experts define a taxonomic structure with the glossary terms. If there is an agreement in both structure and classified terms, the taxonomy is defined and we have the backbone on the EISB ontology.
- **Reference Ontology Building:** This is the phase where the reference ontology is actually built, and unlike the first phase, has only one step. Using a Protégé[1] based environment, and based on acquisition of the taxonomic backbone structure created in the previous phase, a discussion and voting process about the reference ontology rules

takes place with experts in the Enterprise Interoperability constituency, so as to enable inference/reasoning mechanisms. This process may result in the iterative update of the taxonomy and/or classification which therefore needs to be reflected as well in the Wiki. If the backbone is kept harmonized at all times, the contents collection for the ontology knowledge base can be done automatically from the EISB Wiki

## EISB Knowledge Representation Elements (KREs)

As evidenced before, the goal of the EISB knowledge base is to gather the tacit knowledge that Enterprise Interoperability experts hold into machine interpretable knowledge bases. To reach that objective, the EISB reference ontology embraces terms and concepts classification related to its Enterprise Interoperability properties, with the EISB Lexicon, which in turn embodies the reference concepts and semantics. This leads to a knowledge architecture definition where the integrated knowledge is composed by three Knowledge Representation Elements (KREs): the EISB Ontology, the EISB Taxonomy, and the EISB Glossary (Figure 3).

For a good explicit knowledge representation, it is necessary to have significant input from the tacit source (i.e., domain experts). This requires a knowledge architecture enabling the management of the evolution between the KREs:

- **Lexicon Establishment:** The evolution of the first two KREs leads to the EISB Lexicon establishment. This is an abstract KRE because it does not have a physical representation by itself. In this case we can say that the Wiki will act as the knowledge environment for the lexicon;
- **EISB Explicit Knowledge:** Is another abstract KRE since it is composed by the ad-

*Figure 3. EISB knowledge architecture*

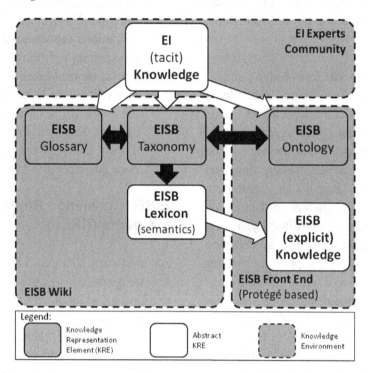

dition of the lexicon to the ontology. The EISB explicit knowledge represents all the EI machine interpretable knowledge and can be interfaced by Web front-end.

The Glossary KRE is a list (mostly in alphabetic order) of specialized terms, sometimes unique to a specific subject. Each term is supported by its corresponding description, and the glossary includes descriptive comments and explanatory notes, such as definitions, synonyms, references, etc.. A glossary can be used when communicating information in order to unify knowledge sharing. It is understood as a set of terms and their definitions, and is bound to the source document or domain where these definitions are set. The EISB glossary is the output of the first and second steps of the methodology for EISB ontology building.

A Taxonomy KRE is a classification system that categorizes all the information in a class/ subclass relationship, representing a simple tree structure. At the top of this structure is a single

classification, the root node that applies to all objects. The root node represents the most general category of all things that the domain is related to. Nodes below this root are more specific classifications that apply to subsets of the total set of classified objects (Malone, 1988). The EISB taxonomy is the output of the third step of the methodology for EISB ontology building.

The Ontology KRE uses the Taxonomy as the basis for the collaborative construction of an EISB reference ontology. An ontology is an explicit specification of a conceptualization (Gruber, 1993), and so ontologies provide a basis for expressing and structuring the knowledge of an organization. They are used to standardize terminologies, classify different concepts, map requirements, and organize them systematically thus facilitating integration of systems (Edgington, Choi, Henson, Raghu, & Vinze, 2004), (Gruber, 1995), (Kitamura, Kashiwase, Fuse, & Mizoguchi, 2004), (Ramaprasad & Prakash, 2009).

Ontologies are related to but different from taxonomies, typologies, concept hierarchies, thesauri, and dictionaries (Gilchrist, 2003). They are tools for systematizing the description of complex systems, which in turn, facilitate in the formalization of the EISB, the output of the final step of the methodology for EISB ontology building.

As stated before, the main purpose of the existence of the EISB is to identify, classify, and conduct a deeper research in the major issues of Enterprise Interoperability with a view to the scientific establishment of a well-defined corpus of material that will act as the fundamental Enterprise Interoperability knowledge. This material will play a very important role not only in the future evolution of the domain of Enterprise Interoperability, but will also support the restructuring of the domain, based on a more scientific approach, clearing out any current inconsistencies and promoting a common understanding amongst all stakeholders.

## Enterprise Interoperability Structural Knowledge

An understanding of knowledge structure is essential to achieving a maintainable and useable knowledge base, since without this, search and recognition of relevant knowledge becomes ineffective and inconclusive. This in turn means that addition and amendment of knowledge cannot be accomplished without risk of duplication, or even contradiction, of pre-existing content. Similarly there can be no confidence that retrieved knowledge is complete, or most relevant to current need. The structure of knowledge in the Enterprise Interoperability Science Base knowledge base is therefore a necessary component of that knowledge base, available to all users. The issues of Enterprise Interoperability Science Base structural knowledge are discussed in detail elsewhere in this book.

## Knowledge from Neighbouring Sciences

No science exists in isolation, and in the Enterprise Interoperability domain, explicitly focusing on interoperability of applications used and developed across a broad technological and disciplinary spectrum, it is not surprising to find that both problems and solutions in Enterprise Interoperability coincide with those of other domains. The structure of the Science base for Enterprise Interoperability therefore explicitly embraces references to knowledge available from such neighbouring domains, directing users to this knowledge where it is relevant to application, and allowing minimization of knowledge and research duplication between the Enterprise Interoperability Science Base and neighbouring domain results already published. These issues too are explored full elsewhere in this book.

## An Evolving Enterprise Interoperability Science Base

To maintain currency the Enterprise Interoperability Science Base must evolve as new knowledge is realized through both research and application. Indeed in the early stages of this evolution, it is necessary to manage an accelerated evolution to ensure that existing Enterprise Interoperability knowledge generated over some 15 years of recognized domain research preceded by perhaps 20 years of pragmatic approaches to the solution of emerging problems of enterprise interoperability.

Within the initial definition of a science base as presented previously and detailed fully in (Popplewell et al., 2012) and (Agostinho et al., 2012), the overall objective in creation of an EISB is to formulate and structure the knowledge gained through pragmatic research in the domain over this period. This establishes that there is indeed a coherent and specific body of scientific knowledge and understanding attributable to that research, and renders it accessible to both future researchers aiming to build on existing knowledge, and to those wishing to use in industrial applications. Without such an EISB there is danger of repeating research, and missing opportunities for application.

At the outset little information was still available on the concept of a science base itself and the elements that would be part of the EISB. Nevertheless the work was framed through the definition of: a problem space that would address the range of application and theoretical problems addressed by the EI domain; a solution space, covering the knowledge available for the solution of EI application problems; and a domain knowledge base that would contain the effective structure and methodological knowledge of the EISB (see Figure 1), all together enabling the acquisition of inputs from practical experience, requirements, research contributions, and producing efficient EISB applications and new research requirements.

Subsequently, through consultation and dialogue with the Enterprise Interoperability constituency, the framework has been further specified, effectively establishing inputs, outputs and supporting elements.

EISB Supporting Elements include:

- **EISB Scientific Areas:** As described earlier.
- **EISB Knowledge Base:** Specifies the relationships and encloses all science base and EI knowledge using precise and semantically meaningful definitions.

EISB Inputs include:

- **Existing EI Methods and Tools:** Are one of the principal inputs for the EISB framework, being part of the solution elements (from proof-of-concept to tools and possible standards), and also highlighting current outstanding needs for a sound scientific framework (problems). It is indubitable

that technology's evolution is accelerating, so the development of new methods of tools must become seamless and comply with the interoperability demands expressed by industry.

- **Existing EI Research Results:** Provide perhaps a more theoretical input explored in some detail in (Popplewell et al., 2012) which includes an extensive analysis on research being developed for each of the EISB Scientific Areas.
- **Neighbouring Domains Methods:** Contribute equally to the problem and solution space, providing formal methods that can be used in the specification of EI problems, and also provide new insights of possible solutions already being addressed within other communities.
- **Enterprise Interoperability Constituency:** Whilst not exactly an input so much as a source of inputs providing contributions in each of the previous elements.

EISB Outputs include:

- **EISB Hypotheses/Laws:** That should be concrete rather than generic, having a specific time horizon and be challenging in order to be tested in forthcoming experiments in which the community will contradict or verify these.
- **EISB Assessment Framework:** A utility that enables measurement of the interoperability level of enterprise systems and applications. With this framework, enterprises will become able to recognize their specific interoperability problems.
- **EISB Supporting Tools:** Which together with the assessment framework, form a toolbox that should be developed and deployed in order to facilitate the verification, the applicability and the expansion of the EISB developments, facilitating the usage of the EISB knowledge base.

- **Problem-Solution Paths:** Which relate in a comprehensible manner the problem and solution spaces, proposing either industrial or research paths to address specific EI problems.
- **Open Research Issues:** As reflected in the FInES Research Roadmap (Missikoff, Charabilidis, Goncalves, & Popplewell, 2012).

## POTENTIAL BENEFITS TO ENTERPRISE INTEROPERABILITY DOMAIN STAKEHOLDERS

Enterprise Interoperability is quintessentially an applied research domain, and therefore must address the needs of a set of stakeholders which includes not only researchers and other research-related entities, but also those whose interest is in application of results. In developing a Science Base for Enterprise Interoperability the potential benefits to categories of stakeholder have been considered.

### Industrial End-Users

The primary interest of industrial end-users of Enterprise Interoperability knowledge is in the rapid resolution of interoperability problems as they arise during the process of commissioning of heterogeneous systems, either with an enterprise or across collaborating enterprises. In this context we see the primary benefit of the Enterprise Interoperability Science Base as forming the basis of rapid and conclusive search for methodologies and supporting interoperability tools which address as closely as possible recognized needs. This can be achieved through application of the EISB problem space to characterize interoperability needs, together with a mapping into the solution space. Furthermore access to and application of standards knowledge provided through the Enterprise

Interoperability Science Base Knowledge Base potentially reduces the incidence of interoperability problems in the first place.

### Interoperability Consultants

End-users from time to time engage the services of consultants in resolution of interoperability problems, usually in the context of a broader systems consultancy. Clearly in this case the benefits available directly to the consultancy, and by implication to the end-user as well, are exactly the same as for the industrial end-user as described earlier.

Additionally, by contributing to the case study content of the Enterprise Interoperability Science Base consultants can effectively market their specific competence in the domain.

### ICT Vendors

ICT vendors are motivated to take interest in interoperability issues in a number of different ways. Just as for the consultants, there is an opportunity to expose to the market competences in the interoperability domain, and beyond this, more direct benefits apply.

Increasingly ICT vendors recognize the market advantage in their software products being capable of use in conjunction with existing legacy systems, or even with other vendors' products to be installed alongside their own. To realize this market advantage it is necessary to design (or where necessary re-engineer) products to facilitate interoperability. The Enterprise Interoperability Science Base provides a "one stop shop" of current domain knowledge, structured for effective search, and so facilitates selection of methodologies and approaches to software design for interoperability. Furthermore, standards knowledge can provide an industry wide accepted approach to interoperability in some application domains.

ICT vendors are also engaged, on occasion, to develop solutions to resolve interoperability problems between existing systems. Here the same considerations arise as for end-users, facilitating solution selection and implementation.

Finally, there remain a number of ICT vendor enterprises who see market advantage in ensuring that there products are interoperable only with one another, and thereby eliminating potential for competition. Whilst such a cynical approach may be undesirable, the Enterprise Interoperability Science Base undeniably offers benefit to such vendors by exposing the capabilities realized by the current state of the art: products may then be engineered to be invulnerable to these capabilities, and indeed reference to the EISB could suggest ways of copyrighting (and then refusing to license) methods that may provide interoperability with their own systems.

## Researchers

Researchers gain clear benefit from access to a single authoritative source of the state of the art of enterprise interoperability, in generating a sound base for future research exploiting previous results, and ensuring that planned research does not duplicate earlier work. Further benefits include of course the exposure of research results through the Enterprise Interoperability Science Base, leading to wider application and opportunities for future research.

## Neighbouring Sciences

Researchers in neighbouring domains have the opportunity to benefit in the same way as Enterprise Interoperability researchers, through EISB access to state of the art knowledge. Whilst this may arise on the margins of a neighbouring science, the use of discipline-crossing methods is well established across sciences, and is facilitated by both providing access to available, proven and applicable solutions, and reducing the risk of research duplication.

## Research Sponsors

Research funding agencies require exhaustive demonstration of the relationship between proposed research and existing state of the art, to avoid duplication and minimize research costs. Whilst the bulk of work on this is done by the proposer, it is incumbent on the sponsoring agency to verify the originality and cost-effectiveness of the proposed work, usually at the expense of engaging expert reviewers. The existence of a recognized current and exhaustive domain knowledge base simplifies this task considerably, at the same time as enhancing its reliability.

## CONCLUSION

We conclude that it is both desirable and possible to construct an EISB to meet the objectives discussed earlier. Whilst many scientific domains have followed a similar path from pragmatic solution of immediate problems, to the establishment of a recognizable corpus of knowledge and interests it is not clear that in any of these cases deliberate attempt has been made to define the domain science base. Rather this has become accepted through custom and practice.

The drivers for this to be attempted as a specific intellectual and philosophical exercise in the case of Enterprise Interoperability arose from several pressures, discussed earlier, and have resulted in the definition of an accepted (within the domain) structure for a science base. This opportunity to take advantage of the crowd-sourcing and consultation capabilities available to the Enterprise Interoperability constituency through recent developments in Internet technology has been exploited, and the need of research funding bodies, as well as industry, to be able to access and assess availably domain knowledge has provided some of the motivation.

The result is an EISB structure together with definition of the tools needed to populate and drive its evolution. The sustainability of the science base is therefore technically achievable, but it remains to be seen whether policy and funding pressures support the Enterprise Interoperability constituency in making full use of the opportunity so presented.

# REFERENCES

Agostinho, C., Goncalves, R., Sarraipa, J., Koussouris, S., Mouzakitis, S., Lampathaki, F., & Assogna, P. (2012). *EISB basic elements report.* Brussels: European Commission.

Agostinho, C., Jardim-Goncalves, R., & Steiger-Garcao, A. (2011). Using neighboring domains towards setting the foundations for enterprise interoperability science. In *Proceedings of International Symposium on Collaborative Enterprises (CENT 2011).* Orlando, FL: CENT.

*Airbus.* (2013). Retrieved 03 27, 2013, from http://en.wikipedia.org/wiki/Airbus

Axelrod, R. (1997). *The complexity of cooperation: Agent-based models of competition and collaboration.* Princeton, NJ: Princeton University Press.

Bellinger, G., Castro, D., & Mills, A. (2004). *Data, information, knowledge, and wisdom.* Retrieved 3 25, 2013, from http://www.systems-thinking.org/dikw/dikw.htm

Berners-Lee, T., & Fischetti, M. (1999). *Weaving the web: The original design and ultimate destiny of the world wide web by its inventor.* San Francisco: HapperOne.

Breiter, A., & Light, D. (2004). Decision support systems in schools – From data collection to decision making. In *Proceedings of AMCIS 2004 - Tenth Americas Conference on Information Systems.* New York: AMCIS.

Charalabidis, Y., Jardim-Gonçalves, R., & Popplewell, K. (2010). Developing a science base for enterprise interoperability. In *Enterprise interoperability IV: Making the internet of the future for the future of enterprise* (pp. 245–254). Berlin: Springer. doi:10.1007/978-1-84996-257-5_23

DODD. (1977). *Standardization and interoperability of weapon systems and equipment within the north Atlantic treaty organization.* DODD.

Dodig-Crnkovic, C. (2002). Scientific methods in computer science. In *Proceedings of the Conference for the Promotion of Research in IT at New Universities and at University Colleges in Sweden* (pp. 126–130). Retrieved from http://www.mrt

Doumeingts, G., & Chen, D. (2013). Interoperability development for enterprise applications and software. In P. Cunningham, M. Cunningham, & P. Fatelnig (Eds.), *Building the knowledge economy: Issues, applications, case studies.* Amsterdam: IOS Press.

Edgington, T., Choi, B., Henson, K., Raghu, T. S., & Vinze, A. (2004). Adopting ontology to facilitate knowledge sharing. *Communictions of the Association for Computing Machinery, 47,* 85–90. doi:10.1145/1029496.1029499

*ENSEMBLE.* (2012). Retrieved 03 27, 2013, from http://www.fines-cluster.eu/fines/jm/FInES-Private-Information/ensemble.html

Figay, N., Steiger-Garcao, A., & Jardim-Goncalves, R. (2006). Enabling interoperability of STEP application protocols at meta-data and knowledge level. *International Journal of Technology Management,* 402–421.

FInES Cluster. (2013). *FInES wiki main page.* Retrieved 03 26, 2013, from http://www.fines-cluster.eu/fines/mw/index.php/Main_Page

*FInES Cluster.* (2013). Retrieved 03 27, 2013, from http://www.fines-cluster.eu

Friedman, A. L., & Peters, T. (2006). Make me a perfect match: Understanding transplant compatibility. *RENALIFE, 21*(5).

Galtuno, J. (1967). *Theory and methods of social research*. New York: Allen and Unwin.

Gharajedaghi, J. (2005). *Systems thinking: Managing chaos and complexity: A platform for designing business architecture*. London: Butterworth-Heinemann.

Gilchrist, A. (2003). Thesauri, taxonomies and ontologies - An etymological note. *The Journal of Documentation, 59*, 7–18. doi:10.1108/00220410310457984

Gordon, J. (2002). *Can sociologists study society in the same way that scientists study the natural world?* Retrieved 03 27, 2013, from http://www.jakeg.co.uk/essays/science.htm

Gruber, T. R. (1993). A translation approach to portable ontology specifications. *Journal of Knowledge Acquisition, 5*(2), 199–220. doi:10.1006/knac.1993.1008

Gruber, T. R. (1995). Toward principles for the design of ontologies used for knowledge sharing. *International Journal of Human-Computer Studies, 43*(5-6), 907–928. doi:10.1006/ijhc.1995.1081

Guarino, N., & D., O. (2009). What is an ontology?. In S. Staab & R. Studer (Eds.), *Handbook on ontologies*. International Handbooks on Information Systems.

Hughes, B., Schmidt, D., & Smith, A. (2006). Towards interoperable secondary annotations in the e-social science domain. In *Proceedings of 2nd International Conference on E-Social Science*. Manchester, UK: E-Social Science.

Hughes, J. (1980). *The philosophy of social research*. London: Longman.

IDABC. (2008). *European interoperability framework draft version 2.0*. IDABC.

*Informal Study Group on Value Proposition*. (2008). Retrieved 03 27, 2013, from http://cordis.europa.eu/fp7/ict/enet/ei-isg_en.html

Jardim-Goncalves, R., Grilo, R., Agostinho, C., Lampathaki, F., & Charalabidis, Y. (2012). *Systematisation of interoperability body of knowledge: The foundation for EI as a science*. Enterprise Information Systems.

Jardim-Goncalves, R., Sarraipa, J., Agostinho, C., & Panetto, H. (2009). Knowledge framework for intelligent manufacturing systems. *Journal of Intelligent Manufacturing*. doi: doi:10.1007/s10845-009-0332-4

Jardim-Goncalves, R., & Steiger-Garcao, A. (2002). Implicit multilevel modelling in flexible business environments. *Communications of the ACM*, 53–57.

Jardim-Goncalves, R., & Steiger-Garcao, A. (2009). *Rowards EI as a science: Considerations and points of view*. Unpublished.

Key, J. J., Boyle, M., & Francis, G. (1999). An ecosystem approach for sustainability: Addressing the challenge of complexity. *Futures, 31*(721).

Kitamura, Y., Kashiwase, M., Fuse, M., & Mizoguchi, R. (2004). Deployment of an ontological framework of functional design knowledge. *Ontology and It's Applications to Knowledge-Intensive Engineering, 18*, 115–127.

Li, M.-S., Cabral, R., Doumeingts, G., & Popplewell, K. (2006). *Enterprise interoperability: A concerted research roadmap for shaping business networking in the knowledge-based economy*. Brussels: Commission for the European Communities.

Malone, J. (1988). *The science of linguistics in the art of translation: Some tools from linguistics for the analysis and practice of translation*. Unpublished.

Mika, P. (2005). Ontologies are us: A unified model of social networks and semantics. *International Semantic Web Conference, 3729*, 552-536.

Missikoff, M., Charabilidis, Y., Goncalves, R., & Popplewell, K. (2012). *FInES research roadmap 2025-v3.0.* Retrieved 3 22, 2013, from http://www.fines-cluster.eu/fines/jm/Publications/Download-document/323-FInES-Research-Roadmap-2025-v3.0.html

Nichols, G., & Prigogine, I. (1989). *Exploring complexity: An introduction.* New York: W.H. Freeman & Company.

Nonaka, I., Konno, N., & Toyama, R. (2001). Emergence of Ba. In I. Nonaka, & T. Nishiguchi (Eds.), *Knowledge emergence: Social, technical, and evolutionary dimensions of knowledge creation* (pp. 13–29). Oxford, UK: Oxford University Press.

Popper, K. (1992). *Conjectures and refutations: The growth of scientific knowledge* (5th ed.). London: Routledge and Keagan Paul.

Popplewell, K., Lampathaki, F., Koussiris, S., Mouzakitis, S., Charalabidis, Y., Goncalves, R., & Agostino, C. (2012). *EISB state of play report.* Brussels: European Commission.

*Proof of Concept.* (n.d.). Retrieved from http://en.wikipedia.org/wiki/Proof_of_concept

Ramaprasad, A., & Prakash, A. (2009). Fostering knowledge sharing in project management. In *Proceedings of the 42nd Hawaii International Conference on System Sciences (HICSS-42).* IEEE.

*Research Areas.* (n.d.). Retrieved 03 27, 2013, from http://www.esf.org/research-areas.html

Sarraipa, J., Jardim-Goncalves, R., & Steiger-Garcao, A. (2010). MENTOR: An enabler for interoperable intelligent systems. *International Journal of General Systems, 39*(5), 557–573. doi:10.1080/03081079.2010.484278

Scholl, H. J., & Klischewsky, R. (2007). E-government integration and interoperability: Framing the research agenda. *International Journal of Public Administration, 30*(8), 889–920. doi:10.1080/01900690701402668

Schrage, M. (2009, February 6). Interoperability: The great enabler. *Financial Times.*

*Scientific Method.* (2010). Retrieved 03 27, 2013, from www.merriam-webster.com/dictionary/scientific%20method

*Scientific Method.* (2013). Retrieved 2013, from http://en.wikipedia.org/wiki/Scientific_method

Shaw, M., & Clements, P. (2006). The golden age of software architecure. *IEEE Software.* doi:10.1109/MS.2006.58

Sriram, R. D., & Fenves, S. J. (2009). A life-saving role: Health care information systems are essential medicine. *Industrial Engineer Magazine,* 34-39.

Steiger-Garcao, A., Jardim-Goncalves, R., & Farinha, F. (2007). An open platform for interoperability of civil engineering enterprises. *Advances in Engineering Software.*

Sugihara, G., & May, R. M. (1990). (n.d.). Nonlinear forecasting as a way of distinguishing chaos from measurement error in time series. *Nature, 344*(734). PMID:2330029

Sullivan, A., & Sheffrin, S. (2003). *Economics: Principles in action.* Upper Saddle River, NJ: Pearson Prentice Hall.

Syed, A., & Shah, A. (n.d.). Data, information, knowledge, wisdom: A doubly linked chain? In *Proceedings of the 101st International Conference on Information and Knowledge Engineering.* IEEE.

*Technical Standard.* (n.d.). Retrieved from http://en.wikipedia.org/wiki/Technical_standard

West, D. M. (2011). *Enabling personalized medicine through health information technology: Advancing the integration of information.* Washington, DC: The Brookings Institution. Retrieved from www.brookings.edu/governance.aspx

Wilson, E. (1999). *Consilience: The unity of knowledge.* New York: Vintage.

Wolfs, S. (2010). *Introduction to the scientific method.* Retrieved 05 2010, from http://teacher.pas.rochester.edu/phy_labs/appendixe/appendixe.html

Wycisk, C., McKelvey, B., & Hulsmann, M. (2008). Smart parts: Supply networks as complex adaptive systems: Analysis and implications. *International Journal of Physical Distribution & Logistics Management, 38*(2), 108–125. doi:10.1108/09600030810861198

## ADDITIONAL READING

Anicic, N., & Ivezic, N. (2005). Semantic web technologies for enterprise application integration. *Computer Science and Information Systems, 2*(1), 119–144. doi:10.2298/CSIS0501119A

Berners-Lee, T., Hall, W., Hendler, J., O'Hara, K., Shadbolt, N., & Weitzner, D. (2006). A framework for web science. *Foundations and Trends in Web Science, 1*(1), 1–130. doi:10.1561/1800000001

Berners-Lee, T., Hendler, J., & Lassila, O. (2001). The Semantic Web. Scientific American magazine.

Bernus, P., Mertins, K., & Schmidt, G. (1998). *International handbook on information systems.* Berlin: Springer.

Berre, A., Elvesæter, B., Figay, N., Guglielmina, C., & Johnsen, S. karlsen, D., Lippe, S. (2007). The ATHENA Interoperability Framework. The ATHENA Interoperability Framework (pp. 569-580).

Charalabidis, Y., Jardim Gonçalves, R., & Popplewell, K. (2010). Towards a Scientific Foundation for Interoperability. In *Interoperability in Digital Public Services and Administration.* Bridging E-Government and E-Business. doi:10.4018/978-1-61520-887-6.ch019

Chen, D. (2003). European initiatives to develop interoperability of enterprise applications–basic concepts, framework and roadmap. *Annual Reviews in Control, 27*(2), 153–162. doi:10.1016/j.arcontrol.2003.09.001

Chen, D., Doumeingts, G., & Vernadat, F. (2008). Architectures for enterprise integration and interoperability: Past, present and future. *Computers in Industry, 59*(7), 647–659. doi:10.1016/j.compind.2007.12.016

Griffith, T. (2001). *The Physics of Everyday Phenomena: A Conceptual Introduction to Physics.* New York: McGraw-Hill Higher Education.

Panetto, H. (2007). Towards a Classification framework for interoperability of enterprise applications. International Journal of Computer Integrated manufacture, 20(8), 727-740.

Spohrer, J., Maglio, P., Bailey, J., & Gruhl, D. (2007). Steps Toward a Science of Service Systems. *IEEE Computer, 40*(1), 71–77. doi:10.1109/MC.2007.33

## KEY TERMS AND DEFINITIONS

**Enterprise Interoperability:** The ability of an enterprise to interact other organizations, to exchange information and to use the information that has been exchanged.

**Enterprise Interoperability Knowledge Base:** The domain knowledge base contains both structuring and methodological knowledge.

**Methodological Knowledge:** Maintains understanding of how problems (both in research and application) may be addressed in the domain.

**Problem Space:** A taxonomy of the spectrum of application and theoretical problems addressed by the domain, organized so as to be used to characterize real applications and to link these to elements of the solution space.

**Science Base:** A structured, ordered, and semantically searchable body of knowledge defining the underlying principles and applications of a scientific domain, together with its relationship with knowledge arising from other, related domains.

**Solution Space:** The converse of the problem space, as it provides a taxonomy of knowledge available for the solution of domain application problems. In turn this links to methodologies and tools in the domain knowledge base.

**Structuring Knowledge:** Defines the structure of the domain as perceived by the Enterprise Interoperability constituency.

## ENDNOTES

[1]     http://protege.stanford.edu/

# Chapter 2
# A Taxonomy of Scientific Areas Driving Assessment of Organisations Readiness

**Sotirios Koussouris**
*National Technical University of Athens, Greece*

**Spiros Mouzakitis**
*National Technical University of Athens, Greece*

**Fenareti Lampathaki**
*National Technical University of Athens, Greece*

## ABSTRACT

*Enterprise Interoperability is one of the most crucial research domains of the modern information age, as it is directly linked with the competitiveness of enterprises as it defines at a large extent the ability of an enterprise to take advantage of the productivity gains offered by the ICT solutions available. However, although various solutions and best practises are emerging on a daily basis, it is the fragmented analysis of the domain that restrains the birth of holistic solutions that will provide the needed leverage to enterprises. Motivated by this situation, this chapter provides an analysis of the different scientific areas that can be found under the Enterprise Interoperability landscape and proposes an assessment framework which may support the identification of the current interoperability profile of an organisation while it reveals various solution paths that could be developed in order to gradually improve the interoperability status of the latter.*

## INTRODUCTION

Today an enterprise's competitiveness is to a large extent determined by its ability to seamlessly interoperate with others. The advantage of one enterprise over another stems from the way it manages its process of innovation. Enterprise Interoperability has therefore become an important area of research to ensure the competitiveness and growth of European enterprises.

Research has significantly advanced the field of Enterprise Interoperability in a number of areas over the past few years. Nowadays, this is a well-established applied research area, studying

DOI: 10.4018/978-1-4666-5142-5.ch002

the problems related with the lack of interoperability in the organisations, and proposing novel methods and frameworks to contribute with innovative solutions for Enterprise Interoperability problems. Pragmatically, in spite of the research developed so far, nowadays we are still missing concrete results regarding the laying of the scientific foundations of Enterprise Interoperability. This is a deficit recognised by the Enterprise Interoperability research community, disabling the generalisation and complete reuse of the methods and tools that have been developed (ENSEMBLE Support Action, 2010).

This chapter is organised as follows: the upcoming section provides a short background on the need for Enterprise Interoperability while the following section provides an analysis of the Enterprise Interoperability and a decomposition of the domain to its main ingredients which are titled as "Scientific Areas" (SA). Moving on, an Assessment Framework is presented which maps the different Scientific Areas to the readiness of each organisation and this section is complemented with three use cases which provide examples on how such an approach may support organisations to improve their interoperability profile. Finally, future research directions are presented and the conclusions of this chapter are presented.

## BACKGROUND

Interoperability is defined as "the ability of systems, units, or forces to provide services to and accept services from other systems, units, or forces and to use the services so exchanged to enable them to operate effectively together" (Cooperstock, 2009). IEEE defines interoperability as "the ability of two or more systems or components to exchange information and to use the information that has been exchanged." Interoperability means the ability of information and communication technology (ICT) systems and of the business processes they support to exchange data and to

enable the sharing of information and knowledge. Through the years, however, interoperability tends to obtain a broader, all-inclusive scope of a repetitive, well organised, and automated at ICT level feature of organisations, as indicated in the definition of the draft EIF 2.0 (European Commission, 2010): "Interoperability is the ability of disparate and diverse organisations to interact towards mutually beneficial and agreed common goals, involving the sharing of information and knowledge between the organisations via the business processes they support, by means of the exchange of data between their respective information and communication technology (ICT) systems" and the Enterprise Interoperability Research Roadmap (Charalabidis, Gionis, Moritz Hermann, & Martinez, 2008) "Interoperability is a utility-like capability that enterprises can invoke on the fly in support of their business activities." In our view, the most appropriate definition introduces Enterprise Interoperability as "the capacity of two or more enterprises, including all the systems within their boundaries and the external systems that they utilise or are affected by, in order to cooperate seamlessly in depth of time for a common objective" (Lampathaki, Koussouris, Mouzakitis, Charalabidis, & Psarras, 2011).

Modern sciences introduce a paradigm shift since, unlike the traditional philosophy of science, they usually do not apply to a single domain, being interdisciplinary and eclectic. They search their methods and raise research questions in broad areas, crossing borders and engineering different scientific fields. For example, the modern computer science embraces formalisms and algorithms created to support particular desired behaviour using concepts from physics, chemistry, biology (Dodig-Crnkovic, 2002), (America Mathematical Society, 2010). Thus, being also a multi-disciplinary domain by nature, the establishment of Enterprise Interoperability scientific base should be developed comprising concepts and theories from related neighbouring sciences and scientific domains (Charalabidis, Jardim Gonçalves, & Popplewell, 2010).

Achieving interoperability requires resolution of issues at various distinct interoperability layers as argued by various authors in the last decade and depicted in Figure 2. As it can be easily deduced from the Interoperability Layers defined in EIF (Technical, Semantic, Organisational, Legal & Political Context Interoperability), there is no consensus reached and often the various layers are interconnected among themselves. The different layers, as currently proposed in the bibliography, define at a high level the necessary stack for interoperable systems, however, their abstraction level hinders researchers and practitioners to really identify problems and provide solutions, as those levels do not only overlap in many cases, but they also hide important low level aspects that deal with technologies and methods that span across all levels. For example, when we talk about data interoperability, semantic interoperability is applied as far as the concepts and their relations are concerned and technical interoperability is also related as far as the syntax and the data exchange is concerned.

## ANALYSIS OF CURRENT ENTERPRISE INTEROPERABILITY CHALLENGES

Dealing with the main challenges of Enterprise Interoperability requires the detailed analysis of the ingredients of the domain which will provide to researchers and practitioners a detailed map of the various issues and their interrelations. Therefore it is essential to identify the structure of Enterprise Interoperability, which can at a second stage be mapped to the four layers adapted by the European Interoperability Framework (EIF), in order to possess a common reference point that is well accepted by the different communities.

In this quest, the initial step one has to take is to focus on the real object of observation, which is the "Enterprise," and then move on to analyse its core components to identify the interoperability needs within them. An Enterprise, as defined in (Sullivan & Sheffrin, 2003) is "...an organisation designed to provide goods, services, or both to consumers." The main ingredients of such a system are the following:

- Infrastructures referring to all the facilities and non-human assets possessed by an enterprise, which are used for their operation. Under infrastructures, software platforms, hardware systems, building facilities, automobiles, etc. can be classified.
- Data used for the business transactions within and outside the boundaries of the enterprise. This includes the documents, application forms, transactional data exchanged by the enterprise.
- Processes including all the related, structured activities or tasks that produce a specific service or product.
- Policies embracing the different rules that are applied either due to external (e.g. legislation, business association rules, etc.) or internal factors (e.g. working hours, dress code, etc.).
- People with all the human resources that are part of an enterprise system.

The approach adopted for formulating an inclusive, yet flexible taxonomy for the Enterprise Interoperability domain, which will facilitate focused and targeted research in the domain, bears the following steps:

1.  Consideration of the terms "Enterprise" and "Business Transaction" and decomposition of the enterprise concept in its major ingredients (e.g. people, assets, processes, knowledge, etc.).
2.  Analysis of the major technologies behind the term "Enterprise 2.0" (like Cloud Computing, Social Networks) and of current

technological trends that are related to the Enterprise world (like Internet of Services, Internet of Things, etc.).

3. Identification of the key Enterprise Interoperability challenges, as documented in the Enterprise Interoperability Research Roadmaps

4. Outline of a set of baseline principles and rules indicating a sufficient body of knowledge for each level (higher levels of abstraction are quite immature and thus include less material)

5. Definition of a common Enterprise Interoperability taxonomy glossary in order to pave the way towards a common understanding of the key underlying terms:

  ○ **Level 1:** Scientific Areas (12 Areas deriving out of the combination of the outcomes/findings of Steps 1 to 4)

  ○ **Level 2:** Scientific Sub-Areas. Each Scientific Area contains 5-15 Scientific Sub-Areas. It needs to be noted that they are rather informally recognised now and will be updated and further elaborated during the waves.

During this step, four different abstraction levels for the Enterprise Interoperability taxonomy have been defined based on the prerequisites they require. Those are presented in Figure 1.

It needs to be noted that the proposed scientific areas aim to promote more focused and concrete research attempts towards the goal of establishing interoperable enterprise systems, as they belong to a smaller abstraction level of that of the four fundamental interoperability layers adapted by EIF. Figure 2 presents the mapping of these scientific areas to the four interoperability layers, showing how those areas span through the different layers.

## The Enterprise Interoperability Scientific Areas Taxonomy

Starting from those core ingredients of an Enterprise, and by analysing the current technological trends and the background knowledge of the domain of Enterprise Interoperability, the first SAs are formulated, which are labelled as the fundamental areas and constitute the 1st abstraction level of EI, as following:

*Figure 1. Enterprise interoperability scientific areas overview*

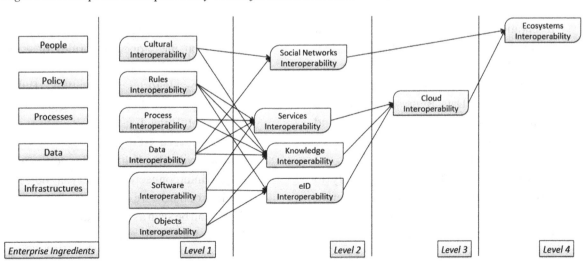

*Figure 2. Enterprise interoperability scientific areas mapping to interoperability layers*

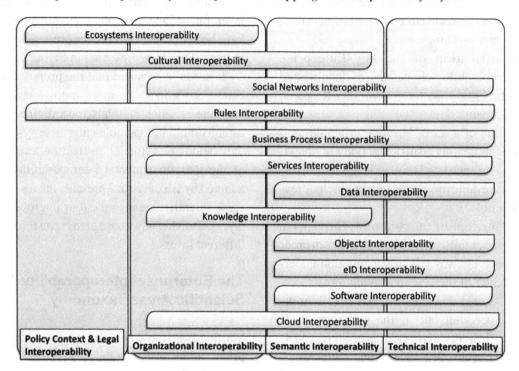

- **Scientific Area 1-Data Interoperability:** Which deals with the ability of data (including documents, multimedia content and digital resources) to be universally accessible, reusable and comprehensible by all transaction parties (in a human-to-machine and machine-to-machine basis), by addressing the lack of common understanding caused by the use of different representations, different purposes, different contexts, and different syntax-dependent approaches. Under this category, the following major sub-categories are identified: Semantic Data Representation, Data Standardisation, Schema Matching, and Data Mediation.

- **Scientific Area 2-Process Interoperability:** Refers to the ability to align and connect processes of different entities (enterprises), in order for them to exchange data and to conduct business in a seamless way. As a scientific area it includes the following sub-areas: Process Modelling, Process Reengineering, Process Standardisation, Process Alignment, Automated Process Execution.

- **Scientific Area 3-Rules Interoperability:** Refers to the ability of entities to align and match their business and legal rules for conducting legitimate automated transactions that are also compatible with the internal business operation rules of each other. Under this category, the following major sub-categories are identified: Rules Modelling, Legislation Homogenisation/ Alignment, Rules Execution.

- **Scientific Area 4-Objects Interoperability:** Which refers to the networked interconnection of everyday objects. Devices or hardware components interoperability can be seen as a particular case of this domain. Under this category, the following major sub-categories are identified: RFID interoperability, Internet-connected objects, Networked media, Factory-of-Things, Smart Objects/Devices.

- **Scientific Area 5-Software Interoperability:** Refers to the ability of an enterprise software application to work with other enterprise software application. Under this category, the following major sub-categories are identified: Component-based software engineering, Service- oriented Architecture (SOA) and Web Services, Software Interoperability Monitoring and Evaluation, Requirements engineering for interoperable enterprises.
- **Scientific Area 6-Cultural Interoperability:** Deals with the degree to which knowledge and information is anchored to a unified model of meaning across cultures. Under this category, the following major sub-categories are identified: Language interoperability, Regional aspects compatibility, Policy Interoperability, Alignment in traditions, religions and ethics.

Those scientific areas, although being the core components and as such the most important areas of Enterprise Interoperability, are however incapable of solving all interoperability related problems, as enterprises are constantly becoming more complex, with disappearing boundaries, loosely coupled architectures and virtual resources. Those changes are very well reflected in the Qualities of Being (QoB) for future enterprises that are pursued by the Grand Objectives of the FInES Roadmap (FInES, 2010), which are the following: Inventive Enterprise, Cloud Enterprise, Cognizant Enterprise, Community-oriented Enterprise, Green Enterprise, Glocal Enterprise.

In the direction of obtaining such qualities, enterprises are restructuring themselves and try to align with new trends they regard as important for their viability, such as the Future Internet. In this direction, the issue of interoperability becomes even more complex, as not only new technologies such as social networks or e-ID are constantly being taken up by enterprises (which have an impact on their overall operation), but also as there is a need for constant and flexible collaboration between all enterprise systems in order to correspond in a timely and effective manner to the requests of the global market.

In order to achieve these transformations and the seamless collaboration, new scientific areas have been developed, which derived through the combination of scientific areas that reside in lower abstraction levels. In other words, the scientific areas that belong to a higher abstraction level are regarded as super-sets of areas that belong in a lower level.

Following this approach, the 2nd abstraction level, which is populated with scientific areas that derive by the combination of the core scientific areas of the 1st level includes:

- **Scientific Area 7-Knowledge Interoperability:** Which area is defined as the ability of two or more different entities to share their intellectual assets, take immediate advantage of the mutual knowledge and utilise it, and to further extend them through cooperation. This area consists of elements coming out of "Data Interoperability," "Process Interoperability," "Rules Interoperability" and "Cultural Interoperability." Under this category, the following major sub-categories are identified: Knowledge Sharing & Knowledge Repositories, Transportation of Knowledge, Business Units Alignment, Smart Infrastructures, Knowledge embedded systems, Context-aware systems, Ontology Matching
- **Scientific Area 8-Services Interoperability:** Which focuses on the ability of an entity to seamlessly and automatically discover, aggregate and utilise a service that belongs to another entity.

Services Interoperability incorporates facts from "Process Interoperability," "Data Interoperability," "Rules Interoperability" and "Software Interoperability" and under this category, the following major sub-categories are identified: Automatic service discovery, description, composition, negotiation, Service Deployment, Service Engineering, Service Mediation, Enterprise Mashups, Service-oriented Architectures (SOA) and Web Services.

- **Scientific Area 9-Social Networks Interoperability:** Which is defined as the ability of enterprises to utilise social networks for collaborations and interconnection purposes, by aligning part of their internal structure and functions to the characteristics of the social networks. As such, this Scientific Area consists of elements coming out of "Cultural Interoperability" and "Data Interoperability." Under this category, the following major sub-categories are identified: Social Network Integration, Social Analytics & Social Cross-Networks Analysis, Social Business Models

- **Scientific Area 10-Electronic Identity Interoperability:** Dealing with the ability of different eID systems to collaborate in order to automatically authenticate entities and to pass on security roles and permissions to eID holders, regardless the system they originate from. This area is strongly related with "Objects Interoperability," "Software Interoperability" and "Rules Interoperability." Under this category, the following major sub-categories are identified: Digital Signatures Interoperability, Federated Identity Management Systems Interoperability, Electronic Identity Security, Electronics ID Cards Infrastructures & Services, Single Sign On Architectures

In the same way, the 3rd abstraction level of Enterprise Interoperability includes:

- **Scientific Area 11-Cloud Interoperability:** Refers to the ability of cloud services to be able to work together with both different cloud services and providers, and other applications or platforms that are not cloud dependant. In essence, this area tackles the provision of services and knowledge over distributed secure infrastructures and as such it includes elements from "Services Interoperability," "Knowledge Interoperability" and "eID Interoperability" and tries to infuse them with cloud characteristics, and under this category, the following major sub-categories are identified, Cloud Application Interoperability, Cloud Orchestration, Unified Cloud Interfaces, Cloud Federation

Lastly, the 4th abstraction level of Enterprise Interoperability includes only one scientific area, which is:

- **Scientific Area 12-Ecosystems Interoperability:** Concerns the ability of instant and seamless collaboration between different ecosystems, ecosystems and independent entities, entities within the ecosystems and the ability of different. - Ecosystems Interoperability, which deals with virtual and digital enterprises and is related to "Cloud Interoperability," and "Social Networks Interoperability," that includes all the other characteristics of the previous levels. Under this category, the following major sub-categories are identified: Cloud Application Interoperability, Cloud Orchestration, Unified Cloud Interfaces, Cloud Federation

## Hypotheses for the Scientific Areas

The above presented analysis and the observation of the Enterprise Interoperability domain and of the various problems and solutions available can lead to the definition of a series of hypotheses which seem logical and true, but need to be verified through further experimentation in order to prove their actual applicability.

Some of the most important and fundamental hypotheses that have led to the development of this taxonomy are the following:

- SAs belonging to the same abstraction level are independent of each other.
- Achieving high degree of Interoperability in a SA belonging to an abstraction level >1 requires to have high degrees of Interoperability in the SAs which are back-linked to the one examined. The degree of Interoperability in a SA is related to the degree of the SAs that are back-linked to the area under examination.
- Although SAs that belong to different abstraction levels are related, it is not required that the underlying SAs have to be of a higher degree than the SA under examination.
- Interoperability Barriers (Conceptual Technical, Organisations) are highly related with each other and thus the degree of Interoperability in each IB is highly affecting the other IBs.
- There are many Solution Paths to resolve an Interoperability problem.
- The use of multiple, connected Solution Paths can provide a solution for an Interoperability Problem as well as an individual Solution path can.

Apart from the generic hypotheses listed above, there are hypotheses present in the different SAs which also need to be checked for their validity. Some of these hypotheses are the following (we are presenting 1 per Scientific Area as examples):

**SA 1:** The degree of interoperable data structures in an enterprise is highly related to the intention of an enterprise to share its data and its data models.

**SA 2:** Business Process Standardisation lowers the effort for interconnecting the processes of enterprises.

**SA 3:** The more business and legal rules exist, the highest the effort to ensure interoperation is.

**SA 4:** Objects Interoperability can be solved by the use of unique but registered object identifiers (IDs).

**SA 5:** Web Services offer high degree of Interoperability and enable developers to interconnect any kind of software systems.

**SA 6:** Language Semantics will enable the instant transformation of textual meanings.

**SA 7:** Enterprises that pose high amounts of business knowledge are more difficult to interoperate due to organisation issues, as compared to enterprises with less business knowledge.

**SA 8:** Services that allow auto discovery and addressability are by nature interoperable with other ones.

**SA 9:** The degree of Interoperability is not affected by the size of the social graph of an enterprise.

**SA 10:** The utilisation of certificates from trusted and interconnected authentication providers is a step towards higher degrees of Interoperability.

**SA 11:** Enterprise Interoperability over the Cloud is a matter of PaaS solutions and not IaaS.

**SA 12:** The more enterprises are willing to expose and share their complete operational assets, the easier they can team up and build virtual ecosystems and digital alliances.

## ASSESSING THE ENTERPRISE INTEROPERABILITY READINESS OF ORGANISATIONS

### Specification of an EI-Specific Assessment Framework

Based on all the above, trying to solve any interoperability issues should be considered as a part of a thorough and methodological process rather than an ad-hoc activity trying to make two different entities interoperate. Such practices of the past had little success, as they indeed solved significant peer to peer interoperability problems, but resulted in proprietary and one time/one case solutions, fragmenting even more the domain and in increased degrees of difficulty when it came to solve problems where new organisations were introduced in the picture.

Following this concept, and having in mind the work that has been carried out the previous years in the domain, alongside with the effort of developing a Science Base for Enterprise Interoperability, it seems that a structured way of identifying, analysing and addressing Interoperability issues is a necessity. Only in this way the community will be able to address Enterprise Interoperability issues in a common and unanimous way, reusing the knowledge and experience of the past, providing evidence-based solutions and further improving already successful approaches.

In this context, an Enterprise Interoperability Assessment Framework is needed as a very first

step, which will be able to identify the status quo of an organisation, and classify it based on its performance on the different Enterprise Interoperability Scientific Areas. The proposed Assessment Framework is in the form of an assessment matrix, where an organisation is in turn assessed based:

- On the Enterprise Interoperability Maturity Level (ML) (ranging from 0 to 4). Each of these levels has a different interpretation depending on each IB and of course on each SA, as maturity cannot be measured in a universal way for scientific areas that possess different characteristics.
  - On each Interoperability Barrier (IB) (Conceptual, Technological, Organisational)
    - On every one of the twelve Scientific Areas (from SA.1 to SA.12)

Following on this procedure, a 12x4 matrix is generated, where each cell represents the ML of each IB in every SA. At the end, each SA is characterised by an SA Interoperability Index (SA.I.I.), which presents at a very high level the assessment of an organisation regarding every SA. It has to be noted, that the SAII ranges from 0 to 12, however it maybe be that not all SA.I.I. have a max value of 12, as it might turn out that in the cases of some SAs, not all IB are present.

Table 1 presents the Enterprise Interoperability Assessment Framework Matrix. Cells that have

*Table 1. Assessment framework matrix*

| | SA.1 | SA.2 | SA.3 | SA.4 | SA.5 | SA.6 | SA.7 | SA.8 | SA.9 | SA.10 | SA.11 | SA.12 | IL.I.I. |
|---|---|---|---|---|---|---|---|---|---|---|---|---|---|
| IB.1 Conceptual | ML[0-4] | ML[0-4] | ML[0-4] | ML[0-4] | ML[0-4] | ML[0-4] | ML[0-4] | ML[0-4] | ML[0-4] | ML[0-4] | ML[0-4] | ML[0-4] | [0-48] |
| IB.2 Technological | ML[0-4] | ML[0-4] | ML[0-4] | ML[0-4] | ML[0-4] | ML[0-4] | ML[0-4] | ML[0-4] | ML[0-4] | ML[0-4] | ML[0-4] | ML[0-4] | [0-48] |
| IG.3 Organisational | ML[0-4] | ML[0-4] | ML[0-4] | ML[0-4] | ML[0-4] | ML[0-4] | ML[0-4] | ML[0-4] | ML[0-4] | ML[0-4] | ML[0-4] | ML[0-4] | [0-48] |
| SA.I.I | [0-12] | [0-12] | [0-12] | [0-12] | [0-12] | [0-12] | [0-12] | [0-12] | [0-12] | [0-12] | [0-12] | [0-12] | |

been left blank show the absence of the notion of each respective IL to a specific SA.

This matrix enables the investigation of Enterprise Interoperability issues from both a SA and an IB perspective, as the more perspectives are available to researchers, the easier it is to diagnose problems and specify with more detail where these issues are occurring. Based on this matrix, the Enterprise Interoperability problem/solution model could be employed in order to derive to a better interoperability status, utilising the previous experience and the various methods and tools that are available. In such a way, a direct mapping between the various tools and methods and the improvement of the interoperability status can be drawn.

## Moving from the Problems to the Solutions

As witnessed in every aspect of life, the way to move from the problem to the solution space is a progressive and repetitive method where various steps are taken, and does not resemble a brutal transition from the as-is to the to-be situation. The same is a reality also for the Enterprise Interoperability domain, where organisations that are considering improvement need to go through various paths in order to gradually reach the desired situation.

The main steps to be taken, as shown in Figure 3 and described in the following:

*Figure 3. Moving from the problem to the solution space*

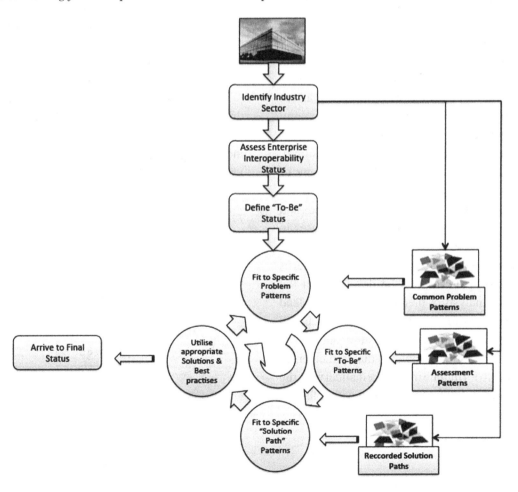

1. Identification of the industry sector the enterprise under investigation belongs to
2. Assessment of Enterprise Interoperability Status
3. Definition of the desired "to-be" status
4. Fitting to existing problem patterns which resemble the current problem
5. Fitting to existing "to-be" patterns based on the solution path chosen
6. Identification of existing solution paths that bring the current "as-is" status closer to the desired "to-be."
7. Repetition of steps 1 to 6 until one reaches the anticipated status.

The iterative process illustrated above is a necessity (at least until there is a vast population of the various problem solution registries), as it will be quite impossible to find exact matching problem and solution patterns. For this case, the arrival to the anticipated "to-be" status will be gradually achieved, through following solution paths that gradually improve the Enterprise Interoperability status of an organisation, with the aim to arrive closer to the desired destination. The problem/solution space refers to a space where known cases and issues regarding interoperability are stored, presenting a "before-after" situation for any of those issues, alongside with the solution paths (mainly referring to the utilisation of methods and tools) that have been employed in such cases in order to reach the optimised situation.

As constantly more and more problem patterns and solution patterns will be developed in the future, the analysis of their comparison will lead to the creation of new selection paths which will populate the solution paths repository and will be applicable in similar problems that will emerge.

Trying to formulate in a mathematical way, the process for connecting the problems with solutions can be seen in the following way:

- Let $i=1…12$ representing the different SAs and $j=1...3$ representing the different IBs
- Then $A=[aij]$ be the initial assessment matrix of an organisation and $D=[dij]$ the destination status, where $aij<=dij<=4$, for each $i=1...12$, $j=1…3$
- The solution path SP connecting the problem space (A) with the desired status (D) is $SP=D-A = [spij]$ (see Figure 4) (Note that there can be various SPs connecting A and D)
- Each SP can be built from partial solution paths $PSP = [pspij]$, and $SP=\Sigma PSPy$, where $y=1…n$ and $0<=[pspij]<= [spij]<=4$, for each $i=1...12$, $j=1…3$

The vast identification of patterns and paths will eventually lead to a huge number of combination which would however tend to stabilise and as a result emerging problem will be tackled in less time with less effort, as the already identified paths will indicate the most compelling and convenient ways to get closer to the solution.

The following sections present examples from three case studies where the above described process took place and we identified how the indicative problem space can be connected with various solution elements.

*Figure 4. Example of problem/solution model*

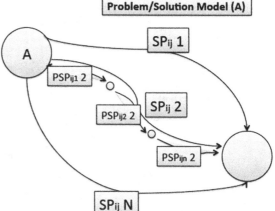

## Applying the Assessment Framework on Real Life Use Cases

This section presents three indicative cases as captured in the Enterprise Interoperability Assessment Framework based on the feedback received from three real enterprises where high level employees comletes a questionnaire. It has to be noted, that the Enterprise Interoperability Assessment Framework would include more detailed data coming from more detailed questions than the high level ones of the questionnaire.

## Case #1: A Small Technological SME Providing Services for the IT Sector

Based on the assessment framework results (Table 2), the SME which filled in the questionnaire is above average in most scientific areas, which can be explained both by the size and the use of small and flexible systems within the organisation, but also on the fact that the SME's main activity is in providing services. Also, the SME confirmed that it is active in Scientific Areas SA.10, SA.11, SA.12, however the degree of integration of social networks in the structure of the organisation and their interoperation with the SME's other systems seems quite low.

Judging from the aforementioned facts, the SME under observation should firstly deal with its Rules Interoperability Issues at the all levels in order to increase its interoperability status. To this, the modelling of its own Business Rules and the utilisation of Decision Support Systems and of Rule Execution Systems would allow a highest degree of interoperation. Regarding SA.9, the SME needs to transfer the social networks mentality to its own structure, thus it needs to work towards Social Network Integration prior to utilising other tools. Last but not least, as technical interoperability is missing in SA.10, Single Sign On and eID Infrastructures are expected to increase the SMEs performance in this domain.

*Table 2. The case of a technological SME*

| | SA.1 | SA.2 | SA.3 | SA.4 | SA.5 | SA.6 | SA.7 | SA.8 | SA.9 | SA.10 | SA.11 | SA.12 | IL.I.I. |
|---|---|---|---|---|---|---|---|---|---|---|---|---|---|
| IB.1 Conceptual | 3 | 3 | 2 | 3 | 3 | 2 | 3 | 3 | 1 | 2 | 3 | 2 | 30 |
| IB.2 Technological | 3 | 2 | 1 | 3 | 2 | 2 | 2 | 2 | 1 | 1 | 3 | 3 | 25 |
| IG.3 Organisa-tional | 2 | 3 | 2 | 3 | 3 | 2 | 3 | 2 | 1 | 1 | 4 | 2 | 28 |
| SA.I.I | 8 | 8 | 5 | 9 | 8 | 6 | 8 | 7 | 3 | 4 | 10 | 7 | |
| Max Potential | 12 | 12 | 12 | 12 | 12 | 12 | 12 | 12 | 12 | 12 | 12 | 12 | |
| SA.I.I Margin | 66.67% | 66.67% | 41.67% | 75.00% | 66.67% | 50.00% | 66.67% | 58.33% | 25.00% | 33.33% | 83.33% | 58.33% | |
| SA.I.I Deficit | 33.33% | 33.33% | 58.33% | 25.00% | 33.33% | 50.00% | 33.33% | 41.67% | 75.00% | 66.67% | 16.67% | 41.67% | |

## Case #2: Large Manufacturing Industry

Based on the assessment framework results (Table 3), the large manufacturing enterprise which filled in the questionnaire is quite below average in most scientific areas. Apart from an average degree of software systems integration and interoperability and from exposing and being able to interconnect its processes, all other aspects suffer severely when it comes to interoperability. This low degree of interoperability can be explained by the very nature of the company, as it focuses on manufacturing, however increased interoperability in some areas would benefit her communication with her clients and the flow of information from/to its partners.

In order to increase its interoperability status, this enterprise should tackle first of all fundamental SAs such as Process Interoperability and Rules Interoperability. In the former, the enterprise should start with modelling its existing processes and trying to align them with existing standards and if necessary proceed to re-engineer them to transform them to new ones which are commonly used by its partners or competitors. Moreover, business and legal rules should be modelled and included into a rule engine for enabling the automatic execution of transactions. Moreover, automatic translation systems are needed to increase the degree of Cultural Interoperability, as the enterprise has a vast number of suppliers from around the world, and translation of technical documents is a major bottleneck in the overall performance of tis supply chain network.

## Case #3: Large IT Integrator Active in One Country

As anticipated, the large IT integrator who completed the questionnaire showed a high level of interoperability capacity in every single Scientific Area. This behaviour is quite expected, as IT industries have since long invested in making their processes and data interoperable (see Table 4).

*Table 3. The case of a large manufacturing industry*

| | SA.1 | SA.2 | SA.3 | SA.4 | SA.5 | SA.6 | SA.7 | SA.8 | SA.9 | SA.10 | SA.11 | SA.12 | I.L.I. |
|---|---|---|---|---|---|---|---|---|---|---|---|---|---|
| IB.1 Conceptual | 3 | 1 | 1 | 3 | 2 | 1 | 2 | 1 | - | 0 | 1 | 0 | 15 |
| IB.2 Technological | 3 | 0 | 0 | 1 | 2 | 0 | 1 | 1 | - | 1 | 0 | 1 | 10 |
| IG.3 Organisa-tional | 2 | 1 | 0 | 3 | 2 | 0 | 1 | 2 | - | 0 | 1 | 1 | 13 |
| SA.I.I | 8 | 2 | 1 | 7 | 6 | 1 | 4 | 4 | - | 1 | 2 | 2 | |
| Max Potential | 12 | 12 | 12 | 12 | 12 | 12 | 12 | 12 | - | 12 | 12 | 12 | |
| SA.I.I Margin | 66.67% | 16.67% | 8.33% | 58.33% | 50.00% | 8.33% | 33.33% | 33.33% | - | 8.33% | 16.67% | 16.67% | |
| SA.I.I Deficit | 33.33% | 83.33% | 91.67% | 41.67% | 50.00% | 91.67% | 66.67% | 66.67% | - | 91.67% | 83.33% | 83.33% | |

*Table 4. The case of a large IT integrator active in one country*

| | SA.1 | SA.2 | SA.3 | SA.4 | SA.5 | SA.6 | SA.7 | SA.8 | SA.9 | SA.10 | SA.11 | SA.12 | IL.I.L. |
|---|---|---|---|---|---|---|---|---|---|---|---|---|---|
| IB.1 Conceptual | 4 | 3 | 2 | 3 | 2 | 1 | 3 | 4 | 4 | 3 | 3 | 1 | 33 |
| IB.2 Technological | 4 | 4 | 4 | 1 | 0 | 0 | 3 | 4 | 3 | 4 | 2 | 3 | 32 |
| IG.3 Organisa-tional | 3 | 3 | 2 | 1 | 3 | 0 | 3 | 3 | 3 | 3 | 3 | 1 | 28 |
| SA.I.I | 11 | 10 | 8 | 5 | 5 | 1 | 9 | 11 | 10 | 10 | 8 | 5 | |
| Max Potential | 12 | 12 | 12 | 12 | 12 | 12 | 12 | 12 | 12 | 12 | 12 | 12 | |
| SA.I.I Margin | 91.67% | 83.33% | 66.67% | 41.67% | 41.67% | 8.33% | 75.00% | 91.67% | 83.33% | 83.33% | 66.67% | 41.67% | |
| SA.I.I Deficit | 8.33% | 16.67% | 33.33% | 58.33% | 58.33% | 91.67% | 25.00% | 8.33% | 16.67% | 16.67% | 33.33% | 58.33% | |

Areas that show medium interoperability levels are those that of software systems, Objects, Rules and Ecosystems. Especially for the Software interoperability, one would expect a large IT industry to score high, however as companies take strategic decision to work with specific products, their ability to interoperate with other systems from other vendors is quite limited.

In order to increase its performance in those areas, the IT integrator needs to align its whole systems with existing standards that allow interoperation with a broader audience. For example, regarding Software the enterprise should deploy standard-based Web Services and work with generic system development methodologies in order to increase the compatibility, and thus the interconnection, of its systems with external ones. The same should happen with existing sensors, which should be based on globally accepted communication protocols to be able to interoperate with third systems. Regarding cultural issues, there is a complete lack of interoperability, mainly due to the fact that the enterprise is active in only one country. Nevertheless, tactics focusing on language interpretation and regional aspects compatibility would enable the enterprise to have a better collaboration with other companies coming from third countries.

## FUTURE RESEARCH DIRECTIONS AND CONCLUSION

Reaching consensus in definitions, analyzing state-of-the art solutions and problem patterns, and mapping a concrete action plan for the stakeholders are the most important aspects that should be considered for eventually establishing an Enterprise Interoperability Science. Making this a reality will enable enterprises to be systematically assisted in exploiting the benefits of interoperability at strategic, organisational, semantic and technical levels, yielding innovative products and services of unprecedented quality, return on investment and sustainability

In this context, the ultimate vision of a Science Base for Enterprise Interoperability making explicit the knowledge and skills, which industry and academia have empirically observed over the last decade, can only be realised by carefully analysing the domain and discovering the different areas and the interelations between them. Such an analysis will also result in a detailed mapping of future research directions in the domain Future Internet and of modern ICT powered enterprise infrastructures.

Taking into account that new scientific knowledge may lead to new applications, that new technological advances may lead to new scientific discoveries, and that potential applications actually motivate new scientific investigations, Enterprise Interoperability has the credentials to gradually evolve into a more rigorous scientific discipline (or sub-discipline). It is well acknowledged that an underlying scientific discipline typically evolves over several decades in incremental stages before being established as a science and there is actually no role model for showing that there is a successful way to initiate a new scientific discipline using a linear "push approach." In this context, the work presented in the previous sections of this chapter should not be regarded as a static result. It should be in constant movement and evolution and it needs to accommodate the dynamicity of the Enterprise Interoperability domain. Therefore a constant update of the different scientific areas is more than necessary. To this extend, the engagement of the domain's community is pivotal in order not only to validate these results, but to strengthen them and turn them into a live body of knowledge that should become a reference point for common research attempts.

Therefore, we believe that it is fundamental to build a large operational and users network around this effort to boost the potential impact it may have next to the target groups (e.g. researchers, enterprises, etc.). These attempts should be recorded in

a sustainability strategy, where organisations like the EC or other large organisations should continue to support the initiative whenever possible. However, it is only time that will eventually prove the Enterprise Interoperability actual positioning and real perspective in relation to its neighbouring scientific disciplines that are already established and well accepted as sciences.

## REFERENCES

America Mathematical Society (AMS). (2010). *Mathematics subject classification*. Retrieved on March 15, 2013 from http://www.ams.org/mathscinet/msc/msc2010.html

Charalabidis, Y., Gionis, G., Moritz Hermann, K., & Martinez, C. (2008). *Enterprise interoperability research roadmap* (Draft Version 5.0). Retrieved on March 15, 2013 from ftp://ftp.cordis.europa.eu/pub/fp7/ict/docs/enet/ei-roadmap-5-0-draft_en.pdf

Charalabidis, Y., Jardim Gonçalves, R., & Popplewell, K. (2010). Towards a scientific foundation for interoperability. In Y. Charalabidis (Ed.), *Interoperability in digital public services and administration: Bridging e- government and e-business*. Hershey, PA: Information Science Reference. doi:10.4018/978-1-61520-887-6.ch019

Commission, E. (2010). *Interoperability solutions for European public administrations*. Retrieved on March 15, 2013 from http://ec.europa.eu/isa/documents/isa_annex_ii_eif_en.pdf

Cooperstock, F. (2009). *General relativistic dynamics: Extending Einstein's legacy throughout the universe*. Singapore: World Scientific. doi:10.1142/7243

Dodig-Crnkovic, G. (2002). *Scientic methods in computer science*. Promotion of Research in IT at New Universities and at University Colleges in Sweden.

FInES. (2010). *Research roadmap* (version 3.0). Retrieved on March 15, 2013 from http://www.fines-cluster.eu/fines/jm/Download-document/2-FInES-Cluster-2010-Research-Roadmap.html

Lampathaki, F., Koussouris, S., Mouzakitis, S., Charalabidis, Y., & Psarras, J. (2011). Digging into the real-life enterprise interoperability areas – Definition and overview of the main research areas. In *Proceedings of CENT 2011: Collaborative Enterprises 2011 – Platforms, Processes, and Practices Advancing the Enterprise 2.0 Science Base for Enterprise Interoperability in the advent of the Future of Internet*. Orlando, FL: CENT.

Sullivan, A., & Sheffrin, S. (2003). *Economics: Principles in action*. Upper Saddle River, NJ: Pearson Prentice Hall.

ENSEMBLE Support Action. (2010). *Description of work*.

## ADDITIONAL READING

Agostinho, C., Goncalves, R., Sarraipa, J., Lampatahki, F., Koussouris, S., & Charalabidis, Y. (2012). *EISB Models & Tools Report*. European Commission.

Berners-Lee, T., Hall, W., & Hendler, J., O'Hara, k., Shadbolt N., & Weitzner, D. (2006). A framework for web science. *Foundations and Trends in Web Science, 1*(1), 1–130. doi:10.1561/1800000001

Berre, A., Elvesæter, B., Figay, N., Guglielmina, C., Johnsen, S., & Karlsen, D. et al. (2007). The ATHENA Interoperability Framework. *Enterprise Interoperability, II*(Part VI), 569–580. doi:10.1007/978-1-84628-858-6_62

Goncalves, R., Agostinho, C., & Steiger-Garcao, A. (2012). A reference model for sustainable interoperability in networked enterprises: towards the foundation of Enterprise Interoperability Science Base. *International Journal of Computer Integrated Manufacturing*, 1–19.

Goncalves, R., Grilo, A., Agostinho, C., Lampathaki, F., Charalabidis, Y. (2012) Systematisation of Interoperability Body of Knowledge: The foundation for Enterprise Interoperability as a science. Accepted for publication in the Special Issue Information Systems for Enterprise Integration, Interoperability and Networking: Theory and Applications to appear in Enterprise Information Systems

Goncalves, R., Popplewell, K., & Grilo, A. (2012). Sustainable Interoperability: The Future of Internet Based Industrial Enterprises. *Computers in Industry*.

Lampathaki, F., Koussouris, S., Agostinho, C., Jardim-Goncalves, R., Charalabidis, Y., & Psarras, J. (2012). Infusing Scientific Foundations into Enterprise Interoperability. *Computers in Industry*. doi:10.1016/j.compind.2012.08.004

Panetto, H. (2007). Towards a Classification framework for interoperability of enterprise applications [Taylor & Francis.]. *International Journal of CIM, 20*(8), 727–740.

Peristeras, V., & Tarabanis, K. (2006) The Connection, Communication, Consolidation, Collaboration Interoperability Framework (C4IF) For Information Systems Interoperability. In Interoperability in Business Information Systems 1(1).

## KEY TERMS AND DEFINITIONS

**Enterprise Interoperability:** The capacity of two or more enterprises, including all the systems within their boundaries and the external systems that they utilise or are affected by, in order to cooperate seamlessly in depth of time for a common objective.

**Enterprise Interoperability Knowledge Base:** The domain knowledge base contains both structuring and methodological knowledge.

**Problem Space:** A taxonomy of the spectrum of application and theoretical problems addressed by the domain, organised so as to be used to characterise real applications and to link these to elements of the solution space.

**Scientific Area:** A technology area that consists of elements that are all dealing with similar concepts and altogether can be grouped under a higher concept.

**Solution Space:** The converse of the problem space, as it provides a taxonomy of knowledge available for the solution of domain application problems. In turn this links to methodologies and tools in the domain knowledge base.

# Chapter 3
# Underpinning EISB with Enterprise Interoperability Neighboring Scientific Domains

**Carlos Agostinho**
*Centre of Technology and Systems (CTS) – UNINOVA, Portugal*

**Ricardo Jardim-Goncalves**
*Centre of Technology and Systems (CTS) – UNINOVA, Portugal*

**Adolfo Steiger-Garcao**
*Centre of Technology and Systems (CTS) – UNINOVA, Portugal*

## ABSTRACT

*Over the last decade, interoperability appeared as a key enabler towards unlocking the full potential of enterprises, products, processes, and systems. With methods to support their lifecycle, contributing towards removing communication barriers, and fostering a new-networked business culture in industrial domains, Enterprise Interoperability (EI) requires tangible scientific foundations. This chapter recognizes that, in terms of content, any scientific field exists in an ecosystem of neighboring domains and presents a methodology to identify EI's relationship with its neighbors, thus supporting the foundations of EI Science Base (EISB). It can be agreed that formalisms like logic and mathematics are an integrant part of every science, but others also share relationships such as application fields' boundaries, methodologies, techniques, or even tools. With the support of the European Commission, through the Future Internet and Enterprise Systems (FInES) cluster of research projects, the authors have initiated an analysis of comprehensive domains (e.g. complexity and software).*

## INTRODUCTION

As enterprise information systems evolve and become more complex, the need for interoperable operation, automated data interchange and coordinated behavior of large scale infrastructures

DOI: 10.4018/978-1-4666-5142-5.ch003

becomes highly critical (Agostinho, Jardim-Goncalves, & Steiger-Garcao, 2011; Athena IP, 2007; INTEROP NoE, 2007). In fact, Interoperability of Enterprise Systems and Applications (I-ESA) has been a strong focus of research in the latest years both motivated from industry and research community alike, and is recognized as a high-impact productivity factor within the private and the public sectors (Charalabidis, Lampathaki, Kavalaki, & Askounis, 2010; Jardim-Goncalves, Grilo, Agostinho, Lampathaki, & Charalabidis, 2013).

Worldwide researchers, working on interoperability domains such as data, process, software and other issues, are exploiting the core components of EI (Koussouris, Lampathaki, Mouzakitis, Charalabidis, & Psarras, 2011). However, due to the increasingly fuzzy boundaries of each domain, the loosely coupled architectures, and virtual resources of enterprises, interoperability is becoming even more complex. Not only new technologies such as social networks or e-ID are constantly being taken up by enterprises, but also as there is a need to address interoperability at knowledge, services, clouds, and even enterprise ecosystems. Whereas in the past it was said that EI was unachievable until seamless interaction could take place at the technical, semantic, and organizational levels of the enterprise (Jardim-Goncalves, Grilo, & Steiger-Garcao, 2006), today this vision is extended, foreseeing that EI will be fully achieved only when the benefits brought by the new technology paradigms are harvested, including those of the Future Internet (http://www.future-internet.eu), e.g., Internet of Things, Internet of Services.

Notwithstanding the research developed so far, only recently have the scientific foundations of EI begun to be formulated (Lampathaki et al., 2012). Following a methodological approach based on two development axes, the Enterprise Interoperability Science Base (EISB) is being defined according to two parallel-running processes, under constant bi-lateral communication and coordination. They ensure proper execution and alignment for the specifications of the areas and the contents to be included in the EISB. As explained by Jardim-Goncalves et al. (2013), axis I is focused on the definition of the contents and structure of the EISB considering the EI neigh-

boring scientific domains, while axis II is strictly concentrated on the internal domains of EI and Future Internet Enterprise Systems (FInES). This chapter reports advances of the activities of axis I.

The classical concept of science is generally related with observable knowledge, described in the form of testable laws and theories (Morris, 1992; Wilson, 1999). Nevertheless, there is a plurality of sciences that differ very much from each other. Formalisms like logic and mathematics are integrant part physics, less important for natural sciences, and their significance continues to decrease towards the more social and humanistic sciences spectrum. Thus, it can be agreed that in terms of content, scientific domains exist in an ecosystem of neighboring domains, and should recognize their relationship with these neighbors and with formal definitions of science bases already established for them. Normally, this relationship includes boundaries between application fields, which may be sometimes fuzzy, shared methodologies, techniques and tools, as well as conflicts in approach.

Acknowledging the existence of these, the authors, supported by the FInES cluster of EU research and most specifically the ENSEMBLE project (ENSEMBLE CSA, 2011), have initiated an analysis of EI neighboring scientific domains in search for commonalities and contributions to the EISB formulation. In this context, *Fluid Knowledge* is a designation proposed to accommodate all that is located within the fuzzy borders of EISB under the frame of development axis I. Section 2 includes a background analysis of the activities conducted towards the development of the EISB. Section 3 includes a literature review on a small set of neighboring domains, which will be used to formulate the Fluid Knowledge in the form of relationships with EI, in section 4. Lastly, sections 5 and 6 conclude the chapter with some final remarks and considerations to the future.

## BACKGROUND

### Raising an EI Science Base

The need to develop an EISB was first documented in the Enterprise Interoperability Research Roadmap (Enterprise Interoperability Cluster, 2008), specifying it as one of four main grand research challenges in the domain. Being identified as a barrier to the generalization and full use of the methods and tools developed so far, the European Commission (EC) DG Information Society and Media initiated a Task Force on EISB, which announced an initial agenda within 2009 (Charalabidis, Jardim-Goncalves, & Popplewell, 2010). Late in 2010, the ENSEMBLE project was launched to provide an official support on establishing the backbone towards the EISB formulation.

Upon studying the fundamentals in creating a science as depicted in the history of science and epistemology, ENSEMBLE defined an action plan for the EISB (Lampathaki et al., 2011). It evolves in 3 waves for which corresponding objectives and actions are identified along the

two axes, one more focused on the analysis of EI/FInES domains and the other concerned with the neighboring knowledge:

- **Wave 1-Basic Elements:** Including the foundational principles and the EISB core concepts formulation;
- **Wave 2-Hypothesis and Experimentation:** With special emphasis on the EISB framework development and enhancement of the problem and solution spaces;
- **Wave 3-Empowerment:** Providing external exploration and popularization to the wider community.

Admitting it could not cover the full extension of the activities defined in the waves, ENSEMBLE kicked-off all of them, taking into account that they would need to be completed with post project activities. To be realistic, as illustrated in Figure 1, the waves were not independent from each other and the methodology was iterative. Thus at the end of the project, ENSEMBLE achieved

*Figure 1. ENSEMBLE EISB waves methodology*

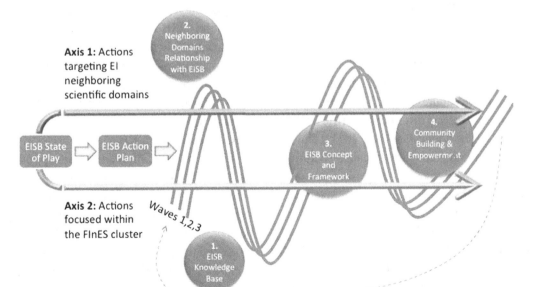

a significantly larger percentage of the activities scoped under Wave 1 than the ones under Wave 3 (ENSEMBLE Partners, 2011, 2012a, 2012b). Bellow is included a short description of the main activities identified in the figure.

## 1. EISB Knowledge Base

As there is no common view of the definition of a science base, it can be agreed it is to a degree dependent on the nature of the domain and the purpose for which it is designed and maintained. Indeed, the definition for a particular domain will evolve as the needs of the domain evolve with its maturity. To keep all this knowledge integrated, the waves' methodology proposes the creation of an EISB knowledge base, starting with an overall taxonomy of the EI domain that is currently evolving to an EISB ontology.

The EISB Knowledge Base (KB) is an activity that keeps all knowledge integrated and synchronized with the FInES wiki (http://www. fines-cluster.eu/fines/mw/) to enable bidirectional information feed and enhanced querying capabilities on the domain.

## 2. Neighboring Domains Relationship with EISB

Unlike the traditional philosophy of science, they usually do not apply to a single domain, being interdisciplinary and eclectic. Methods and research questions address broad areas, crossing borders and engineering different scientific fields (Agostinho, Jardim-Goncalves et al., 2011). Thus, being also a multi- disciplinary domain by nature, the EI science base should comprise concepts and theories from related neighboring sciences and scientific domains, i.e. from those scientific fields where theories and methods can be used or extended, opening its scope to fit the EI requirements (Charalabidis, Jardim-Goncalves et al., 2010). Special attention is given on scientific

knowledge from distributed enterprise systems, shared data and semantics, evolutive applications, dynamics, and adaptation of networked systems on a global scale. These are all directly related with major requirements for interoperability, such as rapid evolution of technology and applications, plug and play instruments, self monitoring capabilities, benchmarking and evaluation of degrading processing, automatic and on-demand reprocessing, recompiling, and fixing of components and processes

From the several reference neighboring scientific domains, theories, and methods identified and classified by ENSEMBLE as potentially relevant for the development of EISB, four scientific domains are analyzed more extensively in this chapter as part of this activity, i.e. complexity science, software engineering, design science, and service science.

## 3. EISB Concept and Framework

Formalization and structured descriptions will not answer all questions nor solve all problems, but methods play a central role in assessing the correctness of a solution to a conceptual problem or empowering researchers to similarly identify, describe and resolve EI problems. This activity tailors the EISB framework, delimiting some of the concepts such as the problem and solution spaces, their connectivity and introducing the EI guiding principles. With these spaces defined and the formal methods identified, EISB has the grounds to begin providing solid and properly defined input to the KB

Following the initial iterations of the EISB methodology, the EISB concept needs to be organized in an easy to understand manner. Thus, this step envisages not only to consolidate what has been presented before including examples of how to use the theoretical EISB foundations, but also to clarify the concept of hypothesis/laws for EISB.

## 4. Community Building and Empowerment

In parallel, this methodology aims to enlarge the research community, communicating the results to a broader community, (re)distributing the accomplishments and attracting the interest of major stakeholders of the domain, other external experts and stakeholders. The community also validates and contributes towards the results of the previous activities.

## LITERATURE REVIEW ON NEIGHBORING DOMAINS

### Complexity Science

Over the last few decades, much has been learned about the nature of complexity and the role that complexity plays in our lives (Courtney, Merali, Paradice, & Wynn, 2008). Complexity Science has become a broad ranging subject appreciated in a variety of ways and illustrated in many books such as (Anderson, Arrow, & Pines, 1988; Holland, 1996; Kauffman, 1996; Mainzer, 1996; Nicolis & Prigogine, 1989; Papadimitriou, 1994; Waldrop, 1992), just to point some of the most referenced.

Nowadays, it is viewed as a source of concepts for enabling the trans-disciplinary exploration of complex organizations in the networked economy and society, and for explaining the dynamics of networked systems at different levels of description (from the micro- to the macro-level). It offers a powerful set of methods for explaining non-linear, emergent behavior in systems. Being such inter-disciplinary, Complexity Science is approached differently by three major schools (Mckelvey, 1999; Merali & McKelvey, 2006), i.e.:

- **European:** A mathematical intensive school, which focuses on the discovery that certain levels of negentropy in physical systems at the "edge of chaos," cause aggregate structures to emerge from a stochastic "soup" of microstates. According to the European school, these structures evidence predictability, thus providing scientific explanations to complexity at the edge of chaos.

- **American:** Which focuses on how new order arises in biological and social systems. Represented by the "The Santa Fe Institute," it studies the so-called "edge of chaos" where order emerges when heterogeneous agents – such as biomolecules, organisms, people or social systems – are motivated, by a drive for improved fitness or learning, to initiate connections with other agents.

- **Econophysics:** Where the focus is on how the order creation actually unfolds once the forces of emergent order creation by self-organizing agents are set in motion. Key parts of this third aspect are fractal structures, power laws and scale-free theory.

The science of complexity is, therefore, the study of emergent order in very disorderly systems. Spirals in whirlpools, flocks of birds, are all examples of orderly behavior in systems that are neither centrally planned nor centrally controlled. In fact, understanding complexity's influence on the performance of enterprises could lead to major gains in driving businesses (McElroy, 2000). Complexity Science introduces a new way of studying. It posits simple causes for complex effects, with rules that typically determine how a set of artificial agents will behave in their virtual environment over time, including their interaction with other agents. Unlike traditional science, it does not predict an outcome for every state; instead, it uses feedback and learning algorithms to enable complex adaptive systems (CAS) to adapt to its environment over time. The application of these rules to a large population leads to emergent behavior that may bear some resemblance to real-world phenomena (Phelan,

2001). In fact, complex networks are referred to as "adaptive" or "dynamic," and the phenomena where multiple components dynamically interact and give rise to complex structures exhibiting common behavior across multiple disciplines, is designated as "emergence."

Complexity Science, namely the research available under aggregate complexity has been important when applied to economics and organizational management, and can also be relevant to the study of enterprise and systems interoperability. In fact, the authors, as in Merali and McKelvey (2006) believe that the information systems researchers should do a paradigm shift towards a more dynamical theoretical and methodological framework better suited to support idiosyncratic aspects of information, business and organizational domains. In that sense, aggregate complexity can be the answer since it illustrates how relationships are more important than attributes in defining the nature of components (Manson, 2001):

- It contains mature concepts and methodologies focused on accessing the holism and synergy resulting from the interaction of system components, as occurs in Enterprise networks;

- If one considers that a system is a very broad concept that can enclose Software, Services, Enterprises, and even Networks, then it can be closely related to many of the EISB areas, understanding the interactions between: information models; business processes; software applications and services; ontologies; clouds of services and enterprise ecosystems; people, etc.;

The domain of Complexity addresses a number of inter-related concepts, summarized in Table 1.

## Software Engineering

Software Engineering (SE) is an engineering discipline that is concerned with all aspects of software production (Sommerville, 2007). According to the IEEE Computer Society, SE is the application of a systematic, disciplined, quantifiable approach to the development, operation, and maintenance of software, as well as the study of such approaches. It is characterized as the appli-

*Table 1. Complexity science core features and properties*

| Complexity Core Features and Properties | Summary | References |
|---|---|---|
| Dimensionality | The dimensionality of a complex system is defined as the degree of freedom that individual agents within the system have to enact behavior in a somewhat autonomous fashion. A system with high dimensionality tends to be difficult to control. On the other hand, controls act as a form of negative feedback, effectively reducing dimensionality, e.g. rules and regulations or budgetary restrictions, ensure that an individual agent's behavior is greatly limited, thus, changing the complexity and helping systems to behave more predictably and cybernetically. | (Choi, Dooley, & Rungtusanatham, 2001) |
| Non-linearity | In a complex system, it is often true that the only way to predict how the system will behave in the future is to wait literally for the future to unfold. Non-linear relationships are relationships in which a change of given magnitude in the input to the system is not matched in a linear fashion to a corresponding change in output | (Choi et al., 2001) |
| Decomposability | Modularity or near decomposability shows up in many scientific disciplines in a matter of degrees, e.g., it may refer merely to the ability to delineate one system module from another (recognizing the boundaries of the module), or to the ability to actually separate components from one another. This decomposability also enables the complexity of a system (or process) to be reduced into more controllable agents that work together to produce emergent properties. | (L. Chen & Li, 2004; Honour, 2008; Simon, 1962, 1995) |

*continued on following page*

*Table 1. Continued*

| Complexity Core Features and Properties | Summary | References |
|---|---|---|
| Reflexivity | As given by the degree of dimensionality, the only constant in complex networks and systems is "change." Each agent acts, and its actions have impacts on the other agents around it. A common way for changes to occur is by altering the boundaries of the system, which change as a result of including or excluding particular sub-system agents and by adding or eliminating connections among them, thereby changing the underlying patterns of interactions. However, other agents act in response to the change in their own environment, thereby changing the environment for the original agent. Furthermore, the environment can impose new rules and norms. Thus, on response to change, adaptation includes structural, physiological and/or behavioral response that increases the expected long-term success of a system and its reflexive nature. | (Choi et al., 2001; Honour, 2008; Maturana & Varela, 1980; Wycisk, McKelvey, & Hülsmann, 2008) |
| Ability to Learn | A complex system (e.g. an enterprise) is not behold to the environment (e.g. a collaboration network or the market economy) - it actively shapes, reacts, and anticipates, remembering through the persistence of internal structures. Therefore, systems are able to adapt by modifying their individual capabilities and change their rules of action to improve their performance as experience accumulates. In doing so, system agents can deal with novel situations, searching the so-called "building blocks" for a set of plausible rules enabling them to interact within a CAS. | (Holland, 1992, 1996; Honour, 2008; Wycisk et al., 2008) |
| Emergence | A process by which a number of lower level systems (considered as parts) self-organize into a higher lever autonomous complex system (a whole) with transcendent macro behaviors. Related to dimensionality, emergent phenomena may lie beyond our ability to predict or control, thus, a system is considered to have emerged when coherent actions at the macro-level dynamically arose from the interactions between the parts at the micro-level. Emergence occurs between the edges of order and chaos via processes of interaction and self-organization | (Bak, Tang, & Wiesenfeld, 1988; Holland, 1998; Honour, 2008; Kauffman & Clayton, 2006; Manson, 2001; Phelan, 2001) |
| Self-Organization | Allows a system to change its internal structure in order to better interact with its environment. This process results from the autonomous interaction of single agents within a system giving rise to bottom-up (new) order creation by a system itself, as opposed to structure and process imposed on the system by outside entities (controllers). Self-Organization is often linked to emergence. | (Manson, 2001; Nicolis & Prigogine, 1989; Wycisk et al., 2008) |
| Quasi-equilibrium | Equilibrium is a state of a system that, if not subjected to perturbation, will remain unchanged. Normally a CAS tends to oscillate between a state of equilibrium and non-equilibrium due to the action of attractors that are sensitive to change as the CAS is pulled away from quasi-equilibrium state to a far-from-equilibrium state. The term "self-organized criticality" also refers to the ability of complex systems to balance between randomness and stasis. | (Bak et al., 1988; L. Chen & Li, 2004; Choi et al., 2001) |

cation of engineering to software because it integrates significant mathematics, computer science and practices whose origins are in engineering (ACM, 2006). Currently, Computer engineering, Project management, Computer science, Quality management, Management, Software ergonomics, Mathematics, and Systems engineering are recognized as disciplines that share boundaries and often a common intersection, with SE.

In summary, the major features that define SE are summarized in Table 2, and the knowledge areas that fall within its scope and boundaries are, as following (IEEE Computer Society, 2005; Wasserman, 1996):

- **Software Requirements:** Including the elicitation, analysis, specification, and validation of requirements for software.
- **Software Design:** As the process of defining the architecture, components, interfaces, and other characteristics of a system or component.

*Table 2. Software engineering core features and properties*

| SE Core Features and Properties | Summary | References |
|---|---|---|
| Abstraction | Abstraction is a common intellectual technique for managing the understanding of a complex item; it allows concentrating on a problem at some generalized level without regard to irrelevant low-level details so that the software engineer can focus on a few concepts at a time. It is the process by which data and programs are defined with a representation similar in form to its meaning (semantics), while hiding away the implementation details. | (Wasserman, 1996) |
| Agility | Agile software development focuses on early and fast production of working code, frequent, small, incremental changes, pair programming, short iterations, rapid and continual user feedback and interaction. Agile methods stress two concepts: the working code and the effectiveness of people working together with goodwill. | (Dyba & Dingsoyr, 2008; Highsmith & Cockburn, 2001; Vijayasarathy & Turk, 2012; Williams, 2010) |
| Design Patterns | A design pattern is a general reusable solution to a commonly occurring problem within a given context in software design. A design pattern is not a finished design that can be transformed directly into code. It is rather a description or template for how to solve a problem that can be used in many different situations. There are many types of design patterns, like Algorithm strategy patterns, Computational design patterns, Execution patterns, Implementation strategy patterns, and Structural design patterns. | (Fowler, 2002; Gamma, Helm, Johnson, & Vlissides, 1995; Hasheminejad & Jalili, 2012; Schmidt, Stal, Rohnert, & Buschmann, 2000) |
| Encapsulation | Encapsulation allows the "layering" of new components on top of existing components, using only information about the functionality and interfaces provided by the existing components. It refers to the design of classes and objects to restrict access to the data and behavior by defining a limited set of messages that an object can receive. | (Armstrong, 2006; Rick Lutowski, 2005; Zweben, Edwards, Weide, & Hollingsworth, 1995) |
| Systematization | Methods impose structure on the SE activity with the goal of making the activity systematic and ultimately more likely to be successful. Methods usually provide a notation and vocabulary, procedures for performing identifiable tasks, and guidelines for checking both the process and the product. Such methods are divided into: heuristic methods dealing with informal approaches, formal methods dealing with mathematically based approaches, model-based methods and prototyping methods dealing with software development approaches based on various forms of prototyping.<br>Implementing some of the above principles, SE tools, also known as Computer-aided software engineering (CASE) tools, allow repetitive, well-defined actions to be automated, reducing the cognitive load on the engineer who is then free to concentrate on the creative aspects of the process. | (Fuggetta, 1993; IEEE Computer Society, 2005) |
| Lifecycle approach | The software lifecycle process defines all the standardized processes and tasks required for specifying, developing, testing and maintaining software. | (ISO/IEC, 2008; Wasserman, 1996) |
| Object Orientation | Object Orientation refers to a programming paradigm using "objects" – data structures consisting of data fields and methods together with their interactions – to design applications and computer programs. | (Armstrong, 2006; Booch, 1994; Larman, 2004; Schach, 2006; Sommerville, 2007) |
| Polymorphism | Polymorphism is the ability to create a variable, a function, or an object that has more than one form and to hide different implementations behind a common interface. It is defined as the ability of different classes to respond to the same message and each implement the method appropriately. | (Armstrong, 2006) |
| Prescriptive Principles | The software engineering principles are the fundamental statements of the discipline formulated in a prescriptive manner in order to direct actions, and susceptible of being checked in terms of their consequences and by experiment. Such principles take into account that software is an intangible product that is not constrained by the laws of physics, and that software engineering is still emerging as an engineering discipline, having only recently been recognized as such. | (Séguin, Abran, & Dupuis, 2010) |

*continued on following page*

*Table 2. Continued*

| SE Core Features and Properties | Summary | References |
|---|---|---|
| Service Orientation | Service-orientation is a design paradigm to build computer software in the form of services. Like other design paradigms (e.g. object-orientation), service-orientation provides a governing approach to automate business logic as distributed systems. What distinguishes service-orientation is its set of design principles to ensure the manner in which it carries out the separation of concerns in the software. | (Booch, 1994; Gold, Mohan, Knight, & Munro, 2004; Larman, 2004; Schach, 2006; Sommerville, 2007) |
| Usability | The usability of a software system is the capability in human functional terms to be used easily and effectively by the specified range of users, given specified training and user support, to fulfill the specified range of tasks, within the specified range of scenarios. | (Folmer & Bosch, 2004) |

- **Software Construction:** With the detailed creation of working, meaningful software through a combination of coding, verification, unit testing, integration testing, and debugging.

- **Software Testing:** Which includes the dynamic verification of the behavior of a program on a finite set of test cases, suitably selected from the usually infinite executions domain, against the expected behavior.

- **Software Maintenance:** Representing the totality of activities required to provide cost-effective support to software.

- **Software Configuration Management:** Identifying the configuration of a system at distinct points in time for the purpose of systematically controlling changes to the configuration, and maintaining the integrity and traceability of the configuration throughout the system life cycle.

- **SE Management:** Embracing the application of management activities - planning, coordinating, measuring, monitoring, controlling, and reporting - to ensure that the development and maintenance of software is systematic, disciplined, and quantified.

- **SE Process:** That reflects the definition, implementation, assessment, measurement, management, change, and improvement of the software life cycle process itself.

- **SE Tools:** Intended to assist the software life cycle processes, and methods that impose structure on the software engineering activity with the goal of making the activity systematic and ultimately more likely to be successful.

- **Software Quality:** As the degree to which a set of inherent characteristics fulfill requirements.

## Design Science

Design Science (DS) is grounded in the book of Simon (1996) "The Science of the Artificial," in which a distinction is made between the natural sciences and the sciences related to man-made artifacts. The key characteristic of natural sciences is that they are explanatory in nature, being engaged in the quest for truth. On the other hand, design sciences, like architecture, engineering, software (as analyzed in the previous section), medicine and law, are prescriptive in nature and are engaged in solving field problems through the creation of new and innovative artifacts (Hevner, March, Park, & Ram, 2004). DS is based on both design thinking, providing its pragmatic and normative orientation, and system thinking, providing the capability to analyze and understand complex relationships (Aken, 2004).

Design theories, grounded on the paradigm of Design Science, are based on the combination of artifacts (i.e. actions, structures, processes, systems, etc.) and methods (i.e. design processes, design roles, specific methods, etc.). Their purpose is to produce new and innovative artifacts that are created to solve field problems regarding the construction of a "better" reality. This aspect makes design theories different from both descriptive theories and explanatory theories of natural and social sciences in terms of ethical issues. In fact, disinterestedness and consensual objectivity, which represent key values for natural and social sciences, lose their role in Design Science where the ethical dimension becomes a central issue (e.g. Friedman (1997); Lessig (1999); Nissenbaum (1998)). Introna and Nissenbaum (2000), in their article on the political issues of search engine design, claim "the commitment we hope to inspire among the designers and builders of search engine technology is a commitment to the value of fairness as well as to the suite of values represented by the ideology of the Web as a public good." Therefore translating these ideas

into practice they claim that information systems' professionals can build better systems (that better respect important social values) if they build them with an explicit commitment to values (Table 3).

According to Hevner et al. (2004), Design Science relies on 7 guidelines.

1. **Design as an Artifact:** Design Science research must produce viable artifacts in the form of constructs (vocabulary and symbols), models (abstractions and representations), methods (algorithms and practices), or instantiations (implemented and prototype systems).

2. **Problem Relevance:** Where the objective of design-science research is to develop technology-based solutions to important and relevant business problems.

3. **Rigorous Evaluation Methods:** For the design, i.e., the utility, quality, and efficacy

*Table 3. Design science core features and properties*

| Design Science Core Features and Properties | Summary | References |
|---|---|---|
| Artifact Production | Natural sciences study natural systems and environments, while design science is related to man-made artifacts. These artifacts can be material or immaterial and can consist of any form of designed intervention that can solve a field problem. | (Simon, 1996) |
| Design and System Thinking | Design science is based on both design thinking and system thinking. The first requires a pragmatic and normative orientation the second the analysis of complex relationships. | (Aken, 2004; Walls, Widermeyer, & Sawy, 2006) |
| Ethical Dimension | This ethical dimension has been addressed and widely debated by philosophers of technology, engineers and experts in cyberlaws, who have recognized the intricate connection between technology and social, political, and moral values. | (Friedman, 1997; Introna & Nissenbaum, 2000; Lessig, 1999; Nissenbaum, 1998) |
| Problem Relevance | The objective of design-science research is to develop technology-based solutions to important and relevant business problem. | (Hevner et al., 2004) |
| Rigor | It is fundamental the use of rigorous evaluation methods for the design. Specifically, the utility, quality, and efficacy of a design artifact must be rigorously demonstrated via well-executed evaluation methods | (Hevner et al., 2004) |
| Academic Importance | Each design exercise must be considered as a contribution to the academic world. | (Hevner et al., 2004) |
| (Nested) Problem Solving | The Design Science framework details how design and research problems can be rationally decomposed by means of nested problem solving. The tight connection between problem solving (the core of design science research), rigor and relevance is fundamental for successful design. | (Hevner, 2007; Wieringa, 2009) |

of a design artifact must be rigorously demonstrated via well-executed evaluation methods.

4. **Contribution to the Academic World:** Effective DS research must provide clear and verifiable contributions in the areas of the design artifact, design foundations, and/or design methodologies.

5. **Research Rigor:** Applying exact methods in the construction and evaluation of the design artifact.

6. **Design as a Search Process:** i.e., the search for an effective artifact requires utilizing available means to reach desired ends while satisfying laws in the problem environment.

7. **Publishing:** In both the academic and practitioner's community.

The tight connections between problem solving at the core of Design Science research, rigor and relevance has been illustrated by Hevner (2007) in his "three cycle view": The *relevance cycle* bridges the contextual environment of the research project with the DS activities; The *rigor cycle* connects DS activities with the knowledge base of scientific foundations, experience, and expertise that informs the research project; And the *central design cycle* iterates between the core activities of building and evaluating the design artifacts and processes of the research. Indeed, the outcomes of Design Science research are not design exemplars, but generic artifacts like methods, reference models or ontologies, which are positioned between "fundamental understanding" and "actual application."

Design, prototyping and evaluation of an ESA (enterprise software application) is based on the knowledge of users, technology and tasks, that comes in the form of analytical, explanatory or predictive rules resulting in design prescriptive rules. Methodologies are indeed theories for design and action focusing on "how to do something" and differing from those aimed at analyzing, explaining, and predicting, which belong to the natural sciences, although they are tightly connected with them.

The connection among the paradigms of science described so far takes place within the so called "rigor cycle" of Design Science (Hevner et al., 2004), in which researchers explore the existing knowledge base seeking the foundations for building and evaluating design artifacts and processes among available scientific theories and methods, experience and expertise, and meta-artifacts, i.e., the methods and tools for designing the former. These foundations are often referred to as kernel theories in the information systems (IS) design research literature, and the nature of their relationship with IS meta-artifacts determines the positioning of existing design theories in different streams of design research (Fischer, Winter, & Wortmann, 2010).

## Service Science

Service Science is emerging as the study of value co-creation in a globally integrated and connected world where diverse entities generate, utilize, configure, and share resources and relationships to co-create benefits with and for each other, both as individuals and collectives, and addressing short and long-term needs (Spohrer, 2009). It is an interdisciplinary approach to the engineering of services systems in which specific arrangements of people and technologies take actions that have value for others.

Service systems, the basic unit of a services science, emphasize collaboration and adaptation, and establish a balanced and interdependent framework for systems of reciprocal service provision. Such systems may be business entities that survive, adapt, and evolve through mutual exchange and application of resources – particularly knowledge and skills (Spohrer, Maglio, Bailey, & Gruhl, 2007). Indeed, as identified by Maglio & Spohrer (2008), entities within service systems exchange competence along at least four dimensions: *information- sharing*, *work-sharing*, *risk-sharing*, and *goods-sharing*, and engage in three main activities in order to co-create value: *proposing value, accepting a proposal*, and *realizing the proposal*. Thus, at least two service systems must engage in both applying and integrating resources in order for service to be realized and for value co-creation to occur (S. L. Vargo & Akaka, 2009). They exchange with others to enhance adaptability and survivability.

Today, certain dimensions of our life have been affected dramatically by information technology, in particular by the Internet that eventually imposed novel service conception based on grid and cloud technologies (Dragoicea & Borangiu, 2013). Together, these two technological concepts refer to specific distributed networks of interoperability services that sustain new ways of gathering, processing, publishing and accessing information in a smarter world that becomes more interconnected, instrumented and intelligent. Pursuing smarter and more sustainable systems, the innovative potential of IT-services in different service industries has been definitely drawn in the new approach of Service Science and its related procedural approaches like Service Oriented Computing, Service Oriented Software Engineering, or Model Driven Service Oriented Architectures (Papazoglou, 2003; Strosnider, Nandi, Kumaran, Ghosh, & Arsnajani, 2008; Tsai, 2005).

The emergence of the new Service Science creates in fact a distinctive body of knowledge on improving new business models based on commoditized IT services that may create cost benefits. Today customers strive for accessing services instead of owning their systems and/or goods (Dragoicea & Borangiu, 2013). As IT is more and more seen as a commodity, new models of IT-based service production and delivery can be imagined and implemented. In this line, one can identify two different service(s) orientations (S. L. Vargo & Akaka, 2009):

1. Grounded in the traditional view of economic exchange and value creation as primarily involving goods (tangible products), with services conceptualized relative to goods;

2. Alternatively, where services can be considered in their own right (i.e., without reference to goods).

Some service-related fields, e.g., Information Systems, have associated to network science to analyze social networking and other economic activities. However, by and large, Service Science has not yet fully engaged with this field to further our understanding on connected value co-creation. As addressed by Hsu (2009), one reason may be the fact that service systems and networks are artificial in nature and hence subscribing more to design than to discover. But more fundamentally, the state of the art may be such that network science has not yet considered the full scale of complexity of service networks, and hence hindered its application to service design (Table 4).

## Open Research Questions for EISB and the Neighboring Domains Body of Knowledge

Based on the findings and discussions conducted during recent years inside the FInES community, and the considerations presented in the above sections, the authors propose the following key open research questions as a priority to be answered with the establishment of EI based on scientific oriented methods (Jardim-Goncalves, Agostinho, & Steiger-Garcao, 2012):

- Why is there so much effort wasted on the development of dedicated technical solutions for interoperability problems? How can this be reduced using the available body of knowledge in EI and neighboring sciences?
- Why do certain interoperability problems appear to be very complex until one finds a dedicated solution for them? How can these solutions be generalized and formalized to guarantee reusability and repeatability?

*Table 4. Service science core features and properties*

| Service Science Core Features and Properties | Summary | References |
|---|---|---|
| The Concept of Value | This concept is central to Service Science, which adopts a concept of value-in-use rather than value-in-exchange. Much research has been devoted to understanding how value-in-use provides understanding of service value, as related to utility. | (Stephen L Vargo & Lusch, 2008) |
| Value Co-Creation | In the concept of value, one finds the opportunity for value co-creation, where service suppliers and consumers must work synergistically to generate value, as without doing so there is no way to generate value in use. | (Grönroos, 2008) |
| Value Networks | Value networks can be defined as complex sets of social and technical resources, which work together to create economic value in the form of value-in-exchange and/or value-in-use. This gives rise to several methodologies assigning service values, including e3-value, ECOLEAD, Allee's Value Conversion Strategy Model, and Caswell's et al. formal model for calculating the total value realized by all value exchanges within a value network. | (Allee, 2008; Camarinha-Matos & Afsarmanesh, 2007; Caswell et al., 2008; Gordijn & Wieringa, 2003) |
| Service Systems | The study of service systems emphasizes collaboration and adaptation in value co-creation, and establishes a balanced and interdependent framework for systems of reciprocal service provision. These systems can be business entities that survive, adapt, and evolve through exchange and application of resources – particularly knowledge and skills – with other systems. | (Spohrer et al., 2007) |
| Service Modeling | Service modeling seeks to formalize the concept of a service, largely through definition on the participants in service value creation (providers and consumers). Proposed models include those by Garschhammer and Baida, Kohlborn's generic business service management framework, and the service process/service package (SP/SP) matrix. | (Baida, Gordijn, Akkermans, Sæle, & Morch, 2007; Garschhammer et al., 2001; Kohlborn, Korthaus, & Rosemann, 2009) |
| Service Description | There are a great many of service description languages proposed, which include some addressing only IT service description issues as well as those that include definition of business processes. | (Oberle, 2010) |
| (Business) Service Management | Business service management is the business discipline dedicated to the holistic management of business services in an organization, i.e. to ensure alignment between customer needs and value offerings of the organization. It includes issues of contracting and performance management, | (Angelov & Grefen, 2008; Camacho, Guerra, Galeano, & Molina, 2005) |

- How to reduce complexity in EI, providing services that can be used universally throughout seamless "plug-and-play" mechanisms, independent of the EI level/area for which they are designed?
- How can one predict and guarantee the long-term knowledge and behavior of interoperability in engineering systems? And as an extension, can the principles of complexity science, namely systems self-organization, be applied in dynamic business networks, to contribute to a sustainable interoperability?

EI does not envisage to become an exact science. Nevertheless, scientific theories are foreseen as integral to EI practice, promotion, and research. The choice of theory, although often unacknowledged, shapes the way practitioners and researchers collect and interpret evidence. In the analyzed neighboring scientific domains, theories range from explicit hypotheses to core features/properties, working models and frameworks of thinking about reality. Some could powerfully influence understandings of EI problems and solutions spaces. Thus, methods coming from both EI and neighboring domains will help to identify the needs of the domain and contribute towards the resolutions of the above questions.

With the EISB, interoperability for enterprises is no longer about basic interconnectivity at the level of technology, or classic information exchange between two entities in static contexts of "universal" business models. Instead, interoperability is closely coupled with the changing nature of business needs, at the level of the enterprise and the community of enterprises, the individual, and the economy (Informal Study Group on Value Proposition for Enterprise Interoperability, 2008). One of the aims of EI is to allow different systems to be integrated in seamless collaborative networks that enable them to advance according to their own needs without risking existing interoperable relationships (Jardim-Goncalves, Agostinho, & Steiger-Garcao, 2010). Disciplines such as Complexity, Software Engineering, Design Science and Services Science can be preeminent contributors to the EISB framework.

## EISB FLUID KNOWLEDGE

The authors designate by "Fluid," all knowledge that is located within the fuzzy borders of EISB.

This knowledge is analyzed in a holistic form, explaining in detail how it relates to the remaining EISB components. Figure 2 illustrates that relationship, evidencing the fact the "Fluid" is the borderline of EISB but can "contribute to" and "learn from" EI specific knowledge.

Following a recursive strategy to recognize neighboring scientific domains and their relationship with EISB (i.e. the waves methodology – axis I), a small set of domains has been selected among the panoply of available neighbors, for a more detailed insight. As a conclusion of wave 2, the authors, supported by the ENSEMBLE project, have identified potential contributions for the EISB both in terms of shared issues/values and also in the form of theories, methods and systemic approaches. During this wave and the next, the EISB Scientific neighboring Domain Reference Glossary (EISB-SDRG) has been elaborated defining domain terminology that is considered relevant or potentially interesting towards the EISB.

As part of the EISB Knowledge Base, the FInES Wiki is the front-end to the EISB "Fluid" Knowledge, which provides access the EISB com-

*Figure 2. The EISB "Fluid Knowledge" elements composition*

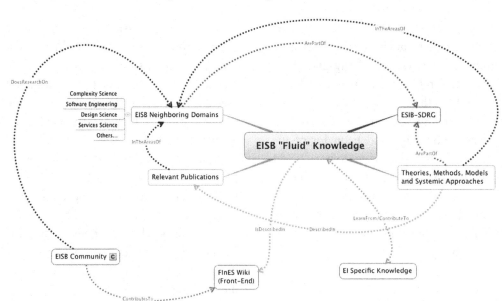

munity (in this case the neighboring community) to contribute with their research and potentially interesting concepts, methods, etc.

## ESIB Scientific Neighboring Domain Reference Glossary (EISB-SDRG)

The classification of neighboring scientific domains under specific categories must be faced with the proper flexibility of any classification exercise. Borders are fuzzy and, as explained, certain scientific disciplines crosscut social, natural and applied sciences (e.g. economics has branches in all of them). The distinction between disciplines is not always sharp and they share a number of cross-discipline fields, e.g. physics plays a significant role in the other natural sciences, as represented

by astrophysics, geophysics, chemical physics and biophysics. For these reasons, the EISB-SDRT (Scientific Domain Reference Taxonomy/Model) published in Jardim-Goncalves et al. (2012) has been flattened to a glossary of potential neighboring scientific domains – the EISB-SDRG.

The terminology enumerated in the glossary is too large to be analyzed in detail along this paper, but the purpose of this exercise is to keep record of all domains and methods that are neighbors to EI, whether they are focused theories or more comprehensive areas (sciences) that enclose several theories of their own. Table 5 exemplifies of the information gathered, which is mostly helpful for the compilation of the atomic knowledge of the neighboring areas in the FInES wiki (Figure 3).

*Table 5. Subset of EISB-SDRG*

| Domain, Theory, Method, Model and Concept | Description |
|---|---|
| Agent-Based Modeling | Agent-Based computational Modeling (ABM) is used to study the dynamics of systems interactions and to reveal emergent structures and patterns of behavior. ABM has characteristics that are particularly useful for studying embedded systems, since agent-based models deploy a diversity of agents to represent the constituents of the focal system (Courtney et al., 2008; Gilbert, 2007). |
| Service-Oriented Architectures (SOA) | A set of principles and methodologies for designing and developing software in the form of interoperable services. (e.g., WS-*, UDDI, SoaML) (Athena, 2005; Oberle, 2010). |

*Figure 3. Snapshot of the EISB-SDRG at the FInES wiki*

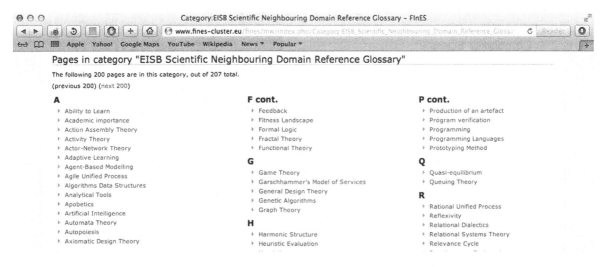

## Analyzing the Relationship with EI

In order to understand its proximity to EI, the neighboring domains literature reviewed before, needs to be analyzed with regards to the scientific areas of Enterprise Interoperability (Koussouris et al., 2011). This can be executed in 3 complementary steps, namely:

1. **Matching:** To identity the high-level relationship between each neighboring domain core features and the EISB scientific areas;

2. **Learning (Neighboring → EISB):** To examine what can in fact contribute to the EISB, namely to the solution space, and thus become part of the EISB Fluid knowledge. The "learning" analysis enables to identify, form a large panoply of methods and systemic approaches available in the EISB-SDRG, which of them can in fact provide something concrete in the specification and design of interoperable solutions.

3. **Extensibility (EISB → Neighboring):** To evaluate if there is evidence of interoperability-based solutions in the neighboring domains, and therefore determine whether EI is relevant in the context of each scientific domain. The rationale of this exercise is opposite to the one of "learning," i.e. instead of looking for formal contributions from the neighboring domains to the EISB, one is envisaging to identify for which domains EI is relevant. An initial analysis to validate the usefulness of this exercise has been conducted within the ENSEMBLE project and presented at different workshops (e.g. Samos 2011 Summit).

This analytical process confirms the inter-relationship(s) that EI has with other domains, namely its interdisciplinary nature. As illustrated in Figure 4 and Table 6 (with more detail), this clearly enables to comprehend the proximity of each neighboring domain by the number of

*Figure 4. Neighboring domains relationship with EI*

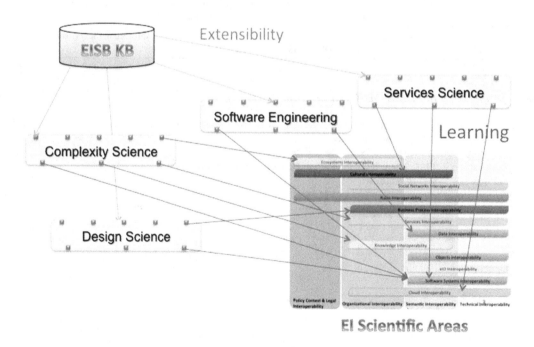

*Table 6. Matching and learning from neighboring domains core features and properties*

| Neighboring Domain | Core Features and Properties | EISB Scientific Area (Koussouris et al., 2011) | Learning: Formal Methods and Systemic Approaches (Indicative) | Comment on the Relationship |
|---|---|---|---|---|
| Complexity Science | Dimensionality | Rules | • Non-cooperative games<br>• Fitness Landscape<br>• Organizational Management methods<br>• Decentralized control<br>• Scalable traffic control<br>• Intelligent Agents | In EI, cooperation is fundamental and companies benefit from participation in cooperative networks where they can maximize their return of investment. Nevertheless, enterprise systems with high dimensionality levels tend to be too uncooperative while, on the opposite side, too much control tends to diminish innovation and chances of succeeds. Complexity can provide EISB, methods and approaches that help measuring and maintaining enterprises freedom in efficient levels. Rules and regulations or budgetary restrictions, ensure that a system's behavior is greatly limited, changing its complexity and helping to behave more predictably, thus fitting to different organization structures. |
| | Non-linearity | N/A | • Monitoring<br>• Edge of Chaos | Non-linear systems are unpredictable thus their interoperation cannot be controlled externally. Whereas this can be important characteristic at business strategy level insuring some degree of surprise to competitors, it is disastrous at information systems level invalidating attempts to cooperate and interoperate. Complex systems that are not erratic (e.g. CAS), manage to control non-linearity by constantly monitoring their status and the environment, maintaining themselves in a quasi equilibrium. |
| | Quasi-equilibrium | All | • Feedback | Is closely related to monitoring, feedback and self-organization capabilities. Only using them is possible to detect when a system is approaching non-equilibrium and prevented from collapsing into randomness. This way, in one sense quasi-equilibrium is an issue for all EISB areas, but on the other way, it is software interoperability that categorizes conformance and interoperability testing which can detect when systems are approaching dangerous situations. |
| | Decomposability | • Data<br>• Process<br>• Software<br>• Ecosystem | • Agent-Based Modeling<br>• Exploratory Analysis<br>• Self-similar traffic modeling | EI is closely related to modeling. Either the full enterprise, products, processes or plain data, models intent to represent and reduce the complexity behind the major enterprise activities. When software systems or data models are divided into modules and components, decomposability is being used in the separation of concerns. Decomposed parts evidence lower complexity values, but the aggregate system needs to manage all the relationships. Decomposability also enables the complexity of a system to be reduced into more controllable agents, thus methods applied may be very similar. |

*continued on following page*

*Table 6. Continued*

| Neighboring Domain | Core Features and Properties | EISB Scientific Area (Koussouris et al., 2011) | Learning: Formal Methods and Systemic Approaches (Indicative) | Comment on the Relationship |
|---|---|---|---|---|
| Software Engineering | Reflexivity | • Process<br>• Service<br>• Software | | Enterprises are frequently changing to respond to new market requirements or internal needs for evolution. Frequently, when that happens they might need to realign their business processes, service compositions, and sometimes even software systems which, in turn, may impact their relationships with other enterprises. These may have the need to adapt as well and might cause a reflexive behavior. |
| | Ability to Learn | • Objects<br>• Knowledge | • Heuristics<br>• Feedback<br>• Adaptive learning<br>• Holland's generic algorithms | The learning ability of physical entities requires the newest information and communication technologies (e.g. multi-agent-based models, RFID tags, etc.), and knowledge intensive data repositories that retain past knowledge used in the learning process. |
| | Self-Organization | • Knowledge<br>• Software<br>• Service | • Kauffman NK and NKC models<br>• Autopoiesis<br>• Decentralized control | Self-organization within EI is related to the capability for a system to adapt automatically to external changes, based on a certain degree of intelligence and the previous acquired knowledge. |
| | Emergence | • Service<br>• Cloud<br>• Social Networks<br>• Ecosystem | • Power Law functions (e.g., Pareto Principle, Fractals, etc.)<br>• Power Law distributions (e.g. Pareto, Kolmogorov–Smirnov)<br>• Strange Attractor | The degree of freedom that individual agents are allowed in information system is rather reduced, but still they can emerge into higher level systems, e.g. mashups created using automatic service discovery and composition; or cloud federation. Nevertheless, if the system depends on a human activity, it tends to exhibit positive feedback and enable complex phenomena such as social networks emergence or ecosystems. Complexity topics such as reflexivity, ability to learn, self-organization and emergence are very closely coupled, thus the methods that apply to one, apply to the majority of them. Feedback is an example, i.e. being one the most important processes used in complexity, it is both an effect of a system's past activity and an influence on its future activity, contributing to reflexivity and emergence. Mathematic equations of deterministic complexity allow for dynamic behavior, by incorporating feedback in most of the systematic ideas about the actions of a system in its environment, i.e. learning, adaptation, evolution. |
| | Abstraction | • Software<br>• Services<br>• Knowledge<br>• Identity<br>• Social Networks<br>• Cloud<br>• Ecosystem | | The concept of abstraction may particularly be aligned to the context of services, knowledge, identity, cloud and ecosystems, apart from software systems. It allows for the specification of the problems and solutions at the specific levels without regard to the interoperability issues that lie beneath (i.e. for data, process, rules, objects, etc.). |
| | Agility | • Software<br>• Cultural<br>• Social Networks<br>• Ecosystem | Agile Unified Process (AUP) | The paradigm of agile software through its provision for rapid and continual user feedback and interaction during software development may contribute to the social-oriented aspects of interoperability related to cultural, social networks and ecosystems issues. The agile techniques including test driven development (TDD), Agile Modeling, agile change management, which fall under the AUP umbrella provide examples on how to drive interoperability. The philosophy on which they are based, especially with regard to simplicity and tool independence, are very much related to interoperability. |

*continued on following page*

*Table 6. Continued*

| Neighboring Domain | Core Features and Properties | EISB Scientific Area (Koussouris et al., 2011) | Learning: Formal Methods and Systemic Approaches (Indicative) | Comment on the Relationship |
|---|---|---|---|---|
| | Design Patterns | All | • Creational Patterns<br>• Structural Patterns<br>• Behavioral Patterns<br>• Concurrency Patterns | Patterns can be applied to all EISB scientific areas in order to document solutions to known problems:<br>• The adaptability to create objects in a manner suitable to each situation embedded in Creational Patterns can be applied to the interoperability areas both as a philosophy and as a practice. Existing patterns may be appropriately extended to provision for interoperability aspects, as well;<br>• Structural patterns which ease the software design by identifying a simple way to realize relationships between entities, could well guide the design of specific interoperability patterns among enterprises;<br>• Behavioral patterns provide increased flexibility in carrying communication between systems and enterprises;<br>• The multi-threaded programming paradigm supported by concurrency patterns may inspire patterns related to interoperability. |

*continued on following page*

relationships, i.e. many relationships identified means that the neighboring scientific domain is close to EI.

Complexity offers a number of new insights, analytical methods, and conceptual frameworks, and it may offer a synthesis on how enterprises adapt to their environments and population. The most exciting characteristic is, perhaps, the promise that complexity theory will help understanding how systems can learn more effectively, and spontaneously self-organize into more structured and sophisticated forms that are better adapted to their environments. Although most of these findings are yet preliminary and confined to computer simulations, management scientists are claiming to be able to apply complexity principles to bring enterprises to "the edge of chaos," enhancing creativity, learning, and adaptation (Lewin, 1999). Following these findings, the application of complexity theory to EI, information systems (IS) design, implementation, testing, installation, and maintenance is under research as well.

For instance, when looking at complexity in ICT, one cannot overlook the organizational structures that technology supports. ICT underlies a huge part of the operations of modern enterprises, so by extrapolation, the role of IS in enterprises is under the scope of complexity science. In this area, the idea that the "whole is greater than the sum of the parts" is fundamental. Thus, complexity cannot be foreseen just from an examination of the constituent parts of an IS. It is, instead, a characteristic that emerges after the parts are tangled in a way that subsequent separation would destroy the whole, creating integration and interoperability problems (McElroy, 2000). Therefore, many of the complexity features are related and can bring value to areas recognized by EI (see Table 6).

In terms of "extensibility," by definition, no external controller can be applied to regulate internal systems behavior. They need to be self-aware and responsive to the surrounding stimuli.

*Table 6. Continued*

| Neighboring Domain | Core Features and Properties | EISB Scientific Area (Koussouris et al., 2011) | Learning: Formal Methods and Systemic Approaches (Indicative) | Comment on the Relationship |
|---|---|---|---|---|
| | Systematization | All | • Unified Modeling Language (UML)<br>• Z notation<br>• Vienna Development Method Specification Language (VDM-SL)<br>• pi-calculus<br>• Petri nets<br>• Model-driven Architecture (MDA)<br>• Programming languages<br>• Computer-Aided Software Engineering (CASE)<br>• Software Requirements Elicitation<br>• Integrated Software Development<br>• Software Testing<br>• Problem Tracking | Domain-specific languages (DSL) are dedicated to a particular problem domain, a particular problem representation technique, and/or a particular solution technique. Formal, algebraic or model-based methods for eliciting requirements, as well as for rigorously and abstractly defining software component interfaces and behavior, may well be customized and applied in interoperability problem definition and problem/solution matching:<br>• A modeling language as UML is used to specify, visualize, modify, construct and document the artifacts of a system under development and provides the baseline to identify and solve interoperability problems from the design phase;<br>• Specification languages are used during systems analysis, requirements analysis and systems design. They can be studied in depth in order to understand how interoperability concerns are embedded in the "what" descriptions;<br>• In MDA, the separation of design from the architecture, as well as the definition of system functionality using a platform-independent model (PIM) and an appropriate domain-specific language (DSL), are fully aligned with the concept of interoperability;<br>• Programming languages from Pascal and C to Perl provide directly executable formal ways used to implement a system. With appropriate extensions, they mat incorporate interoperability by design during software development.<br>CASE tools are software systems designed to support routine activities in the software process (such as editing design diagrams, checking diagram consistency and keeping track of program tests which have been run) may be extended and applied to monitor interoperability across all scientific areas:<br>• The consistent view of SE for defining education and training requirements, certification rules, and accreditation policies for university curricula also represents an example for Enterprise Interoperability and may incorporate the EI directions in a win–win manner. Especially, the SWEBOK represents a systematic paradigm for Enterprise Interoperability on how to promote a consistent view of a discipline worldwide, to set its boundaries with respect to other disciplines and to characterize its contents;<br>• Software requirements tools provide a systematic and automated way to elicit, analyze and trace the requirements, with interoperability often being listed as one of them;<br>• IDEs (Integrated Development Environments) providing program editors, compilers and code generators, interpreters and debuggers provide insight to understand the software building process and the existence of interoperability aspects in each of them;<br>• Software testing methods and tools have strong relation with EI assessment issues;<br>• Problem tracking tools in SE provide best practices on which interoperability problem tracking tools may be developed. |

*continued on following page*

*Table 6. Continued*

| Neighboring Domain | Core Features and Properties | EISB Scientific Area (Koussouris et al, 2011) | Learning: Formal Methods and Systemic Approaches (Indicative) | Comment on the Relationship |
|---|---|---|---|---|
| | Encapsulation | • Software<br>• Services<br>• Social Networks<br>• Cloud<br>• Ecosystem | | From an interoperability perspective, encapsulation is of particular importance when it comes to software systems, services, social systems, cloud and ecosystems. |
| | Lifecycle Approach | Software | • Rational Unified Process (RUP)<br>• ISO/IEC 12207:2008. Systems and software engineering -- Software life cycle processes<br>• Waterfall Method<br>• Spiral Method<br>• Prototyping Method | The rationale behind the software lifecycle process - from inception and requirements elicitation to the implementation, testing and maintenance – lays the grounds to infuse the interoperability dimensions of software systems on more concrete grounds. Waterfall, Spiral and Prototyping are methods that impose structure on the development of a software product, and need to be studied in order to understand the exact stages in which interoperability solutions should be infused. The best practices for modern software engineering identified by an iterative software development process framework like RUP include explicitly or implicitly interoperability concerns and need to be carefully studied to understand how the interoperability requirements can be modeled in a homogenized way and embedded properly. Also, ISO/IEC 12207:2008 establishes a common framework for software life cycle processes, with well-defined terminology, that can be referenced not only by the software industry, but by the EISB with regard to software systems interoperability. |
| | Object Orientation | • Software<br>• Data<br>• Objects | OOA (Object-oriented Architectures) | The object-oriented thinking is beneficiary to the software systems interoperability, as well as to objects and RFID-enabled things in general. OOA model a system as a group of interacting objects, each of which object represents some entity of interest in the system being modeled, and is characterized by its class, its state (data elements), and its behavior. It is particularly beneficiary for EI to learn how coordination, interaction and eventually interoperability can be achieved by and through such an architecture |
| | Polymorphism | • Software<br>• Rules<br>• Process<br>• Services<br>• Cloud | | Enterprises are particular prone to change and to situations that demand different manipulations. In this respect, the ability that polymorphism brings is related not only to software systems, but to rules, processes, services and the cloud, as well. |
| | Prescriptive Principles | All | • Conway's Law<br>• Ninety-ninety Rule<br>• Sixty-sixty Rule | Philosophies, principles and constraints recognized in Software Engineering apply to Enterprise Interoperability. Indicative heuristics that may also apply to EI are:<br>• Align incentives for developer and customer;<br>• Build with and for reuse;<br>• Define software artifacts rigorously;<br>• Establish a software process that provides flexibility;<br>• Grow systems incrementally;<br>• Invest in understanding the problem;<br>• Know software engineering techniques before using development tools; |

*continued on following page*

*Table 6. Continued*

| Neighboring Domain | Core Features and Properties | EISB Scientific Area (Koussouris et al., 2011) | Learning: Formal Methods and Systemic Approaches (Indicative) | Comment on the Relationship |
|---|---|---|---|---|
| Design Science | Service Orientation | • Software<br>• Services<br>• Cloud | • SOA (Service-oriented Architectures)<br>• Web Services | The emerging service-orientation in software design affects the interoperability among software systems themselves, the services they invoke and the cloud on which they are deployed. The principles and methodologies for designing and developing software in the form of interoperable services that expose well-defined business functionalities formulate a solid basis that can be extended and applied for interoperability purposes. The loose coupling of business logic (services) and technology is an example of interoperability that can be applied in various scientific areas as well. The tenets and specifications of Web services reduce or even eliminate interoperability concerns at technical level. Web Services Interoperability (WS-I) also guidelines and tests for interoperability that are beneficiary at least at the Services Interoperability level. |
| | Usability | • Software<br>• Cultural | • Usability testing<br>• Cognitive walkthrough<br>• Heuristic evaluation | The usability parameters in software systems will affect their interoperability and the understanding enterprises have regarding their fulfillment of enterprise operations and their alignment to their strategy. Usability Engineering Methods (UEMs), which are generally concerned with human-computer interaction, provide a systematic way to deal with software systems and cultural-related issues. |
| | Artifact Production | • Objects<br>• Process | • Requirements Engineering<br>• Process Modeling<br>• Concept of Viable Artifact | The methodologies involved in the analysis of requirements and of available resources, and in the proposal of solutions are important for the research of viable/optimal interaction mechanisms between objects and processes. The inter-relation of technical aspects with human factors influences the degree of lack of determinism in most of the interoperability issues. The relevant solutions need to incorporate the capability of life with this unavoidable fuzziness. |
| | Design and System Thinking | • Data<br>• Process<br>• Rules | • Complex systems analysis<br>• Model driven architecture<br>• Contextual pro-activity | Design is almost always a re-combination of (complex) systems, and it is very important to gain a thorough knowledge of systems components like data, processes, rules of interaction. The approach of combining a pragmatic and normative orientation with system thinking provides the capability to analyze and understand the complex relationships typical of interoperability issues. |
| | Ethical Dimension | • Cultural<br>• Knowledge<br>• Social Networks | Ethical dimension evaluation | Interoperability issues can be divided broadly into technological and social. In relation to the latter category all the methods and approaches can be incorporated into EISB. The importance of keeping under control the human aspects of design (both in relation to the developers and to the users-to-be) has to be reflected in these interoperability aspects, where the human factor is prevalent in respect to technology. |
| | Problem Relevance | • Knowledge<br>• Cultural | • Requirements Engineering<br>• Relevance cycle | The concept of relevance of the problem to be solved is very important when analyzing interoperability issues related to knowledge and cultures, as the degree of relevance very often needs to be reconciled and aligned. As interoperability issues will be afforded in time by different research teams, a continuous relevance analysis should be carried on, in order to optimize efforts. |
| | Rigor | Rules | • Requirements Tracking<br>• Rigor cycle | The rigorous approach is very important in relation to the "soft" aspects related to the human side of the issues. In fact, the rigor of approach is particularly needed when aligning or inter-relate rules. |

*continued on following page*

*Table 6. Continued*

| Neighboring Domain | Core Features and Properties | EISB Scientific Area (Koussouris et al., 2011) | Learning: Formal Methods and Systemic Approaches (Indicative) | Comment on the Relationship |
|---|---|---|---|---|
| | Academic Importance | • Cultural<br>• Knowledge<br>• Ecosystem | • Data Mining<br>• Knowledge Discovery | It is important that interoperability research, both on the technical and on the human side, is actively related to the academic world, for mutual advantage. Particularly in these non-technical areas, relevant research advances can be achieved when implementing interoperability, as the related issues imply many cross-disciplinary analyses. A specific consideration of this opportunity has to be pursued. |
| | (Nested) Problem Solving | • Software<br>• Process<br>• Cultural<br>• Knowledge<br>• Services<br>• Cloud<br>• Ecosystem | • Complex systems engineering<br>• Agent based Modeling<br>• Social data analytics<br>• Central design cycle | The nesting of issues is typical of complex systems, and the regulative cycle (problem investigation, solution design, design validation, solution implementation, and implementation evaluation) applies perfectly to the issues encountered particularly in these interoperability areas, level by level in a fractal-like structure. In this way every single local solution can be exploited in other systemic exercises, in a sort of mash-up solution development. The methodology of keeping a parallel control of all three aspects of design is to be strongly affirmed in the interoperability exercises in these areas, characterized by different levels of prominence of technological and human factors. The tight connections between problem solving, rigor and relevance can help in putting in perspective the different interoperability issues and in orienting research efforts. |
| | The Concept of Value | All | | This concept has informed the EISB knowledge base content on Value Scenarios and Business Models. |
| | Value Co-Creation | • Service<br>• Process<br>• Cultural<br>• Knowledge<br>• Cloud<br>• Ecosystem | • Value Concept Models<br>• Value Scenarios<br>• Business Models | Value co-creation is an important concept to be applied to service, process, cloud and ecosystems. Nevertheless, to achieve effective value co-creation, issues of cultural differences must be addressed and resolved, at least between local enterprises, and frequently between globally distributed enterprises. Also, managed knowledge sharing is an essential requirement in achieving value co-creation. |
| | Value Networks | • Service<br>• Process<br>• Software<br>• Ecosystem | Methodologies assigning service values (e.g., e³-value) | The effective functioning of value networks is dependent on the interoperability of enterprise systems. Value networks are conceptually related directly to value networks. |
| | Service Systems | • Service<br>• Software<br>• Cloud | | Service systems are an approach to providing interoperability between software elements. |

Service Science

*continued on following page*

*Table 6. Continued*

| Neighboring Domain | Core Features and Properties | EISB Scientific Area (Koussouris et al., 2011) | Learning: Formal Methods and Systemic Approaches (Indicative) | Comment on the Relationship |
|---|---|---|---|---|
| | Service Modeling | • Service<br>• Cloud<br>• Data | • Agent based Modeling<br>• Garschhammer's model of services (Garschhammer et al., 2001)<br>• Baida's model of needs and demands (Baida et al., 2007)<br>• Kohlborn's generic business service management framework (Kohlborn et al., 2009)<br>• Service process/service package (SP/SP) matrix (Kellogg & Nie, 1995) | In the cases where service systems support interoperating enterprises, it is necessary to include models of the services to be used at all levels of design and development. Service modeling and agent based modeling have close conceptual relationships, and mathematical morphism concepts offer a route to abstraction and re-instantiation of data. |
| | Service Description | • Service<br>• Process<br>• Data | *Service-oriented architectures:* WS-*, UDDI, SoaML, UPMS, SOA-RM, SOA Ontology, WADL, Core Ontology of Web Services<br>*Semantic Web Services:* OWL-S, WSMO, SAWSDL, SA-REST, RO-SOA, WSMO-Lite, MicroWSMO, Minimal Service Model | Several, only marginally compatible, service descriptions standards are in common and competing use among process and service data. Service description languages require underlying ontologies, which are essential to interoperation of services. |
| | (Business) Service Management | • Service<br>• Cultural<br>• Process<br>• Rules | *Software-as-a-Service:* SML, SaaS-DL<br>*Service Network Models:* OBELIX service ontology, e³Value, SNN<br>*Service System Standards:* Alter, Reference Architecture Foundation of SOA, Service Design Model, Ontological Foundations of Service Science, TEXO Service Ontology, DIN PAS 1018, USDL | Service management structures and procedures must be compatible with organization structures and procedures. This is particularly true in the value co-creation scenario, where management (service and organizational) must cross enterprise boundaries to support a virtual organization. Indeed, achieving and assuring business process interoperability is dependent on maintenance of interoperability of individual enterprise processes which compose virtual enterprise collaborative processes. Formal and structural rules are imposed by legislative aspects of collaboration, e.g. establishing legal contracts. |

In fact, living organisms are adaptive by nature and interoperability is innate, but enterprise information systems need interoperability as means to ensure good feedback, capable of triggering proper responses and avoiding erratic behavior. Therefore, traditional complexity is analytic and does not need EI solutions; however, when being applied to other areas such as management strategies or artificial intelligence, it needs EISB as much as it contributes to it, e.g.:

- **Objects Interoperability and Tagging:** Contribute with the learning ability through the use of embedded physical objects (e.g., RFID tags, etc.);
- **Ontologies:** Provide a common language for sharing and reusing environment generated knowledge.

Moving towards the software industry, today, one of the key challenges faced by any software engineer or ICT expert in general, is to build information systems that can cope with heterogeneous platforms and execution environments in order to work together with multiple systems from different vendors. Indeed, interoperability among software systems has remained among the main priorities in the software engineering research for the last two decades. Nevertheless, despite the plethora of available interoperability solutions and best practices, the actual task of making newly designed software interoperable is still solely assigned to the designers and the developers, as a set of abstract specifications to abide with by the release of the service, without much specific support in tools or methods. These groups of people tend to make software interoperable to the ecosystem that is known to them, which usually results into software that is "remade as interoperable" thus simply limiting cooperation within the same platform neighborhood.

In opposition to Complexity that is related with EI mostly through "learning" relationships, Software Engineering is greatly related through "ex-

tensibility" relationships as well. In fact, EI, being defined as the capacity of two or more enterprises (including all the systems within their boundaries and the external systems that they utilize) have of cooperating seamlessly over a sustained period of time to pursue a common objective, has repercussions on Software Engineering mostly through the "Software Interoperability" scientific area. This area represents the ability of an enterprise system or a product to work with other enterprise systems or products without special effort from the stakeholders (Lusk, Desai, Bradshaw, Lusk, & Butler, 2006). Some of the EISB knowledge that can be extended to Software Engineering accounts for example:

- **Software Systems Interoperability Methods and Tools:** Software Engineering may particularly benefit from the EISB KB that provides access to methods and tools for specific EI problems;
- **Interoperability Assessment Solutions:** Provides the means to evaluate the modularity and interoperability level of information systems and software applications.

Even if not as much ICT intensive as software, Services Science is a similar case, and is closely extended by the "Service Interoperability" scientific area. With the help of the EISB, products and service results can be made "interoperable by design" in any ecosystem rather than being embedded at the development or configuration stages. Thus, to conclude, the design activity is probably one of those that more than others, has the need for EISB, particularly as the designed artifacts are getting more and more complex. Interoperability by Design means that there is the need to rethink how IS are designed keeping as central issue the (non functional) requirement of interoperability. In essence, Interoperability by Design means to develop a system having in mind that in the future it will need to exchange information and services with other applications that were not originally conceived to cooperate together. To better understand the implication and the background of this line of research, it is useful to acquire further knowledge (learning) in the emerging Design Science (Table 6).

## Formal and Other Descriptive Methods Already Broadly Used in the EI Research Community

Formal methods in information systems are best described as the application of a variety of theoretical fundamentals, but also type systems and algebraic data types to problems in software and hardware specification and verification (Monin, 2003). For example, formal approaches in the area of computer science include a collection of methods stemming from mathematical formulation, such as First Order Logic, Category Theory, or Pattern Theory. However, unlike the formal methods in ICT domains, which are mostly mathematically based techniques for the specification, development and verification of systems (Butler,

2001), EI needs to consider other descriptive methods to address the human and organizational levels of interoperability.

Not disregarding the fact that many mathematical topics support sciences formalization, and it is neither possible nor desirable to avoid them when pursuing formal methods; as in Fleck (Fleck, 2006), the EISB will not pursue the approach that applying discrete mathematics to everything assures relevant formal methods. While mathematically rigorous descriptions promise to improve system reliability, design time and comprehensibility, they do so at the cost of an increased learning curve. For this reasons the authors are considering native EI methods complemented with the ones from the Fluid Knowledge, and formalization attempts include systemic approaches, such as Model Driven Architecture (MDA), Business Process Management (BPM) or even Service Oriented Architecture (SOA) elements. Table 7 highlights some of them already integrating the EISB body of knowledge.

*Table 7. EISB systemic approaches*

| EISB Area | Systemic Approaches | Benefits and Contributions for EISB |
|---|---|---|
| Data Interoperability | Model Morphisms (MoMo) | MoMo is the application to systems interoperability and information models of the mathematical morphism method, i.e. an abstraction of a structure. By defining model morphisms, it becomes possible to formalize schema mappings and transformations enabling companies to exchange data in the correct format (Agostinho, Sarraipa, Goncalves, & Jardim-Goncalves, 2011; INTEROP Partners, 2005). |
| | Data Modeling and Standardization | Modeling is quickly becoming the primary enabler system design, since it can represent knowledge in an intricate and complex way and at various abstraction levels allowing automated analysis In the same line, standards are of key importance to enable EI (Mosterman & Vangheluwe, 2004). They are great enablers to the agreement of terminology, thus allowing communication and cooperation between software components, processes, organization units and humans (D. Chen & Vernadat, 2002). |
| Process Interoperability | Process Modeling and alignment | Creation of generic process models accompanied with the underlying mapping procedures towards enabling interoperability between processes (e.g. business processes) belonging in different enterprises. |
| | Enterprise Architectures & Models | Are organized in a way that supports reasoning about the structure, properties and behaviour of the system (D. Chen, Doumeingts, & Vernadat, 2008)thus defining its components and providing a blueprint of the enterprise that enable the definition of interoperable relationships |
| Rules Interop. | Organizational Management methods (e.g. organizat. charts) | Identify different organization structures and define business rules |

*continued on following page*

*Table 7. Continued*

| EISB Area | Systemic Approaches | Benefits and Contributions for EISB |
|---|---|---|
| Objects Interop. | Tagging | Providing objects with metadata tags (either RDIF, bar codes, etc.) helps in uniquely identifying them using Web-based tools or large metadata repositories. |
| Software Interoperability | Model-Driven Development (MDD) Model-Driven Architectures (MDA) | To specify an information system at three different levels of abstraction (CIM – computation independent model, PIM – platform independent model, PSM – platform specific model), thus enabling to observe an analyze it from different perspectives and unifying every step of the development of an application or integrated suite from its start as the application's business functionality and behavior, through one or more PSMs, to generated code and a deployable application (OMG, 2003) |
| Software Interoperability | Model-Driven Interoperability (MDI) | A methodological framework, which provides a conceptual and technical support to make enterprises interoperable, by using ontologies and semantic annotations, following the MDA principles (INTEROP Partners, 2007) |
| Software Interoperability | Service-oriented architecture (SOA) | Provide a set of design principles used during the phases of systems development and integration in computing. A system based on a SOA will package functionality as a suite of interoperable services that can be used within multiple, separate systems from several domains (Gorton, 2006). |
| Cultural Interop. | Cross-language semantic matching | Semantic mapping techniques applied to graph-like structures, based for example on WordNet or on cross-language ontologies, identifying those nodes in the two structures which semantically correspond to one another. |
| Knowledge Interoperability | Ontologies | Can be used to describe the problem domain, business semantics and a number of problems - an E/R ontology description can be used for expressing interoperability problems between enterprises. In fact, an ontology produces a common language for sharing and reusing knowledge about phenomena in a particular domain (Gruber, 1995) |
| Knowledge Interoperability | Semantic Annotation | Helps to bridge the ambiguity of the natural language when expressing notions and their computational representation in a formal language. By telling a computer how data items are related and how these relations can be evaluated automatically, it becomes possible to process complex filter and knowledge-based search operations. |
| Services Interoperability | Service Level Agreements | Define a contract between a network service provider and a customer that specifies, recording a common understanding about services, priorities, responsibilities, guarantees, and warranties (Blokdijk, 2008). |
| Services Interoperability | Web Service Orchestration (WSO) | Web Service Orchestration (WSO) is a process of collaboration of the Web services in predefined patterns based on decision about their interaction with one another at the message level and at the execution level. |
| Services Interoperability | Agents and Agent based models | Software agents act for a user or other program in managing a relationship among systems. They have the ability to negotiate and act with some degree of intelligence. |
| Social Networks Interop. | Network Analysis methods | Can be used for identifying the value flows between entities and the various barriers that exist. |
| All | Model-Based Systems Engineering (MBSE) | Applies modeling to support an interoperable systems engineering processes, namely requirements, design, analysis, verification and validation activities, beginning at the conceptual design phase and continuing throughout development and later LC stages (INCOSE & OMG DSIG, 2011). |
| All | Conformance and Interoperability Testing methods | Conformance testing can evaluate if the systems implementation is in conformity with all the requirements, and interoperability testing proves that end-to-end functionality between two or more systems is satisfiable. |

## FUTURE RESEARCH DIRECTIONS AND CONSIDERATIONS

As evidenced in the EISB development methodology and the various waves addressed by project ENSEMBLE, the EISB is not a static result. It has fluid boundaries and is in constant evolution, accommodating the dynamicity of the Enterprise Interoperability domain and by and large, its neighbors.

In the future, it can be important to look beyond the usual focuses of EI, and indeed beyond science, seeking insight into the structures that might be recognized as additional knowledge for the EISB.

Creative arts such as music or dancing can also be of interest and explored inside the wider area of interoperability. In fact, a lot of research has been developed concerning psychology of music and performance, performance sciences, etc.

During the 3rd ENSEMBLE wave, and part of the validation of the results here presented for the domains of Complexity, Software, Design and Services, other domains have been suggested as potentially relevant neighbors and contributors for the EISB. Among them are "Management," "Information Science" and "Innovation Research." This confirms the need to revisit the 3 EISB development waves, so that results can be complemented and validated by an increasingly larger community. It is fundamental that a large operational and users network is built around this effort to boost the potential impact it may have next to the target groups (e.g. researchers, enterprises, etc.). In fact, a key issue of the EISB sustainability strategy is that the EC continues to support the initiative whenever possible, but also that major organizations join, thus somewhat supporting the funding and ensuring a faster EISB establishment.

## CONCLUSION

Despite of the importance of Enterprise Interoperability in the global economy, there is yet no generally accepted scientific base for EI. Due to this fact, situations such as network harmonization breaking with loss of interoperability have a great impact on the enterprise turnover, since nowadays generalization and full re-use of the methods and tools that have been developed so far, is still a great challenge due to the lack of an EISB. Therefore, it is of utmost importance to establish a scientific-base solid enough that embodies lessons learnt from the neighboring domains to demonstrate the interdisciplinary nature of EI.

The authors, supported by the ENSEMBLE project have identified within a set of EI neighboring domains, contributions for the EISB both in terms of shared issues/values and also in the form of methods and systemic approaches. The aim is to be able formalize interoperability problems and solutions, ultimately guaranteeing reusability and repeatability. During the 3 waves, the EISB Scientific neighboring Domain Reference Glossary (EISB-SDRG) has been elaborated defining domain terminology, methods, theories and concepts. The study of neighboring scientific domains and the identification of the "learning" and "extensibility" knowledge leads to the conclusion that those most closely relevant to EI include formal sciences as represented by Complexity but also applied sciences as Software Engineering. Social sciences should not be disregarded as Management, Innovation Research, or even areas from the creative arts could still prove to be relevant.

## REFERENCES

ACM. (2006). *Computing degrees & careers.* Retrieved March 22, 2013, from http://computingcareers.acm.org/?page_id=12

Agostinho, C., Jardim-Goncalves, R., & Steiger-Garcao, A. (2011). Using neighboring domains towards setting the foundations for enterprise interoperability science. In *Proceedings of International Symposium on Collaborative Enterprises (CENT 2011) in the Context of the 15th World-Multi-Conference on Systemics, Cybernetics and Informatics: WMSCI 2011.* Orlando, FL: CENT.

Agostinho, C., Sarraipa, J., Goncalves, D., & Jardim-Goncalves, R. (2011). Tuple-based semantic and structural mapping for a sustainable interoperability. In *Proceedings of 2nd Doctoral Conference on Computing, Electrical and Industrial Systems (DOCEIS'11).* Caparica, Portugal: Springer.

Allee, V. (2008). Value network analysis and value conversion of tangible and intangible assets. *Journal of Intellectual Capital, 9*(1), 5–24. doi:10.1108/14691930810845777

Anderson, P. W., Arrow, K., & Pines, D. (1988). *The economy as an evolving complex system.* Reading, MA: Addison-Wesley Longman.

Angelov, S., & Grefen, P. (2008). An e-contracting reference architecture. *Journal of Systems and Software, 81*(11), 1816–1844. doi:10.1016/j.jss.2008.02.023

Armstrong, D. J. (2006). The quarks of object-oriented development. *Communications of the ACM, 49*(2), 123–128. doi:10.1145/1113034.1113040

Athena, I. P. (2007). *Advanced technologies for interoperability of heterogeneous enterprise networks and their application* (FP6 IST-507849). Retrieved May 30, 2011, from http://interop-vlab.eu/ei_public_deliverables/athena-deliverables/list-of-public-deliverables-submitted-during-the-athena-project

Athena. (2005). *Deliverable D.A5.1: Perspectives in service-oriented architectures and their application in environments that require solutions to be planned and customisable.* Athena IP Project (FP6 IST-507849). Retrieved from http://interop-vlab.eu/ei_public_deliverables/athena-deliverables/A5/d-a5.1/

Baida, Z., Gordijn, J., Akkermans, H., Sæle, H., & Morch, A. (2007). How e-services satisfy customer needs: A software-aided reasoning. In I. Lee (Ed.), *E-business innovation and process management* (pp. 198–233). Hershey, PA: IGI Global. doi:10.4018/978-1-59904-277-0.ch009

Bak, P., Tang, C., & Wiesenfeld, K. (1988). Self-organized criticality. *Physical Review A., 38*(1), 364–374. doi:10.1103/PhysRevA.38.364 PMID:9900174

Blokdijk, G. (2008). *Service level agreement 100 success secrets: SLA, service level agreements, service level management and much more.* New York: Emereo Publishing.

Booch, G. (1994). *Object oriented analysis and design with applications* (Vol. 2, p. 720). The Benjamin Cummings Publishing Co. Inc.

Butler, R. W. (2001). NASA langley formal methods. In *What is formal methods?* Retrieved June 03, 2013, from http://shemesh.larc.nasa.gov/fm/fm-what.html

Camacho, R., Guerra, D., Galeano, N., & Molina, A. (2005). An integrative approach for VO planning and launching. In *Proceedings of Sixth IFIP Working Conference on Virtual Enterprises (PRO-VE 2005)* (Vol. 186, pp. 81–88). Valencia, Spain: IFIP. doi:10.1007/0-387-29360-4_8

Camarinha-Matos, L. M., & Afsarmanesh, H. (2007). A framework for virtual organization creation in a breeding environment. *Annual Reviews in Control, 31*(1), 119–135. doi:10.1016/j.arcontrol.2007.03.006

Caswell, N. S., Nikolaou, C., Sairamesh, J., Bitsaki, M., Koutras, G. D., & Iacovidis, G. (2008). Estimating value in service systems: A case study of a repair service system. *IBM Systems Journal*, *47*(1), 87–100. doi:10.1147/sj.471.0087

Charalabidis, Y., Jardim-Goncalves, R., & Popplewell, K. (2010). Towards a scientific foundation for interoperability. In Y. Charalabidis (Ed.), *Interoperability in digital public services and administration: Bridging e-government and e-business*. Hershey, PA: IGI Global. doi:10.4018/978-1-61520-887-6.ch019

Charalabidis, Y., Lampathaki, F., Kavalaki, A., & Askounis, D. (2010). A review of electronic government interoperability frameworks: Patterns and challenges. *International Journal of Electronic Governance*, *3*(2), 189. doi:10.1504/IJEG.2010.034095

Chen, D., Doumeingts, G., & Vernadat, F. (2008). Architectures for enterprise integration and interoperability: Past, present and future. *Computers in Industry*, *59*(7), 647–659. doi:10.1016/j.compind.2007.12.016

Chen, D., & Vernadat, F. (2002). Enterprise interoperability: A standardisation view. In *Proceedings of IFIP TC5/WG5.12 International Conference on Enterprise Integration and Modeling Technique: Enterprise Inter- and Intra-Organizational Integration: Building International Consensus*. IFIP.

Chen, L., & Li, S. (2004). Analysis of decomposability and complexity for sedign problems in the context of decomposition. In *Proceedings of DETC'04 ASME 2004 Design Engineering Technical Conferences and Computers and Information in Engineering Conference*. Salt Lake City, UT: ASME.

Choi, T., Dooley, K. J., & Rungtusanatham, M. (2001). Supply networks and complex adaptive systems: Control versus emergence. *Journal of Operations Management*, *19*(3), 351–366. doi:10.1016/S0272-6963(00)00068-1

Courtney, J., Merali, Y., Paradice, D., & Wynn, E. (2008). On the study of complexity in information systems. *International Journal of Information Technologies and Systems Approach*, *1*(1), 37–48. doi:10.4018/jitsa.2008010103

Dragoicea, M., & Borangiu, T. (2013). A service science knowledge environment in the cloud. In T. Borangiu, A. Thomas, & D. Trentesaux (Eds.), *Service orientation in holonic and multi agent manufacturing and robotics* (Vol. 472, pp. 229–246). Berlin, Germany: Springer. doi:10.1007/978-3-642-35852-4_15

Dyba, T., & Dingsoyr, T. (2008). Empirical studies of agile software development: A systematic review. *Information and Software Technology*, *50*(9-10), 833–859. doi:10.1016/j.infsof.2008.01.006

ENSEMBLE CSA. (2011). *Envisioning, supporting and promoting future internet enterprise systems research through scientific collaboration* (FP7-ICT-257548). Retrieved May 31, 2011, from http://www.fines-cluster.eu/fines/jm/ENSEMBLE-Public-Category/ensemble-project.html

ENSEMBLE Partners. (2011). *Deliverable D2.3: EISB basic elements report*. Retrieved from http://www.fines-cluster.eu/fines/jm/Publications/ENSEMBLE-Deliverables/View-category.html

ENSEMBLE Partners. (2012a). *Deliverable D2.4: EISB models & tools report*. ENSEMBLE CSA Project (FP7-ICT-257548). Retrieved from http://www.fines-cluster.eu/fines/jm/Publications/ENSEMBLE-Deliverables/View-category.html

ENSEMBLE Partners. (2012b). *Deliverable D2.5: EISB empowerment actions report*. Retrieved from http://www.fines-cluster.eu/fines/jm/Publications/ENSEMBLE-Deliverables/View-category.html

Enterprise Interoperability Cluster. (2008). *Enterprise interoperability research roadmap, version 5.0* (pp. 1–29). Brussels: European Commision. Retrieved from http://cordis.europa.eu/fp7/ict/enet/ei-research-roadmap_en.html

Fischer, C., Winter, R., & Wortmann, F. (2010). Design theory. *Business Information Systems Engineering*, *2*(6), 387–390. doi:10.1007/s12599-010-0128-2

Fleck, A. C. (2006). *22C/55:181 formal methods in software engineering*. University of Iowa. Retrieved from http://homepage.cs.uiowa.edu/~fleck/181.html

Folmer, E., & Bosch, J. (2004). Architecting for usability: A survey. *Journal of Systems and Software*, *70*(1-2), 61–78. doi:10.1016/S0164-1212(02)00159-0

Fowler, M. (2002). Patterns of enterprise application architecture. In M. Fowler (Ed.), *Source* (Vol. 48, p. 560). Reading, MA: Addison-Wesley Professional.

Friedman, B. (1997). *Human values and the design of computer technology*. Chicago: Chicago University Press.

Fuggetta, A. (1993). A classification of CASE technology. *Computer*, *26*(12), 25–38. doi:10.1109/2.247645

Gamma, E., Helm, R., Johnson, R., & Vlissides, J. (1995). Design patterns: Elements of reusable object-oriented software. In *Design* (Vol. 206, p. 395). Reading, MA: Addison-Wesley.

Garschhammer, M., Hauck, R., Hegering, H.-G., Kempter, B., Radisic, I., & Rolle, H. … Nerb, M. (2001). Towards generic service management concepts a service model based approach. In *Proceedings of 2001 IEEE/IFIP International Symposium on Integrated Network Management Proceedings* (pp. 719–732). IEEE. doi:10.1109/INM.2001.918076

Gilbert, N. (2007). Agent-based models. In *Environment and planning A* (Vol. 32). Thousand Oaks, CA: Sage Publications, Inc.

Gold, N., Mohan, A., Knight, C., & Munro, M. (2004). Understanding service-oriented software. *IEEE Software*, *21*(2), 71–77. doi:10.1109/MS.2004.1270766

Gordijn, J., & Wieringa, R. (2003). A value-oriented approach to e-business process design. In *Proceedings of the 15th International Conference, CAiSE 2003*. CAiSE.

Gorton, I. (2006). *Essential software architecture*. Berlin: Springer-Verlag.

Grönroos, C. (2008). Service logic revisited: Who creates value? And who co-creates? *European Business Review*, *20*(4), 298–314. doi:10.1108/09555340810886585

Gruber, T. R. (1995). Toward principles for the design of ontologies used for knowledge sharing. *International Journal of Human-Computer Studies*, *43*(5-6), 907–928. doi:10.1006/ijhc.1995.1081

Hasheminejad, S. M. H., & Jalili, S. (2012). Design patterns selection: An automatic two-phase method. *Journal of Systems and Software*, *85*(2), 408–424. doi:10.1016/j.jss.2011.08.031

Hevner, A. R. (2007). A three cycle view of design science research. *Scandinavian Journal of Information Systems*, *19*(2), 87–92.

Hevner, A. R., March, S. T., Park, J., & Ram, S. (2004). Design science in information systems research. *Management Information Systems Quarterly*, *28*(1), 75–105. doi: doi:10.2307/249422

Highsmith, J., & Cockburn, A. (2001). Agile software development: The business of innovation. *IEEE Computer*, *34*, 120–127. doi:10.1109/2.947100

Holland, J. H. (1992). Complex adaptive systems. *Daedalus*, *121*(1), 17–30.

Holland, J. H. (1996). *Hidden order: How adaptation builds complexity*. Perseus Books.

Holland, J. H. (1998). Emergence: From chaos to order. In *Complexity* (pp. XIII, 258). Perseus Books. Retrieved from http://video.yahoo.com/watch/111582/992708

Honour, E. (2008). Systems engineering and complexity. *INCOSE Insight*, *11*(1), 20.

Hsu, C. (2009). Editorial column--Service science and network science. *Service Science*, *1*(2), i–ii. doi:10.1287/serv.1.2.i

IEEE. Computer Society. (2005). *Guide to the software engineering body of knowledge 2004 version*. IEEE Computer Society. Retrieved from http://www.computer.org/portal/web/swebok/htmlformat

INCOSE, & OMG DSIG. (2011). Model based systems engineering. *MBSE Wiki*. Retrieved February 26, 2012, from http://www.omgwiki.org/MBSE/doku.php

Informal Study Group on Value Proposition for Enterprise Interoperability. (2008). *Unleashing the potential of the european knowledge economy value proposition for enterprise interoperability*. Brussels: European Comission. Retrieved from http://cordis.europa.eu/documents/documentlibrary/100123101EN6.pdf

INTEROP NoE. (2007). *Interoperability research for networked enterprises applications and software* (FP6 IST-1-508011). Retrieved May 30, 2011, from http://interop-vlab.eu/ei_public_deliverables/interop-noe-deliverables

INTEROP Partners. (2005). *Deliverable DTG3.1 (MoMo.2), MoMo roadmap*. INTEROP NoE Project (FP6 IST-1-508011). Retrieved from http://interop-vlab.eu/ei_public_deliverables/interop-noe-deliverables/tg3-model-morphisms/DTG3.1/

INTEROP Partners. (2007). *Deliverable DTG2.3: Report on model driven interoperability*. INTEROP NoE Project (FP6 IST-1-508011). Retrieved from http://interop-vlab.eu/ei_public_deliverables/interop-noe-deliverables/tg2-model-driven-interoperability/dtg2-3-report-on-model-driven-interoperability/

Introna, L. D., & Nissenbaum, H. (2000). Shaping the web: Why the politics of search engines matters. *The Information Society*, *16*(3), 169–185. doi:10.1080/01972240050133634

ISO/IEC. (2008). *Systems and software engineering -- Software life cycle processes (ISO/IEC 12207:2008)*. ISO/IEC.

Jardim-Goncalves, R., Agostinho, C., & Steiger-Garcao, A. (2010). Sustainable systems' interoperability: A reference model for seamless networked business. In *Proceedings of 2010 IEEE International Conference on Systems Man and Cybernetics (SMC)*. Istanbul, Turkey: IEEE.

Jardim-Goncalves, R., Agostinho, C., & Steiger-Garcao, A. (2012). A reference model for sustainable interoperability in networked enterprises: Towards the foundation of EI science base. *International Journal of Computer Integrated Manufacturing*, *25*(10), 855–873. doi:10.1080/0951192X.2011.653831

Jardim-Goncalves, R., Grilo, A., Agostinho, C., Lampathaki, F., & Charalabidis, Y. (2013). Systematisation of interoperability body of knowledge: The foundation for enterprise interoperability as a science. *Enterprise Information Systems*, *7*(1), 7–32. doi:10.1080/17517575.2012.684401

Jardim-Goncalves, R., Grilo, A., & Steiger-Garcao, A. (2006). Challenging the interoperability industry with MDA between computers in and SOA. *Computers in Industry*, *57*(8-9), 679–689. doi:10.1016/j.compind.2006.04.013

Kauffman, S. (1996). *At home in the universe: The search for laws of self-organization and complexity*. Oxford, UK: Oxford University Press.

Kauffman, S., & Clayton, P. (2006). On emergence, agency, and organization. *Biology and Philosophy*, *21*(4), 501–521. doi:10.1007/s10539-005-9003-9

Kellogg, D. L., & Nie, W. (1995). A framework for strategic service management. *Journal of Operations Management*, *13*(4), 323–337. doi:10.1016/0272-6963(95)00036-4

Kohlborn, T., Korthaus, A., & Rosemann, M. (2009). Business and software lifecycle management. In *Proceedings of 2009 Enterprise Distributed Object Computing Conference (EDOC '09)*. EDOC.

Koussouris, S., Lampathaki, F., Mouzakitis, S., Charalabidis, Y., & Psarras, J. (2011). Digging into the real-life enterprise interoperability areas definition and overview of the main research areas. In *Proceedings of International Symposium on Collaborative Enterprises (CENT 2011) in the Context of the 15th World-Multi-Conference on Systemics, Cybernetics and Informatics: WMSCI 2011*. Orlando, FL: CENT. Retrieved from http://www.iiis.org/CDs2011/CD2011SCI/CENT_2011/PapersPdf/ZB589UA.pdf

Lampathaki, F., Koussouris, S., Agostinho, C., Jardim-Goncalves, R., Charalabidis, Y., & Psarras, J. (2011). Towards an interoperability science: Cultivating the scientific foundations for enterprise interoperability. In *Proceedings of International Symposium on Collaborative Enterprises (CENT 2011) in the Context of the 15th World-Multi-Conference on Systemics, Cybernetics and Informatics: WMSCI 2011*. Orlando, FL: CENT.

Lampathaki, F., Koussouris, S., Agostinho, C., Jardim-Goncalves, R., Charalabidis, Y., & Psarras, J. (2012). Infusing scientific foundations into enterprise interoperability. *Computers in Industry*, *63*(8), 858–866. doi:10.1016/j.compind.2012.08.004

Larman, C. (2004). *Applying UML and patterns: An introduction to object-oriented analysis and design and iterative development* (3rd ed.). Upper Saddle River, NJ: Prentice Hall.

Lessig, L. (1999). *Code and other laws of cyberspace*. New York: Basic Books.

Lewin, D. L. (1999). Application of complexity theory to organization science. *Organization Science*, *10*(3), 215. doi:10.1287/orsc.10.3.215

Lusk, E., Desai, N., Bradshaw, R., Lusk, A., & Butler, R. (2006). An interoperability approach to system software, tools, and libraries for clusters. *International Journal of High Performance Computing Applications*, *20*(3), 401–407. doi:10.1177/1094342006067473

Lutowski, R. (2005). *Software requirements: Encapsulation, quality, and reuse*. Boca Raton, FL: CRC Press. doi:10.1201/9781420031317

Maglio, P. P., & Spohrer, J. (2008). Fundamentals of service science. *Journal of the Academy of Marketing Science*, *36*(1), 18–20. doi:10.1007/s11747-007-0058-9

Mainzer, K. (1996). *Thinking in complexity: The complex dynamics of matter, mind, and mankind.* Berlin: Springer-Verlag. doi:10.1007/978-3-662-03305-0

Manson, S. M. (2001). Simplifying complexity: A review of complexity theory. *Geoforum, 32*(3), 405–414. doi:10.1016/S0016-7185(00)00035-X

Maturana, H., & Varela, F. (1980). Autopoiesis and cognition. *The Review of Metaphysics, 42,* 141.

McElroy, M. W. (2000). Integrating complexity theory, knowledge management and organizational learning. *Journal of Knowledge Management, 4*(3), 195–203. doi:10.1108/13673270010377652

Mckelvey, B. (1999). Complexity theory in organization science: Seizing the promise or becoming a fad? Bottom-up organization science. *Emergence, 1*(1), 5–32. doi:10.1207/s15327000em0101_2

Merali, Y., & McKelvey, B. (2006). Using complexity science to effect a paradigm shift in information systems for the 21st century. *Journal of Information Technology, 21*(4), 211–215. doi:10.1057/palgrave.jit.2000082

Monin, J.-F. (2003). *Understanding formal methods.* Berlin: Springer. doi:10.1007/978-1-4471-0043-0

Morris, C. G. (1992). *Academic press dictionary of science and technology.* New York: Academic Press.

Mosterman, P. J., & Vangheluwe, H. (2004). Computer automated multi-paradigm modeling: An introduction. *Simulation, 80*(9), 433–450. doi:10.1177/0037549704050532

Nicolis, G., & Prigogine, I. (1989). *Exploring complexity: An introduction.* W.H. Freeman.

Nissenbaum, H. (1998). Values in the design of computer systems. *Computers & Society,* 38–39. doi:10.1145/277351.277359

Oberle, D. (2010). *Report on landscapes of existing service description efforts.* Retrieved from http://www.w3.org/2005/Incubator/usdl/wiki/D1

OMG. (2003). *MDA guide version 1.0.1 (omg/2003-06-01).* Object Management Group. Retrieved from http://www.omg.org/cgi-bin/doc?omg/03-06-01.pdf

Papadimitriou, C. H. (1994). *Computational complexity.* Reading, MA: Addison-Wesley.

Papazoglou, M. P. (2003). Service-oriented computing: Concepts, characteristics and directions. In *Proceedings of the Fourth International Conference on Web Information Systems Engineering (WISE'03).* Roma, Italy: IEEE.

Phelan, S. E. (2001). What is complexity science, really? *Emergence, 3*(1), 120–136. doi:10.1207/S15327000EM0301_08

Schach, S. (2006). *Object-oriented and classical software engineering* (7th ed.). New York: McGraw-Hill.

Schmidt, D., Stal, M., Rohnert, H., & Buschmann, F. (2000). Pattern-oriented software architecture volume 2: Patterns for concurrent and networked objects. In Event London (Vol. 2, pp. 1–482). Hoboken, NJ: Wiley.

Séguin, N., Abran, A., & Dupuis, R. (2010). Software engineering principles. In *Proceedings of the Third C\* Conference on Computer Science and Software Engineering - C3S2E '10* (pp. 59–65). New York: ACM Press. doi:10.1145/1822327.1822335

Simon, H. A. (1962). The architecture of complexity. *Proceedings of the American Philosophical Society, 106*(6), 467–482. Retrieved from http://www.jstor.org/stable/985254

Simon, H. A. (1995). Near decomposability and complexity: How a mind resides in a brain. In H. J. Morowitz, & J. L. Singer (Eds.), *The mind the brain and complex adaptive systems* (pp. 25–44). Reading, MA: Addison-Wesley.

Simon, H. A. (1996). *The sciences of the artificial.* Cambridge, MA: MIT Press.

Sommerville, I. (2007). *Software engineering* (8th ed.). Harlow, UK: Pearson Education.

Spohrer, J. (2009). Editorial column--Welcome to our declaration of interdependence. *Service Science, 1*(1), i–ii. doi:10.1287/serv.1.1.i

Spohrer, J., Maglio, P., Bailey, J., & Gruhl, D. (2007). Steps toward a science of service systems. *Computer, 40*(1), 71–77. doi:10.1109/MC.2007.33

Strosnider, J. K., Nandi, P., Kumaran, S., Ghosh, S., & Arsnajani, A. (2008). Model-driven synthesis of SOA solutions. *IBM Systems Journal, 47*(3), 415–432. doi:10.1147/sj.473.0415

Tsai, W. T. (2005). Service-oriented system engineering: A new paradigm. In *Proceedings of IEEE International Workshop on Service-Oriented System Engineering (SOSE'05)* (pp. 3–8). IEEE. doi:10.1109/SOSE.2005.34

van Aken, J. E. (2004). Management research based on the paradigm of the design sciences: The quest for field-tested and grounded technological rules. *Journal of Management Studies, 41*(2), 219–246. doi:10.1111/j.1467-6486.2004.00430.x

Vargo, S. L., & Akaka, M. A. (2009). Service-dominant logic as a foundation for service science: Clarifications. *Service Science, 1*(1), 32–41. doi:10.1287/serv.1.1.32

Vargo, S. L., & Lusch, R. F. (2008). Service-dominant logic: continuing the evolution. *Journal of the Academy of Marketing Science, 36*(1), 1–10. doi:10.1007/s11747-007-0069-6

Vijayasarathy, L., & Turk, D. (2012). Drivers of agile software development use: Dialectic interplay between benefits and hindrances. *Information and Software Technology, 54*(2), 137–148. doi:10.1016/j.infsof.2011.08.003

Waldrop, M. M. (1992). *Complexity: The emerging science at the edge of order and chaos.* New York: Simon & Schuster.

Walls, J. G., Widermeyer, G. R., & el Sawy, O. A. (2006). Assessing information system design theory in perspective: How useful was our 1992 initial rendition? *Journal of Information Technology Theory and Application, 6*(2). Retrieved from http://aisel.aisnet.org/jitta/vol6/iss2/6/

Wasserman, A. I. (1996). *Toward a discipline of software engineering.* Reading, MA: Addison Wesley Longman, Inc.

Wieringa, R. (2009). Design science as nested problem solving. In *Proceedings of the 4th International Conference on Design Science Research in Information Systems and Technology DESRIST 09* (pp. 1). ACM Press. doi:10.1145/1555619.1555630

Williams, L. (2010). Agile software development methodologies and practices. *Advances in Computers, 80*(10), 1–44. doi:10.1016/S0065-2458(10)80001-4

Wilson, E. O. (1999). *Consilience: The unity of knowledge.* New York: Vintage.

Wycisk, C., McKelvey, B., & Hülsmann, M. (2008). Smart parts supply networks as complex adaptive systems: Analysis and implications. *International Journal of Physical Distribution & Logistics Management, 38*(2), 108–125. doi:10.1108/09600030810861198

Zweben, S. H., Edwards, S. H., Weide, B. W., & Hollingsworth, J. E. (1995). The effects of layering and encapsulation on software development cost and quality. *IEEE Transactions on Software Engineering, 21*, 200–208. doi:10.1109/32.372147

## KEY TERMS AND DEFINITIONS

**EISB Fluid Knowledge:** All knowledge that is located within the fuzzy borders of EISB. It can be used in the domain of EI being originated in the neighboring domains, or vice-versa, i.e. EI specific knowledge that is used in neighboring domains.

**Enterprise Interoperability (EI):** Ability of enterprises and entities within those enterprises to communicate effectively. Interoperability is considered as significant if the interactions can take place at least on the three different levels of an enterprise: data, services and processes, with semantics carefully defined for a given context.

**Enterprise Interoperability Science Base (EISB):** Scientific foundations to the domains of EI, comprising a new set of concepts, theories and principles derived from established and emerging sciences, with a view to long-term problem solving as opposed to short-term solution provisioning. EISB formulates and structures the knowledge gained through pragmatic research over the last decades.

**Formal Methods:** Mathematically rigorous techniques and tools for the specification, design and verification of systems. Providing a variety of theoretical fundamentals to describe problems, solutions, patterns identification, critical research question, etc., they enable to symbolically examine the entire state space of a design and establish a universal correctness.

**Interoperability:** The ability of two or more systems or components to exchange information and to use the information that has been exchanged.

**Neighboring Domain:** Scientific domain that shares with another, boundaries between application fields, as well as methodologies, techniques and tools that enable a close relationship between the different problem and solution spaces.

**Systemic Approaches:** Extension to formal methods with other descriptive methods that include methodical approaches, which are repeatable and learnable, but not necessarily mathematical intensive.

# Chapter 4
# The Multidimensional Business Value of Information Systems Interoperability

**Euripidis Loukis**
*University of Aegean, Greece*

**Yannis Charalabidis**
*University of Aegean, Greece*

**Vasiliki Diamantopoulou**
*University of Aegean, Greece*

## ABSTRACT

*The creation of complete scientific foundations in the IS interoperability domain necessitates not only the development of mature and widely applicable interoperability architectures, methods, and standards, but also the systematic investigation of the business value they generate. This chapter initially analyses the theoretical foundations of the multi-dimensional business value of IS interoperability and then reviews the quite limited empirical literature on it. Next, it presents an empirical study of the business value generated by the adoption of three main types of IS interoperability standards: industry-specific, proprietary, and XML-horizontal ones. It is based on a large dataset from 14065 European firms (from 25 countries and 10 sectors) collected through the e-Business Watch Survey of the European Commission. It is concluded that all three types of IS interoperability standards increase considerably the positive impact of firm's ICT infrastructure on two important performance dimensions: business processes performance and innovation. However, the effects of these three types of standards differ significantly: the adoption of industry-specific IS interoperability standards has the highest positive impacts, while proprietary and XML-horizontal ones have similar lower impacts. Furthermore, it is concluded that the industry-specific and the proprietary interoperability standards also have positive impacts even at the level of firm's financial performance.*

DOI: 10.4018/978-1-4666-5142-5.ch004

## INTRODUCTION

The creation of complete scientific foundations in the information systems (IS) interoperability domain necessitates not only the development of mature and widely applicable interoperability architectures, methods and standards, but also the systematic investigation of the business value they generate (Legner & Lebreton, 2007; Lampathaki et al., 2012; Jardim-Goncalves et al., 2012). Since big investments are made for the development of various interoperability technologies, and then for their implementation at firm level, it is necessary to study the resulting business benefits and value. This is going to be quite useful for providing guidance to the technological IS interoperability research, in order to focus on the most valuable directions, and also to the individual firms for making more informed decisions concerning their IS interoperability related investments, taking into account not only technical, but also business value factors as well. Furthermore, it will assist firms in maximizing the value they derive from these investments.

IS interoperability, defined by IEEE as the 'ability of two or more systems or components to exchange information and to use the information that has been exchanged' (IEEE, 1990), has been regarded for long time as highly beneficial. In this direction there has been theoretical literature analyzing the business value of IS interoperability, however there is limited empirical literature on it, as explained in more detail later in the following section. Only a very small number of empirical studies have been conducted concerning the business value of IS interoperability, and all of them are based on small datasets. Therefore more empirical research is required concerning all the dimensions of the business value that IS interoperability generates, in order to assess their importance and magnitude in 'real life' and also identify ways of increasing them.

This chapter initially analyses the theoretical foundations of the multi-dimensional business value of IS interoperability, based on a review of relevant theoretical literature, and also of literature in the area of business networks, and then reviews the limited empirical literature in this area. Next it presents an empirical study of the effects of adopting three different types of IS interoperability standards on:

1. The impact of firm's information and communication technologies (ICT) infrastructure on two important performance dimensions: business processes performance and innovation, and

2. On firm's financial performance.

It is based on a large dataset collected from 14065 European firms (from 25 countries and 10 sectors) through the e-Business Watch Survey of the European Commission. In particular, this empirical study is focusing on three main types of IS interoperability standards (Nurmilaakso, 2008a, 2008b; Lampathaki et al., 2009):

- The industry-specific (or vertical) standards, which are usually created by industry associations or sectoral standardization bodies, in order to enable the electronic exchange of important business documents (e.g. quotations, orders, shipment notes, invoices, payment notes) between firms of a specific industry, their suppliers, customers and business partners. As a typical example we can mention the health sector specific standards published and maintained by organizations like the Clinical Data Interchange Standards Consortium (CDISC) (see http://www.cdisc.org/). Such industry-specific standards usually are 'tailored' to meet the needs of the firms of the specific sector, so they have exactly the whole needed "depth and breadth": they include all the range of the required documents and elements of them, and at the same time they do not carry additional elements that would serve neighbouring or even irrelevant domains.

- The proprietary standards, which are typically created and maintained by large and strong firms, who can impose such de-facto specifications for business documents' exchange to their own customers, suppliers or business partners. Such interconnection standards are still very popular in several sectors, e.g. in the large, multinational supermarket chains for accepting electronic invoices from myriads of small and medium suppliers. As a typical example we can mention the TESCO electronic invoicing specifications (see Tesco Invoice Delivery Service at http://tesco.gxs.co.uk). They usually have extensive depth and breadth, but fulfil mainly the needs of (i.e. include mainly the documents and elements required by) the strong creator firm.

- The XML-horizontal standards, which are mainly open cross-sectoral (horizontal) specifications of business documents' interchange formats, aiming to be used by firms of all sectors, which have been based on the XML (eXtensible Markup Language). Typical examples of such standards are the Universal Business Language (UBL) specifications (providing a library of standard XML specifications for the most frequently used business documents to be used in general procurement and transport contexts – see https://www.oasis-open.org/committees/tc_home.php? wg_abbrev=ubl), or the eXtensible Business Reporting Language (XBRL) (supporting financial information exchange – see http://www.xbrl.org). They are broad enough to cover many important aspects of the documents that need to be exchanged among firms, but due to their horizontal nature they lack the needed depth for representing sector-specific characteristics and information elements, as they have been developed

with a 'least common denominator' logic, i.e. they include mainly elements that are common across sectors. It should be mentioned that recently, due to the fast adoption of XML, many industrial standards (and also some proprietary ones) have been ported to XML as well. However, at the time when the data of this study were collected (2006) XML was used mainly for cross-sectoral (horizontal) standards, so XML-based standards were mainly horizontal, therefore the three types of standards we examine in this empirical study were disjoint.

Our study is structured in seven sections. In the next section the theoretical foundations of the business value of IS interoperability are analysed, while in the following section the limited relevant empirical literature is reviewed. Then the research hypotheses of our empirical study are developed. The data and method of the study are described in the next section, followed by the results. In the final section the conclusions are summarized.

## THEORETICAL FOUNDATIONS

There has been some theoretical literature analysing and discussing various dimensions of business value generated by IS interoperability. The most important of them is definitely a report titled 'Unleashing the Potential of the European Knowledge Economy – Value Proposition for Enterprise Interoperability' (Li et al., 2008), which has been written by a high level Informal Study Group (ISG) launched by the European Commission. It concludes that IS interoperability has the potential to improve efficiency dramatically, which has been the main focus in the past, and additionally it can also drive the collaborative development of significant value innovation by 'value networks', defined (based on Allee, 2002) as 'webs of relationships that generate tangible and intangible value through complex dynamic exchanges between two or more individuals, groups, or organizations'. In this direction it defines this new dimension of the value proposition of IS interoperability as "Value innovation derived from new forms of open collaboration and channels targeting new, global and highly customized niches, and grounded in interoperable complex ecosystems, connecting end-users, producers, suppliers, software vendors, telecommunication companies, public bodies and citizens; empowering employees; and sustaining stronger economic growth." The same report proposes an 'Enterprise Interoperability Value Framework' (EIVP), which identifies five types of interaction among firms that can be supported and enhanced by interoperability: communication (exchange of information), coordination (alignment of activities for mutual benefit, avoiding gaps and overlaps, in order to achieve efficiency gains), cooperation (obtaining mutual benefits by sharing or partitioning work, or by establishing supply chain visibility, where manufacturers and distributors allow each other's visibility of stocks, sales and production plans in order to optimize value chain stocks), collaboration (an engagement to work together in order to achieve results and innovative solutions that the participants would be unable to accomplish alone) and channel ("selling less of more products," according to Anderson (2006), which means producing a wider range of products and gaining greater access to small niche markets for selling these products). While the first interaction types support mainly 'red ocean strategies' the last ones support and facilitate 'blue ocean strategies' (using the terminology introduced by Kim and Mauborgne (2005): firms pursuing 'blue ocean strategies' do not aim to out-perform the competition in the existing market, but to create new market space or a "blue ocean," making the competition irrelevant, by introducing radical innovations in the products, services and processes; on the contrary firms pursuing 'red ocean strategies' compete through lower prices or marginal innovations). Also, according to this framework

the scope of exploitation of IS interoperability can vary considerably, and is a significant determinant of the magnitude of the business value generated. So it can be used only for achieving internal information integration (i.e. for making interoperable the applications of different organizational units of the firm), or have a wider scope and use it for supporting specific dyadic business relationships, a hub-spokes structure, or even business networks; widening the scope of exploitation will result in more business value. The above EIVP framework has already been successfully used for analyzing IS interoperability in the Architecture, Engineering and Construction (AEC) sector (Grilo, Jardim-Goncalves, & Cruz-Machado, 2009; Grilo & Jardim-Goncalves, 2010).

Previously Choi and Whinston (2000) had argued that IS interoperability is highly important for maximizing the potential benefits of computing and digital networking technologies. In particular, they argue that it is the key enabler of a new generation of advanced and highly beneficial business practices, such as supply chain management, logistics management, knowledge management, online retailing and auction markets. Also, IS interoperability allows market participants to communicate, exchange information, deliver and use products and services in real time, and this results in significant business benefits. It allows gaining big efficiencies in managing multipartner transactions, in which multiple trades occur among numerous participants who are very often dispersed geographically. Furthermore, it can significantly improve efficiency in product design, manufacturing and distribution, and at the same time increase customers' choices and satisfaction. The business value that interoperability generates is not limited to efficiency gains, since it can be a fundamental driver and enabler of important innovations; it enables the personalization of offerings to customers and the composition at a low cost of new complex products/services by bundling complementary products/services from many different suppliers who are active in traditionally separated markets.

Grilo et al. (2007) argue that firms today increasingly tend to be active in several countries, so they have to cooperate with more and geographically dispersed suppliers and customers; also, they have to change the way they innovate and produce, to increase productivity and flexibility, to achieve higher levels of integration of their internal value chain and of the supply chains in which they participate, and to exploit better the information rich supplier and distribution chain. Establishing IS interoperability with trading partners is of critical importance for meeting the above highly important requirements. The same paper identifies three main functions of IS interoperability that generate significant business value: informational function (exchange of information of various complexity levels), transactional function (electronic execution of the whole life-cycles of various types of transactions) and collaboration function (collaborative products/services design and development).

IS interoperability constitutes a valuable infrastructure, which facilitates and supports various advanced and highly beneficial business practices, making them less costly and more easy and quick to implement and beneficial. One of them is definitely the Electronic Data Interchange (EDI) (Jimenez-Martinez & Polo-Redondo, 2004), which allows the electronic exchange of various types of structured business documents with customers, sales channels, suppliers, business partners, etc. (e.g. quotations, orders, shipment notes, invoices, payment notes), resulting in significant operational and strategic benefits. Another beneficial business practice that can be facilitated and supported by IS interoperability is Collaborative Planning, Forecasting and Replenishment (CPFR) (Dudek & Stadtler, 2007; Stadtler, 2009), defined as the combination of data and the intelligence of multiple trading partners across the supply chain in order to improve planning and fulfilment of customer demand, which can provide important benefits, especially in cases of goods and services characterised by unstable demand. Similarly, Vendor-Managed Inventory (VMI) (Kuk, 2004), defined as a new approach to inventory management, in which the supplier assumes the responsibility of tracking and replenishing firm's inventory, can also be facilitated and supported by IS interoperability of the involved firms, and lead to customers' service improvements and at the same time inventory cost reductions. It should be emphasized that the extent of exploiting the above capabilities finally determines the extent of value generation from IS interoperability.

Furthermore, it should be strongly emphasized that interoperability of firm's IS can facilitate, support and reduce the cost and time required for its participation in 'business networks', defined as structures comprising different and heterogeneous organizations (e.g. firms having different resources and capabilities, suppliers, customers, universities, research centers, etc.), having various types of relationships among them and also economic and social exchanges, which aim at the design, production, marketing and distribution of mainly complex products and services (Hakansson & Johanson, 1992; Hakansson & Snehota, 1995). Business networks have become of critical importance in the modern economy (Rycroft, 2007; Busquets, 2010; Zeng et al., 2010), so competition in many industries tends to be more among business networks than among individual firms. The participation of a firm in business networks offers significant business benefits (Kodama, 2005; Baraldi & Nadin, 2006; Kajikawa et al., 2010; Zeng et al., 2010): access to complementary resources and capabilities, new markets and technologies, diverse knowledge, and also opportunities to achieve economies of scale, to focus on their core competencies, to share the costs and risks of their activities, and to coordinate them in order to cope with market and technological complexities that characterise modern economy.

Furthermore, business networks facilitate learning through transfer of knowledge among participating firms, so they act as 'conduits' for moving and processing knowledge, and increasingly become the 'locus' of combination of diverse knowledge and complementary resources, creation of novel knowledge and innovation at a network level, rather than within the firms of the network. Extensive previous research in the innovation domain has shed light on the increasing importance of business networks for innovation activity in the last decade (Cumbers, 2003; Dewick & Miozzo, 2004; Mancinelli & Mazzanti, 2009; Zeng et al., 2010; Huizingh, 2011; Salavisa et al., 2012). It has revealed that there has been a fundamental change in the way firms design and implement innovation; while previously this has been viewed as a predominantly internal task, in the last decade it increasingly becomes a more 'open' and collaborative process based on interactions among different firms. Interorganizational mainly cross-sectoral networks, which facilitate the flows of information, knowledge, and resources, have emerged as a highly effective strategy.

Therefore firm's business performance today depends critically on its participation in multiple business networks, having variable compositions, objectives and time-horizons (some of them having long term orientation, while some others having shorter term orientations, focusing mainly on the exploitation of individual business opportunities), and this can be greatly facilitated and supported by IS interoperability. The relationships among firms as part of such networks necessitate specific actions at three layers (Hakansson & Snehota, 1995; Baraldi & Nadin, 2006): 'activity links' (i.e. mutual adaptations in their activities), 'resource ties' (i.e., technical connections and mutual orientations of their physical and organisational resources) and 'actor bonds' (i.e. social interactions between individuals and organisational units of cooperating firms). These require extensive exchanges of information, both 'structured' and 'unstructured', with cooperating firms in multiple networks; the exchange of the former (structured information) can be significantly facilitated by IS interoperability.

## EMPIRICAL LITERATURE

However, the business value of IS interoperability has been only to a very limited extent empirically investigated, so it has not been sufficiently examined to what extent the abovementioned expectations of the relevant theoretical literature are realised; only a very small number of empirical studies have been conducted concerning IS interoperability business value, and all of them are based on small datasets.

Boh, Xu, and Soh (2008) investigate empirically the effects of the extent of deployment of a single industry-specific standard (the RosettaNet, a standard aiming to facilitate B2B electronic transaction in high-tech industries, e.g. semiconductor manufacturing, telecommunications, etc.), and its integration in firm's processes, on the operational and strategic benefits that adopting firms obtain; it is based on dataset collected from 62 firms from China, Japan, Malaysia, Singapore and Taiwan. It has concluded that the extent of integration and deployment of this standard have both similar positive effects on the strategic benefits obtained, while the former is the main determinant of the operational benefits.

Mouzakitis, Sourouni, and Askounis (2009) investigate empirically the effect of five levels of interoperability (network, data, process, application and business interoperability) on the required B2B integration effort; it is based on a dataset collected from 239 Greek firms, which had successfully completed at least one B2B integration project in a predefined time period. It was concluded that interoperability at the data, process and business levels is negatively associated with integration effort.

We remark that these few empirical studies do not investigate the multiple dimensions of the business value generated by IS interoperability, i.e. its impacts on various aspects of firm's operation and performance, do not examine its effect on firm's innovation activity, and also do not examine and compare these effects for different types of standards. Our study contributes to filling this empirical research gap, by investigating the effects of the three main types of IS interoperability standards on several business performance variables (both 'final' and 'intermediate' ones, as explained in the following section), based on a large dataset collected from 14065 European firms.

## RESEARCH HYPOTHESES

Since business performance depends on a large number of 'internal' and 'external' variables (associated with the internal resources and organization of the firm, and its external environment respectively), our first two research hypotheses concern the effect of adopting IS interoperability standards on two 'intermediate' business performance variables (impact of firm's ICT infrastructure on business processes performance and innovation), while our third research hypothesis concerns a 'final' business performance variable (financial performance). Previous IS literature has emphasized that ICT affects positively firms' business performance mainly through two mechanisms: by increasing the performance of their business processes, and by driving and facilitating innovations in their business processes and in their products and services (e.g. Brynjolfsson & Hitt, 2000; Brynjolfsson & Saunders, 2010); so for this reason we have focused our first two research hypotheses on the effects of IS interoperability on these two mechanisms.

In particular, as mentioned previously, IS interoperability standards allow the easy and low cost exchange of various types of data between the firm and its customers, suppliers and business partners (Li et al., 2008), without the need of developing complex data conversion programs. These data can be at the informational or transactional mode (using the terminology introduced by Grilo et al. (2007)), and concern both descriptions of products and services at various levels of detail, and also quotations, orders, shipments, receipts,

invoices, payments and returns, leading to process efficiency (Wu & Chang, 2011). Also, these data can be oriented towards supporting and enhancing coordination and collaboration, for instance data on stock levels, production plans and sales forecasts, or on common projects, supporting various highly efficient business practices (Choi & Whinston, 2000). Furthermore, IS interoperability standards can facilitate the participation in business networks, the exploitation of physical resources of other firms, the achievement of economies of scale, resulting finally in important operational benefits (Kajikawa et al., 2010; Baraldi & Nadin, 2006). The above will increase the impact of firm's ICT infrastructure on the performance of its business processes. Therefore our first research hypothesis is:

**H1:** The adoption of IS interoperability standards increases the impact of firm's ICT infrastructure on business processes performance

Furthermore, the establishment of IS interoperability with existing and potential customers, suppliers and business partners that these standards enable can be very useful for the design and implementation of innovations. Today the innovation process becomes increasingly 'open' and collaborative, based on extensive interactions with business partners, customers and suppliers (Zeng et al., 2010; Huizingh, 2011); among them should be exchanged initially ideas and then structured documents (e.g. with designs of new products). The latter flows can be greatly facilitated and supported by IS interoperability. Furthermore, IS interoperability can be of critical importance for the quick and low cost production, marketing and distribution of the designed innovative products, through a close cooperation with multiple suppliers, sub-contractors, wholesalers and retailers, and exchange of various electronic documents with them. Also, as mentioned previously, IS interoperability facilitates the participation in business networks, which have been recognized as important sources of innovation, as they enable extensive sharing of diverse sources of knowledge, combination of them and creation of innovative products and services (Baraldi & Nadin, 2006; Kajikawa et al., 2010; Salavisa et al., 2012), and at the same time allow gaining access to small niche markets for selling to them wider ranges of products (Li et al., 2008). Therefore our second research hypothesis is:

**H2:** The adoption of IS interoperability standards increases the impact of firm's ICT infrastructure on its innovation activity

Finally, as the adoption of IS interoperability standards will increase the business benefits provided by firm's ICT infrastructure concerning both its business processes performance and its innovation activity, we expect that it will finally affect positively its financial performance. So our third research hypothesis is:

**H3:** The adoption of IS interoperability standards has positive impact on firm's financial performance

## DATA AND METHOD

For this empirical study we used a large dataset collected in the 'e-Business Survey 2006', which was conducted by the European e-Business Market W@tch (www.ebusiness-watch.org), an established observatory organization supported by the DG Enterprise and Industry of the European Commission. This survey aimed to assess the extent of adoption and use of various types of ICT infrastructures, applications, standards and practices, the impacts of ICT use, and also the innovation in the member states of European Union, the acceding and candidate countries and also the countries of the European Economic Area (EEA). It was based on computer-aided telephone interview (CATI) technologies, and included

14,065 telephone interviews with decision-makers of firms from 29 countries from the above areas. The target population of this survey included all firms of the above countries which are active in one of the following ten selected highly important economy sectors:

- Food and Beverages (S1),
- Footwear (S2),
- Pulp and Paper (S3),
- ICT Manufacturing (S4),
- Consumer Electronics (S5),
- Shipbuilding and Repair (S6),
- Construction (S7),
- Tourism (S8),
- Telecommunication Services (S9) and
- Hospital Activities (S10).

A stratified sample by company size and sector was randomly selected from this population, including a 10% share of large firms (with 250+ employees), a 30% share of medium sized firms (with 50-249 employees), a 25% share of small firms (with 10-49 employees), while the remaining 35% were micro firms (with less than 10 employees). In the Appendix (Table 3) we can see the questions we used from the above questionnaire for this study.

In order to test research hypotheses 1 and 2, using the above data we estimated the following regression models M1 and M2, having as dependent variables the main variables of these hypotheses: the impact of firm's ICT infrastructure on business processes performance (ICT_BPRO) and on innovation activity (ICT_INNO); as main independent variables they have the adoption of the three types of standards examined in this study, the industry-specific standards (IND_ST), the proprietary standards (PRO_ST) and the XML-horizontal standards (XMLHOR_ST), and also the degree of development of firm's internal IS (that support its internal processes) (INT_IS) and e-sales IS (ESAL_IS):

$$ICT\_BPRO = bo + b1 * IND\_ST + b2 * PRO\_ST + b3 * XMLHOR\_ST + b4 * INT\_IS + b5 * ESAL\_IS \quad (M1)$$

$$ICT\_INNO = bo + b1 * IND\_ST + b2 * PRO\_ST + b3 * XMLHOR\_ST + b4 * INT\_IS + b5 * ESAL\_IS \quad (M2)$$

The impact of ICT on business processes performance (ICT_BPRO) was measured as the average of two items (ICT_BPRO1 and ICT_BPRO2 – see Appendix) assessing whether ICT had positive influence, no influence or negative influence on the efficiency of business processes and on internal work organization respectively. Such items assessing the perceived influence of ICT on various aspects of business performance have been extensively used in previous empirical IS research (Martinez-Lorente et al., 2004; Sanders, 2007; Kearns & Sabherwal, 2007). The impact of ICT on firm's innovation activity (ICT_INNO) was measured as the average of two items (ICT_INNO1 and ICT_INNO2 – see Appendix) assessing whether the firm had introduced in the last 12 months any ICT-based product/service or process innovation. These items have also extensive previous literature support (Koellinger, 2008; Soto-Acosta & Meroño-Cerdan, 2008).

Our main independent variables are three dichotomous items (IND_ST, PRO_ST and XMLHOR_ST) assessing whether the firm uses industry-specific standards, proprietary standards and XML-horizontal standards respectively in order to exchange data with its customers and suppliers. Furthermore, taking into account that the impact of firm's ICT infrastructure on business performance depends critically on the degree of its development, i.e. the extent of using IS for supporting firm's internal processes and for interacting with the external environment (i.e. lower extent of ICT use for these purposes results in lower ICT impact on business performance), we have also included two additional independent variables; they correspond to the two most widely used types of IS: the intra-organizational/internal and the e-sales ones. The first variable was the degree of development of firm's internal IS (INT_IS), which was measured as the average of six items (INT_IS1 to INT_IS6 – see Appendix) assessing whether the firm has a basic internal infrastructure: the Intranet, and also five important applications supporting fundamental internal functions: Enterprise Document Management (EDM) system, Enterprise Resource Planning (ERP) system, software for tracking working hours or production time, capacity or inventories management software and software for sharing documents between colleagues or performing collaborative work in an online environment. Such items have been used extensively in previous empirical IS research for measuring internal IS use (Koellinger, 2008; Soto-Acosta & Meroño-Cerdan, 2008; Brews & Tucci, 2004). The second additional variable was the degree of development of e-sales IS (ESAL_IS), which was measured as the average of four items (ESAL_IS1 to ESAL_IS6 – see Appendix) assessing whether the firm uses IS for the four main stages of sale's lifecycle: for publishing offers to customers, answering calls for proposals or tenders, receiving orders from customers and enabling customers to pay online. These items have also extensive previous literature support (Soto-Acosta & Meroño-Cerdan, 2008; Brews & Tucci, 2004; Hashim, Murphy, & Law, 2007). Finally, in order to control for other sector-specific factors affecting the impact of ICT on business performance, we also included for the abovementioned ten sectors covered by our survey nine sectoral dummies (while one sector was used as a reference group).

Similarly, in order to test research hypothesis 3 we estimated the following regression model M3, having as dependent variable the main variable of this hypothesis: firm's financial performance (FINP); it has the same independent variables with the above M1 and M2 models (the adoption of the three examined types of standards and the degree of development of firm's internal and e-sales IS), and also an additional one concerning firm's human capital (HCAP), which is widely recognised as an important determinant of its financial performance (Arvanitis & Loukis, 2009):

$$FINP = b_0 + b_1*IND\_ST + b_2*PRO\_ST + b_3*XMLHOR\_ST + b_4*INT\_IS + b_5*ESAL\_IS + B_6*HCAP \qquad (M3)$$

Financial business performance (FINP) was measured as the average of three items (FPIN1, FINP2 and FPIN3 – see Appendix) assessing whether firm's turnover, marketshare and productivity increased, stayed roughly the same or decreased in the last financial year in comparison with the previous one. Finally firm's human capital (HCAP) was quantified through the percentage share of firm's employees having a college or university degree (see Appendix). Such items have been used extensively in previous empirical management research for measuring financial business performance and human capital respectively (Martinez-Lorente et al., 2004; Hyvonen, 2007; Koellinger, 2008). For the estimation of this M3 model the data from the 834 Hospital Activities sector (S10) were not used, because of missing data for some financial performance items.

## RESULTS

### Effects on Business Impact of ICT Infrastructure

In Table 1 we can see the results of the estimation of the M1 and M2 regression models – for each model we can see the standardized coefficients of the independent variables, which allow a comparison of their effects on the dependent variable. We remark that in both models the standardized coefficients for all the three examined types of IS interoperability standards (variables IND_ST, PRO_ST and XMLHOR_ST) are positive and statistically significant. This indicates that the

adoption of industry-specific, or proprietary or XML-horizontal standards for establishing IS interoperability with cooperating firms (e.g. customers, suppliers, business partners) increases the positive impact of firm's ICT infrastructure on the performance of its business processes (dependent variable ICT_BPRO) and on its innovation activity (dependent variable ICT_INNO). Therefore our first two research hypotheses H1 and H2 are supported for all three examined types of IS interoperability standards. These results provide a strong empirical evidence of the multi-dimensional business value generated by IS interoperability, with respect to both business processes performance and innovation activity. Also, we can see that in both models the standardized coefficients of the degree of development of firm's internal IS (variable INT_IS) and e-sales IS (variable ESAL_IS) are positive and statistically significant as well, as expected. Finally, we remark that most of the coefficients of the sectoral dummies are statistically significant, which indicates that there are

*Table 1. Estimated regression models of the impact of firm's ICT infrastructure on business processes performance and innovation*

|  | ICT_BPRO | ICT_INNO |
|---|---|---|
| IND_ST | 0.156*** | 0.119 *** |
| PRO_ST | 0.039*** | 0.043 *** |
| XMLHOR_ST | 0.038*** | 0.103 *** |
| INT_IS | 0.219*** | 0.173 *** |
| ESAL_IS | 0.074*** | 0.176 *** |
| DUM_1 | -0.063*** | -0.036 *** |
| DUM_2 | -0.076*** | -0.032 *** |
| DUM_3 | -0.026*** | -0.029 *** |
| DUM_4 | -0.011 | 0.020 ** |
| DUM_5 | -0.009 | 0.029*** |
| DUM_6 | 0.003 | -0.030 *** |
| DUM_7 | -0.014 | -0.068 *** |
| DUM_9 | 0.017* | 0.117 *** |
| DUM_10 | -0.015* | 0.023 *** |

sector-specific factors that affect the impact of ICT on business processes performance and innovation, and this necessitates the inclusion of sectoral dummies in such regressions.

It is interesting to compare between the effects of these three types of IS interoperability standards by examining the corresponding standardized coefficients of these two regression models in Table 1 – we can also see them in Figure 1 normalised as percentages of the corresponding standardized coefficients of the degree of internal IS development in the three models. We remark that the effects of these three types of standards differ significantly. In particular, we can see that the adoption of industry-specific standards leads to the highest increase of the impact of ICT infrastructure on business processes performance and innovation: the corresponding standardized coefficients in the two models (0.156 and 0.119) are higher than the ones of the proprietary standards (0.039, 0.043 respectively) and the XML-horizontal ones (0.038, 0.103 respectively). This is because, as mentioned in the Introduction, industry-specific standards have the following two important characteristics:

1. They have exactly the whole needed "depth and breadth": they cover almost all the electronic documents exchanged between a firm in the industry and its suppliers, customers, sales channels, business partners, etc. (such as orders, invoices, payments, returns, product designs, production plans, demands, etc.), and also for each of them include the whole range of required elements, but do not include additional data elements (Nurmilaakso 2008, 2008; Lampathaki et al., 2009).

2. They also have high level of applicability, as they are usually adopted by most of the firms belonging to the particular industry (e.g. suppliers, competitors, customers, sales channels, etc.), so they can be used for establishing IS interoperability with most of the firms we have transactions and cooperation with.

On the contrary, the proprietary standards usually have extensive 'depth and breadth', but cover mainly the needs (documents and elements) of the strong creator firm. Also, they are charac-

*Figure 1. Normalised effects of independent variables in the ICT_BPRO (M1), ICT_INNO (M2) and FINP (M3) models as percentages of the effects of internal IS (INT_IS)*

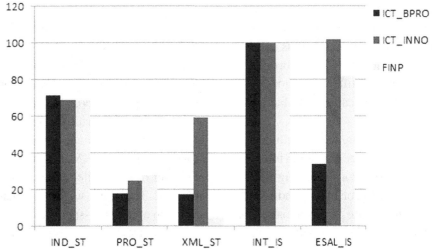

terized by much lower levels of applicability, as such a standard can be used for establishing IS interoperability only with the creator firm and a relatively small number of firms that adopt it. For these reasons the adoption of proprietary standards leads to lower increase of the impact of firm's ICT infrastructure on business processes performance and innovation than the industrial ones.

Finally, the XML-horizontal standards, as mentioned in the Introduction, are mainly cross-sectoral (horizontal) at the time when the data of this study were collected, so they are characterized by higher levels of applicability, since they can be used for exchanging electronically business documents with firms not only of the same industry, but also of other industries as well. However, they lack the needed depth and breadth for representing sector-specific characteristics and information elements, as they have been developed with a 'least common denominator' logic, so they cover mainly business documents and elements of them that are common across sectors, and do not provide a 'perfect match' with needs. For these reasons the adoption of XML-horizontal standards results in a lower increase of the impact of firm's ICT infrastructure on the business processes performance and innovation in comparison with the industrial standards. However, the difference between the effects of these two types of standards (industry-specific and XML-horizontal ones) is much smaller with respect to innovation, since according to previous innovation literature (e.g. Castellacci, 2008) important innovations require extensive interactions and therefore information exchange among firms of different sectors, and XML-horizontal standards can greatly facilitate and support this.

It is interesting to compare the magnitudes of the above effects of these three types of IS interoperability standards with the corresponding effects of the degree of development of internal and e-sales IS using Table 1 and Figure 1. We remark that the effect of the industry-specific standards in the first business processes performance model is 71%

(=0.156/0.219) and in the innovation model it is 69% (=0.119/0.173) of the effect of the degree of development of the internal IS, which is regarded as the fundamental determinant of the business impact of ICT. Therefore the effects of adopting industry-specific standards on the impacts of firm's ICT infrastructure on business processes performance and on innovation seem to be quite strong, about two thirds of the corresponding ones of the degree of development of the internal IS. For the proprietary and the XML-horizontal standards the above percentages are lower: 18% and 25% respectively for the former, and 17% and 60% respectively for the latter.

We can make a similar comparison with the effects of e-sales IS. We remark that the effect of industry-specific standards in the first business processes performance model is 211% (=0.156/0.074) and in the innovation model 68% (=0.119/0.176). Therefore the effects of adopting industry-specific standards on the impact of firm's ICT infrastructure on business processes performance (innovation) is more than double (two thirds of) the one of the degree of development of e-sales IS. For the proprietary standards and the XML-horizontal standards the above percentages are lower: 53% and 24% respectively for the former, and 51% and 58% respectively for the latter.

## Effects on Financial Performance

In Table 2, we can see the results of the estimation of the M3 regression model.

We remark that the standardised coefficients of the industry-specific and the proprietary standards (variables IND_ST and PRO_ST) are positive and statistically significant, while the standardised coefficient of the XML-horizontal standards (variable XMLHOR_ST) is positive as well, but much smaller and statistically non-significant. Therefore we can conclude that the adoption of industry-specific or proprietary standards for establishing IS interoperability with cooperating firms (e.g. customers, suppliers, busi-

*Table 2. Estimated regression model of firm's financial performance*

|  | FINP |
|---|---|
| IND_ST | 0.069 *** |
| PRO_ST | 0.028 *** |
| XMLHOR_ST | 0.005 |
| INT_IS | 0.100 *** |
| ESAL_IS | 0.082 *** |
| HCAP | 0.058 *** |
| DUM_1 | -0.017 |
| DUM_2 | -0.122 *** |
| DUM_3 | -0.019 * |
| DUM_4 | -0.052 *** |
| DUM_5 | -0.042 *** |
| DUM_6 | -0.001 |
| DUM_7 | -0.007 |
| DUM_8 | -0.024 * |

ness partners) has positive impacts even at the level of firm's financial performance. Therefore our third research hypothesis H3 is partially supported (only for two of the three examined types of IS interoperability standards). Also, we remark that the standardised coefficients of the degree of development of firm's internal IS (variable INT_IS) and e-sales IS (variable ESAL_IS), and also of the human capital (variable HCAP), are positive and statistically significant as well, as expected.

A comparison of the magnitudes of the standardised coefficients of the independent variables (using Table 2 and Figure 1) shows that the degree of development of the internal IS has the strongest effect on financial performance (standardised coefficient 0.100), followed by the degree of development of the e-sales IS (0.082), and then the adoption of industrial standards (0.069) and the human capital (0.058), while much weaker is the effect of the adoption of proprietary standards (0.028). These results provide additional empirical evidence of the high business value

that IS interoperability generates: the adoption of industry-specific standards has a strong impact even at the level of financial performance, which is 69% (=0.069/0.100) of the effect of the degree of development of the internal IS, and 84% (=0.069/0.082) of the effect of the degree of development of the e-sales IS (so it is comparable with the effects of the main ICT-related determinants of firm's financial performance). The adoption of proprietary IS interoperability standards has also statistically significant impact at the level of financial performance, but of lower magnitude, about 40% (=0.028/0.069) of the effect of the industry-specific standards; this is probably due to the lower applicability of the proprietary standards in comparison with the industry-specific standards, as the former can be used for establishing IS interoperability only with the strong creator firm and the small number of adopting firms. On the contrary, the adoption of XML-horizontal IS interoperability standards does not have statistically significant impact at the level of financial performance; this probably happens because they cover mainly business documents and elements of them that are common across sectors, having been developed with a 'least common denominator' logic, so they do not fulfil important industry-specific requirements.

## CONCLUSION

The progress towards a scientific maturity of the information systems (IS) interoperability domain and the creation of complete scientific foundations of it will require balanced research both at the technological and the business level: it necessitates both the development of mature and widely applicable interoperability architectures, methods and standards, and at the same time the systematic investigation of the business value they generate. This chapter makes a contribution in this direction. Initially it analyses the theoretical foundations of the multi-dimensional business value of IS interoperability: they include i) previous theoretical literature discussing various possible contributions of IS interoperability to different aspects of business performance, and also ii) previous literature in the area of business networks, as IS interoperability can be an important facilitator of this increasingly important element of modern economy. Then, the quite limited empirical literature on IS interoperability business value is reviewed.

Furthermore, we contribute to filling this research gap by presenting an empirical study of the business value generated by the adoption of three fundamental types of IS interoperability standards: industry-specific, proprietary and XML-horizontal ones. We examine their effects on several business performance variables, both 'intermediate' and 'final' ones. In particular, as intermediate performance variables we have used the impacts of firm's ICT infrastructure on its business processes performance and innovation, while as final business performance variable we have used firm's financial performance. This empirical study has been based on a large dataset collected from 14065 European firms (from 25 countries and 10 sectors) through the e-Business Market W@tch Survey of the European Commission.

The results provide empirical evidence of the multidimensional business value generated by IS interoperability, its big magnitude and its strong dependence on the type of IS interoperability standards adopted. In particular, it has been concluded that the adoption of all these three types of standards for establishing IS interoperability with cooperating firms (e.g. customers, suppliers, business partners) increase the positive impact of firm's ICT infrastructure on the performance of its business processes and its innovation activity. Furthermore, it has been found that the effects of the above three types of standards differ significantly: the adoption of industry-specific IS interoperability standards has the highest impact on business performance, while proprietary standards and XML-horizontal ones have similar

lower impacts. Furthermore, it has been concluded that the industry-specific and the proprietary interoperability standards have positive impacts even at the level of firm's financial performance. All the above effects of the industry-specific IS interoperability standards are quite strong, having a level of about two thirds of the corresponding effects of the degree of development of internal IS (regarded as the main determinant of business benefits from ICT).

The findings of our study have interesting implications for IS research and management. It provides theoretical foundations and also an empirical framework for future empirical research on the business value of various IS interoperability architectures, methods and standards. Also, the strength of the effects of adopting such standards indicates that future research on IS business value should take into account not only the degree of development of various types of firm's IS (as it happened with most of the previous research in this area), but also their interoperability with the ones of other cooperating firms. With respect to IS management practice, our conclusions indicate that it is necessary to place strong emphasis on establishing interoperability of firm's IS with the ones of other cooperating firms, due to the high business value that interoperability seems to generate; this emphasis should be similar to the one placed on the development of the functionality of various types of firm's IS. In order to maximize this business value IS managers should adopt standards characterized by wide applicability (so that they can be used for establishing IS interoperability with a large number of other firms) and also sufficient "depth and breadth" (so that they enable a fully automated exchange of numerous electronic business documents including all required elements), such as the industry-specific standards.

Further empirical research is required on the business value that IS interoperability generates, examining from this viewpoint various existing and emerging IS interoperability architectures, methods and standards. Also, it is necessary to extend this research towards other 'interoperability layers', and investigate empirically the business value not only of the 'technical' interoperability, but also of the 'organizational' interoperability as well, and their complementarities. Finally, it is necessary to identify and understand the moderators (both 'internal' and 'external' ones) and the mediators of the effects of the adoption of various IS interoperability architectures, methods and standards on various dimensions of business performance.

# REFERENCES

Allee, V. (2002). A value network approach for modelling and measuring intangibles. In *Proceedings of Transparent Enterprise Conference*. Madrid, Spain: TEC.

Anderson, C. (2006). *The long tail: Why the future of business is selling less of more*. New York: Hyperion.

Arvanitis, S., & Loukis, E. (2009). Information and communication technologies, human capital, workplace organization and labour productivity in Greece and Switzerland: A comparative study based on firm-level data. *Information Economics and Policy*, *21*, 43–61. doi:10.1016/j.infoecopol.2008.09.002

Baraldi, E., & Nadin, G. (2006). The challenges in digitalising business relationships: The construction of an IT infrastructure for a textile-related business network. *Technovation*, *26*, 1111–1126. doi:10.1016/j.technovation.2005.09.016

Boh, W. F., Xu, Y., & Soh, C. (2008). VIS standards deployment and integration: A study of antecedents and benefits. In *Proceedings of the International Conference on Information Systems (ICIS) 2008*. ICIS.

Brews, P., & Tucci, C. (2004). Exploring the structural effects of internetworking. *Strategic Management Journal*, *25*, 429–451. doi:10.1002/smj.386

Brynjolfsson, E., & Hitt, L. M. (2000). Beyond computation: Information technology, organizational transformation and business performance. *The Journal of Economic Perspectives*, *14*(4), 23–48. doi:10.1257/jep.14.4.23

Brynjolfsson, E., & Saunders, A. (2010). *Wired for innovation – How information technology is reshaping the economy*. Cambridge, MA: The MIT Press.

Busquets, J. (2010). Orchestrating smart business network dynamics for innovation. *European Journal of Information Systems*, *19*(4), 481–493. doi:10.1057/ejis.2010.19

Castellacci, F. (2008). Technological paradigms, regimes and trajectories: Manufacturing and service industries in a new taxonomy of sectoral patterns of innovation. *Research Policy*, *37*, 978–994. doi:10.1016/j.respol.2008.03.011

Choi, S., & Whinston, A. (2000). Benefits and requirements for interoperability in the electronic marketplace. *Technology in Society*, *22*, 33–44. doi:10.1016/S0160-791X(99)00034-2

Cumbers, A., Mackinnon, D., & Chapman, K. (2003). Innovation, collaboration, and learning in regional clusters: A study of SMEs in the Aberdeen oil complex. *Environment & Planning A*, *35*(9), 1689–1706. doi:10.1068/a35259

Dewick, P., & Miozzo, M. (2004). Networks and innovation: Sustainable technologies in Scottish social housing. *R & D Management*, *34*(4), 323–333. doi:10.1111/j.1467-9310.2004.00342.x

Dudek, G., & Stadtler, H. (2007). Negotiation-based collaborative planning in divergent two tier supply chains. *International Journal of Production Economics, 45,* 465–484. doi:10.1080/00207540600584821

Grilo, A., & Jardim-Goncalves, R. (2010). Value proposition on interoperability of BIM and collaborative working environments. *Automation in Construction, 19,* 522–530. doi:10.1016/j.autcon.2009.11.003

Grilo, A., Jardim-Goncalves, R., & Cruz-Machado, V. (2007). A framework for measuring value in business interoperability. In *Proceedings of the IEEE International Conference on Industrial Engineering and Engineering Management,* (pp. 520-524). IEEE.

Grilo, A., Jardim-Goncalves, R., & Cruz-Machado, V. (2009). Analysis of interoperability value proposition in the architectural, engineering and construction sector. In *Proceedings of the IEEE International Conference on Industrial Engineering and Engineering Management 2009,* (pp. 2217 – 2221). IEEE.

Hakansson, H., & Johanson, J. (1992). A model of industrial networks. In *Industrial networks–A new view of reality.* London: Routledge.

Hakansson, H., & Snehota, I. (Eds.). (1995). *Developing relationships in business networks.* London: Routledge.

Hashim, N., Murphy, J., & Law, R. (2007). A review of hospitality website design frameworks. In M. Sigala, L. Mich, & J. Murphy (Eds.), *Information and communication technologies in tourism* (pp. 219–230). New York: Springer Wien. doi:10.1007/978-3-211-69566-1_21

Huizingh, E. (2011). Open innovation: State of the art and future perspectives. *Technovation, 31,* 2–9. doi:10.1016/j.technovation.2010.10.002

Hyvonen, J. (2007). Strategy, performance measurement techniques and information technology of the firm and their links to organizational performance. *Management Accounting Research, 18,* 343–366. doi:10.1016/j.mar.2007.02.001

Institute of Electrical and Electronics Engineers (IEEE). (1990). *IEEE standard computer dictionary: A compilation of IEEE standard computer glossaries.* IEEE.

Jardim-Goncalves, R., Popplewell, K., & Grilo, A. (2012). Sustainable interoperability: The future of internet based industrial enterprises. *Computers in Industry, 63,* 731–738. doi:10.1016/j.compind.2012.08.016

Jardim-Goncalves, R., Popplewell, K., & Grilo, A. (2012). Sustainable interoperability: The future of internet based industrial enterprises. *Computers in Industry, 63,* 731–738. doi:10.1016/j.compind.2012.08.016

Jimenez-Martinez, J., & Polo-Redondo, Y. (2004). The influence of EDI adoption over its perceived benefits. *Technovation, 24,* 73–79. doi:10.1016/S0166-4972(02)00047-0

Kajikawa, Y., Takeda, Y., Sakata, I., & Matsushima, K. (2010). Multiscale analysis of interfirm networks in regional clusters. *Technovation, 30,* 168–180. doi:10.1016/j.technovation.2009.12.004

Kearns, G. S., & Sabherwal, R. (2007). Strategic alignment between business and information technology: A knowledge-based view of behaviors, outcome and consequences. *Journal of Management Information Systems, 23*(3), 129–162. doi:10.2753/MIS0742-1222230306

Kim, W., & Mauborgne, R. (2005). *Blue ocean strategy–How to create uncontested market space and make competition irrelevant.* Boston: Harvard Business School Press.

Kodama, M. (2005). Knowledge creation through networked strategic communities: Case studies on new product development in Japanese companies. *Long Range Planning*, *38*, 27–49. doi:10.1016/j.lrp.2004.11.011

Koellinger, P. (2008). The relationship between technology, innovation, and firm performance: Empirical evidence from e-business in Europe. *Research Policy*, *37*, 1317–1328. doi:10.1016/j.respol.2008.04.024

Kuk, G. (2004). Effectiveness of vendor-managed inventory in the electronics industry: Determinants and outcomes. *Information & Management*, *41*, 645–654. doi:10.1016/j.im.2003.08.002

Lampathaki, F., Koussouris, S., Agostinho, C., Jardim-Goncalves, R., Charalabidis, Y., & Psarras, J. (2012). Infusing scientific foundations into enterprise interoperability. *Computers in Industry*, *63*, 858–866. doi:10.1016/j.compind.2012.08.004

Lampathaki, F., Mouzakitis, S., Gionis, G., Charalabidis, Y., & Askounis, D. (2009). Business to business interoperability: A current review of XML data integration standards. *Computer Standards & Interfaces*, *31*, 1045–1055. doi:10.1016/j.csi.2008.12.006

Legner, R., & Lebreton, B. (2007). Preface to the focus theme section: Business interoperability research: Present achievements and upcoming challenges. *Electronic Markets*, *17*(3), 176–186. doi:10.1080/10196780701503054

Li, M. S., Crave, S., Grilo, A., & Van den Berg, R. (Eds.). (2008). *Unleashing the potential of the European knowledge economy – Value proposition for enterprise interoperability*. Brussels: European Commission, Information Society and Media.

Mancinelli, S., & Mazzanti, M. (2009). Innovation, networking and complementarity: Evidence on SME performances for a local economic system in North-Eastern Italy. *The Annals of Regional Science*, *43*(3), 567–597. doi:10.1007/s00168-008-0255-6

Martinez-Lorente, A. R., Sanchez-Rogriguez, C., & Dewhurst, F. W. (2004). The effect of information technologies on TQM: An initial analysis. *International Journal of Production Economics*, *89*, 77–93. doi:10.1016/j.ijpe.2003.06.001

Mouzakitis, S., Sourouni, A. M., & Askounis, D. (2009). Effects of enterprise interoperability on integration efforts in supply chains. *International Journal of Electronic Commerce*, *14*(2), 127–155. doi:10.2753/JEC1086-4415140205

Nurmilaakso, J. M. (2008a). Adoption of e-business functions and migration from EDI-based to XML-based e-business frameworks in supply chain integration. *International Journal of Production Economics*, *113*, 721–733. doi:10.1016/j.ijpe.2007.11.001

Nurmilaakso, J. M. (2008b). EDI, XML and e-business frameworks: A survey. *Computers in Industry*, *59*, 370–379. doi:10.1016/j.compind.2007.09.004

Rycroft, R. W. (2007). Does cooperation absorb complexity? Innovation networks and the speed and spread of complex technological innovation. *Technological Forecasting and Social Change*, *74*, 565–578. doi:10.1016/j.techfore.2006.10.005

Salavisa, I., Sousa, C., & Fontes, M. (2012). Topologies of innovation networks in knowledge-intensive sectors: Sectoral differences in the access to knowledge and complementary assets through formal and informal ties. *Technovation*, *32*, 380–399. doi:10.1016/j.technovation.2012.02.003

Sanders, N. R. (2007). An empirical study of the impact of e-business technologies on organizational collaboration and performance. *Journal of Operations Management*, *25*(6), 1332–1347. doi:10.1016/j.jom.2007.01.008

Soto-Acosta, P., & Meroño-Cerdan, A. L. (2008). Analyzing e-business value creation from a resource-based perspective. *International Journal of Information Management*, *28*, 49–60. doi:10.1016/j.ijinfomgt.2007.05.001

Stadtler, H. (2009). A framework for collaborative planning and state-of-the-art. *OR-Spektrum, 31,* 5–30. doi:10.1007/s00291-007-0104-5

Wu, I., & Chang, C. (2011). Using the balanced scorecard in assessing the performance of e-SCM diffusion: A multi-stage perspective. *Decision Support Systems.*

Zeng, S. X., Xie, X. M., & Tam, C. M. (2010). Relationship between cooperation networks and innovation performance of SMEs. *Technovation, 30,* 181–194. doi:10.1016/j.technovation.2009.08.003

## KEY TERMS AND DEFINITIONS

**Blue Ocean Strategies:** Strategies aiming to make the competition irrelevant by creating new market spaces, termed as 'blue ocean', through the introduction of radical innovations in the products, services and processes.

**Business Networks:** Structures comprising different and heterogeneous organizations (e.g. firms having different resources and capabilities, suppliers, customers, universities, research centers, etc.), having various types of relationships among them and also economic and social exchanges, which aim at the design, production and marketing of complex products and services.

**Industry-Specific Standards:** Standards created mainly by industry associations or sectoral standardization bodies, in order to enable the electronic exchange of important business documents (e.g. quotations, orders, shipment notes, invoices, payment notes) between firms of a specific industry, their suppliers, customers and business partners.

**Information Systems (IS) Interoperability:** The ability of two or more IS or components to exchange information and to use the information that has been exchanged.

**Proprietary Standards:** Standards typically created and maintained by large and strong firms, which impose de-facto specifications for business documents' exchange with their own customers, suppliers or business partners.

**Red Ocean Strategies:** Strategies based on competition through lower prices in existing established products and services or marginal innovations in them.

**XML-Horizontal Standards:** Standards based on the XML (eXtensible Markup Language), used for open cross-sectoral (horizontal) specifications of business documents' interchange formats to be used by firms of all sectors (though recently many industrial standards, and also some proprietary ones, have been ported to XML as well).

# APPENDIX

*Table 3. Survey questions used for measuring each variable*

| Variable | Items |
|---|---|
| Impact of ICT on business processes performance (ICT_BPRO) | **ICT_BPRO1:** Has ICT had a positive, negative or no influence on internal work organisation quality of customer service? |
| | **ICT_BPRO2:** Has ICT had a positive, negative or no influence on the productivity of your company? |
| Impact of ICT on innovation (ICT_INNO) | **ICT_INNO1:** During the past 12 months have you launched any new or substantially improved product or services directly related to or enabled by information or communication technology? |
| | **ICT_INNO2:** During the past 12 months have you introduced any new or substantially improved internal processes directly related to or enabled by information or communication technology? |
| Financial performance (FINP) | **FINP1:** Has the turnover of your company increased, decreased or stayed roughly the same when comparing the last financial year with the year before? |
| | **FINP2:** Has the share of your company in its most significant market increased, decreased, or remained the same over the past 12 months? |
| | **FINP3:** Has the productivity of your company increased, decreased or stayed roughly the same when comparing the last financial year with the year before? |
| Industry-specific standards adoption (IND_ST) | Do you use industry-specific standards agreed between you and your business partners for exchanging data with them? |
| Proprietary standards adoption (PRO_ST) | Do you use proprietary standards for exchanging data with buyers and suppliers? |
| XML-horizontal standards adoption (XMLHOR_ST) | Do you use XML-based standards for exchanging data with buyers and suppliers? |
| Internal IS degree of development (INT_IS) | **INT_IS1:** Do you use an Intranet? |
| | **INT_IS2:** Do you use an EDM (Enterprise Document Manage-ment) system? |
| | **INT_IS3:** Do you use an ERP (Enterprise Resource Planning) system? |
| | Do you use online applications other than e-mail … ? |
| | **INT_IS4:** to share documents between colleagues or to perform collaborative work in an online environment |
| | **INT_IS5:** to track working hours or production time |
| | **INT_IS6:** to manage capacity or inventories? |
| E-Sales IS degree of development (ESAL_IS) | Do you use IT solutions for... ? |
| | **ESAL_IS1:** Publishing offers to customers |
| | **ESAL_IS2:** Answering calls for proposals or tenders |
| | **ESAL_IS3:** Receiving orders from customers |
| | **ESAL_IS4:** Enabling customers to pay online for ordered products or services |
| Human Capital (HCAP) | What is the percentage share of firm's employees with a college or university degree? |

# Section 2
# Advanced Methods and Tools for Enterprise Interoperability

# Chapter 5
# Hybrid Modeling:
## An Instrument for Conceptual Interoperability

**Robert Woitsch**
*BOC Asset Management, Austria*

## ABSTRACT

*Enterprise Interoperability can be identified on cultural, rule, process, data, software, object, social network, services, knowledge, electronic ID, cloud, and ecosystem level, whereas the challenge is the conceptual integration across those layers in a flexible way. Meta Modeling as a concept is a proven technology to enable such conceptual integration for both machine computation and human-oriented interpretation for information value creation. Hybrid Modeling is a realization approach to merge different meta models and hence enable the interoperability between conceptual models. Stability is provided by the meta modeling platform whereas flexibility is ensured by hybrid modeling via a holistic integration framework. This approach has been successfully implemented in a list of EU-research projects. This chapter introduces (a) concept models as an instrument for interoperability, (b) a meta model approach as a flexible but stable platform, and (c) hybrid modeling as an approach to flexibly compose the conceptual integration. After discussing this theoretical background, the chapter introduces different realization scenarios of hybrid modeling. Each scenario is supported differently by the underlying meta modeling platform ADOxx®. Here, the experience of a list of EU-research projects is explained and reflected to enterprise interoperability requirements. Sample solutions are introduced, showing different hybrid modeling implementations. Technical overviews of the ADOxx® meta modeling platforms are introduced and references to open development communities are provided to invite readers to realize their own modeling solutions.*

DOI: 10.4018/978-1-4666-5142-5.ch005

# 1. INTRODUCTION

Industry 4.0 (Fraunhofer IAO, 2013) describes the ongoing paradigm shift in production industry towards networked enterprises. Future Internet Enterprise Systems (FInES), virtual enterprises and networked IT-infrastructure are keywords indicating current and upcoming challenges of future enterprises facing (FINES Cluster, 2010) agility, sensing, community-orientation, liquidity and globalism.

Enterprise Interoperability is hence defined "as a field of activity with the aim to improve the manner in which enterprises, by means of Information and Communications Technologies (ICT), interoperate with other enterprises, organization, or with other business units of the same enterprise, in order to conduct their business. This enables enterprises to, for instance, build partnerships, deliver new products and services, and/or become more cost efficient."(Popplewell, Lampathaki, Koussouris, Mouzakitis, Charalabidis, Goncalves, & Agostinho, 2012).

Conceptual models such as business process models, value process chains or e3value models are commodity and hence the conceptual modeling approach is a promising candidate to support enterprise interoperability. This chapter sees the result of conceptual modeling not only to be used for software generation, but also to act as an Enterprise Knowledge Platform (Karagiannis, 2012) by enabling information value creation for human interpretation out of models. Hence conceptual modeling approach is argued to be applied for the so-called Next Generation Enterprise System in order to conceptualize relevant parts and to support different layers of interoperability. This approach results in a list of modeling requirements dealing with the modeling language, the modeling steps as well as algorithms and mechanisms that are required to describe the Next Generation Enterprise Systems.

Depending on the complexity of the requirements, those modeling requirements may be covered by one meta model but most likely require the interplay of several meta models focusing on different viewpoints. Domain-specific modeling languages are context-specific and hence designed to optimally support domain experts within that particular domain. Often interoperability issues require the involvement of several domains and hence raise the issue of interoperability of different domain-specific languages. Such interplay between different domain-specific meta models is defined as hybrid modeling, where different viewpoints are commonly applied to create a holistic observation of a Next Generation Enterprise System.

Hence, hybrid modeling is seen as an appropriate technology to observe the different layers of interoperability between different enterprises in order to holistically describe this interoperability in a conceptualized way.

After this introduction, the second section indicates the different levels of enterprise-interoperability and identifies different layers that can be individually supported via conceptual modeling. Samples from previous and currently running EU-projects are briefly mentioned to demonstrate the wide area of hybrid modeling with concrete application samples for the benefit of enterprise interoperability.

The third section discusses challenges when applying conceptual models in form of hybrid modeling. Meta models are a well-established realization approach for conceptual models, hence background is provided on meta models, before hybrid modeling is introduces.

Interoperability between layers is commonly a vertical integration of meta models, whereas interoperability between enterprises is most commonly a horizontal integration. The proposed technical realizations using the ADOxx® meta modeling platform are briefly introduced and relevant parts of the used technologies are underlined.

The fourth section introduces the sample from the EU-project BIVEE in more detail showing the challenges of a complex meta model covering several aspects of enterprise interoperability within a virtual enterprise.

The fifth section discusses approaches, solutions and lessons learned with respect to enterprise interoperability. The last section depicts the concluding remarks mainly pointing to open development communities using enterprise models (Open Models, 2013), developing meta models (Open Models Laboratory, 2013) or in providing technology and platforms (ADOxx.org, 2013).

## 2. INTEROPERABILITY AND CONCEPTUAL BACKGROUND

This section introduces the application domain enterprise interoperability. Hence the characteristics of enterprise interoperability is briefly introduced but mainly referenced to publications of the FInES Cluster and corresponding projects. Some practical samples from current and past research projects are elaborated.

## 2.1. Enterprise Interoperability Raising Requirements

This section is based on the findings of the enterprise interoperability survey from the project ENSEMBLE (Ensemble, 2012) within the FInES Cluster activities. Enterprise interoperability can be traced back till the 1990ties discussing interoperability of information systems. In the last two decades interoperability viewpoints became more complex introducing cultural, organizational, as well as business and legal aspects. The Enterprise Interoperability Science Base State of Play Report from ENSEMBLE in the context of the FInES Cluster observed in a literature research the different aspects of interoperability and depicted the different interoperability aspects and their different granularity levels. For a detailed discussion on the different aspects we refer to the corresponding document, but want to highlight different layers and viewpoints of Enterprise Interoperability from (Popplewell et al., 2012) in Figure 1.

*Figure 1. Enterprise interoperability scientific areas overview*
*Source: EISB State of Play Report (Popplewell et al., 2012), Figure 4-1, p. 48*

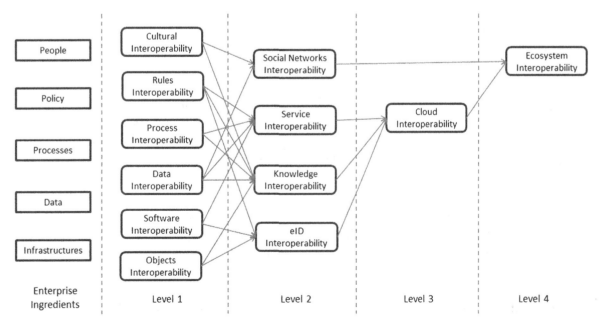

The framework starts from the ingredients of an enterprise (a) people, (b) policy, (c) processes, (d) data and (e) infrastructures. Level 1 derives (1.1) data interoperability dealing with common representations of data to be commonly accessible, (1.2) process interoperability concerned with the connectivity of processes between different enterprises, (1.3) rule interoperability ensuring transaction between enterprises to be compliant within legal and business context, (1.4) object interoperability reflects the vision of the Internet of Thing, where everyday objects are interoperable and traceable, (1.5) software interoperability refers to enterprise software applications that work with other enterprise software applications as well as (1.6) cultural interoperability deals with the context of information and knowledge to avoid misunderstandings between enterprises.

Level 2 considers (2.1) knowledge interoperability dealing with different semantic abstraction of content to enable human or machine based interpretation, (2.2) service interoperability reflects the vision of Internet of Services enabling the usage of distributed services in the Internet, (2.3) social network interoperability considers internal enterprise adaptations to enable the use of social networks and (2.4) electronic identity interoperability has its focus on the exchange of identity data. Third level reflects (3.1) cloud interoperability enabling cloud services to be ideally deployed and used anywhere as well as finally the forth level (4.1) ecosystem interoperability enabling the establishment of digital, business and innovation ecosystems in a global world.

It is clearly stated that although aforementioned interoperability aspects evolved maturity to be elaborated individually there are strong dependencies, overlaps and common issues between them when analyzed in more detail. Conceptual modeling can be identified in all aforementioned interoperability dimensions. Hence it is plausible that different conceptual models are designed to support different dimensions of interoperability. Domain specific business process modeling enables process interoperability, whereas workflow management may focus on service interoperability. Business models, supply chains or e3value models may describe rule interoperability, whereas enriched versions of that models may support ecosystem interoperability.

Hence different conceptual models may support different dimensions of enterprise interoperability. Hybrid modeling enables a plug-in framework that allows the use of different conceptual models for different dimensions of enterprise interoperability within a holistic platform that shares those parts that are in common and enable a specialization of those parts that are specific.

## 2.2. Conceptual Model-Based Solutions in Past and Current EU-Research Projects

Conceptual modeling is an established research field and found its way to industrial applications some decades ago. Meta modeling as an instrument also found its way to industry and is also established in research. In the following scenarios from EU-projects (BOC, 2013) are introduced, where ADOxx® was used to realize hybrid modeling for enterprise interoperability.

In the application domain of "collaboration in factories of the future," the projects ComVantage, BIVEE and e-Save are using ADOxx®.

ComVantage implements a holistic meta model for supply chain, production and logistics, and merge it with IT relevant meta models. A sample is the use case specification of mobile apps within the overall supply chain. Semantic lifting enables to support linked data approach for data interoperability.

BIVEE realizes a similar meta model for supply chain. It merges virtual enterprise models with innovation specific meta models such as a whiteboard enabling creative knowledge techniques and addressing knowledge interoperability.

e-Save uses the same aforementioned holistic meta model but introduces special algorithms for the travelling salesman problem to optimize energy savings using a graph-based conceptual model. Such energy saving properties is merged into the existing process models addressing process interoperability.

In the application domain of "eGovernment and Interoperability" the project FIT, LD-Cast and Immigration Policy are applying conceptual models with ADOxx®.

LD-Cast used public administration processes and transferred those processes to technical workflows. Additionally the meta model was extended by a service pool that registers the corresponding services. Semantic lifting enabled the annotation of services and workflows addressing service interoperability.

FIT also used public administration processes but complementary merged business rules as an alternative representation of processes. Hence meta models for business processes and for business rules have been merged into one holistic meta model dealing with rules and process interoperability.

Immigration Policy is based on legal immigration processes. A harmonization service has been implemented that conceptually compares processes for legal residents within different European states. Although the legal aspects of harmonization cannot be covered, the harmonization service of corresponding processes indicates similarities and addresses process interoperability.

In the "Service and Software Architecture" application domain the projects Akogrimo, BREIN and MOST realized hybrid meta models addressing mainly service interoperability.

Akogrimo investigated to bridge domain-specific business processes with low level workflow orchestration and telecommunication network interaction. The meta model was based on the e-business methodology (Bayer, Junginger, & Kühn, 2000) and merged with different meta models to provide a holistic view enabling to drill down business requirements to either service requests or software development requirements.

BREIN relied on the findings of Akogrimo, introduced semantic lifting and goal-based modeling for agents. The resulting holistic meta model is called "BPM4SOA," links high level business models down to concrete technical use cases or Web-service orchestrations.

MOST merged different meta models in order to support model driven architecture, integrating an ontology and inference mechanisms into the model driven architecture. Besides pure semantic lifting, there is also a semantic enrichment as the resulting software design is ontology-aware.

In the application domain of "Technology Enhanced Learning" the projects MATURE and NEXT-TELL applied hybrid modeling reflecting knowledge interoperability.

MATURE described knowledge maturity within an organization using knowledge management processes enriched with technical models to specify a knowledge-based service bus. The resulting meta model reflected both, knowledge management and technical infrastructure aspects.

NEXTELL describes the course planning for teachers and integrates evaluation models to tightly couple the course planning and the evaluation of courses by using a merged meta model. The result is a holistic meta model incorporating course planning and course evaluation models.

In the domain "Manage your Enterprise Knowledge" the project plugIT, AsIsKnown and eHealthMonitor used hybrid modeling to deal with knowledge interoperability.

AsIsKnown merged a meta model describing knowledge management processes and external ontologies. The application domain was a home textile online shop where customer interaction has been observed and relevant changes have been reflected in the knowledge management processes. Ontological description was added, as the data have been separated in an external ontology management system.

plugIT had the vision of plugging business into IT, hence meta model describing business, IT and knowledge have been integrated. The approach was to "servicify" meta models and hence apply an extreme loose coupled approach, where meta models are connected via semantic lifting. This scenario also addressed aspects of service interoperability.

eHealthMonitor follows the path of hybrid modeling in the domain of knowledge techniques, by applying hybrid modeling for e-health specific modeling, like knowledge management processes, agent goal modeling and semantic lifting. Current solution is therefore a mixture of merged meta models to enable cooperative decision support.

## 2.3. Hybrid Modelling for Enterprise Interoperability

Aforementioned samples of past and current EU projects apply conceptual modeling in a holistic way and hence are in the need to merge different meta models. Conceptual models are used to enable interaction between different domains.

Hybrid modeling is the approach to flexibly combine different meta models and hence enable a flexible interaction between different domains. Hybrid modeling can be applied for vertical and horizontal integration of meta models. Vertical integration is used to vertically align different domains such as business and IT alignment, where business processes, workflows and IT resources are aligned. Horizontal integration is used to horizontally align different domains such as business processes of different enterprises to ensure that processes are aligned along a supply chain.

Conceptually spoken, enterprise interoperability takes place on the concrete level, which means that it takes place in the real world. It is then observed and conceptualized by modelers.

Abstractions in form of models and meta models provide functionality and technology with the aim to support this type of interoperability. In the following chapter the basic functionality and technologies are introduced that enable such enterprise interoperability support.

## 3. HYBRID MODELLING AS A SOLUTION FOR INTEROPERABILITY

Conceptual modeling is a knowledge representation with the aim to observe relevant parts of the real world. Meta modeling is a common realization approach to merge different conceptual models and is therefore briefly introduced. Hybrid modeling enables the creation of one holistic conceptual model using different meta models, hence enables to merge different viewpoints of the real world. As conceptual modeling became commodity and technical solutions rely on such knowledge representation the corresponding hybrid modeling gained importance.

## 3.1. Conceptual Modeling as an Instrument

The term "model" has an extremely ambiguous nature and hence is interpreted with the meaning discussed in the feasibility study of the Open Models Laboratory (Karagiannis, Grossmann, & Höfferer, 2008), where a model is "a representation of either reality or vision" (Whitten, Bentley, & Dittman, 2004), that are created "for some certain purpose" (OMG, 2003).

Hence the benefit of models can be described in four types:

1. Models act as a clear specification of desired target, reduce complexity, allow a structured approach and due to a common understanding support a participative creation. (Whiteman, Huff, & Presley, 1997);
2. Models target semi-automatic implementation of software like in the context of workflow orchestration or model driven architecture (MDA). Models are therefore seen to provide "execution support" (Kokol, 1993).
3. Models are well suited for documentation especially for human interpretation and hence support knowledge management tasks.

4.   Models evaluate current status against modeled targeted goals.

Conceptual models belong to the family of linguistic models that use an available set of pre-defined descriptions to create a model, and enrich the pure textual models (such as mathematical formula) with diagrammatic notations.

Hence, targeting aforementioned enterprise interoperability with conceptual models, means that pre-defined diagrammatic concepts are available that have a specific meaning enabling to reconstruct relevant parts of the reality with these concepts in order to either (1) specify, (2) support execution, (3) represent knowledge or (4) evaluate the different dimensions of enterprise interoperability.

The generic framework introduced in Figure 2 enables the specification of conceptual models.

The framework considers three building blocks:

1.   The modeling language that is most prominently associated with conceptual models, as available concepts to be used for such models are pre-defined according their semantic, their syntax and their graphical notation,

2.   The modeling procedure defines the stepwise usage of the modeling language and hence is not always available, this means there are modeling languages that have not a pre-defined way of usage but leave the modeler freedom during model construction,

3.   Mechanisms and algorithms enable the computer-based processing of models and hence provide an IT support for the aforementioned modeling scenarios – specification, execution support, knowledge representation and evaluation.

Those three main building blocks are composed to achieve different levels in form of a modeling technique or modeling method of a concept model approach. Although there is a discussion on the different terms, it helps to classify the different approaches. The traditional Entity Relationship (ER) diagram for example has a modeling language, a modeling procedure and algorithms that enable the transformation from model into a relational database schema. UML in contrast has

*Figure 2. Modeling method framework based on (Karagiannis & Kühn, 2002)*

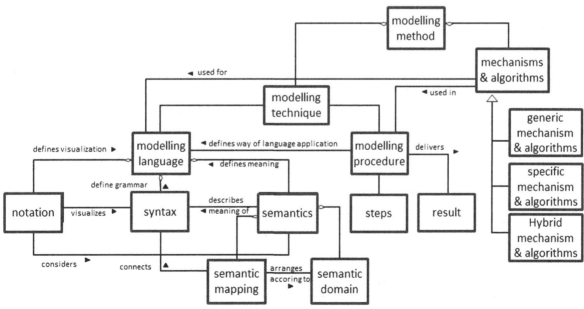

an expressive modeling language but no modeling procedure explaining the stepwise approach how to create a model. OWL for example defines its concepts in form of a modeling language and provides extensive algorithms for ontology inferences, but does not provide a procedure how to define a model. So the argumentation is that all conceptual model approaches can described with aforementioned framework and vice versa, every new conceptual model approach needs to first reflect, how to realize the relevant building blocks.

## 3.2. Meta Models as Realization Approach

Meta modeling is introduced as a realization approach to develop domain-specific modeling tools and hence enable IT-supported concept modeling. Based on (Strahringer, 1996), (Karagiannis & Höfferer, 2006) and (Kühn, 2004) Figure 3 introduce the different layers.

Relevant parts of the real world – in our case the enterprise interoperability – is seen as layer 0 and observed according previous introduced enterprise interoperability dimensions. For this purpose a set of concepts – in form of a modeling

language -, a stepwise procedure – in form of modeling procedure – and a set of software functionality – in form of mechanisms and algorithms - are provided to enable the creation of a model on layer 1. The modeling language is understood as the meta model, as it is a model of the concepts available for the model. This meta model is for example defined in a meta model language like ALL (ADOxx Library Language (ADOxx.org, 2013)). The specification of the meta model can again be defined by a model – the so called meta meta model or as a synonym meta2model.

Meta Model approaches have been analyzed in (Karagiannis & Höfferer, 2006) and can be distinguished in:

- Domain,
- Design – macro and micro level – as well as
- Integration.

Samples for macro-level design are:

- Business Rules (Herbst, 1996),
- Decision Support, (Aalst, Weske, &Grünbauer, 2005),

*Figure 3. Meta model layers*

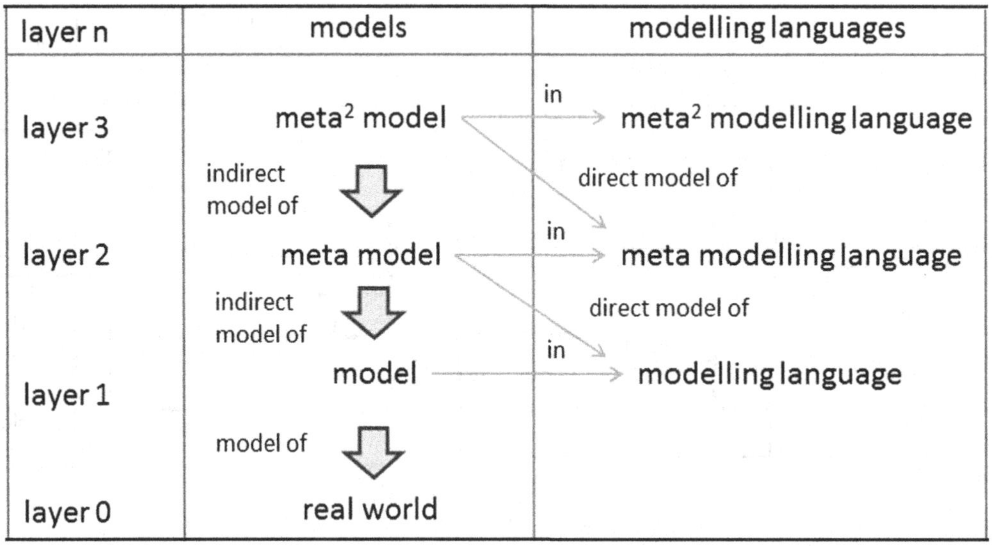

| layer n | models | modelling languages |
|---------|--------|---------------------|
| layer 3 | meta$^2$ model | meta$^2$ modelling language |
| layer 2 | meta model | meta modelling language |
| layer 1 | model | modelling language |
| layer 0 | real world | |

- Business process and - Workflow Management (Chiu, Li, & Karlapalem, 1999), (Rolland, Souveyet, & Moreno, 1995),
- Information systems: Web-based Systems (Nikolaidou & Anagnostopoulos, 2005), Agent-oriented Systems (Wagner, 2003), as well as
- Data Processing (Vassiliadis, Simitsis, Georgantas, Terrovitits, & Skiadopoulos, 2005).

Sample for micro-level design in different domains are:

- Knowledge representation (Mylopoulos, Borgida, Jarke, & Koubarakis, 1990),
- Data Processing mit TIGUKAT (Peters & Ozsu, 1993), FORM (Kim & Park, 1997) or ULD (Bowers & Delcambre, 2006).

Meta Models for integration and interoperability are:

- Object Modelling Framework (Hillegersberg & Kumar, 1999),
- Situational Method Engineering (Brinkkemper, Saeki, & Harmsen, 1999),
- Integrated requirement analysis (Nissen & Jarke, 1999) or
- Data processing schema mapping (Zaniolo & Melkanoff, 1982), (Cheung & Hsu, 1996).

All aforementioned meta models can be specified with a meta modeling language that is derived from an meta meta model. In the following the most prominent meta meta models based on (Kern, Hummel &Küne, 2012) are mentioned:

- Ecore from the Eclipse platform (Budinsky, Steinberg, Merks, Ellersick, & Grose, 2004),

- GOPRR from MetaEdit+ Platform (Kelly, 2008) and
- MS DSL Tools and MS Visio (Cook, Jones, Kent, & Wills, 2007).

Additionally the following meta meta models are introduced:

- MOF (OMG, 2013), which is realised on different UML Profile platforms
- ADOxx based on the equally named platform ADOxx (ADOxx.org, 2013),
- Obeo Designer on Eclipse (Obeo, 2013) and
- Generic Model Environment GME (GME, 2013).

The challenge is now to find the most appropriate modeling approach that covers aforementioned enterprise interoperability dimensions. As the application field of data, software, objects, processes, rules, culture, social networks, services, knowledge, electronic ID, cloud and ecosystem interoperability is too heterogeneous for one domain-specific modeling approach, this chapter argues to apply hybrid modeling by merging different meta models using meta model plug-ins, in order to use different modeling approaches for different enterprise interoperability dimensions.

## 3.3. Hybrid Modeling as Enterprise Interoperability Solution

Hybrid modeling is a concept that merges several meta models and hence applies a similar approach in meta modeling than service orientation applies in software engineering. First the different meta models are classified according to:

- Their domain,
- The level of technical granularity,
- The degree of formalization, and finally
- The cultural dependency of the applying community.

In the project plugIT a list of meta models was classified developing a Wiki (plugIT, 2013) according aforementioned dimension, whereas:

- The domain were the different perspectives of the Zachmann framework,
- The level of technical granularity were the different aspects of the Zachmann framework,
- The degree of formal expressiveness and
- The cultural dependency of applying community was seen as so-called language families, indicating the common philosophy of meta models.

Hence this WiKi listed a set of meta models for each dimension, which can be composed to a holistic modeling approach. So called meta model merging is seen as the composition of such meta models, and distinguish in:

- Loose integration of meta models,
- Strong integration, and
- Hybrid integration.

Based on the PhD thesis of (Kühn, 2004), meta modeling merging patterns are introduced ranging from loose coupled to fixed coupled meta models. Loose coupling is very flexible, whereas fixed coupled enables the realization of additional functionality.

Meta modeling merging patterns can be summarized:

1. Reference pattern, where two meta models are complementary and should not or cannot be changed. There exist different ways to enable a reference depending on if the meta model can be adapted or because of technical or other reasons an adaptation is not possible. Corresponding to requirements raised in section 2.1 meta models for Cloud interoperability may point to concepts from meta model for cultural interoperability.

The semantic distance between these meta models are so big that intermediate or even strong integration is not appropriate.

2. Transformation pattern, where two meta models are in principle complementary but part of one meta model correspond or can be created out of parts of the target meta model. The transformation rules for both the meta model and the corresponding models need to be built in. Reflecting requirements rose in section 2.1 a meta model for process interoperability may be transformed into a meta model for service interoperability. Concepts like processes may be transferred in identified services.

3. Use or aggregation pattern use part of the meta model in another meta model or aggregate them into a new meta model. In case a particular aspect that is covered with one meta model is required also in another meta model, the original meta model is used. Hence similar to software libraries different meta models are included to create a holistic and hence bigger meta model. Referring to requirements discussed in section 2.1 a meta model describing data interoperability may be used in a meta model concerned with knowledge interoperability, as data interoperability issues are seen as part of knowledge interoperability.

4. Merge and extension patterns of meta models are applied if meta models are closely related and cover similar issues. The challenge is to develop a new or extended meta model that still keeps the same concepts of the original meta model, so the original behavior and coverage is not disturbed. Additionally the complexity in merging several meta model would easily raise to an non-applicable amount. Applying merging or extension patterns in enterprise interoperability, may lead to a meta model for knowledge interoperability including a meta model for cultural, for rules, for process, for data, and for object

interoperability. Reflecting the complexity of each meta model the resulting meta model may be inappropriate to be handled by a user. A meta model for ecosystem interoperability including all aspects will most likely be not manageable.

Semantic Lifting of meta models is a special way of meta model merging, as a domain specific meta model is merged with the semantic meta model – in most cases an ontology. Hence all aforementioned types of meta model merging patterns are potentially possible for semantic lifting, but by the nature of the aim of semantic lifting, the reference patterns – in all its variation – is the selected choice, as typically concepts of the meta model are annotated – hence reference – to a particular ontology concepts.

Research in semantic lifting in the domain of enterprise interoperability can be found in the projects ComVantage (ComVantage, 2013) and BIVEE (BIVEE, 2013).

## 3.4. Realization Technology with ADOxx®

This section introduces the development platform adoxx.org (ADOxx.org, 2013) enabling the implementation of hybrid modeling approaches. It is therefore seen as a short tutorial overview on how to implement an individual hybrid modeling solution for enterprise interoperability. Due to space restriction a brief overview is provided with the intension to raise the interest for detailed reading in the tutorial sections of adoxx.org.

### 3.4.1. Introduction on Basic Terms

The meta model is realized in form of a tool configuration, in form of an application library. The model type is a package of modeling classes, enabling the separation of concerns within the meta model. Modeling classes are concepts of the meta model that are populated by the user while modeling and inherited from the domain-specific pre-define meta model. Those instances are model objects that are stored as elements of a concrete model. Each class defines its attributes, which are populated while modeling. The user interface and interaction is defined in the so-called notebook by each class (AttrRep). Graphical representation (GraphRep) is the diagrammatic definition of the notation. The semantic of a model class is defined by its inheritance of the pre-defined meta model. The pre-defined meta model has an operational semantic – in the current version directed graphs for dynamic aspects and trees for static aspects – hence depending from the inheritance of a class the corresponding object inherits the operational semantic. Additional semantic may be provided by hidden attribute that enable annotation to a domain ontology.

### 3.4.2. Relevant Technology for Modelling Languages

Modeling Languages are specified as meta models by inheriting from pre-defined meta models. The semantic as well as algorithms and mechanisms of the pre-defined meta model are automatically inherited to the developed meta model. In the following the two pre-defined meta models of ADOxx® are discussed. First, the dynamic meta model realizes a directed graph and hence provides start, activity, decision, parallelism, merging, and graph-end. Additional to these elements with operational graph-based semantic, there are two classes with container semantic the aggregation and the swim lane that automatically groups elements that are inside. Beside these two groups of classes there are some additional objects.

The static meta model realizes an organizational structure with persons and resources. Similar to the above mentioned containers there are aggregations and swim lanes. A new meta model is developed, when inheriting from the pre-defined classes. In case graph-based algorithms are used, the concepts are inherited from the dynamic meta model. In case a tree-based algorithm is used the classes are inherited from the static meta model. In case no corresponding class is found an own class hierarchy must be implemented.

### 3.4.3. Relevant Technology for Mechanisms and Algorithms

In order to upgrade a simple model editor to a full fletched modeling tool, the previously defined modeling language is enriched with corresponding mechanisms and algorithms. Generic functionality is provided for (a) modeling, (b) query, (c) transformation and (d) simulation. Some features need no configuration like querying a model or running a path analysis, whereas some functionality needs domain specific configurations like the transformation of a model into another format.

Basic components and their configurations can be extended by a script language called ADOscript that provide more than 400 APIs in form of message ports for: (i) acquisition, (ii) modeling, (iii) analysis, (iv) simulation, (v) evaluation, (vi) import/export, (vii) documentation and (viii) query. Ports for user interfaces are (i) ADOscript language, (ii) Core user interface and the (iii) Explorer, whereas APIs for manipulating the models are (i) the Core – the actual model representation, (ii) the data base and (iii) the user management. Finally the application API of the modeling tool is provided in form of (i) drawing and (ii) application.

This set of APIs provide the functionality that can be implemented either within or from outside the tool.

In case communication is established from outside the application there are three concepts:

1.   File based communication that triggers the export in a specific format (e.g. XML),
2.   Batch mode, where an ADOscript is invoked from outside the application, or

3.   Via a Web-service that enables the invocation of all ADOscripts APIs.

In this way also SOAP messages can be exchanged and the modeling tool can be integrated into a modeling environment.

### 3.5. Implementation Approaches for Hybrid Modeling with ADOxx®

Strong and intermediate integration of meta models is performed before modeling tools are deployed, whereas loose integration enables deployment of modeling tools before the integration takes place.

### 3.5.1. Strong and Intermediate Integration of Meta Models

Technical realization of merging two meta models, extending one meta model with another meta model, using part of one meta model in another meta model or aggregating concepts from two meta model into one new concept of the new meta model is supported by using the meta model development environment. The meta model designer using the meta model language ALL, is capable to merge, extend, use or aggregate one meta model with or into another meta model. A set of development tools are provide.

### 3.5.2. Strong Integration of Corresponding Models

The user should not be aware of the fact that actually two meta models are used. The separation of concern is realized by model types, whereas each group of model types represents one meta model. The graphical notation of meta models enable different views, so the user is guided by the view, which model type to use for which concern. This technical realization enables to share objects in form of so-called repository objects, or reference objects with pointers across models.

### 3.5.3. Loose Integration of Meta Models

This type of loose integration is elaborated in more detail as its implementation depends strongly on the user friendliness and applicability. Strict loose integration has no changes in the meta model at all, but this usually lacks of user friendliness. Other solutions point from one concept of one meta model to another concept of another meta model and hence requires changes of the meta model but raises the user friendliness and applicability.

There are different implementation variants:

1.  Non supported direct linkage requires no changes in the meta models, the user needs to manually enter the linkage in an existing suitable attribute. Such suitable attributes may be added into the meta model in form of minor changes of the meta model. Modeling with this solution is error prone.

2.  Supported direct linkage, can be realized by an ADOscript that accesses the other modeling tool and enables the selection of an object. Cardinalities of this linkage can be implemented in ADOscript. This linkage is also called tunnel, as two modeling tools exchange their information using this conceptual tunnel. Direct links can be enriched by additional context information such as pre-defined keywords, or context specific keywords that are identified during modeling and made available to the tunnel through hidden attributes.

3.  Indirect linkage can be realized using a so-called transit model type. Concepts of the corresponding other meta model are included. Hence user friendly mechanisms to reference a model objects (e.g. a pointer in form of an interref) can be used. This results in redundant data storage; hence the redundancy must be managed. A common solution is to write-protect the transit model type and allow only the complete import of new concepts from the original

source. More advanced mechanisms with notification mechanisms can be realized using ADOscript events.

4.  Loose coupling is a special form of indirect linkage, as the concepts that are referenced too are not the target concepts but a reference ontology, which is referenced by both the source and the target concept. The technical implementation is similar to the indirect linkage.

5.  Direct and indirect linkage is a combination of supported and non-supported linkage, by supporting a fixed core set of concepts but leave flexibility to agile evolving concepts using the non-supported implementation.

### 3.5.4. Loose Integration of Models

In non-supported realizations, users need to physically change modeling tools to copy and paste content like URIs or ids from a model in one tool into a model in the other tool. Supported linkages enable the user to model without noticing that the content the user is working with comes from another tool. The reason for not extending such supported scenario is the fact that domain-specific modeling tools have a domain-specific characteristic, the overuse of support between meta models leads to strong coupling and hence to unmanageable and for the user too complex modeling tools. Hence the level of support when integrating meta models, is based on the requirements for user-friendliness and applicability. Aforementioned loose integration leads to different levels of user friendliness and hence need individual assessment for a particular application scenario.

## 4. THE BIVEE PROJECT AS A USE CASE SAMPLE

BIVEE is an EU-project dealing with the "innovation of the innovation" by integrating the so-called "Virtual Innovation Space" into traditional so-called "Value Production Spaces." The integrative element is a component called PIKR (Production and Innovation Knowledge Repository) that provides semantic descriptions to enable knowledge exchange between the production and innovation components. Hence, Value Production Space must be integrated with PIKR by combining the two meta models.

Although this seems to be a simple merge of two meta models – one for the Value Production Space and one for the PIKR – the concerns that need to be managed by the Value Production Space are so heterogeneous that hybrid modeling is required. In the following the Value Production Space and the PIKR are briefly explained and technical solutions are discussed.

## 4.1. The Hybrid BIVEE Meta Model

Value Production Space of BIVEE considers the different viewpoints to enable users to manage virtual enterprises. Hence a so-called modeling stack has been developed that presents the different concerns and identifies different meta models. The Valued Production Space Chart is an extended e3value model that deals with the concerns products, processes and virtual networks. IT-system pool and artifact pool are pool models. KPIs are reflected across the framework. A plug-in mechanism for domain specific conceptual models like energy saving, bull-wipe effect simulations and the like are necessary. The semantic transit implements the aforementioned semantic lifting.

The modeling-stack in BIVEE indicates several aspects of hybrid modeling. The Value Production Space Chart is based on the e3 value model and is enriched with geographical features. Processes are using the BPMN notation and are extended by so called process maps. Product models are concerned with the product composition, whereas the network model is concerned with the composition of the virtual enterprise. From a model perspective, although different meta models are available, these concerns are managed by one user,

hence those meta models have been merged using strong meta model merging. The two pool models are integrated as supporting models.

KPIs are proposed to be modeled with a Balanced Scorecard meta model, although it includes aspects that are not necessary for BIVEE. Hence a reduced meta model was created and strongly merged into the BIVEE meta model. The plugin approach is a type of loose coupled meta models, where transit models are used to establish the link to smaller but focused modeling approaches. Semantic lifting of the complete meta model, applies a loose coupling with a transit model, hence a direct and indirect linkage has been implemented to the PIKR.

## 4.2. The Realization of Hybrid Modeling in BIVEE

This section indicates, how BIVEE realized aforementioned hybrid meta model to fulfill the requirements raised by the Value Production Space.

Figure 4 depicts an overview of hybrid meta models for the Value Production Space in BIVEE on class level showing the different model types, their different views and the list of classes that have been realized. The relations between the meta models are only indicative for simplification reasons as detailed references are from class level and would make the picture unreadable.

Value Production Space Chart extends the e3value model – that is implemented as value flow view, with geographic view. Process meta model aggregates three meta models, by using BPMN, the thread model and the process map. Network meta model aggregates the organizational structure and the scope model as views. The product model has been developed from scratch and the helping pool meta models are used for supporting reasons. KPI meta model is realized in three abstractions, the KPI formula defining the formula of concrete measures to result in an key performance indicator, the KPI pool that collects and specifies the different indicators and

*Figure 4. BIVEE meta model on class level*

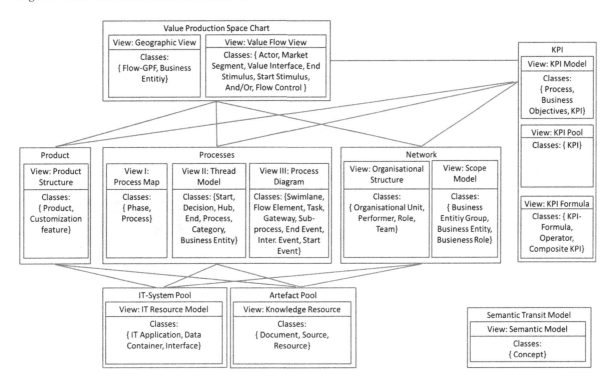

finally the KPI model that enables the linkage between processes, business objectives and concrete indicators.

The semantic transit meta model only realizes the class "concept" that is interpreted as an ontology concept and hence establishes the link to the PIKR. The BIVEE meta model is described in more detail in deliverable D3.1 of BIVEE and supporting material, showing a detailed level on relations, pointer and attributes can be accessed from the project Webpage. In this paper the focus was less on the concrete realization of the meta model but on demonstrating a sample on hybrid modeling and discussing different realization approaches.

## 4.3. The Integration of Domain Specific and Semantic Transit Model

This scenario provides a functionality to annotate any modeling object from the domain specific part of the meta model with a set of concepts available as an external resource. First, a so-called transit model type needs to be developed that represents the ontology concepts that are used for the annotation. This transit model type does not require the full set of concepts, instead focuses on a relevant selection.

Second, the remaining concepts are accessible via a Web-service invocation. Hence the user first selects a concept from the transit model and can then invoke a user interface to access the PIKR Web-service that provides – corresponding to the initial selection of concepts – the related set of additional ontology concepts out of the ontology. Concepts that are accessible through the semantic transit models are used to identify the relevant part of the ontology. Those concepts selected from the user interface of the Web-service enable the annotation with concepts of an ontology that is kept in another system.

Figure 5 indicates a model in the left bottom corner and shows a notebook of a modeling object. The notebook uses two properties for the annota-

*Figure 5. Symbolic screen shot of semantic integration*

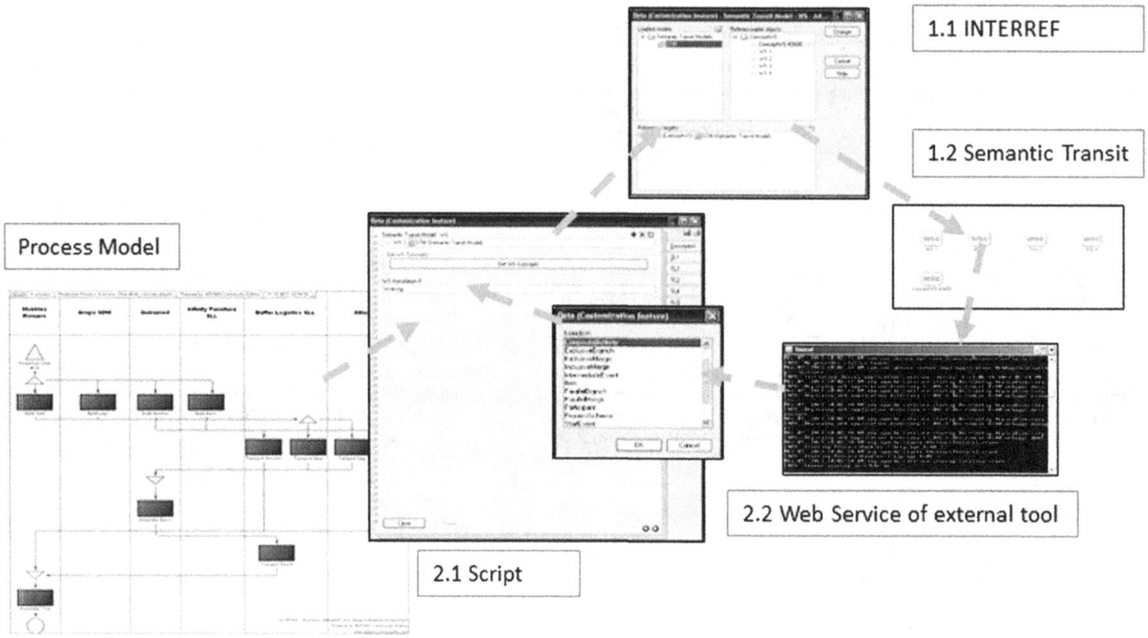

tion, first the Semantic Transit Model – WS is a pointer to concepts of the transit model. This is represented with a user interface to select the corresponding concepts out of the semantic transit model indicated on the right side. Once this pointer is selected, the second property of the notebook can be edited. An ADOscript is invoked opening the user interface –indicated on the lower part of the figure - to access the PIKR Web-service. The Web-service is indicated with the command lines and the corresponding user interface is shown in front of the notebook representing the list of concept from the ontology. Now the user can select content for modeling form another tool without noticing.

In Box 1 the ADOscript code is shown to demonstrate, how such a semantic lifting can be realized in ADOxx using the message-based implementation.

This section introduced the challenges of hybrid modeling in a concrete application scenario and indicated how hybrid modeling has been used considering knowledge interoperability in virtual enterprises in a prototype and demonstration setting. A reflection and lessons learned based also on previous experiences is discussed in the next chapter.

## 5. LESSONS LEARNED

Considering the interoperability aspects cultural, rule, process, data, software, object, social network, services, knowledge, eID, cloud and ecosystem interoperability there are three observations.

First observation, in the list of aforementioned research projects, meta model were used covering most of the individual dimension like processes –BPMN, BPEL, EPC, BPMS -, data – like ERM, SDBD, LOM, ebXML, UBL -, software – UML and iStar – as well as knowledge – PROMOTE, OWL, OPAL. A brief survey on Open Models laboratory (OMiLAB, 2013) or similar platforms and standardization consortiums reveals that there are additional meta model for aforementioned and remaining dimensions. Hence meta model for the

*Box 1.*

```
SET my_objid: (STR objid)
SET myobjid: (VAL my_objid)
CC „Modeling" GET_ACT_MODEL
SET myModelID: (modelid)
CC „Core" GET_CLASS_ID objid: (myobjid)
CC „Core" GET_ATTR_ID classid: (classid) attrname: („Semantic Transit Model -
WS")
CC „Core" GET_INTERREF objid: (myobjid) attrid: (attrid) index: 0
CC „Core" GET_ATTR_VAL objid:(tobjid) attrname:(„WS Endpoint")
SET txtWS:(val)
SYSTEM („C:\SemLift.bat \""„+txtWS+"\"„)
SET txt:(„C:\getConceptsWS")
CC „AdoScript" FREAD file: (txt)
SET text_new: (text)
CC „AdoScript" LISTBOX entries: (text_new) toksep: „@"
IF (endbutton = („ok"))
{     CC „Core" GET_CLASS_ID objid:(myobjid)
      SET myclassid: (classid)
      CC „Core" GET_ATTR_ID classid: (myclassid) attrname: „WS Annotation II"
      SET myattrid: (attrid)
      FOR mySelectedID in: (selection)
      { CC „Core" SET_ATTR_VAL objid:(myobjid) attrid:(myattrid)
val:(mySelectedID)
      CC „AdoScript" FILE_DELETE file:(„C:\getConceptsWS")
      EXIT
      }
      CC „AdoScript" FILE_DELETE file:(„C:\getConceptsWS")
}
ELSE
{ CC „AdoScript" INFOBOX („You cancelled the dialog without selecting detailed
annotation!\
      CC „AdoScript" FILE_DELETE file:(„C:\getConceptsWS")
}
```

individual aspects of enterprise interoperability are available.

Second observation, is that merging meta model for all aspects, will result in an heterogeneous meta model that needs special mechanisms to keep the concerns separated as one end user is most likely not dealing with all aspects. Hence, either strict loose coupling or merged meta models

with additional user and access right management is required. From practical experiences an intermediate approach, is proposed to enable the maintenance of the meta model. Considering that one meta model has between 8.000 and 40.000 lines of ALL code – of course depending on the complexity – a merged meta model may result between 100.000 and 200.000 lines of ALL code.

Hence source code management mechanisms known from software engineering are required to maintain those meta models.

Third observation is that the holistic view on enterprise interoperability will most likely observe one part of the real world – e.g. one virtual enterprise. Hence holistic models that are created with the holistic viewpoint should be available in form of a repository so that meta models dealing with a different concern can refer, re-use or access the information that has been created through another meta model – hence through another perspective.

There are following directions. Domain specific modeling for enterprise interoperability has a variety and cannot be exclusively covered by a standard or a small set of standards. Hence UML and BPMN are prominent players but are not capable to cover all aforementioned aspects, there is the need to develop and adapt new meta models.

The complexity indicated above requires stable and mature meta modeling platforms that rely on stable databases, user and access management and provide appropriate functionality to support the development of own meta models, but also provide functionality for hybrid modeling and enable the combination of different modeling tools.

Screening aforementioned dimension it becomes obvious that current IT and software driven modeling approaches have their important place in enterprise interoperability, but human-oriented aspects like knowledge or culture must not be neglected when dealing with enterprise interoperability. Hence meta models that are valuable for software design may be inappropriate for designing human behavior and cultural interoperability. Hence, new pre-defined meta models and meta meta models need to be developed to perfectly support the full range of dimensions.

Reflecting aforementioned project results leads to the lessons learned that introduced technological solutions sufficiently cover use cases from the different scenarios. However the compilation of the meta model, the decision on the selected hybrid modeling approach and implementation

strategy still strongly depend on the involved method engineer and the domain experts. Tight and interactive development, following an agile development approach from the method engineer with the domain experts, has been found most suitable. The different ways of hybrid modeling approaches are seen as the tool box of the method engineer that must be carefully selected during the development phase.

## 6. CONCLUSION AND OUTLOOK

The chapter started with the observation on enterprise interoperability, their dimensions and their corresponding requirements on model-based approaches. Conceptual modeling has been introduced as a mature field of knowledge representation. A list of EU-projects have been discussed that successfully applied the hybrid modeling approach with ADOxx® and hence can act as a reference for similar approaches.

Hybrid modeling as an instrument has been introduced to show how complex systems, such as enterprise interoperability, can be supported using knowledge representation with conceptual models. Different patterns have been introduced on how hybrid modeling can be used to deal with high complex systems.

The ADOxx® platform as an open use meta modeling platform has been briefly introduced in order to explain how hybrid modeling approaches from theory, can be implemented into a software platform.

This has been demonstrated in more detail with the EU-project BIVEE acting as a sample implementation in the domain of virtual enterprises concerned with knowledge interoperability.

Finally some lessons learned have been raised that need to be considered when realizing hybrid modeling for enterprise interoperability. Based on experiences hybrid modeling is proposed as a possible path to enterprise interoperability.

The Open Knowledge Model Initiative runs a laboratory (www.omilab.org) supporting communities to develop meta models. Hence approaching enterprise interoperability via hybrid modeling is supported by the open development environment of the OMIlab.

Tool development on ADOxx.org (www.adoxx.org) provides platform, technology and tools to create a hybrid modeling tool for enterprise interoperability.

# REFERENCES

Aalst, W. M. P. d., Weske, M., & Grünbauer, D. (2005). Case handling: A new paradigm for business process support. *Data & Knowledge Engineering*, *53*(2), 129–162. doi:10.1016/j.datak.2004.07.003

*ADOxx.org.* (2013). Retrieved, June 24, 2013 from http://www.adoxx.org

Bayer, F., Junginger, S., & Kühn, H. (2000). A business process oriented methodology for developing e-business applications In *Proceedings of the 7th European Concurrent Engineering Conference (ECEC'2000)*. Leicester, UK: ECEC.

*BIVEE Project.* (n.d.). Retrieved 24, June, 2013 from http://www.bivee.eu

*BOC Research Projects.* (n.d.). Retrieved 24, June, 2013 from http://www.boc-group.com

Bowers, S., & Delcambre, L. (2006). Using the unilevel description (ULD) to support data-model interoperability. *Data & Knowledge Engineering*, 59.

Brinkkemper, S., Saeki, M., & Harmsen, F. (1999). Meta-modelling based assembly techniques for situational method engineering. *Information Systems*, *24*(3), 209–228. doi:10.1016/S0306-4379(99)00016-2

Budinsky, F., Steinberg, D., Merks, E., Ellersick, R., & Grose, T. J. (2004). *Eclipse modeling framework*. Reading, MA: Addison Wesley.

Cheung, W., & Hsu, C. (1996). The model-assisted global query system for multiple databases in distributed enterprises. *ACM Transactions on Information Systems*, *14*(4), 421–470. doi:10.1145/237496.237499

Chiu, D. K. W., Li, Q., & Karlapalem, K. (1999). A meta modeling approach to workflow management systems supporting exception handling. *Information Systems*, *24*(2), 159–184. doi:10.1016/S0306-4379(99)00010-1

*ComVantage Project.* (n.d.). Retrieved 24, June, 2013 from http://www.comvantage.eu

Cook, S., Jones, G., Kent, S., & Wills, A. C. (2007). *Domain specific development with visual studio DSL tools (Microsoft.Net Development)*. Reading, MA: Addison-Weseley Longman.

*Ensemble EU-Project (concluded 2012.08).* (n.d.). Retrieved, June 24, 2013 from http://www.fines-cluster.eu

FInES Cluster. (2010). *FInES research roadmap*. Retrieved, June, 24, 2013 from http://cordis.europa.eu/fp7/ict/enet/documents/fines-researchroadmap-final-report.pdf

Fraunhofer, I. A. O. (n.d.). *Industrie 4.0*. Retrieved, June, 24, 2013 from http://www.iao.fraunhofer.de/lang-de/geschaeftsfelder/unternehmensentwicklung-und-arbeitsgestaltung/1009-industrie-40.html

*Generic Model Environment (GME)*. (n.d.). Retrieved 20, February, 2013 from http://www.isis.vanderbilt.edu/Projects/gme

Harald, K. (2004). *Methodenintegration im business engineering*. PhD Thesis.

Herbst, H. (1996). Business rules in systems analysis: A meta-model and repository system. *Information Systems, 21*(2), 147–166. doi:10.1016/0306-4379(96)00009-9

Hillegersberg, J. V., & Kumar, K. (1999). Using metamodeling to integrate object-oriented analysis, design and programming concepts. *Information Systems, 24*(2), 113–129. doi:10.1016/S0306-4379(99)00008-3

Karagiannis, D. (2012). *Presentation at FInES workshop in Aalborg*. Retrieved, June 24, 2013 from http://www.fines-cluster.eu/fines/jm/news-section/past-news/fines-workshop-in-aalborg-may-9th-2012-presentations-videos-available.html

Karagiannis, D., Grossmann, W., & Höfferer, P. (2008). *Open model initiative: A feasibility study*. Retrieved June 24, 2013, from http://cms.dke.univie.ac.at/uploads/media/Open_Models_Feasibility_Study_SEPT_2008.pdf

Karagiannis, D., & Höfferer, P. (2006). Metamodels in action: An overview. In *Proceedings of ICSOFT 2006 – First International Conference on Software and Data Technologies*. Insticc Press.

Karagiannis, D., & Kühn, H. (2002). Metamodelling platforms In *Proceedings of the Third International Conference EC-Web 2002 – Dexa 2002* (LNCS), (vol. 2455). Berlin: Springer.

Kelly, S., & Tolvanen, J.-P. (2008). *Doaminspecific modelling: Enabling full code generation*. Hoboken, NJ: John Wiley & Son, Inc. doi:10.1002/9780470249260

Kern, H., Hummel, A., & Kühne, S. (2011). Towards a comparative analysis of meta-metamodels. In *Proceedings of the 11th Workshop on Domain-Specific Modeling*. Retrieved, 01. January, 2011 from http://www.dsmforum.org/events/DSM11/Papers/kern.pdf

Kim, D. H., & Park, S. J. (1997). FORM: A flexible data model for integrated CASE environments. *Data & Knowledge Engineering, 22*(2), 133–158. doi:10.1016/S0169-023X(96)00042-0

Kokol, P. (1993). Metamodeling: How, why and what? *SIGSOFT Softw. Eng. Notes, 18*, 2. doi:10.1145/159420.155834

Mylopoulos, J., Borgida, A., Jarke, M., & Koubarakis, M. (1990). Telos: Representing knowledge about information systems. *ACM Transactions on Information Systems, 8*(4), 325–362. doi:10.1145/102675.102676

Nikolaidou, M., & Anagnostopoulos, D. (2005). A systematic approach for configuring web-based information systems. *Distributed and Parallel Databases, 17*(3), 267–290. doi:10.1007/s10619-005-6832-0

Nissen, H. W., & Jarke, M. (1999). Repository support for multi-perspective requirements engineering. *Information Systems, 24*(2), 131–158. doi:10.1016/S0306-4379(99)00009-5

*Obeo Designer*. (n.d.). Retrieved 20, February, 2013 from http://www.obeo.fr/pages/obeo-designer/en

Object Management Group (OMG). (2003). *MDA guide version 1.0.1, 2007-01-22*. OMG.

OMG. (n.d.). *Meta object facility*. Retrieved at 24, June 2013 from http://www.omg.org/mof/

OMiLAB. (n.d.). *Open models initiative laboratory*. Retrieved 24, June, 2013 from http://www.omilab.org

Peters, R. J., & Ozsu, M. T. (1993). Reflection in a uniform behavioral object model. In *Proceedings of the 12th International Conference on Entity-Relationship Approach*. Academic Press.

*plugIT*. (n.d.). Retrieved 24, June, 2013, from http://plug-it.org/plugITwiki/

Popplewell, K., Lampathaki, F., Koussouris, S., Mouzakitis, S., Charalabidis, Y., Goncalves, R., & Agostinho, C. (2012). *EISB state of play report, deliverable D2.1 ensemble*. Retrieved, June 24, 2013 from http://www.fines-cluster.eu/fines/jm/Publications/Download-document/339-ENSEMBLE_D2.1_EISB_State_of_Play_Report-v2.00.html

Rolland, C., Souveyet, C., & Moreno, M. (1995). An approach for defining ways-of-working. *Information Systems*, *20*(4), 337–359. doi:10.1016/0306-4379(95)00018-Y

Strahringer, S. (1996). *Metamodellierung als instrument des methodenvergleichs: Eine evaluierung am beispiel objektorientierter analyse-methoden*. Aachen, Germany: Shaker.

Vassiliadis, P., Simitsis, A., Georgantas, P., Terrovitis, M., & Skiadopoulos, S. (2005). A generic and customizable framework for the design of ETL scenarios. *Information Systems*, *30*(7), 492–525. doi:10.1016/j.is.2004.11.002

Wagner, G. (2003). The agent-object-relationship metamodel: Towards a unified view of state and behavior. *Information Systems*, *28*(5), 475–504. doi:10.1016/S0306-4379(02)00027-3

Whitman, L., Huff, B., & Presley, A. (1997). Structured models and dynamic systems analysis: The integration of the IDEF0/IDEF3 modeling methods and discrete event simulation. In *Proceedings of the 29th Conference on Winter Simulation*. IEEE Computer Society. http://doi.acm.org/10.1145/268437.268559

Whitten, J. L., Bentley, L. D., & Dittman, K. C. (2004). *System analysis and design methods* (6th ed.). Boston: McGraw-Hill Irwin.

Zaniolo, C., & Melkanoff, M. A. (1982). A formal approach to the definition and the design of conceptual schemata for database systems. *ACM Transactions on Database Systems*, *7*(1), 24–59. doi:10.1145/319682.319695

## KEY TERMS AND DEFINITIONS

**Conceptual Models:** Models are a simplified representation of a selected reality. Physical models use physical objects to create a physical model in a smaller and simplified way that the reality is. Conceptual model however represent the reality in form of symbols and concepts. Hence they do physically not exist and exist only in the mind in form of concepts and may be drawn with pen and pencil.

**Domain Specific Modelling Language:** Modelling languages can either be constructed to serve several purposes or to serve purposes for only one particular domain. If a modelling language is more meaningful and semantically more expressive, it is typically specialized for a particular domain. Such specialized modelling languages are meant by the term "domain specific modelling language."

**Hybrid Modelling:** Hybrid modelling is a term that indicates that domain specific modelling languages have a specific focus. In case different viewpoints are integrated into one holistic view, those individual modelling methods are integrated to a holistic modelling method. This compilation of different specific modelling methods is understood as hybrid modelling.

**Information Value:** Information is only useful, if the consumer can derive any benefit out of this information. In this context, models are not only a representation of the reality but this representation has to result in a concrete value for the consumer of the model.

**Mechanisms and Algorithms:** Mechanisms and algorithms define the processing of models. Algorithms are mathematically justifiable, whereas mechanisms incudes elements that are not able to be described formally.

**Meta Model:** The term "meta" indicates that this model is on a different abstraction layer. Meta model is commonly understood as a model of a model. There are different interpretations that either the meta model is part of the model, or the meta model defines separately the model. In this chapter we use the latter interpretation that meta models are models of modelling languages, hence they define the modelling language that can be used to create models.

**Modelling Language:** Modelling languages typically consists of syntactical objects that represent the alphabet of the modelling language, the semantic that expresses the meaning for each object as well as the graphical notation that is applied when drawing the model.

**Modelling Method:** Modelling method is understood to enrich modelling languages with functionalities and an intended way of applying the modelling languages. It is therefore not only the conceptual representation of a model but also the processing capabilities as well as the intended way of usage.

**Semantic Lifting:** Semantic lifting in this context is understood as a semantic enrichment of a model. Typically semantic expressions or references are introduced to the model in order enrich the semantic expressiveness and hence semantically lift a model.

# Chapter 6
# Interoperability in Service-Oriented Production Networks:
## Managing n:n Relationships with xRM

**Spiros Alexakis**
*CAS Software AG, Germany*

**Johannes Britsch**
*University of Mannheim, Germany*

**Markus Bauer**
*CAS Software AG, Germany*

**Bernhard Kölmel**
*Hochschule Pforzheim University, Germany*

## ABSTRACT

*How can complex relationship structures be managed? When collaborating in networks, the diversity of stakeholder relationships is increasing. Most times, this leads to interoperability issues that need to be addressed. In this chapter, the authors show how Anything Relationship Management (xRM) can increase interoperability in many-to-many (n:n) relationships. Building upon relationship management theory, they firstly categorize different types of relationships and link them with fitting IT solutions. The authors then give a brief introduction to the xRM concept. Following and more specifically, they present the EU research project GloNet[1] and propose three technical xRM approaches (collaboration spaces, integration of external services, and synchronization framework) in order to improve social network interoperability, services interoperability, and data interoperability. The chapter closes with a conclusion, an example of application, and a research outlook.*

## 1. INTRODUCTION

*The corporation as we know it is unlikely to survive the next 25 years. Legally and financially yes, but not structurally and economically (Peter Drucker, 2000, in: Shuman, Twombly, 2010, p. 1).*

DOI: 10.4018/978-1-4666-5142-5.ch006

The twelve-year old prediction made by business guru Peter Drucker is becoming reality today. As Jay Deragon puts it: due to social computing and social network solutions, economy is changing drastically –with an impact similar to the impact of the 19th century Industrial Revolution (Allen et al., 2008). On various levels a shift towards a primary relationship-based economy can be found:

the old business-centric company model turns into a relationship-centric model, win-lose strategy turns into win-win strategy, the control approach turns into transparency, branding efforts turn into reputation, mass communication turns into conversation, financial targets turn into multifaceted value-based goals, and separate contact silos turn into networks of relationships (Allen et al., 2008).

Naturally, production is also increasingly taking place in networks. While through networks, highly complex and service-enriched product lines can be realized, more and more stakeholder groups are involved in the underlying processes. This leads to issues in the orchestration of the corresponding relationships and to the question how information exchange can be achieved between stakeholders and their multifold information systems. In general, a central challenge of a system (or a product) in the industrial or manufacturing context is its ability to be connected to other systems (or products) without requiring additional user input – it is one of the key factors to maintain high quality and to allow customization, and on the other hand, to offer a quick production at low cost. Interoperability is thereby needed on different levels between internal and external stakeholders. Besides, a new and important success factor is seen in the installation of a management layer across the collaborative network (Cutting-Decelle et al., 2012).

In this chapter, we propose Anything Relationship Management (xRM) as a possible answer to these challenges. Following a classification of different relationship constellations, we outline the xRM concept and show its typical platform architecture. Furthermore, we describe first promising results of the EU research project GloNet. In GloNet, xRM is used to ensure interoperability and a seamless value creation process in a production virtual organization consisting of small and medium-sized enterprises (SMEs) and involving end-to-end collaboration with customers and local suppliers (co-creation). In sum, the three main questions tackled in this chapter are:

1. What kinds of relationships structure are there and which IT solutions suit them?
2. What is the structure of a suitable xRM architecture?
3. How to solve typical interoperability issues in production networks?

# 2. RELATIONSHIP TYPES IN RELATIONSHIP MANAGEMENT

One of the origins of the relationship based view of firms lies in the marketing domain. Until today, the research areas relationship management and its subset relationship marketing play an important role in explaining the mechanisms of organizational relations and networks. The following classification of relationship types is therefore based on a differentiation scheme of relationship marketing perspectives by Coviello et al., 1997. Similar to our classification, Coviello et al. (1997) distinguish between the practices of transaction (see 2.1), database (see 2.2), interaction (see 2.3, 2.4), and network marketing (see 2.5). As an extension, our classification takes into account the historical development of IT tools for relationship management (Britsch & Kölmel, 2012).

## 2.1. Transactional Relationship: Short Term View

The transactional orientation was predominant in the industrial era. Growing markets fostered a strong focus on sales. With McCarthy's (1960) marketing-mix concept and its focus on the Four Ps (Product, Price, Place, and Promotion) new customers should be attracted. The transactional marketing model was overall built around shot-term maximization of profit. "As competition intensified with excess capacity, sales transactions further increased. Many engaged in aggressive selling and competitive warfare." (Sheth & Parvatiyar, 1995, p. 406) In their struggle for market share, firms served the anonymous mass market or particular market segments and communicated to – not with – the customer in order to conclude "discrete, arms-length transactions" (Brodie et al., 2008, p. 85). Instead of establishing an on-going exchange, the relationship with the customer was rather seen to be limited to an episodic and impersonal event.

## 2.2. 1:1 Relationship: Long Term View

Due to the advancing market saturation and the shift from seller's to buyer's markets, more and more marketers began to realize the importance of repeated sales and customer loyalty. In the 1970s, producers of consumer goods were among the first to implement key account management in order to create long term relationships with important customers (Ehrlinger, 1979). The idea quickly expanded to relationship marketing and therefore, to all customer groups (Berry, 1983). Instead of single transactions, the concept is centered on two parties, usually on one buyer and one seller (1:1 relationship). By interacting over a longer period of time, profiles of actors can be generated, and on this basis, a customized sales approach can be realized. IT solutions were the enablers of the 1:1 approach, first in form of simple databases, then as computer aided selling software, and finally as customer relationship management (CRM) systems that helped tracking, analyzing and managing relationships. In the following years, the ideas of 1:1 marketing were adapted to upstream markets. However, solutions for e.g. supplier relationship management (SRM) (Campelo & Stucky, 2007) have stayed behind CRM and enterprise resource planning (ERP) in terms of popularity levels.

## 2.3. 1:n Relationship: Customer Community

Like all relationship types, one-to-many (1:n) relationships are addressed in both informatics and marketing. While in databases, 1:n relations

occur when a record in a table a can reference to multiple records in table b (and, vice versa, references are limited to one record), in the marketing area, 1:n relationships can be interpreted in a slightly different way. Traditionally, 1:n marketing was defined through media like TV, radio, or print, where a message was sent by one content provider and reached many passive content receivers, neglecting interaction among them (Hoffman & Novak, 1996). In today's networked society, these communication processes have changed. The transmitter of a message rather provides a communication "spark" which then "catches fire" in the exchange of knowledge and opinions among its receivers. "[W]ord of mouth is no longer an act of intimate, one-on-one communication. Today, it also operates on a one-to-many basis: product reviews are posted online and opinions disseminated through social networks." (Bughin, Doogan, & Vetvik, 2010, p. 2). Following this reasoning, we propose a definition of 1:n relationships viewing the "many" (n) as a community of interacting members, typically on the customer side. This type of relationship can be managed using Social Customer Relationship Management (SCRM) systems. SCRM typically includes the monitoring of interaction in social networks in order to provide data for CRM solutions. As such, SCRM describes a somewhat hybrid model of platform (e.g. social networks) and system (CRM).

## 2.4. n:1 Relationship: Partner Ecosystem

From the informatics point of view, n:1 relationships are the inversion of 1:n relationships. Interestingly, the n:1 concept has been widely ignored in management literature under this label. Also when looking into the education sector, Schacht, Botzenhardt, and Maedche (2012, p. 21) resume: "[T]he usage of so-called many-to one communication, where a number of persons transmit their messages to one recipient, has been considered only rarely." However, especially in the last years, the notion of "business ecosystem" has gained momentum in theory and practice as an "economic community supported by a foundation of interacting organizations and individuals [...] produc[ing] goods and services of value to customers" (Moore, 1993, p. 26). Consistent with our definition of 1:n relationships, we consider ecosystems as an expression of n:1 relationships. Many collaborators interact and exchange information, typically with and for one dominant member of the ecosystem, and for one common goal, e.g. a co-developed product. This target orientation can mostly be found at inbound stakeholders groups like suppliers or partners. Since these groups usually need a deeper level of integration of their shared processes, they increasingly tend to use social project management solutions or – like in the following collaboration networks – Anything Relationship Management (xRM) platforms for their interaction.

## 2.5. n:n Relationship: Collaboration Network

In informatics and database theory, the term "n:m relationship" is used instead of the marketing term "n:n relationship." N:m relationships are typically composed in databases using a intermediate table (table a_b) that joins two source tables (table a and table b). For example, there may be multiple reasons (table a) for customers to make a purchase (table b) and, vice versa, multiple purchases for one reason (Microsoft, 2012). Similarly in marketing, n:n relationships describe relationships of groups of entities in networks.

For example, a part of a consumer network may interact with a supplier network and, vice versa, a part of the supplier network may collaborate with a consumer network. Consequently, Gummesson (2004, p. 2) defines: "Many-to-many marketing describes, analyzes and utilizes the network properties of marketing." Interaction takes place among various stakeholder groups as well as directly between these groups. In such networks of different actors, value-creation is not limited to business-to-business (B2B) or business-to-customer (B2C), but could result from transaction models like "B2B2C2C2B2B" (Gummesson, 2004, p. 7). Gummesson lists the following advantages of the n:n concept:

- **Complexity:** The complexity of relational structures is recognized. Building on network theory, the many-to-many approach views co-operation as relationships and interaction between network nodes which can consist of individuals as well as organizations. At the same time, it is taken into account that networks are not limited in size; that basically "everything influences everything" (Gummesson, 2004, p. 3). Along the value chain, a variety of stakeholders interacts with each other in many ways, providing valuable feedback and idea input for organizations. As Gummesson (2008, p. 16) concludes: "The number of unique situation [sic] is unlimited, [...] change is a natural state of affairs, and [...] processes are iterative rather than linear." Therefore, with the many-to-many concept, it is possible to draw a more realistic picture of organizational relationship structures. These structures again should serve as a basis when managing parts of the relational network.

- **Context:** Looking at "the big picture of relationships," the approach offers context to analytics. Gummesson (2004, p. 3) compares this to information provision in the media: "When newspapers print an interview statement out of context and makes [sic] it a headline, the statement may be perceived as something else than was originally intended. In the same sense, loose statements, concepts, strategies and models in marketing need a context." An isolated management of 1:1 relationships therefore has a high risk of overlooking critical factors for the decision-making. For instance, there may be intervening effects between actors by other (groups of) actors or there may be different (or similar) actors that depend on each other within a production process. These interrelations must be considered in order to achieve and maintain successful networks.

- **Balanced Centricity:** The many-to-many concept does not exclusively address customer satisfaction, but stakeholder satisfaction. Gummesson (2008) questions whether the efforts of a firm should always concentrate on customer satisfaction. Since collaboration with different stakeholders often has a great influence on the success of a firm, he suggests that the interests of all parties should rather be balanced. Consequently, Gummesson (2008, p. 17) also calls for a refocusing of marketing and management: "[...] I am convinced that if we keep fragmenting marketing and other business functions and duck complexity, context and dynamics, we will not move ahead. A change requires that we reconsider marketing basics and abandon mainstream methodological rigidity and move toward a more pragmatic and holistic research agenda."

# 3. ANYTHING RELATIONSHIP MANAGEMENT

## 3.1. Relationship Types and (x)RM

To make this holistic view on organizational relationships become reality and to support collaboration among all stakeholders, both, new types of management concepts and software tools are needed. In sum, with the growing complexity of inter-firm relationships, interoperability barriers are rising. Among those barriers identified in the INTEROP framework (conceptual, technological, and organizational barriers) (Chen, Doumeingts, & Vernadat, 2008), especially the dimensions of technological and organizational barriers must be considered simultaneously when pursuing an integrated solution approach.

Table 1 encapsulates the close collection between the management layer and technical layer throughout the historical development of relationship types, showing that emerging IT solutions act as enablers as well as drivers of management. The table also illustrates the broad view of new platform based xRM solutions versus the limited view of traditional system-based solutions: in contrast to the rather passive support of relationship management in CRM, xRM focuses on actively designing and transforming

*Table 1. Relationship types and (x)RM (based on Mirovsky, 2013)*

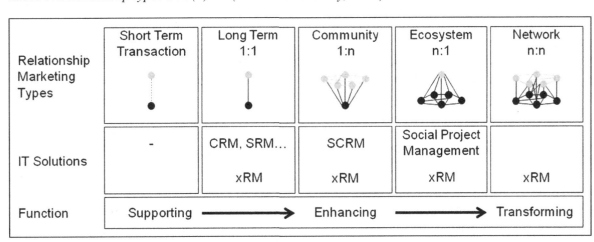

| Relationship Marketing Types | Short Term Transaction | Long Term 1:1 | Community 1:n | Ecosystem n:1 | Network n:n |
|---|---|---|---|---|---|
| IT Solutions | - | CRM, SRM… xRM | SCRM xRM | Social Project Management xRM | xRM |
| Function | Supporting ➔ Enhancing ➔ Transforming | | | | |

relationship structures. xRM allows to maintain a functioning, interoperable supply chain throughout the combined evolution of companies in networks, where multiple firms collaborate, share knowledge, and stakeholder compositions constantly change (Blanc, 2005).

Using a simple sample calculation, we want to demonstrate the extend of interoperability challenges arising from evolving networks and changing n:n relationships. Mathematically, the triangular number $n(n - 1)/2$ expresses the number of connections that can be formed between n network nodes. For a network with 5 participants, there are 10 unique exchange connections between them and, thus, 10 possible interoperability problems (given that all participants use different IT systems). For a network with 50 participants, this results in 1225 possible interoperability issues, and for a network with 500 participants, 124.750 interoperability issues could arise. Every time one participant is added to a network of n participants, the possible connections and interoperability problems grow by n. Now, since the increase in number of network nodes between a 1:n or n:1 network and an n:n network is typically larger than 1, there is a significant jump in possible interoperability issues. For example, if until now you have managed an n:1 ecosystem with 10 suppliers, you have 55 possible interoperability problems to handle. If in a next step you want to add 10 customers and form a co-creation network, you will end up facing 210 possible interoperability problems. Although we are aware that this calculation is a very simplified form of the actual problem, we think that these numbers can act as a first indicator for the urgency of platform implementations when managing n:n relationships in collaboration networks.

## 3.2. User-Side Drivers of xRM

Apart from the necessity of platform concepts for technological and organizational interoperability, these concepts correspond with a range of trends which can be observed in the enterprise IT sector. From a user perspective, the trends covered by xRM include:

- Due to the high popularity of social networks in the private environment, benefits like direct messaging, status updates in real-time, or simple sharing of content have been presented to a broad audience. As an effect, users increasingly expect business software to support similar functionalities. This "consumerization of [business] IT" (Gartner, 2011) is reflected in the aim of xRM to facilitate an uncomplicated maintenance of all organizational relationship strings.

- "Consumerization" is linked closely with a rising attention towards usability and user experience of software products: business software is more and more requested to offer intuitive user interfaces and also to satisfy hedonistic demands ("joy of use"). In contrast to separate software systems, xRM platforms provide users with a consistent and therefore easy to learn interface design across different relationship-based applications (Greenbaum, 2011).

- The growing availability of Internet-capable mobile devices has raised the demand for external hosted Software-as-a-Service solutions (SaaS). For organizations, these services are very interesting because they provide information regardless of location and – at the same time – promise high flexibility at low initial investment costs. xRM as a platform concept is predestinated for such a model since it allows to combine multiple apps for relationships with various stakeholders to an enterprise specific relationship management bundle.

- With regards to market requirements one can observe a strong dynamic progress. Globalization and disruptive technologies have the consequence that organizations need to react to environmental changes immediately. If business models are changed, new relationship constellations emerge that must be mapped. By standardizing relationship functions in the core platform, new xRM apps which build on the platform can be developed fast and cost efficiently.

## 3.3. xRM Definition

Since its first mentioning more than a decade ago (Radjou, Orlov, & Child, 2001), the term xRM is defined in different ways depending on the background of the particular writers. Business administration researchers focus rather on the managerial side of xRM. They describe xRM as "CRM beyond the customers," referring to the possibility not only to apply it in marketing, but for managing all kinds of business relationships, e.g. those with suppliers or partner organizations. Thereby, "[t]he XRM approach allows a holistic communication strategy [… that] includes the explicit consideration of processes, players and positioning" (Schubert, 2005, p. 155). Software manufacturers and computer scientists on the other hand put the technical aspects of xRM in the spotlight of their definitions. xRM is seen as an IT platform with customized apps which "are needed to define inter-enterprise relationships [... and] can be used to configure a whole supply chain or virtual enterprise" (Zwegers, Wubben, & Hartel, 2002, p. 157).

A common ground of most definitions, however, is that xRM build on the logic of CRM: establishing and maintaining good relationships with business partners is regarded as profitable strategy in the long run. Well-managed business relationships, building the basis of successful collaboration and knowledge exchange, are considered as a central factor of value creation. As such, xRM is positioned as the central software solution for managing the relationships both within a firm and with its surrounding network. We build upon these previous definition approaches and define xRM as:

*xRM is the concept of managing n:n relationships in collaboration networks by connecting all related parties through a common IT platform. The typical xRM platform/app architecture and its deployment in the cloud allow a scalable integration of systems, stakeholders, things, and services, while at the same time guaranteeing interoperability and seamless processes between all companies of the network.*

Looking at the software market, most of the leading CRM producers have realized that specialized relationship management solutions for different industries offer new business chances. Subsequently, there is a shift from CRM systems to xRM platforms: Microsoft's Dynamics CRM is sold as an xRM framework which can easily be customized according to customer's needs. Salesforce.com offers a cloud hosted platform named Force.com that includes a market place where various apps can be purchased and combined to custom solutions (Salesforce, 2011). For the OEM market, SugarCRM has introduced Sugar Platform Edition in order to facilitate the development of xRM products. Based on the CAS Open xRM platform, CAS Software AG sells branch-specific solutions for relationship management. Furthermore, a number of smaller software producers and consultancies offer specialized xRM solutions based on various platforms. The state of art of current solutions regarding interoperability issues is outlined in the next chapter (for an overview of xRM use cases see e.g. Britsch, Schacht, & Mädche, 2012).

## 3.4. Interoperability Requirements

From a technical standpoint, the above described concept requires that enterprise systems and applications need to be interoperable in order to achieve seamless business interaction across organizational boundaries and realize networked organizations. IEEE (IEEE, 1990) defines interoperability as "the ability of two or more systems or components to exchange information and to use the information that has been exchanged." Adopting the classification of interoperability areas as indicated by the EN-SEMBLE project, the xRM concept concentrates on problems positioned in the field of stakeholder collaboration and social network interoperability, in the field of service and object interoperability, as well as in the field of data and software interoperability (Popplewell et al., 2012).

Heterogeneous applications adopted for the operation of enterprise, either at business or at manufacturing levels, need to share information to cooperate: this can be critical to the whole enterprise performance. With xRM, apps have to handle a multitude of relationships as different logical steps of the same transaction. They must allow users to assume different roles across communities and, hence, support cross-firm collaborations (Radjou, Orlov, & Child, 2001). Adding external services (Yamamoto et. al., 2011) and physical objects into relationship patterns, xRM platforms need to contain comprehensive on-demand integration services and to provide data to all different layers of business networks (e.g. operational units, IT networks).

In order to understand the related state of the art, we have analyzed the leading xRM platforms. Table 2 summarizes the results in the three categories social network, service and data interoperability.

In the following chapter, we show how the described interoperability fields (social networks, services, data) are tackled within the proposed xRM architecture.

## 4. USE CASE GLONET: XRM AND INTEROPERABILITY

### 4.1. Project Overview

GloNet is an EU research project co-funded by the European Commission under the ICT scheme within the EU's Seventh Framework Programme. Partners of the project are, among others, UNI-NOVA – Instituto de Desenvolvimento de Novas Tecnologias (Portugal), UvA – Universiteit van Amsterdam (Netherlands), and CAS Software AG (Germany).

*Table 2. State of the art: xRM platforms*

|  | Social Network Interoperability | Service Interoperability | Data and Software Interoperability |
|---|---|---|---|
| Microsoft | Not built-in, but can provide public services using Microsoft SharePoint. | Not built-in, but.NET open technologies can be used to provide integration between both Microsoft and non-Microsoft applications. | Contact records synchronization from social applications. |
| Salesforce.com | Salesforce Chatter allows the sharing of information files and having discussions in groups. However, user management is limited to a single domain, whereby the first user creating the collaboration community is assigned as the moderator. Furthermore, the platform provides limited permission security to shared data, granting all users in the group access. | Partly supported offering a mash-up service (SOAP, REST, Bulk, Metadata API). | Uses SKYVVA integration suite offering a data loader functionality to upload data. States of the records are not maintained. |
| SugarCRM | Provides collaboration of e-mail, schedules, calls, meetings and tasks. | Partly supported, using a cloud connector/external API that allows the integration of data from external Web services. | Uses a GUID algorithm that avoids primary key collisions across databases. |

The GloNet project aims at designing, developing, and deploying an agile virtual enterprise environment for networks of SMEs involved in highly customized and service-enhanced products through end-to-end collaboration with customers and local suppliers (co-creation). GloNet intends to implement the "glocal" (global and local) enterprise notion with value creation from global networked operations and involving global supply chain management, product-service linkage, and management of distributed manufacturing units.

There is a growing trend in manufacturing to move towards highly customized products, ultimately one-of-a-kind, which is reflected in the term "mass customization." At the same time, customers demands the timely delivery of associated services to the purchased product. GloNet refers to a customer co-design process of products and services which meet the needs and choices of each individual customer. When focusing on co-operation and customizable complex products, European SMEs might have the chance to gain a competitive advantage over regions that are more competitive in mass production of standardized products.

To achieve this goal, GloNet intends to support the operation of virtual organisations where companies are essentially part of value chains composed of a series of distinct value creation activities, including production, installation, maintenance, monitoring and other activities. The project's objective of creating an agile virtual enterprise environment for SMEs thereby follows a holistic approach which is based on three interacting pillars:

1. Organizational structures,
2. Technological platform, and
3. Governance models.

The overall idea and structure of a glocal, collaborative value-chain, interlinking networks of manufacturers and networks of customers and, thus, enabling collaborative innovation, is shown in Figure 1 (for further information see Bauer, 2012).

As illustrated, GloNet adopts a cloud-based approach, implementing a platform for the deployment of xRM services. The platform offers two virtual spaces:

- **Collaborative Solution Space:** Where manufacturers, local suppliers and customers meet to co-design the product (and associated services).
- **Service Provision Space:** A "registry" of the products, along their life-cycle, where the customer can have access to the specific services associated to the customized product.

In the following sections we will give an overview of the IT architecture of GloNet and describe how we have approached interoperability issues.

## 4.2. xRM Platform Concepts

Isolated enterprise software is not any more appropriate for SMEs acting in the global economy. Future tools and systems like those planned in GloNet have to support the SMEs in a flexible manner, ensuring interoperability between the particular systems of the stakeholders involved. GloNet is based on server-side OSGi-technology which enables building of highly modularized applications that consisting of multiple bundles each encapsulating a specific business case.

Figure 2 provides a more detailed view on the software architecture of the GloNet platform. Essentially each layer is implemented using a number of modules. The GloNet platform uses an OSGi run-time to provide an infrastructure for defining, deploying and running independent software modules. Working with that OSGi run-time is structured and simplified using the well-proven Spring framework, which manages the different application modules and their dependencies.

*Figure 1. GloNet glocal production network*

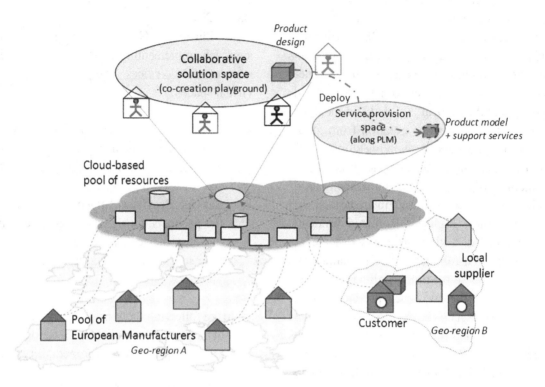

*Figure 2. GloNet system overview*

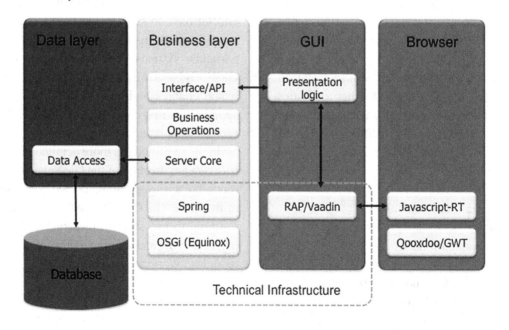

GloNet offers a framework for building Web- and service-enabled cloud solutions. Such solutions typically consist of features to represent and handle data in a flexible way, perform business process related logic with the help of that data and interact with the users through some user interface. The GloNet platform simplifies the creation of new applications and solutions, offering reusable core components, supporting the customization of existing components and providing mechanisms to extend the functionality of the framework by adding new components to it.

Interoperability of enterprises is a strategic issue in the context of networked organizations. Therefore, the GloNet platform provides mechanisms for the efficient collaboration between different tenants (social interoperability), the integration of externally deployed services (service interoperability) and the automatic synchronization of data with external systems (data interoperability). Thus, the platform allows for the harmonized execution of collaborative processes within the virtual organization, involving people and systems. The following sections give an overview.

### 4.2.1. xRM Collaboration Spaces

Multi-tenancy is the capability of a software system to serve multiple customers or tenants (which in turn comprise multiple users) from a single consolidated software system.

In essence, cloud solutions have to address two potentially conflicting requirements: On one hand they need to leverage the economy of scale principle by employing a consolidated architecture that handles all customers uniformly, on the other hand customers demand that the software they use can be tailored to meet their specific requirements and match with their highly-individual business and the processes they work with. This implies that both data and customizations have to be isolated on a tenant-based level.

GloNet employs a *one schema per tenant approach:* each of the tenants is mapped into separate logical unit, called *schema*, within a single physical database (Figure 3).

In a SaaS system, a customer (a company or an organization) is typically associated with one tenant. This approach has the advantage of clearly separating data from different customers. In collaborative scenarios, sharing information between different organizations is a key concept. The GloNet platform therefore introduces a mechanism called collaboration spaces for that. A collaboration space is a shared space in the database that is accessible by an arbitrary number of tenants at the same time. All collaboration spaces are placed in some dedicated tenant, as illustrated in Figure 4.

To share information (e.g. data object or documents) between tenants and collaboration spaces, replicas of the object are created in each tenant and in each collaboration space. The platform implementation maintains links between all replicas of the object. The platform can be configured to automatically propagate changes between the replicas; alternatively changes can be propagated in an on-demand mode.

*Figure 3. Tenant specific database schemas*

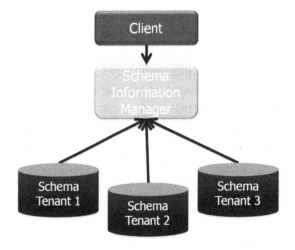

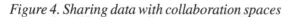

*Figure 4. Sharing data with collaboration spaces*

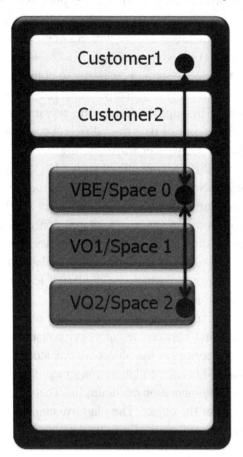

## 4.2.2. Integration of Externally Deployed Services

Externally deployed services are independently developed and share no infrastructure with the GloNet platform. Service interoperability requires more than just calling a service; it requires integration into the surrounding application or platform logic. Since external services can have arbitrary interfaces (syntax, protocol, semantics, user interfaces), it is necessary to map GloNet platform concepts onto those of the external services. In order to integrate an external service, the GloNet platform provides two different mechanisms:

- A proxy-based approach (Figure 5) where each external service has a proxy within the

GloNet platform that performs the mapping between the GloNet platform and the external service. Since in most cases these plugins will need to provide glue code to implement both data and protocol mediation, the codebase of the GloNet platform must be extended. Thus, this approach is a rather heavyweight integration. However, a seamless integration into GloNet platform-based applications is possible, since the proxy runs within the same context as the GloNet platform core. It is even possible to add new user interface components that can be used to control and manage the external service (e.g. service specific data input forms).

- A mashup-based approach (Figure 6) where an external service is aware of the GloNet platform, e.g. the external service uses the external Webservice interfaces (REST, SOAP) of the GloNet platform to push/pull data to/from the platform. Data and protocol mediation is performed in the external service. The GloNet platform provides a thin integration interface that exposes some basic state of the current application using RESTful services. User interface composition is done within the end user's browser by rendering the external service's user interface into dedicated frames within the applications. Since no additions to the GloNet platform's code base (e.g. proxy implementations) are required, this is a rather lightweight integration.

Scenarios that involve service integration do often require end-users to authenticate against multiple service providers, obliging the user to remember and enter different credentials for each provider. This fact does not only have a significantly negative impact on the usability. Since no identity information is shared among the involved services, it is impossible for the service providers to make collaborative access decisions based on

*Figure 5. Proxy-based external service integration*

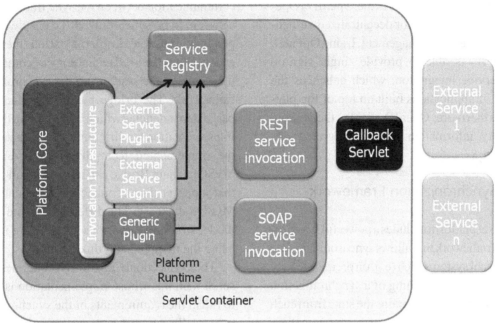

*Figure 6. Mashup-based external service integration*

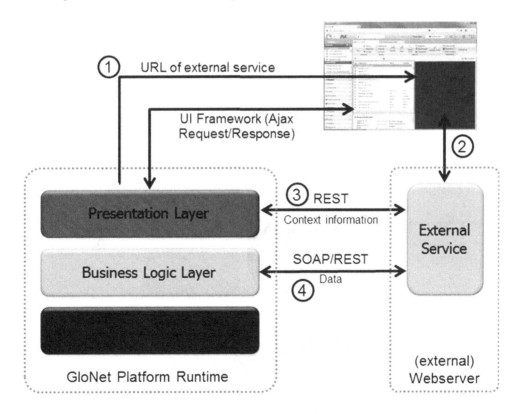

the user's identity. To circumvent these problems, the GloNet platform supports the OpenID (OpenID Foundation, 2012) for decentralized authentication and identity management. Using OpenID, the platform is able to provide single sign-on (SSO) service integration, which enhances the usability of applications built on top of the platform. Furthermore, OpenID enables the sharing of identity information among integrated services.

### 4.2.3. Synchronization Framework

The GloNet platform includes a powerful synchronization framework that allows synchronizing data with external systems such (e.g. on premise legacy software). At the beginning of a synchronization session the framework obtains the state from each of the synchronized systems and compares them with the known state of the last session. The synchronization architecture is depicted in Figure 7.

The *ConnectionBridge* module controls the communication between the sync framework and a system to be synchronized. To ensure an independent, reusable implementation the bridge encapsulates the used technology of communication between the system and the synchronization framework. The bridge has no domain model-based dependencies which allows using the same implementation for different systems that support the implemented technology. For example, a MySQL Client Bridge can be used for all systems that support a direct connection to the underlying MySQL database. The differences in the domain model structure of various systems are resolved using the mapping and link definitions.

The ConnectionBridge interface defines a small set of methods whose implementation is needed to fulfill the requirements of the synchronization process. To support new systems, this interface needs to be implemented but the synchronization process itself need not be changed. This keeps the cost of supporting multiple external Systems low.

*Figure 7. Bird's eye view on the GloNet synchronization framework*

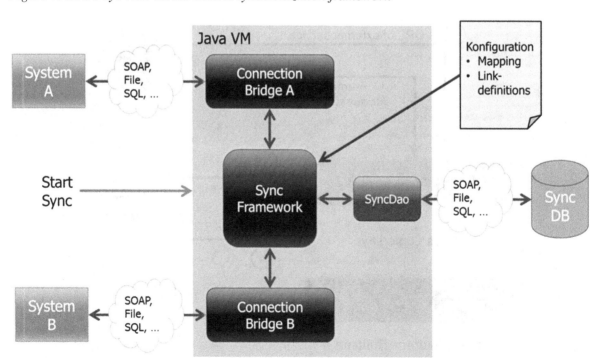

The *Sync Framework* itself manages the workflow of the entire synchronization session and manages the communication to the Connection-Bridges. It contains the logic of the synchronization, which includes the ability to determine the states of the records to synchronize, the creation of the operations based on the record pair state and the strategy.

## 5. CONCLUSION

### 5.1. Summary

This chapter is divided into three main parts. In the first section, relationship types were described. We explained the advantages of many-to-many relationships, being able to better deal with complexity, to offer context to analytics, and to support balanced centricity when managing relationships. Ultimately, this led to the conclusion that new concepts which go beyond CRM are needed for those many-to-many relations (e.g. between communities of suppliers and customers). In the second section of the paper, we then introduced xRM as such a concept. We presented drivers of the xRM trend, proposed an xRM definition, and listed first xRM solutions. In the third section, we continued the list of xRM use cases by giving an in-depth analysis of the GloNet project which deploys xRM for creating an agile virtual enterprise environment for networks of SMEs. In our technical description of the GloNet xRM platform, we especially highlighted the ability of the platform to provide system interoperability between stakeholders. We reasoned: using xRM as a common IT platform, applied in combination with its managerial tasks, gives SMEs the opportunity to build successful global value chains, fostering inter-organizational collaboration and co-innovation.

### 5.2. Example of Application

One example of such a collaborative value chain among SMEs is the use case "iPlon Parters" within the GloNet project. iPlon Partners, a SME network consisting of ca. 20 partners, is specialized on the construction of solar parks, provision of control technologies, and the operation and maintenance of solar park units. Naturally, a variety of stakeholders are involved in solar energy projects: management, service companies, contractors, project developers, lenders, investors, insurance companies, etc. Until now, collaboration between these partners was limited to coordination via telephone, fax, and e-mail. With the GloNet xRM approach, collaboration was unified into one common cloud platform leading to positive effects on the process performance: both quality and speed of customer projects were improved, new services could be created and bundled to modules, co-offered to customers, and invoiced according to the time invested by each partner involved (Tamburaj, Camarinha-Matos, & Maltesen, 2013; Surajbali et al., 2013).

### 5.3. Future Research

Since xRM still is a widely unexplored scientific subject, future research must be conducted in several directions. Firstly, hand-on experience with xRM – like the GloNet project – has to be collected and thoroughly analyzed. The three interoperability approaches introduced (collaboration spaces, service integration, synchronization framework) are designed to be reusable in different industry contexts and are currently tested within the use case "iPlon Partners." As a next step, a further practical application in the context of building automation is planned. Parallel to this, from a theoretical perspective, the different management approaches of stakeholder relationships have to be systemized. One of the key questions here is called: What does xRM mean for organization structures? Also, regarding the technological side of xRM, procedure models for a stepwise introduction of xRM platforms have to be developed. Looking at xRM again from a managerial point of view, the problem of how to integrate relationship quality of different stakeholder networks into an overall objective function is still largely unsolved. Combining all research stings, finally a "grand model" and general framework for xRM must be elaborated.

## ACKNOWLEDGMENT

The authors would like to thank the European Commission for the financial support of the R&D project GloNet (7. Framework Programme, grant 285273), the organizators of the FInES cluster, and the GloNet consortium members for the fruitful collaboration.

## REFERENCES

Allen, S., Deragon, J. T., Orem, M. G., & Smith, C. F. (2008). *The emerge of the relationship economy*. Cupertino, CA: HappyAbout.

Bauer, M. (Ed.). (2012). *D3.1 glonet platform design specification*. Retrieved February 25, 2013, from https://sites.google.com/site/glonetproject/8-download/GloNet-D3.1.pdf?attredirects=0&d=1

Berry, L. L. (1983). Relationship marketing. In L. L. Berry, G. L. Shostack, & G. Upah (Eds.), *Emerging perspectives on services marketing* (pp. 25–28). Chicago, IL: American Marketing Association.

Blanc, S. (2005). Interoperability problems: Management of evolution of collaborative enterprises. In *Proceedings of Interoperability for Enterprise Software and Applications Conference, I-ESA* (Vol. 5). I-ESA.

Britsch, J., & Kölmel, B. (2012). Anything relationship management as basis for global process management in networked enterprises. In M. Zelm, R. Sanchis, R. Poler, & G. Doumeingts (Eds.), *Enterprise interoperability I-ESA'12 proceedings* (pp. 227–234). London, UK: Wiley. doi:10.1002/9781118561942.ch33

Britsch, J., Schacht, S., & Mädche, A. (2012). Anything relationship management. *Business & Information Systems Engineering, 4*(2), 85–87. doi:10.1007/s12599-012-0208-6

Brodie, R. J., Coviello, N. E., & Winklhofer, H. (2008). Contemporary marketing practices research program: A review of the first decade. *Journal of Business and Industrial Marketing, 23*(2), 84–94. doi:10.1108/08858620810850191

Bughin, J., Doogan, J., & Vetvik, O. J. (2010). *A new way to measure word-of-mouth marketing*. New York, NY: McKinsey Quarterly.

Campelo, E., & Stucky, W. (2007). The supplier relationship management market trends. *Proceedings of the World Academy of Science, Engineering and Technology, 22*, 105-110.

Chen, D., Doumeingts, G., & Vernadat, F. (2008). Architectures for enterprise integration and interoperability: Past, present and future. *Computers in Industry, 59*(7), 647–659. doi:10.1016/j.compind.2007.12.016

Coviello, N. E., Brodie, E., Roderick, J., & Munro, H. J. (1997). Understanding contemporary marketing: Development of a classification scheme. *Journal of Marketing Management, 13*(6), 501–522. doi:10.1080/0267257X.1997.9964490

Cutting-Decelle, A.-F., Barraud, J. L., Veenendaal, B., & Young, R. I. M. (2012). Production information interoperability over the internet: A standardised data acquisition tool developed for industrial enterprises. *Computers in Industry, 63*(8), 824–834. doi:10.1016/j.compind.2012.08.010

Ehrlinger, E. (1979). Kundengruppenmangement. *Die Betriebswirtschaft, 39*(2), 261–273.

Gartner Inc. (2011). *Gartner says consumerization of BI drives greater adoption.* Stamford, CT: Gartner. Retrieved February 22, 2013, from http://www.gartner.com/it/page.jsp?id=1748214

Greenbaum, J. (2011, June). *Is CRM + xRM the new ERP?* Paper presented at the Decisions Spring Virtual Conference. New York, NY.

Gummesson, E. (2004). From one-to-one to many-to-many marketing. In B. Edvardsson et al. (Eds.), *Proceedings from QUIS 9 Symposium* (pp. 16-25). Karlstad, Sweden: Karlstad University. Retrieved February 20, 2013, from http://ipam5ever.com.sapo.pt/profile/QUISeg2004.pdf

Gummesson, E. (2008). Extending the service-dominant logic: From customer centricity to balanced centricity. *Journal of the Academy of Marketing Science, 36*(1), 15–17. doi:10.1007/s11747-007-0065-x

Hoffman, D. L., & Novak, T. P. (1996). Marketing in hypermedia computer-mediated environments: Conceptual foundations. *Journal of Marketing, 60*(3), 50–68. doi:10.2307/1251841

IEEE. (1990). *IEEE standard computer dictionary: A compilation of IEEE standard computer glossaries.* New York, NY: Institute of Electrical and Electronics Engineers.

McCarthy, J. E. (1960). *Basic marketing – A managerial approach.* Homewood, IL: Richard D. Irwin.

Microsoft. (2012). Defining a many-to-many relationship. *Microsoft SQL Server.* Retrieved February 20, 2013, from http://technet.microsoft.com/en-us/library/ms170463.aspx

Mirovsky, D. (2013). *Relationship marketing of startups – An empirical analysis of commercial and social startups' management of stakeholder relationships.* (Unpublished master thesis). University of Mannheim, Mannheim, Germany.

Moore, J. F. (1996). *The death of competition: Leadership & strategy in the age of business ecosystems.* New York, NY: HarperBusiness.

Open, I. D. Foundation. (2012). *The OpenID foundation.* Retrieved February 24, 2013, from http://openid.net/foundation

Radjou, N., Orlov, L. M., & Child, M. (2001). *The Forrester report – Apps for dynamic collaboration.* Cambridge, MA: Forrester Research.

Salesforce Inc. (2011). *Salesforce appexchange.* Retrieved February 23, 2013, from http://appexchange.salesforce.com/browse?type=Apps

Schacht, S., Botzenhardt, A., & Maedche, A. (2012). AskEris – A many-to-one communication platform for higher education. In Proceedings of System Science (HICSS), 2012 45th Hawaii International Confherence, (pp. 21-30). IEEE.

Schubert, V. A. (2005). *XRM: Integrated customer relationship management for pharmaceutical innovation.* (Doctoral Dissertation). University of Berlin, Berlin, Germany.

Sheth, J. N., & Parvatiyar, A. (1995). The evolution of relationship marketing. *International Business Review, 4*(4), 397–418. doi:10.1016/0969-5931(95)00018-6

Shuman, J., & Twombly, J. (2010). Collaborative networks are the organization: An innovation in organization design and management. *Vikalpa, 35*(1), 1–14.

Surajbali, B., Bauer, M., Bär, H., & Alexakis, S. (2013). A cloud–based approach for collaborative networks supporting serviced-enhanced products. In *Proceedings of PRO-VE 2013 Conference 2013.* PRO-VE.

Tamburaj, V., Camarinha-Matos, L. M., & Maltesen, T. (2013). *D6.1 detailed specification of the pilot demonstrator.* Retrieved June 24, 2013, from https://sites.google.com/site/glonetproject/8-download

Yamamoto, H., Sameshima, S., Sekiguchi, T., Kato, H., Yura, J., & Takashio, K. (2011). Interoperability of middleware for context-aware services. *Electronics and Communications in Japan, 94*(2), 67–74. doi:10.1002/ecj.10260

Zwegers, A., Wubben, H., & Hartel, I. (2002). Relationship management in enterprise networks. In V. Marik, H. Afsarmanesh, & L. M. Camarinha-Matos (Eds.), *Knowledge and technology integration in production and services* (pp. 157–164). Norwell, MA: Kluwer Academic Publishers. doi:10.1007/978-0-387-35613-6_17

## KEY TERMS AND DEFINITIONS

**Anything Relationship Management (xRM):** The concept of managing n:n relationships in collaboration networks by connecting all related parties through a common IT platform.

**n:n Relationship:** A relationship of groups of entities in networks, e.g. a consumer network interacting with a supplier network.

**Stakeholder:** An individual, group or organization that is affected by the actions of an enterprise.

**Production Network:** A temporary, target-driven affiliation of multiple enterprises in order to jointly create a product.

## ENDNOTES

[1]   GloNet - Glocal enterprise network focusing on customer-centric collaboration. R&D project within the FInES cluster, see https://sites.google.com/site/glonetproject/.

# Chapter 7
# Collaboration and Interoperability within a Virtual Enterprise Applied in a Mobile Maintenance Scenario

**Tobias Münch**
*SAP AG, Germany*

**Jan Hladik**
*SAP AG, Germany*

**Angelika Salmen**
*SAP AG, Germany*

**Werner Altmann**
*Kölsch and Altmann Software and Management Consulting GmbH, Germany*

**Robert Buchmann**
*University of Vienna, Austria*

**Dimitris Karagiannis**
*University of Vienna, Austria*

**Jens Ziegler**
*TU Dresden, Germany*

**Johannes Pfeffer**
*TU Dresden, Germany*

**Leon Urbas**
*TU Dresden, Germany*

**Oscar Lazaro**
*Innovalia Association, Spain*

**Patricia Ortiz**
*Innovalia Association, Spain*

**Oscar Lopez**
*Nextel S. A., Spain*

**Etxahun Sanchez**
*Nextel S. A., Spain*

**Frank Haferkorn**
*RST Industrie Automation GmbH, Germany*

## ABSTRACT

*This chapter presents an infrastructure approach for virtual enterprises developed by the consortium of the European research project ComVantage and discusses its impact with respect to the mobile maintenance domain. The approach focuses on the core aspects of interoperability, which are data interoperability and process interoperability. Regarding the interorganisational access to enterprise data, the authors propose a semantic abstraction layer that is completely decentralised and therefore meets the key requirement of virtuality. The execution of business processes and workflows across organisational boundaries are addressed by the unique App Orchestration Concept.*

DOI: 10.4018/978-1-4666-5142-5.ch007

# INTRODUCTION

In order to master the competition in a global market, companies do not only have to operate more efficiently but need to be much better cross-linked among each other. Moreover, agility in terms of networking and process execution is important (Kim, et al. 2006). The execution of business processes across organisational boundaries as well as cross-linking data sets of collaboration partners are key success factors and initiate the transformation of isolated individual companies towards an integrated, agile virtual enterprise.

By definition of Barnett, et al. (1994), a virtual enterprise is based on a temporary alliance of several businesses. It takes advantage of a market opportunity and dissolves, when it has passed. A virtual enterprise does not have own major resources but it consists of the resources and core competencies of its individual partners.

The European research project *ComVantage*, which is funded by the European Commission within the Framework Programme No. 7, has the goal to develop an architecture as well as a working prototype of a distributed infrastructure for virtual enterprises. In this chapter, the architecture and the functionality of core components is explained. Moreover, technical and organisational improvements as well as scientific and social impacts are discussed with respect to a specific application area – the domain of mobile maintenance.

# CHALLENGES FOR A VIRTUAL ENTERPRISE IN A MOBILE MAINTENANCE SCENARIO

In the following section a representative use case is outlined including a description of pain points, an explanation of an application scenario, a list of aggregated high-level requirements connected with this scenario and finally a description of improvements provided by the application of our prototype.

Mobile Maintenance is a term used for performing maintenance of embedded systems (machines) remotely by using Internet technologies. Today, mobile maintenance is characterised by a couple of pain points. First, a very heterogeneous environment of different machine types and interfaces causes high training costs for service staffs. Second, the current on-site processes related to mobile maintenance are very ineffective. The main cause is an error-prone communication between the client and the maintenance service provider which is currently not well supported by a proper tooling. This often results in improper and imprecise error descriptions and leads later to a wrong pre-selection of spare parts. Regarding the high resource investment in terms of time and money of travelling engineers with high specialisation, unnecessary maintenance operations should be avoided.

As response to the listed pain points and under consideration of the capabilities of a collaboration platform for virtual enterprises using active machines, a comprehensive requirements and scenario analysis has been conducted within *ComVantage*. Figure 1 visualizes a scenario that describes the application of our prototype in the mobile maintenance domain. The scenario involves three different stakeholders: the manufacturer that produces the machine, the customer that purchases and runs the machine and finally a maintenance service provider.

A central aspect of the scenario is the use of active machines that are equipped with sensors and actuators to permanently monitor their operational status. Thus, active machines are able to identify problems (e.g. sensor values out of thresholds) and send a notification to the service company in order to initiate a maintenance request automatically. In a service landscape that is characterised by heterogeneous machine types, a maintenance coordinator is required to assign appropriate resources (e.g. technicians with relevant skills) to individual maintenance requests. The maintenance coordinator is able to decide on

*Figure 1. Interorganisational collaboration within a virtual enterprise in a mobile maintenance scenario*

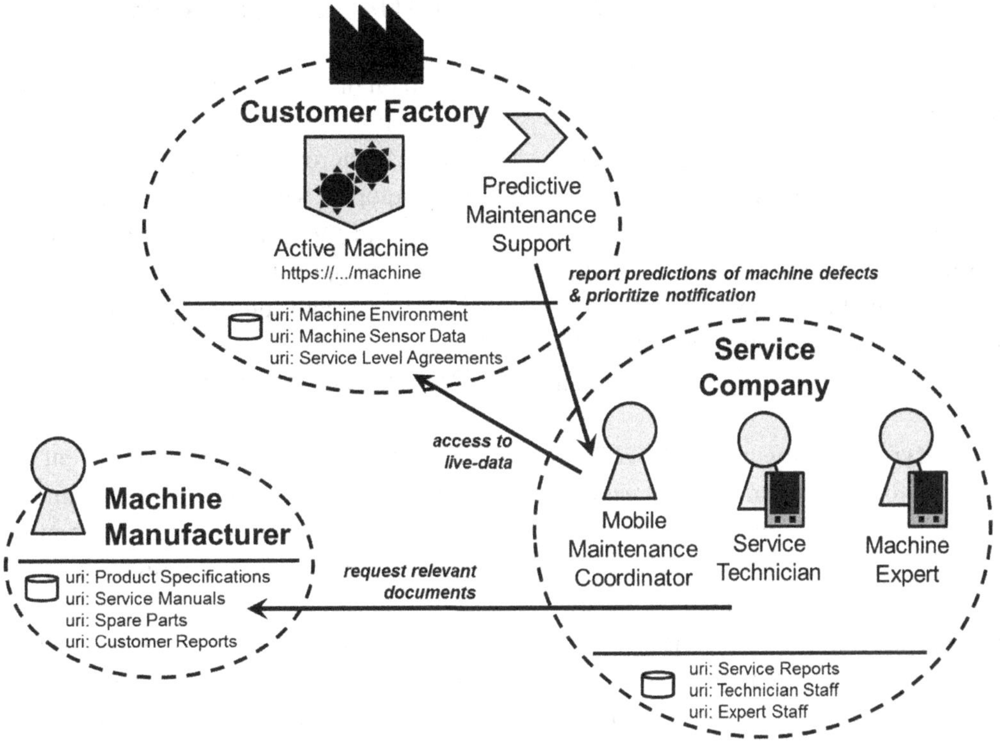

the basis of the identified machine and available historian data of similar machines, if the warning is serious and which concrete actions need to be taken. In case of a serious issue that needs immediate reaction, the maintenance coordinator is able to select a service technician with appropriate skills and expertise regarding the identified problem. The service technician is able to further analyse the problem without being on-site by using the capabilities of the collaboration infrastructure. First, he is able to use data of his own company. These are mainly former service reports with information about symptoms and possible solutions. Moreover he is able to identify experts for specific machine types within his company in case he needs further support. Due to the capabilities of the collaboration infrastructure, he is also able to access data of partners. Regarding the maintenance operation, service specifications,

user manuals and recommendations for spare parts provided by the manufacturer are of additional value. Finally, live access to the machine at the customers place can reveal further helpful information about the current state of the machine. On the basis of the analysis results, the service technician is able to do a pre-selection of necessary spare parts and a precise planning of the on-site maintenance operation. Finally, the service technician is able to solve the problem on-site on the basis of his pre-analysis and the selected spare parts. Due to the very accurate analysis and machine diagnosis enabled by the *ComVantage* platform, the maintenance operation will be successful and no additional travel of the service technician is needed. Thus, the whole maintenance operation is very straightforward and efficient in terms of costs and time investment. As result of a requirements analysis and generalisation among all the *ComVantage* use cases and scenarios, the following 6 high-level requirements need to be addressed:

- **Virtuality:** Use of distributed data sources and processes among the collaboration partners and avoiding central management components.
- **Mobility:** Compatibility with affordable, commercial mobile devices.
- **Usability:** Offering intuitive user interfaces and handy tool support for on-site workers.
- **Flexibility:** Flexibility in terms of collaboration platform configuration and easy adaptation of generic components to specific application scenarios.
- **Collaboration:** Processing of workflows among organisational boundaries.
- **Security:** Securing local datasets of unauthorised access of external stakeholders.

These requirements will be addressed in the architecture description in the sections below including an explanation of their individual influence on the design of generic components.

The application of our prototype in the mobile maintenance scenario results in a couple of improvements. First, the utilisation of mobile devices results in a better integration of workflows into the native working environment of a service technician. Second, the identification and localisation of errors gets easier by enabling live access to sensor data and running diagnostic software directly on the machine. Third, the machines become active parts in the future scenarios by automatically reporting potential failures on the basis of conspicuous sensor data. This may avoid complete breakdowns of machines which creates higher costs and a loss of production. Moreover, the holistic approach of semantic technologies allows abstract access to heterogeneous data sources and different machine types which leads to a dramatic reduction of complexity of the scenario for the user.

## ARCHITECTURE OF A VIRTUAL ENTERPRISE

Based on the consolidated requirements (refer to the section above) an architecture for data- and process interoperability in virtual enterprises is developed within the *ComVantage* research project. In this section, the architecture and its central components is explained regarding the design-time and run-time perspective.

### Design-Time Aspects

Following the definition of virtual enterprises as temporary alliance of single companies (refer to the introduction section) four different processes are of main relevance at design-time.

- Initial set up of a virtual enterprise
- Integration of new partners
- Integration of new data sources of a partner
- Development of new use case specific client applications

Following our architecture, the very basic component to set up a virtual enterprise consists in a definition of tasks and roles according to the actual application scenario. This *Task & Role Model* is used to define access rights on data sources as well as defining responsibilities in collaborative workflows among organisational boundaries.

As a next step, individual partners using specific workflows and local data sources need to be integrated into the collaboration network. In order to address the key requirement of "flexibility," we need to provide a uniform interface for applications to access these data sources. Technically this can be achieved by using an abstraction layer performing a data harmonisation among all connected data sources. Within the *ComVantage* project, a semantic approach based on ontologies, RDF and Linked Data (Bizer, Heath, & Berners-Lee, 2009) is used for data harmonisation. A first step towards realising such a semantic approach is the development of an ontology which describes all relevant entities and relations in the domain of the application partner. Within *ComVantage*, we call this ontology the *Domain Data Model*. Since the development of such ontologies is often a huge effort when you have to do everything from scratch, the *ComVantage* consortium envisions an alternative approach. Within the collaboration network of a virtual enterprise a common foundation of used entities already exists. Regarding our selected use case of the mobile maintenance domain, service providers, customers and machine manufacturers are already using very similar terms and relations in between. New members should be able to reuse semantic definitions of collaboration partners as much as possible and only provide new definitions for areas that are not yet modelled to complement their own data model. Of course, if the data structure of a partner is not compatible to an already existing definition, he can define his own model. In this case, he needs to provide a mapping to the already existing definitions. In the *ComVantage* architecture, this functionality will be covered by the *Model Mappings*. Using this approach, the necessity of complicated schema matching is avoided and the effort of initial schema definition is reduced if applicable. In order to complete the ramp up process of a new partner, access control policies need to be created. Using these policies, the domain owner keeps full control of his valuable data and actively decides, which external partners are allowed to access individual data units. According to our comprehensive requirements analysis – "security" is the most important requirement in the business domain.

Once a partner has finished the ramp up process and has modelled his *Domain Data Model*, the *Model Mappings* and the *Access Control Policies*, it's time to make concrete data sources available to the external partners. Regarding our semantic approach, this means mapping the data structures of legacy systems to the *Domain Data Model*. In order to cover a wide range of het-

erogeneous data source types, the *ComVantage* consortium proposes a set of semantic adapters, which will perform the mapping. Once again, the "flexibility" of the approach is a key requirement. Therefore, the adapters are developed as generic components which can be configured in order to be used in a specific context. The *Linked Data Adapters* allow for an internal mapping of data sources for single partners. Having in mind the key requirement of "collaboration," an approach for interlinking datasets across organisational boundaries is needed as well. The functionality of the individual adapters and the related security concept on top of Linked Data are described in detail in section "Interorganisational Access to Information."

Using the proposed infrastructure for interorganisational data access, collaboration partners of a virtual enterprise are able to securely share all types of structured enterprise information. However, on top of this infrastructure, a design for consuming this information in collaborative workflows among organisational boundaries is required. Regarding the use cases of the *ComVantage* project and especially in the mobile maintenance domain, the demands for "mobility" and "usability" are high and mobile clients are of particular importance in order to provide relevant information anytime and everywhere – also to non-expert users. Within *ComVantage* we are using a model driven design approach in order to cope with the complexity of business process dependencies on the individual workflows and the development of mobile application itself. Moreover we adopted the very successful paradigm of simple and single-purpose apps. However, in order to cover complex and interorganisational workflows which can be usually found in professional use cases, these single purpose apps need to be orchestrated on design-time. In the sections "Modelling Support for Interorganisational Business Processes" and "Mobile Tools for Interorganisational Collaboration" these processes are explained in detail.

## Run-Time Aspects

After the configuration and adaptation of all generic components of the infrastructure is done, the following two run-time aspects do matter.

- Secure interorganisational access to enterprise data
- Execution of interorganisational business processes

As described by (Barnett, Presley, Johnson, & Liles, 1994), the added value of a virtual enterprise consists in an integration of business data and processes among collaboration partners to pursue a market opportunity. The architecture proposed by the *ComVantage* consortium is shown in Figure 2. It represents a fully decentralised approach that consists only of partner-specific components and therefore aligns itself with the key requirement "virtuality."

The core part of this design is the *Domain Access Server*, which acts as single point of access for the resources of each collaboration partner. Its main functionalities are data harmonisation, access control and domain-specific configuration. The Domain Access Server has a lean design that provides three different layers offering its main functionalities. The *Web Layer* contains a uniform interface for information requests based on SPARQL queries. Moreover, it provides an interface for access control, which will be explained more detailed in the section "Interorganisational Access to Information." The *Data Integration Layer* is responsible for distributing an information request to the relevant data sources that are connected within this particular domain. Furthermore it merges all results to a combined result set and eliminates duplicates for instance. The *Domain Configuration Layer* provides all components that are necessary for a domain specific configuration of the Domain Access Server. These components

*Figure 2. The architecture for virtual enterprises from a run-time perspective*

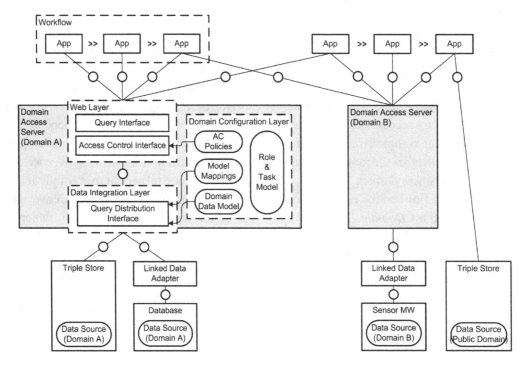

have been explained already in the section about design-time aspects of the architecture.

The important task of harmonisation among all data sources of a collaboration partner is done outside of the Domain Access Server within the individual Linked Data Adapters. Their main task is to map data sources of heterogeneous technology (e.g. database, excel file) and arbitrary data schema to the uniform data model of the Domain Access Server that is realised in RDF and uses the Domain Data Model as common data schema. Despite of the fact that the mapping is defined at design-time, the advantage of the *ComVantage* approach consists of an execution of these mappings at run-time. This way, redundant semantic data and the connected problem of keeping it synchronized is avoided as Linked Data is extracted on demand only. Thus, the Linked Data cloud of the virtual enterprise is a distributed and virtual one rather than a permanent persistent one. More details about the functionality of the Linked Data Adapters will be provided in the section "Interorganisational Access to Information."

Additionally to the data harmonisation for one partner, the "flexibility" in consumption of information at run-time is a key requirement. Each partner is responsible to develop client applications to support his own workflows. Of course, some of these workflows are interorganisational. The application of a maintenance service provider requests for his own data (e.g. history of defects of similar machines, HR data of technicians), data from the customer (e.g. location of the machine, operational parameters) and data from the machine manufacturer (e.g. specifications and service manuals of the machine type). As we are proposing a highly decentralised approach based on semantic technologies, each application must be developed using a Domain Data Model of a specific partner. In case the application requests data from another domain, the Domain Data Model used for the query might be different to the Domain Data Model of the receiving Domain Access Server. In

this case, each Domain Access Server is able to resolve conflicts in schema definitions by looking up the Model Mappings. These Model Mappings map the local schema definitions of a partner to the deviating ones of other collaboration partners. The result of this activity is a rewritten query that fully matches the local Domain Data Model and produces valid results on the local data sources.

Finally, the process of executing interorganisational business processes by using single purpose client applications in an orchestrated manner is of interest. It is described in more detail in section "Mobile Tools for Interorganisational Collaboration."

## INTERORGANISATIONAL ACCESS TO INFORMATION

There are numerous challenges that usually have to be met in order to enable business partners to collaborate effectively and efficiently. Each partner has to understand the meaning of the data residing in the other partners' systems. Moreover, entities that occur in the systems of several partners, but are referenced by different names have to be identified and matched so that all information about this entity can be obtained upon request. Accessing this data must be possible using just one access point, and all pieces of data returned must be in a common format, independent of the system they originate from. Obviously, access restrictions and security measurements also have to be applied for all data sources.

Without these requirements, developing an application using data from different partners is extremely complex: different data sources have to be read, the underlying data models understood, the data matched and consolidated, before it is finally presented to the user. If a new partner joins the network, the application has to be substantially modified, even if only a new data source is added, in order to reflect the source's data model.

Moreover, for an application lacking a consistent universal data model, displaying the data to the user in an easily understandable and consistent way is almost impossible.

## Linked Data and RDF

Within our virtual enterprise setting, we decided in favour of the RDF data format (RDF Working Group, 2004) and the Linked Data principles (Bizer, Heath, & Berners-Lee, 2009). In RDF, statements are made in the form of data triples:

```
<Subject> <Predicate> <Object>
```

An application example from the mobile maintenance domain is presented below:

```
<Machine01> <hasReport> <ServiceRe-
port01>
<ServiceReport01> <hasAuthor> <Servi-
ceTechnician01>
```

Similar to a database, a triple store allows for storing, modifying, and querying triples. Queries can be formulated in the SPARQL (W3C, 2013) language, whose syntax is influenced by SQL.

According to Tim Berners-Lee, the "Linked Data Web" should satisfy the following demands:

1.  Use URIs to identify things.
2.  Use HTTP URIs so that these things can be referred to and looked up ("dereferenced") by people and user agents.
3.  Provide useful information about the thing when it's URI is dereferenced, using standard formats such as RDF/XML.
4.  Include links to other, related URIs in the exposed data to improve discovery of other related information on the Web.

The subject and the predicate of an RDF triple are always URIs, whereas the object can either also be a URI (if the object is a "thing") or a lit-

eral (if the object simply is a text or a number). Additionally to RDF and Linked Data example above, a HTTP URI example from the mobile maintenance application area representing the concept of the service technician is shown below:

```
<http://www.comvantage.eu/ontologies/
mma/rppm/ServiceTechnician>
```

Thus, we obtain a framework that enables us to represent all kinds of information in a single format that is based on the widely adapted HTTP standard and thus is compatible with a large number of existing software systems. Moreover, in the years since the term "Linked Data" was coined, many tools have been developed in order to generate, publish, organise, or modify Linked Data sets. Additionally, there exists a huge amount of Linked Open Data, i.e. datasets that are in Linked Data format and are freely available (see e.g. DBpedia (Bizer, et al. 2009)). These tools and datasets especially allow small companies to join a virtual enterprise and profit from existing information without requiring a significant upfront investment.

## Linked Data for Collaboration Networks

Representing a company's data as Linked Data requires several steps. First, the terms for the entities (Berners-Lee's "things") have to be defined, along with relations between them. The result of this endeavour is called an ontology, and is stored in a triple store. Second, the company's existing systems and data sources have to be made accessible as well. Since a complete migration to the Linked Data format would disrupt the current processes and also would make it impossible to use specialised software, it is a better alternative to transform data from such legacy systems into RDF on-the-fly, i.e. upon a reading request. The software component performing this task is called *Linked Data Adapter*. Finally, it is important to integrate the company data with existing data, i.e. to find existing entities that correspond to or are related with the company data and make these connections visible.

For the first step – the data model development – it is necessary that people with expert knowledge about the company and its business (the "domain experts") work together with people who are experienced with representing knowledge and generating ontologies (the "ontology engineers"). Several methodologies have been developed for structuring this process, like Tove (Grüninger & Fox, 1995), Enterprise (Uschold & King, 1995), and Methontology (Fernandez Lopez, Gomez Perez, & Juristo, 1997). The ontology itself is formalised using a tool like Protege (Stanford Center for Biomedical Informatics Research, 2013), and loaded into a triple store like Sesame (Aduna Software, 2012), Jena (Apache Jena, 2012), or Virtuoso (OpenLink Software, 2013).

For the second step – the integration of existing data sources and IT-systems – Linked Data Adapters are readily available for many popular data formats: D2RQ (Cyganiak & Bizer, 2012) for databases, XLwrap (Langegger, 2013) for spreadsheets, or Any23 (Apache Any23, 2012) for a variety of semantic formats, like RDFa, Microformats, or HTML5 Microdata. If the company uses systems for which no adapters are readily available, the adapters have to be written from scratch. We will discuss examples for both kinds of adapters below.

For the third and final step – the interlinking of information across organizational boundaries – one has to find relations between the newly generated entities and those that already exist in the Linked Data web. If the new entity A is exactly identical with an already existing one B, this can be expressed with the triple A owl:sameAs B. For other relations, one uses an appropriate predicate: e.g. if A is a special kind of B, one can say: A rdfs:subClassOf B. If there is no appropriate predicate, but one still wishes to include a relation, on can use the rdfs:seeAlso predicate.

This makes it possible to interlink data between different companies or between a company and a public source. Exemplary data from the mobile maintenance application area is shown below:

```
PREFIX owl: <http://www.
w3.org/2002/07/owl#>
PREFIX rdfs: <http://www.
w3.org/2000/01/rdf-schema#>
PREFIX rppm: <http://www.comvantage.
eu/ontologies/mma/rppm/>
PREFIX mop: <http://www.comvantage.
eu/ontologies/mma/mop/>
<rppm:WaterPump01> <owl:sameAs>
<mop:Machine04>
<rppm:ServiceTechnician>
<rdfs:subClassOf> < rppm:Employee>
```

This "glue data" has to be stored in a triple store for each collaboration partner. The Open Source project Silk (Isele et al., 2012) is a tool for discovering relationships between data items within different Linked Data sources. It supports RDF link generation with flexible link conditions expressed in a declarative language. SPARQL endpoints are used to access the datasets and provide the generated links.

## Linked Data Adapters

The *ComVantage* approach utilizes adapters in order to make data sources and IT systems available for collaboration partners. Generic adapters for specific data source technologies are provided. In order to transform data from a database into RDF, it is necessary to transform the database entities (like customers or products) into URIs; to assign these entities to their respective RDFS classes; and to transform each line of a table into a set of RDF triples. This transformation is done using the D2RQ system mentioned above. D2RQ reads data from a relational database, converts it into RDF using a set of rules (which logically contain the semantics of the database) and exports this data in RDF or HTML format. It also offers a SPARQL endpoint for queries.

Figure 3 visualizes an example application of the Linked Data Adapter for databases from the mobile maintenance application area. The example database at the top lacks semantic information. This means that for the numbers in the tables, it is not clear which ones are foreign keys (e.g. address) and which ones actually represent numeric values (e.g. number or zip code). Moreover, since no universally accepted vocabulary for names within databases exists, human intelligence is required to interpret the meaning of the corresponding columns: in other tables, "first name" might be

*Figure 3. Application of a Linked Data adapter to access a customer database*

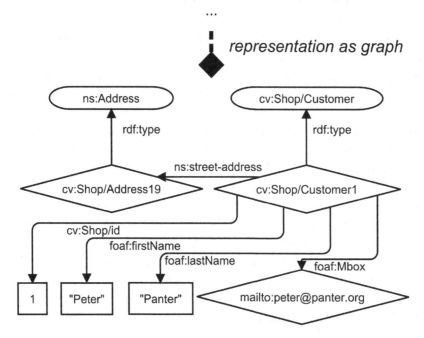

called "given name" or "Christian name." Also the email address is not in URI format, which makes it difficult to use by computer software.

Figure 3 shows moreover a textual and a graph representation of the transformation result. First and last name of the customer are identified using the Friend of a Friend (FOAF) vocabulary, one of the most frequently used RDF ontologies, thus making the links easily machine processable. All foreign keys have been replaced with direct links between the entities, thus resolving the ambiguity of numbers. The email address is in URI format (and connected with the individual it belongs to by a FOAF predicate), which makes it immediately understandable and usable by computer programs. Additionally, each individual refers to its class via an rdf:type link allowing the user to obtain more information about this kind of individuals.

Integrating live sensor data from a machine middleware into the Linked Data environment is a more complex task: from a practical point of view, since no adapter system is readily available, but also from a technical point of view, since the sensor data is not static, and thus an access to an entity referencing a sensor or an actuator has to be transformed into an access to the current reading of that sensor or an instruction to the actuator. The Data Harmonisation Middleware (DHM) adapter consists of the following parts.

The middleware itself provides access to sensor data of one or several machines. The Linked Data Publisher (LDP) extracts parts of the machine semantics from the configuration information within the middleware. This machine semantics describes the structure of the production units and the available sensors and actuators (using URIs). The Linked Data Server (LDS) stores the machine semantics provided by the LDP and provides a SPARQL endpoint. Thus those parts of the machine semantics that are relevant for access to sensors can be queried via SPARQL. The History Data Server (HDS) allows accessing previously stored values and results of tests. The MW-Log component logs changes of sensors and actuators in the HDS. The Live Data Access Component allows read/write access to sensors and actuators. The Test Execution Environment (TEE) component is responsible for executing tests and storing their results in the HDS. The Job Controller (JC) dispatches access requests to the resources, e.g. if a test running for an extended time, it prevents writing access to actuators.

## Secure Access Control for Linked Data Collaboration

Interorganisational access to information is at the very core of collaboration. Interorganisational collaboration success revolves around the ability to leverage light-weight and agile interoperability solutions that facilitate the information sharing across the network of collaborators in a secure and controlled manner for implementation of agreed business processes. The use of Linked Data has so far proven a very effective means to manage open Webs of Data. However, the deployment of Linked Data solutions in the context of the enterprise collaboration demands to develop the ability to create private Linked Data clouds. So the implementation of interorganisational product-centric collaboration spaces demand that suitable mechanisms to control the access to information are proposed. The open nature of current Web of Data information and the consumption of Web resources on the go may give data providers the impression that their content is not safe, thus preventing further publication of datasets, at the expense of the growth of the Web of Data itself (Heath & Bizer, 2011). Hence, facilitating trust in controlled access to information published in the Web of Data is of strategic importance to the development of Linked Data-based data interoperability solutions for enterprise collaboration. In a collaborative environment, where a set of interlinked data will be shared and consumed by different agents, ensuring that Linked Data information remains secure and only accessible to authorised members is a crucial issue.

Multi-domain access control solutions based on XACML standards are well-established solutions to govern information access control in distributed and federated environments. Traditionally, XACML architectures allow decisions to be made in terms of access permit/deny to a number of resources based on a set of access policies. However, coarse-grained XACML decisions (permit/deny) to control SPARQL requests for information access to graph stores supporting the Linked Data resources may prove insufficient to deal with the requirements of industrial collaboration. It is essential that access control should be supported at a fine granularity (i.e., RDF minimum information entity which is the tuple or triple), and not only at a coarse-grained level (i.e., repository level), as done by XAML standards. Implementation of effective access control solutions for Linked Data access in the context of enterprise collaboration raises three major challenges:

1. How to define a fine-grained access control model for heterogeneous Web of Data resources; i.e. semantic data in RDF, live data from enterprise sensors, or typical documents;
2. How to allow a controlled mobile consumption of such information; and finally
3. How to deal with exceptional requests for information access.

Addressing these security challenges should leverage more agile and effective forms of collaboration.

Over the last few years, an increasing interest has been generated in terms of providing access control solutions to Linked Data stores. The access control methods provide different levels of granularity – triple (Costabello, Villata, Delaforge, & Gandon, 2012), document (Sacco &

Passant, 2011) or graph level –, they implement different approaches to integration with Graph Stores – plugged-in solutions (Costabello, Villata, Delaforge, & Gandon, 2012), layered control store independent (Abel, De Coi, Henze, & Koesling, 2007) –, they use different languages for access control policy specification – high-level syntax (Abel, De Coi, Henze, & Koesling, 2007), RDF metadata (Corradi, Montanari, & Tibaldi, 2004), context algebra (Cuppens & Cuppens-Boulahia, 2008), semantic Web languages (Finin, y otros, 2008), (Hollenbach, Presbrey, & Berners-Lee, 2009), (Shen & Cheng, 2001), (Toninelli, Montanari, Kagal, & Lassi, 2006) – or they use different approaches to specify policies – user based (Giunchiglia, Zhang, & Crispo, 2009), attribute based (Finin, et al, 2008) (Sacco & Passant, 2011).

The SHI3LD mobile access control framework for Linked Data has been recently proposed (Costabello, Villata, Delaforge, & Gandon, 2012). It protects RDF stores by changing the semantics of the incoming SPARQL queries, whose scope is restricted to triples included in accessible named graphs only. However, to determine the list of accessible graphs, it is necessary to evaluate predefined access policies against the context of the requester, which may create scalability issues as the size of users and the data space increases. Furthermore, the proposed approaches fail to deliver mechanisms that allow a controlled and delegated exceptional access to information and support for real-time Linked Data access.

To overcome such limitations, the *ComVantage* approach relies on the concept of data view generation, which does not require policy reevaluation at the SPARQL processing stage. A view is defined as a set of triples, where a triple will be the smallest unit that could be protected. The proposed approach infers new facts from the original RDF data, by applying access control policies, which employ a predefined vocabulary for access control schema generation. The language Notation3 (Berners-Lee & Connolly, 2013), which is a readable RDF syntax, is selected for defining the set of rules/formulas concerning the RDF data and supports the organisation of original RDF data in a set of views with different access types; e.g. canSee, canUse. Views are then created inferring new facts from access control schemas and importing them into RDF data stores, replacing the original data. As a result of this process a new set of RDF data with inferred facts is created and organised in views. Based on this data, the SPARQL processing, i.e. SPARQL re-writing, is handled. Indeed, as a relevant distinguishing feature from other existing Liked Data access control methods, within the *ComVantage* approach, this SPARQL rewriting time cost does not depend on the amount of data to protect and on the number of policies to apply to those data, thus facilitating a time efficient security method.

## Security Architecture for Mobile Linked Data Collaboration

The *ComVantage* mobile collaboration approach relies on the implementation of the Domain Access Servers, which will offer an HTTP interface to mobile client applications. The central element in the Domain Access Server is the Query Interface that receives either HTTP requests with embedded SPARQL queries or requests for single dereferenceable URIs that the module transfers to the distribution service.

From a security perspective, "product-centric inter-organisational collaborative environments" are referred to independent administrative domains that engage in an information exchange process to complete a particular set of business processes. So as to being able to perform an access request to the information in the target domain(s), the target domain will need to trust the requester. This is achieved by defining a "circle of trust" among the collaborative partners/enterprises.

To generate such "circle of trust" *ComVantage* relies on the security architecture depicted below. Moreover, *ComVantage* provides an integrated

authentication and authorisation framework based on the SAML (Security Assertion MarkUp Language) standard. This standard, defined by OASIS SSTC (OASIS, 2013), provides on the one hand, an XML schema for security assertions and on the other hand, protocols to exchange these assertions. Thus, business entities can make assertions regarding the identity, attributes and entitlements of a subject to other entities, such as a partner company or another enterprise application.

The *ComVantage* security architecture, as depicted by Figure 4, relies on 5 major elements

1. **Domain A IdP (Identity Provider):** Provides authentication services according to SAML standard. It includes a LDAP repository where users' credentials/attributes are stored. Domain A can implement any type of authentication method, e.g. user/password, multi-factor authentication, etc. It is responsible for issuing security tokens.
2. **Domain Authenticator:** This module is in charge of user authentication on the mobile device as part of the Industrial App Framework and issuing of secure resource access requests.
3. **Service Provider:** A module in the Domain Access Server responsible for protecting the resources and dealing with reception of resource access requests according to the SAML standard.
4. **Query Rewriting Access Control:** A module that grants access based on the available RDF data views.
5. **XACML based Access Control:** A module to control access to non RDF data, using HTTP requests.

The proposed solution to limit the access to an SPARQL endpoint follows a simple procedure:

1. The role of the requester of the SPARQL query is known as a result of the SAML au-

*Figure 4. ComVantage security architecture*

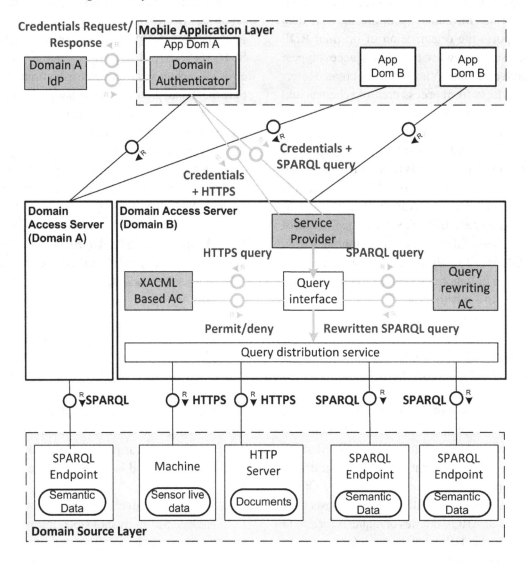

thentication protocol implemented between the Domain IdP and the mobile Domain Authenticator;

2. An inferring process has added out of band access control facts to original RDF data, creating data views associated with roles/groups and applying particular access constrains;

3. Original SPARQL queries are rewritten based the user role and by adding access control checks composed by triple patterns and constraints.

As a result, rewritten queries that include requester roles/groups will limit the access to data contained into the views associated only with those roles/groups.

## MODELLING SUPPORT FOR INTERORGANISATIONAL BUSINESS PROCESSES

*ComVantage* envisions a run-time architecture that is complemented with design-time modelling support for collaborative businesses aiming to deploy their IT infrastructure on the *ComVantage* technical guidelines. The *ComVantage* modelling method aims to tackle some of the research challenges defined by the FInES Roadmap (FInES, 2013), particularly *RC1. Unified Digital Enterprise* (the digital image of the enterprise is model-driven); *RC2. Linked Open Knowledge* (the ontological intension of Linked Open Data can be related to our "models as Linked Data" approach) and *RC3. Complex Systems Modelling* (knowledge generated by complexity management can be externalised and communicated as conceptual models). Process-oriented supply chain modelling is being provided by tools such as (ARIS, 2013), which has been involved in Semantic Web-related research: (Ang et al., 2005) proposed a transformation of EPC models in Semantic Web Services described with OWL-S (OWL-S, 2013); ARIS was also used in the SUPER project (SUPER, 2013), where focus was placed on Semantic Web Services for process automation purposes. Compared to these approaches, our modelling method is not so concerned with inferences and service discovery, as with model linking and querying, and it is app-focused rather than service-focused. Mobile apps are treated as essential enablers for human-controlled business process execution (as necessary in our mobile maintenance context), while the approaches based on Semantic Web Services focus on service capability modelling for full automation. Tools such as those provided by Metastorm/OpenText (OpenText, 2013) or (ADOLog, 2013) also support design of business processes linked to models of their execution environment, but using generic IT resources, while *ComVantage* focuses on process-based mobile app requirements.

Aspects of model interoperability have been tackled mainly in the context of model-driven engineering. Various model serialisation formats are tool-specific, such as the ADL format of (ADONIS, 2013), or problem-specific, such as (XPDL, 2013) for business process models.

General purpose exchange formats such as OMG's XMI (OMG, 2013) fuelled the paradigm of model-driven engineering, as basis for code generators. Our immediate aim is not code generation, but rather the exposure of models linked at modelling tool level in a Linked Data environment where they can be used for various purposes: as injected data structures (if mapped on execution/instance data), as starting point for ontology development or, in the specific case of mobile apps, for model-driven app orchestration (as indicated in the next section of the chapter).

The state-of-the-art in business process modelling also revolves around standard languages such as BPMN or general purpose flowchart languages (e.g. UML activity diagrams). Compared to these, we distinguish the wider notion of "modelling method" (see its building blocks in the next section), we favour community-oriented customization against standardization and domain specificity captured by integrating the process models with aspects regarding their execution requirements (app-oriented) and context (supply chain-oriented). For integration purposes, a common metamodel enables models of different types to be navigable along semantic links and exportable as linked models.

## The ComVantage Modelling Method: An Overview

The "building blocks" of a modelling method are as follows, according to (Karagiannis & Kuhn, 2012).

*The modelling procedure* comprises the steps to be taken towards the modeller goals. In *ComVantage*, it concerns both the initial and final stages of the lifecycle. An early modelling procedure has been defined in order to identify modelling goals and requirements (after they were derived from domain-specific use cases during the requirements analysis phase of the run-time platform). A late modelling procedure is to be refined as guidelines to document the modelling tool, after its implementation phase.

*The modelling language* comprises the actual modelling constructs (concepts, relations and their attributes) grouped in model types, which are further grouped on a modelling stack (Figure 5). The layers of the modelling stack further group the model types on different levels of detail and abstraction. In *ComVantage* these layers cover two types of problems:

- *Product-centred supply chain management issues* with some adaptation to the application areas (customer-oriented production, plant engineering/commissioning and mobile maintenance);
- *Business-IT alignment*, in the form of capturing requirements for mobile apps consuming Linked Data, with an approach that mixes aspects of goal-oriented, feature-oriented and usability requirements modelling (which gives the "hybrid" nature of the method as a whole).

*The mechanisms and algorithms* comprise functionality necessary for transforming or evaluating models. This covers the interoperability support, to be detailed in the next subsection.

We present here the modelling procedure in parallel with the envisioned modelling stack, depicted in the slogan view from Figure 5.

- The Know layer supports the high level design of business models reusing the established modelling language for value constellations, e3 value (Gordijn & Akkermans, 2001);
- The Identify layer supports the modelling of high level resources and knowledge structures, which are necessary to deploy the business model. This includes product configurations (customisations) that are built around a base product. The product configurations follow principles of feature-oriented modelling (Kang et al., 1990),

*Figure 5. The ComVantage modelling stack*

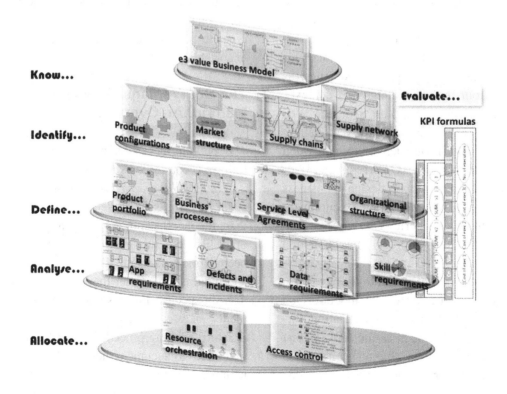

with features classified according to Kano's attributes (Kano et al., 1984), mapped on needs/goals from the market structure models (derived from assumed market analysis effort). Each product configuration is assigned to a supply chain process model similar to the thread models popularised by SCOR (Supply Chain Council, 2013), describing the process map involved in production, with references to participating organisations. The participants to the virtual enterprise are modelled according to the practice of scope modelling, which is also suggested by SCOR. They reflect the business entities and their geographical locations involved in a particular supply chain;

- The Define layer drills down the resources and parties that are previously identified: products are organised in a product portfolio, with configurations that can be manually linked by association rules (to be used, potentially, for recommender systems); supply chain processes are detailed down to the level of operational business and technical processes; business entities are drilled down as organisational structures reflecting units, roles and performers responsible with the execution of processes; requirements of service level agreements can be defined (as alternative to product configurations, for service-oriented businesses);

- The Analysis layer covers: a) skill requirements, used to match roles with performers in the organisational model; b) SIPOC (Simon, 2010) modelling of process paths, redesigned to express data requirements and Linked Data ownership during the execution of a process; c) defects and incidents to capture specificities of the mobile maintenance application area (by assigning maintenance processes and roles to particular defect models); d) mobile app requirements assigned to tasks from business processes;

- The Allocate layer is concerned with the pool of resources and artefacts that are required for the business process execution, and the level of control that is necessary for accessing them. Here, the mobile apps that are designed with a model-driven approach are of a particular importance (described more detailed in the next section);

- Finally, the Evaluate (horizontal) dimension must be covered by a mechanism for generic KPI formulas (not designed yet) that are envisioned to cover both standard (SCOR) and custom KPIs, to be associated to goals on various abstraction levels.

For the purposes of this chapter, we focus on the lower layers, with the specific case of mobile app support, in order to provide a bridging towards the next section. We take examples from the mobile maintenance application area, for which the method supports elicitation of mobile app requirements with linked models of different model types, as depicted in Figure 6 (top half):

- A business process model describing maintenance tasks and decisions during a maintenance process;

- A pool of resources linked to various process steps (in this case, roles and mobile app requirements);

- Models detailing the relations involving those resources: for *roles*, of particular interest are the organisational model structure (where performers from various business units are assigned to roles and required skill models); for *mobile IT support*, app functionality is further described in terms of provided interaction and capabilities.

The links between models are valuable on several levels:

*Figure 6. Maintenance process model example mapped on its resource requirements (top) and its translation to Linked Data structures (bottom)*

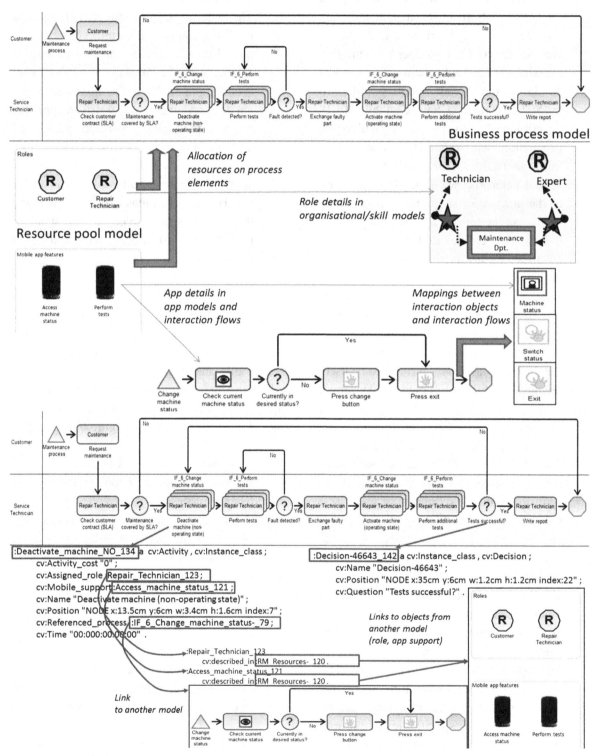

1. As a *usability feature* in the modelling tool (allowing the user to navigate between related models);
2. As a *conceptual feature* helping us to link constructs that have been grouped in different model types and support queries based on them (similar to the table joins in relational databases);
3. As a basis for *exporting the models* as Linked Data, enabling their interconnectivity, transformation and federation via SPARQL regardless of purpose.

## Interoperability-Oriented Functionality in the ComVantage Modelling Method

T*he mechanisms and algorithms* building block comprise functionality that takes as input attributes and structures found in the models. This is functionality meant to automate some of the procedure steps, to provide model analysis (querying), transformation (including import/export) and simulation. In *ComVantage*, the model "interoperability" aspects are defined on this level, supported by an RDF vocabulary designed for model export. This is a mechanism that exposes diagrammatic models as Linked Data, thus enabling model querying and transformation outside the modelling tool, and, potentially, a bridge to model-driven code generation. Relative to the interoperability areas defined by the ENSEMBLE project (ENSEMBLE, 2012), this can be positioned as *data interoperability*, since it is a matter of exchanging models serialised in Linked Data structures, but also lays foundations for *business process interoperability* and *knowledge interoperability*, if we consider the specific subvocabularies derived from the metamodel of each particular model type. As Figure 6 (bottom half) suggests, the serialisation relies on:

- A meta-meta-vocabulary (with concepts such as *cv:Model_class, cv:Instance_class, cv:Relation_class*);
- Vocabularies derived from the metamodel for each particular model type, here the business process model type (*cv:Activity, cv:Activity_cost, cv:Sequence_relation* etc.);
- As well as resources captured from the model instances (*:Repair_technician_123, :Decision-46643* etc.).

The example indicates RDF fragments describing an activity and a decision from the maintenance process depicted in the top half of Figure 6. The full model export groups such fragments in a named graph, together with the relations between the modelling objects (in the case of a business process model, the flows) and the metamodel elements (classes for each object). Also, the cross-model links, with resources belonging to other models, are captured. The example depicts *links to objects from other models* (from activity to the role responsible with performing it – via *cv:Assigned_role*; from activity to a mobile support feature – via *cv:Mobile_support*) and *links to other models* (from activity to a subprocess representing the interaction process relative to the UI design of the mobile support – via *cv:Referenced_process*).

## MOBILE TOOLS FOR INTERORGANIZATIONAL COLLABORATION

In the last section an app-centred approach for mobile collaboration is presented. The App Orchestration Concept proposed by *ComVantage* extents the current App deployment process for mobile systems with methods and tools that allow an automation of the App deployment and management process. The concept largely increases reusability, consistency and usability of professional Apps for industrial use while keeping the flexibility and cost-efficiency of the existing App deployment process.

## Requirements for Mobile Collaboration

Mobile systems are changing the way people use electronic devices and digital information. The "information every time, everywhere" paradigm has become reality as nearly any relevant information is available on the Internet; and wireless networks provide instant access to this information with mobile and pervasive devices wherever and whenever needed. Small applications, so-called Apps, provide optimised task-specific functionality and a highly usable user interface for a particular mobile device. As millions of Apps are offered in huge app repositories, often called App Stores, users can customise their mobile systems according to their particular tasks and needs. The workflows, tasks and context of mobile users are manifold, and so are the configurations of their devices. Today, the selection, adaptation and arrangement of Apps are highly individual and entirely manual tasks. Although sufficient for consumer products, this lack of support or automation of the customisation process is a main hinderer of a large-scale exploitation of App-centred mobile infrastructures in professional IT environments. Business process models, planning systems or standard operating procedures contain detailed information on tasks, workflows and their actual context, and provide detailed models of the information needs of the tasks. Formal domain-specific data models contain detailed information on the amount and structure of the relevant data. Human performance models and a large body of empirical data provide reliable information on human behaviour of professional users. Today, none of this information can be used to automate the App deployment and management process for professional mobile systems.

## The App Orchestration Concept

The *ComVantage* project has developed an App Orchestration Concept (AOC) that overcomes these limitations (Pfeffer et al., 2012; Ziegler et al. 2012). Unlike Service Orchestration (Erl, 2005), App Orchestration is about explicit user interfaces. However, it does not cope with distributed UIs (Daniel et al. 2010) but with native apps installed on a mobile device. The concept employs a pragmatic model-driven approach that makes use of the available models in the *ComVantage* collaboration space and allows for partial or complete automation of the deployment and management process. Core of the concept is the insight that many existing apps share common structures and design elements, serve similar purposes, and use similar data. Business processes, data structures, visual appearance and human factors contain typical patterns that are invariant to a particular task. These invariants can be used to generalise apps from supporting a single specific task to supporting an abstract type of tasks. Such a Generic App implements a particular set of data, process, and human-factors specific invariants and can be reused for all tasks that call for this set of invariants. To do so, each Generic App is accompanied by a formal app description notated in an App Description Language. Core of the AOC is a process for selection of appropriate Generic Apps, their specialisation and adaptation to the actual task and context, and the management of all selected apps as an integrated App Ensemble. In the Select Step, a set of Generic Apps is selected from the App Pool that supports the type of tasks given in the current business process. To increase reusability, the generic apps are not yet adapted to a specific use case or information source. Instead, they are adaptable to various specific tasks. This is done in the Adapt Step. Adaptation may include the visual appearance, the interaction style, the actual data source, and more. In the Manage Step, the Adapted Apps are connected according to a navigation design model which is derived from the business process model. Navigation might be implicit or explicit. For implicit navigation, app switches are generated automatically when a certain system event occurs. For explicit navigation, appropriate navigation elements are added to the user interfaces of the apps to enable the user to switch between the apps. Since the navigation model is derived from the business process model, only useful navigation paths are available for the user, whereas all other possible paths are being omitted. An orchestration approach was chosen above a choreography approach because a central management component has the advantage of being able to load a navigation design as a rule set for specific workflows. Thus, no further modifications or adaptations in the involved apps are necessary.

The entire process of the App Orchestration is shown in Figure 7. The result of the process is an App Ensemble accompanied by a special management component that manages the navigation and exchange of information among the App Ensemble. This component is realised as an app as well, and is deployed along with the adapted apps. At runtime, each app of the ensemble runs independently with the management component as its only communication partner. Once deployed, the App Ensemble receives no further changes or online adaptation, in order to ensure consistency and dependability of the application, and to allow for software certification for safety critical applications.

The *ComVantage* project has implemented an Industrial App Framework that implements the App Orchestration Concept for a Linked Data

cloud and a Google Android target platform. The proposed collaboration environment of *ComVantage* provides business process models, a common vocabulary and a shared information space. As can be seen in Figure 8, the Industrial App Framework retrieves the available information from the same information space at design time as the later App Ensemble does at runtime. After the App Orchestration process has been completed, the App Ensembles are automatically deployed to the mobile target devices. At runtime, the Ensembles can access the shared information space using secured SPARQL endpoints. For this purpose, the overall architecture of *ComVantage* provides a decentralised dynamic access control model as described in the previous sections.

Figure 9 shows three exemplary apps from the mobile maintenance application area that have been adapted from Generic Apps that share the same invariants regarding visual appearance and context. The shown App ensemble allows authorisation of the user using the Login App, browsing of reversible neighbourhood relations in Linked Data, and the visualisation and comparison of discrete and continuous time series as trend charts. It thus allows maintenance personnel to quickly obtain information about the assets and the process of a plant or factory. Another Orchestration scenario in the area of mobile maintenance was presented by Ziegler et al. (2012) applying the Industrial App Framework on a Smartphone as target device. At this stage of development, the selection and adaptation of the apps was done by hand according to specified business processes

*Figure 7. The process of app orchestration*

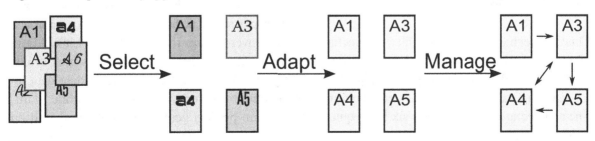

*Figure 8. Linked Data and the Industrial App Framework for mobile collaboration in virtual enterprises (Ziegler et al., 2012)*

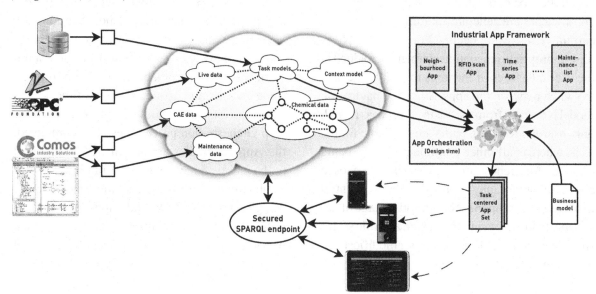

*Figure 9. Implementation of Apps for mobile maintenance implementing the same invariants regarding visual appearance and context but different invariants regarding the data structures; left: login app; middle: neighbourhood-browser; right: trend chart app (Pfeffer et al., 2011)*

and formalised design guidelines for visualisation and interaction. For future releases, this process will be automated step by step with the final goal of a mainly automated App Orchestration process.

## CONCLUSION

This Chapter has presented a detailed architecture of an IT-infrastructure for virtual enterprises including detailed descriptions of core components for realizing data- and process interoperability. The architecture is based on the six key require-

ments, virtuality, mobility, usability, flexibility, collaboration and security and represents a fully decentralised approach.

In order to realise adequate data interoperability, a semantic approach for data harmonisation based on RDF and Linked Data was chosen. Using Linked Data, datasets of different collaboration partners can be interlinked. Our approach moreover realises the derivation of Linked Data from legacy systems at run-time, which avoids synchronisation problems of redundant data. In addition, a security approach to mobile multi-domain product centric collaboration based on two steps was developed. First, data is organized in separated views following access control constraints. Second, SPARQL queries are rewritten according to the applied access control policies. Thus, it is possible to filter the access to Linked Data without the need to continuously evaluate the set of access control policies on the available data sets and making the space of data sets to be explored by mobile applications highly extensible without the need of application re-coding. Hence, the benefits of mobile app stores and Linked Data can be jointly exploited in a secure manner.

Process interoperability is achieved by an app-centric and model-driven development approach. First, business process models are used to define interorganisational workflows. Second, these models are serialized to Linked Data. Third, each workflow is segmented into individual activities and each activity is mapped on a generic mobile app. Finally, these generic apps are adapted to the concrete application context and are orchestrated according to the navigation model of the business process.

The presented design represents a holistic approach of enterprise interoperability based on enterprise data and business processes. The feasibility of performing data harmonization with semantic technologies and Linked Data has already been proved, especially in the area of Linked Open Data and public information. In the European research project *ComVantage*, the appropriateness of these new technologies shall be demonstrated in an enterprise environment. Therefore, an architecture for virtual enterprises is designed and implemented in prototypes for three different application areas in the manufacturing domain. This chapter focuses on results from the application area of mobile maintenance and includes current pain points, a scenario description, derived key requirements and envisioned improvements. The following social, economic and environmental impact is predictable for the application area of mobile maintenance: First, a longer uptime of machines due to more efficient

and more precise maintenance operations as well as the prevention of failures due to early recognition of potential problems. Second, less costs due to better preparation of on-site maintenance operations caused by more precise and versatile information and symptom descriptions. This includes a more accurate pre-selection of spare parts and finally results in less travel for the executing maintenance technician. Of course, the two last mentioned facts do also have a positive environmental impact. Regarding a more general application context, the *ComVantage* approach offers easier means for SMEs to establish collaboration networks, represents a light-weight and secure mean to share business data and enables professional users to exploit business data for mobile collaboration.

In terms of breakthrough innovations, especially for the domain of mobile maintenance, our design offers active machines with self-diagnostic capabilities and their seamless integration into virtual enterprises. Moreover, breaking technologies like Linked Data and affordable mobile devices from the consumer products market are utilised for real-world industrial application scenarios.

Future research directions beyond the *ComVantage* project should focus towards more effective policy management frameworks for efficient data view management that derive into optimised inferring processes and data view maintenance each time a RDF data set is changed. Research directions should provide mechanisms to limit and control the explosion of RDF data store size that may result from application of rich access control policies or the increase in collaboration networks managed by the enterprise. Intelligent graph management and policy organisation may result in simpler view arrangements and the need for partial inferring processes, with the inherent performance and management advantages.

The approach taken by the *ComVantage* modelling method facilitates interoperability on the level of conceptual modelling, which can be further developed in several research directions: first, process-aware information systems can benefit from the levels of interoperability and data integration promised by the Linked Data paradigm; second, modelling tools may be turned into knowledge acquisition tools capable of exposing captured knowledge as Linked Data structures. Additionally, ontology engineers may use metamodels exported as Linked Data as a starting point in their ontology development efforts, bringing closer the worlds of prescriptive metamodelling and descriptive ontology engineering.

The presented App Orchestration Framework is a highly dynamic framework. The App Description language will be refined and extended as new invariants will be discovered and formalised. Several selection and adaptation mechanisms will render useful for different purposes. Other target platforms may require different implementation concepts. As more data and tools will become available, more and more subtasks of the process will be automated, which may finally lead to a fully automated App Orchestration.

Along with the increasing exploitation, more and more Generic Apps will become available for orchestration, which calls for sophisticated tools for App Pool management. It is thinkable that professional Generic App developers will come up with Generic App sets and orchestration support for various application domains. This will allow Industrial App Framework users to concentrate on their task being the improvement of business processes and workflows rather than app development. This separation of concerns might significantly increase the business value of the presented App Orchestration Concept.

## REFERENCES

Abel, F., De Coi, J., Henze, N., & Koesling, A. (2007). Enabling advanced and context-dependent access control in RDF stores. In *Proceedings of the 6th Int. Semantic Web Conf. (ISWC-2007)* (LNCS), (vol. 4825). Berlin: Springer.

*ADOLog - Supply Chain-Management mit ADOlog*. (2013). Retrieved February 25, 2013, from http://www.boc-group.com/products/adolog/

*ADONIS – Community Ed*. (2013). Retrieved February 25, 2013, from http://www.adonis-community.com/

Aduna Software. (2012). openRDF.org - Home of Sesame. *Aduna Software*. Retrieved February 25, 2013, from http://www.openrdf.org/

Ang, C. L., Gu, Y., Sourina, O., & Gay, R. K. L. (2005). An ARIS-based transformation approach to semantic web service development. In *Proceedings of Cyberworlds Conference* (pp. 8-16). IEEE Computer Society Press.

Apache Any23. (2012). *Apache software foundation*. Retrieved February 25, 2013, from http://any23.apache.org/

Apache Jena. (2012). *Apache software foundation*. Retrieved February 25, 2013, from http://jena.apache.org/

ARIS. (2013). *ARIS community Ed. official product page*. Retrieved February 25, 2013, from http://www.ariscommunity.com/aris-express

Barnett, W., Presley, A., Johnson, M., & Liles, D. (1994). An architecture for the virtual enterprise. In *Proceedings of the IEEE International Conference on Systems, Man, and Cybernetics*. San Antonio, TX: IEEE.

Berners-Lee, T., & Connolly, D. (2013). *Notation3 (N3), a readable RDF syntax*. Retrieved from http://www.w3.org/TeamSubmission/n3/

Bizer, C., Heath, T., & Berners-Lee, T. (2009). Linked data - The story so far. *International Journal on Semantic Web and Information Systems*, *5*(3), 1–22. doi:10.4018/jswis.2009081901

Bizer, C., Lehmann, J., Kobilarov, G., Auer, S., Becker, C., Cyganiak, R., & Hellmann, S. (2009). DBpedia – A crystallization point for the web of data. *Journal of Web Semantics: Science. Services and Agents on the World Wide Web*, 7, 154–165. doi:10.1016/j.websem.2009.07.002

ComVantage EU Project Page. (2012). *Deliverable D3.1.1 – Specification of modelling method including conceptualization outline.* Retrieved February 25, 2013, http://www.comvantage.eu/

Corradi, A., Montanari, R., & Tibaldi, D. (2004). Context-based access control management in ubiquitous environments. In *Proceedings of the 3rd IEEE Int. Symposium on Network Computing and Applications (NCA-2004)*, (pp. 253-260). IEEE.

Costabello, L., Villata, S., Delaforge, N., & Gandon, F. (2012). Linked data access goes mobile: Context-aware authorization for graph stores. In *Proceedings of the 5th Workshop about Linked Data on the Web (LDOW2012)*. LDOW.

Cuppens, F., & Cuppens-Boulahia, N. (2008). Modeling contextual security policies. *International Journal of Information Security*, 7(4), 285–305. doi:10.1007/s10207-007-0051-9

Cyganiak, R., & Bizer, C. (2012). *D2RQ - Accessing relational databases as virtual RDF graphs.* Retrieved from http://d2rq.org/

Daniel, F., Soi, S., Tranquillini, S., Casati, F., Heng, C., & Yan, L. (2010). From people to services to UI: Distributed orchestration of user interfaces. In R. Hull, J. Mendling, & S. Tai (Eds.), *Business process management* (pp. 310–326). Berlin: Springer. doi:10.1007/978-3-642-15618-2_22

ENSEMBLE EU Project. (2012). *Deliverable D2.1 – Envisioning, supporting and promoting future internet enterprise systems research through scientific collaboration.* Retrieved February 25, 2013, from http://www.fines-cluster.eu/fines/jm/Publications/Download-document/339-ENSEMBLE_D2.1_EISB_State_of_Play_Report-v2.00.html

Erl, T. (2005). *Service-oriented architecture: Concepts, technology, and design.* Upper Saddle River, NJ: Prentice Hall PTR.

Fernandez Lopez, M., Gomez Perez, A., & Juristo, N. (1997). METHONTOLOGY: From ontological art towards ontological engineering. In *Proceedings of the AAAI97 Spring Symposium.* AAAI.

FInES Cluster Task Force. (2013). *FInES research roadmap 2025.* Retrieved February 25, 2013, from http://www.fines-cluster.eu/fines/jm/Deliverables/Download-document/323-FInES-Research-Roadmap-2025-v3.0.html

Finin, T., Joshi, A., Kagal, L., Niu, J., Sandhu, R., Winsborough, W., et al. (2008). ROWLBAC: Representing role based access control in OWL. In *Proceedings of 13th ACM Symposium on Access Control Models and Technologies (SACMAT-2008)*, (pp. 73-82). ACM.

Giunchiglia, F., Zhang, R., & Crispo, B. (2009). Ontology driven community access control. In *Proceedings of the 1st Workshop on Trust and Privacy on the Social and Semantic Web (SPOT-2009)*. SPOT.

Gordijn, J., & Akkermans, H. (2001). E3-value: Design and evaluation of e-Business model. *IEEE Intelligent Systems*, 16(4), 11–17. doi:10.1109/5254.941353

Grüninger, M., & Fox, M. S. (1995). Methodology for the design and evaluation of ontologies. In *Proceedings of Workshop on Basic Ontological Issues in Knowledge Sharing, IJCAI-95.* Montreal, Canada: IJCAI.

Heath, T., & Bizer, C. (2011). *Linked data: Evolving the web into a global data space.* San Francisco: Morgan & Claypool. doi:10.1007/978-1-4614-1767-5_4

Hollenbach, J., Presbrey, J., & Berners-Lee, T. (2009). Using RDF metadata to enable access control on the social semantic web. In *Proceedings of the Workshop on Collaborative Construction, Management and Linking of Structured Knowledge (CK-2009).* CK.

Isele, R., Jentzsch, A., Bizer, C., & Volz, J. (2012). *Silk - A link discovery framework for the web of data.* Retrieved from http://wifo5-03.informatik.uni-mannheim.de/bizer/silk/

Kang, K., Cohen, S., Hess, J., Novak, W., & Peterson, A. (1990). *Feature-oriented domain analysis (FODA) feasibility study* (Technical Report CMU/SEI-90-TR-021). Pittsburgh, PA: Software Engineering Institute.

Kano, N., Nobuhiku, S., Fumio, T., & Shinichi, T. (1984). Attractive quality and must-be quality. *Journal of the Japanese Society for Quality Control, 14*(2), 39–48.

Karagiannis, D., & Kühn, H. (2002). Metamodelling platforms. In *Proceedings of the Third International Conference EC-Web 2002 – DEXA 2002* (LNCS), (vol. 2455, pp. 451-464). Berlin: Springer.

Kim, T. Y., Lee, S., Kim, K., & Kim, C. H. (2006). A modeling framework for agile and interoperable virtual enterprises. *Computers in Industry, 57*(3), 204–217. doi:10.1016/j.compind.2005.12.003

Langegger, A. (2013). *XLWrap – Spreadsheet-to-RDF wrapper.* Retrieved from http://xlwrap.sourceforge.net/

OASIS. (2013). *Standards.* Retrieved from https://www.oasis-open.org/standards#samlv2.0

OMG. (2013). *MOF 2 XMI mapping.* Retrieved February 25, 2013, http://www.omg.org/spec/XMI/

OpenLink Software. (2013). *Virtuoso universal server.* Retrieved from http://virtuoso.openlinksw.com/

OpenText. (2013). *OpenText business process management.* Retrieved February 25, 2013, from http://bps.opentext.com/bpm-and-case-basics/

OWL-S. (2004). *OWL-S: Semantic markup for web service.* Retrieved February 25, 2013, from http://www.w3.org/Submission/OWL-S/

Pfeffer, J., Graube, M., Ziegler, J., & Urbas, L. (2012). Browsing reversible neighborhood relations in linked data on mobile devices. In *Proceedings of 2nd International Conference on Pervasive Embedded Computing and Communication Systems* (PECCS). PECCS.

RDF Working Group. (2004). *Resource description framework (RDF).* Retrieved from http://www.w3.org/RDF/

Sacco, O., & Passant, A. (2011). A privacy preference ontology (PPO) for linked data. In *Proceedings of the 4th Workshop about Linked Data on the Web (LDOW-2011).* LDOW.

Shen, H., & Cheng, Y. (2001). A semantic context-based model for mobile web services access control. *International Journal on Computer Network and Information Security.*

Simon, K. (2010). *SIPOC diagram.* Retrieved February 25, 2013, from http://www.isixsigma.com/tools-templates/sipoc-copis/sipoc-diagram

Stanford Center for Biomedical Informatics Research. (2013). *Protege.* Retrieved from http://protege.stanford.edu/

SUPER. (2012). *Integrated project SUPER.* Retrieved February 25, 2013, from http://www.ip-super.org/

Supply Chain Council. (2013). *Supply chain operations reference*. Retrieved February 25, 2013, from http://supply-chain.org/scor

Toninelli, A., Montanari, R., Kagal, L., & Lassi, O. (2006). A semantic context-aware access control framework for secure collaborations in pervasive computing environments. In *Proceedings of the 5th Int. Semantic Web Conf. (ISWC-2006)* (LNCS), (vol. 4273, pp. 473-486). Berlin: Springer.

Urbas, L., Pfeffer, J., & Ziegler, J. (2011). iLDapps: Usable mobile access to linked data clouds at the shop floor. In *Proceedings of Workshop on Visual Interfaces to the Social and the Semantic Web* (VISSW). VISSW.

Uschold, M., & King, M. (1995). Towards a methodology for building ontologies. In *Proceedings of Workshop on Basic Ontological Issues in Knowledge Sharing, held in conjunction with IJCAI-95*. IJCAI.

W3C. (2013). *SPARQL 1.1 query language*. Retrieved February 25, 2013, from http://www.w3.org/TR/sparql11-query/

XPDL. (2013). *XML process definition language*. Retrieved February 25, 2013, http://www.xpdl.org/

Ziegler, J., Graube, M., Pfeffer, J., & Urbas, L. (2012). Beyond app-chaining: Mobile app. orchestration for efficient model driven software generation. In *Proceedings of 17th International IEEE Conference on Emerging Technologies & Factory Automation* (ETFA). IEEE.

## ADDITIONAL READING

Allemang, D. (2010). Semantic Web and the Linked Data Enterprise. In D. Wood (Ed.), *Linking enterprise data* (pp. 3–23). New York, NY, USA & Heidelberg, Germany: Springer. doi:10.1007/978-1-4419-7665-9_1

Bizer, C., Heath, T., & Berners-Lee, T. (2009). Linked Data - The Story So Far. In T. Heath, M. Hepp, & C. Bizer, (Eds.) International Journal on Semantic Web and Information Systems (IJSWIS), Vol. 5(3) (pp. 1–22).

Breslin, J. G., Harth, A., Bojārs, U., & Decker, S. (2004). Towards Semantically-Interlinked Online Communities. In *The 2nd European Semantic Web Conference (ESWC '05)*. LNCS 3532 (pp. 500–514).

Dumas, M., Recker, J., & Weske, M. (2012). Management and engineering of process-aware information systems. *Information Systems*, *37*(2), 77–79. doi:10.1016/j.is.2011.09.003

Erl, T. (2005). *Service-Oriented Architecture: Concepts, Technology, and Design*. Upper Saddle River, NJ, USA: Prentice Hall PTR.

Fill, H.-G., Redmond, T., & Karagiannis, D. (2012), FDMM: A Formalism for Describing ADOxx Meta Models and Models. In Maciaszek, L. A., Cuzzocrea, A., Cordeiro, J. (eds.) *Proceedings of ICEIS* (pp. 133-144), SciTePress.

Gašević, D., Kaviani, N., & Hatala, M. (2007), On metamodeling in megamodels, Engels G. (Ed.), *Proceedings of MoDELS 2007*, LNCS 4735 (pp. 91–105), Springer-Verlag, Berlin

Graube, M., Pfeffer, J., Ziegler, J., & Urbas, L. (2012). Linked Data as Integrating Technology for Industrial Data. [IJDST]. *International Journal of Distributed Systems and Technologies*, *3*(3), 40–52. doi:10.4018/jdst.2012070104

Guizzardi, G. (2005). *Ontological Foundations for Structural Conceptual Models*. Enschede, The Netherlands.

Henderson-Sellers, B. (2011). Bridging metamodels and ontologies in software engineering. *Journal of Systems and Software*, *84*(2), 301–313. doi:10.1016/j.jss.2010.10.025

Hepp, M., Leymann, F., Domingue, J., Wahler, A., & Fensel, D. (2005). Semantic business process management: a vision towards using semantic Web services for business process management. In *IEEE International Conference on e-Business Engineering* (pp. 535–540).

Hyland, B. (2010). Preparing for a Linked Data Enterprise. In D. Wood (Ed.), *Linking Enterprise Data* (pp. 51–64). Springer, US. doi:10.1007/978-1-4419-7665-9_3

Junginger, S., Kühn, H., Strobl, R., & Karagiannis, D. (2000). Ein Geschäftsprozessmanagement-Werkzeug der nächsten Generation - ADONIS: Konzeption und Anwendungen. [in German]. *Wirtschaftsinformatik, 42*(5), 392–401. doi:10.1007/BF03250755

Karagiannis, D., Grossmann, W., & Höfferer, P. (2008), Open Model Initiative – A Feasibility Study, ISBN 978-3-902826-00-8, Retrieved February 25, 2013, from http://cms.dke.univie.ac.at/uploads/media/Open_Models_Feasibility_Study_SEPT_2008.pdf.

Karagiannis, D., & Höfferer, P. (2006). Metamodels in Action: An Overview. In J. Filipe, B. Shishkov, M. Helfert (eds.), *ICSOFT 2006 - First International Conference on Software and Data Technologies*. IS-27 - IS-36, Insticc Press.

Katasonov, A., & Palviainen, M. (2010). Towards ontology-driven development of applications for smart environments. In *Proceedings of the 8th IEEE International Conference on Pervasive Computing and Communications (PERCOM Workshops)* (pp. 696-701).

Knublauch, H. (2004). Ontology-driven software development in the context of the semantic web: An example scenario with Protegé/OWL. *In 1st International Workshop on the Model-Driven Semantic Web (MDSW2004)*.

Mehandjiev, N., & Grefen, P. (Eds.). (2010). *Dynamic Business Process Formation for Instant Virtual Enterprises*. Berlin: Springer. doi:10.1007/978-1-84882-691-5

Milanovic, N., Cartsburg, M., Kutsche, R., Widiker, J., & Kschonsak, F. (2009). Model-Based Interoperability of Heterogeneous Information Systems: An Industrial Case Study. In R. F. Paige, A. Hartman, & A. Rensink (Eds.), *Model Driven Architecture - Foundations and Applications* (Vol. 5562, p. 325). Berlin, Heidelberg: Springer Berlin Heidelberg. doi:10.1007/978-3-642-02674-4_24

OASIS XACML v3 (2013). eXtensible Access Control Markup Language (XACML) Version 3.0. Retrieved from http://docs.oasis-open.org/xacml/3.0/xacml-3.0-core-spec-cs-01-en.pdf

Pousttchi, K., & Thurnher, B. (2007). Adoption and Impact of Mobile-Integrated Business Processes - Comparison of Existing Frameworks and Analysis of their Generalization Potential. 8. Internationale Tagung Wirtschaftsinformatik 2007 - Band 1 (pp. 273-290).

Schenker, J. L. (2010). *Cloud Services Hasten The Rise of The Virtual Company*. Retrieved from http://www.informilo.com/20100312/cloud-services-hasten-rise-virtual-company-257

Studer, R., Benjamins, R., & Fensel, D. (1998). Knowledge engineering: Principles and methods. *Data & Knowledge Engineering, 25*(1–2), 161–198. doi:10.1016/S0169-023X(97)00056-6

Thompson, K. (2008). *The Networked Enterprise. Competing for the Future Through Virtual Enterprise Networks*. Tampa, FL, USA: Meghan Kiffer.

van Heck, E., & Vervest, P. (2007). Smart business networks: how the network wins. [ACM.]. *Communications of the ACM, 50*, 28–37. doi:10.1145/1247001.1247002

Ventures, A. K. (2008). *Collaboration across borders.* Retrieved from http://www.corp.att.com/emea/docs/s5_collaboration_eng.pdf

Verclas, S., & Linnhoff-Popien, C. (2012). *Smart Mobile Apps.* Springer. doi:10.1007/978-3-642-22259-7

## KEY TERMS AND DEFINITIONS

**App:** Informal computing abbreviation for application program. Today, it mainly refers to a single or limited purpose mobile application, often product, service or task-specific, which can be deployed and executed on the target architecture on its own right.

**App Orchestration:** The process of selecting, adapting and managing a set of instances of generic apps to implement complex workflows. The result of App Orchestration is an Orchestrated App Ensemble.

**Linked Data:** Describes a recommended best practice for exposing, sharing, and connecting pieces of data, information, and knowledge on the Semantic Web using URIs and RDF.

**Modelling Method:** A knowledge structure describing how to model a domain, comprising a modelling language, functionality to use and evaluate models and a procedural way of modelling.

**Modelling Procedure:** The series of steps describing "how to model," driven towards the goals of the modeller.

**Multi-Domain Access Control:** Information access control method devised for federated trust relationship enforcement.

**Ontology:** A formal, explicit specification of a shared conceptualisation. In RDF ontologies contain information about classes and properties. RDF ontologies describe how these concepts have to be used for modelling individuals.

**RDF Graph Store Access Control:** Information access control method addressing Linked Data store needs.

**Virtual Enterprise:** Coordinated actions of multiple companies to take advantage of a market opportunity (e.g. produce special goods in a cross company production chain).

# Chapter 8
# Interoperable Process Engineering System for Collaborative Optimization of Product Life–Cycle

**Alberto Armijo**
*TECNALIA R&I, Spain*

**Mikel Sorli**
*TECNALIA R&I, Spain*

## ABSTRACT

*Most of the industrial organizations, including SMEs, need to quickly react and adapt to the changing market conditions imposed by globalization, such as new sustainability directives or new type of customers. The fulfillment of these requirements on time is a must so as to remain competitive in the global markets. Since data management information systems are already present in almost all the corpus of industrial enterprises as custom developments or standard PLM solutions, the natural technical evolution that aims to provide an effective answer to these changing market conditions comprises the shifting from a data management perspective towards a process management view. Hence, the challenge is how to manage business processes that build upon existing information systems so as to encourage business agility, efficiency, and interoperability. The proposed approach roots on the Business Process Management (BPM) discipline and leverages process optimization through the systematic modeling and reengineering of business processes accompanied by supporting interoperable and configurable eco-services, which are conceived as sustainability-aware services designed to optimize some aspects of the product life-cycle through eco-constraints management.*

DOI: 10.4018/978-1-4666-5142-5.ch008

## INTRODUCTION

Thirty years ago, organizations' main goal focused on managing their business data, the "what," with the help of informatics systems, which were conceived following a Structured Analysis (Senn, 1992) approach. The use of tools such as data flows, data models, structure charts and state models was considered appropriate enough to document and develop those monolithic systems integrated with normalized databases. As a result, the business logic of those IT systems was centered in data management.

Nowadays, data and functions that manage data are still equally important, but the focus is more centered on how to work more efficiently with data through process management. The main difference with respect to the previous scenario resides in the fact that information systems are already present in almost all the corpus of organizations as custom developments or standard software solutions. This technical capability allows an evolutionary shift of paradigm in the sense that organizations are able to react to the continuous market changes imposed by globalization, such as new types of customers or incoming sustainability regulations. The challenge is how to evolve from the "what" or data perspective to the "how" perspective more focused on processes, that is to say, how to manage business processes that build upon existing data management so as to leverage interoperability among processes. In this regard, Business Process Management (BPM) (ABPM, 2009) is a "disciplined approach to identify, design, execute, document, measure, monitor, and control both automated and non-automated business processes to achieve consistent, targeted results aligned with an organization's strategic goals. BPM involves the deliberate, collaborative and increasingly technology-aided definition, improvement, innovation, and management of end-to-end business processes that drive business results, create value, and enable an organization to meet its business objectives with more agility."

Consequently, BPM is regarded as a discipline that allows the integration of manual processes with automated processes that involve the support of IT. It leads to the overall efficacy through the definition of control flows that enable the orchestration and choreography of the modeled processes that take place either within a specific area in an organization, across different areas or even between organizations, such as suppliers' and customers' processes.

The BPM discipline roots on three major business process traditions (Harmon, 2010) i.e. the Quality Control tradition, the Business Management tradition and the Information Technologies (IT) tradition. The *Quality Control tradition*, whose practitioners have been engineers and quality control specialists, focuses on the continuous improvement of the isolated productive process by means of process analysis, measurements and statistical quality control techniques application. This tradition was reinforced with quality control and quality assurance methodologies such as Total Quality Management (TQM), Lean and Six Sigma. On the other hand, the *Business Management tradition* extends the Quality Control tradition and incorporates business people's (executives) worries about the improvement of the whole operation of the companies, in addition to the traditional economic and financial concerns. Thus, not only the productive processes are taken into account, but also the supporting processes, including those involving clients' satisfaction. The main emphasis is on aligning the processes of the company with the business strategy by means of the implementation of the company operations under a process perspective that enables the measurement of process performance towards a continuous improvement. In this sense, the Balanced Scorecard methodology provides a systematic so as to determine if the modeled and implemented operations are aligned towards the business strategy. In order to identify and model enterprise operations, several Business Process Frameworks (also called Operation Reference

Frameworks) were developed during the last decade. Examples of these frameworks include the Supply Chain Operations Reference (SCOR) and the more comprehensive Value Reference Model (VRM) that covers the wider scope of the value chain (COMVANTAGE, 2013). SCOR framework provides a structured and quick way to establish a high level process architecture comprising production and supporting processes. It is built around two basic sets; a standard visual library for modeling operations under a processes view, which allows companies to set-up environments for leveraging collaboration and process alignment, and a standardized set of semantically defined metrics that allows executives to quantify and benchmark processes and drive business strategies. The visual library is comprised of a three level structure for describing supply chain processes in more detail. Each level 1 element is decomposable in level 2 subsets and each subset is, in turn, decomposable in level 3 subsets. Each of the elements of level 3 can be treated as a sub-process further detailed in a level 4, which is not described by the SCOR standard. Level 4, visualization, is company specific and can be modeled by any modeling language that has enough expressivity, such as BPMN, UML, IDEF or EPC. The use of process frameworks were driven initially by the growing interdependency of company supply chains and by the need of a taxonomy that enables the communication among company processes to easily react to rapid market changes. To finish with, the *IT tradition* involves the use of computers and Internet technologies as communication media that facilitates radically new business models on the way to automate work processes. Business people have realized during the last decade that IT is no longer a support service but a fundamental service in the strategy of the company that help implement business processes. IT managers, in turn, have decided to stop focusing on IT as a peripheral supporting service and to concentrate on how IT can help implement business processes. As a result of this IT-Business alignment, software tools that

traditionally were described as workflow tools (that help automate document driven processes), Business Intelligence (BI) tools, Rules Engines, Expert Systems, Enterprise Resource Planning (ERP) or Enterprise Application Integration (EAI) tools are now evolving towards the Business Process Management Systems (BPMS) concept. A BPMS not only should enable the description and execution of a process involving human interaction, but also should go far beyond. It should allow the management of these processes, such as the description of the interconnections of processes including outputs and inputs, the elaboration and tracking of strategic and process metrics including current and targeted values (BI), the management of data elements created by the processes, the choreography with external processes, the management of roles and actors associated with the processes, the connection with IT systems through integration frameworks (EAI), the framing of the processes within collaborative spaces or projects and the provision of shared semantics to promote interoperability among organizations.

The approach presented in this chapter contributes to the *IT tradition* towards the conceptualization of a methodology that facilitates the technical implementation of the business processes modeled as a result of the application of a Business Process Framework, such as SCOR or VRM. The approach incorporates the modeling of business processes with the support of the BPMN 2.0 standard, the modeling of simulation and optimization capabilities that build up interoperable eco-services that can be leveraged by the business processes instances, and Sustainability Intelligence concepts, as an extension to Business Intelligence. The scientific area targeted by the approach is Process Interoperability, as identified in the EISB State of the Play Report produced by ENSEMBLE project (ENSEMBLE, 2012). Since interoperability requires an alignment of inter-organizational processes, the elaboration of a systematic approach for modeling and re-engineering business processes is expected to leverage interoperability. Consequently, the main objective is to introduce a holistic BPM method for supporting the systematic design, process modeling, collaborative execution, monitoring and optimization and reengineering of business processes accompanied by the application of portable eco-services that integrate simulation and optimization software services, enabling a foundation for interoperability among business processes deployed within the Virtual Factory.

## BACKGROUND

During the years, many enterprise modeling techniques, which support the technical implementation of models derived from Business Process Frameworks, have been developed and evolved. These, can be formally grouped into two classifications; techniques based on *scripting languages* and techniques based on *diagramming techniques*. The former techniques are very close to programming languages (for instance BPEL) and contain very precise syntax. However, since their visual expressivity is very low, the involvement of business users would be cumbersome. The latter techniques, those based on diagramming, open the possibility of involving actors with different backgrounds (either business users or technical users) in the enterprise modeling process. Methodologies based on diagramming techniques can be classified in data flow, control flow and object oriented techniques (Gadatsch, 2010). The use of data flow techniques, such as Structured Analysis, is decreasing in favor to UML diagramming (object oriented techniques). A survey realized by Gadatsch (Gadatsch, 2010) in 2007 to big organizations lead to the conclusion that the Event Driven Process Chain (EPC) technique (control flow), Swimlane Diagram (control flow) and UML (object oriented) were the most used for process modeling.

The Event Driven Process Chain (EPC) notation achieved a great diffusion during the Nineties

and became an industrial standard in German countries. Until the year 2008, EPC was the most popular process modeling notation. However, the introduction of the BPMN standard (control flow technique) turned the balance in favor of this notation.

According to the Object Management Group (OMG) (OMG, 2011) definition, "BPMN provides businesses with the capability of understanding their internal business procedures in a graphical notation and will give organizations the ability to communicate these procedures in a standard manner." Furthermore, the graphical notation will facilitate the understanding of the performance collaborations and business transactions between the organizations. This will ensure that businesses will understand themselves and participants in their business and will enable organizations to adjust to new internal and B2B business circumstances quickly.

Recent interviews in the BPM community (Freund, 2011) show a huge growing towards BPMN adoption along with a reduction of the employment of other mainstream modeling techniques. The main reason for this shift of paradigm lies on the fact that the BPMN, standardized by the OMG, became an official industry standard for modeling business processes and, the new version 2.0 contains also a metamodel for interchanging models between different modeling tools and a metamodel for execution of the process models directly by a Process Engine. While BPMN 1.x enabled the process analyst to model a business process, the process engineer had to convert the model into an executable business process with an execution language, such as BPEL, in order to execute it in a Process Engine. The BPMN 2.0 extends this scope formalizing the execution semantics for all the BPMN constructs and enabling the portability of process definitions between different vendors' environments. Consequently, BPMN 2.0 enables business oriented individuals and IT developers talk each other with the same vocabulary and share the business models, even between organizations, without the need for conversion, bridging the gap between business and IT layers, and leveraging round-trip-engineering.

## BUSINESS PROCESS MANAGEMENT

Ideally and as a precondition to effectively adopt the BPM approach, the organizational structure should be oriented to processes and functional areas so as to streamline the future assignation of manual tasks to the involved actors. This involves the promotion by the senior management of a corporate cultural change through leadership and a consistent process management policy in line with the corporate vision. This cultural adaptation includes the establishment of a breeding environment, where knowledge sharing and, therefore, collaboration is promoted and compensated. In this sense, well defined roles should be created to support the introduction of the new approach. Furthermore, organizations collaborating in a Virtual Factory environment have to be aware that they are sharing data, documents, information and knowledge outside the boundaries of their enterprises and this knowledge may be protected under Intellectual Property Rights (IPR).

The actors participating in the process oriented management are the process owner, the process manager, the process participant, the process analyst and the process engineer. These roles span from the business oriented to the most IT oriented role. The process owner is responsible for defining the process strategy under the business perspective, aligning it with the organization's strategic targets. In the majority of organizations, the process owner belongs to the management board or is in charge of a business line or area. The process manager is the one that reports directly to the process owner and is responsible for introducing process improvements at descriptive level. A process participant is a business user, who operates in the process, that is to say, is the user of a functional area, such

as the sales department, finances, engineering or manufacturing area. Referring to the process analyst, the duties expected are knowledge in Business Process Management in general, and specifically, knowledge in the BPMN 2.0 model and notation. The analyst supports the process manager as an internal or external assessor and can be a member of the process area of the organization or belong to the informatics area. Rarely, the process analyst is in charge of the technical implementation of the processes, despite of the IT skills the analyst may have. Extensive knowledge about the BPMN 2.0 notation is expected and is considered a key role, since acts as a coordinator between business and IT people. To finish with, the process engineer develops and implements the technical model starting from the specification and the operational design validated by the process analyst.

When it comes to design, document, execute, measure, monitor, and control both automated or a non-automated business process, a number of systematic steps have to be performed around a continuous improvement BPM cycle, that is to say, design, modeling, execution, monitoring and optimization steps. Throughout the execution of these iterative steps, a BPMN 2.0 structural framework (Freund, 2011) is applied in order to model a business process and implement a business execution model following the BPMN 2.0 standard. This modeling framework comprises three levels, a descriptive level, an operative level and a technical level, being the first two businesses oriented and the third one technically oriented. The ultimate aim of this framework is to systematically help practitioners close the gap between business and IT worlds and leverage the automation of business processes and interoperability capabilities. The next epigraphs will introduce the reader the systematic to apply the *BPMN 2.0 structural framework* by means of iterating through the five steps that embrace the continuous improvement BPM cycle, as described in Figure 1. For each of the steps, a mapping to the relevant level of the structural framework

*Figure 1. Interoperability interaction models and applicable BPM steps*

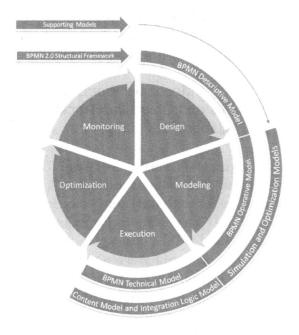

will be done. In addition to the business process model, supporting interaction models are built, such as the augmented simulation and workflow optimization models, the integration logic model and the content model. These *supporting models*, contributed by this chapter as an extension to the structural framework, provide a systematic to build eco-services, which can be leveraged by the business model instances. These eco-services, which are influenced by external requirements derived from sustainability intelligence networks, are considered sustainability aware, since they are based on simulation models augmented with social and environmental metrics and provide the business process with sustainability assessment capabilities.

## Design

The continuous improvement BPM cycle starts with the design step, which comprises the next tasks.

## Creation of a Virtual Factory Infrastructure

An important precondition that a BPM approach will require for its successful and effective application is the establishment of a Virtual Breeding Environment (VBE) (Camarinha-Matos, 2008) or a Virtual Factory infrastructure, which enables the distribution of the process participants into collaborative networks. The aim of these networks is to achieve business goals through the capturing, sharing and reusing of the generated knowledge by means of the collaborative execution of the modeled business processes. This infrastructure can be conceived as a collaborative Enterprise Content Management (ECM) system that provides document and Web content management, human to human tacit interaction for sharing content, and workflow execution capabilities, which may involve content transformation.

The collaborative network may contain process participants that belong to a single organization or participants that belong to several organizations. In this latter case, the business process may involve the exchange of data between two or more processes, for instance, the collaboration between a provider and a client. In this regard, the BPMN 2.0 specification extends the capability of the BPMN 1.2 specification with the definition of a choreography model that leverages collaboration and interoperability among different organizations, and with the capability of exchanging the same modeling notation, which is directly executable by different vendors' environments compliant with BPMN 2.0. Thus, the collaboration capability facilitated by the standard along with the Virtual Factory infrastructure that supports the business process automation, promote process interoperability, referred as the "ability of interconnecting heterogeneous services towards the formation of cross organization joint collaborative processes" (ENSEMBLE, 2012, p. 61).

## Creation of a Mechanism for Business Optimization Opportunities Tracking (BOOT) in the Business Community

The main network derived from the Virtual Factory infrastructure is conceived as a Business Community, which involves and contains the organizations within the Virtual Factory domain, such as users, suppliers, clients, governmental agencies and RTD partners. Based on the tracking and identification of business optimization opportunities within the Business Community, the infrastructure enables the creation of new organizational alliances, so-called Collaborative Spaces, inside the Business Community, focused on answering the identified opportunities. The process of surveillance and identification of these optimization opportunities involves the application of data mining and social network analysis techniques upon the content allocated in the Virtual Factory, upon the tacit knowledge generated interactively by the users and with the support of external sustainability intelligence sources.

A Virtual Collaborative Network (VCN) or a Collaborative Space represents a specific temporary goal-oriented network aimed at the optimization and improvement of key business processes. The managers of these networks are able to enroll stakeholders, who can contribute with their insight to the optimization. Reciprocally, stakeholders interested in participating in a network are able to request to join it. These temporal alliances involve collaboration processes, rather than the cooperation processes found at the Business Community level.

This establishment mechanism can be observed as an enabler of a knowledge based heterarchical fishnet structure (Schatten, 2007), where Collaborative Spaces, symbolized as lifted nodes in the fishnet, are observed as dynamically created ad-hoc hierarchies anchored in the responded business optimization opportunities. The aim of the Collaborative Spaces is to jointly develop the optimization opportunities by means of the automation of related key business processes through the application of the five steps that comprise the BPM continuous improvement cycle.

## Creation of a Mechanism for Eco-Constraints and Objectives Tracking in the Collaborative Spaces

With the support of collaborative Web 2.0 capabilities, open data and sustainability intelligence sources tracking, and content management features of the Virtual Factory infrastructure, stakeholders who are linked to the Collaborative Spaces are able to track and investigate eco-constraints and objectives that influence a particular business process. The process of automated identification of these requirements may involve the application of text mining and social network analysis techniques such as n-grams and word frequency calculation, high-confidence association rules recognition, similarity between documents calculation, clustering or classification of documents into classes and discovery of with words/terms are relevant for the identification and processing of eco-constraints. These analytic techniques allow process managers to gather and classify sustainability directives, local regulations or sectorial recommendations in order to process and encode them into eco-constraints and objectives readable by people and computers. These constraints and objectives are the basis for the identification and tracking of sustainability KPIs involving profit, environmental and social measurements. In addition, they can be regarded as elements aimed at shaping the business process towards more sustainable practices as described in the Modeling step. Business Process compliance levels will be finally evaluated by the continuous monitoring of these KPIs within the Monitoring step.

## High Level Description of the Business Model (BPMN 2.0 Descriptive Model)

During this task, the activities that comprise a business process are drafted. This means that the high level activities are identified, possible organizational changes are discussed, service level agreements are defined and process details such as actors, notifications and escalations are specified. This task of the design stage is intended to complete the descriptive level of the BPMN 2.0 structural framework, where the process is described and documented at high level by the process owner and the process manager. Thus, this descriptive level defines the context of the process that will eventually be designed, documented, modeled, implemented and redesigned based on sustainability constraints and objectives. One of the aims in this level is the definition of the scope and the main functionality of the process that is going to be automated under the BPM approach. In order to do so, the normal flow of the high level process is defined with a simple palette of BPMN constructs, without taking into account process exceptions or errors. The main objectives related to this first level of the structural framework are:

- Definition of the process scope, in the sense of delimiting clear from/to boundaries.
- Assignment of process responsibilities and resources.
- Extraction of initial eco-constraints and objectives that the process must fulfill.
- Based on these constraints, identification of associated sustainability KPIs involving performance, social and environmental measurements. The monitoring of the sustainability KPIs will help process manager assess the compliance of the process with respect to eco-constraints and objectives that come from external sustainability intelligence networks.

During the descriptive level, the BPMN 2.0 syntax should be strictly maintained, while small execution semantic inconsistencies may be allowed. These business logic inconsistencies will be corrected by the process analyst during the next stage.

## Modeling

The modeling step involves the elaboration of several models that will enable the automation and leverage the interoperability of the key business process at issue, aiming at theoretically fulfilling the eco-constraints and objectives identified in the design step and during the Monitoring step. On the one hand, the business process model (described in BPMN notation) is promoted to the operative level and, on the other hand, simulation and optimization models are built and published as Web services so as to support the business process.

## Augmented Simulation Model and Optimization Workflow Model

The enhancement of the design of a business process comprises the simulation of certain activities, mostly related to the productive process, such as the design of a new plant layout, the scheduling of a manufacturing plant or the planning of maintenance activities. Most of the business processes depend on decision making tasks with respect to the selection of the best alternative among several ones. The simulation model helps process participants assess sustainability to-be indicators (KPIs) that theoretically satisfy the process requirements with respect to the fulfilment of eco-constraints and objectives. Accordingly, the process analyst, supported by simulation experts, creates a simulation model and its associated execution framework, involving Discrete Event Simulation techniques or other Operational Research methods. This simulation model is augmented with sustainability metrics assessment capabilities, such as the evaluation of environmental and social metrics, i.e. energy consumption and carbon footprint, in addition to the assessment of traditional performance based metrics, i.e. utilization of resources or manufacturing rate.

The augmented simulation model is handled by the optimization workflow model, which implements Multi Objective Optimization capability. This model allows performing an automated batch of simulations under controlled conditions driven by an optimization algorithm. This algorithm performs a search in the configuration space guided by the performance on analysed points. Performance is defined through the so-called objective functions, which corresponds to sustainability indicators derived from objectives. A single function resulting from the aggregation of sustainability indicators can be used as the objective function, producing a single solution as outcome of the optimization. However, to consider all sustainability indicators as independent objectives is preferred in order to perform a better exploration of the search space. In this case, the outcome of the optimization is not a single solution, but a set of trade-off configurations, where no sustainability indicator can be enhanced without a deterioration of at least one of the others (the so-called Pareto Front). The optimization can also be influenced by sustainability eco-constraints, which are considered by the algorithm in order to reduce the search space by considering only feasible configurations.

The process analyst can define an optimization session by specifying the process configuration parameters, sustainability objectives and sustainability eco-constraints, and by selecting a design of experiments strategy and the optimization algorithm. Other elements, like robust sampling or response surface models, which are in many cases required in industrial applications, can also be considered. The aim of a design of experiments is to test specific configurations regardless the sustainability objectives of the optimization run, but rather considering their pattern in the configurations space. It provides an a-priori exploration and analysis, which is of primary importance when a rigorous statistical analysis through Business Intelligence tools has to be performed later on. The optimization algorithm implements the mathematical strategies, or heuristics, which are designed to obtain a good approximation of the actual Pareto front.

These augmented simulation and optimization models are eventually wrapped-up as an optimization service and published as a Web Service by the process engineer. The optimization service can be conceived as a network level capability promoted from the traditionally confined desktop perspective that can be remotely leveraged from the process business layer. The optimization service focuses on complying with external sustainability requirements dictated by local regulations, sectorial recommendations or business intelligence networks via the augmentation of the integrating models with sustainability indicators.

In order to support the elaboration of optimization services, the next state of the art methods regarding Simulation, Multi Objective Optimization and Decision Making can be leveraged:

### Simulation

According to Banks, "Simulation is the imitation of the operation of a real-world process or system over time. Simulation involves the generation of an artificial history of the system, and the observation of that artificial history to draw inferences concerning the operating characteristics of the real system that is represented" (Banks, 1996).

Modelling and simulation are considered efficient tools for continuous improvements (e.g. TOC). Although simulation as a service is not yet a common practice, first commercial tools are already on the mainstream market as shown here. Sustainability aspects and data can be integrated to the simulation analysis in order to augment the simulation models with sustainability assessment capabilities. Web-based simulation is one relatively new concept that has evolved in the new Web era. The appearance of the network-oriented programming language, e.g. Java and of distributed object technologies has had major effects on the state of simulation practice. These technologies have the potential to significantly alter the way we think of, develop, and apply simulation as a problem solving technique and a decision support tool.

Three approaches for Web-based simulation have been identified in the literature already in 1998 (Whitman, 1998):

- Server-hosted simulation allows existing simulation tools to be hosted on a Web server and accessed by clients via normal HTML pages. This approach has the advantage of using a familiar tool and enables the reuse of existing models. The disadvantage is that the communication power provided by animation in these tools is not visible over the Web.
- Client-side simulation allows simulation tools to use an applets-based approach that minimizes the learning curve, but on the expense of power and flexibility. The performance of this type of simulation is also limited by the client machine capabilities. Java is an example of programming languages that may be used to develop simulation applications that may be executed on the client machine.
- Hybrid client/server simulation attempts to combine the advantages of server hosted and client executed simulations. The approach relies on hosting the simulation engine on the server and using Java for visualization of the animation to provide a dynamic view on the client machine.

Current developments in ICT and Web technologies (e.g. HTML5) provide enhanced communication performance, and some of disadvantages reported in 1998 are not valid anymore. Until recently, the technologies used in Modeling & Simulation (M&S) have remained stubbornly non-Web-based. Nowadays, most major M&S tools, or Commercial-off-the-shelf (COTS) Simulation Packages, such as AnyLogic and Simul8, have Web-based aspects. However, these have aspects more commonly associated with Groupware and certainly do not seek to take advantage of model/component discovery, composition, interoperability and reuse (Taylor, 2011).

Integration of sustainability and environmental aspects to simulations is one of the on-going development efforts in many research institutes. VTT development in the SIMTER project (Lind, 2009), was made using Visual Components 3DCreate DES software and EU LCA platform database. Other similar efforts based on use of commercial software e.g. Anylogic, Arena, AutoMod and so on exist. Some of the development is based on research institutes' own simulation software. Commercial tools are also entering the market. Simul8, for example, includes a carbon monitoring option and the WITNESS simulation tool from Lanner includes a module for energy optimization. NIST (National Institute of Standards and Technology) has used also system dynamics for sustainability modeling (Jain & Kibira, 2010).

## Multi Objective Optimization

It is important to stress that real-world optimization problem are solved through rigorously proven converging methodologies only in very few cases, since the high number of input parameters and the low smoothness of objective functions involved limit the possible usage of classical mathematical algorithms. Optimization Algorithms implement the mathematical strategies, or heuristics, which are designed to obtain a good approximation of the actual Pareto front.

A Design of Experiments (DoE) session usually precedes the optimization stage (Santner, 2003). The aim of a DoE is to test specific configurations regardless the objectives of the optimization run, but rather considering their pattern in the input parameters space. It provides an a-priori exploration and analysis which is of primary importance when a statistical analysis has to be performed. For example, a reduced factorial DoE can be the basis for a principal components analysis, since it avoids correlations among input parameters and therefore highlights input-output relationships. Moreover, almost all optimization algorithms require a starting population of designs to be considered first and the DoE can provide it, eventually generating random input values if no other preference has emerged yet.

The most widely used Multi Objective Optimization methods can be classified in the following groups.

## Traditional Multi Objective Optimization

Traditional optimization methods follow the gradient information (direction of improvement) in order to achieve a fast and accurate convergence towards the optimal solution. Well-established mathematical bases guarantee their efficiency. These algorithms need some computational efforts for calculating derivatives, unless their analytical formulation is given, but as a benefit, it can reach quadratic local convergence rate. The most used general-purpose tool for solving smooth nonlinear optimization problems is Sequential Quadratic Programming (SQP) (Fletcher, 2006). Within a SQP method, the original optimization problem is iteratively solved by approximating it with a suitable quadratic model. The crucial element is gradient computation, since the effort paid for the approximation is rewarded by a super-linear convergence rate (under standard hypothesis).

## Evolutionary Multi Objective Optimization

Evolutionary Algorithms (EA) were introduced to solve technical optimization problems where no analytical objective functions are usually available (Deb, 2001; Branke, 2008). EA has been success-

fully applied in many different fields, making EA recommended for scalable to high-dimensional optimization problems and particularly well-suited for evolutionary improvement of designs. EA may be used for continuous, discrete and binary variables, and even when a large number of constraints are present. The advantages are that EA always converge to a good enough solution in successive, self-contained stages, which are cut for parallelization and that no gradients are necessary guarantying robustness against noisy objective functions.

The most famous and important techniques are Genetic Algorithms (GA) and Evolution Strategies (ES). The backbone of GA is based on the following scheme: a parent population produces through appropriate genetic operators a child population; a new parent population is selected among children and/or parents, depending on the chosen elitism procedure and the loop is iterated. ES are optimization technique based on ideas of adaptation and evolution. In this sense ES are similar to GA, but on ES, the main search procedure is a smart mutation operator.

## Synthetic Models-Based Multi Objective Optimization

In real case applications, the simulation is usually computationally expensive since every single simulation can take hours or even days. Therefore multi objective optimization algorithms are required to face the demanding issue of finding a satisfactory set of optimal solutions within a reduced number of evaluations. Response Surface Models (RSM), also known as meta-models, can help in tackling this situation by speeding up the optimization process. Previously evaluated designs can be used as a training set for building surrogate models, allowing a subsequent inexpensive virtual optimization to be performed over these meta-models of the original problem. Clearly the candidate solutions found in this way need to be validated, i.e., evaluated by means of the real solver (validation process). This process can be iterated in an automatic way. At each iteration, the newly evaluated designs enrich the training database permitting more and more accurate meta-models to be built in an adaptive way. The virtual optimization, which represents an exploitation process, should be accompanied by a virtual run of a suited space-filler algorithm for exploration purposes, increasing the robustness of the optimizers.

## Decision Making

Ranking between alternatives is a common and difficult task especially when several solutions are available or when many objective or decision makers are involved. The decision makers choose one reasonable alternative from among a limited set of available solutions; design decisions usually reflect the competencies of each decision maker. When more than one decision attribute exists, making coherent choices can be a very difficult task. The following Decision Making methods represent the state of the art.

### Multivariate Analysis (MvA)

Multivariate Analysis (MvA) refers to any statistical techniques used to analyze and visualize data arising from many variables. MvA essentially models a reality, where each situation, product or decision, involves more than one variable. Many techniques do exist for MvA. For example, Self-Organizing Maps (SOM) can be used to establish and visualize the correlation between inputs and outputs (Kohonen, 1982).

### Principal Component Analysis (PCA)

Principal Component Analysis (PCA) computes the most meaningful basis to re-express a noisy data set by reducing the dimensionality of variables. Multi-Dimensional Scaling (MDS) produce a low-dimensional coordinate representation of multivariate datasets preserving, as much as possible, the inter point distances of the input data (Cox & Cox, 2003).

### Cluster Analysis

Cluster Analysis tries to identify homogeneous subgroups of samples in a data set such that they both minimize within-group variation and maximize between-group variation (Jain, 1999). Several approaches to cluster analysis can be found in literature, which mainly differ in their concept of cluster and how efficiently they are found. Different concepts exist to merge pairs of clusters at each step, each of which will result in different cluster patterns: Single Linkage works well when the clusters are chain-like, Complete Linkage is used when the clusters form distinct clumps, Average Linkage is suitable when clusters homogeneity is needed, Centroid Linkage base the distance between two clusters with the distance between cluster centroids.

### Computer Aided Principle (CAP)

Computer Aided Principle (CAP) is a support tool for design principle extraction proposed by Prof. Qiang Yu from Yokohama National University. While conventional sensitivity and contribution analysis focus on effects of a single variable, CAP focuses on effects (trends) of combinations of multiple variables. CAP at first classifies data into groups based on their characteristic value (clustering) and then visually represents trends in description variables. The characterization of each cluster and variations in the trends in the description variables can be seen when visually moving between clusters. CAP provides concepts that offer an interactive guide to the physical meaning of the trends based on visual representations.

### Smoothing Spline ANOVA (SS-ANOVA)

Smoothing Spline ANOVA (SS-ANOVA) is a statistical modeling algorithm based on the decomposition of the function, which is similar to the classical analysis of variance (ANOVA) decomposition and the associated notions of main effects and interactions (Chong, 2002). Each term (main effects and interactions) exposes an interesting measure: the percentage of its contribution to the global variance. For this reason SS-ANOVA represents a suitable screening technique for detecting, for each output of the model, important variables in a given dataset. Since SS-ANOVA terms sum to one, they could be sorted and plotted in a cumulative chart. This chart might provide a very useful and direct view of SS-ANOVA terms and help designers to filter and choose the most important input variables for each output.

### Reliability Analysis

Randomness and variability in structural materials and applied loads result in an uncertainty which affects the reliability of engineering systems. The reliability analysis aims to estimate the probability that a structure, a mechanical component (or other) will fail to meet a predefined criterion represented by a limit state function of the system random variables. This function marks the boundary between the safe design domain and the failure set. Various techniques have been developed over the years to estimate the failure probability, e.g. first or second order reliability methods (FORM and SORM), importance sampling techniques, and response surface models.

The capability of assessing reliability is very useful within a design optimization context. Reliability-based design optimization methods are popular approaches for finding the optimal (lightest, least expensive, etc.) design for an engineered component that meets or exceeds a specified reliability level. These methods may be applied across a wide spectrum of engineering fields.

### Multi Criteria Decision Making

Multi-Criteria Decision Making (MCDM) methods allow the user to classify all the available alternatives through pair-wise comparisons on attributes and designs, assisting the Decision Maker in finding the best solution from among a set of reasonable alternatives. They allow the correct grouping of outputs into single utility function that is coherent

with the preferences expressed by the user and it does not have the same drawbacks of a weighted function. The most well-known algorithms are: Linear MCDM that can be used when the number of decision variables is small, GA MCDM that does not perform an exact search but is more efficient, Hurwicz, which is used for uncertain decision problems and Savage MADM used for uncertain decision problems, where both the decision states and their likelihoods are unknown.

The above described simulation, optimization and decision making methods and tools support the elaboration of sustainability aware simulation and optimization models that can be wrapped, integrated with an integration logic model and consumed by a BPMS framework as interoperable, self-configuring and reusable eco-services.

A substantial value this approach aims to deliver is to bring environmental and social KPIs available to decision makers in addition to traditional economic KPIs. Traditionally, sustainability related factors have required specific LCA tools, and couldn't be coupled to simulation functionalities. In this regard, this approach allows augmenting the simulation and optimization models with Sustainability Intelligence, with the purpose of taking into account these factors. As a general rule, Business Intelligence domain has been using for years traditional KPIs so as to assess the current business performance status and to prescribe future action lines. However, the increasing importance of sustainability and Corporate Social Responsibility (CSR) should also be assessed. Hence, process managers should take into account not only increased sales and profits and/or decreased costs, but also sustainable development of the business itself and of the surrounding context. Sustainability Intelligence is the augmentation of Business Intelligence concepts with sustainable development concepts, where the traditional economic-financial bottom line is coupled with environmental and social bottom lines. Sustainability Intelligence Triple Bottom Line (TBL) system allows users, who may not be familiar with all the metrics and concepts of sustainable development, to make strategic sound decisions based on systematic data gathering, monitoring, analysis and distribution.

## BPMN 2.0 Operative Model

This task of the modeling step focuses on completing the operative level of the BPMN structural framework. Thus, the BPMN descriptive model initiated by the process manager and process owner is further elaborated by the process analyst in order to build an operative model, which involves the definition of the full process logic, including the handling of process errors and exceptions, in addition to the normal flow defined during the descriptive level. The model includes the association of manual tasks to the different process participants and the definition of optimization services that will be leveraged by the model during the execution step. The elaboration of the operative model implies the use of a great range of BPMN 2.0 constructs, for instance, those related to error handling. The skill of the process analyst is a key factor that will allow creating a business process model that comprises the whole business logic and that is easily transferrable to the next level. The main objective related to this second level is that the logic of the operative model belongs to the logic that will be technically implemented. Therefore, during the operative level, the BPMN 2.0 execution semantic should be strictly maintained. This means that a good alignment between the business layer and the IT layer can be achieved, the elaborated documentation is valid for communicating changes in both directions and business and IT people can comment and build upon the same model.

The design and modeling steps are accomplished to cover the Business Collaboration Level, which is based on the description and modeling of user's interaction required to accomplish business process activities through manual tasks and automated tasks involving IT.

## Execution

The execution step comprises the execution of the next tasks. Some of them include the elaboration of models that support the interoperability of the whole system.

## Integration Logic Model

The process engineer is in charge of building the integration logic, which includes the configuration of the optimization service that eventually can be leveraged from the executed instance of a BPMN 2.0 workflow. The integration logic involves the provision of simulation and optimization parameters to the optimization service (e.g. simulation model, simulation parameters, objectives and eco-constraints) needed to configure and wrap the optimization service as an eco-service interoperable at business level. Once this logic is orchestrated, the eco-service is eligible to be remotely accessible from to the BPMN model service tasks, which link the business process with the service consumption capability, allowing the connection of the Business layer with the IT layer. In order to streamline the integration, the next technical services should be available; capability that allows the import of Open Data; Extraction, Transformation and Loading (ETL) functionality required so as to permit the extraction of data from existing PLM operational databases (e.g. ERPs, CRM, SCM and CMMS). This data can be transformed and loaded into an analytical database for later analysis and monitoring of as-is KPIs through Sustainability Intelligence tools; data interaction capability from and to the Virtual Factory repository, enabling the retrieval of simulation configuration parameters and eco-constraints, or saving optimization results.

The ultimate aim of the integration logic is to leverage the scaling-up of the augmented simulation and optimization capabilities from a desktop confined approach into intra-enterprise and inter-enterprise wide interoperable eco-services to enable non-expert industrial practitioners to configure and run optimization scenarios anywhere in the Virtual Factory, stimulating collaborative and intelligent decision making, and providing advice on the configuration of what-if scenarios.

## Content Model (EKR)

Process management requires an effective content model that supports the execution of eco-services. The content model can be built upon the Enterprise Knowledge Resource (EKR) concept (Bermell-García, 2012). One subdivision of the EKR is dedicated to the "Knowledge" and contains the corporate managed assumptions, constraints, rules or standards derived from best practices required to execute an eco-service. They can be considered as inputs to the simulation and optimization models. Another section of the EKR, the "Process," captures the business process steps required to execute the eco-service. This section may contain a pointer to the BPMN model that will leverage the eco-service. Finally, the "Process history" section contains the historical use of the service, such as optimization results and KPIs.

## Build Technical BPMN Model

The third level of the BPMN 2.0 structural framework is located behind the line that delimits the business layer and the IT layer. This level, also known as technical model, involves the steps required by a process engineer to technically transform the operative model into an executable model via the addition of technical details. The different steps required to transform the operative model into a technical model include:

- Decision about a platform and technological architecture where the business model will be executed. If a Business Process Management System (BPMS) compliant with BPMN 2.0 standard is used to execute the business model, it should only be technically updated with complete ex-

ecution semantics prior to the deployment into the BPMS. On the other hand, if another technical model is used, e.g. BPEL, it will be necessary to realize a mapping between BPMN to the particular execution language.

- Iteratively redesign the operative model in case there are problems that do not allow implementing the business model.

- Test and assess the technical model according to software engineering current practices.

- Provide a data structure according to the technology that will be used. The technical model should provide a specification of the data formats that will be used by the process instances, such as XML, Java or Core Manufacturing Simulation Data – XML Representation (SISO, 2012).

- Implement the interface for the connection of the service tasks of the BPMN 2.0 model with the eco-services, or with an Enterprise Service Bus (ESB) or integration framework (EAI) that provides enterprise services. This service interface can be implemented with Web Services technology (RESTful, SOAP, etc.). The connection to external systems or eco-services can be synchronous or asynchronous. If the service call is synchronous, the emitting service waits until it obtains an answer from the remote system. In contrast, if the service call is asynchronous the emitting service does not block the process execution, which continues towards the next BPMN element.

- Define details of the manual tasks, such as roles, user groups and rights. An important aspect to consider in the technical model is the configuration of the human interaction in a manual task. The manual or user tasks are managed through a list of activities, which are received by the process participants. If the user selects one task, the process will continue once the user has finished its processing.

- Define service tasks error handling and exceptions. In the operative level, the process analyst considered errors and exceptions related to the business process. These errors and exceptions are modeled with specific BPMN constructs. However, in order to complete the technical model, the process engineer extends the casuistic of potential errors to technical errors that may happen. This involves exception handling within the service tasks using programming language logic.

- Define process instantiation. The instantiation of a process can be achieved with start events triggered manually by process participants. However, for complex choreographies that involve the instantiation of different processes through the exchange of message flows or message events it is necessary to establish a methodology that allows the process engine to find the process that has to be instantiated.

Another alternative approach to the technical model development involves the elaboration of a specification for the development. If a BPMS is not used for the execution of a business process, the business logic has to be developed in a programming language. Thus, a technical specification has to be developed starting from the operative BPMN model. The notation has to be translated into the appropriate specification, e.g. UML diagrams, for the selected programming environment. Once the specification is elaborated, the workflow is implemented in a traditional platform. On the other hand, if a BPMS is used, just the technical model has to be developed in terms of enriching the operative model with technical aspects. Once the technical model is implemented and well designed, it is directly deployable into a Process Engine. The technical model is like source code for the process engine, what means that the model

must be formally correct, i.e. syntactically and semantically, in order to be successfully interpreted by the engine.

## Deploy and Execute the BPMN Technical Model

The modeled business process is deployed in a business process application through a Business Process Management System (BPMS). One of the core components of BPMS is the Process Engine, which provides the core capabilities to execute BPMN 2.0 processes and create new workflow tasks. When such a process definition is deployed on the process engine and a new process instance is started, the BPMN 2.0 elements are executed one by one. Thus, once the process engineer deploys the BPMN model into the Virtual Factory Collaborative Space domain, the process participants are able of running the business process, and in turn the optimization and simulation routine by means of triggering the eco-service, in a collaborative and automated way, allowing the continuous improvement of the business process and hiding the optimization complexity to the end-user.

## Monitoring

The monitoring step consists of the iterative application of the next tasks aiming at the identification and follow-up of process optimization metrics:

- Application of the mechanism for Business Opportunities Tracking within the Business Community established in the Design step. The systematic research on sustainability intelligence networks with the help of social network analysis techniques accelerate the identification of business optimization opportunities, which will leverage the establishment of Collaborative Spaces focused on the automation of key business processes. The collaborative nature of these networks, involving the Virtual

Factory value chain, leverages the intra-organizational business process exchange and fosters interoperability.

- Application of the mechanism initiated in the Design step for eco-constraints and objectives tracking within the Collaborative Spaces. The continuous surveillance of sustainability related requirements lead to the identification of the eco-constraints and objectives an automated business process has to fulfill. The aim of those constructs is twofold: on the one hand sustainability indicators (traditional and eco-KPIs) are derived out of them that will enable the process monitoring and tracking. On the other hand, they are employed to create a to-be model that satisfies them. The implementation of the to-be model and the comparison of the as-is and to-be indicators between the real and the theoretical model enables the adoption of optimization measures that will lead to a modification of the current process model.

- Tracking and analysis of KPIs with Sustainable Intelligence tools. These tools can be used to generate reports and to show analytics on different dimensions of multidimensional data through graphical tools (e.g. OLAP cubes). They support process managers on the decision making process so as to leverage more sustainable business processes. Sustainability Intelligence provides organizations the translation of their objectives in study-indicators for the construction of models by which to predict future models. These monitoring and analysis tools allow process managers and analysts to detect deviations between the current executed process instance and the theoretical model. If a deviation with respect to the desired outcome occurs, the optimization step is followed to introduce changes in the process.

## Optimization

Based on new knowledge generated within the BPM steps, such as environmental constraints, objectives, changing business requirements and monitoring results, the implemented business process will need to be optimized. This step retrieves process performance information from the monitoring phase, identifies the potential or actual bottlenecks and the potential opportunities for sustainability improvements, and then, applies those enhancements in the design of the process through the creation of a to-be model. This step implies the adjustment of some of the tasks in the modelling step to improve the business process, e.g. to augment the simulation model with new Sustainability Intelligence capabilities to comply with a new eco-constraint or objective. When the process has become un-reactive to modeling upgrades, a process reengineering may be required. Thus, the business process goes into the design phase again and completes the whole circle.

## FUTURE RESEARCH DIRECTIONS

The emerging trends on some of the most relevant topics related to interoperability in engineering systems, from the perspective of the presented BPM approach, are introduced in the following text:

## Virtual Collaborative Networks (VCN)

While cooperation refers to the working ties of individual organizations, network refers to the huge number of cooperating partners. However, differentiating between the terms cooperation and network is not always applied with sufficient distinction, they are occasionally viewed as interchangeable, and the terms used synonymously.

The main concepts involved in collaboration and the main differences between all of them are the following ones:

- Networking: involves communication and information exchange for mutual benefit.
- Coordinated Networking: in addition on communication and exchanging information it involves aligning/altering activities so that more efficient results are achieved.
- Cooperation: involves not only information exchange and adjustments of activities, but also sharing resources for achieving compatible goals. A VBE is considered a cooperative network.
- Collaboration: a process in which entities share information, resources and responsibilities to jointly plan, implement and evaluate a program of activities to achieve a common goal. Regarding this, a VCN is considered a collaborative network.

Collaborative networks appear in a diversity of forms and show a variety of behavioral patterns. Different collaboration forms can be identified according both structure and duration. In terms of structure, three collaborative network topologies seem to appear frequently in literature:

- Chain topology; this is the case of the supply chains in manufacturing industries.
- Star topology, with a dominant member, which is typically the case in construction or automotive industries.
- General network topology, project oriented, which is typically used for creative and knowledge industries. This is the case of Virtual Breeding Environments (VBE) and Virtual Collaborative Networks (VCN).

In terms of duration, we can find two different types of networks:

- Short-term networks, typically triggered by a collaboration opportunity, such as an optimization. This is the case of Virtual collaborative networks (VCN).

- Long-term networks. This is the case of strategic alliances or supply chains. This is the case of Virtual Breeding Environment (VBE).

Virtual Collaborative Networks (VCNs) are timely limited, dynamic coalitions of organizations that may be tailored within a VBE to respond to a single collaboration (business optimization) opportunity, and dissolve once their mission/goal has been accomplished, and whose collaboration is supported through computer networks. The establishment of VCNs around a VBE infrastructure with the purpose of optimizing BPMN 2.0 compliant business processes driven by sustainability intelligence networks, is anticipated to leverage process interoperability practices, not only at intra-organizational, but also at inter-organizational level.

## System Integration/Interoperability

Table 1 presents a selection of tools supporting systems integration/interoperability.

The addition of an integration framework system to the BPMS architecture provides a clear separation between the Business Process logic and the integration logic. Although it's theoretically possible to implement integration logic within the business process logic (service tasks) to communicate with external PLM systems, such as databases, ERPs or CRMs, or with eco-services, the natural approach is to delegate the data transformation and interfacing logic to an integration platform. Thus, all that closely relates to process logic, like assignment of manual tasks to people, process events handling, process tasks orchestration and choreography among processes, or working with process variables, is carried out within the BPMS framework, while the communication with PLM systems should be carried out with the help of an integration framework.

Regarding future work on the process interoperability approach presented here, the research will continue under the frame of EPES project (EPES,

*Table 1. System integration/interoperability supporting tools (alphabetical order)*

| Tool \ Features | Open Source | License | Type |
|---|---|---|---|
| **Apache Camel** | Yes | Apache Software License | Rule-based routing, mediation engine |
| **Apache Synapse** | Yes | Apache Software License | ESB, mediation engine |
| **JBoss Enterprise Service Bus** | Yes | LGPL | ESB |
| **JBoss Enterprise SOA Platform** | Yes | LGPL | ESB, SOA |
| **Mule ESB** | Yes | CPAL | ESB, integration framework |
| **OpenESB** | Yes | CDDL | ESB, SOA |
| **ServiceMix** | Yes | Apache Software License | ESB, SOA |

2013), which proposes a novel eco-process system that will provide organizations with a high degree of interoperability with internal and external information systems and will focus on a low integration effort by the industrial end-users, including SMEs. This goal will be achieved through the application of well-established enterprise modeling standards, which will assure that the end-users will not be stuck to a particular vendor's rules. This approach leverages the Business Process Management (BPM) discipline presented above and will help industrial organizations design, model and implement systematic collaboration, data sharing and data transfer patterns within the organization and with other organizations that belong to the value chain, whenever business processes are performed across organizational limits.

EPES will be built on top of the interaction models introduced in the Business Process Management chapter, as displayed in Figure 2. These models span from the business to the IT domain, which is represented in the figure as the most inner layers. The content model, augmented simulation and optimization models, and the integration logic model comprise an interoperable eco-service, which can be leveraged by a Business Process model instance. This BPMN model is, in turn, able to interface with other organizations' Business Processes through a choreography model, fostering interoperability and collaboration within the Virtual Factory domain.

Following this approach, one of the main capabilities of EPES will be fulfilled, i.e. publish complex services that will be easily accessed by non-experts once they are configured in order to optimize the product life-cycle management. EPES project will be focused on the application of an end-user driven approach, through the specification of three Business Cases or demonstrators, which will be used to implement and validate the results of the project. Thus, the industrial partners, supported by the RTDs, identified for which business processes within the life cycle they intend to explore the developed software components so as

*Figure 2. Interaction models represented as encapsulated layers*

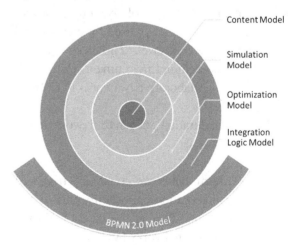

Content Model

Simulation Model

Optimization Model

Integration Logic Model

BPMN 2.0 Model

to optimize the selected processes towards sustainability. The project concept is being applied to the following sectors:

- Wind mill engineering: Generate and develop high value added services to the windmill farms maintenance.
- Energy: Supporting services easily adaptable to customer specific needs, which facilitate the analysis and maintenance of cable systems with respect to a secure use of increasing cable capacity, due to the increasing share of renewable energy in the European Union.
- Aeronautics: The project will identify eco-constraints relevant to the manufacturing systems assessment capability at the right point in time in aeronautics sector.

Regarding the application of EPES solution to the wind mill engineering sector, TAMOIN is the industrial company that acts as Business Case provider and demonstrator. This company is focused on developing high added value engineering maintenance services through the collaboration with RTDs and the other industrial BCs. The main objective is expected to be achieved by improving the data capture and knowledge management through the EPES eco-process engineering system, which will extend the functionalities of TAMOIN current maintenance software with new designed eco-services, comprising a service for the development and monitoring of business indicators for supporting continuous improvement activities and a service for planning and programming short term maintenance activities, which takes into account the optimal time frame for the maintenance of each component according to the failure probability of each of them, the human and material resources availability, forecasted weather conditions and eco-constraints and objectives that come from sustainability intelligence networks, such as those related to the optimization of the availability of the wind turbines, the minimization of maintenance costs or improvement of environmental impact.

These eco-services will help the company to overcome present maintenance management software limitations and will be configured and composed to optimize the company Wind Farm Maintenance Engineering services, offering to the customers a wider range of high added value services covering areas such as technical support, spare parts management, operation efficiency improvement, quality, environment and health & safety.

In addition to the eco-services development and in order to capture TAMOIN maintenance operations and allow the triggering of the eco-services in a distributed fashion, the maintenance process will be automated and systematized with the help of BPMN 2.0 and, eventually, will be deployed into the Virtual Factory Collaborative Space domain. Consequently, TAMOIN maintenance operations will be captured in order to enable process managers the measurement of process performance. On the other hand, the process participants will be capable of running the business process and, in turn, the optimization and simulation routines by means of triggering the eco-services in a collaborative and automated way, allowing the continuous improvement of the business process and hiding the optimization complexity to the end-user.

EPES system will include Web 2.0 features for collaborative design, an extended enterprise knowledge repository, business process modeling tools and a simulation and decision-making platform with the ultimate objective of integrating a set of readily available tools into a modular and extendable system that facilitates the use, reuse, storage, analysis and sharing of knowledge within the Virtual Factory. Planned industrial demonstrations, derived from the above mentioned Business Cases, cover different stages of the technical product life-cycles, such as product and production system conceptual design stage, as well as at the operational and service stage.

As such, EPES project does not aim to develop any of the present technologies alone to further levels, but, instead, to innovatively combine them for achieving novelty functionality and more comprehensive interaction. As for including the simulation and optimization into the mix, the target for EPES project optimization is moving from large static, spread sheet models to more flexible dynamic, collaborative and integrated modeling. The same trend of moving from static isolated systems to more flexible loosely coupled system is largely present in the whole EPES concept. Thus, instead of having desktop applications and "engineering islands of analysis," EPES aims to fulfill integration of assessment methods and provide them as a service for non-simulation experts (but simulation models will remain domain specific).

EPES is one of the first attempts to provide a holistic methodology and supporting tools to directly link Eco-driven engineering with generation of interoperable eco-services around manufacturing products. Eco-constraints concept itself is expected to be very useful to shape the environmental "modus operandi" of a company, as a new kind of scenario for decision making. This concept could be extended rapidly in the overall market. Furthermore, the fact of working within distributed ICT platforms to manage intelligence would cause overall cost reduction in the Virtual Factory along the value chain because of sharing same needs or at least similar ones. This aspect is quite relevant for SMEs, which are represented in most of these value chain structures. In addition, the effect of sharing information, and having the feedback on it, could push more than one company to extend the relationships among them to other aspects as design collaboration, commercial complementary and so on.

## CONCLUSION

The chapter begins with an introduction that describes how the industrial enterprises have been changing their focus during the last 30 years from the concept of managing data "the what" with the support of informatics systems to the concept of managing business processes "the how" that build upon existing data management systems. Most of the industrial enterprises, which already have such data management systems, need to react and adapt to the changing market conditions, such as new sustainability directives, to stay competitive. This shift of paradigm involves the adoption of a Business Process Management (BPM) approach that includes, on the one hand, the Enterprise Modeling through, for instance, Business Process Frameworks and, on the other hand, the technical modeling and automation of concrete business processes. The proposed approach introduced roots on the BPM discipline and leverages process optimization and interoperability through the systematic modeling of business processes and their associated, exchangeable and configurable eco-services, which optimize some aspects of the product life-cycle through eco-constraints management.

Next, the evolution of the different enterprise modeling techniques is discussed, such as the traditional techniques oriented to data flow, e.g. Structured Analysis, and novel techniques oriented to manage the control flow, e.g. BPMN. In this regard, the advantages of adhering to the recent BPMN 2.0 industry standard are described, such as the capability of interchanging models between different modeling tools and the potential of directly executing these models in different BPMN 2.0 compliant Process Engines without the need for conversion, leveraging communication between business-oriented individuals and IT developers using a single model and bridging the gap between business and IT layers. Last but not least, another benefit lies on the capability of choreographing different business processes, which may belong to different organizations, leveraging interoperability and collaboration.

After introducing the standard BPMN 2.0, the preconditions required to successfully apply the proposed BPM approach are presented. These comprise the establishment of an organizational structure oriented to processes and the promotion of a corporate cultural change towards collaboration and knowledge sharing through collaborative networks. Next, the actors and roles that participate in the process oriented management are introduced.

The design, documentation, execution, monitoring and control of a business process comprise the performance of a number of systematic steps around a continuous improvement BPM cycle (design, modeling, execution, monitoring and optimization). Along with the implementation of these steps, a BPMN structural framework is incrementally applied to model the business process. The aim of the structural framework concept is to build up the business model starting from the business perspective and eventually reaching the technical level, which allows the direct execution of the business model in a BPMS. On the other hand, during the implementation of the BPM steps, additional interaction models are built to support the business model, such as the simulation and optimization models, the integration logic model and the content model. The aim of these models is to provide a structured approach to assemble interoperable eco-services. These eco-services are sustainability aware, meaning that they are based on augmented models that feature sustainability assessment capability.

To finish with, the future research directions are addressed. In this regard, the current work on the FP7 project EPES is introduced, where the BPM approach presented in will be applied to three Business Cases to test and validate the concepts.

# REFERENCES

ABPMP. (2009). *Guide to business process management common body of knowledge (BPM CBOK)* (2nd ed.). New York: Association of Business Process Management Professionals.

Banks, J., Carson, J. S., & Nelson, B. L. (1996). *Discrete-event system simulation* (2nd ed.). Upper Saddle River, NJ: Prentice Hall.

Bermell-García, P., Verhagen, W., Astwood, S., Krishnamurthy, K., Johnson, J. L., & Ruiz, D. et al. (2012). A framework for management of knowledge-based engineering applications as software services: Enabling personalization and codification. *Advanced Engineering Informatics*, *26*, 219–230. doi:10.1016/j.aei.2012.01.006

Branke, J., Deb, K., Miettinen, K., & Slowinski, R. (2008). Multiobjective optimization, interactive and evolutionary approaches, multiobjective optimization. *Lecture Notes in Computer Science*, 5252.

Camarinha-Matos, L. M., & Afsarmanesh, H. (2008). Collaborative networks: Reference modelling. Berlin: Springer Science+Business Media, LLC.

Chong, G. (2002). *Smoothing spline ANOVA models*. New York: Springer-Verlag.

COMVANTAGE FP7 Project Consortium. (2012). *D3.1.1 specification of modelling method including conceptualization outline*. Retrieved June 4, 2013, from http://www.comvantage.eu/

Cox, T. F., & Cox, M. A. A. (2003). Multidimensional scaling. *Technometrics*, *45*(2).

Deb, K. (2001). *Multi-objective optimization using evolutionary algorithms*. Hoboken, NJ: Wiley-Interscience Series in Systems and Optimization, John Wiley & Sons.

ENSEMBLE FP7 Project Consortium. (2012). *D2.1 enterprise interoperability science base state of play report*. Retrieved March 18, 2013, from http://www.fines-cluster.eu

EPES FP7 Project Consortium. (2012). *D100.3 EPES concept* (FP7-FoF-ICT-2011.7.3-285093). Retrieved March 18, 2013, from http://www.epes-project.eu

Fletcher, R., Leyffer, S., & Toint, P. L. (2006). A brief history of filter methods (Preprint ANL/MCS-P1372-0906). Argonne National Laboratory, Mathematics and Computer Science Division.

Freund, J., Rücker, B., & Hitpass, B. (2011). *BPMN 2.0 manual de referencia y guía práctica.* Santiago de Chile: RPI Chile.

Gadatsch, A. (2010). Grundkurs geschäftsprozess-Management. Wiesbaden, Germany: Vieweg+Teubner.

Harmon, P. (2010). *The scope and evolution of business process management.* Berlin: Springer-Verlag. doi:10.1007/978-3-642-00416-2_3

Jain, A. K., Murty, M. N., & Flynn, P. J. (1999). Data clustering: A review. *ACM Computing Surveys, 31*(3). doi:10.1145/331499.331504

Jain, S., & Kibira, D. (2010). A framework for multi-resolution modeling of sustainable manufacturing. In *Proceedings of the 2010 Winter Simulation Conference* (pp. 3423–3434). Retrieved from http://www.informs-sim.org/wsc10papers/316.pdf

Kohonen, T. (1982). Self-organized formation of topologically correct feature maps. *Biological Cybernetics, 43*(1), 59–69. doi:10.1007/BF00337288

Lind, S., Johansson, B., Stahre, J., Berlin, C., Fasth, Å., Heilala, J., et al. (2009). *SIMTER – A joint simulation tool for production development.* Retrieved from http://www.vtt.fi/inf/pdf/workingpapers/2009/W125.pdf

Object Management Group (OMG). (2011). *Business process model and notation (BPMN) version 2.0.* Retrieved March 18, 2013, from http://www.omg.org/spec/BPMN/2.0/

Santner, T. J., Williams, B., & Notz, W. (2003). *The design and analysis of computer experiments.* Berlin: Springer Verlag. doi:10.1007/978-1-4757-3799-8

Schatten, M., & Žugaj, M. (2007). Organizing a fishnet structure. In *Proceedings of the ITI 2007 29th International Conference on Information Technology.* Zagreb: SRCE University Computing Centre.

Senn, J. A. (1992). *Análisis y diseño de sistemas de información* (2nd ed.). Mexico City, Mexico: McGraw Hill.

Simulation Interoperability Standards Organization (SISO). (2012). *Standard for core manufacturing simulation data – XML representation.* Retrieved March 20, 2013, from http://www.sisostds.org

Taylor, S. F. E. (2011). Challenges for web simulation science. In *Proceedings of the 2011 Winter Simulation Conference.* Retrieved from http://www.informs-sim.org/wsc11papers/259.pdf

Whitman, L., Huff, B., & Palaniswamy, S. (1998). Commercial simulation over the web. In *Proceedings of the 1998 Winter Simulation Conference* (pp. 335–339). Retrieved from http://www.informs-sim.org/wsc98papers/046.PDF

## ADDITIONAL READING

Baumann, H., & Tillman, A.-M. 2004. The Hitch Hiker's Guide to LCA. An orientation in life cycle assessment methodology and application. Studentlitteratur AB. ISBN 91- 44-02364-2

Bosilj-Vuksic, V., Ceric, V., & Hlupic, V. (2007). *Criteria for the Evaluation of Business Process Simulation Tools.* Interdisciplinary Journal of Information, Knowledge, and Management. Vol. 2, pp. 73–88. Available at: http://ijikm.org/Volume2/IJIKMv2p073-088Bosilj396.pdf

Camarinha-Matos, L., Afsarmanesh, H., & Ollus, M. (2008). *Methods and Tools for Collaborative Networked Organisations.* Springer. doi:10.1007/978-0-387-79424-2

Deming, W. E. (1986). *Out of the crisis: quality, productivity and competitive position*. Cambridge University Press.

EPES FP7 project consortium. (2012). *D100.1 EPES State of the Art Analysis*. Retrieved March 20, 2013, from http://www.epes-project.eu

Fasoli, T., Terzi, S., Jantunen, E., Kortelainen, J., Sääski, J., & Salonen, T. (2011). *Challenges in Data Management in Product Life Cycle Engineering, Glocalized Solutions for Sustainability in Manufacturing*, Proceedings of the 18th CIRP International Conference on Life Cycle Engineering, CIRP International Conference on Life Cycle Engineering, LCE/CIRP 2011, Braunschweig, Germany, May 2nd–4th, 2011. Springer-Verlag, pp. 525–530

Feng, S. C., & Joung, C. B. (2009). *An Overview of a Proposed Measurement Infrastructure for Sustainable Manufacturing*. In Proceedings of the 7th Global Conference on Sustainable Manufacturing. December 2–4, Chennai, India. Available at: http://www.nist.gov/manuscript-publication-search.cfm?pub_id=904166

Fowler, J. W., & Rose, O. (2004). Grand Challenges in Modeling and Simulation of Complex Manufacturing Systems. *Simulation*, *80*(9), 469–476. doi:10.1177/0037549704044324

Giaglis, G. M. (2001). A Taxonomy of Business Process Modeling and Information Systems Modeling Techniques. *International Journal of Flexible Manufacturing Systems*, *13*, 209–228. doi:10.1023/A:1011139719773

Gold-Bernstein, B., & Ruh, W. (2006). *Enterprise integration: the essential guide to integration solutions*. Addison Wesley.

Halog, A., & Manik, Y. (2011). Advancing Integrated Systems Modelling Framework for Life Cycle Sustainability Assesment. *Sustainability*, *3*(2), 469–499. doi:10.3390/su3020469

Hambleton, L. (2008). *Treasure chest of six sigma: Growth methods, tools and best practices*. Upper Saddle River, NJ, USA: Pearson Education Inc.

Harrell, C., & Tumay, K. (1996). *Simulation made easy. A manager's guide*. Norgross, GA: Industrial Engineering and Management Press, Institute of Industrial Engineers.

Havey, M. (2005). *Essential Business Process Modeling, Chapter Seven: The Workflow Management Coalition (WfMC)*. O'Reilly.

Heilala, J., Montonen, J., Järvinen, P., Kivikunnas, S., Maantila, M., Sillanpää, J., & Jokinen, T. (2010). *Developing Simulation-Based Decision Support Systems for Customer-Driven Manufacturing Operation Planning*. Proceedings of the 2010 Winter Simulation Conference, WSC '10, Baltimore Marriot Waterfront, Baltimore, Maryland, USA, December 5–8, 2010. Johansson, B. Jain, S. Montoya-Torres, J.

Hochschorner, E., & Finnveden, G. (2003). Evaluation of two simplified Life Cycle assessment methods. *The International Journal of Life Cycle Assessment*, *8*(4), 119–128. doi:10.1007/BF02978456

Hohpe, G., & Woolf, B. (2003). *Enterprise Integration Patterns: Designing, Building, and Deploying Messaging Solutions*. Addison Wesley, Inc.

IBM. (2008). *SOA in manufacturing guidebook*. White paper 27. A MESA International, IBM Corporation and Capgemini co-branded white paper. Available at: ftp://ftp.software.ibm.com/software/applications/plm/resources/MESA_SOAinManufacturingGuidebook.pdf

Jammes, F., Smit, H., Martinez Lastra, J. L., & Delamer, I. (2005). *Orchestration of Service-Oriented Manufacturing Processes*. Proceedings of the 10th IEEE International Conference on Emerging Technologies and Factory Automation, Vol. 1, pp. 617–624

Jawahir, I. S. (2010). *Sustainable Manufacturing: The Driving Force for Innovative Products, Processes and Systems for Next Generation Manufacturing.* Lexington, KY, USA: University of Kentucky, Department of Mechanical Engineering, and Institute for Sustainable Manufacturing.

Jayal, A. D., Badurdeen, F., Dillon, O. W. Jr, & Jawahir, I. S. (2010). Sustainable manufacturing: Modeling and optimization challenges at the product, process and system levels. *CIRP Journal of Manufacturing Science and Technology, 2,* 144–152. doi:10.1016/j.cirpj.2010.03.006

Jeswiet, J. A. (2003). *Definition of life cycle engineering.* In Bley H, editor. Proceedings of the thirty-sixth CIRP international seminar on manufacturing systems. Saarbrücken. Pp. 17–20

Koukkari, H., & Nors, M. (Eds.). (2009). *Life Cycle Assessment of Products and Technologies.* LCA Symposium. Espoo, VTT. 142 p. VTT Symposium 262. Available at: http://www.vtt.fi/inf/pdf/symposiums/2009/S262.pdf. ISBN 978-951-38-7585-5, 978-951-38-7586-2

Krajnc, D., & Glavic, P. (2003). Indicators of Sustainable Production. *Clean Technologies and Environmental Policy, 5*(3), 279–288. doi:10.1007/s10098-003-0221-z

McLean, C., Jain, S., Riddick, F., & Lee, Y. T. (2007). *A Simulation Architecture for Manufacturing Interoperability Testing.* In Henderson, S.G., Biller, B., Hsieh, M-H., Shortle, J., Tew, J.D., & Barton, R.R. (Eds.). Proceedings of the 2007 Winter Simulation Conference, Piscataway, New Jersey: Institute of Electrical and Electronics Engineers, Inc

Newcomer, E., & Lomow, G. (2004). *Understanding SOA with Web Services.* Addison-Wesley Professional.

Paju, M., Heilala, J., Hentula, M., Heikkilä, A., & Johansson, B. Leong, S., & Lyons, K. (2010). *Framework and Indicators for a Sustainable Manufacturing Mapping Methodology.* Proceedings of the 2010 Winter Simulation Conference, B. Johansson, S. Jain, J. Montoya-Torres, J. Hugan, and E. Yücesan, (Eds.), pp. 3411–3422. 2010 Winter Simulation Conference 2010, WSC '10, Baltimore Marriot Waterfront, Baltimore, Maryland, USA, 5–8 Dec. 2010

Papazoglou, M. P., & van den Heuvel, W.-J. (2007). *Service Oriented Architectures: Approaches.* Technologies and Research Issues. Springer [VLDB]. *The International Journal on Very Large Data Bases, 16*(3), 389–415.

Rademakers, T. (2012). *Activiti in Action. Executable Business Processes in BPMN 2.0.* Shelter Island, NY: Manning Publications Co.

Rademakers, T., & Dirksen, J. (2008). *Open-Source ESBs in Action. Example Implementations in Mule and ServiceMix.* Shelter Island, NY: Manning Publications Co.

Riddick, F., & Lee, Y. T. (2008). *Representing Layout Information in the CMSD Specification.* In Mason, S.J., Hill, R.R., Mönch, L., Rose, O., Jefferson, T., & Fowler, J.W. (Eds.). Proceedings of the 2008 Winter Simulation Conference. Piscataway, New Jersey: Institute of Electrical and Electronics Engineers, Inc

Silver, B. (2011). BPMN Method and Style, 2nd Ed., with BPMN Implementer's Guide: A Structured Approach for Business Process Modeling and Implementation Using BPMN 2.0. Cody-Cassidy Press. ISBN: 0982368119

# KEY TERMS AND DEFINITIONS

**BPMN 2.0:** Business Process Model and Notation (BPMN) is a standard for business process modeling that provides a graphical notation. The objective of BPMN is to support BPM, for both process analysts and process engineers, by providing a notation that is intuitive to business users and useful to technical users, since is able to represent complex process execution semantics.

**Business Process Management (BPM):** Business Process Management is a corporate discipline aimed at improving the business performance (efficiency and efficacy) through the management of the different business processes, which have to be documented, designed, modeled, executed, monitored, optimized and reengineered. BPM refers to the shift of paradigm from a functional view towards a process view.

**Collaborative Space:** A Collaborative Space is a network created within the Virtual Factory that allows their members share information, resources and responsibilities to jointly achieve a common goal, such as the development of a business optimization opportunity.

**Eco-Constraint:** An eco-constraint is a requirement that an eco-service targets to fulfill. It is derived from the research on sustainability intelligence networks.

**Eco-Service:** Sustainability aware service designed to optimize some aspects of the product life-cycle through eco-constraints management. An eco-service is a portable service that can be leveraged from instances of an executed technical business process.

**Process Interoperability:** Business Process Interoperability is the ability to align and connect organizational business processes among different organizations in order to improve the overall business collaboration. In this regard, process modeling and process optimization/reengineering BPM steps support the formal representation of business processes and their adaptation to leverage seamless collaboration.

**Sustainability Intelligence:** Sustainability Intelligence is the blend of Business Intelligence concepts with those related to Sustainable Development, where the traditional economic-financial bottom line is coupled with environmental and social bottom lines to achieve a Triple Bottom Line (TBL) system capable of tracking people-profit-planet KPIs. This TBL system will assist managers in dealing with Corporate Social Responsibility requirements, local regulations and other eco-constraints.

**Virtual Factory (Business Community):** A Virtual Factory is a community of industrial organizations connected by an electronic network, which allows them to cooperate, not only in sharing and exchanging information, but also in sharing resources for achieving compatible goals.

# Chapter 9
# A Case for Enterprise Interoperability in Healthcare IT:
## Personal Health Record Systems

**Mustafa Yuksel**
*Software Research Development and Consultancy Ltd. (SRDC), Turkey & Middle East Technical University (METU), Turkey*

**Asuman Dogac**
*Software Research Development and Consultancy Ltd. (SRDC), Turkey*

**Cebrail Taskin**
*Argela Software and Informatics Technologies, Turkey*

**Anil Yalcinkaya**
*Argela Software and Informatics Technologies, Turkey*

## ABSTRACT

*The PHR systems need to be integrated with a wide variety of healthcare IT systems including EHRs, electronic medical devices, and clinical decision support services to get their full benefit. It is not possible to sustain the integration of PHRs with other healthcare IT systems in a proprietary way; this integration has to be achieved by exploiting the promising interoperability standards and profiles. This chapter provides a survey and analysis of the interoperability standards and profiles that can be used to integrate PHRs with a variety of healthcare applications and medical data resources, including EHR systems to enable access of a patient to his own medical data generated by healthcare professionals; personal medical devices to obtain the patient's instant physiological status; and the clinical decision support services for patient-physician shared decision making.*

## INTRODUCTION

The Personal Health Record (PHR) systems have evolved from Web pages where patients entered their own data manually to the systems giving patients access to their electronic health records

DOI: 10.4018/978-1-4666-5142-5.ch009

(EHRs) from a healthcare provider. The latter is called a provider-tethered PHR system, and the data from a healthcare provider's information system such as an EHR or a laboratory system is entered into the PHRs automatically via the data exchange interfaces established among these systems. There are also employer/payer portals providing patients access to claims data and more recently third party PHR systems such as Microsoft HealthVault (http://www.healthvault.com) that provides a secure storage for PHR data together with data exchange interfaces so that third parties can develop applications to upload patient data from a specific system or source, for example, home health devices.

The intent of all of these systems is to give patients better access to their own healthcare data (Halamka et al., 2008). The PHR is defined as "a tool for collecting, tracking and sharing important, up-to-date information about an individual's health or the health of someone in their care" (American Health Information Management Association et al., 2007, p. 1). It typically contains information about an individual's diagnoses, medications, allergies, procedures, lab test results, immunization records and other personal health information. Many PHR systems also provide linkages to convenience tools such as requesting appointments, requesting prescription renewals, asking billing questions and communication tools to assist the patient in connecting with various healthcare professionals.

However, currently all this integration is achieved mostly in a proprietary way and in a fragmented fashion rather than using the standard interfaces. A recent survey investigating the major 48 PHR systems on the market discovered that almost none of the PHRs use existing medical standards for the storage and communication of their data (Helmer et al., 2011). Given the existing semantic and technical diversity of eHealth platforms, each integration effort with a new system will be an expensive process unless standard interfaces are used for data exchange.

In this chapter, we present a survey and analysis of interoperability standards to connect the PHR systems to healthcare applications and medical data resources including EHR systems, personal medical devices and clinical decision support services. Some of these standards are specifically developed for the PHR systems; some are general standards that can also be used in the PHR sys-

tems. Additionally, because PHR systems contain a summary of EHR data, some EHR standards directly apply. For the sake of completeness, we present an analysis of all these standards as they apply to the PHR systems.

The chapter is organized as follows: A motivating example based on a visionary scenario is presented in the next section. Then, a classification of the PHR interoperability standards is provided, which is followed by a section on the EHR-PHR interoperability content standards and profiles. The succeeding section classifies the terminology systems based on the underlying structure and the knowledge representation formalism which determine the way they express the semantics and hence help with the interoperability. After that, the medical device interoperability standards and profiles for importing medical device data to patient's PHR are introduced. The standards relevant for clinical decision support services are covered in another section. Finally, the last section concludes the chapter.

## A MOTIVATING EXAMPLE

Mr. Smith visits his general practitioner (GP) with the symptoms of pain in his joints. The results of laboratory tests as well as radiographs indicate rheumatoid arthritis with high risk of damage in the joints. The GP refers the patient to a rheumatologist in the local hospital.

The local hospital that Mr. Smith is referred to has a care management system for rheumatoid arthritis, which provides a care plan for shared decision making between the physician and the patient to help them monitor the progress jointly. The care plan is a workflow based on "National clinical guideline for management and treatment of rheumatoid arthritis in adults," and it is processed and visualized through a clinical decision support service.

Mr. Smith decides to enroll in this program, and a care plan is created for him using this guideline, which specifies all the decision, action, branch and synchronization steps including medical tests, medications, home monitoring and follow-up appointments recommended for the care of his condition. To execute these steps, the care management workflow needs to retrieve data from the Electronic Medical Record (EMR) system at the GP's office; the Electronic Health Record (EHR) system at the hospital; the Laboratory Information System (LIS) at the local lab, and from the PHR of the patient. Fortunately for Mr. Smith, his PHR system provides a single point of access and control to all this information because it is interoperable with all the mentioned systems based on relevant standards. Additionally, the consent management mechanism of the PHR controls access to this data according to his privacy consent.

The rheumatologist goes over the steps of the care plan and describes them to Mr. Smith. He also wants Mr. Smith to record the symptoms and signs of the disease, his emotional state and side effects of the medications to his PHR.

At his next appointment with the GP, standard physical exam reveals that Mr. Smith suffers from hypertension, which is the side effect of his arthritis medication. For hypertension control, the GP recommends him benazepril. The PHR system of Mr. Smith has standard interfaces to external decision support services, one of which checks drug-to-drug interactions. When this medication record appears in his PHR, the drug-to-drug interaction checker recommends medication replacement because his current drug for rheumatoid arthritis, namely ibuprofen, might decrease the antihypertensive efficacy of benazepril. The rheumatologist replaces the drug and recommends blood pressure measurements to Mr. Smith four times daily. The PHR system uses standard interfaces for importing medical device data and therefore the off-the-shelf blood pressure device he purchases is capable of automatically uploading his measurements to his PHR so that both the patient himself and the GP can follow the results.

The GP monitors remotely both the progress of the care plan, the measurements provided by the medical device and status updates provided by Mr. Smith, and confirms that everything is under control. He motivates Mr. Smith through the instant messaging service of the PHR for his continuous dedication to the care plan, and notifies him for his next regular appointment.

## CLASSIFICATION OF THE INTEROPERABILITY STANDARDS FOR THE PHR SYSTEMS

PHRs are not only electronic repositories of health information controlled or accessed by patients. They are also integrated with a wide variety of healthcare information technology systems. Therefore, the interoperability standards for the PHR systems can be categorized according to the systems they are communicating with:

- Electronic Health Record standards,
- Personal Medical Device standards, and
- Clinical Decision Support Service (CDSS) standards.

It should be noted that the interoperability of IT systems can be assessed on different layers, from the lowest physical layer in the ISO/OSI model to the behavior of the system as perceived by the end users. It is feasible to organize these into three major layers in the case of interoperability of healthcare IT systems: the communication layer, the content layer and the business process layer. The communication layer covers the messaging specifications that are built on top of the application layer of the ISO/OSI model or the TCP/IP model, such as HL7 SOAP Web Services Profile; or rarely some lower layers such as the OSI session layer in the case of HL7 Minimal Lower Layer Protocol (MLLP). The content layer involves the format of the exchanged clinical messages and documents as well as their semantics expressed through the clinical terminology systems used. The business process layer involves the choreography of the interactions among the healthcare IT systems, by defining high-level transactions and then binding them to specific standards from the communication layer and content models from the content layer.

This article focuses mainly on the standards in the content layer. It also covers the profiling approach that corresponds to the business process layer as described above. The communication layer is not directly within the scope of the article, as it is built on top of very well known standards such as Web services and used similarly in other domains. However, relevant healthcare communication standards are referred within interoperability profiles.

## Enterprise Interoperability Perspective

Building on the well-established state of the art, the interoperability layers are specified as legal, organizational, semantic and technical interoperability within the European Interoperability Framework (EIF) (European Commission, 2004). This classification is adopted by several initiatives including the European Interoperability Architecture (EIA), which explores the need for a European interoperability architecture facilitating the establishment of European public services (Van Langenhove et al., 2011). Although interoperability in PHR systems covers all four layers of enterprise interoperability, this chapter focuses specifically on two layers: technical and semantic interoperability.

In parallel with this layered approach, in order to identify a proper structure dedicated to enterprise interoperability, the ENSEMBLE project (Envisioning, Supporting and Promoting Future Internet Enterprise Systems Research through Scientific Collaboration) has formulated 12 scientific areas of enterprise interoperability in 4 granularity levels by analyzing the technologi-

cal trends and the background knowledge (Popplewell et al., 2012). Among the 6 fundamental scientific areas that constitute the 1st granularity level, the interoperability standards and profiles presented in this chapter address directly all but one; i.e. data, process, rules, objects and software interoperability are covered, but cultural interoperability is not. Most of the remaining areas in other granularity levels (e.g. eID interoperability at 2nd level or cloud interoperability at 3rd level) are not addressed directly but since these levels are derived by iterative combination of core scientific areas at the 1st level, they are addressed indirectly.

As a highly interdisciplinary domain, interoperability in PHR systems affects and is affected by a number of neighboring scientific domains. Inspired by the needs of enterprise interoperability and several state of the art classification structures, the ENSEMBLE project provides a reusable classification of the scientific domains, which is termed as Enterprise Interoperability Science Base - Scientific Domain Reference Taxonomy (EISB-SDRT). Social sciences, applied sciences and formal sciences are recognized in the three-level general classification of this taxonomy. Within the social sciences category, we have identified sociology, economics and political science as the neighboring scientific domains since management of healthcare data by the patients themselves as the true owners of their data has social and legal aspects, as well as financial implications such as reducing costs by reducing the number of unnecessary physical patient visits through remote monitoring and communication. Among the main scientific domains within the applied sciences, medicine and engineering are directly involved in establishing interoperability in PHR systems. Finally, a majority of the scientific areas within the formal sciences category as the fundamentals of enterprise interoperability are again neighboring domains of interoperability in PHR systems. These can be listed as mathematics (logic especially for semantic interoperability), computer science (almost all sub-domains like data structures, software engineering, information theory) and other interdisciplinary sciences (systems, network, Web...). Since our work in this chapter focuses on technical and semantic interoperability layers, following sections detail the interoperability problems by considering the neighboring scientific domains within applied and formal sciences categories.

In order to address the semantic and technical interoperability problems in establishing interoperability among PHR systems and several other healthcare information technology systems by making use of reusable patterns, we prioritize the work done by following the profiling approach. Profiling starts with analyzing the required use cases in a specific domain. As the next step, the actors, transactions among them and the requirements of these transactions are identified in detail. Finally, instead of developing technical data exchange specifications from scratch, the identified technology independent transactions are bound to the most appropriate state of the art interoperability standards, which are further refined or extended when necessary. It is also possible to switch technology bindings of or provide several technology bindings to these technology independent transactions. The profiling approach is widely used by Integrating the Healthcare Enterprise (IHE) initiative (http://www.ihe.net/), several interoperability profiles of which are presented in the following sections. The profiling approach is also totally in line with the European Interoperability Architecture guidelines of the European Commission.

## PHR-EHR INTEROPERABILITY STANDARDS

### PHR/EHR Content Standards

Electronic Health Record (EHR) is defined as "digitally stored health care information about an individual's lifetime with the purpose of sup-

porting continuity of care, education and research, and ensuring confidentiality at all times" (Iakovidis, 1998). EHR data is stored in a multitude of medical information systems, which are used by health professionals but not directly accessible by the patients. A PHR contains the summary of the patient's EHR data. Therefore PHR content standards, just like EHR content standards (Eichelberg et al., 2005), define document structures consisting of document components such as sections, entries and data elements and are in fact based on the EHR content standards most of the time.

One of the most widely used standards that define PHR summary data is the E2369-05 Standard Specification for Continuity of Care Record (CCR) (ASTM International, 2005) by the American Society for Testing and Materials (ASTM) International. CCR defines a core data set for the most relevant administrative, demographic, and clinical information facts about a patient's healthcare, covering one or more healthcare encounters. It contains various sections such as patient demographics, insurance information, diagnosis and problem list, medications, allergies and care plan. CCR specification has its own XML schema definition; but it is also used in constraining other EHR content standards to obtain PHR/EHR content templates.

Generic EHR content standards that can also be used for EHR-PHR interoperability include HL7 Clinical Document Architecture, Release 2 (CDA) (Health Level Seven, 2005), ISO/CEN 13606-1: Reference Model (International Organization for Standardization et al., 2008) and openEHR (The openEHR Foundation, 2006). Unlike CCR, all these standards define quite generic structures such as folder, section, entry, observation and substance administration that can be used to represent any kind of clinical statement. The specialization of these generic structures is done by refining their semantics through the use of coded terms and/or free text explanations. For example, a 13606-1 section can be declared to be an allergies section by setting its name (free text) and meaning (coded value) attributes accordingly. Formal expressions of such specializations result in content templates as explained in *PHR/EHR Content Templates* Section.

Another PHR content standard is the Health-Vault Thing Types that are defined by Microsoft. Instead of using the existing content standards, Microsoft preferred defining a simple proprietary XML syntax for each possible clinical statement (e.g. blood glucose measurement, body dimension, insulin injection, etc.). Yet, the underlying information model of these Thing Types is compatible with the data types and structures of the well-known standards such as CCR and CDA which facilitates the interchange of clinical data complying with these standards in HealthVault.

## Analysis of PHR/EHR Content Standards

All PHR/EHR content standards serve similar purposes, that is, consistent and machine processable representation of healthcare information. The main distinguishing property among various content standards is the specificity (expressivity) of the underlying information model; that is, how generic or specific their schemas are (Table 1).

ISO/CEN 13606 and openEHR provide the most generic schema. It is possible to represent any kind of clinical statement with the combination of just three classes, namely Entry, Cluster and Element. HL7 CDA R2, on the other hand, has multiple structures each specialized for a group of medical activities; hence it has a more specialized schema. It has nine entry classes derived from the HL7 v3 Reference Information Model (RIM) (Health Level Seven, 2010c), such as Act, Observation, SubstanceAdministration and En-

counter. It is possible to classify ASTM CCR schema similarly with CDA. Some CCR classes like Immunization, Plan and Alert are more specific than CDA classes but still, there are no dedicated structures for representing individual medical events such as blood pressure or insulin injection, which are provided by HealthVault.

The advantage of a specialized schema such as HealthVault is that it is self-explanatory and easy to implement at first. However, in the long run, they might create maintenance issues for the implementers because each time the information model of a dedicated clinical event is modified or a new one is created, the syntax completely changes as well. Consider for instance, a Web service endpoint that accepts HL7 CDA R2 documents; this single endpoint can accept any CDA document, perform XSD validation on it, and then invoke the corresponding validation procedure according to the content, actually according to the content template (*PHR/EHR Content Templates* Section). When there is a change in the content template, the endpoint stays the same and the validation rules are modified. This is not easily achievable with specialized schemas.

The disadvantage of the generic and semi-generic schemas is that the footprint of clinical documents can become quite large. There can be many repeating constructs and attributes for representing a very simple medical event, especially with fully generic schemas. Therefore, it is better to have at least some common structures for modeling a group of medical activities, as in the case of CDA. Even with CDA, the experience shows that it is not easy to deal with tens of attributes just for modeling a diagnosis with an ICD-10 code for instance. In order to overcome these issues, recently greenCDA (Health Level

*Table 1. Comparison of PHR/EHR content schema expressivities*

| Totally Generic Schema | Semi-Generic Schema | Specialized Schema |
| --- | --- | --- |
| ISO/CEN 13606, openEHR | HL7 CDA R2, ASTM CCR | HealthVault Thing Types |

Seven, 2011a) has been proposed by the HL7 CDA community. greenCDA is the strategy of hiding certain CDA complexities such as fixed attributes (e.g. classCode, moodCode) and generic XML tags by introducing an intermediary XML schema with clinically meaningful XML element and attribute names, such as resultId, procedureType and problemCode. This intermediary schema is supported with transformation rules expressed in XSLT to automatically convert greenCDA instances to valid CDA instances. It is more meaningful to implement greenCDA together with content templates such as Continuity of Care Document (CCD) and Patient Care Coordination (PCC) templates (*PHR/EHR Content Templates* Section). The first release of greenCDA implementation guide by HL7 provides an intermediary greenCDA schema conforming to Health Information Technology Standards Panel (HITSP) C32/C83 content modules (Healthcare Information Technology Standards Panel, 2009) and generating CDA instances through transformation that comply with the corresponding CCD templates.

Finally regarding the analysis of existing PHR/EHR content standards, in order to foster unique representation and hence interoperability, there has to be a normative computer processable schema of a content standard. To remain technology independent, ISO/CEN states that compliance to 13606 standard is achieved by implementing the 13606 UML model. However, because XML is the de facto data exchange standard, it would be good to have a normative XML Implementation Technology Specification of the 13606 UML model. In this way, when two 13606 implementing systems need to interoperate, the implementers can directly skip interoperability at the syntactic level and concentrate on the actual clinical content. It should be noted that, although it is not official, there is an XML schema of ISO/CEN 13606 for the last three years, maintained by the EN 13606 Association (2010).

## PHR/EHR Content Templates

The content templates are built on top of the well-accepted content standards to further refine these standards by:

- Restricting the alternative hierarchical structures to be used within the instances,
- Constraining optionality and cardinality of some elements,
- Defining the code systems and codes used to classify parts of the content, and also
- Describing the specific data elements that are included.

One of the most prominent PHR content templates, namely Continuity of Care Document (CCD) (Health Level Seven, 2008) is defined by constraining an EHR content markup standard, namely, HL7 Clinical Document Architecture, Release 2 (CDA) with requirements set forward in ASTM CCR. CCD defines a single document template, but there are several section templates and clinical statement templates to be used within this main document template. IHE Patient Care Coordination (PCC) Technical Framework further details and multiplies the CCD templates at the document, section and clinical statement levels according to the content module requirements of its integration profiles such as Exchange of Personal Health Record Content (XPHR) (Integrating the Healthcare Enterprise, 2010d) and Query for Existing Data (QED) (Integrating the Healthcare Enterprise, 2008b). For example, currently PCC has six main document templates (Discharge Summary, Medical Document, Medical Summary, PHR Extract, PHR Update, Scanned Document) in comparison to the single CCD document template. Similarly, HITSP has defined CDA content modules that reuse and further restrict the IHE PCC templates and the underlying CCD templates according to the requirements in the US (Healthcare

Information Technology Standards Panel, 2010). In December 2011, within the US Office of the National Coordinator's (ONC) Standards and Interoperability (S&I) Framework, through the joint efforts of HL7, IHE, ONC and the Health Story Project (2011), the Consolidated CDA Templates guide was released as the single source incorporating and harmonizing CDA templates from CCD, PCC, HITSP C32, HL7 Health Story guides and Stage 1 Meaningful Use. Consolidated CDA is by far the most comprehensive and complete single source library of CDA templates, which makes it very valuable for CDA implementers all over the world.

As a result, although the CCR specification itself defines an XML schema as a content template for the exchange purposes, the HL7 CDA implementation of CCR, that is the HL7/ASTM CCD, and the other templates building on top of the CCD, are more widely-accepted than CCR's own XML schema.

In all CDA based templates, the most common way of formally expressing the constraints defined in templates and checking these constraints on clinical document instances is to create machine processable versions of templates as schematron rules, which then can be executed on the instances and present validation results automatically. Recently, model based validators that are implemented with Model Driven Health Tools (MDHT) (https://mdht.projects.openhealthtools. org/) have become popular as well. In MDHT, the validation rules are executed as Java and Object Constraint Language (OCL) code generated from the UML models.

ISO/CEN 13606 and openEHR adopt the concept of archetype, which is a computable expression of a domain level concept (e.g. blood pressure, physical examination or laboratory result) in the form of structured constraint statements, based on a reference information model (Beale et al., 2007). Hence, openEHR archetypes are based on the openEHR reference model, and

13606 archetypes are based on the 13606 reference model (i.e. 13606-1). It should be noted that the term "template" in openEHR has a more specific meaning than its generic usage in the HL7 and IHE domains; it corresponds to a directly usable definition that composes archetypes into larger structures such as a screen form, document or report. It can be said that clinical statement templates and section templates of ASTM/HL7, IHE and HITSP correspond to archetypes of ISO/CEN and openEHR; while document templates in the former correspond to templates in the latter. Both 13606 and openEHR use the ISO/CEN standardised Archetype Definition Language (expressed in ADL syntax or its XML equivalent) to formally define archetypes. openEHR also maintains the openEHR Clinical Knowledge Manager (CKM) (http://www. openehr.org/knowledge/) as a collaborative environment to build and host archetypes, templates and termsets. CKM is a valuable repository not only for openEHR and 13606 implementers, but for all; since it serves hundreds of archetypes in various representations (tabular, mindmap, ADL and XML) and languages, and all these archetypes are a result of harmonization of contributions from healthcare professionals all around the world.

Finally, HealthVault Thing Types can be considered as content templates as well, since they are specific to domain level concepts as in the case of CDA based templates and openEHR archetypes.

## Analysis of PHR/EHR Content Templates

Content standards are not enough for interoperability because there can be many different ways of organizing the same clinical information even when the same PHR/EHR content standard is used: the same information can be expressed through different components and these components can be nested differently. Therefore, the templates/ archetypes are necessary to constrain the structure and format of generic PHR/EHR content standards.

There is already much effort in defining content templates on top of content standards as explained in the previous section.

However, overlapping terminology systems as well as the structural differences in document templates create semantic interoperability problems in content templates which can be categorized as follows:

- Different terminology systems used by different healthcare applications in the same compositional structure within the same document template; and
- Different compositional structures within the same document template that express the same meaning differently.

As an example, consider the glucose measurement representations in HL7/ASTM CCD given in Figure 1. In this figure, there are two instances of the "CCD result organizer" template for reporting 104 mg/dL glucose in the plasma of a patient,

which is measured in a laboratory setting. Both instances present the same information, are valid CCD result organizer extracts and can be used in various integration profiles of IHE, such as XPHR (Exchange of Personal Health Record Content), XDS-MS (Cross Enterprise Sharing of Medical Summaries) or XD-LAB (Sharing Laboratory Reports).

In the following subsections, we investigate these types of interoperability problems and address possible solutions.

## Different Terminology Systems in the Same Compositional Structure

Consider the third shaded block of the first instance in Figure 1, which states that the observed value is within the normal ranges by using SNOMED CT code for "within reference range" (281301001) as the interpretation code of the observation class. Because, there is no CCD constraint on the value of interpretation code, in the second instance, this

*Figure 1. An example on some of the semantic interoperability problems in content templates*

**CCD Result Entry 1**

```
<organizer classCode="BATTERY" moodCode="EVN">
  <!-- Result organizer template -->
  <templateId root="2.16.840.1.113883.10.20.1.32"/>
  <id root="7d5a02b0-67a4-11db-bd13-0800200c9a66"/>
  <!-- SNOMED CT code for Plasma glucose measurement procedure -->
  <code code="119958019" codeSystem="2.16.840.1.113883.6.96"
    displayName="Glucose measurement, plasma"/>
  <statusCode code="completed"/>
  <effectiveTime value="200003231430"/>
  <component>
    <observation classCode="OBS" moodCode="EVN">
      <!-- Result observation template -->
      <templateId root="2.16.840.1.113883.10.20.1.31"/>
      <id root="107c2dc0-67a5-11db-bd13-0800200c9a66"/>
      <!-- SNOMED CT code for Blood glucose status -->
      <code code="405176005" codeSystem="2.16.840.1.113883.6.96"
        displayName="Blood glucose status"/>
      <statusCode code="completed"/>
      <effectiveTime value="200003231430"/>
      <value xsi:type="PQ" value="104" unit="mg/dL"/>
      <!-- SNOMED CT Code for Within Reference Range (Qualifier)-->
      <interpretationCode code="281301001"
        codeSystem="2.16.840.1.113883.6.96"/>
    </observation>
  </component>
</organizer>
```

**CCD Result Entry 2**

```
<organizer classCode="BATTERY" moodCode="EVN">
  <!-- Result organizer template -->
  <templateId root="2.16.840.1.113883.10.20.1.32"/>
  <id root="7d5a02b0-67a4-11db-bd13-0800200c9a67"/>
  <!-- SNOMED CT code for Laboratory test procedure (generic) -->
  <code code="15220000" codeSystem="2.16.840.1.113883.6.96"
    displayName="Laboratory Test"/>
  <statusCode code="completed"/>
  <effectiveTime value="200003231430"/>
  <component>
    <observation classCode="OBS" moodCode="EVN">
      <!-- Result observation template -->
      <templateId root="2.16.840.1.113883.10.20.1.31"/>
      <id root="107c2dc0-67a5-11db-bd13-0800200c9a67"/>
      <!-- LOINC Code for Glucose in serum or plasma -->
      <code code="2345-7" codeSystem="2.16.840.1.113883.6.1"
        displayName="Glucose in serum or plasma"/>
      <statusCode code="completed"/>
      <effectiveTime value="200003231430"/>
      <value xsi:type="PQ" value="104" unit="mg/dL"/>
      <!-- HL7 ObservationInterpretation code for Normal -->
      <interpretationCode code="N"
        codeSystem="2.16.840.1.113883.5.83"/>
    </observation>
  </component>
</organizer>
```

time the HL7 ObservationInterpretation code for "normal" (N) is used for the same purpose. Semantically, this code is an exact match with the SNOMED CT code used in the first instance.

## Possible Solutions for Addressing Different Terminology Systems in the Same Compositional Structure

When different terminology systems are used in the same compositional structure, it is necessary to semantically mediate them for interoperation. There are some repositories of biomedical vocabularies that also provide mapping information among the terms of these vocabularies, such as the Unified Medical Language System (UMLS) (http://www.nlm.nih.gov/research/umls/) Metathesaurus that integrates over 2 million names for some 900,000 concepts from more than 60 families of biomedical vocabularies, as well as 12 million relations among these concepts. Similarly, BioPortal initiative (http://bioportal.bioontology.org/) serves more than 290 biomedical ontologies including ontological representations of major terminology systems like SNOMED CT, LOINC, ICD-10 and MedDRA, as well as mapping information between the coded terms of these terminology systems through ontological constructs. Such repositories can be exploited for automated or semi-automated mapping of coded terms from different terminology systems.

Yet, neither UMLS, nor BioPortal is perfect regarding the quality of the terminology mappings they provide. There are some mappings between the terms that are not at the same hierarchical level. For example, in one BioPortal mapping, "bronchitis" in one terminology system is matched with "respiratory diseases" in another terminology system. Furthermore, some of the mappings provided by these repositories are automatically generated with the help of NLP based methods, and they need to be validated.

Therefore, it is necessary to involve clinical terminology experts to increase the quality of the mappings, during both the mapping creation phase and the clinical statement translation phase. Creation of mapping definitions among entire terminology systems is an ambitious task. Instead, focusing on particular sub-topics such as cardiovascular diseases with the involvement of related experts is more achievable. When the quality of the mappings is not assured, semi-automatic translation of clinical statements should be preferred over fully automatic translation. In this case, the translation mechanism can be a living system that can be improved with the integration of feedback received from terminology experts.

### Different Compositional Structures

Another type of semantic interoperability challenge comes from different compositional structures for encoding the same medical information.

Consider the first shaded block of the first instance in Figure 1. The result organizer code is the SNOMED CT code for plasma glucose measurement procedure (119958019). In the second instance, the code of the result organizer template is again from SNOMED CT; however, this time the code refers to a more generic meaning, i.e. laboratory test procedure (15220000). Because the CCD constraint for the result organizer code is to use an appropriate code from SNOMED CT or LOINC or optionally CPT-4, by using the codes from SNOMED CT, both of these documents satisfy this constraint.

In the first instance, the second coded attribute presents the topic of the observable entity of the result organizer, and the SNOMED CT code for blood glucose status (405176005) is used for this purpose. This code encodes the meaning for the actual observed value, which is 104 mg/dL glucose.

In the second instance, the code system preferred in the code attribute of observation class is different. Here, the LOINC code for glucose in serum or plasma (2345-7) is used for encoding the meaning of the actual observed value.

As a result, the result organizer codes and the observation codes of the first and second instances do not directly correspond to each other; the first result organizer code is restricted to glucose measurement domain while the second one is generic, and the observation codes are quite similar but not identical. However, when we consider the medical information represented in these instances, the combined meaning of organizer and observation codes are almost identical.

## Possible Solutions for Addressing Different Compositional Structures

This problem is well-known and to address it, terminology bindings (Browne, 2008) have been proposed which specify the association between a data point (node) of an information or data model and the set of terms that can be used to populate that data point's value. The set of permissible values for a data point can be expressed by a query or a rule. As an example, the HL7 TermInfo (Health Level Seven, 2006) guidelines specify how SNOMED CT can be used in HL7 v3 standards, in order to communicate healthcare information in an agreed, consistent and adequately expressive form. In SNOMED CT, concepts are defined by relationships (e.g. method, procedure site, etc.) among them, and they can also be qualified (combined) to represent more precise meanings. Hence, even a single SNOMED CT concept may represent a meaning that the HL7 v3 RIM is able to represent using a combination of classes and attributes. TermInfo identifies options for use of SNOMED CT concepts in various attributes of HL7 RIM classes, and also provides an evaluation of such options. Unfortunately, although TermInfo is a very important project to contribute to consistent usage of terminology systems within content templates, its activities have been suspended for the last few years.

Another practical approach to this type of semantic interoperability has been developed in epSOS (http://www.epsos.eu), which is a pan-European project for piloting cross-border interoperability among national and regional EHR systems in Europe. For this purpose, first, the content templates of the three document types (i.e. patient summary, ePrescription and eDispensation) to be exchanged are defined as pivot documents by using and further restricting IHE PCC templates. Each country defines its own mapping from its national data structures onto these pivot document schemas. For the coded and unique representation of clinical content within these schemas, subsets from existing terminology systems such as SNOMED CT, ICD-10, LOINC and ATC have been selected to create the epSOS Master Value Sets Catalogue (MVC). The latest version of MVC contains 46 value sets. For example, the procedures value set contains 102 terms from SNOMED CT and illnesses and disorders value set contains 1685 terms from ICD-10. Each epSOS participating nation provides mapping of any locally used terminology system to MVC content and also translation of the MVC content into its own language, resulting in the epSOS Master Translation/Transcoding Catalogue. There are plans to provide MVC as an ontology (coded in OWL) to foster semantic interoperability.

As in the case of epSOS, the Clinical Info Model & Vocabulary Work Group of Transitions of Care (ToC) Initiative in the US has defined "Meaningful Use Subsets" of SNOMED CT, ICD-10, LOINC and RxNorm.

## EHR-PHR INTEROPERABILITY PROFILES

### IHE Exchange of Personal Health Record Content (XPHR) Integration Profile

The XPHR profile (Integrating the Healthcare Enterprise, 2010d) provides an interoperability mechanism to exchange data between PHR systems and the healthcare providers' information systems. Two actors have been defined: the "Content Creator" that creates the content to be exchanged and the "Content Consumer" that consumes this content. The data exchange is in both directions: a PHR system can get data from the healthcare information systems and can also feed data to these systems. A PHR system in the "Content Creator" role provides a summary of patient PHR information to providers' information systems, and the providers' systems in the "Content Creator" role can suggest updates to the patient's PHR upon completion of a healthcare encounter.

The content to be exchanged is specified through two content templates, namely PHR Extract Module and the PHR Update Module. The PHR Extract Module describes the document content that summarizes information contained within a Personal Health Record. The purpose of the PHR Update Module is to provide a mechanism to update an existing PHR Extract content to reflect the changes in patient information in other healthcare information systems. Both PHR Extract and Update modules are defined as IHE PCC templates based on HL7/ASTM CCD.

XPHR relies on the previously defined document exchange profiles such as Cross-Enterprise Document Sharing (XDS) (Integrating the Health-care Enterprise, 2010c), Cross-Enterprise Document Media Interchange (XDM) (Integrating the Healthcare Enterprise, 2010a) or Cross-Enterprise Document Reliable Interchange (XDR) (Integrating the Healthcare Enterprise, 2010b).

As an example, in Figure 2 we describe how IHE XPHR profile can be implemented based on IHE XDS Profile. A PHR system in the "Content Creator" role stores patient information to a Content Repository using XDS "Provide & Register Document Set" transaction whose content complies with the "PHR Extract Module" content template (Optionally, the Content Creator and Content Repository actors can be grouped as a single actor as shown by the dotted lines in Figure 2, in which case the "Provide & Register Document Set" transaction becomes irrelevant). Then the metadata of the stored content is sent to the Content Registry by using "Register Document Set" transaction of XDS to facilitate its discovery. Similarly, an EHR system can take the role of a "Content Creator" and store patient information again complying with the "PHR Extract Module" content template. Additionally, an EHR system may provide patient data through "PHR Update Module" to update the PHR Extract.

*Figure 2. IHE XPHR profile based on IHE XDS*

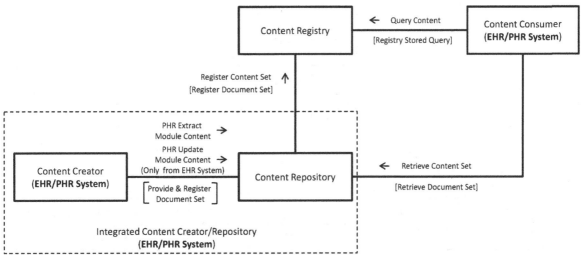

## IHE Query for Existing Data (QED) Integration Profile

Using the Query for Existing Data (QED) Profile (Integrating the Healthcare Enterprise, 2008b), it is possible to access clinical data sources with predefined queries and hence this profile is quite relevant for PHR-EHR data exchange. There are two actors in this profile, namely the "Clinical Data Consumer" and the "Clinical Data Source," and the business process layer involves one transaction, namely, "Query Existing Data" that is used by the consumer to query the source. This transaction gets a number of query parameters such as "patientId," "patientName," "careProvisionCode" and "careRecordTimePeriod." Six different types of queries are defined and each of them is indicated as an option of the "Query Existing Data" transaction. The actor implementing this transaction must support at least one of them:

- Vital Signs Option;
- Problems and Allergies Option;
- Diagnostic Results Option;
- Medications Option;
- Immunizations Option;
- Professional Services Option.

A content template is specified for each result to be returned by the query. Each content template inherits constraints from the CCD and PCC entry level templates, and defines further constraints such as by setting the units to be used and a specific vocabulary.

For example, a "Clinical Data Consumer" that implements the "Problems and Allergies Option" can retrieve all problem entries by specifying the code "MEDCCAT" and the result will conform to the PCC Problem Entry template, or can specify the code "INTOLIST" that will return the results conforming to the PCC Allergy and Intolerance Concern template.

A "Clinical Data Source" that implements the "Problems and Allergies Option" on the other hand, must be able to respond to all vocabulary specified for problems and allergies including "MEDCCAT" and "INTOLIST." An example QED usage scenario is depicted in Figure 3.

For the communication layer, the IHE ITI Web services (Integrating the Healthcare Enterprise, 2010f) and HL7 Web services guidelines (Health Level Seven, 2010b) are used. The "Query Existing Data" transaction is mapped to the Query Care Record Event Profile Query of HL7 v3 Care Record Query topic. It is important to note that

*Figure 3. The use of IHE QED Profile for data exchange*

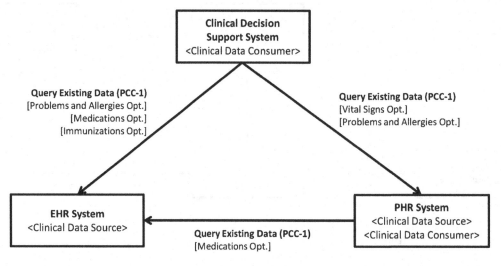

in these transactions that are defined by the HL7 v3 Care Provision domain (used by IHE RCG and CM profiles as well), it is not possible to exchange a complete CDA document instance. The payload of a Care Provision Event instance as used in these transactions can contain only Care Statement instances, which are almost identical with CDA entry classes. Hence, IHE QED (also RCG and CM) profile refers to only entry level PCC templates.

## Analysis of PHR Interoperability Profiles

Being interoperability profiles, both XPHR and QED address all the layers in the interoperability stack. Their difference is that with QED, it is possible to get parts of a patient's EHR as specified through the options such as "vital signs" or "medications." Indeed, such partial queries are important because exchange of a complete patient history is not necessary all the time; it might be necessary to get only the active medications of a patient for example. QED is relevant for decision support services as well; it can be used to retrieve only relevant portions of patient data according to the requirements of the specific decision support service. However, in the future, it might be necessary to extend the existing set of options.

A disadvantage of QED is that it lacks support for asynchronous communication. XPHR on the other hand, when implemented with XDS for instance, can support asynchronous Web services exchange. This issue is further detailed in *Clinical Decision Support Service Standards* Section while describing the Clinical Decision Support Service standards.

## TERMINOLOGY SYSTEMS

In medicine, the clinical data structures such as EHR and PHR content templates refer to "controlled vocabularies" or "terminologies"

to express semantics, i.e., the meaning of the terms used. For example, the observation for a patient can be expressed as a "heart attack" or a "myocardial infarction," and these mean the same thing to medical professionals. But unless the term is associated with a unique code from a terminology system, automated processing of the exchanged term is very difficult because an application, programmed to use "heart attack," would not understand "myocardial infarction." When the observation refers to a medical terminology system such as SNOMED CT and the code 22298006 for "Myocardial infarction" is used to represent the observation, the meaning exchanged can be shared in a consistent and automated way as long as both of the applications use this code.

In this section, we will briefly mention some of the well-known terminology systems and provide an analysis especially for terminology systems' mapping.

## Analysis of Terminology Systems

The terminology systems can be classified based on the underlying structure and related knowledge representation formalism that determine the way they express the semantics of the relationships between the coded terms: Some are plain lists, for example the Standard Terms of the European Directorate for the Quality of Medicines and Healthcare (EDQM); some are terminology systems organized into a hierarchy, for example ICD-10 and hence give the parent-child information among the terms; and some express the relationships between the coded terms through ontological constructs, for example SNOMED CT or semantic networks like Unified Medical Language System (UMLS). This classification together with some example terminology systems and resources is provided in Table 2.

Currently, SNOMED CT is the most comprehensive clinical vocabulary available, in terms of coverage and the relationships among concepts. It contains approximately 350,000 active concepts,

*Table 2. Classification of some medical terminology systems and resources*

| Simple Lists (No Relationship Among the Terms) | Classification Systems (Hierarchical Relationship Among the Coded Terms) | Semantic Relationship Among the Concepts | Mapping Information Among Different Terminology Systems |
|---|---|---|---|
| EDQM Standard Terms | ICD-9, ICD-10, MedDRA | SNOMED CT, UMLS Metathesaurus and Semantic Network | UMLS Metathesaurus, BioPortal |

more than 1 million terms including synonyms and about 1.5 million relations between the concepts. On the other hand, SNOMED CT has both logical and ontological problems as has been discussed in the literature (Heja et al., 2008; Bodenreider et al., 2007; Schulz et al., 2009). The identified problems include mixing the subsumption relation with other relations such as "part of;" redundant concepts; omission of obvious relationships and contracting disjoint entities into one concept. A number of recommendations have been proposed to overcome these problems such as arranging SNOMED CT upper ontology according to a standard upper ontology (Heja et al., 2008; Schulz et al., 2009); assigning SNOMED CT concepts to four disjoint groups such as classes, instances, relations and meta-classes (Schulz et al., 2009) and a high level core reference ontology of shared medical knowledge (Heja et al., 2008). However, the use of SNOMED CT as a terminology service as a plain or loosely structured list does not need substantial restructuring.

To achieve interoperability among terminology systems, not only the mapping information between them but also the semantic relationships among the terms (or, concepts) are necessary because this helps discovering the implicit equivalences between two terms from different terminology systems by using reasoning. As an example, assume a patient's acute heart failure condition is expressed with SNOMED CT code 56675007 in a clinical document and the receiving application understands only the MedDRA terminology system. Through reasoning, it is possible to discover that the equivalent MedDRA code is 10019279 for "heart failure," because

the SNOMED CT class for "acute heart failure" (56675007) is a subclass of the class for "heart failure" (84114007) and given that MedDRA code for "heart failure" (10019279) maps to 84114007 in SNOMED CT; a reasoner can deduce this result by using subsumption reasoning.

Currently, several sources provide terminology system mappings. More than 60 families of biomedical vocabularies together with context and inter-context relationships among these various vocabularies are available within the UMLS. Also, ontological representations of more than 290 terminology systems and their mappings are accessible through BioPortal, which is maintained by the US National Center for Biomedical Ontology. However, not all the mappings are fully reliable. Therefore, as discussed in *Possible solutions for addressing different terminology systems in the same compositional structure* Section, although there is a need to develop tools to map terms from different terminology systems, continuous involvement of terminology experts and healthcare professionals in this process is necessary to guarantee reliable translation of clinical statements/documents.

## STANDARDS FOR EHR-PHR-MEDICAL DEVICE INTEROPERABILITY

Personal medical devices are essential to the practice of modern healthcare services, including the PHR systems. A number of applications have been developed to store personal medical device data to PHR systems.

The prominent standards for the integration of medical device data into electronic and personal health records (EHR/PHR) include the IHE Patient Care Device (PCD) integration profiles (Integrating the Healthcare Enterprise, 2010e) and Electronic/Personal Health Record Network Interface (xHRN-IF) (Carroll et al., 2007) by the Continua Health Alliance.

Both of these standards address how to map the device data obtained through the ISO/IEEE 11073 standard (International Organization for Standardization et al., 2004a) to the healthcare application interfaces. This is because the most widely used standard to obtain data from the medical devices is ISO/IEEE 11073 set of standards. 11073 standards define an object-oriented Domain Information Model (DIM) (International Organization for Standardization, 2004b) to model medical device domain. It is possible to represent a medical device and its measurements with objects using the DIM. However, in order to define interoperable medical devices, the attributes of these objects must consist of codes that are specified in a data dictionary. ISO/IEEE 11073 - 10101: Nomenclature (International Organization for Standardization, 2004c) is a data dictionary of vital signs domain which is used to represent the DIM objects with common codes.

IHE Device Enterprise Communication (DEC) Profile is used for transmitting information from medical devices at the point of care to the enterprise applications. For this purpose, ISO/IEEE 11073 Domain Information Model is mapped to HL7 v2.5 Observation Report and the ISO/IEEE 11073 Data Types are mapped to HL7 v2.5 Data Types. For semantic interoperability, IHE has developed the Rosetta Terminology Mapping (RTM) Profile to provide the mapping between the proprietary device parameters to ISO/IEEE 11073 Nomenclature. Each row of the Rosetta table, which is under development, gives the vendors' displayed name and units of measure together with the equivalent ISO/IEEE 11073

identifier and the unit from the Unified Code for Units of Measure (UCUM) code system (http://www.unitsofmeasure.org/).

The Continua Health Alliance Electronic/Personal Health Record Network Interface (xHRN-IF) is based on the HL7 Personal Health Monitoring Report (PHMR) (Health Level Seven, 2008) document format. The PHMR carries personal healthcare monitoring information including the representation of the measurements captured by devices, notes, summaries and graphs. In order to represent such varying data, templates are defined by reusing HL7 Continuity of Care Document. The health record systems like PHRs need to implement xHRN-IF to be able to exchange personal health information with healthcare entities conforming to this standard.

## Analysis of the Standards for EHR-PHR-Medical Device Interoperability

As already mentioned, the EHR-PHR-Medical Device Interoperability standards address how to map the device data obtained through the ISO/IEEE 11073 standards to the healthcare application interfaces. Considering that there are different EHR/PHR content standards and templates, generating a mapping from ISO/IEEE 11073 Domain Information Model to each of them is not very practical.

A recent work (Yuksel et al., 2011) addresses this challenge by specializing the HL7 v3 Reference Information Model (RIM) to the medical device domain using the ISO/IEEE 11073 Domain Information Model (DIM) to obtain its Refined Message Information Model (RMIM). The novelty of this approach is that it provides a common denominator for different HL7 v3 RIM based interfaces of various EHR/PHR content models rather than using the bilateral mappings between the device models and different application standards. This facilitates EHR/PHR and personal medical device data interoperability because the concepts are derived from a common RIM through a well-defined refinement process and hence the building blocks of the interfaces are similar, and they can be traceable back to the RIM.

## CLINICAL DECISION SUPPORT SERVICE STANDARDS

Clinical Decision Support Services (CDSSs) are used in care management to provide clinicians, staff and patients with knowledge, intelligently filtered or presented at appropriate times, to enhance health and healthcare (Kawamoto et al., 2007). Common uses of CDSSs include computerized provider order entry systems that give patient-specific recommendations as part of the order entry process; listing health maintenance procedures due when patient age, gender, past health maintenance procedures are provided; or laboratory alerting systems that page physicians when critical lab values are detected.

Although the CDSSs are designed primarily to assist patient-specific decision making by clinicians, it is anticipated that CDSSs will be adapted to provide patient guidance services from the PHR systems to be used by patients themselves (European Commission, 2010). In this respect, a relevant topic that is indirectly linked with the CDSS concept is enabling patients' access to evidence-based health information available as text or multimedia resources presented in layman terms, to foster their engagement in the management of their care. Some PHR systems automatically link the key terms or phrases in the patient's records with relevant evidence-based health information on the Web. A further improvement in this direction is provided by the HL7 International Context-Aware Knowledge Retrieval Standard, known as Infobutton (Health Level Seven, 2010a), which rather than providing a direct link, helps a user (not necessarily a patient; can be a health professional as well) to refine his query based on automatically collected contextual information

(e.g. user type, patient age and gender, the term of interest) and user feedback. Then it allows the user to easily access the preferred evidence-based resource through World Wide Web links.

CDSSs generally include a knowledge base containing information such as compiled clinical information on diagnoses, drug interactions and guidelines; a program for combining that knowledge with patient-specific information to draw machine interpretable conclusions regarding patients; and a mechanism to enter or import patient data from the EHR/PHR systems into the CDSS so that the relevant information, such as lists of possible diagnoses, drug interaction alerts, or preventive care reminders can be provided (Berner et al., 2009).

The main challenge to wider use of CDSSs is the need to implement different interfaces when dealing with different CDSSs. There are three major initiatives to address this challenge: the service oriented model by the Healthcare Services Specification Project (HSSP) to expose clinical decision support services in a uniform way, the IHE Request for Clinical Guidance (RCG) Profile and the IHE Care Management (CM) Profile that provides a mechanism for EHR/PHR and other health IT systems to communicate information to care management systems.

HSSP developed first a service functional model (SFM) (Kawamoto et al., 2006) and then a technical specification built upon this SFM for exposing CDSS modules as decision support services. The aim is to let the CDSS client applications have uniform access to different knowledge modules. By using the specified service interfaces, a service client is able to determine which knowledge module to use, what data are needed for requesting a patient evaluation, as well as what will be returned by the CDSS as a result of the patient evaluation request.

IHE has published the Request for Clinical Guidance profile (Integrating the Healthcare Enterprise, 2009b) that describes how to exchange patient data as the payload needed to drive the clinical decision support service for certain decision support modules such as drug and allergy interaction detection, forecasting a vaccine schedule, identifying eligible patients for research or other programs, and cost effective selection of antibiotics based on recent institutional data.

Another related IHE profile is the Care Management profile (Integrating the Healthcare Enterprise, 2008a). This profile is more generic than the RCG profile in that it provides a mechanism for EHR/PHR and other health IT systems to communicate information to care management systems through the use of evidence based guidelines.

## HSSP Clinical Decision Support Service Specification

In 2006, Healthcare Services Specification Project (HSSP), which is a joint effort by Health Level Seven (HL7) and the Object Management Group (OMG), developed a service functional model for exposing CDSS modules as decision support services. The aim is to facilitate CDSS client applications to:

- Identify the knowledge modules that could be used to meet their needs;
- Know what patient data must be submitted to the CDSS in order to obtain an accurate evaluation; and
- Know the meaning and format of any results that will be returned by the CDSS following a patient evaluation (Kawamoto et al., 2006).

In order to realize this functionality, three interface specifications are developed:

- The Meta-data Discovery interface provides operations for discovering and examining meta-data associated with a CDSS or its knowledge modules.
- The Query interface provides operations for discovering and examining knowledge modules of interest. This interface includes operations for identifying the data required for evaluating a patient using a knowledge module.
- The Evaluation interface provides operations for obtaining evaluation results using specified knowledge modules. A CDSS is permitted to return evaluation results using a variety of information constructs including the RIM acts (e.g., an HL7 medication entity with a mood code indicating that the medication should be ordered), dates (e.g., the date that a test was last performed, or the date at which a test will be due), and boolean values (e.g., whether a patient is in need of a pneumococcal vaccine).

Building on this functional model, OMG developed a fully implementable Clinical Decision Support Service (CDSS) specification as a normative standard in 2010 (the latest version is from 2011) (Object Management Group, 2011), which is then proceeded by the HL7 Decision Support Service (DSS) specification (Health Level Seven, 2011b). HL7 DSS and OMG CDSS technical specifications are almost identical; minor differences will be resolved in future releases. They include both a platform-independent model (PIM) for the DSSs as well as a platform-specific model (PSM) for SOAP XML Web services. The PIM represents the platform-independent definitions of the DSS interfaces and the elements used within these interfaces as a UML model. The PSM describes technical details for implementation including WSDLs and XSDs that are generated according to the PIM. The XML syntax of these schemas are mostly custom defined by OMG, but some data elements are built upon the HL7 v3 RIM XSD representation as well. The HL7/OMG Decision Support Service technical specifications also define several profiles and semantic requirements to ensure a minimum level of interoperability among DSSs.

OpenCDS (http://www.opencds.org/) is a multi-institutional, collaborative effort to develop an open-source reference implementation of the HL7/OMG DSS technical specifications, and 1.1 release of the implementation is already available.

## IHE Request for Clinical Guidance (RCG) Profile

The IHE Request for Clinical Guidance (RCG) profile supports integration of clinical decision support into healthcare IT systems by describing how to exchange patient data as the payload needed to drive the clinical decision support service.

There are two actors in this profile, namely, the "Care Manager" and the "Decision Support Service" actors. "Request for Clinical Guidance" transaction requests and returns information between these actors. At the communication layer HL7 v3 Web Services Profile is used, and the Report Care Provision transaction that is defined by the HL7 v3 Care Provision domain is utilized. In general, RCG profile suggests leveraging the existing PCC content modules to deliver information to a CDSS. The CDSS then responds with a suggested care plan or additional clinical information. As an example, consider an immunization forecasting scenario (Integrating the Healthcare Enterprise, 2009b). The "Care Manager" actor obtains patient age, gender, and current immunization status, allergies and problem information from the EHR/PHR system. The "Care Manager" actor submits the relevant portions of this information to the decision support service using "Request for Clinical Guidance" transaction. The "Decision Support Service" actor, which in this case is an immunization forecasting service, processes this information and returns a response to the "Care Manager" actor in the same transaction. The response includes the evaluations of the immunizations and one or more immunization schedules.

It is clear that content templates are needed for describing the payloads used in the request and response messages of the request for clinical

guidance transaction. Currently, only immunization content template is available through the Immunization Content Profile (Integrating the Healthcare Enterprise, 2009a). It is anticipated that additional content profiles that work with these actors will be created in the future.

## IHE Care Management (CM) Profile

The Care Management (CM) profile supports the exchange of information between health IT systems and applications used to manage care for specific conditions. The Care Management profile describes a publish/subscribe mechanism between source and the consumer systems. It is almost the same with the QED profile (*IHE Query for Existing Data (QED) Integration Profile* Section), but rather than getting an immediate response only for once; the source system keeps sending back the new results that matches the criteria as they become available. This query is maintained indefinitely until the requesting system cancels it.

As in the case of QED and RCG profiles, Care Management profile uses transactions and messages that are defined by the HL7 v3 Care Provision domain. For this reason, it is not possible to use document level content templates directly within the CM profile, as Care Provision Event messages allow only entry level instances as the payload.

Unlike QED and RCG, CM profile supports HL7 v2 messaging in addition to HL7 v3 Web services implementation.

## Analysis of the Clinical Decision Support Service Standards

Among the three major initiatives explained above, the HL7/OMG DSS technical specifications, which are defined on top of the HSSP service functional model, cover the widest range of accessible interfaces for the CDSSs. For example, meta-data discovery and query interfaces together provide several methods to find knowledge modules of interest. IHE RCG and CM profiles on the other hand do not provide discovery functionalities. OpenCDS, that is, the collaborative and open-source reference implementation effort for HL7/ OMG DSS technical specifications is another advantage of HSSP functional model.

The main advantage of the Care Management profile over the rest, and also over the IHE QED profile, is that, it enables asynchronous stateful clinical decision support.

The major drawback of all three efforts is their low-profile support for the structured content modules to exchange patient and decision support data. HL7/OMG DSS technical specifications state that ASTM CCR, HL7/ASTM CCD or any other HL7 v3 RIM based syntax can be used to exchange patient data with CDSSs, which in fact is quite a loose restriction. IHE CM and RCG profiles on the other hand, necessitate the usage of messages that are defined by the HL7 v3 Care Provision domain; but the profiles are always explained with IHE PCC content modules that are defined on top of CCD. As explained previously, it is not possible to use PCC document and section level templates in the Care Provision Event messages, and entry level templates are subject to some changes while transforming them to Care Statement instances used within Care Provision Event messages. However, transformation of complete CDA documents to valid Care Provision messages is presented very briefly in the profiles. Such issues impede the use of the CDSS standards and profiles.

## CONCLUSION

Personal Health Records (PHRs) have the potential to dramatically change healthcare over the coming years (Kaelber et al., 2008). It is anticipated that empowering patients with PHRs and thus making their active participation possible in their own healthcare management will produce better health outcomes at lower costs.

A notable report by some of the leading industry organizations including Google, HIMSS, Kaiser Permanente and Microsoft investigates the value of PHR systems in the context of four PHR system architectures: provider-tethered, payer-tethered, third-party, and interoperable PHRs (Kaelber et al., 2008). Provider tethered, payer-tethered, and third-party PHRs all have related examples in the current marketplace. These systems mostly use ad hoc interfaces to pass information from each healthcare application to the PHR system. Given the large number of applications involved, it is not practical or cost effective to design one-off interfaces.

Interoperable PHRs, on the other hand, represent a future type of PHR in which all entities have access to data due to health data communication standards and interoperability. The report concludes that from the perspective of the healthcare system, interoperable PHRs provide the greatest value.

This chapter surveys the interoperability standards that can be used to import/export data to and from the PHR systems to a large number of healthcare applications and medical data resources. It is an analysis harmonizing the state-of-the-art and the authors' experiences in developing systems using these standards which are presented through clear examples rather than a compilation of descriptions from the standards' specifications. The study also aims to provide an entry point for the researchers in this domain.

The interoperable PHRs, when realized, will reinforce patient participation in care processes and health management, improve health outcomes by improved decision support, enhance adherence to treatment by making it possible to measure patients' compliance and to demonstrate their progress and have positive impact on lifestyle diseases by empowering patients with better information, communication and means for shared decision making.

# REFERENCES

American Health Information Management Association (AHIMA) & American Medical Informatics Association. (AMIA). (2007). *The value of personal health records: A joint position statement for consumers of health care.* Retrieved from http://www.amia.org/sites/amia.org/files/ahima-amia-phr-statement.pdf

ASTM International. (2005). *E2369 - 05e1 standard specification for continuity of care record (CCR).* Retrieved from http://www.astm.org/Standards/E2369.htm

Beale, T., & Heard, S. (2007). *Archetype definitions and principles.* Retrieved from http://www.openehr.org/svn/specification/TRUNK/publishing/architecture/am/archetype_principles.pdf

Berner, E. S. (2009). *Clinical decision support systems: State of the art.* Retrieved from http://healthit.portaldev.ahrq.gov/portal/server.pt/gateway/PTARGS_0_1248_874024_0_0_18/09-0069-EF.pdf

Bodenreider, O., Smith, B., Kumar, A., & Burgun, A. (2007). Investigating subsumption in SNOMED CT: An exploration into large description logic-based biomedical terminologies. *Artificial Intelligence in Medicine, 39*(3), 183–195. doi:10.1016/j.artmed.2006.12.003 PMID:17241777

Browne, E. (2008). *openEHR archetypes and terminology.* Retrieved from http://www.openehr.org/wiki/display/healthmod/Archetypes+and+Terminology

Carroll, R., Cnossen, R., Schnell, M., & Simons, D. (2007). Continua: An interoperable personal healthcare ecosystem. *IEEE Pervasive Computing/IEEE Computer Society [and] IEEE Communications Society, 6*(4), 90–94. doi:10.1109/MPRV.2007.72

Eichelberg, M., Aden, T., Riesmeier, J., Dogac, A., & Laleci, G. B. (2005). A survey and analysis of electronic healthcare record standards. *ACM Computing Surveys, 37,* 277–315. doi:10.1145/1118890.1118891

EN 13606 Association. (2010). *Unofficial ISO/CEN 13606 XML schema.* Retrieved from http://www.en13606.org/resources/files/cat_view/53-xml-schemas

European Commission. (2004). *European interoperability framework for pan-European egovernment services.* Retrieved from http://ec.europa.eu/idabc/servlets/Docd552.pdf?id=19529

European Commission. (2010). *FP7 ICT work programme 2011 - Objective ICT-2011.5.3 patient guidance services (PGS).* Retrieved from ftp://ftp.cordis.europa.eu/pub/fp7/docs/wp/cooperation/ict/c-wp-201101_en.pdf

Halamka, J. D., Mandl, K. D., & Tang, P. C. (2008). Early experiences with personal health records. *Journal of the American Medical Informatics Association, 15*(1), 1–7. doi:10.1197/jamia.M2562 PMID:17947615

Health Level Seven. (2005). *Clinical document architecture (CDA), release 2.* Retrieved from http://www.hl7.org/implement/standards/cda.cfm

Health Level Seven. (2006). *TermInfo: Using SNOMED CT in HL7 version 3.* Retrieved from http://www.hl7.org/library/committees/terminfo/TermInfo_Ballot_DRAFT.30Jan2006.doc

Health Level Seven. (2008). *Personal healthcare monitoring report (PHMR).* Retrieved from http://www.hl7.org/documentcenter/ballots/2008SEP/support/CDAR2_PHMRPTS_R1_DSTU_2008NOV.zip

Health Level Seven. (2010a). *Context-aware retrieval application (infobutton), knowledge request, release 1.* Retrieved from http://www.hl7.org/v3ballot/html/domains/uvds/uvds_Context-awareKnowledgeRetrieval(Infobutton).html

Health Level Seven. (2010b). *HL7 version 3 standard: Transport specification - Web services profile, release 2.* Retrieved from http://www.hl7.org/v3ballot/html/infrastructure/transport/transport-wsprofiles.html

Health Level Seven. (2010c). *Reference information model (RIM) release 3.* Retrieved from http://www.hl7.org/v3ballot/html/infrastructure/rim/rim.html

Health Level Seven. (2011a). *greenCDA project.* Retrieved from http://wiki.hl7.org/index.php?title=GreenCDA_Project

Health Level Seven. (2011b). *HL7 version 3 standard: Decision support service, release 1.* Retrieved from http://www.hl7.org/v3ballot/html/infrastructure/dss/HL7_Decision_Support_Service_%20Normative_Specification_Release_1.pdf

Health Level Seven & ASTM International. (2008). *Continuity of care document (CCD) release 1.* Retrieved from http://wiki.hl7.org/index.php?title=Product_CCD

Healthcare Information Technology Standards Panel. (2009). *HITSP C32 - Summary documents using HL7 continuity of care document (CCD) component.* Retrieved from http://www.hitsp.org/ConstructSet_Details.aspx?&PrefixAlpha=4&PrefixNumeric=32

Healthcare Information Technology Standards Panel. (2010). *HITSP C83 - CDA content modules component.* Retrieved from http://www.hitsp.org/Handlers/HitspFileServer.aspx?FileGuid=717d69a5-6bc4-4f8b-a22c-197130b50567

Heja, G., Surjan, G., & Varga, P. (2008). Ontological analysis of SNOMED CT. *BMC Medical Informatics and Decision Making, 8*(S1), S8. doi:10.1186/1472-6947-8-S1-S8 PMID:19007445

Helmer, A., Lipprandt, M., Frenken, T., Eichelberg, M., & Hein, A. (2011). Empowering patients through personal health records: A survey of existing third-party web-based PHR products. *Electronic Journal of Health Informatics, 6*(3), 1–19.

Iakovidis, I. (1998). Towards personal health records: Current situation, obstacles and trends in implementation of electronic healthcare. *International Journal of Medical Informatics, 52*(1-3), 105–115. doi:10.1016/S1386-5056(98)00129-4 PMID:9848407

Integrating the Healthcare Enterprise. (2008a). *Care management (CM) integration profile.* Retrieved from http://www.ihe.net/Technical_Framework/upload/IHE_PCC_Care_Management_CM_Supplement_TI_2008-08-22.pdf

Integrating the Healthcare Enterprise. (2008b). *Query for existing data (QED) integration profile.* Retrieved from http://www.ihe.net/Technical_Framework/upload/IHE_PCC_Query_for_Existing_Data_QED_SupplSuppl_TI_2008-08-22.pdf

Integrating the Healthcare Enterprise. (2009a). *Immunization content (IC) integration profile.* Retrieved from http://www.ihe.net/Technical_Framework/upload/IHE_PCC_Immunization_Content_IC_Supplement_TI_-2009-08-10.pdf

Integrating the Healthcare Enterprise. (2009b). *Request for clinical guidance (RCG) integration profile.* Retrieved from http://www.ihe.net/Technical_Framework/upload/IHE_PCC_Request_for_Clinical_Guidance_RCG_TI_-2009-08-10.pdf

Integrating the Healthcare Enterprise. (2010a). *Cross-enterprise document media interchange (XDM) integration profile.* Retrieved from http://www.ihe.net/Technical_Framework/upload/IHE_ITI_TF_Rev7-0_Vol1_FT_2010-08-10.pdf

Integrating the Healthcare Enterprise. (2010b). *Cross-enterprise document reliable interchange (XDR) integration profile.* Retrieved from http://www.ihe.net/Technical_Framework/upload/IHE_ITI_TF_Rev7-0_Vol1_FT_2010-08-10.pdf

Integrating the Healthcare Enterprise. (2010c). *Cross-enterprise document sharing (XDS) integration profile.* Retrieved from http://www.ihe.net/Technical_Framework/upload/IHE_ITI_TF_Rev7-0_Vol1_FT_2010-08-10.pdf

Integrating the Healthcare Enterprise. (2010d). *Exchange of personal health record content (XPHR) integration profile.* Retrieved from http://www.ihe.net/Technical_Framework/upload/IHE_PCC_TF_Rev6-0_Vol_1_2010-08-30.pdf

Integrating the Healthcare Enterprise. (2010e). *Patient care device (PCD) technical framework, volume 1, revision 1.2.* Retrieved from http://www.ihe.net/Technical_Framework/upload/IHE_PCD_TF_Rev1-2_Vol1_TI_2010-09-30.pdf

Integrating the Healthcare Enterprise. (2010f). *Web services for IHE transactions.* Retrieved from http://www.ihe.net/Technical_Framework/upload/IHE_ITI_TF_Rev7-0_Vol2x_FT_2010-08-10.pdf

International Organization for Standardization & Comité Européen de Normalisation. (2008). *EN 13606-1, health informatics – Electronic health record communication – Part 1: Reference model.*

International Organization for Standardization & The Institute of Electrical and Electronics Engineers. (2004a). *ISO/IEEE 11073 family of standards.*

International Organization for Standardization & The Institute of Electrical and Electronics Engineers. (2004b). *ISO/IEEE 11073-10201:2004(E) health informatics – Point-of-care medical device communication – Part 10201: Domain information model.*

International Organization for Standardization & The Institute of Electrical and Electronics Engineers. (2004c). *ISO/IEEE 11073-10101:2004(E) health informatics – Point-of-care medical device communication – Part 10101: Nomenclature.*

Kaelber, D. C., Shah, S., Vincent, A., Pan, E., Hook, J. M., Johnston, D., et al. (2008). *The value of personal health records.* Retrieved from http://www.citl.org/publications/_pdf/CITL_PHR_Report.pdf

Kawamoto, K., & Esler, B. (2006). *Service functional model specification - Decision support service (DSS).* Retrieved from http://archive.hl7.org/v3ballotarchive/v3ballot2009jan/html/infrastructure/dss/Decision%20Support%20Service%20v1_0.pdf

Kawamoto, K., & Lobach, D. (2007). Proposal for fulfilling strategic objectives of the U.S. roadmap for national action on clinical decision support through a service-oriented architecture leveraging HL7 services. *Journal of the American Medical Informatics Association, 14*(2), 146–155. doi:10.1197/jamia.M2298 PMID:17213489

Object Management Group. (2011). *OMG clinical decision support service (CDSS), version 1.0.* Retrieved from http://www.omg.org/spec/CDSS/1.0/PDF

Popplewell, K., Lampathaki, F., Koussouris, S., Mouzakitis, S., Charalabidis, Y., Goncalves, R., & Agostinho, C. (2012). *ENSEMBLE deliverable D2.1 - EISB state of play report.* Retrieved from http://www.fines-cluster.eu/fines/jm/Publications/Download-document/339-ENSEMBLE_D2.1_EISB_State_of_Play_Report-v2.00.html

Schulz, S., Suntisrivaraporn, B., Baader, F., & Boeker, M. (2009). SNOMED reaching its adolescence: Ontologists' and logicians' health check. *International Journal of Medical Informatics, 78*(S1), 86–94. doi:10.1016/j.ijmedinf.2008.06.004 PMID:18789754

Seven, H. L. Integrating the Healthcare Enterprise, The Office of the National Coordinator for Health Information Technology & Health Story Project. (2011). *Implementation guide for CDA release 2.0 - Consolidated CDA templates (US realm).* Retrieved from http://wiki.hl7.org/images/b/be/CDAConsolidationR12011.zip

The openEHR Foundation. (2006). *Introducing openEHR.* Retrieved from http://www.openehr.org/releases/1.0.2/openEHR/introducing_openEHR.pdf

Van Langenhove, P., Dirkx, M., & Decreus, K. (2011). *European interoperability architecture (EIA), phase 2 - Final report: Common vision for an EIA.* Retrieved from http://ec.europa.eu/isa/documents/isa_2.1_eia-finalreport-commonvisionforaneia.pdf

Yuksel, M., & Dogac, A. (2011). Interoperability of medical device information and the clinical applications: An HL7 RMIM based on the ISO/IEEE 11073 DIM. *IEEE Transactions on Information Technology in Biomedicine, 15*(4), 557–566. doi:10.1109/TITB.2011.2151868 PMID:21558061

## KEY TERMS AND DEFINITIONS

**Clinical Decision Support Service:** An interactive information system to assist health professionals, ideally with the involvement of patients, in their decision making tasks by reusing existing healthcare knowledge.

**Electronic Health Record (EHR):** Digitally stored healthcare information by the care givers about an individual's lifetime with the purpose of supporting care.

**Personal Health Record (PHR):** A tool for collecting, tracking and sharing important, up-to-date information about an individual's health or the health of someone in their care.

**Personal Medical Device:** Portable, wearable or implantable devices that can monitor vital signs and manage chronic diseases of an individual. These devices are able to communicate with other computer systems through electronic means.

**Semantic Interoperability:** The ability of two or more information systems to actually interpret and understand the exchanged data.

**Technical Interoperability:** The ability of two or more information systems to communicate and exchange data.

# Chapter 10
# Attaining Semantic Enterprise Interoperability through Ontology Architectural Patterns

**Rishi Kanth Saripalle**
*University of Connecticut, USA*

**Steven A. Demurjian**
*University of Connecticut, USA*

## ABSTRACT

*Enterprise Interoperability Science Base (EISB) represents the wide range of interoperability techniques that allow the creation of a new enterprise application by utilizing technologies with varied data formats and different paradigms. Even if one is able to bridge across these formats and paradigms to interoperate a new application, one crucial consideration is the semantic interoperability to insure that similar data is reconciled that might be stored differently from a semantic perspective. In support of this requirement, usage of ontologies is gaining increasing attention as they capture shareable domain knowledge semantics. The design and deployment of an ontology for any system is very specific, created in isolation to suit the specific needs with limited reuse in the same domain. The broad proliferation of ontologies for different systems, which, while similar in content, are often semantically different, can significantly inhibit the information exchange across enterprise systems. This situation is attributed, in part, to a lack of a software-engineering-based approach for ontologies; an ontology is often designed and built using domain data, while software design involves abstract modeling concepts that promote abstraction, reusability, interoperability, etc. The intent in this chapter is to define ontologies by leveraging software design pattern concepts to more effectively design ontologies. To support this, the chapter proposes Ontology Architectural Patterns (OAPs), which are higher-level abstract reusable templates with well-defined structures and semantics to conceptualize modular ontology models at the domain model level. OAP borrows from software design patterns inheriting their key characteristics for supporting enterprise semantic ontology interoperability.*

DOI: 10.4018/978-1-4666-5142-5.ch010

# 1. INTRODUCTION

In today's world, the design, development, and deployment of a new enterprise application is no longer taking the prior approach of developing the application from scratch; rather, the emphasis is on the ability to construct a new enterprise application through the usage of existing resources such as enterprise applications, systems, servers, databases, etc., that are brought together to yield a system of systems. Enterprise Interoperability Science Base (EISB, Popplewell et al., 2012) has been promoted in order to address all of the different interoperability concerns including data, process, knowledge, cloud and Web services, rules, objects, APIs, etc. Two related interoperability of issues of particular interest are the ability to deal with: data in varied formats (e.g., XML, JSON, RDF (Allemang & Hendler, 2011), relational database, etc.) and the need to resolve semantics among enterprise systems of data (e.g., in a geospatial application, grid north vs. true north vs. magnetic north and these must be resolved if different do not use consistent formats). Ontologies have emerged to play a pivotal role in the World Wide Web (WWW) to promote the Semantic Web (Allemang & Hendler, 2011) by attaching semantics to electronically represented information thereby assisting users (humans and agents) in various ways such as semantic Web agents, semantic information extraction, semantic search, etc. Currently, ontologies are highly employed in the wide variety of enterprise applications for knowledge representation and reasoning (Baader, McGuinness, Nardi, & Patel-Schneider, 2007), software modeling and development (Demurjian, Saripalle, & Behre, 2009; Kuhn, 2010; Saripalle, Demurjian, & Behre, 2011), semantic information extraction (Wimalasuriya & Dou, 2010), biomedical and clinical informatics (Smith & Ceusters, 2006), databases (Gali, Chen, Claypool, & Uceda-sosa, 2004), geospatial semantics (Janowicz, Scheider, Pehle, & Hart, 2012), etc.

The primary goal of the ontologies is to capture semantics of a domain and tag the semantic concepts to electronically represented information, which in turn will ease *semantic interoperability* for enterprise applications to support both data and knowledge interoperability in EISB, assuming that the exchanging systems (e.g., computer systems, software applications, database records etc.) must come to an agreement on domain semantics in order to build an enterprise application. For example, various ontologies have been developed for capturing knowledge semantics on various aspects of a given domain for easing semantic interoperability issues in enterprise applications. For instance, in the business domain, the semantic Web has influenced various aspects of existing implementations such as: Simple Object Access Protocol (SOAP) (SOAP, 2007), Web Service Description Logic (WSDL) (WSDL, 2001), Service Oriented Architecture (SOA) (Bell, 2008), etc. In all of these approaches, the domain semantics captured in an ontology are tagged to business/service information represented using these standards, facilitating semantic compatibility between interacting enterprise services and easing knowledge interoperability (Nagarajan, Verma, Sheth, Miller, & Lathem, 2006; Burstein & McDermott, 2005). Researchers have also designed and implemented OWL-S (OWL-S, 2004), a semantic Web enabled Web-service model that incorporates all of the aspects of a software Web service lifecycle using ontology frameworks. For example, in the financial enterprise, lack of standard ontologies for capturing the semantics related to the financial domain have created a major bottleneck for information exchange/integration, knowledge extractions, financial reporting, Web services, etc., due to semantic ambiguity in the represented financial knowledge (Makela, Rommel, Uskonem, & Wan, 2007; Hu, 2010). Currently, Object Management Group (OMG) has taken an initiative to develop Financial Industry Business Ontology for capturing semantics related to the financial domain (FIBO, 2012). As another example, in the government domain, semantic technologies such as linked data, semantic Web, ontologies, etc., have become a crucial component for achieving integrated e-government services (Bettahar, Moulin, & Barthes, 2009). These semantic components have been introduced into software architectures, providing semantics to electronically augment government information and facilitate semantic integration/interoperability between the participating government services/departments (Davis, Harris, Crichton, Shukla, & Gibbons, 2008; Fonou-Dombeu & Huisman, 2011), etc.

However, the success of employing ontologies for resolving enterprise semantic interoperability is jeopardized due to *structural* and *semantic interoperability* issues among the domain ontologies that are used for the systems that support a new enterprise application. There are a number of key issues to address. First, the individual ontologies of each constituent system used by a new enterprise application may each organize knowledge in different ways to suit their specific application and organizational processes, meaning that the ontologies across the constituent systems are often incompatible and difficult to integrate. Second, the ontology development and deployment process is predominantly *instance* and *construction* based, often dictated by the talent and expertise of the ontologist rather than using any concrete software development process; such an approach limits the reuse since ontologies end up being very domain centric. For a new enterprise application, the existence of consistent ontologies of the constituent systems will greatly simplify the semantic interoperability. Finally, many existing ontology representational frameworks lack an ability to design solutions that are broader in scope; the end result is often narrowed to not just a single domain, but to a subset of the domain that is very application specific. Thus, the overriding issue is that ontologies solely focus on the

domain knowledge and its usage by constituent systems rather than abstracting back from the problem to consider the enterprise domain ant its appropriate set of ontologies in a more comprehensive and general manner. Such an approach towards ontologies is in direct conflict with the design methodologies in software engineering, databases, and Web settings, where the primary emphasis is on the modeling techniques that can applied to conceptualize the problem in a fashion that promotes characteristics such as modularity, abstraction and reuse, which implicitly eases structural and semantic interoperability issues. In this chapter, we leverage our previous work on extending the Web Ontology Language (OWL) for design and development of ontologies for applications that is more aligned with the software lifecycle and emphasizes a design approach for ontologies (Saripalle, Demurjian, & Behre, 2011; Saripalle & Demurjian, 2012b).

To provide a context for this chapter, we leverage an example in the healthcare domain, where it is necessary to construct an enterprise application for health information exchange (HIE) that is able to pull patient medical information from multiple sources in different formats and using alternative programming paradigms. An HIE enterprise application is constructed by gathering data from: electronic health records (EHRs) which repositories of patient medical records that may exist in provider offices, clinics, and hospitals; personal health records, (PHRs) that allow patients to manage their own health care data; personalized medicine health portals (PMHP) which allows providers to view their own patients' genetic data against their EHR in order to bridge the gap between providers and medical researchers; and, other laboratory, diagnostic, pharmaceutical systems that involve patient care. Note that an HIE enterprise application for many situations provides only read information to patient data or de-identified data sets. In support of an HIE enterprise application, the biomedical field provides a significant variety of high-level XML standards including: the Continuity of Care Record (CCR) (ASTM, 2003), Continuity of Care Document (CCD), the Health Language Seven (HL7) Clinical Document Architecture (CDA) (HL7 CDA R2, 2008), etc. These high-level standards allowed medical providers to seamless *structure*, *integrate*, and *share* the patient's medical data with their respective propriety systems and collaborating environments. For providing enterprise semantic interoperability between the constituent systems (EHRs, PHRs, etc.), there are numerous standards such as: International Classification of Disease (ICD-10) (ICD, 2013), Logical Observation Identifiers Names and Codes (LOINC) (LOINC, 2013), Systematized Nomenclature of Medicine Clinical Terms (SNOMED-CT) (SNOMED CT, 2013), Diagnostic and Statistical Manual of Mental Disorder (DSM) (DSM, 2012), Unified Medical Language System (UMLS) (Bodenreider, 2004), etc. The problem that exists in the health care domain to hinder enterprise semantic interoperability are the inconsistencies in these low-level ontology standards, e.g., Psychoses (DSM, 2102) is a "Mental Disorder" in ICD and a "Psychotic illness" in DSM, while. Spherocytosis (SNOMED CT, 2013) is a "Diseases of Blood and Blood-Forming Organs" in ICD and "Red Blood Cell Shape-finding" in SNOMED-CT. These differences in the health care domain, along with similar cases in other enterprise domains, must be reconciled to achieve enterprise semantic interoperability.

In software engineering, a designer can better understand the domain problem and propose a plausible solution by developing domain model(s) to provide an abstract view of the solution with well-defined structure and semantics and are developed by considering domain instance data as it can influence the design, but not to the point that the design gets tied to the domain instances. One approach to software domain modeling that greatly facilitates reuse are software design pat-

terns (SDP) defined as "a template illustrating a reusable solution to a reoccurring problem in multiple different situations with similar context" (Gamma, Helm, Johnson, & Vlissides, 1994; Freeman, Robson, Bates, & Sierra, 2004). SDPs can influence an enterprise application by allowing these generalized templates to be customized for a specific domain. For instance, the Model-View-Controller (MVC) pattern can be used easily in any enterprise application that requires: a *Model* that manages the behavior and data of the application; a *View* that manages the UI of the application; and, a *Controller* that interprets the user actions and informs the actions to the model and/or the view. Based on the domain application, the domain models replace the respective MVC components. This ability of SDP to divide the complex problem into modular manageable sub-problems and develop solutions that facilitate modularity, reusability, interoperability, etc., has gained them a prominent position in the software community; our intent is to extend SDPs to support enterprise semantic interoperability for ontologies.

In this chapter, the overall goal is to improve the design, development, and deployment of ontologies with syntactic and semantic integration in support of an enterprise application by proposing a set of *Ontology Architectural Patterns (OAPs)* which are abstract reusable architectural patterns influencing the overall development of semantic knowledge involving multiple ontology models that ease interoperability issues and promote a software engineering approach for ontology development. This have been introduced to a limited extent in our prior work on semantic patterns (Saripalle & Demurjian, 2012a), but this chapter dramatically extends that work by leveraging SDP concepts to ease *structural* and *semantic interoperability* issues. In the process, the ontologist is encouraged and guided to design and develop modular ontology models, reusable in multiple domain application settings that share similar contextual requirements. As a result, the ontologist can focus on constructing reusable ontology models, moving future reconciliation and integration of different ontologies for an enterprise application from the current labor-intensive instance level to a more abstract and conceptual domain model level. The OAP extensions are illustrated using an HIE enterprise application that brings together different systems (EHRs, PHRs, etc.) in support access across multiple sources for two types of users: medical providers that are interested in obtaining a full picture of a patient's medical data collected from varied sources to facilitate clinical care; and, researchers that seek to analyze data from the HIE Repository that has been de-identified to conduct disease related, public health surveillance, and other research. HIE is a complex enterprise application that must marshal data from multiple sources and can be greatly benefited by OAPs to model a solution that can resolve and reconcile syntactic and semantic differences among the ontologies of its constituent systems.

Towards this goal, the reminder of this chapter is divided into five sections. Section 2 provides additional background and motivation on the role of ontologies in the design and development process, a review of software design patterns, their classification, and usage in the software development process, and a brief introduction to enterprise interoperability (EI) and the role that ontologies can play, particularly in regards to our proposed OAPs. Section 3 proposes the developed Ontology Architectural Patterns (OAP) which are explained in terms of name, motivation, description, context & usage, and application & implementation; examples in both health care and other enterprise domains are provided Section 4 reviews related research in ontology patterns and ontology frameworks, comparing and contrasting to our work presented in Section 3. Section 5 discusses the future direction of knowledge development for facilitating enterprise interoperability. Finally, the last section concludes the chapter.

## 2. ONTOLOGIES, SOFTWARE DESIGN PATTERNS, AND ENTERPRISE INTEROPERABILITY

This section provides additional explanation on motivation and background for the paper. First, Section 2.1 reviews additional motivation on ontologies regarding the role that they can plan in systems design and development, with an example in the health care domain that further motivates the need for Ontology Architectural Patterns (OAP). Using this as a basis, Section 2.2 briefly examines Software Design Patterns (SDP) in terms of their inception, categories, and role in the software development process. Finally, Section 2.3 introduces the domain of Enterprise Interoperability (EI), its concepts and relationship with Sections 2.1 and 2.2, to place the work of this chapter into a proper perspective with EI.

## 2.1. Role of Ontologies in Systems Design and Development

The discussion in Section 1 provided an initial motivation for the need and usage of Ontology Architectural Patterns (OAP) for enterprise interoperability through a discussion of the status of ontologies, design, and modeling approaches of knowledge and software engineering and software design patterns. This section further clarify the motivation to precisely position the work on OAP with respect to traditional ontology development and its need for a higher level abstract approach akin to software design patterns. The end result provides a means to more precisely and generally define ontologies (and their components) with an aim towards potential reusability in a domain (or program family).

Current approaches to ontology development today are conducted using tools such as Protégé (Protege, 2012), Java Ontology Editor (JOE) (Java Ontology Editor, 1998), etc. These tools allow an ontology developer to work with domain experts with a focus on building an ontology that maximizes the domain knowledge by capturing the knowledge concepts for a given domain of disclosure. This leads to a current ontology development practice that is predominantly *instance* and *construction* based (Kuhn, 2010; Saripalle, Demurjian, & Behre, 2011; Saripalle & Demurjian, 2012b), totally focused on the application and its specific domain and system requirements. Such a process is highly influenced by the ontology developer's experience, input from domain experts, and based on the actual data that is to be modeled within the ontology rather than defining a structure for the ontology that is more reusable across enterprise systems. As a result, ontologies created for different systems of the same domain can be quite different. For example, constructing a set of ontologies for enterprise application such as Amazon would require a very broad set of ontologies to capture all of its products characteristics (books, electronics, household, fashion, etc.), while a set for Barnes & Noble may be limited much more to books. The two resulting sets of ontologies developed for Amazon and Barnes & Noble may be difficult to integrate, with human intervention need to understand equivalences across the two sets, a laborious task with at best semi-automatic methodologies and reuse of the ontology is obscure. The OAP and an emphasis on that ontology design would allow a more generalized ontology for "books" to be created that would have the potential to be utilized in all enterprise applications where book sales are a part of their business process.

Second, ontologies cannot be created in a vacuum without consideration of concepts that may cut across different solutions (different enterprise applications) and require sophisticated modeling to abstract domain specific materials out of the ontology to yield an ontology schema (akin to an XML schema) that is reusable across multiple enterprise applications of a given domain. Further, a single ontology may not suffice for the structural and knowledge requirements of the enterprise application, but may require multiple interacting ontologies to correctly represent the required medical knowledge. Continuing with the earlier example, there may be an ontology architectural pattern that can be applied at a higher level across the Amazon and Barnes & Noble enterprise applications that is able to capture ontology similarities at a higher abstraction level that promotes reuse. In the health care domain, there could be many enterprise applications that would need to utilize the same ontology. For example, a clinical researcher trying to identify genes responsible for mental disorders might want to have an enterprise application to access genomic and clinical (patient) databases that would require the integration of the Gene Ontology (Ashburne & Lewis, 2002) and the Diagnostic and Statistical Manual of Mental Disorders (DSM) to develop a Gene-Mental Disorder ontology. Likewise, another enterprise application could provide the ability to allow queries to cross the International Classification of Diseases (ICD-10) codes with Logical Observation Identifiers Names and Codes (LOINC) ontology to develop a Disease-Laboratory Test correlation ontology to be used by combining ICD-10 and LOINC with de-identified patient data for mining. However, the reconciliation process between these ontologies will be arduous, performed on the instance level rather than at a higher-level of abstraction that would involve the structure of the ontologies. Even, if an expert ontologist develops a massive single ontology by integrating the required multiple ontologies, the large-scale nature of this massive ontology (defined and then integrated at an instance level) sacrifices fundamental software characteristics such as modularity, reusability, abstraction, minimal coupling, etc. The integration/mapping rules between these participating ontologies are contextually based on an organization application goals, meaning that their integration may not be easily accomplished if their purposes are so diverse as to make it difficult to identify linkages and commonalities. We note again that the current ontology integration methodologies focus on integrating ontology instances using linguistic and statistical techniques that often ignore semantics. Such an approach can result in a merging that cannot be syntactically and semantically verified. This is evident from studies on the UMLS (Krauthammer, 2002; Kohler, 2007) and SNOMED-CT (Chiang, Hwang, Yu, et al., 2006) medical standards where they have been attempts to integrate two ontologies that have significantly different nomenclature. This is true for many other domains.

Finally, while the existing medical ontologies previously discussed have an overwhelming knowledge overlap among them, the way that each ontology deals with that knowledge can be quite different. Further, since these ontologies have often been built in isolation (e.g., by different standard committees and other organizations), having an ontologist that can understand all of them is unrealistic. For example, if there are one or two features a newly developed ontology needs that are not in the standard, the solution to develop yet another ontology occurs, often replicating information from multiple ontologies and having a vocabulary that may be in conflict with other standards the "same" information (semantically). Thus, the

existing ontologies, the newly development ontologies, and any future customized ontologies have to be constantly monitored and integrated with one another in order to remain consistent. This is a monumental task in any enterprise application, further compounding the structural and semantic interoperability issues with ontologies. Imagine the difficulty it would be to get the organizations (and their enterprise applications) for Amazon, Barnes & Noble, eBay, etc., to all work towards a common shared ontology. Obtaining agreement from such a large number of stakeholders will be difficult to achieve in practice. Figure 1 supports this argument by illustrating the domain knowledge overlap between medical ontologies. Notice in Figure 1 that the OMIM and Gene Ontologies have overlapping knowledge on Gene domain. In addition ICD and DSM have a knowledge overlap on the domain of Mental Disorders, with SNOMED-CT and ICD having a major knowledge overlap on multiple domains such as Disease, Symptom, Procedure, etc. Further, SNOMED-CT, ICD and OMIM have a knowledge overlap on domain of Disease. More significantly, UMLS is attempting to encompass all of the standards under one umbrella via its own theory and model

*Figure 1. Domain knowledge overlap between various standard medical ontologies*

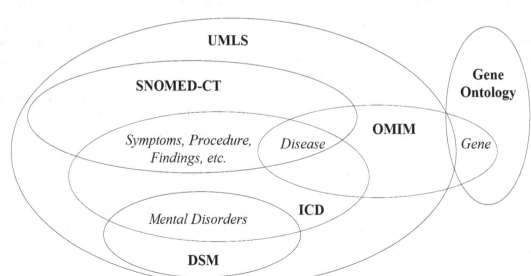

for achieving its goal, but fails to provide modular domain models for respective domains which can reused independent of the domain application. Thus, failing to reuse existing knowledge sources and developing new ontologies for targeting the same domain knowledge leads to chaotic structural and semantic interoperability issues.

## 2.2. Software Design Patterns

In software engineering, Software Design Patterns (SDP) arose when developers noticed that they were using the same software structure in terms of classes, interfaces, and interactions in multiple settings, tweaking them to handle difference in domain data. SDPs expand the concept of generics (used to capture a lower level component like a stack that can be instantiated for any data type) to a higher-level pattern that captures the generalized structure, semantics, direction and usage at of a set of classes, interfaces, and their interactions that represents a major component of a system. As a result, SDPs are adaptable to work in varied settings for enterprise applications that have similar design requirements or behavioral characteristics. The primary components of a SDP are: *context* that explains when the design pattern is applicable by defining environment parameters and the usage of the pattern itself; *problem* that illustrates the kind of problems the pattern can applied to; and, *solution* to explain the way to use the pattern as a viable software engineering solution to the encountered domain problem. Apart from these components, a design pattern also may have the following essential elements: *name* of the pattern; examples to illustrate the application of the pattern to a multiple domain specific problems; *rationale* for the logic explanation of the pattern and its application; *related patterns* that have the same or varying categories or types; and *known uses* for successful industrial usecase scenarios. SDPs have gained importance since they are generalized artifacts from multiple solutions they are domain independent making them interoperable between

heterogeneous domain application problems. The use of SDPs in Web-based solutions are foundational regardless of the implementation platform.

SDPs are classified into three broad categories that are based on the functionality, interactions, and purpose of the SDP (Freeman, Robson, Bates, & Sierra, 2004). The first category, the *Creational SDP*, deals with a software entity's (mostly classes) creation in a manner suitable to the given application context. Sample creational SDPs include: the Abstract Factory Pattern that provides a way to encapsulate a group of individual factories that have a common theme without specifying their actual classes; the Factory Method pattern that defines the interface for creating an object, but allows subclasses to decide which class to instantiate; and, the Builder Pattern that separates the concerns of construction of a complex object from its representation,. The second category, the *Behavioral SDP*, is used to identify the common communication patterns between objects. Sample behavioral SDPs include: the Chain of Responsibility Pattern consisting of a source of command objects and a series of processing objects where each processing object contains logic that defines the types of command objects that it can handle; the Command Pattern in which an object is used to represent and encapsulate all of the information needed to call a method at a later time; and, the Observer Pattern where an object, called the subject, maintains a list of its dependents, called observers, and notifies them automatically of any state changes, usually by calling one of their methods. The third category, *Structural SDP*, provides a simple way to realize relationships between multiple entities. Sample structural SDPs include: the Adapter Pattern that allows classes to work together that normally could not because of incompatible interfaces; the Bridge Pattern that decouples an abstraction from its implementation so that the two can vary independently; and, the Composite Pattern which describes that a group of objects are to be treated in the same way as a single instance of an object, with the intent to compose objects into a tree structure to represent part-whole hierarchies. SDPs play a significant role in enterprise applications; our intent is to expand this concept to include knowledge modeling which will allow the specification of ontology architectural patterns (OAP) that can play a major role in achieving enterprise semantic interoperability.

## 2.3. Enterprise Interoperability (EI)

Enterprise Interoperability (EI) (Charalabidis, Goncalves, & Popplewell, 2010; Jardim-Goncalves, Grilo, Agostinho et al., 2013) is defined

*... as a field of activity with the aim to improve the manner in which enterprises, by means of information and communications technologies, interoperate with other enterprises, organizations, or with other business units, in order to conduct their business (Popplewell et al., 2012).*

The reality is that new enterprise applications are built today by the cobbling together of functionality from multiple sources (via APIs, Web services, cloud services, JSON calls, etc.) and their interoperation requires addressing different facets associated with enterprise development. The overriding object of EI is to support the ability of enterprises to communicate and interact seamlessly. The term Enterprise can be defined as "an organization that provides open/paid services to clients" (Charalabidis, Goncalves, & Popplewell, 2010) and Interoperability can be defined as

*...the ability of two or more systems or components to exchange information and to use the information that has been exchanged (Popplewell et al., 2012).*

EI as a generalized concept, subsumes other interoperability issues from differing perspectives, detailed in ESIB Report (Popplewell et al., 2012): Data Interoperability, Process Interoperability, Knowledge Interoperability, Services Interoperability, Rules Interoperability, Objects Interoperability, Software Interoperability, Cultural Interoperability, Social Networks Interoperability, Electronic Identity Interoperability, Cloud Interoperability, and Ecosystems Interoperability. These noted interoperability issues are interweaved with one another at a conceptual level. For example, there is a strong dependency between Data and Knowledge Interoperability, Process and Knowledge Interoperability, and Process and Service Interoperability, to name a few. When one addresses the issues for a given interoperability, there is a corresponding ripple effect on other interoperability issues.

The proposed ontology architectural patterns (OAP) in this chapter has the primary goal to solve semantic interoperability among domain ontologies and is primarily targeting Knowledge Interoperability and is closely related to Data Interoperability. Hence, providing a software-engineering-based solution to semantic interoperability among ontologies has an impact on the Knowledge and Data Interoperabilities of EI. Additionally, in support of OAP, we leverage the related works of Gangemi's (Gangemi, 2005; Gangemi & Presutti, 2009) proposed Conceptual Ontology Design Pattern (CODeP), Clarks's (Clark, Thompson, & Porter, 2004) abstract Knowledge Patterns (see Section 4) for designing more effective ontology models at a high abstraction level via ontology semantic patterns. For example, multiple enterprise systems can employ a Time-Indexed Participation CODeP for defining their own open-source/proprietary ontology model for online services, where: Object in the CODeP pattern can represent physical items, online Web services, person/semantic agent, etc.; Event can be cast as service orders, automated triggers, internal events, etc.; and, Time Interval can represent a time frame. Even though the service ontology model(s) and respective implementation vary between the enterprises, the ontology models that are utilized refer to the same semantic pattern (including the semantic context). This results in reusing the patterns concepts (classes, attributes and associations) and application context thereby easing Knowledge Interoperability when enterprises need to collaborate.

## 3. ONTOLOGY ARCHITECTURAL PATTERNS (OAP)

The emergence of the eXtensible markup language (XML) as a near defacto standard for information representation and exchange has had a significant impact on the ontology and enterprise interoperability research and development areas. XML dominates standards in computing and other fields, in addition to all of the aforementioned healthcare standards (HL7 CDA, CCR, etc.) there are many other standards that have the potential to impact enterprise applications including: HR-XML (HR-XML, 2013) for personnel and developers to have a common terminology for all aspects of human resources; the Oasis Open Office XML (Brauer & Schubert, 2013) document format for representing documents, presentations, etc., more easily; a wide variety of standards for libraries (LOC, 2012) such as the METS standard for tracking metadata on objects in digital collections; the Oasis LegalXML (LegalXML, 2008) standard for the electronic exchange of legal data and documents; and so on. In addition, ontologies can capture and attach semantic knowledge to represented information thereby aiding users (humans and agents) in knowledge engineering and representation, domain modeling, database and object-oriented analysis, natural language processing, biomedical and clinical informatics, etc. These efforts are supported by a wide variety of knowledge representation frameworks such as Resource Description Framework (RDF) (Powers, 2003), Web Ontology Language (OWL) (OWL Guide, 2004; Lacy, 2005), KIF (Genesereth, 1991), DAML+OIL (Horrocks, 2002), etc. Clearly, all of these standards and frameworks are available for

a wide range of enterprise applications, and will be more and more important over time.

In this section, the work on ontologies as discussed in Section 2.1 and issues related to enterprise interoperability in Section 2.3 provides a strong justification to extend and apply software design pattern concepts so that they are suitable for ontology design. Specifically, this section details our developed *Ontology Architectural Patterns* (OAP) defined as abstract reusable architectural patterns that can assist the domain designer to define reusable modular ontology models at a higher abstraction level in order to support enterprise interoperability. The primary aim of developing OAP is twofold. First, OAP as a modeling construct eases the ontology architectural design process by providing the ability to define a more general solution for a domain application that attains required domain knowledge. Second, these OAPs promote development of modular domain ontology models encouraging knowledge abstraction, minimizing coupling, facilitating reuse, etc., which has the end result of easing *interoperability* issues between ontologies thereby facilitating enterprise interoperability of data and knowledge. In order to achieve these goals, we have developed three OAPs. The *Linear Ontology Architectural Pattern (LOAP)* is presented in Section 3.1 and represents a linear/parallel architectural arrangement of multiple ontology models for achieving the required knowledge goal in a manner where the captured knowledge is accessible in an ordered manner. Then, in Section 3.2, the *Centralized Ontology Architectural Pattern (COAP)* is explained, defining a global ontology model (higher-level abstraction) under which multiple component ontology models interact akin to a centralized hub. Lastly, in Section 3.3, the *Layered Ontology Architectural Pattern (LaOAP)* in defined to support a layered arrangement of the components organized from the innermost to outermost layer as: the Ontology Conceptual Model (innermost layer) within the Axiom and Rule for the Model within the

Mapping of the Model within the Terminology (vocabulary) of the Model within the Query and Web Services (outmost layer).

To standardize the discussion in the remainder of this section, the presentation follows a consistent ordering for each *Ontology Architectural Patterns* (OAP) expressed with: the *Pattern Name* which identifies the OAP by name; the *Pattern Motivation* which is utilized to more fully motivate the need of the proposed pattern and the influence of various SDP, ontologies, and their frameworks from other domains; the *Pattern Description* which explains the operational and functional interactions of each pattern; the *Pattern Context & Usage* which represents the contextual requirements for applying the pattern and its usage in an enterprise application; and, the *Pattern Application & Implementation* which illustrates an instantiation of the pattern and its realization in an enterprise application. Throughout the discussion, we provide examples using the domains of biomedical informatics, e-commerce, e-services, e-government etc.; again, we note that these patterns are general and can be applied to any domain.

## 3.1. Linear Ontology Architectural Pattern

**Pattern Name:** Linear Ontology Architectural Pattern (LOAP).

**Pattern Motivation:** The *Linear Ontology Architectural Pattern (LOAP)* is primarily motivated and influenced by the Pipe & Filter and Chain of Responsibility SDPs that are categorized under structural SDPs as defined in Section 2.2. The primary goal of these patterns is to divide the large complex problem into smaller modular problems and develop generic reusable solutions. The *Pipe & Filter SDP* as shown in Figure 2a has two primary components: Filter which holds the logical modules (e.g., file readers, boot loaders, memory units, etc.) that accept the given input(s), processes them, and generates an output; and, Pipe which interconnects two or more Filters (i.e., the output of one Filter is fed in as input to another Filter). For example, compliers might utilize Pipe & Filter SDP where the complex problem of compiling

*Figure 2. The Pipe & Filter SDP and its implementation*

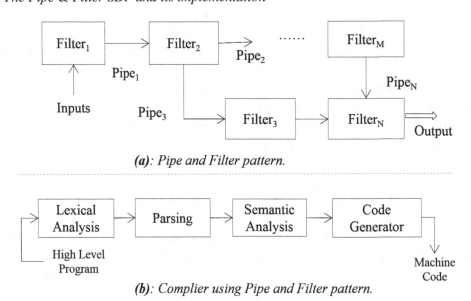

*(a): Pipe and Filter pattern.*

*(b): Complier using Pipe and Filter pattern.*

a program is divided into smaller problem modules such as Lexical Analysis, Parsing, Semantic Analysis, and Code Generator. These modular components are connected and executed accordingly to obtain the final output that is machine executable code as shown in Figure 2b.

Similarly, the *Chain of Responsibility SDP*, as shown in Figure 3a, also has two primary components: Logical Handlers, which are generally governed by a superior interface (Handler Interface) to manage the application logic; and, the Relationship that handles the interactions between the participating Logical Handlers.

For example, as shown in Figure 3b. when a patient arrives at the clinic practice there may be several steps: nurse or medical assistant brings the patient to a room, reviews the medications, measures BP, pulse, temperature, etc., and notes on the purpose of the patient's visit; physician visits the patient, makes an assessment, and comes up with a treatment plan that may be a diagnosis (e.g., has strep throat take Augmentin) or require further evaluation (blood work and/or x-rays); the nurse or medical assistant may return to answer any follow-up questions and to provide appropriate prescriptions or other treatment instructions. In the example, all of the individuals involved in this process take up their responsibility (acting as Logical Handlers) and communicate (Relationship) the information to the next individual (nurse review→ physician assessment→ medical assistant/nurse action) to finally arrive at the outcome (successful treatment of the patient). The main difference between Chain of Responsibility and Pipe & Filer is for the latter to allow cyclical connections and bi-directional flow.

**Pattern Description:** The *Linear Ontology Architectural Pattern (LOAP)* as shown in Figure 4 is an architectural arrangement of ontology models (Ontology$_1$, Onotology$_2$,..., Ontology$_N$) which are connected (Link$_1$, Link$_2$,...,Link$_N$) in a sequential and/or in parallel order for achieving the

*Figure 3. Chain of Responsibility SDP and its implementation*

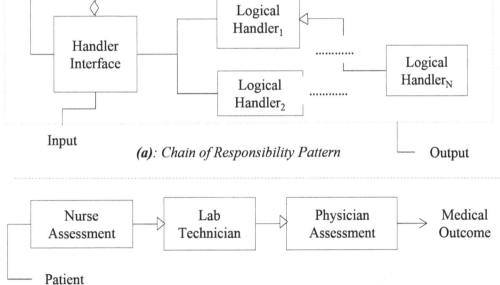

*(a): Chain of Responsibility Pattern*

*(b): Example illustrating Chain of Responsibility Pattern.*

*Figure 4. Linear Ontology Architectural Pattern (LOAP)*

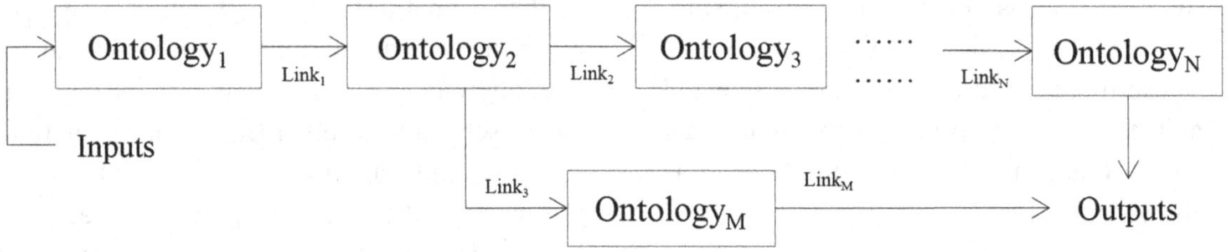

desired knowledge goal. The LOAP is developed by combining Pipe & Filter and Chain of Responsibility SDPs, where the ontology models (Ontology$_1$, Onotology$_2$,… ,Ontology$_N$) are aligned to Filters (Filter$_1$, Filter$_2$, …,Filter$_N$, Figure 2a) and Logical Handlers (Logical Handler$_1$,…,Logical Handler$_N$, Figure 3a), and the connecting links (Link$_1$, Link$_2$,…,Link$_N$) correspond to Pipes (Pipe$_1$, …,Pipe$_N$, Figure 2a) and Relations (Figure 3a). The output is primarily a query result performed on the multiple ontology models based on the inputs (initial inputs or previous ontological outputs). The connections (Link$_1$, Link$_2$, …Link$_N$) between the ontology models are generally unidirectional but can also be a loop within an ontology model or between ontology models, where the data flows from the previous ontology model (Ontology$_1$) to the next ontology model (Ontology$_2$) and so on until the final output is generated. The initial input is given to Ontology$_1$, then the output of Ontology$_1$ is fed as input to Ontology$_2$ through Link$_1$ and the chain continues as the result is finally obtained at Ontology$_N$ to generate an output. One step with LOAP can also generate intermediate results from an entire other OAP (i.e., for some M, Ontology$_M$). The desired knowledge goal is achieved by developing modular reusable ontology models to ease semantic interoperability issues during the ontology models integration/reconciliation process.

**Pattern Context and Usage:** The LOAP pattern is applicable to any enterprise domain application where the required domain knowledge is obtained by connecting multiple source ontology models or a single large ontology has to be divided into multiple modular ontology models that will then be connected in sequential/parallel fashion. The ability to separate a larger ontology into different logical component ontologies has an advantage in an enterprise interoperability context to allow the separation of various data and knowledge components. The links (Link$_1$, Link$_2$,…., Link$_N$ in Figure 4) between the ontology models is primarily *programmatic* consisting of the software logic that is written using languages such as Java, C++, etc., or *semantic* where the link semantics are captured in another ontology model. By designing and connecting reusable ontology models for capturing the required domain knowledge, the LOAP and its component ontology models are reusable in multiple enterprise application settings.

As an example, recall Figure 3 for the treatment of a patient in multiple steps. Underlying this process is the need to organize the information that is used into different ontology models that would be utilized in different steps of Figure 3. By analyzing the treatment process, an ontologist can design a Triage LOAP (pattern name) as shown in Figure 5a that has three Ontology Models (Diagnosis, Anatomy, and Test) with associated links (Link$_{Disease-Anatomy}$ and Link$_{Disease-Test}$). In Figure 5a, the Diagnosis Ontology model captures the knowledge on various Disease, Symptom, and Injury models, an Anatomy Ontology model captures the domain knowledge of the human body, and a Test Ontology model captures the knowledge on blood tests, imaging tests, cardiac tests, etc. Figure 5b expands each of the Ontology model blocks of Figure 5a demonstrating that within each step resides a significant ontology (that may

also be an OAP). By modularizing the domain knowledge into multiple ontology models, the domain ontology models have the potential to be reusable in different enterprise applications, e.g., the Disease and Symptom Ontology models may only be needed for one enterprise application, with the Anatomy model used by another application.

Similarly, in the domain of e-government, there is constant need to exchange information between various departments such as public administration

*Figure 5. Instance of a triage LOAP*

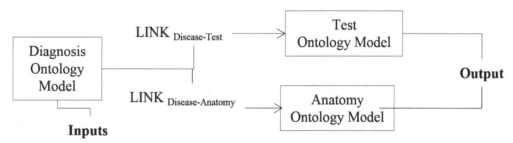

*(a). LOAP implementation using Diagnosis, Test and Anatomy Ontologies.*

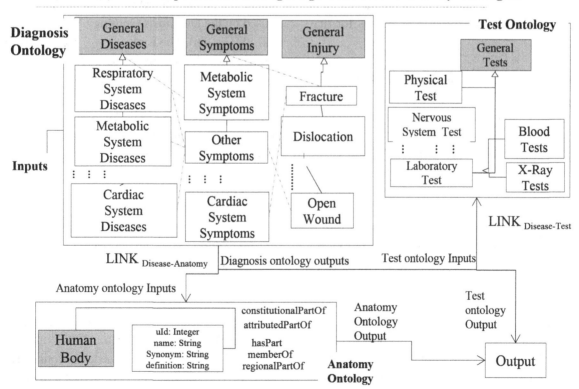

*(b). Diagnosis, Test and Anatomy Ontology Models.*

229

services, immigration services, tax department, immigration law bureau, etc. The ontology designer for the e-government domain can modularize the needed ontology models for maximizing the reuse of semantic knowledge among the government services. For example, a Public Service Ontology model captures the semantics (e.g., codes, description, definitions, eligibility, etc.) of the government public services, an Immigration Ontology model captures the semantics (e.g., types of visas, statuses of visa, etc.) of the government immigration domain, a Tax Ontology model captures knowledge about the tax codes of the government, and an Immigration Law Ontology model captures sematic knowledge about various laws involving immigration. Thus, based on the required knowledge goal, the e-government ontology models can be interconnected or linked (e.g., $Link_{Tax-Immigration}$, $Link_{Service-Immigration}$, $Link_{Immigration-Law}$, etc.) with one another similar to Figure 5a. Once the ontologies is developed for the e-government domain, subsets can then be applied to other enterprise applications for that domain.

**Pattern Application and Implementation:** The Triage LOAP in Figure 5 can be realized as shown in Figure 6 using a combination of: the OWL Framework (Lacy, 2005) for defining the three ontology models; the Protégé Ontology Editor (Protege, 2012) for building OWL based ontology models; the SPARQL (Lacy, 2005) query language to interrogate the Triage LOAP and its ontology models; and, Java for UI and program logic. The implementation of Figure 6 for an enterprise application as shown in Figure 7 adopts a three-layered approach where: Layer 1 holds the Java based UI for the user to enter the inputs, Layer 2 holds the logic of the application implemented using Java and SPARQL, and Layer 3 holds the actual OWL ontology instances for each model. The layered approach allows each layer to

be independent and reusable from the other layers. The flow of the Triage LOAP (Figure 5) and its implementation (Figure 6) begins when the user (e.g., nurse, physician assistant, etc.) types in symptoms such as fever, cold, and fatigue (Layer 1) that are read using a Java program (Layer 2) and then fed into the SPARQL query engine (Layer 2). Next, the SPARQL engine feeds the user inputs to the Diagnosis Ontology Model whose outputs are given as inputs to both the Test and Anatomy Ontology Models.

The query performed on the Diagnosis Ontology model (LOAP_Diagnosis.owl, Figure 6a) by the SPARQL engine is shown in Figure 8a, which queries the model for known diseases for the given input symptoms. The links $Link_{Disease-Test}$ between the Diagnosis and Test Ontology Models (Figure 6) are implemented as a SPARQL query as shown in Figure 8b, which queries the Test Ontology Model (LOAP_Test.owl, Figure 6b) based on the Diagnosis Ontology Model outputs (d1, d2,...., dn). The $Link_{Disease-Anatomy}$ between the Diagnosis and Anatomy Ontology Models (Figure 6) is also implemented as a SPARQL query as shown in Figure 8c, which queries the Anatomy Ontology Model (LOAP_Anatomy.owl, Figure 6c) based on the Diagnosis Ontology Model outputs (d1, d2,...., dn).

## 3.2. Centralized Ontology Architectural Pattern

**Pattern Name:** Centralized Ontology Architectural Pattern (COAP).

**Pattern Motivation:** The *Centralized Ontology Architectural Pattern (COAP)* is influenced by the Façade SDP, the Local As View (LAV) methodology (Lenzerini, 2002), and the MAFRA framework (Maedche, Motik, Silva, & Volz, 2002). The Façade SDP provides a unified higher-level global interface/system developed from a set of complex heteroge-

*Figure 6. OWL implementation of triage LOAP shown in Figure 5*

**General_Diseases**
- Skin_Diseases
- Nervous_System_Diseases
- Digestive_System_Diseases
- Circulatory_System_Diseases
- Cardiac_System_Diseases
- Metabolic_System_Diseases
- Respiratory_System_Diseases
- Mental_Disorders

**General_Injuries**
- Burns
- Dislocations
- Fracture
- Open_Wound
- Poison
- Sprain
- Surgical_Injuries
- Toxic_Effects

**....**

**General_Symptoms**
- Cardiac_System_Symptoms
- Metabolic_System_Symptoms
- Other_Symptoms
- Nervous_System_Symptoms
- Respiratory_System_Symptom
- Digestive_System_Symptoms
- Skin_Symptoms

**Medical_Name**

**topObjectProperty**
- isCausedBy
- hasGeneralDiagnostics
- hasGeneralSymptoms
- hasNervousSystemSymptoms
- hasRespiratorySystemSymptoms

**....**

- hasCardiacSystemSymptoms
- performXRay

**topObjectProperty**
- hasMedicalName

**....**

- hasName

**topDataProperty**
- providerID
- phramaceuticalName
- patientId
- commonName
- firstName
- lastName
- midName
- suffix
- references

**(a) Diagnosis Ontology Model**

**General_Test**
- **Laboratory_Test**
  - Cardiac_System_Test
  - Respiratory_System_Test
  - Nervous_System_Test
  - Blood_Tests
  - Mental_Disorder_Test
  - X-Ray_Tests
- Physcical_Test

**topObjectProperty**
- hasRespiratoryTest
- hasNervousTests
- hasBloodTest
- hasCardiacTests
- hasGeneralTreatments

**topDataProperty**
- hasUniqueId
- references

**topObjectProperty**
- hasMedicalName
- hasName

**(b) Test Ontology Model**

**Thing**
- Human Parts

**topObjectProperty**
- constitutionalPartOf
- atributedPartOf
- regionalPartOf
- memberOf
- partOf

**topDataProperty**
- commonName
- hasSynonyms
- hasDefinition
- hasMedicalName
- hasUniqueId

**(c) Anatomy Ontology Model**

- ● Class
- ■ Attribute
- ■ Association
- ■ Datatype

*Figure 7. Layered implementation of triage LOAP shown in Figure 5*

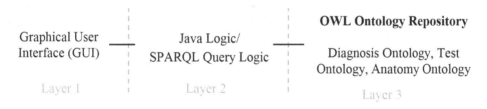

| Graphical User Interface (GUI) | Java Logic/ SPARQL Query Logic | **OWL Ontology Repository** Diagnosis Ontology, Test Ontology, Anatomy Ontology |
|---|---|---|
| Layer 1 | Layer 2 | Layer 3 |

*Figure 8. The SPARQL queries representing the Diagnosis Ontology Model query, Link$_{Disease-Anatomy}$, and Link$_{Disease-Test}$ between the ontology models as show in Figure 6*

```
PREFIX LOAP:
<http://www.owl-ontologies.com
       /LOAP_Diagnosis.owl/>

SELECT ?commonName
WHERE {
    ?disease LOAP:hasSymptom "Fever".
    ?disease LOAP:hasSymptom "Cold".
    ?disease LOAP:hasSymptom "Fatigue".
}
```

*(a): SPARQL Symptom query.*

```
PREFIX LOAP:
<http://www.owl-ontologies.com
       /LOAP_Test.owl/>
SELECT ?commonName
WHERE {
    ?t LOAP:hasGeneralTreatments ?d1.
    ?t LOAP:hasGeneralTreatments ?d2.
    ....
    ?t LOAP:hasGeneralTreatments ?dn.
}
```

*(b): SPARQL query representing the LinkDisease-Test.*

```
PREFIX LOAP:
<http://www.owl-ontologies.com/
       LOAP_Anatomy.owl/>
SELECT ?commonName
WHERE {
    ?a LOAP:effects ?d1.
    ?a LOAP:effects ?d1.
    ....
    ?a LOAP:effects ?dn.
}
```

*(c): SPARQL query representing the LinkDisease-Anatomy.*

neous source interfaces/subsystems making these local sources easier to utilize for the clients. As shown in Figure 9a, the Façade SDP abstracts common features or functional implementation from multiple complex subsystems ($SS_1$, $SS_2$... $SS_N$) and provides a unified simple global system (Façade) to access these complex subsystems for multiple clients, thus hiding the complexity of the subsystems. For example, the compiler example from the Pipe & Filter in Figure 2 can also be implemented using Façade as shown in Figure 9b, where the clients will call the simplified complier's functionality (function call - compile) which in turn performs the complex process of invoking other subsystems such as Lexical Analysis, Parser, SemanticAnalysis and codeGenerator in an appropriately defined order.

The LAV methodology is a data integration approach where a set of local schemas ($LS_1$, $LS_2$, $LS_3$... $LS_N$) are expressed as database views ($V_1$, $V_2$... $V_N$) over a global schema ($G_S$) as shown in Figure 10a. The mapping between the global schema and each local schema is expressed by associating the concepts in the local schemas as a view $V_N$ over the global schema. For example, in Figure 10b, the global schema is defined as Global Disease Schema ($G_S$) (id, Name, severityLevel, medName) which captures various diseases in terms of their unique identifier, commonly referred name, disease severity level, and medication name which acts as a treatment for this disease. The data for this global schema is obtained from the two local schemas and their respective views: a local schema $LS_1$ Local Disease Schema$_1$ ($LDS_1$) (id, commonName, severityLevel), captures diseases in terms of identifier,

*Figure 9. Facade software design pattern and its implementation*

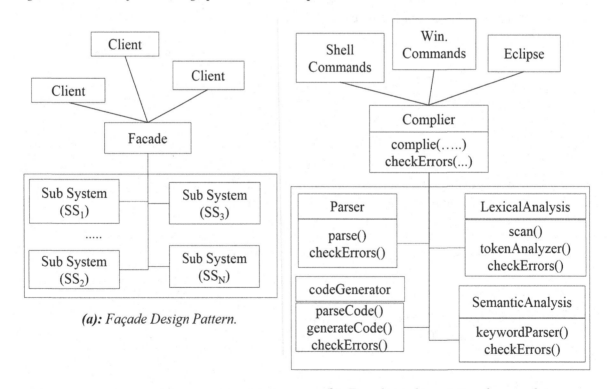

*(a): Façade Design Pattern.*

*(b): Façade implementation for complier.*

*Figure 10. The LAV methodology and its implementation*

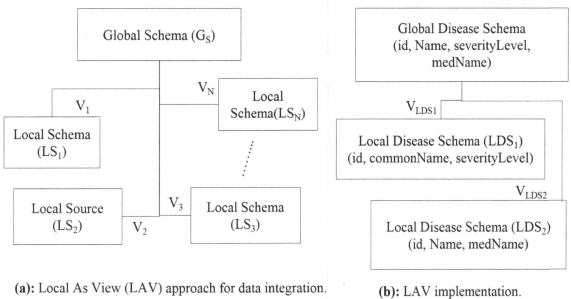

**(a):** Local As View (LAV) approach for data integration.

**(b):** LAV implementation.

commonly referred name, and disease severity level, respectively, and, its view $V_{LDS1}$ is defined as a mapping (represented as ~) between $LDS_1$(commonName, severityLevel) ~ $G_S$(name, severityLevel). The second local schema $LDS_2$, Local Disease Schema$_2$ $(LDS_2)$(id, name, medName), captures the medications for respective diseases in terms of identifier, disease name, and medication name, respectively, and its view $V_{LDS2}$ is defined as mapping between $LDS_2$(name, medName) ~ $G_S$(name, medName).

The MApping FRAmework (MAFRA) provides a conceptual framework for building semantic mappings between heterogeneous ontology models using *semantics bridges* as shown in the Figure 11a. A semantic bridge is a construct that allows the connections to have different meanings based on the needed interactions of the models. The mapping framework provides various types of semantic bridges such as RelationBridge, ConceptBridge, AttributeBridge, etc. For example, consider Local Disease Model (LDM) and the Global Disease Model ($G_M$) in Figure 11b. The semantically equivalent concepts between these

models are mapped using attributeBridge i.e., LDM (id) ~ $G_M$(id), and as LDM(commonName) ~ $G_M$(Name) as shown in the Figure 11b; as a result, we are able to represent this higher level dependencies among different ontologies.

**Pattern Description**: The *Centralized Ontology Architectural Pattern (COAP)* as shown in Figure 12 consists of a Global Ontology Model ($O_G$), multiple local source ontology models ($LO_1, LO_2, LO_3, ....., LO_N$), and the respective mappings ($OM_1, OM_2, ...., OM_N$) between local ontology models and the global ontology ($O_G$). Conceptually, the COAP in Figure 12 can be aligned as: the Global Ontology Model ($O_G$) (similar to a Façade in Figure 9a), a global schema in Figure 10a, or an Ontology ($O_1$) in Figure 11a; the local source ontology models ($LO_1, LO_2, LO_3, ......, LO_N$) can be local subsystems in Figure 9a, a local schemas from Figure 10a, or ontologies ($O2, ..., O_N$) in Figure 11a; and, the mappings ($OM_1, OM_2, ...., OM_N$) are similar to function calls

*Figure 11. The MAFRA framework and its implementation*

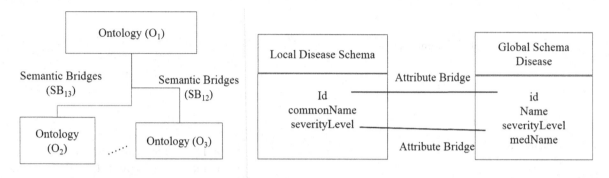

**(a):** MAFRA Framework.　　　　　　　　　**(b):** MAFRA implementation.

between subsystems in Figure 9a, views $(V_1,..,V_N)$ in Figure 10a, or semantic bridges in Figure 11a. The queries are generally performed on the Global Ontology Model $(O_G)$ of COAP and the local sources are extracted using the mappings $(OM_1, OM_2, ...,OM_N)$ which are primarily *semantic* in nature, i.e., the mappings are mostly semantic queries similar to views in Figure 11b or semantic mappings in Figure 14. The global ontology model acts as a centralized reference model for mapping the local source ontology models which can also be traversed using the mapping to the global ontology model, thus eliminating the semantic interoperability issues between heterogeneous

local ontology models. An enterprise application can use the Global Ontology Model supplemented by zero or more Local Ontology Models based on its needs.

**Pattern Context and Usage:** The COAP pattern is applicable where an enterprise application has an existing ontology acting as a global ontology and other ontology models (from potentially different enterprise applications) are to be integrated/mapped with the global ontology, or a single knowledge ontology model has to be built from existing multiple ontology models. An ideal example of the COAP is the Unified Medical Language System (UMLS) (Bodenreider, 2004) knowledge system developed and maintained by

*Figure 12. Centralized Ontology Architectural Pattern*

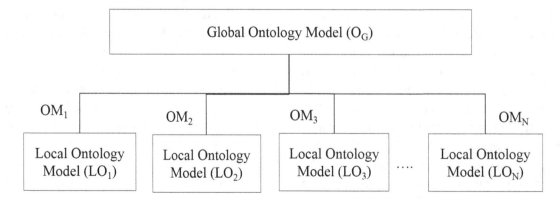

*Figure 13. Unified Medical Language System as instance of COAP*

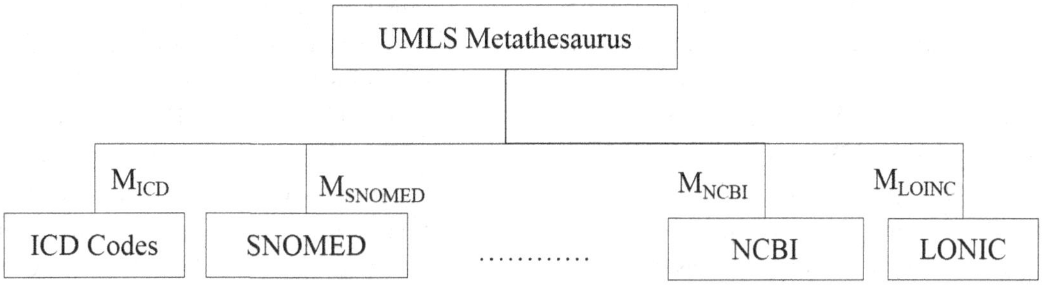

National Institute of Health (NIH) which has two primary tools: UMLS Semantic Network (UMLS-SN) and UMLS Metathesaurus (UMLS-Meta). The UMLS-Meta holds the medical vocabulary obtained by aggregating existing medical standard ontologies such as ICD, DSM, OMIM, SNOMED-CT, etc., and also providing the mappings between these aggregated ontologies. As shown in Figure 13, the UMLS-Meta (UMLS Metathesaurus) can be viewed as a global ontology model ($O_G$, Figure 12), obtaining its medical vocabulary from various local source ontologies such as ICD Codes,, SNOMED-CT, NCBI, LOINC, etc., which are local ontology models ($LO_1$, $LO_2$,...,$LO_N$, Figure 12).

Using the mappings ($OM_1$, $OM_2$,...,$OM_N$) and the global ontology model ($O_G$) as the reference, the semantic mappings (implicit mappings) between the local source ontology models can be deduced. The semantic interoperability issues among the ontologies are eased by employing the defined mappings ($OM_1$, $OM_2$, ..., $OM_N$) and the implicit mapping.

Another enterprise domain that could use COAP is e-commerce. While each e-commerce enterprise is unique from the perspective of its business model, sales strategies, software architecture, data management, user experience, etc., in total, a majority of them may overlap on the types of the merchandize/services offered (e.g., electronics, apparel, tools, books, materials, music, could

space, streaming music, etc.). However, each enterprise system may structure the semantic knowledge about the merchandize/services offered differently, as it's primarily influenced by the interests of the enterprise and talent of the ontology developer. For example, an e-commerce service ($ES_1$, e.g., Amazon, Barnes & Noble, eBay, etc.) may have an ontology model(s) ($O_{E1}$) capturing the semantics knowledge about the merchandize/services offered by the enterprise system. Similarly, other e-commerce services ($ES_2$, $ES_3$, $ES_4$,........,$ES_N$) will have their own ontology models ($O_{E1}$, $O_{E2}$, $O_{E3 ......}$,$O_{EN}$) capturing the semantic knowledge of their merchandize/services offered. When two enterprises, say $ES_1$ and $ES_2$, need to collaborate/merge, the semantic knowledge in the ontology models ($O_{ES1}$ and $O_{ES2}$) has to be mapped to one another to ease the semantic interoperability issues (both Knowledge and Data). However, individual one-to-one mappings between different ESs are not a feasible solution, since it would require a custom bi-direction exchange in varied formats. For providing a more scalable and feasible solution, the enterprises need to collaborate to define a global ontology model ($O_{EG}$) and map their respective local ontology models ($O_{E1}$, $O_{E2}$, $O_{E3 ......}$,$O_{EN}$) to the global ontology model. Thus, when multiple enterprises need to collaborate/merge, they can use the $O_{EG}$ ontology model as a reference to ease semantic interoperability issues. The global ontology model $O_{EG}$ will also act as a foundational platform for new enterprise systems and to interact with existing systems.

**Pattern Application and Implementation:** The NIH has provided open access to the UMLS system as previously discussed and shown in Figure 14 through a Web browser for online services and a Java Swing based UI supported with MySQL and Oracle database scripts for standalone applications as show in Figure 14. The sample database query diagrams between the UMLS-Meta schemas are shown in Figure 15, where the user can query: the *MRCONO* table for a common name for a given Concept Unique Identifier (CUI) for identifying medical concepts) as shown in Figure 15a; the *MRCONO* and *MRSTY* tables for finding all of the semantic types (UMLS-SN) for a given CUI as shown in Figure 15a; the MRCONO and MRDEF for obtaining the definition of a CUI as shown in Figure 15a; and, the MRCON and MRREL tables for obtaining all of the relationships a given concept is participating in using the Source Concept Unique Identifier (SCUI) that uniquely identifies the source of the medical concept as shown in Figure 15b. The UMLS acts as a global reference ontology model that can be utilized to obtain medical semantics and the system provides mappings between integrated local ontologies.

*Figure 14. Unified Medical Language System as instance of COAP and its implementation*

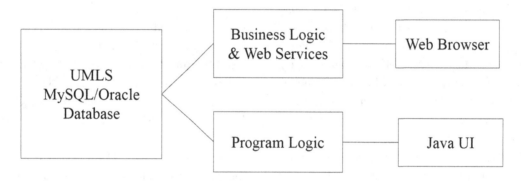

*Figure 15. Sample database query diagrams for querying UMLS for a given CUI and SCUI*

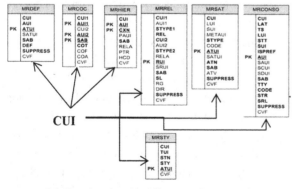

**(a)** Database query diagram for querying information for a given concept CUI.

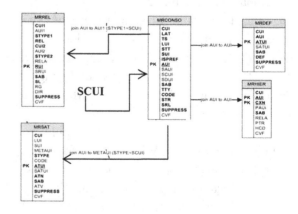

**(b)** Database query diagram for querying information for a given source concept SCUI.

## 3.3. Layered Ontology Architectural Pattern

**Pattern Name:** Layered Ontology Architectural Pattern (LaOAP)

**Pattern Motivation:** The *Layered Ontology Architectural Pattern (LaOAP)* focuses on the underlying conceptual models for databases, software, and development in order to structure the ontology and its components in a layered manner. To motivate, we use a health care example in Figures 16a, 16b, and 16c, and an e-commerce/cloud example in Figures 16d, 16e, and 16f. First, if we start with databases, where an Entity Relationship Diagram (ERD) (Chen, 1976) is employed for modeling entities with respective attributes and associations limited by constraints (cardinality, primary key, etc.) on attributes and association in order to achieve the desired database behavior. As shown in Figure 16a, the entities Disease and Symptom are described using attributes id and name, and are connected using the has Symptom association with a many-to-many constraint. Similarly, in Figure 16d, the entities Customer (described with attributes cId and cEmail), CloudSpace (described using attributes location and space) and ContentAllowed (an enumeration) are connected with hasCloudSpace, and cloudAllows associations respectively with a many-to-many constraint imposed on them. The ERD models in Figure 16a and 16d can be modeled from an object-oriented perspective using UML Class Diagrams as shown in Figure 16b and 16e, respectively, where Disease, Symptom, Customer, CloudSpace, and ContentAllowed are all classes; id, cId, space (type Integer), and Name, Location (type String) are all attributes; and, they are all connected using the associations hasSymptom, hasCloudSpace, and cloudAllows. The OWL framework allows developers to add complex axioms such as disjoint, subset, union, not, etc., on the modeling elements themselves to further constrain and control behavior and data values. As shown in Figure 16c and 16f, Disease, Symptom, Customer, CloudSpace, and ContentAllowed are OWL Classes that are connected using the links hasSymptom, hasCloudSpace, and cloudAllows that are of type OWL objectProperty (equivalent to an association in UML), with an additional constraint stating that the pairs of classes Disease and Symptom and Customer and CloudSpace are disjoint. The OWL framework also allows experts to define Semantic Web Rules and Fuzzy Logic on the defined concepts. The ability of ERD, UML, and OWL to model from differing perspectives or layers can be employed to define an OAP that takes advantage of the layering of conceptual models, akin to ISO layers.

**Pattern Description:** The *Layered Ontology Architectural Pattern (LaOAP)* organizes various participating modules in the ontology in a layered fashion that separates the ontology from a functional perspective as shown in Figure 17a. The LaOAP pattern has five layers where the heart of the pattern is the *Conceptual Model Layer*. This layer holds the ontology conceptual model capturing the structure and semantics of the intended domain. The second layer is the *Axiom & Rule Layer* that captures the rules and constraints for semantically interpreting the ontology conceptual model entities. The third layer is the *Mapping Layer* that captures any semantic mapping between the current ontology model and any other target ontology models. The fourth layer is the *Terminology Layer* that contains the vocabulary for the ontology model captured in the Conceptual Model Layer and adhering to the rules of the Axiom & Rule Layer. Finally, the fifth layer is the *Query and Web Service Layer* that allows users to query the conceptual model for its terminology or Web service API for serving Web-based requests.

For illustrating the five layers of the LaOAP pattern, consider the conceptual model for a health care application developed in OWL (Figure 16c and 16f) as shown in the Figure 17b. From the bottom up in Figure 17b, the *Conceptual Model Layer* holds the domain model (Disease Ontology Model) with classes (Disease, Symptom, etc.), associations (hasSymptom, hasMedication, etc.), and attributes (id, commonName, etc.). The *Axiom & Rule Layer* holds the first-order descriptive axioms for domain model entities such as the disjointness between Disease and Symptom classes. These axioms are defined in a new workspace by importing the ontology model from the *Conceptual Model Layer* to provide limited coupling between these two participating layers. The ontology designer can exploit this limited coupling to define multiple set of Axioms & Rules on the same ontology conceptual model. Continuing upward in Figure 17b, the *Mapping Layer* holds any mappings that are relevant and/or have been loaded to the current ontology model imported from *Conceptual Model Layer*. The attribute semantic bridge defined in the MAFRA framework (Figure 11) is utilized for illustrating an attribute equivalent mapping between the current Disease entity attribute id (Figure 16c) and the Disease entity attribute uid from a different conceptual Disease model. The *Terminology Layer* captures all of the instance data of the ontology model such as Heart Attack (instance of Disease class), Fever (instance of Symptom class), etc. Finally, at the top of Figure 17b, the *Query & Web Service Layer* has the domain model query logic (example OWL SPARQL queries, see Figure 9) for interrogating the Disease Ontology Model. In LaOAP, the outer layer may use the content defined in the inclusive inner layers. For example, the *Axioms and Rules Layer* will use the conceptual

model defined in *Conceptual Model Layer*; the *Terminology Layer* and the *Query & Web service Layer* imports the *Conceptual Model Layer* and import *Axiom and Rules Layer*. The *Conceptual Model Layer* is required to define this pattern and all of the other layers are optional.

**Pattern Context and Usage:** The LaOAP can be used when an ontology developer requires minimal coupling between various participating ontological modules (Figure 17a), maximizing their reuse especially for the core ontology model in the *Conceptual Model Layer*. The intent is that the layers of functionality build upon one another from the Conceptual Model Layer to the Query & Web Service Layer. For instance, as shown in Figure 18, the UMLS-Meta schema can be reused by multiple health care institutions (Hospital$_1$, Hospital$_2$, …,Hospital$_N$) in order to develop customized sets of mapping and axioms specific to their enterprise application on top of the shared UMLS-Meta model. LaOAP allows maximum reuse of the core conceptual model of the ontology, thereby mitigating interoperability issues.

**Pattern Application and Implementation:** The implementation of LaOAP employing OWL (see Figures 16c and 16f again) to represent the ontology is shown in Figure 19. Starting from the bottom of Figure 19, the *Conceptual Model Layer* holds the domain model (classes Disease, Symptom, CloudSpace, etc.), associations (hasSymptom, hasCloudSpace, etc.), and attributes (id, commonName, spaceAllocated, etc.). The *Axiom & Rule Layer* holds the first-order descriptive axioms for model entities such as the disjointness between Disease and Symptom, the spaceAllocated attribute has an integer range, etc. These axioms are defined in a new workspace by importing the ontology model from the *Conceptual Model Layer* to provide limited coupling between these two

*Figure 16. Domain models using ERD, UML and OWL*

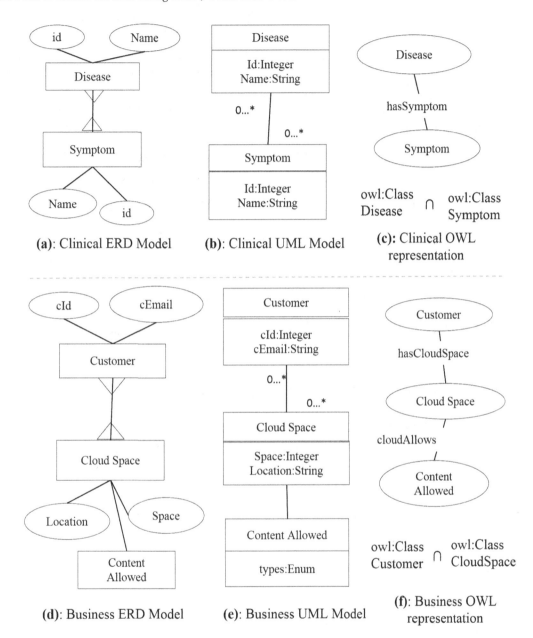

**(a)**: Clinical ERD Model    **(b)**: Clinical UML Model    **(c)**: Clinical OWL representation

**(d)**: Business ERD Model    **(e)**: Business UML Model    **(f)**: Business OWL representation

participating layers. The ontology designer can exploit this limited coupling to define multiple sets of Axioms & Rules on the same ontology conceptual model. For example, one business enterprise can define a range for the space attribute (CloudSpace class) between 2GB – 10GB, while another can define a different range between 5GB – 9GB.

Note that both enterprises use the same ontology model, but can customize that from a constraint perspective.

Similarly, the enterprise can define various accepted values to ContentAllowed based on the business goals. The *Mapping Layer* holds any mappings that are relevant and/or have been

*Figure 17. Layered Ontology Architectural Pattern and its implementation*

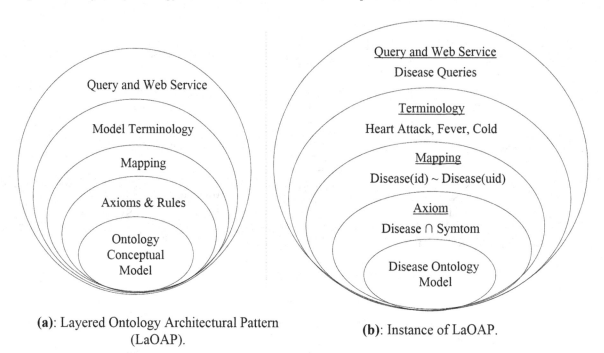

**(a)**: Layered Ontology Architectural Pattern (LaOAP).

**(b)**: Instance of LaOAP.

*Figure 18. Illustrating LaOAP using UMLS-Metathesaurus (UMLS-Meta)*

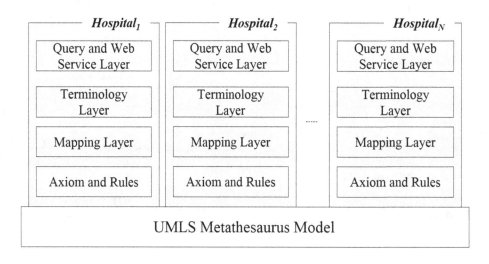

loaded to the current ontology model imported from *Conceptual Model Layer*. The attribute bridge defined in the MAFRA framework (Figure 10) is used for illustrating an attribute equivalent mapping between the current Disease entity (Figure 16c) and the Illness entity from a different conceptual model. The *Terminology Layer* captures all of the instance data of the ontology model such as Asthma (instance of Disease class), High Fever (instance of Symptom class), Heart Attack (instance of Disease class), 50GB (value of space attribute), etc. The ontology model and Axiom & Rules are imported into Terminology Layer to define the required domain vocabulary.

Finally, at the top of Figure 19, the *Query & Web Service Layer* can hold SPARQL query logic for interrogating the OWL conceptual model in the *Conceptual Model Layer*.

## 4. RELATED WORK

The work in this chapter has been influenced by a number of efforts and has ties to other work in ontology frameworks. First, in knowledge engineering, ontologies play a pivotal role in providing semantics to data, converting information into knowledge for a specific domain. To date, researchers have taken an approach to ontology patterns that implements different aspects of software design patterns (SDPs) in the domain of ontologies. The work of (Gangemi, 2005; Gangemi & Presutti, 2009) has defined Ontology Patterns (OP) and classified them into six categories: Structural OP, Correspondence OP, Content OP, Reasoning OP, Presentation OP, and Lexico-Syntactic OP. The Structural OP is equivalent to the structural SDP and further divided into Logical OP to handle the problem of expressivity and Architectural OP to affect the overall shape of the ontology either internally or externally. The Correspondence OP encompasses the Reengineering OP and provides a designer with a solution to the problem of transforming the ontology conceptual model. The

*Figure 19. Implementation of LaOAP using OWL*

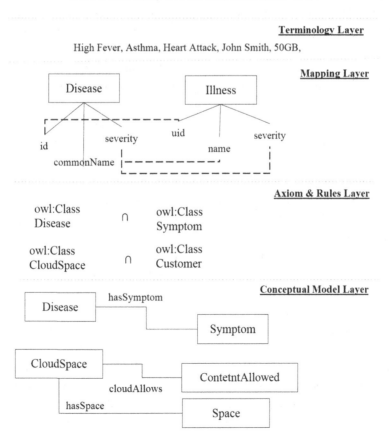

Mapping OP refers to the possible semantic relations between mappable ontology model elements. Content OPs have gained priority as they solve knowledge design problems in terms of domain classes and properties, similar to Creational and Behavioral SDP. Our OAPs presented in this chapter can be positioned within the classification the six categories in (Gangemi, 2005) by placing the developed OAPs (LOAP, COAP and LaOAP) under Architectural OP, as they influence the architectural design of the ontology for an enterprise application. Our approach operates at a slightly higher level than their work which is more closely aligned to SDPs.

Second, the work on Ontology Patterns (Gangemi, 2005; Gangemi & Presutti, 2009) has proposed the Conceptual Ontology Design Pattern (CODeP) categorized as a Content OP to capture a generalized use case scenario acting as a template to solve domain knowledge design issues and offering a number of different patterns that target varied capabilities. For example, Time Indexed Participation is a CODeP that represents time indexing for the relation between persons and roles they play. The Role Task Pattern is also a CODeP representing temporary roles that objects can play, and the tasks that events/actions that are allowed to execute. The Participation Pattern is a CODeP extracted from the DOLCE ontology that illustrates participation relation between objects and events. The CODeP are knowledge-level abstractions that primarily influence the design of the ontology content and can be employed by OAPs to define ontology knowledge for the participating ontology models (Ontology$_1$, Figure 4; Global Ontology, Figure 12 and Layered Ontology, Figure 18). Similarly, both the paradigms CODeP and OAP provide abstractions at different levels, i.e., the former provides knowledge abstraction and the latter provide architectural abstraction.

Third, the work of (Clark, Thompson, & Porter, 2004) has proposed the concept of knowledge patterns defined as a semantic structure representing reoccurring patterns similar to SDP, but morphing the knowledge pattern entities onto domain classes instead of instantiating them. For example, a simple distribution knowledge patterns consists of a Producer P, a Switch mechanism S, and a Consumer C that are connected. This knowledge pattern is applicable to any domain model, e.g., P can represent a battery, generator, etc., S can be a common electrical switch, and C can be any electrical device such as light, heater, computer, etc. There is a close association among our LOAP and their knowledge pattern, since they are both similar to Pipes & Filters and Chain of Responsibility SDPs. However, their knowledge pattern primarily targets ontological concepts similar to CODeP for a domain across multiple enterprise applications that follows a similar knowledge structure.

Fourth, our work on a framework for ontologies has proposed extensions to the OWL framework to provide additional modeling features and introduce the concept of an ontology schema to evolve OWL to align to the UML meta-model (Saripalle, Demurjian, & Behre, 2011) with an associated software engineering process (Saripalle & Demurjian, 2012a) that elevates ontologies to be more design-oriented as opposed to instance based, allowing ontologies to be reused in an enterprise setting. As a foundation for the Ontology Architectural Patterns (OAP) in this chapter, our work (Saripalle & Demurjian, 2012) has introduced a Semantic Design Pattern defined as a modular domain knowledge pattern at the meta-model level which can be referenced while developing concrete domain models. The work in this chapter significantly extends the semantic design pattern concept to Ontology Architectural Patterns, promoting a design process for ontologies that has a much higher abstraction level than existing ontology frameworks.

Finally, there are a number of efforts underway in ontology frameworks related to Enterprise applications, where our work on OAP can be utilized to augment their approaches. The Enterprise Ontology (Uschold, 1995) project provides an approach to model ontologies at the enterprise level, and is part of a larger Enterprise Project (Uschold, 1998) that is aimed at supporting a framework to collaboratively model enterprise applications. Our work in this chapter dovetails with this effort by providing the means to define OAPs within their framework to have a higher-level modeling (OAP) not currently supported by their work. Another effort, the Toronto Virtual Enterprise (TOVE) project (Gruninger & Fox, 1995) is an enterprise model that is able to generate common sense enterprise data models that has the ability to deduce answers to common sense queries regarding the enterprise. Our work on OAP in this chapter can augment TOVE and EO enterprise projects by promoting a higher-level abstract design process for ontologies (source of enterprise application knowledge for the projects) that supports knowledge reusability through ontology modeling coupled with architectural concepts. Additionally, the concept of OAP can easily be integrated into TOVE's project lifecycle model to tackle any interoperability issues. For the field of Ontology Based Information Extraction (OBIE) (Maynard, Yankova, Kourakis, & Kokossis, 2005; Saggion, Funk, Maynard, & Bontcheva, 2007; Wimalasuriya & Dou, 2010), the construction of an application for an enterprise domain heavily relies on ontology models that capture the required domain knowledge using information and knowledge extracted from unstructured and semi-structured sources (e.g., Web, texts, data streams, etc.). Our work on OAP can provide OBIE with the ability to model knowledge at a higher level of abstraction, providing another means to organize the needed knowledge into an ontology via a pattern. Similarly, in enterprise data warehousing architecture (Blechner, Saripalle, & Demurjian, 2012), ontologies play a key role of attaching semantics to the stored data for: providing meaning to information, support querying of the stored data using the shared standard concept semantics, and providing the ability to present the stored information as human readable knowledge

through semantic definition. We envision that our OAP architectural pattern framework will assist ontology designers to make better ontology architectural decisions in the initial phases of the ontology life cycle process that will influence the usage of the ontology models in multiple enterprise application setting, thus primarily targeting enterprise interoperability.

## 5. FUTURE RESEARCH DIRECTIONS

Over the span of the last 30 years, the computing field has evolved to be more domain independent and device agnostic trending towards the development of software, database, and Web applications that are easily modified and evolved as requirements change over time. There have been many examples in computing where industry and academia have come together towards generalized solutions. The 1980s provided a transition from procedural to object-oriented languages (objective-C, Eiffel, GNU C++, AT&T C++, etc.). Standards eventually coalesced C++ into a single solution. During the same time, there was a wide (and confusing) collection of object-oriented design models with different (and often conflicting) concepts and terminology that were eventually unified into UML. The Object Management Group (OMG) took control of the standard, which included a UML meta-model and the ability to generate an XML instance of a UML design with both the content of the design and the positioning of the graphical objects in each UML diagram that was easily ported. There was a similar convergence in the database community, first on standardizing the Structure Query Language (SQL) and later in the use of XML and XMI to export/import both a database schema and the tuples themselves from one database system to another. In the late 1990s, Java came on the scene to revolutionize programming (write once, run anywhere), and today its dominance throughout computing and our daily lives is significant particular in regards to mobile devices. This history serves as a strong justification as to why there needs to be improvements in the ontology development process towards a design-oriented approach where reuse can be facilitated and interoperability can be achieved.

In order to ease structural and semantic interoperability issues among knowledge sources, we need to analyze and implement the lessons learned from software engineering, programming languages, and computing. *First*, there is definitely a lack of *commitment* and *agreement* by knowledge developers and domain experts towards a common knowledge source. This is evident in the health care domain as shown in Figure 1 and for many other domains such as e-commerce, digital collections (METS), human resource applications (HR-UML), legal applications (LegalUML), document exchange (Open Office XML), where multiple standards are developed for providing semantic knowledge on the same domain with minimal knowledge reuse. We need to strive towards a *formal standard* for knowledge sources, primarily ontologies, as they are currently the key source of knowledge semantics. This process encompasses the development of standard knowledge models and, most importantly, employing up-to-date technologies such as UML 2.0, RDF, OWL, etc. For example, many existing medical standards are implemented using outdated technologies such as XML DTDs, KIF, Frames, Semantic Networks, etc.; the future will require knowledge representation frameworks to demonstrate the same evolution as UML tools and databases towards a common context.

*Second*, even with the existence of multiple standard models for a given domain, there would still be disagreement on the semantics on the elements defined in the standard. For example, the health care domain has various representational standards such as CCD, CCR, HL7 CDA for patient data and ontologies with similar domain interests such as SNOWMED-CT, LOINC, ICD, DSM, etc. However, these standards lack the agreement on semantics of the defined concepts; CCD and CCR

store the same information in different ways and as a result infer different semantic relationships among the information that comprises a patient's medical record. Further, it is nearly impossible to take data form one vendor's EHR to another vendor's EHR since data formats and ontologies are all proprietary. We need to understand the existing standards from both structural and semantic perspectives, and define an agreed standard *meta-model* for enterprise domains with sound structure and semantics that can be utilized in a unification process. The structure and semantics for this meta-model can be defined based on existing domain model standards supplemented with additional concepts. This developed meta-model will then act as a standard framework for developing multiple standard models. For example, the UML meta-model provides a UML Profile feature which is a generic lightweight extension mechanism allowing developers to tailor the UML metamodel to domain specific requirements. The extension allows refining the standard UML semantics according to user requirements in a strictly additive manner without contradicting the defined metamodel semantics. The OMG employs this feature to define profiles (Fuentes-Fernández & Vallecillo-Moreno, 2004) in various domains such as Service oriented architecture Modeling Language (SoAML), Distributed Data Systems (DDS), Advanced and Integrated Telecommunication Services (TelcoML), etc. These UML Profiles based on the UML metamodel act as a domain specific standard metamodel with well-defined concepts from respective domains for developing multiple domain models. Thus, developing a generic or domain specific metamodel for domains such as e-commerce, human resources, legal field, medicine, finance, business, biology etc., will ease interoperability issues as the *structure* and *semantics* defined in the metamodel are well agreed among the domain experts.

*Third*, we need to encourage domain experts to develop and standardize *knowledge patterns* which can be referred to while developing knowledge models for specific domains. When multiple knowledge models refer to the same knowledge pattern, the semantics of the defined model can easily be understood, closing the gap for any semantic misinterpretations. As a result, knowledge patterns supplement ontology patterns and strive towards a process that emphasizes design rather than development. For example, the well-defined Task-Role CODeP proposed by Gangemi in Figure 20 in Section 4 can be referenced for developing any domain applications involving tasks (such as financial transactions, prescription writing, changes to Web services, etc.), roles (such as manager, physician, developer, etc.), object (such as currency, patient, software code), etc. Similarly, the domain experts need to develop, document, maintain, and share domain knowledge patterns for easing semantic interoperation.

## CONCLUSION

This chapter has addressed a serious disconnect between ontologies for enterprise applications that are primarily focused on encoding the captured domain knowledge concepts and their respective relationships at the instance level and software-engineering-based approaches focused on developing domain models which provide abstract view of the solution employing software design patterns. The current approach chosen by ontologists focuses on the development of specific instance-level ontologies to capture knowledge requirements of specific domain application but with the side effect of causing potential *structural* and *semantic interoperability* conflicts when one attempts to integrate two or more ontologies from different contexts. For two or more enterprise application that need to share data and knowledge via their respective ontologies, this is a significant roadblock to facilitate interoperation. There is a clear need to support Enterprise Interoperability (EI) particularly in regards to the interoperation of data and knowledge across multiple enterprise

applications. The major premise of this chapter is that there needs to be an upgrade from an ontology development process to one that is focused on abstraction and the leveraging of design models (UML and ER) and approaches (SDPs). Through this enhanced design and modeling process, ontologies will be able to be more clearly and abstractly defined with the potential for reuse in multiple settings. The work of this chapter applied and extended the concept of SDPs in order to propose a set of Ontology Architectural Patterns (OAPs) that would provide ontologists with a significant abstraction capability to be able to more effectively design ontologies that can promote enterprise interoperability in terms of both data and knowledge.

Towards this objective, Section 2 presented background and motivation on the different ways that ontologies can be exploited in the design and development process, reviewed software design patterns, and provided a context for the work of this chapter by exploring enterprise interoperability (EI) with a particular emphasis on data and knowledge integration via ontologies. Using this as basis, in Section 3, we presented three Ontology Architectural Patterns (OAPs): the Linear Ontology Architectural Pattern (LOAP) in Section 3.1 for modeling the linear/parallel architectural arrangement of ontology models for achieving the required knowledge goal; the Centralized Ontology Architectural Pattern (COAP) in Section 3.2 which supported the definition of a centralized ontology model and its interactions with multiple local/other ontology models; and, the Layered Ontology Architectural Pattern (LaOAP) in Section 3.3 that defined a layered architectural arrangement of participating modules in the ontology model. The discussed OAPs applied concepts from structural and architectural software design patterns in order to define the three OAPs that allow ontologies to be both modeled and related to one another at a higher conceptual level. As a result, OAPs promote the design of domain knowledge semantics into a modular concept that can then yield reusable ontology models for enterprise applications to more effectively address *structural* and *semantic* enterprise interoperability. To place our work into its proper perspective, Section 4 explored related work in ontology patterns and ontology frameworks, comparing their efforts to our OAPs thereby demonstrating the inclusion of our OAPs in practice. Section 5 focused on future directions by first providing a discussion of the history of programming languages, software models, and databases, and that the standards have shaped their evolution over time. This in turn serves as a basis for discussing improvements in regards to ontology design and development to work towards a knowledge representation framework that operates in a more abstract perspective through the proposal of OAPs. While the chapter demonstrated the developed OAP in the health care domain, the work is more general in nature and applicable to interoperability issues among ontologies for, any enterprise domain. This argument was supported by providing additional and complementary examples of LOAP, COAP, and LaOAP for e-government, e-services, and e-commerce domains. If we can continue to move the ontology process to embrace a more conceptual and design level perspective, there is great potential to allow ontologies to be more easily integrated leading to an ability to share information across a domain.

# REFERENCES

Allemang, D., & Hendler, J. (2011). *Semantic web for the working ontologist: Effective modeling in RDFS and OWL* (2nd ed.). Waltham, MA: Morgan Kaufmann.

Ashburne, M., & Lewis, S. (2002). On ontologies for biologists: The gene ontology-untangling the web. In *Proceedings of the Novartis Found Symposium* (pp. 66-80). Novartis Found.

ASTM. (2003). *Standard specification for continuity of care record (CCR)*. Retrieved from www.astm.org/Standards/E2369.htm

Baader, F., McGuinness, D., Nardi, D., & Patel-Schneider, P. (2007). *The description logic handbook: Theory, implementation and applications.* New York, NY: Cambridge University Press. doi:10.1017/CBO9780511711787

Bell, M. (2008). *Service-oriented modeling: Service analysis, design, and architecture.* Hoboken, NJ: Wiley & Sons. doi:10.1109/EDOC.2008.51

Bettahar, F., Moulin, C., & Barthes, J. (2009). Towards a semantic interoperability in an e-government applications. *Electronic. Journal of E-Government*, 7(3), 209–226.

Blechner, M., Saripalle, R., & Demurjian, S. (2012). Proposed star schema and extraction process to enhance the collection of contextual & semantic information for clinical research data warehouses. In *Proceedings of the 2012 International Workshop on Biomedical and Health Informatics*. Philadelphia: Academic Press.

Bodenreider, O. (2004). The unified medical language system (UMLS), integrating biomedical terminology. *Journal Nucleic Acids Research*, 32(1), 267–270. doi:10.1093/nar/gkh061

Brauer, M., & Schubert, S. (2013). *The OpenOffice.org XML project*. Retrieved from http://www.openoffice.org/xml/

Burstein, H. M., & McDermott, V. D. (2005). Ontology translation for interoperability among semantic web services. *AI Magazine*, 26(1), 71–82.

Charalabidis, Y., Goncalves, R. J., & Popplewell, K. (2010). Developing a science base for enterprise interoperability. In K. Popplewell, J. Harding, C. Ricardo, & R. Poler (Eds.), *Enterprise interoperability IV: Making the internet of the future for the future of enterprise* (pp. 245–254). Springer Publications. doi:10.1007/978-1-84996-257-5_23

Chen, P. (1976). The entity-relationship model: Toward a unified view of data. *ACM Transactions on Database Systems*, *1*(1), 9–36. doi:10.1145/320434.320440

Chiang, M. F., Hwang, J. C., Yu, A. C., Casper, D. S., Cimino, J. J., & Starren, J. (2006). Reliability of SNOMED-CT coding by three physicians using two terminology browsers. In *Proceedings of the 2006 AMIA Annual Symposium* (pp. 131-135). AMIA.

Clark, P., Thompson, J., & Porter, B. (2004). Knowledge patterns. In S. Staab, & R. Struder (Eds.), *Handbook on ontologies* (pp. 191–207). Berlin: Springer. doi:10.1007/978-3-540-24750-0_10

Davis, J., Harris, S., Crichton, C., Shukla, A., & Gibbons, J. (2008). Metadata standards for semantic interoperability in electronic government. In *Proceedings of the 2nd International Conference on Theory and Practice of Electronic Governance* (pp. 67-75). Academic Press.

Demurjian, S., Saripalle, R., & Behre, S. (2009). An integrated ontology framework for health information exchange. In *Proceedings of the 21st International Conference on Software Engineering and Knowledge Engineering* (pp. 575-580). Boston: Academic Press.

DSM. (2012). *DSM-5 implementation and support*. Retrieved from http://www.dsm5.org/

FIBO. (2013). *Financial report ontology*. Retrived from http://financialreportontology.wikispaces.com/home

Fonou-Dombeu, J. V., & Huisman, M. (2011). Semantic-driven e-government: Application of uschold and king ontology building methodology for semantic ontology models developments. *International Journal of Web & Semantic Technology*, *2*(4), 1–20. doi:10.5121/ijwest.2011.2401

Freeman, E., Robson, E., Bates, B., & Sierra, K. (2004). *Head first design patterns*. Sebastopol, CA: O'Reilly Media.

Fuentes-Fernández, L., & Vallecillo-Moreno, A. (2004). An introduction to UML profiles. *European Journal for the Informatics Professional*, *5*(2).

Gali, A., Chen, C. X., Claypool, K. T., & Uceda-Sosa, R. (2004). From ontology to relational databases. In S. Wang (Ed.), *ER workshops (LNCS)* (Vol. 3289, pp. 278–289). Berlin: Springer-Verlag.

Gamma, E., Helm, R., Johnson, R., & Vlissides, J. (1994). *Design patterns: Elements of reusable object-oriented software*. Boston, MA: Addison-Wesley.

Gangemi, A. (2005). Ontology patterns for semantic web content. In *Proceedings of the 4th International Semantic Web Conference* (pp. 262-276). Academic Press.

Gangemi, A., & Presutti, V. (2009). Ontology design patterns. In S. Staab, & R. Struder (Eds.), *Handbook on ontologies: International handbooks on information systems* (pp. 221–243). IOS Press. doi:10.1007/978-3-540-92673-3_10

Genesereth, M. (1991). Knowledge interchange format. In *Proceedings of the 2nd International Conference on Priciples of Knowledge Representation and Reasoning* (pp. 238-249). Morgan Kaufman.

HL7 CDA R2. (2008). *HL7/ASTM implementation guide for CDA® R2 -Continuity of care document (CCD®) release 1*. Retrieved from http://www.hl7.org/implement/standards/product_brief.cfm?product_id=6

Horrocks, I. (2002). DAML+OIL: A description logic for the semantic web. *IEEE Computer Society on Data Engineering*, *25*, 4–9.

HR-XML. (2013). *HR-XML consortium*. Retrieved from http://www.hr-xml.org/

Hu, B. (2010). Semantic interoperability for financial information: A component-based approach. In *Proceedings of 3rd IEEE International Conference on Computer Science and Information Technology* (pp. 228- 232). IEEE.

ICD. (2013). *ICD-10*. Retrieved from http://www.cms.gov/Medicare/Coding/ICD10/index.html?redirect=/icd10

Janowicz, K., Scheider, S., Pehle, T., & Hart, G. (2012). Geospatial semantics and linked spatio-temporal data – Past, present, and future. *Semantic Web – Interoperability, Usability. Applicability*, *3*(4), 321–332.

Jardim-Goncalves, R., Grilo, A., Agostinho, C., Lampathaki, F., & Charalabidis, Y. (2013). Systematisation of interoperability body of knowledge: The foundation for EI as a science. *Special Information Systems for Enterprise Integration, Interoperability and Networking. Theory and Applications*, *7*(1), 7–32.

Java Ontology Editor. (1998, May 19). *Java ontology editor (JOE)*. Retrieved from http://cit.cse.sc.edu/demos/java/joe/joeBeta-jar.html

Kohler, M. (2007). *UMLS for information extraction*. (Mater's Thesis). Vienna University of Technology, Vienna, Austria.

Krauthammer, M. (2002). *Brief review of clinical vocabularies*. Retrieved from http://www.cbil.upenn.edu/Ontology/MKreview.html

Kuhn, M. (2010). Modeling vs encoding for semantic web. *Journal of Semantic Web-Interoperability, Usability. Applicability*, *1*(1), 11–15.

Lacy, L. (2005). *OWL: Representing information using the web ontology language*. Victoria, Canada: Trafford Publishing.

Legal, X. M. L. (2008). *Overview of the OASIS LegalXML*. Retrieved from http://www.legalxml.org/

Lenzerini, M. (2002). Data integration: A theoretical perspective. In *Proceedings of the 21st ACM SIGACT-SIGMOD-SIGART Symposium on Principles of Database Systems* (pp. 233-246). ACM.

LOC. (2012). *Standards in the library of congress*. Retrieved from http://www.loc.gov/standards/

LOINC. (2013). *Logical observation identifiers names and codes (LOINC®)*. Retrieved from http://loinc.org/

Maedche, A., Motik, B., Silva, N., & Volz, R. (2002). MAFRA - A mapping framework for distributed ontologies. In *Knowledge engineering and knowledge management: Ontologies and the semantic web (LNCS)* (Vol. 2473, pp. 235–250). Berlin: Springer. doi:10.1007/3-540-45810-7_23

Makela, T., Rommel, K., Uskonem, J., & Wan, T. (2007). *Towards a financial ontology – A comparison of e- business process standards*. Retrived from http://www.soberit.hut.fi/T-86/T-86.5161/2007/FinancialOntology_final.pdf

Maynard, D., Yankova, M., Kourakis, R., & Kokossis, A. (2005). Ontology-based information extraction for market monitoring and technology watch. In *Proceedings of the Workshop Of ESWC, End User Apects of Semantic Web*. Heraklion.

Nagarajan, M., Verma, K., Sheth, A., Miller, J., & Lathem, J. (2006). Semantic interoperability of web services – Challenges and experiences. In *Proceedings of the 4th IEEE International Conference on Web Services* (pp. 373-382). IEEE.

OWL-S. (2004, November). *OWL-S: Semantic markup for web services*. Retrieved from http://www.w3.org/Submission/OWL-S/

Popplewell, K., Lampathaki, F., Koussouris, S., Mouzakitis, S., Charalabidis, Y., Goncalves, R., & Agostinho, C. (2012). *ENSEMBLE: Promoting future internet enterprise systems research.* Retrieved from http://www.fines-cluster.eu/fines/jm/Publications/Download-document/339-EN-SEMBLE_D2.1_EISB_State_of_Play_Report-v2.00.html

Powers, S. (2003). Practical RDF. Sebastopol, CA: O' Reilly Media.

Protege. (2012). *Protege ontology editor.* Retrieved from http://www.protege.stanford.edu

Saggion, H., Funk, A., Maynard, D., & Bontcheva, K. (2007). Ontology-based information extraction for business intelligence. In *Proceedings of the 6th International Conference on Semantic Web.* IEEE.

Saripalle, R., & Demurjian, S. (2012a). Towards a hybrid ontology design and development life cycle. In *Proceedings of the 11th International Conference on Semantic Web and Web Services.* IEEE.

Saripalle, R., & Demurjian, S. (2012b). Semantic patterns using the OWL domain profile. In *Proceedings of the 2012 International Knowledge Engineering Conference* (pp. 3-9). IEEE.

Saripalle, R., Demurjian, S., & Behre, S. (2011). Towards software design process for ontologies. In *Proceedings of the 1st International Conference on Software and Intelligent Information.* IEEE.

Smith, B. A., & Ceusters, W. B. (2006). Ontology as the core discipline of biomedical informatics: Legacies of the past and recommendations for the future direction of research. In G. D. Crnkovic, & S. Stuart (Eds.), *Computing, philosophy, and cognitive science.* Cambridge, UK: Cambridge Scholars Press.

SNOMED CT. (2013). *SNOMED CT® technical implementation guide.* Retrieved from http://ihtsdo.org/fileadmin/user_upload/doc/

SOAP. (2007, April). *Simple object access protocol.* Retrieved from http://www.w3.org/TR/soap/

Wimalasuriya, D. C., & Dou, D. (2010). Ontology-based information extraction: An introduction and a survey of current approaches. *Journal of Information Science, 36*(6), 306–323. doi:10.1177/0165551509360123

WSDL. (2001, March). *Web services description language.* Retrieved from http://www.w3.org/TR/2001/NOTE-wsdl-20010315

## ADDITIONAL READING

Baclawski, K., Kokar, M., Kogut, A. P., Hart, L., Smith, E. J., Letkowski, J., & Emery, P. (2002). Extending the Unified Modeling Language for ontology development. *Journal of Software and System Modeling, 1*, 142–156. doi:10.1007/s10270-002-0008-4

Bendaoud, R., Napoli, A., & Toussaint, Y. (2005). A proposal for an Interactive Ontology Design Process based on Formal Concept Analysis. In *Proceedings of the Formal Information and Ontology System (FIOS).*

Boone, K. (2011). *The CDA book.* New York, NY: Springer. doi:10.1007/978-0-85729-336-7

D'Amore, J. D., Sittig, D. F., Wright, A., Iyengar, M. S., & Ness, R. (2011). The Promise of the CCD: Challenges and Opportunity for Quality Improvement and Population Health. In *Proceedings of the 2011 AMIA Annual Symposium* (pp. 285-294).

Davis, J., Harris, S., Crichton, C., Shukla, A., & Gibbons, J. (2008). Metadata standards for semantic interoperability in electronic government. In *Proceedings of the 2nd international conference on Theory and practice of electronic governance* (pp. 67-75).

Djurić, D., Gašević, D., & Devedžić, V. (2005). Ontology Modeling and MDA. *Journal of Object Technology*, *4*(1), 109–128. doi:10.5381/jot.2005.4.1.a3

Gomez-Porez, A. (1996). A Framework to Verify Knowledge Sharing Technology. *Expert Systems with Applications*, *11*(4), 519–529. doi:10.1016/S0957-4174(96)00067-X

Gruber, R. T. (2005). Toward Principles for design of ontologies used for knowledge sharing. *Journal of Human Computer Studies*, *43*, 90–928.

Guranio, N. (2001). Formal Ontology and Information Systems. In *Proceedings of the 1st International Conference on Foraml Ontology and Infomration System*. Trento, Iltay.

Hartmann, J., Palma, R., & Sure, Y. (2005). OMV–Ontology Metadata Vocabulary for the Semantic Web. In *Proceedings of the International Workshop on Ontology Patterns for the Semantic Web*.

Herre, H., Heller, B., Burek, P., Hoehndorf, R., Loebe, F., & Michalek, H. (2007). *General Formal Ontology (GFO), A Foundational Ontology Integrating Objects and Processes. Part I: Basic Principles. Research Group Ontologies in Medicine (Onto-Med)*. University of Leipzig.

Mazzoleni, P., Crispo, B., Sivasubramanian, S., & Bertino, E. (2008). Xacml policy integration algorithms. [TISSEC]. *ACM Transactions on Information and System Security*, 11.

Nicola, A., Missikoff, M., & Navigli, R. (2005). A Proposal for a Unified Process for Ontology building: UPON. In *Proceedings of the 16th International Conference on Database and Expert Systems Applications*.

OMIM. (2013). Retrieved from Online Mendelian Inheritance in Man: http://www.omim.org/

Trinh, Q. (2007). Semantic Interoperability Between Relational Database Systems. In *Proceedings of the 11th International Database Engineering and Applications Symposium* (pp. 208-215).

Wache, H., Vögele, T. U., Stuckenschmidt, H., Schuster, G., Neumann, H., & Hübner, S. (2001). Ontology-Based Integration of Information - A Survey of Existing Approaches. In *Proceedings of the International Workshop on Ontologies and Information Sharing* (pp. 108-117).

## KEY TERMS AND DEFINITIONS

**Continuity of Care Record (CCR):** A document standard for health information typically used for representing data in Personal Health Records (PHR).

**Electronic Health Record (EHR):** An electronic health record contains all related health information, from medications to procedures, and is managed by the institution in which it is stored (e.g. hospital, private practice, clinic, etc.).

**Enterprise Interoperability (EI):** A field of activity with the aim to improve the manner in which enterprises, by means of information and communications technologies, interoperate with other enterprises, organizations, or with other business units, in order to conduct their business.

**eXtensible Markup Language (XML):** A structured language utilized for information exchange, standards and information validation via the use of schemas. Its extensibility allows developers and experts to design and implement common standards for the use across systems and domains.

**Health Information Exchange (HIE):** The ability to share information among health information technology systems by linking information for the same patient across multiple repositories to provide a complete health care view.

**Health Language Seven Clinical Document Architecture (HL7 CDA):** HL7 CDA is an XML-based markup standard intended to specify the encoding, structure and semantics of clinical documents for exchange.

**Interoperability:** The ability of diverse systems and organizations to work in a collaborative environment.

**Resource Description Framework (RDF):** RDF is as a metadata data model which is used for conceptual description or modeling of information that is implemented in web resources, using a variety of syntax notations and data serialization formats.

**Software Design Patterns (SDPs):** SDPs are general reusable solution to a reoccurring problem in multiple different situations with similar context without involving any application specific objects.

**SPARQL Protocol and RDF Query Language (SPARQL):** SPARQL is an RDF query language that will be able to retrieve and manipulate data stored in RDF/OWL format. SPARQL allows for a query to consist of triple patterns, conjunctions, disjunctions, and optional patterns.

**Systematized Nomenclature of Medicine Clinical Terms (SNOMED-CT):** an organized computer processable collection of medical terms providing codes, terms, synonyms and definitions covering domains such as diseases, findings, procedures, microorganisms, substances, etc.

**Unified Medical Language System (UMLS):** UMLS is defined as a compendium of multiple standard medical vocabularies such as ICD, LOINC, SNOMED-CT, etc., and provides a mapping structure between the integrated standards.

**Web Ontology Language (OWL):** The Web Ontology Language is a knowledge representation languages for defining ontologies.

## Section 3
# Perspectives and Future Research Directions for Enterprise Interoperability

# Chapter 11
# Towards an Enhanced Interoperability Service Utility:
## An Ontology Supported Approach

**Irene Matzakou**
*National Technical University of Athens, Greece*

**Ourania Markaki**
*National Technical University of Athens, Greece*

**João Sarraipa**
*Universidade Nova de Lisboa, Portugal*

**Kostas Ergazakis**
*National Technical University of Athens, Greece*

**Dimitris Askounis**
*National Technical University of Athens, Greece*

## ABSTRACT

*This chapter suggests an innovative approach towards establishing Enterprise Interoperability in the everyday electronic transactions among the contemporary enterprise information systems. Based on the rather cutting-edge concept of the "Interoperability Service Utility (ISU)," enriched with a concrete methodology for ontologies' reconciliation, the authors suggest an enhanced ISU that would serve as a mediator among the incompatible enterprise information systems, providing semantic harmonization of the exchanged knowledge and a fertile ground for achieving Enterprise Interoperability and Collaboration. The authors' proposition and methodology can constitute a high quality scientific and supportive material for any stakeholder in the enterprise field, giving useful directions for any other similar implementation and contributing to the scientific aspect of Enterprise Interoperability.*

## CONTEXT, SCOPE AND OBJECTIVES OF THE CHAPTER

### Introduction

In this chapter we investigate possible ways to *bridge the gap* among the different and heterogeneous ways in which enterprises currently organize

their internal knowledge. The reason for that is the lack of *Enterprise Interoperability* which results into *significant costs* both in terms of time and money, as well as in terms of information loss, which arise during the communication and knowledge exchange among enterprises and their corresponding information systems. Therefore, we suggest combining two innovative concepts in one novel approach. More specifically, we propose the implementation of an ISU, which is currently a

DOI: 10.4018/978-1-4666-5142-5.ch011

rather cutting-edge concept, promoted by the EU in the field of Enterprise Interoperability, especially enhanced with MENTOR, an already rigorous and widely-applied methodology for ontologies' reconciliation. That way, we suggest an enhanced ISU that would serve as an intermediary among enterprises and their corresponding information systems, providing added-value Web Services and supporting the achievement of Enterprise Interoperability, especially on a semantic level. Our proposition of this enhanced ISU is beyond any other similar implementation so far, covering a significant amount of aspects, gathering all specifications of other similar implementations and contributing widely to the scientific foundations of Enterprise Interoperability.

## Structure of the Chapter

The structure of the chapter is the following:

The first section, "Context, Scope and Objectives of the Chapter", includes an introduction to the chapter by shortly giving the context, scope and objectives of this joint research work.

The second section, "Current Business Environment", shortly reviews the current business environment, especially regarding to the barriers that prevent the smooth communication and knowledge exchange among enterprise information systems, suggesting, at the same time, a novel idea of an enhanced ISU, in order to overcome those barriers.

The third section, "The ISU concept", includes a thorough presentation of the ISU concept, starting from the conceptual idea of the ISU, explaining why it is a cutting-edge concept, jointly promoted by the EU and the research community, moving on to the design principles that govern ISUs and closing with a bibliographical review of the so far existing ISU implementations.

In the fourth section, "An Ontology-Based ISU", the authors suggest embedding a concrete, already existing and tested ontologies' reconciliation methodology, called MENTOR, in an ISU

implementation. That way, stems a novel and enhanced ISU that will serve as an intermediary in the semantic harmonization of the different enterprise ontologies.

The fifth section, "The Proposed ISU Platform", gives an in-depth presentation of the suggested by the authors ISU implementation, explaining how it functions and how it would provide semantically harmonized and added-value services to the involved enterprises. It concludes by explaining why the authors' proposed solution is not only the most appropriate, but also an innovative one.

The sixth section, "Application to an Agrofood Business Scenario", includes a scenario of applying the suggested ISU within the everyday and real-life enterprise transactions, grounding and fostering that way, the value of the suggested enhanced ISU.

The seventh section, "Conclusions, Reusable Components and Future Challenges", includes the conclusions of the present research work, highlights the reusable scientific components and acknowledges the future challenges ahead.

# CURRENT BUSINESS ENVIRONMENT

## Introduction

Nowadays, Information and Communication Technologies (ICT) offer to contemporary enterprises a great amount of communication means and channels that enable them to expand their power for communication, collaboration and knowledge sharing and, by extension, their general strategic capabilities and competitiveness. Besides, *fostering collaboration* is a key challenge for today's managers. Connecting enterprises sparks innovation and speeds the development process, thereby helping them maximize their return on research and development activities.

Notably, the current business environment is mainly characterized by the increase of electronic services offered over the Web, a fact that is fueled by the great extension and ubiquitous connectivity of the Internet. Web Services offer a huge amount of business functionalities that may reside anywhere over the Internet. The most important benefit of Web Services is the promotion of Interoperability by enabling different applications to talk to each other and share data and services among them. Besides, web Services typically work outside of private networks, offering developers a *non-proprietary* route to their solutions. Services developed are likely, therefore, to have a longer life-span, offering better Return-On-Investment (ROI) of the developed service. Web Services also let developers use their preferred programming languages. In addition, thanks to the use of standards-based communications methods, Web Services are virtually platform-independent. For example, VB or.NET application can talk to java web services and vice versa. So, Web Services are used to make the application platform and technology independent.

## Current Issues and Problems Faced by Enterprises

However, there are still a lot of barriers that prevent the seamless communication, data transactions and general knowledge exchange among the various enterprise Web Services. These stem from the various different Knowledge Representation schemes and approaches that the various enterprises use. More specifically, enterprises, based on their individual needs, characteristics and context, use different and heterogeneous ways, means and tools in order to organize and represent their internal knowledge and information. Sometimes, knowledge is represented as raw data or is stored using complex structures for representing the necessary relationships among the data.

Therefore, the translation of exchanged data between the different components and information systems of the various enterprises, creates a major non-value-added cost for enterprises, especially the Small-Medium ones (Small-Medium Enterprises - SMEs). This cost is detected in terms of both time and money and stems from the retraining and translation processes that are required to take place between the incompatible software systems, towards the reconciliation of the exchanged knowledge. On top of that cost is also detected in terms of actually losing some information that cannot be translated and mapped between the corresponding communicating information systems.

All these facts, render the processes of representation, manipulation and exchange of knowledge and data, very important issues and constraining factors for the further collaboration, expansion and evolution of enterprises. The most significant outcome, is that these issues and constraints impede the achievement of Enterprise Interoperability and prevent enterprises, especially SMEs, from entering new markets and exploiting new challenges and opportunities.

## Towards a Problem Solution Approach

After recognizing the problem space and the actual dimensions of the problem described, the authors moved on to the process of seeking an approach for dealing with the aforementioned barriers of interoperability. Therefore, given that the authors already have significant research activity in the ontologies domain, they soon came up with the use of ontologies for approaching a possible problem solution space.

Ontologies are one of the most common means of formally representing knowledge as a set of concepts within a domain, along with the relationships between pairs of concepts. Thus, they can be used to model a domain, supporting reasoning about entities. Notably, ontologies, in the form of logical domain theories and their according knowledge bases, offer the richest representations of machine-interpretable semantics for systems and databases in the loosely coupled world, thus ensuring greater semantic interoperability and integration (Obrst, 2003).

From this perception, the interoperability problem, which the authors acknowledge within the exchange of knowledge via Web Services among enterprises, is related to the existence of different and heterogeneous *ontologies* that are used by enterprises to model even the same segment of reality. Therefore, we soon reached to the conclusion that the major challenge that we have to deal with, is bridging the gap among the different enterprise ontologies.

In addition to ontologies and based again on the authors' significant research activity in the domain of Enterprise Interoperability, we also focused on the concept of the Interoperability Service Utility, as both a challenge and a means for achieving Enterprise Interoperability. As it is going to be explained in the next section, the ISU concept is rather a "hot topic" in the domain of Enterprise Interoperability, as it is one of the four Grand Challenges recognized by the EU within the "Enterprise Interoperability Research Roadmap", towards the direction of achieving Enterprise Interoperability (Information Society Technologies, 2008).

Based on these two facts, the ISU Grand Challenge on the one hand and the necessary ontologies' reconciliation on the other, in this chapter the authors propose the integration of an ontologies' reconciliation methodology, called *MENTOR*, within an Interoperability Service Utility, in order to finally suggest an intelligent system that serves as a utility software component to promote interoperability among communicating enterprises.

After shortly reviewing the current achievements available in the field of Interoperability Service Utilities, especially those that also deal with ontologies, the authors go beyond and describe the design and implementation specifications of our novel infrastructure, explaining how MENTOR methodology will enable the proposed

ISU to seamlessly provide the necessary set of Web Services which will deliver and sustain interoperability across the various enterprise users. The authors especially compare it to the existing solutions available in order to prove the current absence of such an intelligent system that embraces such an integrated methodology for ontologies' reconciliation. In order to support its usability and functionality, the authors particularly give an operational example of applying the proposed ISU to a set of common transactions that may take place in the everyday transactions of two enterprises in the agro-food domain. Finally, the authors acknowledge various challenges in the domain, which the research community will have to deal with in the future.

The chapter's main aim is to promote the crucial need for interoperability among enterprises, especially the Small-Medium ones, acknowledging that they should ideally interoperate and exchange data smoothly and seamlessly, achieving real-time collaboration, providing and delivering to each other cost-effective and one-stop shop services. That way, by facilitating the establishment of innovative business partnerships, enterprises will have at their disposal a lot of opportunities to new markets, becoming even more innovative, productive, cost-effective and competitive. The benefits from such an evolution will be further reflected in the final products and services, in their overall quality and price, a fact that will further enhance the overall satisfaction of the final recipient, i.e. the consumers and citizens.

## THE ISU CONCEPT

### Introduction

In 2006, the Enterprise Interoperability Cluster of European projects coined the term ISU as the new IT infrastructure able to provide interoperability services to all SMEs, at low cost and under non-rivalry and non-discriminatory principles

(Gusmeroli, 2012). More recently, the European Commission used the term ISU to denote a basic "infrastructure" that supports information exchange between diverse knowledge sources, software applications and Web Services (Information Society Technologies, 2006 and European Commission, 2010).

It is notable that the ISU has been prescribed within a number of research roadmaps adopted by European Commission research project clusters and support actions. The Enterprise Interoperability Research Roadmap (EIRR) Version 5.0, (Information Society Technologies, 2008) developed within the European Commission/ DG INFSO Future Internet Enterprise Systems (FInES) cluster, sets the ISU concept as a *Grand Challenge* in the quest for achieving Enterprise Interoperability. It stands on top of the Challenges of Future Internet Enterprise Systems and Knowledge-Oriented Collaboration and Semantic Interoperability, focusing on the development and application of a federated infrastructure able to deliver the key services needed by the industry, including SME-specific needs and preconditions. Therefore, we acknowledge the crucial need for establishing enterprise interoperability through the ISU. Finally, the ISU is also recognized as a concept that implements various views of interoperability, thus it can be classified in the following Enterprise Interoperability Science Base (EISB) Scientific Areas: Data Interoperability, Software Interoperability, Knowledge Interoperability and Services Interoperability (ENSEMBLE D2.4 "EISB Models and Tools", 2011),

Moving on, the ISU is a basic software infrastructure that comprises "utility services". It is a new generation of e-business services that supports information exchange between knowledge sources, software applications and web-services, especially among Small and Medium Enterprises (SME) and start-up companies, establishing semantic interoperability between the communicating parties. The ISU is independent of, rather than an extension to,

the existing Enterprise Interoperability solutions available on the market (Li, 2011).

The role of an ISU is to transform information from an entity, according to the format and the ontology of the broadcasting entity, into information described in the format and the ontology of the receiving entity. It is assumed that the ISU uses resources, which evolve with the time to realize the transformations of format and ontology. The information exchanged in collaboration between heterogeneous entities requires transformations between the formats and the ontologies associated, where several types of heterogeneousness must be taken into account (Zbib et al., 2012). Therefore, it is around the capability of providing semantic reconciliation in an ISU to support SMEs to establish business partnerships that this research is focused on.

## ISU Design Principles Followed

As interoperability is more and more considered and treated as a utility-like capability that should be invoked "on the fly" (Information Society Technologies, 2008), the proper preliminary system analysis and design becomes of high importance towards the subsequent actual development of systems, that holds interoperability as an intrinsic concept, i.e. as an embedded property. According to Suh (1990), it is possible in principle to recognize general rules for best performing a given design activity. The design of systems though, to assure their interoperability, is a new area and not an experienced one. In fact, despite the well assessed set of knowledge in the IT domain, this task is still not clearly defined at enterprise level, where different types of systems are involved: technological, organizational, physical, etc.

With the scope to provide a structured path to the design of a generic system so as to be interoperable, Dassisti and Chen (2011) propose an interoperability analysis approach, guided by a set of axioms that have derived on the foundation of the general system theory concepts. Their axiomatic approach, grounded on the Axioms of Analysis (AA), Meta-modelling (MMA), and Modelling (MA), further encompassing the Complexity, Decomposition and Specificity sub-axioms, as well as the Systemic (SA) and Interfacing (IA) axioms, the latter further comprising the Interface feature sub-axiom, provides a high level of abstraction and can be thus generically applied for the analysis and design of any system.

Moving on from the design of generic enterprise systems to the design of an Interoperability Service Utility in particular, we should also recognize, follow and comply with the necessary principles and rules that every ISU must comply with, during the processes of its design, development and implementation.

Thus, according to the EIRR, we bear in mind that an ISU should be "by design" an open infrastructure that supports heterogeneity, flexibility, usability, and continuous evolution, enabling enterprise and ecosystem collaboration. In this frame, our ISU is designed to emphasize on services' pervasiveness and decentralization in accordance with the end-to-end design principles of the internet, following the "peer-to-peer" interconnection of communicating systems. The main principle set by the EIRR is not intervening in vital information or collaboration knowledge exchange, but sustaining interoperability through a mediation center that will provide for coordination, negotiation and delegation functions.

Additionally, when setting the specifications for our ISU, we followed the principle of designing a simple infrastructure that should be offered at a low and affordable initial cost, requiring low maintenance and subsequent investment by the enterprises and especially by the SMEs. We acknowledge that it should be easily adopted by enterprises, regardless of their capabilities, leaving their existing infrastructures unchanged internally or suggesting the least possible alterations and adaptations. We worked towards the direction that states that an ISU should be able to serve

all kinds of enterprises, giving access to all of them, regardless of their size, business sector or geographical location. Furthermore, we take into consideration that the ISU should be in position of guaranteeing the quality of its offered services, comply with a service level agreement and follow a set of common rules.

Moreover, we followed the principle which defines that an ISU should be based on the usage of open standards and specifications in support of information exchange and modular software deployment versus hierarchical layering, transparency and scalability. This principle underpins the ISU nature as a system of systems and enables the development of additional, value-added capabilities to be built on top of an ISU.

Finally, as it will be shown below, our ISU prototype is designed to deliver certain services, basic and value-added ones, supporting not only the end-to-end connectivity and interoperability, but also the co-creation of services that enables innovation and value creation. Such services include:

- Facilitating real-time information sharing and collaboration between enterprises (e.g. reasoning, searching, discovery, composition, assembly, and automatic delivery of semantics)
- Enabling the generation of information-based applications that can among others self-compose, self-declare, self-document, self-integrate, self-optimise, self-adapt, and self-heal,
- Supporting knowledge creation, management, and acquisition to enable knowledge sharing between virtual organisations
- Allowing to connect islands of interoperability by federating, orchestrating, or providing common e-business infrastructural capabilities (e.g. digital signature management, certification, user profiling, identity management, and libraries of templates and interface specifications), and

- Supporting the next generation of e-business services (e.g. among others verification of credentials; reputation management; assessment of e-business capabilities; assessment of collaboration capabilities; facilities for data sourcing, integrity, security and storage; contracting; registration and labelling; and payment facilities).

## State of the Art in ISU Research

Since a decade, although some efforts have been made to develop enterprise interoperability, especially in Europe (ATHENA 2007, INTEROP 2007) where several research projects have been launched under FP5/FP6, there was still not an overall satisfactory solution on interoperability. Research in this area was, until recently, quite fragmented. Most of researches and developments were focused on the technology.

Recently, the ISU concept has evolved from the initial stage of a very ambitious and useful idea to the stage of development and implementation. It is a field of major concern and this fact is justified by several European research projects which provide ISU-like architectures that allow companies to use the ISU as an independently offered intelligent infrastructure to support and help planning, setting-up, and running complex knowledge-based collaboration activities (Popplewell et al., 2008) to solve interoperability problems.

In order to provide an overview of the state of the art in the newly emerged and quite promising field of interoperability service utilities, in this section, the authors present in brief specific implementations of the ISU concept, developed within the context of relevant and recently completed research projects, namely, the COIN (Enterprise COllaboration & Interoperability – ICT-2007: 216256), COMMIUS (Community-based Interoperability Utility for SMEs – ICT-2007: 213876), and iSURF (An Interoperability Service Utility for Collaborative Supply Chain Planning across

Multiple Domains Supported by RFID Devices – ICT-2007: 213031) research projects.

The COIN integrated system is a complex cross-enterprise environment, encompassing several different components, platforms and services and constitutes an ISU implementation that targets the settlement of enterprise interoperability and collaboration (EI/EC) issues, encountered by enterprises within the frame of interconnected or collaborative tasks and processes (Sitek et al., 2011). The COIN ISU is in particular a federation of platforms, services and web interfaces which allow EI/EC services to be searched, discovered, ranked, orchestrated and executed by cross-organizational business processes, and can be schematically represented as a double cloud (COIN butterfly), made up of two distinct clouds, one for service provision (upper cloud - COIN Upper Federation) and the other for service consumption (lower cloud - COIN Collaboration Federation); the two clouds tied together through the COIN Front End integration software. The COIN ISU consists of three main components, as follows:

- The Generic Service Platform (GSP) implemented as an open-source SESA (Semantically Enabled Service Architecture) instantiation, based on the WSMX environment (Web Service Modeling eXecution environment) and specialized in the EI/EC domain, while also empowered with advanced capabilities for trust & security, distribution & scalability, reasoning & negotiation.
- A constellation of COIN EI/EC Services which are able to implement state-of-the-art and innovative technologies to support information, knowledge and business interoperability as well as human collaboration in a collaborative business context of product development, production planning and project management.
- The COIN Collaboration Platform (CP) which is a generic open source web por-

tal encompassing social networking inter-action, knowledge assets accession and business process management in a unique integrated multi-enterprise collaboration environment customized for more or less hierarchical organizational networks.

The COMMIUS Service Utility, a reference implementation of the ISU concept, developed by the COMMIUS project, aspires to support SMEs with a zero, or very low-cost entry into interoperability, by offering an interoperability solution that allows the reuse of existing and familiar applications for electronic communication, such as e-mail and the web. This solution is downloaded with the SME's consent using automated self-installation routines, and then hooks into the formers' e-mail infrastructure proceeding to the establishment of interoperability agreements with the peers of the SME at the levels of system, semantics and processes. From an architectural point of view, the COMMIUS Service Utility comprises an email gateway plugin, responsible for intercepting and post-processing emails, the system's hosting environment, encompassing a series of independent software components that provide functionalities for achieving system, semantic and process interoperability as well as facilities and modules for supporting data management, security and privacy, and module management, and lastly user tools, relying on existing email and web browser infrastructure and aiding the user to perform business tasks and configure the COMMIUS platform.

Finally, the iSURF ISU, a highly dynamic and flexible building block of the iSURF open collaborative supply chain planning environment, developed on the basis of the CPFR (Collaborative Planning, Forecasting, and Replenishment) guidelines (European CPFR Insights, 2002), aims at serving as a semantic infrastructure enabling the establishment of interoperability among enterprise applications across multiple domains, in order to achieve the required planning data exchange for deploying a CPFR process within a supply chain consortium (Dogac et al., 2009). The system architecture consists in particular of the following building blocks, interconnected with each other via an Enterprise Service Bus (ESB):

- The iSURF Service Oriented Collaborative Supply Chain Planning Environment, a graphical tool enabling SMEs to create visual descriptions of their collaborative planning processes and customize them according to their needs.

- The iSURF ISU, accountable as mentioned above, for using semantic information and transforming documents from one standard to another, and provided as a service unit in the ESB, enabling thus parties to communicate with each other within the scope of a supply chain planning process, even when using different planning document standards.

- A Smart Product Infrastructure (SPI), an open source software component, compliant with the EPCglobal standards (EPCglobal Architecture Framework, 2007), allowing the tracking of items across the supply chain historically in a near real-time fashion by using RFID technology, and delivering RFID data to iSURF business applications and services to support their seamless interoperation.

- A Global Data Synchronization Service Utility (GDSSU) that constitutes a mechanism for achieving synchronization and harmonization of the master data used in supply chain transactions, allowing trading partners to share accurate information reliably and efficiently.

- A Transitory Collaboration Service Utility (TCSU), ensuring the unhampered collaboration and decision making among all interested partners in case of unexpected events or other problems within the supply chain.

- A series of legacy adapters, developed by wrapping the needed functionality of the legacy applications as web services, and facilitating thus the transmission of messages and data between the former and the iSURF components via the ESB.

Even though, the information presented above on the selected ISU-related research projects is quite concise and concerns mainly the ISU high level objectives and specific implementations, it is in parallel quite sufficient so as to render clear that the ISU concept is open to several interpretations and may be instantiated through various, even diverse, implementations of different purpose and different scale, depending on the particular context and needs it is required to cover. Beside the settlement of interoperability issues, encountered within the context of enterprise collaboration, the common denominator of the existing ISU implementations seems to be confined in the adoption of some of the ISU design principles, set at policy level, notably scalability, guaranteed quality of service, open standards – at least where applicable, etc. The scope of application as well as the context and types of services to be offered by the ISU are dependent of the particular implementation. In any case, for more information on the ISU implementations presented, the reader is prompted to referring to the relevant research project deliverables.

## AN ONTOLOGY-BASED ISU

### An Ontology-Based Interoperability Service Utility

In line with the ISU design principles as they have been presented above and taking into consideration the existing relative implementations and developments in the field, we have defined a set of design specifications for a novel ISU instantiation. One part of the novelty of our instantiation mainly

lies in the particular methodology for ontologies' reconciliation.

Ontologies allow key concepts and terms relevant to a given domain to be identified and defined in a structure able to represent an explicit specification of a conceptualization (Gruber, 1993). Its recognized capacity to represent knowledge, to facilitate reasoning, use and exchange of knowledge between systems, contributes to promote and facilitate interoperability among ICT systems.

Since various companies that operate in the same domain may have different representations of a same knowledge, when they describe it electronically it will most likely lead to different representation models. Thus semantic interoperability problems, regarding concepts involved, may appear when these different systems try to exchange or share information with one another. For that reason, a wide spectrum of approaches for the ontologies reconciliation that represent the same concept has been proposed.

The authors have identified a set of required characteristics based in (Sarraipa et al., 2009), for a reference ontology building in ISU that are: ontology building from scratch; ontology reengineering; cooperative building and merge methods. This was accomplished with the directive of allowing the enterprises enrolled, to keep their own ontologies or semantics unchanged internally at the same time they contribute with concepts and definitions.

In an analysis performed by the authors it was identified that both MENTOR methodology supported by Protégé and NeOn toolkit aggregates all the above-mentioned characteristics. However in a deeply analysis it was identified that only MENTOR supports enterprises to establish a common view on their semantics at the same time as its related mappings tables, between the proprietary knowledge bases and the new created ontology is built. In additional, such mappings records also facilitate further semantic updates that could come from any new member subscription or service update in ISU.

As a result MENTOR was chosen mainly because it has a collaborative mechanism for building reference ontologies, as it addresses the objective of achieving a shared representation of a domain's knowledge. Besides, since such community reference ontology has to represent all the involved enterprises, the more collaborative this process could be, the easier the community will reach a wider representative ontology.

## The Core of the ISU: The MENTOR Methodology

The ISU proposed approach has the support of the MENTOR, a "Methodology for Enterprise Reference Ontology Development", to establish a common lexicon about the knowledge of all the ISU participants. MENTOR proposes the use of a "reference ontology" to work as an intermediary in the communications between the various communicating enterprises. Thus, it supports the knowledge alignment establishment between each participate enterprise and the ISU knowledge base, providing electronic services for enabling knowledge-based collaboration.

MENTOR methodology is composed by two phases and each phase has three steps, as depicted in the Figure 1.

The first Phase is constituted by three steps, and represents the acquisition of knowledge to accomplish the Lexicon Settlement, about a domain. The Terminology Gathering step represents the knowledge gathering from all actors. They submit all their concepts and definitions on the domain. Then in the Glossary Building, through organized discussions, are established a list of reference concepts with definitions. From this step could be identified semantic mismatches that then are recorded in a Mediator Ontology (MO) using a specific tuple specification for mapping representations defined by Agostinho et al. (Agostinho et al., 2011). These semantic mismatches can be used in further semantic mappings establishment, which in Figure 1 is illustrated by the arrow that goes from the Glossary Building block to the Ontologies Mapping block). The last step (the Thesaurus Building) is composed by a cycle where the participants through discussions organised accordingly to the Delphi method (Sarraipa et al. 2010), define a taxonomic structure establishing an "is a" relationship between the glossary concepts.

In the second phase, the Reference Ontology is built and the semantic mappings between participant' knowledge representation means (ontologies, concepts, etc.) and the new built

*Figure 1. The MENTOR methodology (light view)*

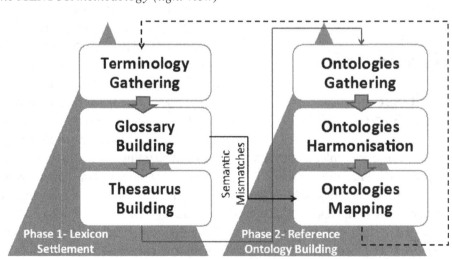

262

ontology are established (Sarraipa et al. 2010). This phase has three steps: Ontologies Gathering, Ontologies Harmonization, and Ontologies mapping. In the Ontologies Gathering step it is gathered the participants' knowledge bases. The Ontologies Harmonization step is comprised by two distinct discussions: the ontology taxonomy definition; and the properties and rules' establishment. This step creates the reference ontology of the involved community. The last step of this phase (Ontology Mapping) establishes the semantic mappings between each participants' knowledge base and the new built (reference) ontology. The mapping tables establishment uses the semantic mismatches identified in the previous steps, as additional information to support the identification of the mappings. MENTOR methodology can be repeated if the semantics is changed at any of its sources, or if any new participant is introduced to the community. Such repetition encloses an entire cycle of the MENTOR methodology. The dashed arrow in Figure 1 represents it.

The ability of proceeding for a next cycle of the entire MENTOR methodology represents its maintenance procedure. Such procedure is represented by the traditional MENTOR phases encircling, which relates to the reference Ontology Learning (OL) phase (Sarraipa et al., 2010) (Figure 2). This encircling phase enables the dynamic learning mechanism for ontologies, which enables the auto-adaptability of the related information systems semantics.

Silva et al., 2011 presented the oLEARCH component that relates to the concept "Ontologies LEArn by seaRCHing", which implements the referred dynamic learning mechanism for ontologies (Silva et al., 2011). It is related to ontologies ability to change or adapt their knowledge (to learn) through their users' patterns of searching/reasoning.

oLEARCH component is a type of a searching engine that learns from users patterns to improve its related knowledge base, which is supported by an algorithm based in an instance-based learning

approach applied to user interaction patterns. In instance-based learning, training examples are stored verbatim, and a distance function is used to determine which member of the training set is closest to an unknown test instance (Witten and Frank, 2005). The mentioned distance function represents the semantic distance, which is the inverse of the semantic relatedness between the users introduced concepts and the products or services classified in the reference ontology. Thus, inside the proposed ISU, oLEARCH provides to the users a set of products or services that are close to their introduced concepts in terms of semantic relatedness. Consequently, users are able to select the most appropriated product or service from a set of possible choices. The users' selections are used, as a feedback, to increase the semantic relatedness weight of the selected products or services associated concepts. In additional, this component integrates the main role of what a folksonomy is, in the sense that it allows the users to describe the ISU available services with a set of keywords of their own choice, in a kind of social context. Thus, at the end each service could has a set of related concepts that integrates a folksonomy of services, which represent services labeling resulted from the users searching interactions.

*Figure 2. The MENTOR encircling phase (Sarraipa et al. 2010)*

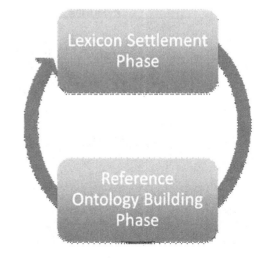

## THE PROPOSED ISU PLATFORM

### Conceptual View

The particular ISU instantiation that we propose in the present chapter can also be described as an intelligent "system of systems" because it is a software system layered upon already existing systems, applications and knowledge sources from various different enterprises, establishing them interoperable. This software system is designed to support and promote the direct exchange of computer meaningful information and knowledge between the end-users by adopting the principle of end-to-end interconnection (peer to peer approach). The proposed ISU aspires not to implement dedicated services but to deliver as services already existing IT functionalities that may reside anywhere and be invoked anytime, according to the business needs of the end users, i.e. the enterprises in our case (Figure 3).

The proposed ISU will provide the so-called "ISU services". In order to define what an "ISU-service" is, we have to define the terms that it consists of, i.e. service and ISU. First, a service is a provider/client interaction that captures and creates value (IBM). Second, the ISU is an infrastructure that composes and orchestrates services coming from diverse sources and stakeholders, providing complete, interoperable end-to-end business services to enterprises (Charalabidis, 2007). Therefore in the context of our envisaged

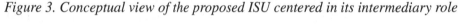

*Figure 3. Conceptual view of the proposed ISU centered in its intermediary role*

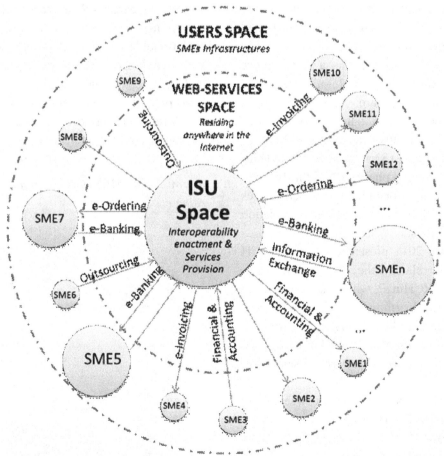

ISU implementation, an "ISU service" is a technical, commoditized functionality, delivered as a service and provided by the ISU, in order to enable the semantic interoperability in knowledge exchange and further enhance collaboration between enterprises.

The proposed ISU platform is to be implemented as a distributed, n-tier software application, bearing two main building blocks: the *Interoperability Engine*, serving as the core building block for managing all the common processes and transactions and the *Service Provision Components*, containing all the necessary service-related software artefacts (Figure 4).

The Interoperability Engine is composed by six blocks, each one accordingly to the process of the submission, classification, integration and provision of the various "ISU-services". Thus, first there is the *Reputation Assessment Engine*, responsible for assessing the reputation of the new ISU-service providers and users, especially in the P2P mode of operation. Then, there is the *Knowl-*

*edge Taxonomy Management* block which manages the process of the classification and integration of the various ISU services. It also holds the overall expandable ontology that carries all the knowledge that is related to the various services offered by the ISU. Following on, there are the *Security and Authentication Mechanisms*, commonly used by all services to provide security enhancement by encrypting the knowledge exchanged and managing the various logging methods and user information (e.g. credentials, cookies). Also, there are the *Contracting and Quality of Service (QoS) Management components*, gathering and presenting information on the quality of each offered service and then, the *Messaging & Transaction Engine*, responsible for managing the store-and-forward transactions passing through the ISU server. Finally, there is the *Process and Document Repository* which holds all the standard processes and business documents in BPEL and XML formats, respectively.

*Figure 4. The ISU platform architecture*

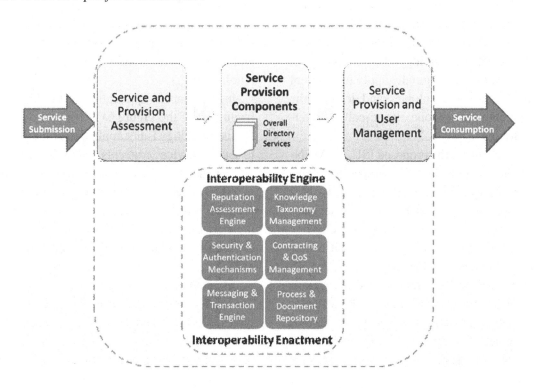

The other building block of the ISU, i.e. the Service Provision Components, mainly includes the Overall *Directory* of the offered ISU-services, which is actually an electronic catalogue where the various interested enterprises can search and easily retrieve the services that they need to use. Also, it includes the *Service and Provider Assessment interface*, used for the initial assessment of the submitted services and finally, the *Service Provision and User Management interface*, used for the continuous assessment of the provided services.

## Reference Ontology Building to Semantically Harmonize the Exchanged Knowledge

MENTOR methodology is proposed in ISU as a semantic interoperability facilitator. Its main goal is to align the various semantic representations of the ISU participants' enterprises within the process of knowledge exchange among them and further to promote its collaboration and interoperability via the services provision of the proposed ISU.

The Knowledge Taxonomy Management block (Figure 4) represents the process of the development of the overall expandable ontology of the ISU, which is based on the principles of the MENTOR methodology. These principles, as presented before, originally apply to different existing enterprise ontologies and lead to the development of a new one, the so-called "reference ontology".

However, within the proposed ISU, the MENTOR methodology is adapted to the special features of the exchanged knowledge and the involved communicating parts related to web services representation. Thus, when an enterprise or any other service provider wishes to submit a new service within the ISU, they have to provide a set of concepts, as well as their related definitions that describe and are relevant to each particular service and its domain. In this way, the various candidate services can be defined or classified and further on, identified in the ontology. This process of providing concepts accomplishes the "Terminology Gathering" step of the MENTOR methodology. After the submission of various enterprises services, it is obtained a substantial set of concepts and definition that characterize them. Afterwards, they are used to obtain a list of reference concepts and definitions, which represents the "Glossary" of the services introduced. Then all these concepts and definitions are organised in a "is a" classification kind tree resulting in the establishment of the "Thesaurus" that becomes the lexicon of such services.

The classical MENTOR methodology, as it was originally conceived and presented by its authors, applies to ontologies, ("$O_a$" in left part of Figure 5) and leads to the development of a reference ontology ("$O_R$" in left part of Figure 5). It leaves the initial ontologies ($O_1$; $O_2$ ... $O_m$ – in Figure 5) unchanged due to various mappings ("$M_{a,R}$") established between these ontologies and the reference one ($O_{R1}$), to be used in their communications. After having a reference ontology accomplished the process allows new enterprise ontologies continuously be added to the knowledge established. The left part of Figure 5 illustrates that through a set of other proprietary ontologies ($O_3$ ... $O_n$) that are added to the community and which result in a second version of the reference ontology ($O_{R2}$).

In the adapted application of the MENTOR (right part of the Figure 5) to the proposed ISU, the methodology is not applied to ontologies, but to sets of services concepts and their definitions, leading also to the creation of a reference ontology ($O_R$). The main difference between both approaches is related to the input sources: in the first there are ontologies; in the second there are concepts able to categorise the ISU introduced services.

In additional, the right part of the Figure 5 also illustrates the oLEARCH component, which is represented here as an extra source of concepts ($C_{OL}$). These concepts come from the users introduced concepts in the ISU services

*Figure 5. Adaptation of the MENTOR methodology*

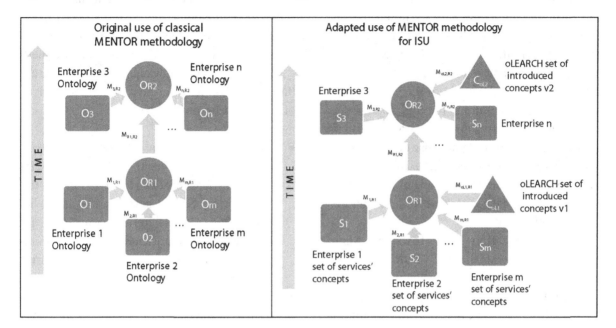

searching functionality. Always this component figure out any relation between the introduced concepts and the reference ones, they receive a link between each other. In such process it is built a network of connections, which is able to receive a statistics value to represent the frequency of its use. Such statistics helps MENTOR to readjust the importance of the concepts, thus in further MENTOR cycles, due to its higher importance or recognition, an high frequency concept could become, for instance, a reference concept in change to another not so often used. This represents the OL capability, which by inheritance contributes for the intelligence increase of the proposed ISU and also contributes for a new reference ontology generation.

If enterprises and/or service providers would like to submit new services to an already populated ISU, it is performed a semantic harmonization of all the involved knowledge. If conceptually equivalent concepts are already present in the ISU reference ontology, it is established semantic mappings between the knowledge of these newly submitted sets of services terms and the knowledge

of the existent reference ontology version. If not, such new services terms are introduced as in a regular merging process.

Ontology mapping is the process that relates the vocabulary of two ontologies that share the same domain of discourse (Goncalves et al., 2007). In the present case, the mapping process relates concepts using "conceptual" links between the services suppliers and the ISU reference ontology, relating this different knowledge views. Thus, a common view ontology is built but allowing different conceptualisations between services suppliers and the ISU. This allows an advanced reasoning over the ontology mainly because it accepts not only the reference ontology concepts but also the others originally introduced by services suppliers, which were recorded through the mentioned mappings establishment on the MO.

Authors have developed specific services to interact with the MO, facilitating ISU to have intelligent systems able to understand each participant's representation view, and allowing them to keep their data and schema of import or export processes.

The right part of Figure 5 shows how each new version of the Ontology is built and how it evolves by embedding new knowledge when new services are being submitted. This new knowledge feed, leads to a sustainable evolutional learning of the ISU knowledge accordingly to the OL concept. In this case, OL feature, through appropriate analysis and machine learning algorithms also in association to statistics, makes use of the patterns obtained from the users interactions related to their search of the services in ISU using oLEARCH, to readjust the mappings established, updating the concepts relevance.

Therefore, the Knowledge Taxonomy Management block, with the MENTOR methodology embedded, establishes semantic bridges between the different representations and forms of the exchanged knowledge, providing ontology interoperability operations. Thus, this knowledge management block particularly contributes to increase the computational intelligence of the proposed system, i.e. the ISU.

## Business Events Based Operation

An enterprise is a living and dynamic organization whose lifetime includes a set of various Business Events and Business Situations that may occur internally or within its close external environment. For this reason, the operation of our ISU approach is based on these Business Events.

In order to define the structure the operation of the proposed ISU and the according ISU services that it will provide, there should be a precise analysis of what the Business Events and Situations exactly are and what kind of Events and Situations that concern an enterprise might possibly take place. For example, during the initial setup and operation (business situation) of an enterprise, various procedures (business events) can take place, invoking internally or externally real-life situations, pertaining to the company operation according to its present status.

Therefore, through precise analysis of these events and situations, the business needs of an SME are gathered, analysed and the needed services from an ISU can be systematically defined.

The following core business events constitute the source of the needs in interoperable e-Services of a typical European SME.

- Company Creation (Figure 6), where typically Government-to-Business (G2B) services are needed for registering the enterprise, getting permits relevant to its operation, establishing the company legal address and representation, establishing relations with Banking and Social Security Institutions.
- The initial set-up (Figure 6) of the supply chain of the enterprise (suppliers, distribution network, subcontractors, B2B customers), where knowledge-related services are typically needed.
- The making of the First Purchase (Figure 6) or sale, where electronic ordering, invoicing and payment services are needed.
- Making a VAT or INTRASTAT declaration (Figure 6), where electronic reporting services are needed, in interconnection with the company financial management or ERP system.

In a similar situation, as depicted in the Figure 6, the same or another SME or organisation may also be operating as service provider to the ISU system: similar business events are now to be dealt with as service provision sources, in a way that ensures easy deployment and standardised interconnection. As an example:

- An SME develops a New Service (Figure 6) to be provided in an electronic form (e.g. electronic assessment of sector-specific financial statements, a service usually provided by consulting firms or specialised

*Figure 6. The ISU business events based operation*

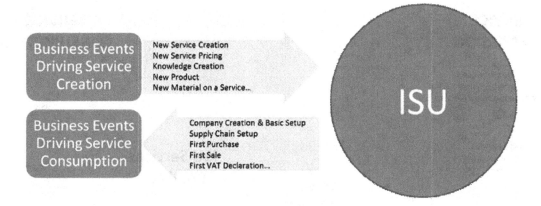

accountants) and deploys that through the ISU platform.

- A company creates new knowledge items (Figure 6) or material relating to an offered service and automatically deploys that through the ISU platform, providing pricing and contractual information.
- Other similar situations may be the new service pricing, the new product, etc. (Figure 6).

Such services are to be provided by the ISU platform, in such a way that automated discovery, service negotiation, orchestration and final electronic provision are dealt with seamless integration between the company and collaborating enterprises or organisations. Thus, enterprises, especially SMEs may exploit the proposed ISU in order to facilitate their everyday life, interactions and communication activities with other enterprises, precisely corresponding and adapted to their whole lifecycle events and situations.

## ISU Services Provision

Based on a service oriented architecture and mode of operation, the proposed ISU offers the possibility of composing, orchestrating and providing a wide set of web-services dedicated to serve and facilitate the everyday transactions

of the contemporary enterprises, especially the SMEs. Without the use of connectors or legacy software components, the proposed ISU platform provides well-defined Web Service Interfaces and the necessary transactional engine support for fulfilling its functionality.

The four types of services that are to be deployed our ISU-benchmark are shown in Figure 7.

First, there are the Core Business Services (Figure 7), which cover the connectivity of the ISU services themselves, following the Service Oriented Architecture (SOA) concept. Technical Interoperability is highly important for this type of Services as it includes the establishment of connectivity among various common Enterprise Application functionality services, i.e. services that typically are deployed by systems like Enterprise Resource Planning (ERP), Supply Chain Management (SCM), Customer Relation Management (CRM), etc. in the form of Software-as-a-Service (SaaS).

Then, there are the Extended Services (Figure 7) which serve, in an interoperable way, the everyday Application-to-Application business needs of an enterprise, such as electronic invoicing, electronic ordering and fulfilment, VAT reporting, Taxation reporting, electronic payments, etc. These services include the exchange of real information and data and for that reason they use standard XML business documents which contain

*Figure 7. The ISU services overview*

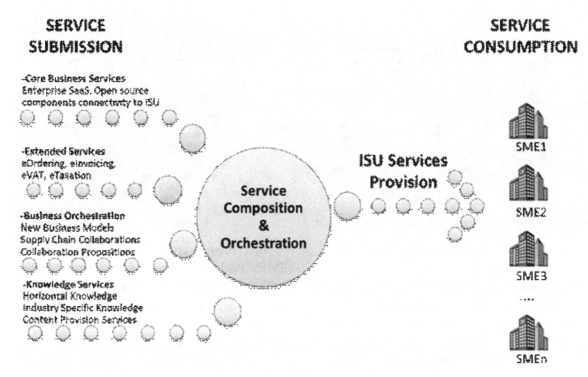

## ISU Services Lifecycle

the necessary data to be exchanged. Therefore, the challenge in the provision of these services is the establishment of semantic Interoperability among the different data structures and underlying ontologies.

Furthermore, there are the Complex Business Orchestration Services (Figure 7), which serve industry-specific needs of finding and handling collaboration propositions, organizing the supply chain or investing in new business models of operation, thus providing Business Interoperability solutions. Finally, the proposed ISU deploys Knowledge-related services (Figure 7), needed for complementing the everyday tasks of the typical enterprise, usually pertaining to organized content provision on everyday tasks (such as financial reporting, accounting, management) or sector-specific operations (e.g. production methods, specialized personnel training, product standardization).

Concerning the service life-cycle, i.e. the deployment and integration of an ISU-service in the proposed ISU, there are three loosely-coupled phases for service composition, orchestration and provision:

- The service submission phase, which includes the submission of any new candidate service to the ISU platform. Then, each new service is categorized and pre-screened for its service quality characteristics.
- The orchestration phase includes complex service composition, directory availability and matching to user profiles, based on ISU users' registry (personalized Universal Description Discovery and Integration (UDDI) mechanisms).

- The provision phase can operate both under a server-based and a Peer-to-Peer model, catering for service discovery by the potential enterprise user, negotiation and charging mechanisms.

## Comparative Analysis and the Added Value of our approach

Following the presentation of the state of the art in ISU research, as well as of the proposed, semantically enhanced Interoperability Service Utility, bringing forth the respective ISU characteristics, architecture and services, and of course the MENTOR ontology component, and thereby justifying its usability, it is now possible to evince the suggested ISU added value, along with the strengths and advantages offered by the latter, as opposed to the ISU implementations, already available. In fact, the added value and strengths of the proposed ISU may be located in three axes, concerned with the types of ISU services offered, the way in which the management of the ISU is handled and the ISU applicability.

Leveraging the classification of ISU services, adopted by our proposed ISU in the categories of core business, extended, complex business orchestration and knowledge-related services, it becomes evident that only COIN covers all types of services, whereas COMMIUS offers functionality that only corresponds to basic connectivity services and application–to–application interoperability, subject still to constraints, since cross-enterprise communication and therefore data exchange is in its context mandatorily conducted via e-mail and the web. In fact, the provision of ISU services via email, touted by the COMMIUS project as an ideal solution for achieving inter-enterprise interoperability at zero cost, is indeed a real advantage, inhibiting though the provision of more complex and collaborative services. iSURF services on the other hand, seem to touch upon all of the above-mentioned types, yet are exclusively restricted to supply chain–related activities, which

only constitute one aspect of the usually versatile operation of enterprises, whereas the proposed ISU covers explicitly the whole life-cycle of the enterprise, from its initial set up and day-to-day operation, encompassing all every-day transactions, such as ordering, invoicing, selling etc., development and value adding activities, such as the development of new products and services etc. to its final closure.

Additionally and contrary to the COIN and iSURF implementations under consideration, the proposed interoperability service utility is ontology-supported, meaning that it embraces a functionally proven methodology for ontologies reconciliation, in order to establish semantic interoperability within the process of knowledge exchange among communicating enterprises, as well as to promote enterprise collaboration within the context of ISU service provision. The ontology reconciliation process leaves the knowledge of the various communicating enterprises unchanged internally, allowing thus the former to avoid internal changes that are both time and money consuming. Moreover, it covers the entire ISU services lifecycle, encompassing all submission, orchestration and provision phases, as indicated by the COIN project as well, but unlike the former it supports scalability and lifelong adaptability of the ISU services, as a result of the maintenance procedure foreseen in the MENTOR methodology. At this point, it should be clarified that the use of ontologies in COMMIUS is only restricted to holding information about document types (Laclavik, 2007) and enabling ways of processing them, as well as that the absence of a complete ISU services lifecycle management perspective within the context of the COMMIUS and iSURF ISUs is justified due to the limited scope of their functionality and the services offered.

Concerning the costs that may be necessary for SMEs to install and setup such an ISU infrastructure, it has to be highlighted that, as it has been shown, the ISU is generally a simple infrastructure with no significant expenses, especially when comparing it to the great return on investment (ROI) during the actual operation of the ISU, when SMEs will register and use it one after another. On the other hand, the cost for an SME to register, enter and consume the ISU-services is also of no significance, comparing it to the fact that SMEs will remain unchanged internally and will avoid all the time, money and data loss that they now have from the current communication and knowledge exchange conditions.

Finally, the most important hallmark of the proposed ISU, concerns its scope of applicability, which, as it has already been explained, covers the whole lifecycle of the enterprise and is not restricted to specific business processes, while it further does not require any modifications to the enterprises' internal and legacy systems. As far as the rest of the implementations studied are concerned, the former constraint is only covered by the COIN ISU, whereas the latter is only met by the COMMIUS ISU, which explicitly claims to offer a zero or very low-cost entry into interoperability.

The aspects in which the proposed ISU resembles, and more importantly, differs from the existing ISU instantiations are cumulatively exposed in Table 1.

## Application to an Agro-Food Business Scenario

The proposed ISU has been applied to a business case scenario for validating its applicability and addressing possible limitations and/or any further appropriate extensions of the intelligent system proposed. The scenario involves e-transactions within the agriculture industry and especially between farmers, agro-food intermediaries and retailers while performing their procurement activities.

The problem within these e-transactions lies first with the capability of searching the intended products, and secondly with the document handling and data checking, resulting in high time consuming tasks, due to the possible errors pro-

*Table 1. ISU implementations' comparison*

| | Types of ISU Services Offered | | | | ISU Management | | ISU Applicability | |
|---|---|---|---|---|---|---|---|---|
| | Core Business Services (e.g. system and application connectivity services) | Extended Services – Document Exchange Services (e.g. e-invoicing, e-ordering and fulfillment, taxation reporting, e-payments) | Complex Business Orchestration Services | Knowledge-related Services | Ontology – supported (i.e. enabling ontology reconciliation) | Supporting scalability and lifelong adaptability of the ISU | Covering the entire enterprise lifecycle/Restricted to specific business processes | Requiring modifications to the enterprises' internal/legacy systems/applications systems/applications |
| COIN ISU | √ | √ | √ | √ | - | - | √/- | √ |
| COMMIUS ISU | √ | √* | - | - | √ | - | -/√ | - |
| iSURF ISU | √ | √* | √* | √* | - | - | -/√ | √ |
| The proposed ISU specification | √ | √ | √ | √ | √ | √ | √/- | - |

*Yes, but only partially

duced by the transmitting media, mainly fax and phone. Nowadays, the seller or supplier staffs have processed data checking manually. On the other hand, end-customers have been asking for special demands, like for organic certified products, which increase complexity to the current searching processes. This provokes an increment in trust, time and data to be transferred between the involved actors. Consequently, the possibility of producing errors in communications and the number of not accomplished orders has increased.

The solution could be achieved by using the proposed ISU which, through the interoperable services that it provides, has the ability to automatically manage the various existing commercial documents, (quotations, orders, certifications, invoices), but also generate and deploy new ones, for non-existent products that could at any moment, be produced and consequently need to be introduced by its business actors.

The first case (ISU-service creation) of the proposed e-Procurement deals scenario is initialized by the farmer and refers to the introduction of a new service (Figure 8) within the ISU. Within this first case of the scenario, suppose that there is the "Farmer A" who wants to submit a new service within the ISU. More specifically, he/she wants to sell massively the various agro products that he/she produces to intermediaries or retailers. Suppose that this service is called "Sell Agro-food". In this case, the process of introducing the new service involves, first of all, the provision of all the concepts, terms and their according definitions of the farmer's products to the ISU: apples, oranges, tomatoes, peppers, and other related products, as well as all their according definitions or descriptions are collected and provided to the ISU. Then, MENTOR collects all these terms and definitions, creates the lexicon and the thesaurus as they have been described in the previous sections and classifies the service "Sell Agro-food" by the "Farmer A" in the electronic catalogue of the ISU's provided electronic services. The same can happen with many other farmers or even agro-food intermedi-

aries that wish to sell their products and wish to submit similar type of selling agro-food services within the ISU. That way, the ISU's electronic catalogue will contain similar services of selling agro-food from various farmers or agro-food intermediaries. In other words, the ISU provides to these actors the "Sell Agro-food" Service. In additional, ISU also supports the aggregation of suppliers to the agro-food intermediaries. Figure 8 illustrates that in the first set of interactions between the agro-food intermediaries and the ISU system. Intermediaries use ISU Overall Directory Services and oLEARCH to find the appropriate farmers for their intended products. With such approach, agro-food intermediaries buy agro products massively from the farmers to then sell them to the retailers.

The second case of the scenario (ISU-service consumption), refers mainly to the Agro-food Retailer, i.e. a shop that sells fruits and vegetables to various end-customers (e.g. households) in a smaller scale than the farmer or the agro-food intermediary. The problem is that in the traditional way, the Agro-food Retailer communicates directly with the various intermediaries and places orders with all specifications needed, stating also other preferences concerning the available payment methods, shipment, etc. But as expected, this procedure involves many communication and general interoperability barriers because of the different knowledge representation means of the communicating parts.

Within the proposed scenario though, suppose that the Retailer decides that he/she needs new products for his/her store. That means that the Retailer wants to "Buy Agro-food" and therefore he/she will make use of the ISU's electronic catalogue of "Agro-Food Vendors", in order to find all the Agro-food Intermediaries that "Sell Agro-food". In other words, the ISU allows the Retailer to consume the "Sell Agro-food" Service. Thus, it provides the Retailer with the listed Manufacturers that "Sell Agro-food". The Retailer navigates to the list (Figure 8) of the Agro-food Intermediaries,

*Figure 8. Use case diagram of the proposed scenario*

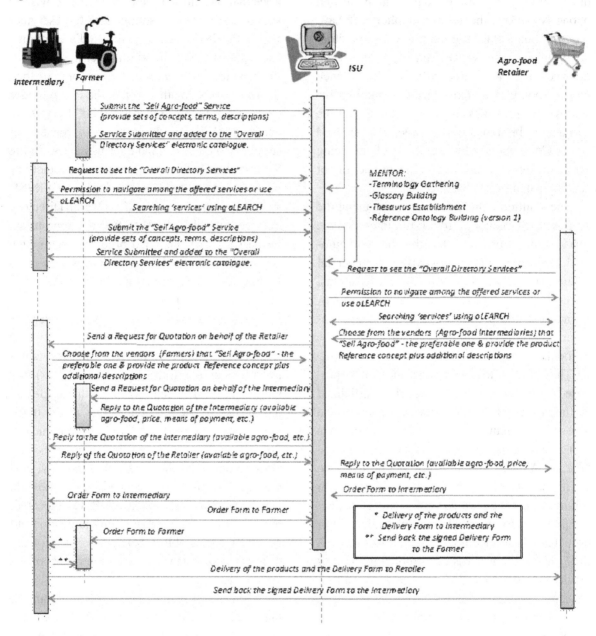

through the oLEARCH component, watching the products that they sell and chooses the preferable one. oLEARCH could make the semantic establishment between the concepts that the retailer use and show the correct product even that could use other nomenclature by the ISU. Since the reference ontology has the reference concepts descriptions, these could be also provided by the system to the

retailer to help them if needed to understand the various semantics used.

Then, the Retailer declares to the ISU the preferable Agro-food Intermediary to buy products, along with the reference name or concept that characterizes the product on the ISU catalogue, accomplished by requested delivery date and other additional descriptions that the buyer would like to transmit to the seller about it. Subsequently, the ISU sends a Request for Quotation to the chosen Agro-food Intermediary, with all the information provided by the Retailer. The MENTOR will translate this request for Quotation, from the ISU Reference's "semantics", into the Intermediary "semantics", if not equal. This process is repeated from the Intermediary to the farmer. Since the agro-food intermediaries buy products from farmers in big quantities it could happen that the Intermediary has the requested product in stock. Thus in that case there is no need to make any request to the farmers in relation to this specific retailer requests.

Therefore, the query from the Retailer is sent to the Intermediary and then it could generate the regular process to choose one vendor (Farmer) that "Sell Agro-food" appropriated to this request. This is then accomplished also by sending a "Request for Quotation" from the Intermediary to the Farmer with the referred product.

The Farmer answers, providing to the ISU the corresponding Quotation. This Quotation includes information about the price the requested delivery date and its own (possible) delivery date of the product that the Intermediary has asked, as well as any other possible characteristics of the requested product. This Quotation is then translated by ISU through the MENTOR reference ontology into the Intermediary's "semantic" and next sent to the Intermediary. This process is afterwards repeated between the Intermediary and the Retailer.

If the Intermediary and then the Retailer agree on the price, the (possible) delivery date and any other possible characteristics of the product, the Retailer sends to the ISU the corresponding "Order" by referencing the previous Quotation. The ISU forwards it to the appropriate Intermediary, which in turn sends an "Order" to the Farmer, using the same approach and system.

The Farmer responds to this Order by sending the "Order Confirmation", which specifies a note about the delivery date and the total amount of the Order representing a final ok.

When the Agro-food product is prepared, it is then delivered to the Intermediary jointly with the Delivery Invoice. In turn the Intermediary checks if there are other requests to the same customer (retailer), and if there are, he makes a package of everything and delivers it to the retailer with the corresponding invoice to the Retailer.

This scenario and the relevant figure validate the proposed ISU as an intelligent system, because, lying upon the existing systems of the communicating parties and leaving their internal semantics unchanged, it successfully manages all the processes of the electronic transactions that take place within the present scenario, facilitating and promoting the Interoperability between the involved systems, overcoming barriers that exist in the traditional version of the proposed scenario. The great enabler for this is the MENTOR methodology that is encapsulated within the ISU and makes the necessary semantic translations and alignments between the different knowledge representation means. The ISU is the mediator system between the enterprises but MENTOR is the core enabler for the seamless communication.

## CONCLUSION, REUSABLE COMPONENTS, AND FUTURE CHALLENGES

The proposed ISU is an indicative example and an initial approach of what an ISU should ideally be. Its conception is unique because it goes beyond other similar existing implementations, in terms of implementing broader features that cover the whole lifecycle of an enterprise, from its establishment and initial set-up, to its actual operation and interaction with other enterprises, until its eventual disintegration and closing. Also, the suggested enhanced ISU offers service-oriented functionalities, regardless of the underlying technologies, ontologies and other local and internal structures, leaving enterprises unchanged internally, leaving all the work to be done by the ISU. Finally, it embraces a rigorous, already well-proven and widely tested methodology for ontologies' reconciliation, i.e. MENTOR, that uniquely includes in only one methodology all major features and functionalities that other similar methodologies may have, but neither of them all-in-one.

The main practical contribution and impact of the present work is the promotion and establishment of semantic interoperability among SMEs. SMEs, which strive to be competitive and innovative, seek more and more to establish new collaborations and virtual organizations with other SMEs, in order to survive and further expand their activities, by entering new markets and chasing new opportunities. SMEs would definitely benefit from such collaborations and for that reason the demand for entering and registering in such an ISU is expected to be extremely high.

Besides, the suggested ISU is a proposition of low cost, either an SME wishes to install the ISU and be the actual mediator for other SMEs or an SME just wishes to register, enter and consume the ISU-services as an external partner. The cost for setting-up such a software infrastructure, compared to the return on investment (ROI) from the attraction of a lot of new SMEs which, as explained before, would massively wish to join and be served by the ISU, is of low significance. On the other hand, the revenue for an SME that wants to enter and register to an ISU would be rather high because, by achieving Enterprise and Semantic Interoperability, it would cover multiple times the current costs in time, money and data loss because of the current incompatibilities among the various enterprise information systems.

However, the authors' suggestion of an enhanced ISU is only another indicative benchmark of what an ISU should ideally be, contributing to the research in this field and paving the way to the evolution of this idea, its further enhancement and development. Notably, the scientific foundations of the proposed approach can also be applied and further cultivated and evolved, by every SME that is interested in implementing such an infrastructure.

It includes all the necessary related information, state-of-the-art, existing implementations and current trends, properly organized, composed and presented, providing an initial scientific framework of design directions and decision support aspects, useful to every stakeholder in SMEs or other settings and industries, that wishes to implement such an ISU, either like the suggested one or a similar one, properly adjusted and adapted to each stakeholder's needs.

Furthermore, its application to a use-case scenario of the real everyday life of the enterprises and the according results of our work are only a first step that gives us the guarantees that our proposed ISU is actually serving its purpose, to such an extent, that when further expanded and improved, it will be more and more efficient and nearly ideal, precisely serving the particular needs of the SMEs.

Thus, concerning the future research directions and activities of our work, apart from improving the various characteristics and parts of our ISU, especially focusing on the specific structural blocks of its architecture and examining the implementation specifications in detail, in order to provide even more accurate solutions. We also acknowledge that there are still a lot of open issues for discussion and further research concerning the ISU concept, which we keep under consideration.

- Issues concerning the public or private body that will own, control, direct and operate the ISU are still pending, with no or only a few ideas to answer this question. Further legal principles in the wider ISU legal framework should be carefully researched.
- Moreover, concerning the cost of using the ISU services, the ideal should is offering them for free or at a low cost. However, such a proposal requires a complete and concrete business plan in advance, defining the ISU business model, in order to investigate the profitability, viability and sustain-

ability of the undoubtedly innovative and useful ISU.

- Also, the view of the ISU, by its nature, should ideally include electronic transactions among enterprises not only in a national, but also in an international, pan-European level. However, such an idea raises other questions that constitute breed for further investigation. For example, when it comes to cross-border transactions, there should be a way to authenticate the enterprises in order to give them access to interoperate with other enterprises across Europe. STORK project (Secure Identity Across Borders Linked - INFSO-ICT-PSP-224993) will constitute for us a first step to study this field and come back with new ideas and features.

Finally, we will constantly keep an eye open to the relevant research field, to all new initiatives and developments and to what the community and the stakeholders suggest that is crucial.

The whole ISU concept is an innovative but also a rather ambitious idea that we will further expand based on certain strategy, serving certain needs of the SMEs, effectively, efficiently and to-the-point.

## ACKNOWLEDGMENT

The joint research work presented in this paper has been financially supported by the European Commission through the FP7 project 'The Greek Interoperability Centre' – 204999. The authors acknowledge the European Commission for their support to the development of the ideas and concepts presented in this paper. Acknowledge to the European funded Project UNITE (FP7 248583), namely its secondment programme coordinated by UNINOVA-GRIS, that supported the development of various ideas and concepts presented in this paper. In additional it is also acknowledge the project ENSEMBLE FP7-ICT – 257548 – for its support on the development of some of these ideas.

## REFERENCES

Agostinho, C., Sarraipa, J., Goncalves, D., & Jardim-Goncalves, R. (2011). Tuple-based semantic and structural mapping for a sustainable interoperability. In *Technological innovation for sustainability - IFIP advances in information and communication technology* (Vol. 349, pp. 45–56). Berlin: Springer. doi:10.1007/978-3-642-19170-1_5

ATHENA. (2003, April). *Advanced technologies for interoperability of heterogeneous enterprise networks and their applications*. FP6-2002-IST-1, Integrated Project Proposal.

Bechhofer, S., Gangemi, A., van Harmelen, N. G., Horrocks, I., Masolo, M. K., & Oberle, D. et al. (2004). Tackling the ontology acquisition bottleneck: An experiment in ontology re-engineering. *Journal of Web Semantics*.

Charalabidis, Y. (2007). *From people to systems interoperability: The interoperability service utility concept*. eChallenges 2007 Conference. Retrieved December, 2011 from ftp://ftp.cordis.europa.eu/pub/ist/docs/ict-ent-net/echallenges2-yc_en.pdf

Commius Consortium. (2009). *Commius architecture (final version, deliverable D3.1.2)*. Retrieved from web http://www.commius.eu/index.php?option=com_remository&Itemid=2&func=startdown&id=84

Dassisti, M., & Chen, D. (2011). Interoperability analysis: General concepts for an axiomatic approach. In *OTM 2011 Workshops (LNCS)* (Vol. 7046, pp. 49–60). Berlin: Springer-Verlag. doi:10.1007/978-3-642-25126-9_13

Dogac, A., Laleci, G., Kennedy, J., Drissi, S., Sesana, M., Gonçalves, R., & Canepa, A. (2009). iSURF: RFID enabled collaborative supply chain planning environment. In *Proceedings of the 4th Mediterranean Conference on Information Systems, MCIS 2009*. Athens, Greece: Athens University of Economics and Business.

Donini, F. M., Lenzerini, M., Nardi, D., & Schaerf, A. (1991). A hybrid system with datalog and concept languages. In *Trends in Artificial Intelligence (LNCS)* (Vol. 549, pp. 88–97). Berlin: Springer Verlag. doi:10.1007/3-540-54712-6_221

ENSEMBLE Project. (2011). *EISB models and tools, deliverable 2.4*. Retrieved from http://www.fines-cluster.eu/fines/jm/Publications/Download-document/303-ENSEMBLE_D2.4_EISB-Models-and-Tools-Report-v1.00.html

*EPCglobal Architecture Framework*. (2007). Retrieved on January 2013 from http://www.epcglobalinc.org/standards/architecture/architecture_1_2-framework-20070910.pdf

*European CPFR Insights*. (2002). Retrieved from web http://www.ecr-institute.org/publications/best-practices/european-cpfr-insights/files/pub_2002_cpfr_european_insights.pdf

Gruber, T. R. (1993). A translation approach to portable ontology specifications. *Journal of Knowledge Acquisition*, *5*(2), 199–220. doi:10.1006/knac.1993.1008

Guarino, N., & Schneider, L. (2002). Ontology-driven conceptual modeling. In CAiSE 2002 (LNCS), (vol. 2348). Heidelberg, Gemany: Springer.

Gusmeroli, S. (2012). From enterprise interoperability to service innovation: European research activities in future internet enterprise systems. In *Enterprise Interoperability: 4th International IFIP Working Conference on Enterprise Interoperability* (LNBIP), (vol. 122). Berlin: Springer Verlag.

Hayek, F. (1945). The use of knowledge in society. *The American Economic Review*, *35*(4), 519–530.

IBM Service Sciences. Management and Engineering. (n.d.). *Services definition*. Retrieved December, 2011 from http://www.research.ibm.com/ssme/services.shtml

Information Society Technologies. (2008). *Enterprise interoperability research roadmap*. Retrieved on January 2013 from ftp://ftp.cordis.europa.eu/pub/fp7/ict/docs/enet/ei-research-roadmap-v5-final_en.pdf

INTEROP. (2007). *Enterprise interoperability-framework and knowledge corpus - Final report, INTEROP NoE, FP6 – contract n° 508011, deliverable DI.3 (May 21, 2007)*. Author.

Jardim-Goncalves, R., Silva, J. P. M. A., Steiger-Garcao, A., & Monteiro, A. (2007). Framework for enhanced interoperability through ontological harmonization of enterprise product models. In *Ontologies: A handbook of principles, concepts and applications, information systems* (Vol. 14, p. 915). Secaucus, NJ: Springer.

Laclavik, M. (2007). *COMMIUS: ISU via email*. eChallenges e-2007. Retrieved on March 2013 from ftp://ftp.cordis.europa.eu/pub/ist/docs/ict-ent-net/echallenges2-ml_en.pdf

Li, M. S. (2011). Utility service infrastructure in the future internet: PPP models and policy impact. *Samos Summit 2011*. Retrieved on December 2011 from https://pithos.grnet.gr/pithos/rest/irematz@ntua.gr/files/SamosSummit2011/Presentations/Session+I/ManSzeLi.pdf

Obrst, L. (2003). Ontologies for semantically interoperable systems. In *Proceedings of the Twelfth International Conference on Information and Knowledge Management (CIKM '03)* (pp. 366-369). New York, NY: ACM.

Popplewell, K., Stojanovic, N., Abecker, A., Apostolou, D., Mentzas, G., & Harding, J. (2008). Supporting adaptive enterprise collaboration through semantic knowledge services. In *Proceedings of IESA, Enterprise Interoperability III* (pp. 381–393). Berlin, Germany: Springer.

Sarraipa, J., Jardim-Goncalves, R., Gaspar, T., & Steiger-Garcao, A. (2010). Collaborative ontology building using qualitative information collection methods. In *Proceedings of Intelligent Systems (IS), 2010 5th IEEE International Conference Proceedings* (pp.61-66). IEEE.

Sarraipa, J., Jardim-Goncalves, R., & Steiger-Garcao, A. (2010b). MENTOR: An enabler for interoperable intelligent systems. *International Journal of General Systems*, *39*(5), 557–573. doi:10.1080/03081079.2010.484278

Sarraipa, J., Silva, J. P., Jardim-Goncalves, R., & Monteiro, A. (2008). MENTOR – Methodology for enterprise reference ontology development. In *Proceedings of Intelligent Systems, 2008 (IS '08), 4th International IEEE Conference* (vol. 1, pp. 6-32, 6-40). IEEE.

Silva, J., Cavaco, F., Sarraipa, J., & Jardim-Goncalves, R. (2011). Knowledge based methodology supporting interoperability increase in manufacture domain. In the *Proceedings of the ASME Congress 2011 - ASME International Mechanical Engineering Congress and Exposition IMECE 2011* (pp. 837-843). Denver, CO: ASME.

Sitek, P., Gusmeroli, S., Conte, M., Jansson, K., & Karvonen, I. (2011). *The COIN book - Enterprise collaboration and interoperability*. Aachen, Germany: Druck und Verlagshaus Mainz.

Suh, N. P. (1990). *The principles of design*. Oxford, UK: Oxford University Press.

Witten, I. H., Frank, E., & Hall, M. A. (2011). *Data mining: Practical machine learning tools and techniques* (3rd ed.). Burlington, MA: Morgan Kaufmann.

Zbib, N., Archimede, B., & Charbonnaud, P. (2012). Interoperability service utility model and its simulation for improving the business process collaboration. [). London, UK: Springer.]. *Proceedings of Enterprise Interoperability*, *5*, 403–413.

## KEY TERMS AND DEFINITIONS

**Enterprise Interoperability (EI):** The capacity of two or more enterprises, including all the systems within their boundaries and the external systems that they utilize or are affected by, in order to cooperate seamlessly in depth of time for a common objective.

**Intelligent System:** A securely managed IT infrastructure which, by being connected to the internet, autonomously executes native or cloud-based applications collects, analyzes and processes the data and knowledge collected.

**Interoperability Service Utility:** A basic IT infrastructure that provides interoperability services to enterprises through enabling and supporting information exchange between diverse knowledge sources, software applications and web services.

**Knowledge Management:** The process of capturing, developing, sharing, and effectively using organisational knowledge. It refers to a multi-disciplined approach to achieving organisational objectives by making the best use of knowledge.

**Reference Ontology:** A domain ontology about ontologies that gathers, describes, relates and has links to already existing ontologies, using a common logical organization.

**Semantic Interoperability:** Refers to the ability of computer systems to transmit data with unambiguous, shared meaning. Semantic interoperability is a requirement to enable machine computable logic, inference, knowledge discovery, and data federation between information systems.

# Chapter 12
# An Enterprise Interoperability Framework based on Compliance and Conformance

**José C. Delgado**
*Instituto Superior Técnico, Universidade de Lisboa, Portugal*

## ABSTRACT

*The existing interoperability frameworks usually take an application-driven, top-down approach, in which the most relevant dimensions of interoperability are optimized for some problem space. For example, The European Interoperability Framework has been conceived primarily to support e-Government services. With the goal of contributing to the establishment of the scientific foundations of interoperability, this chapter presents a multidimensional interoperability framework, conceived in a generic, bottom-up approach. The basic tenet is to add an interoperability dimension (based on the concepts of compliance and conformance) to an enterprise architecture framework with lifecycle and concreteness as its main dimensions, forming a universal core framework. This core is then provided with an extensibility mechanism, based on a concerns dimension, into which the specific characteristics of applications and their domains can be added to instantiate the framework, now in an application-driven fashion. The most relevant concerns, with sufficient applicability breadth, can be promoted to full dimensions and extend the framework. The use of partial compliance and conformance reduces coupling while still allowing interoperability, which increases adaptability, changeability, and reliability, thereby contributing to a sustainable interoperability.*

## INTRODUCTION

Just as any other system, an enterprise is a composition of smaller systems that interact among themselves and with the outside world. In this respect, it must solve the same interoperability problems as any two systems that need to understand each other to achieve meaningful and useful collaboration. In fact, no enterprise can survive alone. It needs to interact with other enterprises and be part of a value network. This means that interoperability is one of the most fundamental issues that any enterprise must deal with, in all its main slants, namely:

DOI: 10.4018/978-1-4666-5142-5.ch012

- **Functionality:** Guaranteeing that one enterprise understands the requests of another and reacts according to what is expected.
- **Non-Functional Aspects:** Ensuring adequate service levels, resource management, security, and so on.
- **Coupling:** Reducing it as much as possible, to avoid unnecessary dependencies.
- **Reliability:** Maintaining interoperability, even in the presence of unanticipated failures.
- **Adaptability:** Maintaining interoperability, even when partners change their characteristics.

What distinguishes an enterprise from other systems is not only its high complexity but also the need to redefine itself constantly and to carve its own place in the global enterprise ecosystem. Beating competition through constant renovation and evolution, playing the right cards by balancing factors such as innovation, quality, governance, competitiveness, marketing, customer satisfaction, and so on, is a matter of survival. Basic data interoperability is not enough. Enterprise collaboration demands higher levels of meaningful interaction.

There is no universally accepted definition of interoperability, since its meaning can vary accordingly to the perspective, context and domain under consideration. Although limited to information, the 24765 standard (ISO/IEC/IEEE, 2010) provides the most cited definition of interoperability, as "the ability of two or more systems or components to exchange information and to use the information that has been exchanged." We can generalize this by defining interoperability as "the ability of two or more systems or components to exchange stimuli and to react to them according to some pattern or contract that fulfills all partners' expectations." However, what does this really mean?

There are several frameworks and initiatives conceived to provide insight into what is involved in interoperability. However, most of these efforts attempt to classify interoperability by a single dimension, from high to low level. For example, the LCIM framework (Wang, Tolk, & Wang, 2009) uses the following levels: conceptual, dynamic, pragmatic, semantic, syntactic, technical and no interoperability.

The one-dimensional, layered approach to complexity in a framework is classic in software and communication systems. It has the advantage of simplicity but can only express the levels of detail, from more abstract to more concrete, and not the different natures of the various aspects and concepts involved. In addition, it does not provide a justification, or foundation, for the levels used in the framework, nor how they can fit a method or a maturity model, nor which are the conditions to actually achieve interoperability at each level, nor the implications for coupling and adaptability.

Other frameworks, such as the Framework for Enterprise Interoperability (ISO, 2011), resort to more than one dimension, but the extra dimensions pertain to the method that is used to solve the interoperability problem in some context or domain, not just to the framework. This is a consequence of the typical, application-driven approach of these frameworks, which start by defining the problem space (set of applications or systems in which the interoperability problems must be solved) and then derive the corresponding solution space, by establishing a set of guidelines to solve those interoperability problems.

This chapter presents an interoperability framework that takes a different, concept-driven approach. We start by defining a domain independent core, then we provide mechanisms to instantiate it to concrete applications and finally we extend it as required by those applications and their domain. This framework is applicable to any system, (be it simple or very complex, such as enterprises), in its interaction with other systems. It includes several dimensions that reflect orthogonal aspects and which are rooted on fundamental concepts, such as:

- **Lifecycle:** (of the enterprise's architecture or of one its components) No system is created in the operation stage. It must go through several stages of development, such as conception, design, implementation and operation, until someday, at the end of its useful life, it is decommissioned or destroyed.

- **Abstraction:** Abstracting details is fundamental to deal with complexity. Any system can be described at a high level of abstraction or at full detail. Going from abstract to concrete is the usual path in system design.

- **Transaction:** In this context, a *transaction* is a set of elementary activities that constitute a basic interaction pattern between two partners, in the roles of *consumer* and *provider*. Typically, it involves one request from the consumer and a response from the provider. It is during a transaction that interoperability must be accomplished.

- **Compliance and conformance:** The two sides of *compatibility*. A system *A* can engage in a transaction (as a consumer) with a system *B* (as a provider) only if *A* is compatible with *B* with respect to that transaction. This implies that *A* must be compliant with *B* (fulfils all the requirements of *B* for placing requests) and *B* must be conformant to *A* (produces responses according to the requirements of *A*).

- **Layers of interoperability:** Which express how much a system must know about the other (how much compatibility is needed) in order to exchange messages meaningfully (in terms of intent, content and reaction).

The main goals of this chapter are:

- To contribute to the scientific foundations of enterprise interoperability, by dissecting it into its main orthogonal components as justified by fundamental concepts in interoperability, while separating the framework from the method.

- To propose and to present a multidimensional framework that caters for this orthogonality.

- To demonstrate the expressive power of this frameworks, by showing that existing frameworks can be mapped onto it.

- To discuss a method in the context of the proposed framework.

This chapter is structured as follows. We start by presenting a multidimensional framework for enterprise architecture. Next, we present the compliance and conformance concepts, in the context of the transactions used to implement interoperability. Then, we incorporate the interoperability dimension in the enterprise architecture framework. We present some guidelines on how a method could exercise the interoperability framework. We also discuss how this framework compares with existing frameworks and how it can contribute to the establishment of a scientific base for enterprise interoperability. Finally, we present guidelines for future work and draw conclusions from this work.

## BACKGROUND

Interoperability has been studied in the most varied domains, such as enterprise collaboration (Jardim-Goncalves, Agostinho, & Steiger-Garcao, 2012), e-government services (Gottschalk & Solli-Sæther, 2008), military operations (Wyatt, Griendling, & Mavris, 2012), cloud computing (Loutas, Kamateri, Bosi, & Tarabanis, 2011), healthcare applications (Weber-Jahnke, Peyton, & Topaloglou, 2012), digital libraries (El Raheb et al, 2011) and metadata (Haslhofer & Klas, 2010).

Interoperability is as old as networking. When two or more systems need to interact, an interoperability problem arises. A typical approach to deal with it is to consider several layers of abstraction and complexity, along a single dimension. Other frameworks consider several dimensions, to detail issues and concerns.

One of the first systematizations of distributed interoperability was accomplished by the Open Systems Interconnection (OSI) reference model, a standard since 1984 (ISO, 1994), which considers seven layers (Table 1). This pertains mostly to communication issues, with the objective of sending data and reproducing it at the receiver. How that data is interpreted by the receiver and how it reacts to it is left unspecified, encompassed by the topmost layer, Application. Since interoperability must not only deal with data exchange but also meaningful use of information (ISO/IEC/IEEE, 2010), we need to detail the Application layer.

Table 1 depicts the basic structure of several interoperability frameworks that use this layered approach, establishing a rough horizontal correspondence between layers.

Peristeras & Tarabanis (2006) proposed a framework (C4IF) based on four layers: Connection (basic use of a channel), Communication (data formats), Consolidation (meaning through semantics) and Collaboration (through compatible processes). It simplifies the lower levels (distinguishing only connectivity and communication) and refines the application layer, distinguishing information semantics from behavior. Lewis, Morris, Simanta & Wrage (2008) proposed a similar framework, with slight differences but basically with the same structure.

Stamper (1996) applied *semiotics* (the study of signs, stemming from linguistics) to the field of information systems and proposed a semiotic ladder, a layered structure in which each layer builds on the previous one (just like a ladder) in increasingly higher levels of abstraction and complexity. Besides the usual syntax and semantics, the pragmatics concept was used to refer to the effect caused by the reception of a message

*Table 1. Comparison between several layered interoperability frameworks*

| OSI (1994) | C4IF (2006) | Lewis (2008) | Stamper (1996) | LCIM (2009) | EIF (2010) | Monfelt (2011) |
|---|---|---|---|---|---|---|
| Application | Collaboration | Organizational | Social world | Conceptual | Political | SWOT |
| | | | | | | Cultural |
| | | | | | | Ethical |
| | | | | | Legal | Legal |
| | | | Pragmatic | Dynamic | Organizational | Managerial |
| | | | | Pragmatic | | Organizational |
| | Consolidation | Semantic | Semantic | Semantic | Semantic (includes syntactic) | Adaptation |
| | | | | | | Application |
| Presentation | Communication | Syntactic | Syntactic | Syntactic | | Presentation |
| Session | | | | | | Session |
| Transport | | Machine | Empirics | Technical | Technical | Transport |
| Network | Connection | | | | | Network |
| Link | | | | | | Link |
| Physical Medium | | | Physical world | | | Physical Medium |

by a receiver. Empirics refer to the lower levels that use the physical world, encompassing details that are well established and less relevant to the understanding of interoperability as a whole. The social world tackle the higher levels, in which people become more involved.

Wang, Tolk & Wang (2009) described the LCIM framework, which follows the semiotic ladder in essence, with the interesting addition of a dynamic layer, which considers evolution along the system lifecycle.

The European Interoperability Framework (EIF, 2010) was conceived as a broad framework for the interoperability of public services and establishes four main interoperability levels (legal, organizational, semantic and technical), with an upper political context that should ensure compatible visions and aligned priorities.

Monfelt, Pilemalm, Hallberg & Yngström (2011) proposed a more detailed framework, by refining the social layer of the semiotic ladder to take care of higher level issues, such as risk (SWOT analysis) and "dependencies on social and organizational aspects concerning cultural, ethical and legal values and existing administrative and managerial issues" (p. 126). This extends the basic OSI reference model with another seven layers. The organizational layer refers to the effect that a message will have (pragmatic meaning of the message) and the adaptation layer refers to the semantics of the message, adapting the new layers to the technical layers provided by the OSI model.

Although shown above the Application layer, the new ones actually refine it by considering the issues that it leaves unspecified (ISO, 1994, p. 33).

Several frameworks are defined more on the maturity of systems' interoperability than on layer structure, by establishing a set of levels that give an indication (usually qualitative) of how far interoperability is considered in the abstraction scale. Table 2 illustrates this. Each framework has its own slant and terminology, but overall they possess rather similar structures, ranging from a complete lack of interoperability to full integration.

Ford, Colombi, Graham, and Jacques (2007) developed a six-step mathematical method of measuring interoperability (i-Score), providing a means to identify the gap between an existing interoperability measurement and its optimal value.

Other interoperability frameworks, particularly those conceived for complex systems, such as enterprises, try to complete the scenario by considering more than one dimension of interoperability.

Berre *et al* (2007) described the ATHENA Interoperability Framework (AIF), which builds on previous research, including the IDEAS and INTEROP projects (Chen, Doumeingts, & Vernadat, 2008). This is a framework developed mainly for enterprise integration, structured into three parts:

- Conceptual integration, at the levels of enterprise/business, process, service and information/data.

*Table 2. Comparison between several interoperability frameworks in terms of maturity levels*

| Level | LISI (C4ISR, 1998) | OIM (Fewell & Clark, 2003) | OIAM (Kingston, Fewell, & Richer, 2005) | MMEI (Guédria, Chen, & Naudet, 2009) |
|---|---|---|---|---|
| 4 | Enterprise | Unified | Dynamic | Adapted |
| 3 | Domain | Combined | Open | Organized |
| 2 | Functional | Collaborative | Accommodating | Aligned |
| 1 | Connected | Ad hoc | Amenable | Defined |
| 0 | Isolated | Independent | Static | Unprepared |

- Application integration, which includes a methodology with methods to support the development of interoperability projects.
- Technical integration, which provides an implementation basis around technologies such as BPEL, Web Services and XML.

Chen (2006) proposed an enterprise interoperability framework, based on three dimensions:

- Concerns (business, processes, services and data), based on the interoperability layers of the Athena framework (Berre *et al*, 2007).
- Barriers, which express the difficulties in making systems interoperable, such as syntactic and semantic differences, and are divided into three categories: conceptual, technological and organizational.
- Approach, the plan to overcome these barriers and to achieve a solution to the interoperability problem. It can be organized in three ways: integrated (a common format is used by all systems), unified (common goals and semantic mapping) and federated (there may be common goals and ontology, but each system must adapt to others dynamically, without any imposed model). This leads to a barrier-driven method (Chen & Daclin, 2007), oriented towards solving the concrete problem of implementing interoperability between two existing enterprises by removing the perceived barriers to achieve the solution.

The CEN EN/ISO 11354-1 standard (ISO, 2011) defines a Framework for Enterprise Interoperability (FEI) and is based on the interoperability framework described by Chen (2006).

Morris *et al* (2004) proposed an interoperability framework (SOSI) that includes not only the operational dimension but also the programmatic and constructive dimensions, which pertain to prior stages in the systems' lifecycle, namely conception and design, respectively.

Ostadzadeh & Fereidoon (2011) presented an interoperability framework conceived for ultra-large-scale systems, with three dimensions. It tries to include interoperability aspects from the previous frameworks, while adding an enterprise framework dimension:

- **Abstract:** Which draws on the Zachman enterprise framework (Sowa & Zachman, 1992) and answers the classical six questions (what, how, where, who, why, when) in the context of interoperability.
- **Perspective:** Expressing layered interoperability concerns (contextual, conceptual, logical, physical and out-of-context).
- **Barriers:** Extending the SOSI framework with a social slant, to take into account the human factor and cultural issues, but collapsing the three SOSI dimensions into one.

The European project ENSEMBLE (Agostinho, Jardim-Goncalves, & Steiger-Garcao, 2011) embodies an effort to formulate a science base for enterprise interoperability. This involves discovering which interoperability problems exist in domains related to interoperability, such as social, applied and formal sciences, and identifying which are the relevant scientific areas underlying interoperability. Twelve areas have been identified in which interoperability is necessary: data, process, rules, objects (in the context of the Internet of Things), software, cultural, knowledge, services, social networks, electronic identity, cloud and ecosystems. In addition, four levels of scientific elements of interoperability (semantics, models, tools and orchestration) have been identified.

Modeling before designing has always been an important tenet. Since the early days of the Zachman framework (Sowa & Zachman, 1992), we understand that enterprise architecture and its underlying principles (Greefhorst & Proper, 2011; Winter & Aier, 2011) are the cornerstones of the enterprises themselves.

Today, several enterprise architecture frameworks exist, with Zachman framework and TOGAF (The Open Group, 2009) as two of the most used, among a wide set (Minoli, 2008) that includes the Department of Defense's Architectural Framework (DoDAF), the Extended Enterprise Architecture Framework (E2AF), the Federal Enterprise Architecture Framework (FEAF), the Treasury Enterprise Architecture Framework (TEAF) and the Integrated Architecture Framework (IAF).

TOGAF is gaining widespread acceptance as a *de facto* standard in the industry (Dietz & Hoogervorst, 2011). This standard establishes a metamodel and a set of best practices for describing architectures, including ontology and requirements for architecture frameworks and architecture description languages.

Since this chapter contends that interoperability starts on the early stages of architecture development, the BMM, or Business Motivation Model (Malik, 2009), is of particular importance. In fact, it has influenced the architecture framework presented in this chapter. Instead of organizing the architecture into layers, from business down to technology (Winter & Fischer, 2007), the BMM emphasizes the motivations (the reasons why an architecture should be the way it is), the ends (the expectations which should be satisfied) and the means (what should be done to achieve those

ends). Each of these types of concerns is derived from the previous one, in a model driven way under a business perspective.

## ENTERPRISE ARCHITECTURE AS THE FOUNDATION FOR INTEROPERABILITY

The frameworks mentioned in Table 1 use a single dimension of interoperability. Although this leads to a simple classification scheme, they fail to acknowledge that not all interoperability levels belong to the same dimension and ignore other relevant aspects.

To understand why, we need first to consider an enterprise in isolation and to establish a framework to characterize its enterprise architecture. We will later extend it with the interoperability perspective.

### The Enterprise Architecture Lifecycle

Figure 1 depicts the typical lifecycle of the conception and animation of an enterprise architecture, with several stages that reflect different perspectives and occupy specific positions in a graph that is part of an overall method. The loops cater for changes and improvements.

The *architectural loop* is inspired by the Business Motivation Model (Malik, 2009) and laid around three main concepts:

*Figure 1. Typical enterprise architecture lifecycle, with stages chained in changeability loops*

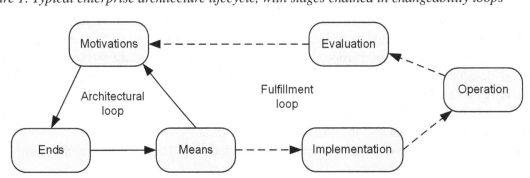

- **Motivations:** Which emphasize the reasons behind the architectural decisions taken, in accordance with the business needs.
- **Ends:** Which express the desires and expectations of stakeholders (e.g., goals and objectives).
- **Means:** Which describe the mechanisms used to fulfill those expectations (e.g., actions).

The *fulfillment loop* in Figure 1 models subsequent stages and is based on the organization adopted by classical development methods, such as the Rational Unified Process (Kruchten, 2004):

- The ends and the means of the architectural loop correspond roughly to the analysis and design stages of those methods.
- The *implementation* includes stages such as development, testing and deployment.
- The *operation* corresponds to animating (executing) the system.
- The *evaluation* measures KPIs (Key Performance Indicators) and assesses how well the system meets the expectations caused by the motivations.

## A Multidimensional Architecture Framework

The lifecycle of Figure 1 corresponds to a dimension (or axis) of the framework, discretized into six stages. There is another implicit dimension, Evolution, discretized into versions, that stems from repeating the loops, expressing that the architecture can be successively changed and improved. This is not enough to capture all the most important aspects. In particular, we need two additional axes:

- **Concreteness:** Each stage in Figure 1 can be seen at a very high, abstract level, or at a very detailed, concrete level. We have discretized this axis into four lev-

els: *Conceptual*, *Strategic*, *Tactical* and *Operational*. It is common to mix these designations with the Lifecycle axis (embedded into the Motivations, Ends, Means and Implementation stages, respectively). However, note that this common usage corresponds to a specific instantiation of the method, in which tactical decisions are made only after the strategy has been laid out and detailed. In other words, the strategy is used as the motivation for the tactics. However, the motivation for the tactics should be a refinement of the motivation for the strategy and not a consequence of strategy design. That is why we separate concreteness from lifecycle. We can have the Implementation stage at a conceptual level (ideas on how to do it) as well as the Motivations stage at an operational level (justification for the lowest level actions). Stages of the lifecycle and their level of concreteness are orthogonal concepts.

- **Concerns:** The focus words (*what*, *how*, *where*, *who*, *when*, *why*) in the Zachman framework (Sowa & Zachman, 1992) are generic but do not address the entire focus range. Other questions can be made, such as *whence* (where from), *whither* (where to), *how much* (quantitative assessment) and *how well* (qualitative assessment). It is important to be able to express the dynamics of the architecture, its quality (how good it is, quantitatively and qualitatively) and other stakeholders' concerns (financial, regulatory compliance, security, interoperability, domain specific, and so on), both functional and non-functional. The architectural principles of TOGAF (The Open Group, 2009) fit in here. This axis can be organized into categories of concerns, from qualitative to quantitative.

We start by laying down the plane formed by the Lifecycle and Concreteness axes, in Figure 2,

*Figure 2. The lifecycle and concreteness plane*

| | Motivations | Ends | Means | Implementation | Operation | Evaluation |
|---|---|---|---|---|---|---|
| **Conceptual** | Purpose | Vision | Mission | Model | Animation | Rationale & assessment |
| **Strategic** | Principles, drivers & risks | Goals | Method | Design | Simulation | Strategic KPIs |
| **Tactical** | Policies & constraints | Objectives | Plan | Blueprint | Rapid prototyping | Metrics & measurements |
| **Operational** | Rules & exceptions | Targets | Procedure | Working system | Execution | Monitoring |

*(Lifecycle axis, horizontal, at top; Concreteness axis, vertical, at left; Tacit threshold above Conceptual; Empiric threshold below Operational)*

and explaining what is the meaning of each cell, which results from crossing the values of both axes and represents one lifecycle stage at a given level of concreteness.

The Concreteness axis (vertical) considers four levels, from Conceptual, more fuzzy and abstract, down to Operational, more detailed and concrete. Each level in this axis is a refinement of the level above it, by including decisions that turn some abstract aspects into concrete ones. This axis has two opposite thresholds:

- **Tacit:** This is the highest level, above which concepts are too complex or too difficult to describe. It encompasses the tacit knowledge and know-how (Oguz & Sengün, 2011) of the people that conceived the enterprise architecture or manage the enterprise, expressing their insight and implicit expectations and assumptions about the business and enterprise governance.
- **Empiric:** The lowest level, below which details are not relevant anymore and we settle for just using something that already exists and is known to work, such as a standard, an organizational unit or a piece of equipment.

The Lifecycle axis (horizontal) lays down the six lifecycle stages in Figure 1, disregarding the loops, which means that it describes the stages of one iteration (version) of the enterprise architecture. Each column, and the cell at each concreteness level, can be described as:

- **Motivations:** This column is the result of contextual requirements for the design of the system, acting as motivation and justification for the ensuing stages. At the top level, we have the *Purpose*, which reflects the essence and the reason for the existence of this architecture. The *Principles, drivers & risks* refine the *Purpose* by establishing not only the basic tenets that this architecture must obey but also the enablers and inhibitors that foster and limit the characteristics of the architecture (resulting probably from a SWOT analysis). The *Policies & constraints* perform a similar role, but at a lower level and greater detail, which in turn are refined into *Rules & exceptions* (special cases), at the *Operational* level.
- **Ends:** This column corresponds to the expectations established for the architecture and that are justified by the *Motivations*.

At the top level, the *Vision* corresponds to the global scenario sought that fulfills the purpose. The vision is refined and decomposed into *Goals*, which express, usually in a qualitative way, a desired state or set of properties to achieve. Goals are in turn refined into *Objectives*, concrete enough to be declared SMART (*Specific*, *Measureable*, *Achievable*, *Realistic* and *Time framed*). *Targets* are lower level and simpler objectives, at the atomic level (which cannot be further decomposed) or close enough.

- **Means:** The cells in this column specify what needs to be done in order to meet the expectations. The *Mission* is the top-level expression of the type of actions to carry out. The *Method* is a refinement of the mission by including the choice of an approach or paradigm. The *Plan* is a graph of steps that make the method concrete by choosing a set of techniques. The *Procedure* is a set of actions that detail the plan by choosing a set of algorithms. The method here refers to the high level plan underlying a specific architecture and should not be mixed up with the architecture development method, which is discussed in section "The method to achieve interoperability."

- **Implementation:** This column specifies the tools, languages and procedures to provide an implementation of the means, by transforming them into workable representations. The *Model* is an overall representation of the architecture chosen to carry out the mission, expressed in some notation, such as UML. The *Design* details the model, structuring it into modules, or subsystems, and establishing their interactions. The *Blueprint* is the detailed description of each module. The *Working system* provides full details (such as data and code).

- **Operation:** This column exercises the system, either to operate it in real conditions or just to get insight about its quality, in both

functional (how well does it fulfill the motivations) and non-functional (how much does it comply with a set of fulfillment criteria) terms. At the conceptual level, we can only imagine what will happen by *Animation* of scenarios and use cases (nevertheless, important to check global behavior). *Simulation* can abstract many details by using statistical models and still obtain meaningful insight into the behavior (in statistical terms). *Rapid prototyping* works with partial specifications (not statistical, but not fully implemented modules, either) and enables exercising some specific concerns (user interfaces, for instance). At the lower level, *Execution* corresponds to exercising the completely implemented system, under real conditions, such as running a program.

- **Evaluation:** This is the assessment of the operation, so that changes and improvements can be introduced, if deemed necessary to better fulfill the purpose in the *Motivations* stage. At the top level, *Rationale & assessment* perform reasoning over the scenario and use case animation. *Simulation* provides the inputs to *Strategic KPIs*, which can be checked against the *Principles, drivers & risks* in *Motivations*. *Metrics & measurements* can check how well and how much the *Policies & constraints* in *Motivations* are satisfied. *Monitoring* checks events and serves as the basis for all higher-level evaluation procedures, assessing whether all *Rules & exceptions* in *Motivations* are dealt with satisfactorily.

The Concerns axis expresses the various aspects under consideration in the system, from a more qualitative to a more quantitative emphasis. Each concern corresponds to a Lifecycle and Concreteness plane. The Evolution axis corresponds to a new batch of planes, expressing a new version of the system. Figure 3 illustrates these axes.

The framework can be extended by promoting concerns to axes, if they are relevant enough. This can happen if the concern:

- Can be discretized into several situations, stages or values.
- Has a variability that is relevant across the entire span of existing axes.
- Refers to issues orthogonal to those dealt with by other axes.

In general, the architecture framework is multidimensional but, for the sake of simplicity, the following sections consider only a subset of axes at a time.

## Discussion and Rationale

Strategy and tactics are usually bound to the notion of course of action (Malik, 2009) and therefore it may seem strange that the Motivations stage, for example, can be described at the strategic, tactic and even operational levels. However, as motivations are progressively detailed and made more concrete, they have to include some notion of approach. The Strategic and Tactical levels of the Motivations stage, for instance, describe the motivations for the strategy and tactics to use in subsequent stages.

In the same way, policies and rules appear in the Business Motivation Model (Malik, 2009) as directives in the course of action stemming from tactics and motivated by a SWOT-type assessment.

*Figure 3. The concerns and evolution axes*

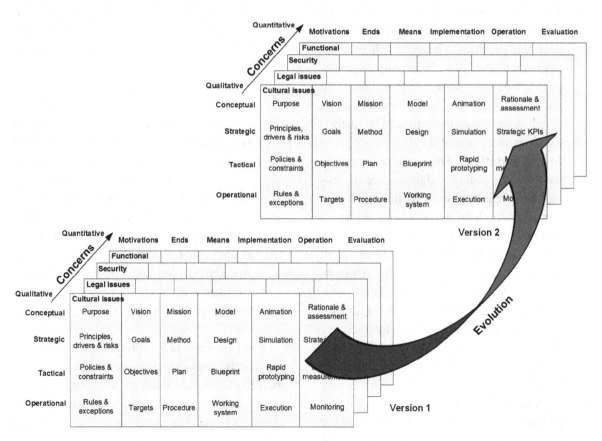

In our opinion, however, they should appear first in the Motivations stage and not just afterwards, in the Means stage.

In fact, we can look at each horizontal plane (parallel to the plane formed by the Concerns and Lifecycle axes) in Figure 3 as global descriptions of the system at increasingly depths of detail and concreteness. The top plane (Conceptual) is a view that describes essentially the main concepts, ideas and features, both in the various stages (Motivations, Ends, Means, and so on) and in stakeholder's concerns. The next plane (Strategic) is a refinement of the previous one, with decisions that reflect a strategic approach by making it partially more concrete. The same happens in the two lower planes (Tactical and Operational), with increasingly level of refinement and detail. Each plane can lead to different lower planes, according to the decisions taken and approach followed.

These planes correspond roughly to the main rows of the Zachman framework (*planner*, *owner*, *designer* and *builder*). TOGAF also includes a dimension of level of detail (and strategy as the top level), but with refinement essentially linked to structure, with the strategic level architecture decomposed into architectural units at the segment (business areas) and capability (business units) levels. Aspect refinement in TOGAF is accomplished by considering different types of architectures, or domains (*business*, *data*, *application* and *technology*), which may have its justification in terms of current technology (namely, by separating data and applications, which assumes the process paradigm) but that in practice tend to act as architectural silos. The Concreteness axis in Figure 2 supports both structural decomposition and aspect refinement.

Note that, in our framework, both the Lifecycle and Concreteness axes reflect features of the system itself (nature of considerations and level of refinement) and not stakeholder's perspectives of the system (Zachman) nor architectural units, types or domains (TOGAF).

Vertical planes that are parallel to the Concreteness-Lifecycle plane correspond to concern oriented views (for example, looking at everything from the security or from the legal point of views). Vertical planes that are parallel to the Concreteness-Concerns plane correspond to considering every issue in each stage (for example, the ends, namely goals and objectives, to achieve under the various concerns and at various levels of detail).

Like most architectural frameworks (Minoli, 2008), ours is recursive (Greefhorst & Proper, 2011), in the sense that progression downwards the concreteness axis can be made by aspect refinement or structural decomposition. In the latter case, each architectural subsystem can be modeled by the same framework. The architecture concept can thus refer to a set of interacting enterprises, an enterprise, a department, a business unit, and so on, down to the level of a small module in an application. It all depends on the granularity envisaged.

## TRANSACTIONS AND CHOREOGRAPHIES

Interactions between enterprises occur in the Operation stage of the lifecycle (Figure 1), in the form of transactions, but the fact is that interoperability starts at the beginning of the lifecycle, with the motivations to interact with other enterprises.

A transaction is a primitive pattern (predefined sequence) of messages exchanged between two interacting partners, one in the role of consumer, which initiates the pattern by a request, and the other in the role of provider, which satisfies that request and typically provides a response. The same enterprise can act as a consumer and as a provider, in bidirectional interactions. A *choreography* (Bravetti & Zavattaro, 2009) is a contract between two or more partners that expresses a composition of transactions.

Figure 4 illustrates a request/response transaction and a multi-partner choreography. Figure 4a shows that the interaction between enterprises

*Figure 4. Illustration of a transaction (a) and of a choreography (b)*

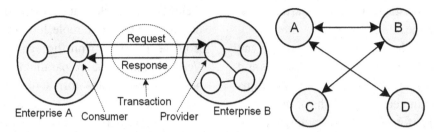

usually involves only specific (sub)systems and not the enterprise as a whole. Nevertheless, since systems are recursively composed of other systems, the rules are the same. Figure 4b shows a simplified representation of a choreography.

Dietz (2006) established a standard basic transaction pattern, in which the provider, upon receiving a request, can either send a *promise* (to honor it) or decline it, whereas the consumer can either accept or reject the response. If the interaction is asynchronous, a *future* (which the provider's response will later replace) can be returned to the consumer immediately, upon sending the request. Table 3 illustrates some of the basic message types that a transaction can entail.

To achieve interoperability, messages need to be accepted and understood at all required levels, within a transaction or a choreography. Some enterprises resort to mediators to convert data formats, protocols or some other aspect. In this case, Figure 4a still applies, with the mediator as just another partner involved, producing two relationships (Enterprise *A* to mediator and mediator to Enterprise *B*).

Meaningfully exchanging a message (the basic component of a transaction) between consumer and provider, in one direction or the other, entails the following main aspects:

*Table 3. Examples of message types*

| Message category/type | | Description |
|---|---|---|
| *Request* | | *Initial request in each transaction* |
| | React | React to message, no answer expected |
| | React & respond | React to message and answer/notify |
| *Amendment* | | *Further information on an already sent request* |
| | Cancel | Cancel the execution of the request |
| *Response* | | *Response to the request* |
| | Answer | A value returned as a response (replaces the future, if any) |
| | Resource fault | A value returned as the result of an exception |
| | Protocol fault | A value resulting from a protocol error (or failure in partner) |
| *Notification* | | *Information of completion status* |
| | Promise | Confirm will to honor the request |
| | Denial | Confirm rejection of request |
| | Done | Request completed but has no value to reply |
| | Cancelled | Confirm cancellation of request |

- **Intent:** Sending the message must have a given intent, inherent to the transaction it belongs to and related to the collaboration sought by two interacting enterprises.
- **Content:** This concerns the generation and interpretation of the content of a message by the sender, expressed by some syntax and semantics (including ontology) in such a way that the receiver is also able to interpret if.
- **Transfer:** The message content needs to be successfully transferred from the context of the sender to the context of the receiver.
- **Reaction:** This concerns the reaction of the receiver upon reception of a message, which should produce effects according to the expectations of the sender (either functionally and non-functionally, including issues such as security and exceptions caused by failures).

This is valid both at higher levels of detail, which typically correspond to business choreographies, and at lower levels, which typically implement data communication protocols.

## COMPATIBILITY: COMPLIANCE AND CONFORMANCE

The ability of two enterprises to engage successfully in a transaction, in the roles of consumer and provider, means that they are *compatible* with respect to that transaction and in those roles. In the same way, an enterprise is said to be compatible with a choreography if it fulfills all the requirements of all the roles that enterprise needs to perform in that choreography. The same enterprise can act both as consumer and as provider at multiple times in a given choreography.

In many cases, systems are made compatible by design, i.e., conceived and implemented to work together. The problem with enterprises is that they are complex and evolve in an independent way,

which means that ensuring compatibility at the enterprise level is not an easy task. A typical and pragmatic solution is to resort to Web Services and XML data, sharing schemas and namespaces.

More flexible solutions involve discovering Web Services similar to what is sought, by performing schema matching with similarity algorithms (Jeong, Lee, Cho & Lee, 2008), and ontology matching and mapping (Euzenat & Shvaiko, 2007). Manual adaptations are usually unavoidable.

The *compatibility* notion introduces a different perspective, stronger than similarity but weaker than commonality (resulting from using the same schemas and ontologies). The trick is to consider partial (instead of full) compatibility, by considering only the intersection between what the consumer needs and what the provider can offer. If the latter subsumes the former, the degree of compatibility required by the consumer is feasible, regardless of whether the provider supports additional features or not.

Compatibility (of a consumer with a provider) entails the following concepts:

- **Compliance:** The consumer must satisfy (*comply with*) the requirements of the provider for sending requests to it, without which these cannot be honored (Kokash & Arbab, 2009).
- **Conformance:** The provider must fulfill all the expectations of the consumer regarding the effects of a request (including eventual responses), therefore being able to take the form of (*to conform to*) whatever the consumer expects it to be (Adriansyah, van Dongen, & van der Aalst, 2010).

In full compatibility, the consumer can use all the provider's features. In partial compatibility, the consumer uses only a subset of the provider's features, which means that compliance and conformance need only be ensured for that subset.

As an example, consider Figure 5a, in which an enterprise *A* (in the role of consumer) has full

*Figure 5. Full (a) and partial (b) compatibility*

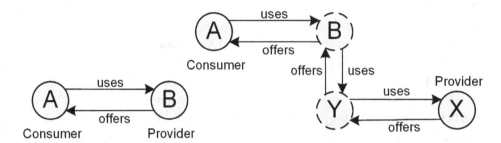

compatibility with enterprise *B*, in the role of provider. *A* uses only the features that *B* offers and *B* offers only what *A* uses. However, in Figure 5b, the provider of *A* is now enterprise *X*, which has been designed for full compatibility with enterprise *Y*, in the role of consumer. The problem is that *A* was designed to interact with a provider *B* and *X* was designed to expect a consumer *Y*. In other words, *B* is how *A* views provider *X* and *Y* is how *X* views consumer *A*. In this case, *B* and *Y* are specifications, not actual systems. How can *A* be made compatible with *X* so that it becomes able to interact with it?

There are two necessary conditions:

- **Compliance:** *B* must comply with *Y*. Since *A* complies with *B* and *Y* with *X*, this means that *A* complies with *X* and, therefore, *A* can use *X* as if it were *B*, as it was designed for.
- **Conformance:** *Y* must conform to *B*. Since *X* conforms to *Y* and *B* to *A*, this means that *X* conforms to *A* and, therefore, *X* can replace (take the form of) *B* without *A* noticing it.

In this example, partial compatibility has been achieved by *subsumption*, with the set of features that *A* uses as a subset of the set of features offered by *X*. This inclusion relationship, without changing characteristics, allows compatibility to be transitive across the interacting partners and specifications in Figure 5b.

Partial compatibility can also be achieved by *translation*, in which a mediator adapts features by changing names, formats, or any other characteristic (including mashups of features) between actual interacting partners. In this case, compatibility is not transitive.

Compatibility is also not commutative, since the roles of consumer and provider are different and asymmetric by nature. However, nothing prevents two interacting partners from switching roles in a symmetric way, by using and offering identical features in a reciprocal fashion, which is typical of certain interaction protocols. These are just special cases.

We should also note that:

- Compliance and conformance are general concepts, in terms of satisfying requirements and expectations, respectively, and can be applied to behavior, data or any other specifications that somehow become related (such as enterprise strategies, for example), either at a high level of abstraction or at a low and detailed level. Wherever there is a relationship, compliance and conformance are present.
- Compatibility, which encompasses both compliance and conformance, is thus a concept that is more general than interoperability, which applies to the Operation stage of the lifecycle, in which the operational interactions occur. Compatibility applies to any relationship in any stage of

the lifecycle, even if the Operation stage is never reached (such as in models and documentation).

The greatest advantage of partial compatibility is the ability to tune up the right level of interoperability, achieving a balance between two opposing goals:

- Enterprises need to cooperate and therefore must share some set of specifications, so that information can flow between them, be properly understood and produce the intended effects.
- However, shared specifications mean coupling and constraints to diversity (universally adopted standards are not always the typical case) and lifecycle evolution;

The more specifications are shared, the greater the coupling. Therefore, compatibility should be reduced to the minimum necessary compliance and conformance and no more than that. On the other hand, an enterprise that needs less compliance and/ or less conformance has better chances of being able to participate in a choreography (Delgado, 2012). This is an important aspect when discovering potential partners for a collaboration contract.

## A MULTIDIMENSIONAL INTEROPERABILITY FRAMEWORK

Armored with the multidimensional enterprise architecture framework of Figure 3 and the concepts of compliance and conformance introduced in the previous section, we now set out to improve on the linear structure of the interoperability frameworks of Table 1 to reach a multidimensional interoperability framework.

## A Linear Perspective of Interoperability

We start by addressing ourselves the following question: if an enterprise A (in the role of consumer) wants to interact with another B (in the role of provider), what must A know about B, and vice-versa?

If we consider again Table 3, which describes the various types of messages that can be used to build a transaction, and the aspects that it entails (intent, content, transfer and reaction), it is easy to assert that a lot needs to be involved to ensure that A complies with what B requires and B conforms to what A expects.

As any complex issue, interoperability may be considered at various levels of abstraction, which means discretizing it into layers. In our framework, we consider the layers described in Table 4, which details and extends the layer schemes used in Table 1.

Table 4 depicts a transaction, in which a consumer sends a request to a provider, which executes the request and sends a response to the consumer. This involves an interoperability ladder, with a set of layers of interoperability, from a very high level of abstraction (each enterprise has assumptions and expectations regarding the nature of the intent of the other in engaging in some interaction) down to a very low level (any message must physically reach the other enterprise). The goal of the U-shaped message paths (in both requests and responses) depicted at the center of the table is twofold:

- To show that two enterprises do not interact directly, except at the lowest level. Any message needs to go down the interoperability ladder all the way to the bottom, at the sender, so that the message flows through the communication channel in

*Table 4. Layers of interoperability in a transaction*

| Category | Layer | Artifact (Consumer) | Interaction Channel | Artifact (Provider) |
|----------|-------|---------------------|---------------------|---------------------|
| Symbiotic (nature) | Coordination | Governance | | Governance |
| | Alignment | Joint-venture | | Joint-venture |
| | Collaboration | Partnership | | Partnership |
| | Cooperation | Outsourcing | | Outsourcing |
| Pragmatic (context) | Contract | Choreography | | Choreography |
| | Workflow | Process | | Process |
| | Interface | Service | | Service |
| Semantic (meaning) | Inference | Rule | | Rule |
| | Knowledge | Semantic network | | Semantic network |
| | Ontology | Concept | | Concept |
| Syntactic (notation) | Structure | Schema | | Schema |
| | Primitive type | Primitive object | | Primitive object |
| | Serialization | Message format | | Message format |
| Connective (protocol) | Messaging | Message protocol | | Message protocol |
| | Routing | Gateway | | Gateway |
| | Communication | Network protocol | | Network protocol |
| | Physics | Equipment | | Equipment |

▬▬Request; ▭▭Response

some physical format, and then needs to be reconstructed at the receiver, climbing the interoperability ladder all the way up until its intent is understood.

- Any message goes through all levels, both in sender and receiver. Whether it pertains to some low level protocol or to some high level business choreography, it must be sent through the lowest level (physical channel communication) but, at the same time, it has been sent with some intent and serves a given purpose. The transaction is just an instantiation of a general interaction pattern, which means that it goes through all layers. Choreographies will be compositions thereof.

The Category column in Table 4 organizes the most interrelated interoperability layers (Layer column) into sets, with the following meaning:

- **Symbiotic:** This category expresses the interaction nature of two interacting enterprises in a mutually beneficial agreement. This can be a tight coordination under a common governance, if the enterprises are controlled by the same entity, a joint-venture agreement, if the two enterprises are substantially aligned, a collaboration involving a partnership agreement, if some goals are shared, or a mere value chain co-operation, instantiated as an outsourcing contract.

- **Pragmatic:** The interaction between a consumer and a provider is done in the context of a contract (the nature of which in not known in this category), which is implemented by a choreography that co-ordinates processes, which in turn implement workflow behavior by orchestrating service invocations.

- **Semantic:** Both interacting enterprises must be able to understand the meaning of the content of the messages exchanged, both requests and responses. This implies compatibility in rules, knowledge and ontologies, so that meaning is not lost when transferring a message from the context of the sender to that of the receiver.
- **Syntactic:** This category deals mainly with form, rather than content. Each message has a structure, composed by data (primitive objects) according to some structural definition (its schema). The data in messages need to be serialized to be sent over the channel, using formats such as XML or JSON.
- **Connective:** The main objective in this category is to transfer a message from one enterprise to the other, regardless of its content. This usually involves enclosing that content in another message with control information and implementing a message protocol (such as SOAP or HTTP) over a communications network, according to its own protocol (such as TCP/IP) and possibly involving routing gateways.

Formally, each transaction must satisfy compatibility (compliance and conformance) at all layers, both in the request and in the response, which can be viewed in two orthogonal directions:

- **Horizontally:** between the same layer in the consumer and in the producer. This is merely an abstraction mechanism, hiding the lower layers, as if the interaction occurred in that layer. Programs 1 and 2, in section "A simple wrap-up example," illustrate the Service and Schema layers.
- **Vertically:** between adjacent layers in each interacting partner. An artifact in an interoperability layer is obtained by (abstracting the details of) the composition of artifacts in the layers below. For example, a

choreography coordinates a set of processes and a process is a set of service invocations. The vertical relationship between the Choreography and Process layers, for example, means that a process must comply with a choreography in the role of consumer and conform to it in the role of provider.

It is interesting to note that these horizontal and vertical relationships have essentially the same principles that have already been stated by the OSI reference model (OSI, 1994). The most relevant changes are the distinction between compliance and conformance and the discrimination of the Application layer into a range of interoperability layers.

In practical terms, it is very difficult to consider all the interoperability layers in a systematic way for all transactions, which means that the tacit and empiric limits, already used in the concreteness axis of the multidimensional framework if Figure 2, are again helpful here. For example, a business-oriented perspective may consider the empiric level (below which details are not that relevant) at the semantic category, whereas a more implementation-oriented perspective may see the pragmatic category as the tacit level (assuming someone is taking care of behavior and intentions of the interacting partners). In practice, only a range of layers is considered explicitly in each context, but Table 4 needs to consider all layers for completeness. The fact that a Web Service, for instance, does not deal explicitly with semantics does not mean that the corresponding interoperability layers are not there. Simply, it is a tacit aspect, unverified by the system.

From bottom to top, each interoperability layer adds new knowledge of one interacting partner about the other partner's interoperability characteristics. For example, at the lowest layer only the physical level protocol is known. Layers up to Choreography have a reasonably universal meaning. Therefore, we detail only the layers above, in the Symbiotic category, which is dealt with explicitly only by interacting partners that understand why they are engaging in an interaction (all others do it tacitly):

- **Cooperation:** This just a marriage of convenience, limited to a contract to supply something at the exchange of something else (such as a payment). Mutual interoperability knowledge is limited to the set of choreographies necessary to implement that contract. This is typical of business interactions in value chains.
- **Collaboration:** This involves an interaction agreement towards some compatible (or even common) goals and not just a supply contract, entailing explicit compliance and conformance between the goals of the interacting enterprises. This is what happens in partnerships.
- **Alignment:** This is even a more profound interaction, in which there must be explicit compatibility not only in goals but also in the motivations to pursue them. Alignment leads to interactions such as those found in joint-ventures.
- **Governance:** This corresponds the highest level of mutual interoperability knowledge, because not only goals and motivations, but also the actual governance, and by extension evolution into new versions of the enterprise architecture, must be compatible. This layer is only found in partners that experience a tight coordination, such as found in merging operations, subsidiary enterprises or departments of the same enterprise.

We also note that:

- The composition ladder across interoperability layers, in the Artifact columns of Table 4, is not necessarily as linear as expressed. For example, the Schema artifact in the Structure layer composes Primitive

objects (necessary in any system), but can also compose higher-level objects, namely the artifacts in the layers of the Semantic category. This is a natural consequence of the recursive nature of system (de)composition. In addition, composition can be both in space (module composition) and time (interaction protocols).

- The relationship between interacting partners needs not be symmetric and the level of mutual interoperability knowledge (highest layer dealt with explicitly) needs not be the same when consumer and provider roles are reversed in subsequent transactions.

These considerations lead to the concept of *interoperability profile*, which is a set of interoperability layers dealt with explicitly in a given interaction (between a tacit and an empiric treatment). Some profiles can occur frequently enough to create a pattern. Examples of interoperability profiles:

- Value-chain, partnership, joint-venture and subsidiary, corresponding to the four symbiotic layers in Table 4.
- Service, corresponding to the Service layer but without the Semantic layers (which are tacit).
- Semantic service, which now includes at least part of the Semantic layers.
- Normative, which involves semantics but not pragmatics (used for documentation).

## Combining Interoperability and Enterprise Architecture in a Framework

How does the linear interoperability framework of Table 4 fit the multidimensional enterprise architecture framework of Figure 3? In other words, how can we combine both into just one multidimensional interoperability framework?

Figure 6 illustrates the answer to this question. The basic tenet is to recognize that interoperability, one of the possible concerns in the enterprise architecture framework of Figure 3, fulfills all the criteria, stated in section "A multidimensional architecture framework," to be promoted to an axis of its own.

The interoperability axis is orthogonal to the others and relates two enterprise architectures (one as consumer, the other as provider) in corresponding features. For simplicity, Figure 6 omits the Concerns and Evolution axes and considers only one plane (Lifecycle and Concreteness axes) for each enterprise architecture. These planes are generic, but they should correspond to the same concern in both enterprise architectures. Again, for simplicity, the details of the provider's plane are omitted but are identical to the consumer's.

The interoperability axis, which relates the two planes, has two directions: compliance (consumer to provider) and conformance (provider to consumer). This is an innovation with respect to other axes and stems directly from the dichotomy between compliance and conformance. This axis is discretized into the interoperability layers of Table 4, in both directions. For simplicity, only the interoperability categories are shown. The highest level is represented at the origin (the middle) of the axis, much like the origin of the Lifecycle and Concreteness axes in Figure 2 are represented at top left of the plane. What makes sense for any method is to start at the origin of the framework at the highest abstraction level and progress outwards by refining and detailing all axes.

Figure 6 raises some interesting questions, such as:

- Where should interoperability fit (in what perspective and at what concreteness level of the planes)?

*Figure 6. A multidimensional interoperability framework. Only three axes are shown and the provider has been simplified.*

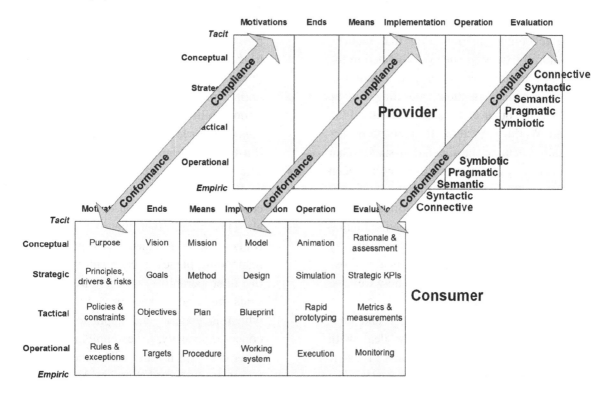

- How do we assert the orthogonality of the axes, or why the interoperability layers are not simply the concreteness axis applied to the interoperability concern?
- How do we cater for the fact that interoperability is usually not dealt with in an uniform and monotonic way across the range of layers? For example, the pragmatic, syntactic and connective layers are the easiest to tackle, with semantic and symbiotic typically left to documentation only;
- Where do we fit in non-functional concerns, such as security and legal issues?

To answer these questions, the interpretation of Figure 6 should be done in the following way:

- Interoperability makes sense in all cells of the consumer and provider planes (not just in the Operation stage) and should be done on a homologous base. For example, the Purpose (motivation, at a conceptual level) of the consumer to send a request to the provider must be compliant with the Purpose (homologous cell) of the provider in accepting and honoring that request. Naturally, the same needs to happen in the opposite direction, but now in relation to conformance. Identical reasoning can be made for other cells, such as Goals, Plan and Working System. If interactions actually occur in the Operation stage, what occurs is a consequence of what has been designed, which means that the interoperability must be considered from the initial stages of the lifecycle. Even the Evaluation stage makes sense for interoperability, by using the adequate metrics (such as those relative to SLAs) to measure how well the interoperability works.
- Although both interoperability and concreteness axes progressively deal with an increasing amount of details (as other axes), they refer to different issues. The concreteness axis measures the refinement in the development of the system, from fuzzy specifications (many decisions yet to take) to full details (everything is known). The interoperability axis is just a way of dealing with complexity, a zoom in or out of the interoperability aspects, according to the various layers. The concreteness level at which each interoperability layer is defined will certainly vary during the executing of the method used to develop the system, but the hierarchical organization of the interoperability layers can be the same right from the start.
- The orthogonality of the interoperability and concreteness axes is also the answer to the third question. Some interoperability layers are easier than others to deal with. Communication protocols, syntax formats and code entail the most well-known aspects, with semantics and organizational issues typically dealt with in a tacit (implicitly assumed) or empiric (based on existing specifications, such as standards) way. The framework must be able to express this reality, because the designers are unable to specify everything at once and intermediate versions must be workable until improvements can be made. Each interoperability layer can be specified at any concreteness level, from tacit to empiric, as illustrated by Figure 6.
- The enterprise architecture framework of Figure 3 includes one plane for each concern, be it functional or non-functional. This means that the interoperability framework interconnects each pair of corresponding planes in each enterprise with the interoperability axis. Figure 6 represents only one of these pair of planes, but which is generic and applicable to any concern. Security, for example, is like any other concern: it must follow the lifecycle stages, be described at various levels of de-

tails and respect the compliance and conformance rules as described above, otherwise interoperability will not be possible in a secure way. Equivalent reasoning can be made about legal issues, including regulatory compliance, or any other concern.

## Interoperability Maturity Model

The main purpose of an interoperability maturity model is to express how well a given enterprise explores the potential of interoperability when interacting with another enterprise. This is typically done in a simple scale, from not being able to interoperate at all to full knowledge of the partner's characteristics relevant to interoperation.

Table 2, in the Background section, summarizes several existing maturity models, which typically use five levels. The number of levels used to discretize the maturity of an enterprise interaction is really not that important. The relevant aspect is that each level brings something substantially new and that the granularity of the levels is not so fine or so coarse that discrimination between levels becomes doubtful or difficult.

In our framework, the maturity level of an enterprise interaction expresses how high it climbed the ladder of interoperability layers of Table 4 before tackling layers at the tacit level. Recall that all layers are always present, although some are dealt with empirically and others tacitly, at the lower

and upper extremes of the range, respectively. This means that the interoperability categories in Table 4 provide a natural classification of maturity level, in a scale of six levels, without the need to resort to a different set of level names. Table 5 expresses this scale. A given interaction is classified in the highest level that it deals with explicitly. If needed, the layers of interoperability in Table 4 provide a refinement of this scale.

The maturity of interoperability is also an expression of the degree attained in the relationship between several fundamental concepts, namely:

- The enterprise architecture is the main architectural component, which defines the enterprises that need to interoperate.
- The interoperability framework provides a means by which the enterprise architectures can be analyzed and systematized from the point of view of their interaction.
- The method (described in the next section) to use the framework to achieve interoperability between two enterprise architectures.

The fact that Table 5 mimics the Category column of Figure 4 is no coincidence. True enterprise integration, up to the highest abstraction levels, can only be achieved through proper design or adaptation of the enterprise architectures, by using a framework and methd such as those proposed in

*Table 5. Interoperability maturity levels*

| Level | Name | Description |
|---|---|---|
| 5 | Symbiotic | Partners understand the nature of the interaction and the intent, purpose and goals of the interlocutor |
| 4 | Pragmatic | Partners are able to specify their reaction to messages and transactions |
| 3 | Semantic | Partners understand the meaning of the a message and reason on it, but not the reaction of the interlocutor to it |
| 2 | Syntactic | Partners can only understand the structure of the messages, but not the meaning of its components |
| 1 | Connective | Partners can exchange messages, but do not understand the format or meaning of their content |
| 0 | Incompatible | There is no compliance and conformance at any level, not even basic communication protocols |

this chapter, which consider all the main aspects and dimensions involved right from the motivations (even before the conception and design) and not as an afterthought solution.

The linear structure of Table 5, with just one value, is a simplification of what the framework can provide. Looking at the maturity concept as an assessment indicator, we could define a more elaborate maturity model, with one indicator for each of the axes in the framework. For simplicity, this is not done in this chapter.

## THE METHOD TO ACHIEVE INTEROPERABILITY

A method is needed to exercise the multidimensional interoperability framework, with the goal of designing, implementing or improving the interaction between two enterprises. The basic goal is to move every axis from its origin (essentially, ideas) to the other extreme, where everything is refined and established, eventually recycling the design through successive versions.

Figure 7 illustrates this, by representing the main axes of the framework for each concern. For simplicity, the Concerns and Evolution axes are not represented and compliance and conformance have been represented in the same direction in the Interoperability axis. The method is pictured as the path taken from the initial steps, near the origin and with very little detail (referred to as *start*), down to the last stages (Operation, Evaluation), full level of concreteness and lowest layer of interoperability (referred to as *end*). Unlike what Figure 7 seems to imply, this path is most likely not linear.

The method should be model driven, with the lifecycle as the main guide, based on the architectural and fulfillment loops of Figure 1. The *consistency*, *alignment* and *traceability* throughout these loops are fundamental. A stage $S_i$ must be derived from the previous one $S_{i-1}$ by adding further detail and turning abstract aspects into concrete ones, but maintaining conformance to $S_i$. This means supporting at least all the requirements imposed on $S_i$, forward propagating any constrains and adding new ones, while maintaining the ability to trace back constraints to the stage that took the decisions that originated them.

Figure 8 represents the front plane of Figure 7 and illustrates the possible transitions along the

*Figure 7. The method as the path taken along the axes of the framework*

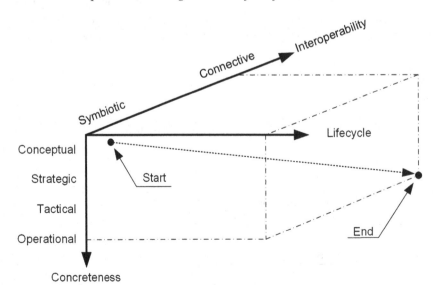

*Figure 8. Transitions along the front plane of the framework*

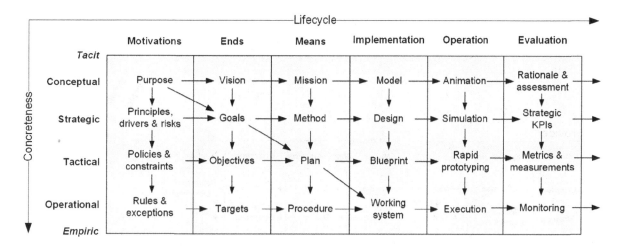

lifecycle, in this plane. Each cell represents one stage at a given level of concreteness and the arrows represent possible transitions between cells. Only rightwards and downwards transitions are represented, but the evaluation stage can loop leftwards to the motivations stage, as indicated in Figure 1.

Transitions are not limited to vertical or horizontal moves, not even to adjacent cells, but that means leaping over intermediate steps and therefore greater effort and less support (from the development method) in performing those transitions. Figure 3 exemplifies this by showing direct transitions from *Purpose* to *Goals*, *Goals* to *Plan* and *Plan* to the *Working system*. Usually, this corresponds to laying down goals and defining and programming processes directly from them.

We describe three of the possible paths in Figure 8:

- **Breadth-First:** Go along the conceptual level until the *Implementation* column is reached and then plunge until the *Working system*. This is the worst path. Initially all goes well, since we are evolving only with concepts, but when we want to detail we have no support from intermediate steps,

so we need to decide everything on the spot and on the fly, without a guiding map.

- **Depth-First:** Work as much as possible at the *Motivations* column, successively detailing from Purpose down to *Rules & exceptions*, and then follow right at this detailed level until the *Working system*. This seems the best path, since everything is thoroughly justified, but crashes into complexity, loses sight of overall picture and takes the risk of deciding everything at high level, unaware of whether the Means support those decisions.

- **Straight Line:** Traverse the front plane in a straight line (*Purpose*, *Goals*, *Plan* and *Working system*). By evolving along the Lifecycle axis at the same time that concreteness is increased, this is a tradeoff between the previous two paths.

Equivalent reasoning can be made when introducing the Interoperability axis in two interacting partners (provider and consumer), as illustrated by Figure 9 (which represents this axis on the right side just to avoid cluttering). Interoperability between the two partners must be achieved in every cell of the front plane and in all layers of interoper-

*Figure 9. Confronting the interoperability frameworks of two enterprises as part of the method to achieve interoperability*

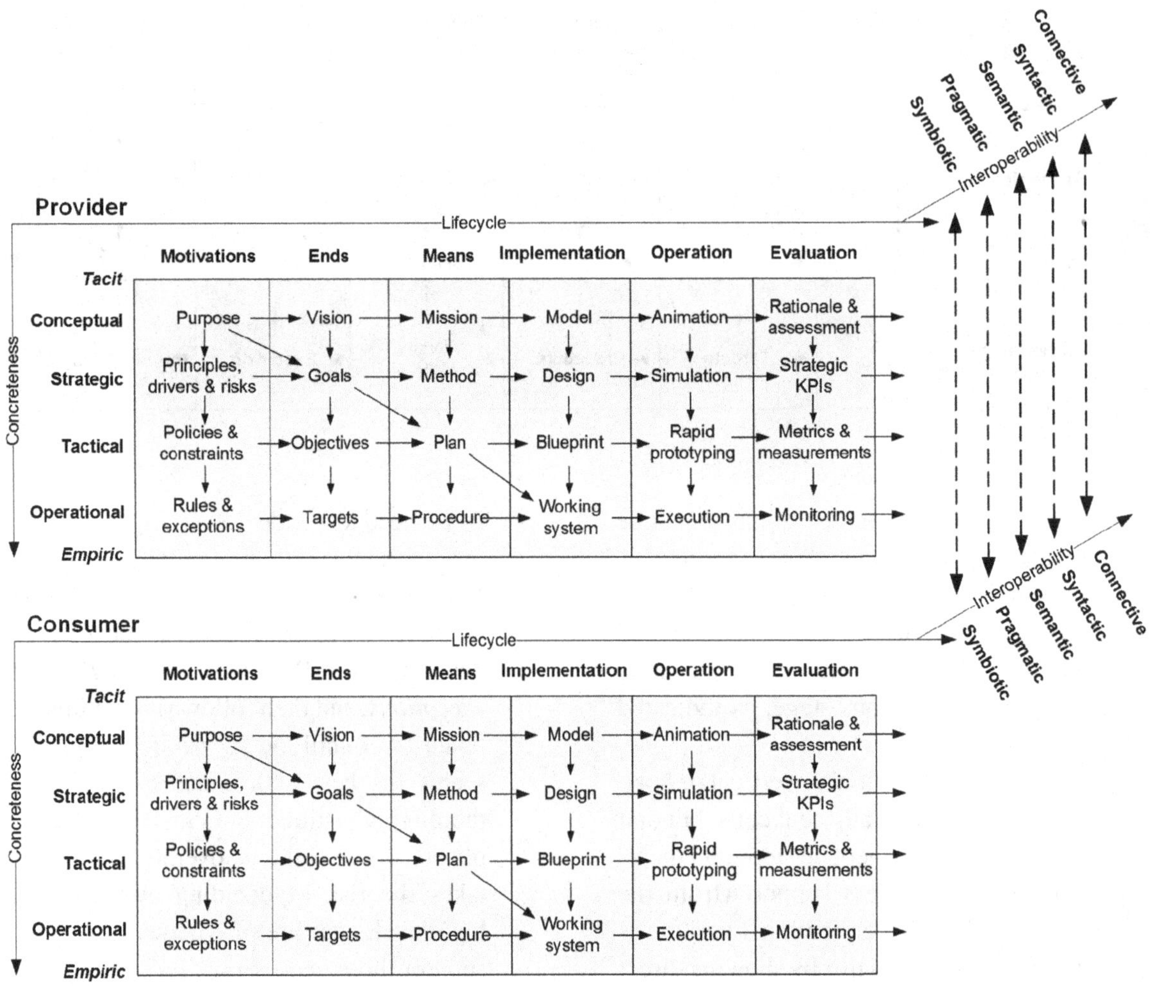

ability. The dashed lines express compliance in the consumer to provider direction and conformance in the provider to consumer direction.

Again, a breadth-first approach can be followed, by staying in the symbiotic layer until the working system is reached and only then dealing with the details of the lower interoperability layers. A depth-first approach, more radical, would involve agreeing on interoperability details right from the conception of the interaction between the partners. A more balanced approach would be following the axes in diagonal, refining them as design moves along.

In practice, the depth-first approach is not so radical. Since interoperability is a difficult issue that in many cases is built as an afterthought over existing enterprise architectures, in many cases existing integration technologies (such as Web Services and REST) take a central role in the method and impose on the remaining aspects, which usually works as a pragmatic approach but diminishes agility and the sustainability of interoperability.

Figure 9 is not the full picture. It should be repeated for every concern, functional and non-functional (see Figure 3) and everything repeated again along the Evolution axis, by iterating the lifecycle into a new version. Since two or more interacting partners are involved, the method would still have to be applied to each of them, but considering their interaction and the influence of each of them on the others (the choreography).

This is a complex scenario and the most adequate path to follow will depend a lot on the enterprise architectures and on the level of integration sought, but a reasonable approach would be to step along the following guidelines:

- The interoperability method should complement the existing enterprise architecture method, not replace it. The cells in the front plane of Figures 8 and 9 should be reasonably identifiable in that method, providing a mapping between the front plane and the framework underlying that method.
- Most likely, the enterprise architecture method will transition from the Purpose to the Working System cells. In each transition, consider the Interoperability axis. This means that compatibility between the consumer and the provider must be checked in cells such as Purpose, Goals, Plan and Working System (if the straight-line path is followed).
- Consider the interoperability layers as low as needed. For example, it is natural to check only at the symbiotic level that the purposes of both enterprises are compatible, but the goals will probably rely on different ontologies and the plan may depend on the architectural model (such as SOA or REST) used to achieve interoperability.
- Consider the most important concerns right from the start, but the rest should be introduced as needed and as possible. Complexity should be dealt with gradually.
- Use interoperability standards (such as Web Services) whenever possible and as adequate.

In practice, Figure 9 does not entail designing the enterprise architectures from scratch, but rather adaptations or the design of adapters and mediators. The method is applicable to a full system or to a subsystem, as well as to a design from scratch or to an adaptation that involves another iteration in the enterprise architecture.

The method also needs to consider the issue of what should come first when modeling and designing: conformance or compliance. Should a consumer comply with an already existing provider, adapting to the provider's interface requirements, or should a provider conform to a role previously specified by a choreography?

Given the discoverable nature usually attributed to the service paradigm, many authors tend to opt for the second option (Diaz & Rodriguez, 2009), in a polymorphic setting. Given a role in a choreography, any discovered service that is found to be conformant to that role can be used to fulfill that role. However, given the variability of software services, in particular if non-functional aspects are considered, how many services can we expect to conform to an independently specified role?

A more realistic scenario, even in a distributed context, considers that designing a system is a combination of top-down and bottom-up strategies, in which the expectations of the system have to be matched against and mapped onto already existing subsystems and the services they offer, with new services needed when there is no match or mapping. This means that conformance (bottom-up) and compliance (top-down) have to be dealt with together, in an overall strategy that constitutes the art and science of design.

## COMPARISON WITH OTHER INTEROPERABILITY FRAMEWORKS

The usefulness of any framework lies in its expressive power. It should be able to describe any instantiation of the problem domain for which it has been conceived. The objective of this section is to show how several interoperability frameworks can be mapped onto ours and be described by it. Although not an exhaustive exercise, it gives a hint on how these mappings can be undertaken.

We start with the frameworks that express a linear perspective of interoperability, such as those described by Table 1. This table presents one dimension of level of detail, from high-level and abstract to low-level and concrete. This suggests a vertical composition mechanism, in which each layer is composed of artifacts in the layers below it. However, the following difficulties arise:

- Composition alone is not sufficient to fully describe a layer in terms of the artifacts in lower layers, particularly in the higher layers (social, cultural, ethical, legal, etc.).
- Not all interoperability layers are dealt with at the same time. Some are more dynamic and pertain to operation time, whereas others are more static and must be dealt with at conception or design time.
- An enterprise (or its subsystem relevant to interoperability) is not a monolithic artifact with a single facet. It has several slants and aspects, under which interoperability may need differentiated treatment. This is usually the case of non-functional aspects, such as reliability, security and context-oriented behavior.

Multidimensional interoperability frameworks, such as those mentioned in the Background section, have appeared to cater for this diversity and variability. Some give more relevance to enterprise architecture than others do, but most are heavily influenced by the interoperability problem-solving issue, which corresponds to the method of making two enterprises or services interoperable. In a way, these frameworks start from the real world, in a set of contexts and domains, identify which types of artifacts need to be made interoperable and conceive an architectural space of dimensions oriented towards the problems to be solved in those contexts and domains.

Our approach is different, guided by the following principles:

- To consider the interoperability as a generic system problem, context and domain independent, but contemplating interacting systems of arbitrarily high complexity, such as enterprises.
- To introduce real world contexts and domains as instantiations of the generic interoperability problem, by not only using the provisions of the framework itself (dimensions, namely Concerns) but also the method that exercises it, to solve a given problem.
- To clearly separate the framework (the organization and classification scheme of the various aspects of the enterprises that are relevant to interoperability) from the method (the plan to make two or more enterprises interoperable). In this chapter we focus on the framework, although the method is generically described.
- To elect the enterprise architecture as the foundation ground for interoperability, by starting with a set of orthogonal dimensions, as illustrated by Figure 3, with life-cycle stages and levels of concreteness as the main structuring guidelines.
- To organize interoperability as a mapping from one enterprise architecture to another, as expressed by Figure 6. In other words, each interoperability issue arises from the need to relate the corresponding issues of two interacting enterprises.
- To separate clearly what is relevant to the interoperability mechanism proper, in a domain independent way (which corresponds to understanding the intent, content and transfer mechanism of a message, as well as the reaction of the interlocutor, in the context of a generic transaction), from

what is domain specific (such as social, cultural, ethical and legal issues).

- To separate clearly the roles of consumer and provider in an interaction, which discriminates compliance from conformance, instead of considering generic, symmetric relationships.

Under these principles, the mapping of the interoperability frameworks of Table 1 in our framework is done essentially in the following way:

- OSI (1994), C4IF (Peristeras & Tarabanis, 2006), Lewis (2008) and LCIM (Wang, Tolk, & Wang, 2009) have a straightforward mapping, with essentially similar layers at the lower levels and with our framework detailed the higher layers in these frameworks. In the case of LCIM, the Dynamic layer corresponds roughly to the Symbiotic category of layers in Table 4 and the Conceptual layer, dealing with documentation, is mapped onto the left side of the Lifecycle-Concreteness plane of our framework, in which the system is designed and models and documentation are produced.
- In the framework of Stamper (1996), there is a good mapping to our framework up to the Pragmatics layer. The Social world layer is mapped onto a plane in the Concerns axis of our framework.
- The political and legal layers in the European Interoperability Framework (EIF, 2010) are also mapped onto planes in the Concerns axis.
- Something similar happens in the case of the framework of Monfelt (2011). The Legal, Ethical and Cultural layers are mapped onto planes in the Concerns axis. The SWOT analysis belongs to the method, which means that it is best mapped onto our method, by performing the analysis in the context of several Concerns planes.

The mapping of the multidimensional frameworks can be done in the following way:

- In the ATHENA framework (Berre *et al*, 2007), the conceptual integration, with the levels of enterprise/business, process, service and information/data, has a straightforward mapping onto our interoperability layers, in Table 4. The application and technical integrations, however, involve activities that are best mapped onto the method, not the framework.
- In the framework proposed by Chen (2006), the concerns dimension (business, processes, services and data) correspond to our interoperability dimension and are mapped onto layers in Table 4. The other dimensions, the barriers to overcome and the approach taken fit better the method than the framework. Nevertheless, there is an interesting mapping from the types of approach to the higher layers of our interoperability dimension, in Table 4. These types are integrated (a common format is used by all systems), unified (common goals and semantic mapping) and federated (there may be common goals and ontology, but each system must adapt to others dynamically, without any imposed model). These can be mapped onto interoperability profiles and therefore be described by the framework prior to exercising the method.
- The SOSI framework (Morris *et al*, 2004) include the lifecycle dimension, which can be easily mapped onto the Lifecycle dimension in our framework.
- The framework of Ostadzadeh & Fereidoon (2011) is based on an enterprise architecture framework, like our own. The Zachman questions map partly onto the Lifecycle stages (Motivations is why, Ends is what, Means is how) and partly onto the Concerns axis (who, where and when). The layered interoperability concerns

(contextual, conceptual, logical, physical and out-of-context) map directly onto our interoperability layers in Table 4 and the remaining dimension is identical to SOSI (expressing the lifecycle), with the addition of a cultural aspect, which we map onto a Concerns plane.

The project ENSEMBLE (Agostinho, Jardim-Goncalves, & Steiger-Garcao, 2011) follows a methodology to establish a scientific base for enterprise interoperability, rather than an interoperability framework. In this respect, the ENSEMBLE's approach is complementary to ours, coming from the opposite direction. Essentially, it adopts a top-down approach by gathering information on the real world domains that pose interoperability problems and then deriving the scientific base to solve them. Our approach, bottom-up, entails establishing a rationale for what interoperability is, as an universal concept relating entities of any level of complexity and domain, and deriving a generic framework that allows us to structure and to organize the aspects in real world interoperability problems, as a tool that can be a precious aid in solving them.

The main challenges in the top-down approach are:

- To deal with the massive scale of interoperability problems.
- To be able to identify which are the basic interoperability elements (the equivalent of a periodic table) that underlie them all in an orthogonal way.
- To derive (de)composition patterns that are able to map typical problems onto those elements, so that a set of commonly used techniques can be applied to solve them.

ENSEMBLE has defined twelve scientific areas of interoperability (Popplewell, 2011), which can be organized into the following categories:

- Data, process, rules and knowledge have a domain and system independent perspective.
- Objects, software, services, cloud and eco-systems are domain independent but refer to systems, with interoperability problems similar to any other system, albeit with varying levels of complexity.
- The cultural, social networks and electronic identity levels are domain dependent, with social networks including a system perspective.

Other areas in which interoperability is relevant and encompassing, such as security, need to fit in and increase the complexity of the scenario.

This variability emphasizes the need to separate concerns, striving for the orthogonality between the meaning of each layer of interoperability, area of concern, domain and class of systems. Therefore, we see the top-down approach as an application-driven effort that ensures that the interoperability problem scenario is complete and the bottom-up approach as an effort to structure that scenario by identifying the orthogonal aspects involved.

The taxonomy developed by the ENSEMBLE project can be mapped onto our framework in the following way:

- Domain independent interoperability areas (data, process, rule and knowledge) map directly onto interoperability layers in Table 4.
- System/module oriented areas (objects, software, services, cloud and ecosystems) map onto system/module composition (Concreteness axis) and interoperability layers.
- Domain oriented areas (cultural, social networks and electronic identity), as well as applications and issues in the three main neighboring domains (social, applied and formal sciences) map onto the Concerns axis.

- Of the scientific elements of interoperability:
  - Semantics maps onto the corresponding category in Table 4.
  - Orchestration maps onto the pragmatic and particularly the symbiotic layers.
  - Models and tools map onto interoperability profiles, which may or may not include actual message exchange, depending on whether the goal is just to have format compatibility (compliance and conformance) or actual interoperation, in tools.

## A SIMPLE WRAP-UP EXAMPLE

Figure 10 considers a simple example of a collaboration between several partners to achieve some common goals. A customer requests a quote for a product from a seller, places an order, pays for it and picks it up at a local distributor when it arrives. The collaboration involves the customer, the seller, the distributor and a transporter. We assume that the customer is a company and elec-

tronic interaction is done by services that have their API available.

The typical way of solving the interoperability problem in such an example entails the following:

- The customer searches for a seller providing the product(s) needed.
- The customer downloads the seller's API (in either SOA or REST) and develops a client matched for it, as well as the necessary adapter(s) to enable its enterprise architecture to deal with this client.
- If semantic information is available, the customer may use it to improve the programmatic treatment of interoperability.
- Same thing for the interface with the distributor.
- The higher levels of interoperability are dealt with manually, through documentation.
- If the seller or the distributor change something in the functionality of their interfaces, the client program at the customer needs to be changed accordingly (to reflect the new schemas).

*Figure 10. A simple example to illustrate the interoperability framework and method*

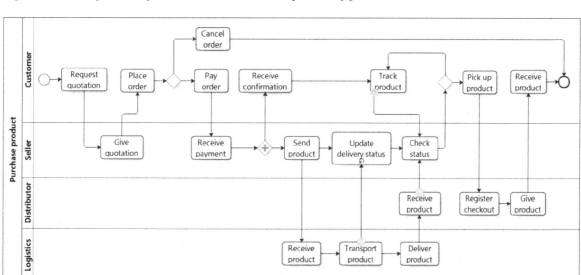

This is a classical view of interoperability as integration, in which the schema of the data exchanged is the centerpiece and partners are made interoperable for the full variability range of that schema, even if the interaction actually exercises only a fraction of that variability. This leads to unnecessary coupling.

The framework and method described in this chapter propose a minimalist vision, reducing interoperability to the minimum coupling needed and, at the same time, widening the range of partners with which interoperability can be established.

To illustrate this claim, consider the interoperability needed between the customer and the seller, in Figure 10. For the customer, this involves not only finding a suitable seller but also avoiding lock-in with that seller, by allowing the seller to be replaced by another with a compatible interface.

Current technologies, such as Web Services and the tools that deal with them, have not been conceived with compliance and conformance in mind, but through an example we can give an idea how that can be done. Consider the seller as a Web Service offering several operations, including one (which we will call getQuote) that allows the customer to implement its RequestQuote activity in Figure 10.

Program 1 contains a fragment of the seller's WSDL file, showing only the relevant parts for the interface. Only the operation getQuote is depicted, to keep it simple. It receives the specification of a product (the model and the seller's department it belongs to) and the information returned includes a quote for each product of that model found, with an optional boolean that indicates whether that product is in stock. A client is needed at the customer to deal with this Web Service.

Now, in Program 2, consider the equivalent WSDL fragment in another seller's Web Service, compatible with this one but not identical. Its getQuote operation provides the same overall functionality and has the same name, so that a syntactical interface match is possible (for simplicity, this example does not tackle semantics).

It also obtains a quote on the product, specified by a description and the product category it belongs to, and returns up to three pairs of product ID and respective price. The description can be made with one or two strings, so that brand and model, for example, can be separated if required, and the category is optional but supports two strings so that the product's division and unit, for example, can be specified.

These two WSDL fragments correspond to two different schemas and the usual way to invoke the respective services would be to generate two different clients, one for each service. However, by looking at both the WSDL fragments, we can notice that:

- The In element of the getQuote operation in Program 1, of type Product, complies with the In element of the operation in Program 2, of type ProductSpec. In other words, supplying a model and department with one string each is within the requirements of the operation in Program 2.
- The Out element of the operation in Program 2, of type ProductInfo, conforms to the Out element of the operation in Program 1, of type ProdInfo. This means that all the values returned by the operation in Program 2 will be expected as if they were returned by the operation in Program 1.

The conclusion is that, although the services are different, a client generated to invoke the service that Program 1 belongs to can also be used, without changes, to invoke the service in Program 2, as long as both getQuote operations are consistent in the interoperability layers above Syntactic.

Compliance and conformance are checked structurally (Delgado, 2012), in which complex types are checked recursively, component by component, until primitive types are reached. Corresponding components need to either have

*Program 1. A fragment of the WSDL of the seller's Web service*

```
<types>
    <xs:schema xmlns:xs="http://www.w3.org/2001/XMLSchema"
            targetNamespace="http://example.com/schema/seller1"
            xmlns="http://example.com/schema/seller1"
            elementFormDefault="qualified">
        <xs:element name="product" type="Product"/>
        <xs:element name="prodInfo" type="ProdInfo"/>
        <xs:complexType name="Product">
            <xs:sequence>
                <xs:element name="model" type="xs:string"/>
                <xs:element name="department" type="xs:string"/>
            </xs:sequence>
        </xs:complexType>
        <xs:complexType name="ProdInfo">
            <xs:sequence minOccurs="0" maxOccurs="unbounded">
                <xs:element name="ID" type="xs:string"/>
                <xs:element name="cost" type="xs:decimal"/>
                <xs:element name="inStock" type="xs:boolean"
                                minOccurs="0"/>
            </xs:sequence>
        </xs:complexType>
    </xs:schema>
</types>
<interface name="Seller_1">
    <operation name="getQuote"
                pattern="http://www.w3.org/ns/wsdl/in-out">
        <input messageLabel="In" element="seller1:product"/>
        <output messageLabel="Out" element="seller1:prodInfo"/>
    </operation>
</interface>
```

the same name in the same ontology or be mapped one to the other when reconciling ontologies. In the general case, compliance and conformance must hold at all interoperability layers, as shown in Figure 9.

The example of Figure 10 can also be used to argue that the multidimensional framework proposed in this chapter is better than one-dimensional frameworks such as those in Table 1, essentially due to the following reasons:

- The enterprise architecture and its lifecycle are always the starting point, guiding the development of interoperability in a model driven way. This is actually nothing new as a good practice, but the organization presented for the front plane in Figure 8, coupled with the rationale for the method, with the set of desirable transitions, provide a modeling map that will emphasize where the relevant subsystems fit and where in-

*Program 2. A fragment of the WSDL of another seller's Web service*

```
<types>
    <xs:schema xmlns:xs="http://www.w3.org/2001/XMLSchema"
               targetNamespace="http://example.com/schema/seller1"
               xmlns="http://example.com/schema/seller2"
               elementFormDefault="qualified">
        <xs:element name="productSpec" type="ProductSpec"/>
        <xs:element name="productInfo" type="ProductInfo"/>
        <xs:complexType name="ProductSpec">
            <xs:sequence>
                <xs:element name="description" type="xs:string"
                            minOccurs="1" maxOccurs="2"/>
                <xs:element name="category" type="xs:string"
                            minOccurs="0" maxOccurs="2"/>
            </xs:sequence>
        </xs:complexType>
        <xs:complexType name="ProductInfo">
            <xs:sequence minOccurs="0" maxOccurs="3">
                <xs:element name="productID" type="xs:string"/>
                <xs:element name="price" type="xs:decimal"/>
            </xs:sequence>
        </xs:complexType>
    </xs:schema>
</types>
<interface name="Seller_2">
    <operation name="getQuote"
               pattern="http://www.w3.org/ns/wsdl/in-out">
        <input messageLabel="In" element="seller2:productSpec"/>
        <output messageLabel="Out" element="seller2:productInfo"/>
    </operation>
</interface>
```

teroperability is needed. Interoperability is clearly not a mere operational issue.

- Making compliance and conformance explicit at all layers, in Table 4, but in an integrated way with the enterprise architecture, as expressed by Figure 9, reminds the designers of that enterprise architecture that no enterprise is isolated and interoperability is an integral part of that enterprise architecture as well.

- An enterprise architecture is not limited to electronic services, but includes physical resources and even human roles, which means that interoperability must be ensured in these areas as well. As an example, the products transported in the Transport process in Figure 10 must comply with the containers used, and these must conform to what the products to transport need.

- Another aspect is the overall choreography expressed in Figure 10. The role performed by each enterprise (as determined by its enterprise architecture) must comply with (as a consumer) and conform to (as a provider) that choreography.

The main conclusion is that interoperability and enterprise architecture are not dissociable.

## CONTRIBUTIONS TO A SCIENTIFIC BASE FOR ENTERPRISE INTEROPERABILITY

The development of a scientific base for any domain involves necessarily the systematization of thought in that domain. This chapter seeks to complement existing efforts towards this purpose (Jardim-Goncalves, Grilo, Agostinho, Lampathaki, & Charalabidis, 2013) by trying to discover which are the fundamental concepts underlying interoperability, much in the same way as Physics goes deep down to the smallest scale to understand the Universe in the largest scale.

In the general sense, interoperability stems from two conflicting goals:

- Systems need to interact to accomplish collaboration, either designed or emergent. Mutually understanding partners creates dependencies on others that hamper system evolution.
- Systems need to be independent to evolve freely and dynamically. Independent systems do not understand each other to be able to interact.

Enterprises are (complex) systems and have exactly the same issue, with the additional problem that agility (which translates to fast evolution) is a critical requirement to the survival of even the largest enterprises. These are actually quite vul-

nerable, because their complex architecture has woven a large web of dependencies.

This chapter contends that, for systems in general and enterprises in particular:

- Compliance and conformance, expressed in Figure 5, are the two basic concepts that underlie all interactions.
- The basic reusable pattern is the transaction, as illustrated by Figure 4a.
- There is a set of primitive message types, as depicted in Table 3, which by composition can yield a set of primitive transaction patterns, which by composition in turn can yield arbitrarily complex choreographies.
- Compliance and conformance extend into non-operational stages of the lifecycle, in which case what is involved is the use of a specification, rather than message interaction, as shown in Figure 5a. Interoperability is then extended into the concept of compatibility. Regulatory compliance is an example.
- Partial compliance and conformance constitute a solution to the conflicting goals mentioned above, allowing to tune up the desired level of interoperability according to the constraints and requirements of the problem at hand. Only the features of the interacting systems relevant to interaction, as depicted in Figure 5b, contribute to dependencies. The principle of substitution, applicable here, shows that inheritance and polymorphism, typical of programming languages, is just another expression of compliance and conformance.

The importance of compliance and conformance can be seen in various examples:

- The fact that interoperability is inherently asymmetric becomes clearer and more explicit. In the literature, interoperability is commonly taken as symmetric and reversible, but this is just a consequence of the fact that an enterprise takes part in choreographies sometimes as a consumer, other times as a provider.

- Partial compliance and conformance reduce coupling between systems because less restrictions are imposed on the systems. This compares very favorably with an interoperability based on schema sharing, such as when using XML, in which interoperability needs to be maintained for the full spectrum of variability of the schema, even if only a very small subset of document types are exchanged.

- Sustainable interoperability is easier with partial compliance and conformance, because they support polymorphism and the substitution principle in a distributed fashion, as Programs 1 and 2 illustrate. The basic tenet is that, by reducing coupling to a bare minimum, all the remaining features are free to change. This increases the ease of design (the range of suitable interacting partners increase), adaptability (adaptations can also be partial and as needed), changeability (the features with dependencies on others are in a smaller number and more explicit) and reliability (if a partner fails, it is easier to get an alternative which ensures compliance and conformance). Delgado (2012) established coupling and adaptability metrics which show the benefits of partial compliance and conformance.

- Strategic alignment is usually seen as a requirement for enterprise interoperability and collaboration. Again, this is just too much coupling. Their strategies and goals just need to be partially compatible (compliant and conformant), not necessarily aligned.

- Structural compliance and conformance (Delgado, 2012) constitute a solution to checking system interoperability in a distributed environment, in which the lifecycles of interacting systems are not synchronized. Using names, even if belonging to a previously agreed ontology, is not adequate due to dynamic changeability. The trick is to agree on some upper ontology (an universal set of concepts), and then to specify everything (data, behavior, goals, and so on) in terms of composition of those concepts. Compliance and conformance can then be verified by checking, recursively, the corresponding structures of the components that are relevant to the interoperability in interacting partners;

This richness of properties justifies that compliance and conformance take a central role in the framework and in the method presented in this chapter.

## FUTURE RESEARCH DIRECTIONS

Compliance and conformance are basic concepts in interoperability and can be applied to all domains and levels of abstraction and complexity. Although work exists on its formal treatment in specific areas, such as choreographies (Adriansyah, van Dongen, & van der Aalst, 2010), an encompassing study needs to be conducted on what is the exact meaning of compatibility (compliance and conformance) at each of the interoperability layers of Table 4. Their formal definition, across all layers, needs to be made in a systematic way, building on previous work.

The interoperability framework presented in this chapter needs to be improved and made more complete, namely in the Concerns axis, to include relevant concerns such as security and common domain-specific aspects and problems, such as those uncovered by other frameworks and those being systematized by ENSEMBLE (Agostinho, Jardim-Goncalves, & Steiger-Garcao, 2011).

The method to exercise the framework needs to be detailed and structured in a systematic way, with a comparative case study regarding other interoperability methods being used today, namely those that are part of specifications promoted by relevant bodies, such as the European Interoperability Framework (EIF, 2010) or standardized, such as the Framework for Enterprise Interoperability (ISO, 2011).

The recognition of interoperability as a science, expressed by efforts such as the ENSEMBLE project, constitutes an opportunity to conduct all these efforts in a systematic and organized way, as a contribution to the establishment of a base to that science.

## CONCLUSION

This chapter has presented an interoperability framework, conceived with the purpose of providing a systematic way to organize and structure the various aspects that interoperability entails, with orthogonality of concepts, domain independence, large-scale complexity and extensibility as the main goals. Their achievement has been sought in the following way:

- Orthogonality, by considering multiple dimensions, each for an aspect or concern orthogonal to others, with all combinations valid and, as a whole, able to support the full spectrum of applications.
- Domain independence, by basing the framework on dimensions with universal applicability (such as lifecycle, level of concreteness and layers of interoperability), with domain dependent aspects as part of a concerns dimension, orthogonal to the others.
- Large-scale complexity, by contemplating not only recursive system composition (any system is a composition of other systems) and but also very complex aspects, up to the tacit, human level of understanding and reasoning.

- Extensibility, by allowing any concern (in the dimension of concerns) to be promoted to a full dimension, if its relevance and applicability breadth justifies it (criteria for this have been described).

The approach taken is generic and bottom-up, from universal architectural concepts to domain and context dependent concerns, as a complement to the more common approach, application-driven and top-down. For example, the European Interoperability Framework (EIF, 2010) has been conceived specifically for e-Government level services. The advantage of the bottom-up approach is that it leads to an open-ended framework, with an universal core that can then be instantiated and extended at will and as required in each context and domain, in which it can be complemented by a top-down approach that systematizes the problems in each context and domain.

We hope that this framework and the approach we took serve as a contribution to the establishment of the scientific foundations of interoperability, in particular in the enterprise context.

## REFERENCES

Adriansyah, A., van Dongen, B., & van der Aalst, W. (2010). Towards robust conformance checking. In *Proceedings of Business Process Management Workshops* (pp. 122–133). Berlin: Springer.

Agostinho, C., Jardim-Goncalves, R., & Steiger-Garcao, A. (2011). Using neighboring domains towards setting the foundations for enterprise interoperability science. In *Proceedings of the International Symposium on Collaborative Enterprises* (CENT 2011). CENT.

Berre, A. et al. (2007). The ATHENA interoperability framework. In *Enterprise interoperability II* (pp. 569–580). London, UK: Springer. doi:10.1007/978-1-84628-858-6_62

Bravetti, M., & Zavattaro, G. (2009). A theory of contracts for strong service compliance. *Journal of Mathematical Structures in Computer Science, 19*(3), 601–638. doi:10.1017/S0960129509007658

C4ISR. (1998). *Levels of information systems interoperability (LISI)*. C4ISR Architecture Working Group (AWG), Department of Defense. Retrieved February 25, 2013, from http://www.eng.auburn.edu/~hamilton/security/DODAF/LISI.pdf

Chen, D. (2006). Enterprise interoperability framework. In *Proceedings of Open Interop Workshop on Enterprise Modelling and Ontologies for Interoperability*. Academic Press.

Chen, D., & Daclin, N. (2007). Barriers driven methodology for enterprise interoperability. In *Establishing the foundation of collaborative networks* (pp. 453–460). New York: Springer. doi:10.1007/978-0-387-73798-0_48

Chen, D., Doumeingts, G., & Vernadat, F. (2008). Architectures for enterprise integration and interoperability: Past, present and future. *Computers in Industry, 59*(7), 647–659. doi:10.1016/j.compind.2007.12.016

Delgado, J. (2012). Structural interoperability as a basis for service adaptability. In *Adaptive web services for modular and reusable software development: Tactics and solutions* (pp. 33–59). Hershey, PA: IGI Global. doi:10.4018/978-1-4666-2089-6.ch002

Diaz, G., & Rodriguez, I. (2009). Automatically deriving choreography-conforming systems of services. In *Proceedings of IEEE International Conference on Services Computing* (pp. 9-16). IEEE Computer Society Press.

Dietz, J. (2006). *Enterprise ontology: Theory and methodology*. Berlin: Springer-Verlag. doi:10.1007/3-540-33149-2

Dietz, J., & Hoogervorst, J. (2011). A critical investigation of TOGAF - Based on the enterprise engineering theory and practice. In *Advances in Enterprise Engineering V* (pp. 76–90). Berlin: Springer-Verlag. doi:10.1007/978-3-642-21058-7_6

EIF. (2010). *European interoperability framework (EIF) for European public services, annex 2 to the communication from the commission to the European parliament, the council, the European economic and social committee and the committee of regions 'towards interoperability for European public services'*. Retrieved June 22, 2013, from http://ec.europa.eu/isa/documents/isa_annex_ii_eif_en.pdf

El Raheb, K. et al. (2011). Paving the way for interoperability in digital libraries: The DL.org project. In *New trends in qualitive and quantitative methods in libraries* (pp. 345–352). Singapore: World Scientific Publishing Company.

Euzenat, J., & Shvaiko, P. (2007). *Ontology matching*. Berlin: Springer.

Fewell, S., & Clark, T. (2003). *Organisational interoperability: Evaluation and further development of the OIM model*. Defence Science and Technology Organisation. Retrieved February 25, 2013, from http://www.dtic.mil/dtic/tr/fulltext/u2/a466378.pdf

Ford, T., Colombi, J., Graham, S., & Jacques, D. (2007). The interoperability score. In *Proceedings of the Fifth Annual Conference on Systems Engineering Research*. Hoboken, NJ: IEEE.

Gottschalk, P., & Solli-Sæther, H. (2008). Stages of e-government interoperability. *Electronic Government: An International Journal, 5*(3), 310–320. doi:10.1504/EG.2008.018877

Greefhorst, D., & Proper, E. (2011). *Architecture principles: The cornerstones of enterprise architecture*. Berlin: Springer-Verlag. doi:10.1007/978-3-642-20279-7

Guédria, W., Chen, D., & Naudet, Y. (2009). A maturity model for enterprise interoperability. In *On the move to meaningful internet systems workshops* (pp. 216–225). Berlin: Springer.

Haslhofer, B., & Klas, W. (2010). A survey of techniques for achieving metadata interoperability. *ACM Computing Surveys, 42*(2), 7:1-37.

ISO. (2011). *CEN EN/ISO 11354-1, advanced automation technologies and their applications, part 1: Framework for enterprise interoperability.* Geneva: International Standards Office.

ISO/IEC. (1994). *ISO/IEC 7498-1, information technology – Open systems interconnection – Basic reference model: The basic model* (2nd Ed.). Geneva: International Standards Office. Retrieved February 25, 2013, from http://standards.iso.org/ittf/PubliclyAvailableStandards/index.html

ISO/IEC/IEEE. (2010). *Systems and software engineering – Vocabulary.* Geneva: International Standard ISO/IEC/IEEE 24765:2010(E).

Jardim-Goncalves, R., Agostinho, C., & Steiger-Garcao, A. (2012). A reference model for sustainable interoperability in networked enterprises: Towards the foundation of EI science base. *International Journal of Computer Integrated Manufacturing, 25*(10), 855–873. doi:10.1080/0951192X.2011.653831

Jardim-Goncalves, R., Grilo, A., Agostinho, C., Lampathaki, F., & Charalabidis, Y. (2013). Systematisation of interoperability body of knowledge: The foundation for Enterprise Interoperability as a science. *Enterprise Information Systems, 7*(1), 7–32. doi:10.1080/17517575.2012.684401

Jeong, B., Lee, D., Cho, H., & Lee, J. (2008). A novel method for measuring semantic similarity for XML schema matching. *Expert Systems with Applications, 34*, 1651–1658. doi:10.1016/j.eswa.2007.01.025

Kim, D., & Shen, W. (2007). An approach to evaluating structural pattern conformance of UML models. In *Proceedings of ACM Symposium on Applied Computing* (pp. 1404-1408). ACM Press.

Kingston, G., Fewell, S., & Richer, W. (2005). *An organisational interoperability agility model.* Defence Science and Technology Organisation. Retrieved February 25, 2013, from http://www.dtic.mil/dtic/tr/fulltext/u2/a463924.pdf

Kokash, N., & Arbab, F. (2009). Formal behavioral modeling and compliance analysis for service-oriented systems. In *Formal methods for components and objects (LNCS)* (Vol. 5751, pp. 21–41). Berlin: Springer-Verlag. doi:10.1007/978-3-642-04167-9_2

Kruchten, P. (2004). *The rational unified process: An introduction.* Boston: Pearson Education Inc.

Lewis, G., Morris, E., Simanta, S., & Wrage, L. (2008). Why standards are not enough to guarantee end-to-end interoperability. In *Proceedings of Seventh International Conference on Composition-Based Software Systems* (pp. 164-173). IEEE Computer Society Press.

Loutas, N., Kamateri, E., Bosi, F., & Tarabanis, K. (2011). Cloud computing interoperability: The state of play. In *Proceedings of International Conference on Cloud Computing Technology and Science* (pp. 752-757). IEEE Computer Society Press.

Malik, N. (2009). Toward an enterprise business motivation model. *The Architecture Journal, 19*, 10–16.

Minoli, D. (2008). *Enterprise architecture A to Z.* Boca Raton, FL: Auerbach Publications. doi:10.1201/9781420013702

Monfelt, Y., Pilemalm, S., Hallberg, J., & Yngström, L. (2011). The 14-layered framework for including social and organizational aspects in security management. *Information Management & Computer Security, 19*(2), 124–133. doi:10.1108/09685221111143060

Morris, E., et al. (2004). *System of systems interoperability (SOSI), final report* (Report No. CMU/SEI-2004-TR-004). Carnegie Mellon Software Engineering Institute. Retrieved February 25, 2013, from http://www.sei.cmu.edu/reports/04tr004.pdf

Oguz, F., & Sengün, A. (2011). Mystery of the unknown: Revisiting tacit knowledge in the organizational literature. *Journal of Knowledge Management, 15*(3), 445–461. doi:10.1108/13673271111137420

Open Group. (2009). *TOGAF version 9 – The open group architecture framework (TOGAF).* The Open Group.

Ostadzadeh, S., & Fereidoon, S. (2011). An architectural framework for the improvement of the ultra-large-scale systems interoperability. In *Proceedings of International Conference on Software Engineering Research and Practice.* Las Vegas, NV: Academic Press.

Peristeras, V., & Tarabanis, K. (2006). The connection, communication, consolidation, collaboration interoperability framework (C4IF) for information systems interoperability. *International Journal of Interoperability in Business Information Systems, 1*(1), 61–72.

Popplewell, K. (2011). Towards the definition of a science base for enterprise interoperability: A European perspective. *Journal of Systemics, Cybernetics, and Informatics, 9*(5), 6–11.

Sowa, J., & Zachman, J. (1992). Extending and formalizing the framework for information systems. *IBM Systems Journal, 31*(3), 590–616. doi:10.1147/sj.313.0590

Stamper, R. (1996). Signs, information, norms and systems. In Signs of work (pp. 349–397). Berlin, Germany: de Gruyter.

Wang, W., Tolk, A., & Wang, W. (2009). The levels of conceptual interoperability model: Applying systems engineering principles to M&S. In *Proceedings of Spring Simulation Multiconference.* San Diego, CA: Society for Computer Simulation International.

Weber-Jahnke, J., Peyton, L., & Topaloglou, T. (2012). eHealth system interoperability. *Information Systems Frontiers, 14*(1), 1–3. doi:10.1007/s10796-011-9319-8

Winter, R., & Aier, S. (2011). How are enterprise architecture design principles used? In *Proceedings of International Enterprise Distributed Object Computing Conference Workshops* (pp. 314-321). IEEE Computer Society Press.

Winter, R., & Fischer, R. (2007). Essential layers, artifacts, and dependencies of enterprise architecture. *Journal of Enterprise Architecture, 3*(2), 7–18.

Wyatt, E., Griendling, K., & Mavris, D. (2012). Addressing interoperability in military systems-of-systems architectures. In *Proceedings of International Systems Conference* (pp. 1-8). IEEE Computer Society Press.

## ADDITIONAL READING

Athanasopoulos, G., Tsalgatidou, A., & Pantazoglou, M. (2006) Interoperability among Heterogeneous Services. In *International Conference on Services Computing* (pp. 174-181), IEEE Computer Society Press

Bell, M. (2008). *Service-Oriented Modeling: Service Analysis, Design, and Architecture.* New York: John Wiley & Sons. doi:10.1109/EDOC.2008.51

Berkem, B. (2008). From the Business Motivation Model (BMM) to Service Oriented Architecture (SOA). *Journal of Object Technology*, 7(8), 57–70. doi:10.5381/jot.2008.7.8.c6

Brocke, J., Schenk, B., & Sonnenberg, C. (2009) Organizational implications of implementing service oriented ERP systems: an analysis based on new institutional economics. In Abramowicz, W. (Ed.) *12th International Conference Business Information Systems*, Poznan, Poland (252–263). Berlin, Germany: Springer-Verlag

Earl, T. (2005). *Service-oriented architecture: concepts, technology and design*. Upper Saddle River, NJ: Pearson Education.

Earl, T. (2007). *SOA: Principles of Service Design*. Upper Saddle River, NJ: Prentice Hall PTR.

Earl, T. (2008). *Principles of service design*. Boston, MA: Pearson Education.

Fricke, E., & Schulz, A. (2005). Design for changeability (DfC), Principles to enable changes in systems throughout their entire lifecycle. *Systems Engineering*, 8(4), 342–359. doi:10.1002/sys.20039

Ganguly, A., Nilchiani, R., & Farr, J. (2009). Evaluating agility in corporate enterprises. *International Journal of Production Economics*, 118(2), 410–423. doi:10.1016/j.ijpe.2008.12.009

Gehlert, A., Bramsiepe, N., & Pohl, K. (2008) Goal-Driven Alignment of Services and Business Requirements. In *International Workshop on Service-Oriented Computing Consequences for Engineering Requirements* (pp. 1-7), IEEE Computer Society Press.

Havey, M. (2005). *Essential business process modeling*. Sebastopol, CA: O'Reilly.

Hoogervorst, J. (2004). Enterprise Architecture: Enabling Integration, Agility and Change. *International Journal of Cooperative Information Systems*, 13(3), 213–233. doi:10.1142/S021884300400095X

Hoogervorst, J. (2009). *Enterprise Governance and Enterprise Engineering*. Berlin: Springer-Verlag. doi:10.1007/978-3-540-92671-9

Juric, M., & Pant, K. (2008). *Business Process Driven SOA using BPMN and BPEL: From Business Process Modeling to Orchestration and Service Oriented Architecture*. Birmingham, UK: Packt Publishing.

Khadka, R., et al. (2011) Model-Driven Development of Service Compositions for Enterprise Interoperability. In van Sinderen, M., & Johnson, P. (Eds.), Lecture Notes in Business Information Processing, 76 (pp. 177-190), Springer Berlin Heidelberg.

Kurpjuweit, S., & Winter, R. (2009) Concern-oriented Business Architecture Engineering. In *ACM Symposium on Applied Computing* (pp. 265-272), ACM Press.

Lankhorst, M., Proper, H., & Jonkers, H. (2009). The Architecture of the ArchiMate Language. In T. Halpin et al. (Eds.), *Enterprise, Business-Process and Information Systems Modeling* (pp. 367–380). Berlin: Springer-Verlag. doi:10.1007/978-3-642-01862-6_30

Läufer, K., Baumgartner, G., & Russo, V. (2000). Safe Structural Conformance for Java. [Oxford University Press.]. *The Computer Journal*, 43(6), 469–481. doi:10.1093/comjnl/43.6.469

Loutas, N., Peristeras, V., & Tarabanis, K. (2011). Towards a reference service model for the Web of Services. *Data & Knowledge Engineering*, 70, 753–774. doi:10.1016/j.datak.2011.05.001

Lovelock, C., & Wirtz, J. (2007). *Services marketing: people, technology, strategy*. Upper Saddle River, NJ: Pearson Prentice Hall.

Markov, I., & Kowalkiewicz, M. (2008) Linking Business Goals to Process Models in Semantic Business Process Modeling. In *International Enterprise Distributed Object Computing Conference* (pp. 332-338), IEEE Computer Society Press.

Papazoglou, P., Traverso, P., Dustdar, S., & Leymann, F. (2008). Service-oriented computing: a research roadmap. *International Journal of Cooperative Information Systems*, 17(2), 223–255. doi:10.1142/S0218843008001816

Patten, K., Whitworth, B., Fjermestad, J., & Mahinda, E. (2005) Leading IT flexibility: anticipation, agility and adaptability. In Romano, N. (Ed.) *Proceedings of the 11th Americas Conference on Information Systems*, Omaha, NE, 11–14, Red Hook, NY: Curran Associates, Inc.

Perepletchikov, M., Ryan, C., Frampton, K., & Tari, Z. (2007) Coupling Metrics for Predicting Maintainability in Service-Oriented Designs. In *Australian Software Engineering Conference* (pp. 329-340), IEEE Computer Society Press.

Quartel, D., Engelsman, W., Jonkers, H., & van Sinderen, M. (2009) A goal-oriented requirements modelling language for enterprise architecture. In *International conference on Enterprise Distributed Object Computing* (pp. 1-11) IEEE Press.

Regev, G., & Wegmann, A. (2005) Where do goals come from: the underlying principles of goal-oriented requirements engineering. In *International Conference on Requirements Engineering* (pp. 353-362) IEEE Press.

Ross, A., Rhodes, D., & Hastings, D. (2008). Defining changeability: Reconciling flexibility, adaptability, scalability, modifiability, and robustness for maintaining system lifecycle value. *Systems Engineering*, 11(3), 246–262. doi:10.1002/sys.20098

Schekkerman, J. (2006). *How to survive in the jungle of enterprise architecture frameworks*. Bloomington: In Trafford Publishing.

Shroff, G. (2010). *Enterprise Cloud Computing: Technology, Architecture, Applications*. Cambridge, UK: Cambridge University Press. doi:10.1017/CBO9780511778476

Spohrer, J., Vargo, S., Caswell, N., & Maglio, P. (2008) The Service System is the Basic Abstraction of Service Science. In Sprague Jr., R. (Ed.) *41st Hawaii International Conference on System Sciences*. Big Island, Hawaii, 104, Washington, DC: IEEE Computer Society

Turnitsa, C. (2005). Extending the levels of conceptual interoperability model. In *IEEE Summer Computer Simulation Conference*. IEEE Computer Society Press

van der Aalst, W. (1999). Process-oriented architectures for electronic commerce and interorganizational workflow. *Information Systems*, 24(8), 639–671. doi:10.1016/S0306-4379(00)00003-X

van Lamsweerde, A. (2001) Goal-Oriented Requirements Engineering- A Guided Tour. In *International Symposium on Requirements Engineering* (pp. 249-262), IEEE Computer Society Press.

Xu, X., Zhu, L., Kannengiesser, U., & Liu, Y. (2010). An Architectural Style for Process-Intensive Web Information Systems. In *Web Information Systems Engineering* (Vol. 6488, pp. 534–547). Lecture Notes in Computer Science Springer-Verlag Berlin Heidelberg. doi:10.1007/978-3-642-17616-6_47

Xu, X., Zhu, L., Liu, Y., & Staples, M. (2008) Resource-Oriented Architecture for Business Processes. In *Software Engineering Conference* (pp. 395-402), IEEE Computer Society Press.

## KEY TERMS AND DEFINITIONS

**Choreography:** Contract between two or more systems, which establishes how they cooperate to achieve some common goal through a composition of transactions.

**Compatibility:** Asymmetric property between a consumer $C$ and a provider $P$ ($C$ is compatible with $P$) that holds if $C$ is compliant with $P$ and $P$ is conformant to $C$.

**Compliance:** Asymmetric property between a consumer $C$ and a provider $P$ ($C$ is compliant with $P$) that indicates that $C$ satisfies all the requirements of $P$ in terms of accepting requests.

**Conformance:** Asymmetric property between a provider $P$ and a consumer $C$ ($P$ conforms to $C$) that indicates that $P$ fulfills all the expectations of $C$ in terms of the effects caused by its requests.

**Consumer:** A role performed by a system $A$ in an interaction with another $B$, which involves making a request to $B$ and typically waiting for a response.

**Enterprise Architecture Framework:** Set of guidelines, best practices and tools to analyze, to classify, to structure and to describe the architecture of an enterprise.

**Interoperability Framework:** Set of principles, assumptions, rules and guidelines to analyze, to structure and to classify the concepts and concerns of interoperability.

**Interoperability Method:** Set of steps to be taken to derive an interoperable enterprise architecture from an initial problem statement or from an already existing enterprise. This is typically used in conjunction with an interoperability framework.

**Interoperability:** The ability of a consumer $C$ to be partially or fully compatible with a provider $P$. By composition, it can also refer to multilateral compatibility between several systems, interacting in the context of some choreography.

**Layers of Interoperability:** Organization of interoperability concepts and concerns along a single dimension, in layers of monotonically varying degree of complexity and abstraction.

**Lifecycle:** Set of stages that a system goes through, starting with a motivation to build it and ending with its destruction. Different versions of a system result from iterations of these stages, in which the system loops back to an earlier stage so that changes can be made.

**Provider:** A role performed by a system $B$ in an interaction with another $A$, which involves waiting for a request from $A$, honoring it and typically sending a response to $A$.

**Transaction:** Primitive pattern (predefined sequence) of messages exchanged between two interacting systems, one in the role of consumer, which initiates the pattern by a request, and the other in the role of provider, which honors that request and typically provides a response.

# Chapter 13
# Science–Base Research for Advanced Interoperability

**H. T. Goranson**
*Sirius-Beta, USA*

**Beth Cardier**
*The University of Melbourne, Australia*

## ABSTRACT

*Studies show that enterprises are severely constrained by their management structures, and that those constraints become more vexing as information technologies are adopted. This is more true as "interoperability engineering" advances; the enterprise is capable of doing simple, ordinary things better, but the form of the enterprise becomes less adaptive, less agile as external firms are integrated in using lowest common denominator standards. The net result is that we are worse off now because of the constraints of integration decisions. A radical advance is required, one based on breakthroughs in the underlying science used by enterprise engineers. This chapter indicates one advanced form of enterprise that current research could make possible and uses it to illustrate desired enterprise engineering tools. It then suggests an agenda for fundamental research to support those goals.*

## INTRODUCTION

Enterprises are the means of large scale collaboration, and so have been with us as long as civilization itself. What enterprises can accomplish is dependent on the technology used to engineer and manage them. Thus the history of such technology is punctuated by events such as Italy's introduction of arithmetic accounting (as double-entry bookkeeping) in the 13th century

(Devlin, 2000); before that, the 'technology' of representing value in the abstraction of bankable currency changed the nature of cooperative business. Just as language is a shaper of thought, certain modeling technologies can be seen as the driver of collaborative structure.

In the modern era, US military research introduced system-wide process metrics during World War II to integrate operations in large manufacturing enterprises. This shift depended on work sponsored through (what is now) Wright-Patterson Air Force Base into the science of

DOI: 10.4018/978-1-4666-5142-5.ch013

coupled process modeling. Defense sponsorship in the three decades ending in the 1980s in process modeling produced other scientific foundations that can directly be traced to the general productivity increase of world-wide manufacturing in those years. A vast array of accounting tools and best management practices resulted (Walker & Wickam, 1986).

Few practitioners, be they managers or enterprise engineers, appreciate this history and the food chain it demonstrates:

- First, basic scientific insights into abstraction, modeling and computation are developed.
- These enable an innovative enterprise arrangement or operation.
- Learning from this, practitioners and their suppliers develop engineering rules of thumb that are considered best practices.
- Enterprises adopt these practices in how they are structured, inevitably producing limits to capability and agility that go largely unnoticed because all competitors use the same infrastructure tools.

Starting in the 1980s, the Pentagon confronted some of these limits. As the world's largest buyer of complex manufactured systems, they were also the most far reaching and practiced enterprise engineer. The so-called Military Industrial Complex was then structured by some very restrictive laws, acquisition practices and legal precedents. The resulting structures were vastly more costly than they could have been, producing weapon systems that were suboptimal and in some cases systems simply could not be designed, manufactured and fielded at any cost.

One example was an air-to-air missile that was essential to military strategy. The US version was not good enough. We knew what to build; an adversary had a superior system. But the enterprise – as a manufactured system itself – had to be designed and engineered simultaneously with the product. Changes in the missile and the system to create the missile were bound in destructive loops. For instance, the integration of key components took much longer than the technology cycles of the individual components; meanwhile, the management processes used to keep track of changes and (partly) adapt were consuming 80% of the project cost (Winner, Pennell, Bertrand, & Slusarczuk, 1988).

In response, Congress funded a Defense Manufacturing Office at the Defense Advanced Research Projects Agency and work on the science base for what is now called *interoperability* focused on product modeling fundamentals (features, abstractions and logics). Most of this work was performed on classified aerospace programs and quietly transferred to vendors servicing the civil sector. Some was channeled through SEMATECH, the consortium addressing the enterprise interoperability crisis in the semiconductor industry. Once again, the food chain was clear: start with the science, the basics of abstraction and its calculus. Only then can significant change be reflected in tools and practices for the engineers (Goranson, 1999).

The ideas presented here were initiated in studies for a planned civil research agency to further that DARPA work, a sort of National Institutes of Health for manufacturing.

## A VISION OF ADVANCED VIRTUAL ENTERPRISES

As a part of the DARPA modeling research, we examined the notion of *agile enterprises*, and particularly the agility enabled by the *virtual enterprise*. A virtual enterprise is a collection of small organizations that are integrated, and operate so as to accomplish what is expected of a traditional enterprise (one comprised of a central, large prime contractor/integrator and a hierarchical supply chain of partners, subcontractors, suppliers and consultants). Virtual enterprises are of interest because:

- Most of the innovation in advanced complex systems originates in small independent groups.
- Most of the job growth in the US and Europe in the last 40 years has been through small businesses.
- Small groups are generally more agile, more productive and more responsive.
- Small businesses can be more flexible in supporting the lifestyle of its workers.
- Small groups are more comfortable for creative people.

The research surrounding such organizations was comprehensive. It identified several models of integrated enterprise that would be desirable, but are constrained by current integration methods. Some examples of these models and their characteristics are:

- Partners may be widely dispersed, have no conventionally auditable trust metrics and are unknown to each other.
- Partners may not exist in the form required for the enterprise, and/or be required to perform a task or use a process that is unknown to them, or does not yet exist.
- Partners are radically heterogeneous in fundamental ways, so as to enhance innovation and competitiveness. These operations are characterized by diverse information systems, models and business practices. Such diversity can also extend to fundamental differences in values, analytical methods and ethnomathematical insights.
- The goals of partners in the enterprise may not be externally quantifiable. Instead they might be participating for market share/introduction, brand building, experience enhancement, competitive blocking or even some seemingly irrational goal.
- A partner might be a virtual enterprise in its own right, with opaque internal structures.

- Partners might play unconventional roles. These could include the ability to intrusively modify the roles and processes of other partners, to add or exclude partners, or even put themselves out of the enterprise.

These characteristics enable *advanced virtual enterprises* that are highly dynamic and frangible. The dynamism may be a continuous optimization, but could also include radical product or service pivots, or major reorganizations among partners. The frangibility can be expressed as lowered costs of an expected dissolution, internal reorganization or graduation to a more conventional model if needed.

The anticipated benefits of these types of advanced virtual enterprises are:

- Reduced costs of failure so that more and greater risks can be taken, radically affecting some markets.
- Increased productivity, based on the assumption that self-organizing methods can reduce the ratio of the costs of management processes compared to processes that create direct value.
- Increased innovation, as small groups create more leverageable intellectual property than large cumbersome organizations.
- Improved upward mobility for organizations and individuals based on their actual added value.
- Greater opportunity for advancement in the developing world, as opposed to neo-colonial exploitation.
- Reduced political power of multinational corporations, making them less likely to compromise responsible government.
- More effective value development strategies emerge, as the methods of management of capital investment become decoupled from the methods of production.
- Happier workers, based on the notion that actual value added is better rewarded, un-

necessary institutional rules are minimized and group processes are more flexible.

- Improved national economies, based on the experience that small businesses are traditionally the basis of economic health (in the US, Europe and much of the rest of the world).
- A return to the coupling of liberal democracy and free markets, as market forces are allowed to do what they do best, without distortions from powerful oligopolies.

Internal studies and some pilot programs in the military sector indicated that radical improvements in innovation, as well as complexity of product integration, product cost and/or time to market can result when some of these advanced virtual enterprise concepts are empowered (by technical, legal and political means). A central requirement for these features was improved novelty in the information infrastructure.

Note that this notion of *virtual enterprise* is radically different from the concept of virtual enterprise (or virtual organization) adopted by a majority of EU-sponsored programs (Camarinha-Matos & Afsarmanesh, 2004). These programs emphasize a notion of:

- Generally collocated,
- Existing small businesses organized and coordinated by a prime contractor or similar agent,
- Who perform known tasks that are stable and clearly advertised,
- And which are prequalified for joining the enterprise, including harmonization of process and business models,
- With pre-arranged legal documents,
- To deliver conventional goods (compared to novel advanced aerospace systems).

Interoperability in this context is much the same as in a unified enterprise (except you use the Web more). It depends on preserving the centers of influence and the definitions of enterprise and operation. Disruptive models cannot emerge from this.

## RADICAL IMPROVEMENTS REQUIRE BASIC SCIENCE

Currently, enterprise integration practitioners have mature tools and techniques supported by a large supplier community. Interoperability is now overwhelmingly based on standards and other homogenizing techniques. When this is the case, maturation of the industry focuses on centralization. In the US, this focus on standards is indicated by the lead agency for integration being the national standards agency, NIST. While the European Union sponsors enterprise integration research, those projects focus on rounding out engineering tools within the existing paradigm, making existing methods available to small businesses or adapting practices for the Web.

In terms of interoperability, the current state isn't especially integrated. We do have better integration in some ways than 30 years ago, but instead of an entire, cooperative enterprise, we have independent islands of integration. A big company is an interweaving of three control systems, each using its own abstractions and ontologies, and using competing modeling abstractions. These three integrating ontologies permeate all operations simultaneously.

In the recommendations below, we recognize this need for true integration and propose a new set of abstractions (value features) that spans the three. This would have to be a new level of abstraction and would require some breakthrough in the science base. Such a new level would have to be a federating, on the fly set of abstractions that both makes sense by itself (what is the value?) and translates to what is used now by the people who need and pay for integration technology.

In the remainder of this section, we review some needs of these three relatively independent islands of integration. Following that, we extract grand challenges for science base research. (There happen to also be three grand challenges, but that is a coincidence.)

## Three Interoperability User Communities

Three kinds of islands of abstraction commonly permeate manufacturing enterprises. The first is *management by numbers*, controlled by financial managers, including those external to the enterprise. A second is management of processes, controlled by what in most enterprises are called 'operations managers.' A third is management of 'the product' and this is controlled by strategists, their product designers and, in turn, their engineers. When we talk of interoperability, we generally talk about interoperability within one of these communities.

Because the fundamental ontologies of the abstractions used by each community are distinct, deep interoperability *among* the communities is impossible. The best we have is a robust consulting industry that devises 'enterprise dashboards' that simultaneously displays information from each. Instead we need a new set of abstractions that span concepts central to each area.

Following is a characterization of the three abstractions used by each of these users of interoperability infrastructure:

- Financiers and their representatives within the enterprise want *accounting* abstractions affixed to fine-grained activities, across what is normally called the 'supply chain.' Integration engineering is accomplished by reducing everything to numbers, and these numbers relate to contractual requirements: cost, quality, responsiveness, risk and time to market. One could call these cost features and so on.
- Product managers and strategists use *product-centric integration*, based on consis-

tent, central product models. Such models depend on widely used standards that are centered on geometric and manufacturing descriptions, and have associated provenance annotations (to note process information). Historically, this kind of integration grew from the aerospace industry and transferred to the automobile sector. The underlying science base for product feature abstraction was created through usually classified US government investment, totaling some billions of dollars in discrete investment.

- *Process management* and *process feature abstraction* is where most recent attention has been given by technologists. The science base here was also sponsored by the US military through the previously mentioned DARPA office. The triggering requirement was to save the US semiconductor business, which had dipped below critical mass under Japanese pressure. Japanese enterprise integration at the time was heavily process driven, leveraging the science base of statistical abstraction and empowered by large stable keiretsu. The challenge was to develop a new generation of process integration engineering bound to competitive market forces as required for the West.

Primary progress on this third type of abstraction, process management, was accomplished through the SEMATECH consortium, accompanied by a Supplier's Working Group that included all the then industrial infrastructure suppliers. Again, the direct science base investment was significant, targeted directly at the fundamental modeling characterizations. At the time, we knew we would be cementing a third integration community and make our problem worse in the long run. But we were in crisis; the industry was saved when it transitioned from a focus on *product* features to *process* features.

(It is also the case that it was important to enfold the processes of building semiconductor fabs with the processes of manufacturing chips, but that is another story not central to the science base.)

Today, most enterprises use an ad hoc synthesis of these three integration abstractions (cost, product and process) with a robust consulting industry integrating the integration techniques using tools based on combined constraints.

Regardless of which of the three abstractions are used, problems with the current state of affairs are:

- Such integration is inflexible. It highlights the need for *agile enterprises,* as currently, the integration of enterprises takes much longer than the market and technology cycles that trigger change.
- Such integration is profoundly expensive, and the resulting management structures cost far more than the organizational components that create the direct value. Moreover, the investment is out of the reach of small businesses.
- Such integration is based on 'one-size-fits-all' standards that in many cases force expert groups in the enterprise to use tools based on abstractions that are less capable than those they would choose if given the chance to do their jobs well.
- Required standards take a long time to develop. Influence of the active participants and the weighting of the votes often produces inappropriate results, sometimes comically so.
- The result favors large, stable, inflexible organizations with strict centralized and hierarchical control: the 'Soviet model.'

Crusading legislators in the US Congress (primarily Republicans) have now made it impossible to advance the science base through government sponsored research, as it has been in the past.

The rationale is that if the free market does not value the work enough to fund it, the work must be inessential.

In Europe, large firms want to maintain the status quo while the sponsorship from Brussels is appropriately targeted at addressing the needs of small businesses. But the process is driven by engineers – those employed to create optimal tools from the existing science base – so no new science base research is supported. The rest of the world follows by exercising the engineering discipline, often expertly.

When weighed by these problems, the discipline of enterprise engineering becomes moribund and drags on the health of enterprises and the societies they were supposed to support. A radical improvement is required, similar to the disruptions enabled by prior advances in enterprise engineering and interoperability tools. It will not suffice to be satisfied with incremental evolution of the existing discipline. This will require, as in the past, a dedicated focus on the science base.

The nature of the advanced virtual enterprise, as described above, can be used to scope the needs for progress in the underlying science base. Such work should be performed by actual scientists and mathematicians, not users or engineers. Contrary to the successful template of past work, it should be open research, internationally based, and likely exploiting modern Web collaboration and publishing tools. As with most successful research endeavors, competing theories should be sponsored with competing efforts differentiated at the most fundamental level. The funding must be stable and long-lived.

## A PROPOSED AGENDA

We propose three grand challenges for the new science base. A new generation of productivity will result, should they be adequately addressed.

## Evolution of the Abstractions

Historically, integration/interoperability is a matter of:

- Adequately shared, structured information (cheap, correct, timely, trusted, useful…),
- That is relevant to the formation, operation and optimization (lean or agile),
- Of all functions in the potential organization that are to be reached.

In this context, integration strategies have evolved in two ways: by increasing the scope of what can be included and by becoming more relevant to activity at the local level. Both of these depend on the nature of the shared information. In turn, the nature of the shared information depends on the scope of the underlying abstractions.

In initial interoperability, the common denominator was *numeric abstractions* that took the outward-facing quantitative baseline – the cost to customers – and used it internally. Today this is called Activity Based Costing. Numeric abstractions have been built into contract boundaries and then extended into internal operations, addressing not only cost but duration of activity, quality, responsiveness and even trustworthiness. In retrospect, we'll call these abstractions *quantitative features*.

Enterprise integration depended on this form of abstraction for centuries, maturing in the period between the two World Wars.

Then with the introduction of numerically-controlled milling machines (and previously, looms) – and the sponsorship of wartime manufacturing research through the ICAM program – these abstractions transitioned from numeric to symbolic (in the computer science sense of 'symbolic'). The evolutionary path is easy to trace as the abstractions moved to what we can call *product feature abstractions*. The shift was from an administrative artifact to a goal-oriented artifact: what was being made.

Because the design and specification of these artifacts happened to be expressed in digitally created engineering drawings, the development of these abstractions was associated with the CAD industry and CAD-centric exchange standards. But that is merely a residue of the previous exchange technology – paper-based drawings. The effect was to move the nature of enterprise models – and hence interoperability abstractions – to the physical goal of the enterprise: the created object.

As with every step of the evolution of abstractions, the new one inherits all the attributes of the old. Even in the early days, product features were primarily characterized by numeric measurements (geometric and other physical properties) and by annotations that carried all the old cost, quality and other metrics.

We've already noted the power structures within the enterprise that require abstractions such as those related to cost and product. It is important to note that the abstractions create the power centers, not the other way around. Until the science base of product features was created, there was no agent in the enterprise who owned that enterprise-wide engineering function. The ability to harness that functionality came from the science base.

More recently, the abstractions and interoperability tools evolved in a different way, from an orientation towards nouns ('what we make') to verbs ('how we make it'). So-called *process feature abstractions* resulted, and this new level of modeling opened complexities and promises that are still being dealt with. The promise is tantalizing because when we integrate a wide-ranging enterprise system we are really trying to put the working pieces together in the best way. We are integrating processes.

Abstractions that describe how the components of the enterprise actually perform the work is the best way to engineer at this level. Once again, however, all the older abstractions have been clumsily accommodated. For example, a process feature is annotated by describing how it transforms or adds a product feature. (In the current state of the art, service attributes can be captured as product attributes. *Service attributes* can include be included in product features. *Brand value* is an example.)

The challenges to designing a new, more incisive set of abstractions are significant. The early, numeric, abstractions can be managed by simple arithmetic, matrix operations, statistics and linear algebra – all of which are simple to comprehend and code. Anyone in the enterprise knows what numbers are and how they combine.

Product features are more complex, but as they are statically-typed and noun-centric, the computational difficulties are relatively trivial, appearing only in scalability. Products are generally physical items that are easy to comprehend. The abstractions derived from them thus become only slightly less intuitive when they must encompass a pervasive vision throughout the enterprise. For example, aircraft are complex systems but the notion of an aircraft and its parts are easy to imagine. (Integration of software and pure service enterprises lacks this advantage.)

But process abstractions present more challenges, because everything is dynamically connected, and involves entire situations of elements. A minor change in one area can produce nonpolynomial-hard or non-deterministic changes in the evolving system. Such permutations populate incomprehensibly huge sets. A requirement that each process 'see' the integrated process model seems optimal, like the way each product agent can (theoretically) 'see' and evaluate its role in an integrated product model. But this is simply impossible from the scalability perspective.

Moreover, until recently, we did not have good formal foundations for process calculus and process ontologies. We are improving in this regard, but the complexity is growing faster than our ability to manage it. The dynamism is just too great.

(And this is before one addresses the problem that potential partners may be fine with modeling and revealing some characteristics of their processes, but unable to describe them all. The core competitive advantage of a business is often captured in these process models, if they are done well.)

What we need is the next logical step in enterprise abstractions. We'll call it *value feature abstraction.*

## Value Feature Abstractions

A value feature abstraction would be drawn from an external view of the enterprise, in order to express what customers really are paying for: what they value. Value feature assemblies would be related to product features, but they are not equivalent; a given array of product features would be only one way to deliver a portfolio of value features. As already noted, product features should include brand value, lifestyle definition and other soft deliveries.

Value features would be complex expressions of why an enterprise exists, or might exist. These expressions can cover influences of what we used to call stakeholders, and include societal values (community and human well-being, ecological sense...). Complex 'statements' composed of these abstractions should be decomposable into the 'nouns' of product features and 'verbs' of process features. These would be related by a higher level abstraction that characterizes how the relations themselves relate – a simpler way to understand this is to think of it as the overall 'story' of the product's purpose. The 'noun' and 'verb' process features should in turn be decomposable into quantitative metrics (cost, quality, agility...). Each decomposition will be lossy in the sense that some ontological richness is lost to gain computational efficiency.

A grand research challenge therefore, is to devise the types, the vocabulary, the ontology, the computational foundations and the mapping to existing abstractions for these *value features.*

## Ontology Federation

We've mentioned that enterprise engineering has traditionally depended on homogenization. The computational root of this homogenization was at first crude standards on data particulars, then on data types and relations. More recently, enlightened efforts have focused on the homogenization of ontologies. This was somewhat inspired by the genome effort. Ontologies are hard and big, but the assumption is that we all live in the same world and once we complete a logically consistent, computationally apt description of that world, then every enterprise component can just use that one ontology. Everyone will be able to understand everyone else.

It is probably unfortunate that the most robust ontology work is being done within the context of the 'Semantic Web.' The goals and assumptions that they started with are not friendly to the integration tasks needed by agile virtual enterprises. The Web assumes a document model with elements constrained by the limits of XML. This is decidedly unfriendly to process ontologies, and nearly impossible for the capture of soft value.

The current state of OWL2, the emerging specification for the next generation Web Ontology Language, allows for several versions to serve specific niches. This is because large or complex ontology worlds can quickly become incomputable, either for practical or theoretical reasons. In order to make searches practicable, Web ontologists have kept their described worlds small. Nonetheless, the community is now working to populate a very large collection of relatively small, *harmonized* ontologies for domains that share some core elements.

The underlying science for ontologies is based on logic. The capabilities and constraints thus result from decisions in defining the underlying *description logic* used. As it happens, research into description logics is very active and hosts many controversies. We are very likely headed toward a situation in which the constraints of practical computation produce innovative organizations that not only have different ontologies, but are built using different description logics. Certain organizations might choose different fundamental abstractions and structured ontologies because it actually improves their work.

Here is an example of why such heterogeneity might be desirable. We studied one large aerospace enterprise that imposed ontological homogeneity across all of its thousands of engineering functions. A result was that nearly everyone was ontologically constrained. For instance, the worlds of thermal and structural engineers overlap, but are distinct. One standard, the process specification language (PSL, ISO 18629-1:2004) tried to address the problem of federating ontologies; a 'process' in this program could be a process that maps one ontology to another. But it ran into foundational problems. A subsequent larger program in the US intelligence community solved some of these problems but uncovered others (Cheikes, 2006).

This second grand research challenge will address the creation of new logical tools to federate ontologies at a number of levels:

- At the user level, between differently populated (open) worlds that use congruent description logics.
- At the definitional level among differently designed description logics.
- In the context where different description logics co-exist, each dynamically evolves and do so in response to interactions among their components.

## Soft Reasoning

Enterprises are not machines divorced from real life; they exist in the context of human interaction, desires, rewards and emotions. Some part of the enterprise can be reduced to logical rules and these are the parts normally integrated. But there are large parts of any interesting, real enterprise that are opaque to current integration technologies.

We have found this in simple collaborative dynamics where personalities come into play, such as in cross-cultural teams where basic assumptions about life and work differ. It can also be found in any area where creative insight is an essential part of the work.

There are other so-called 'soft' areas. The most obvious are behaviors that are central to the interests of the enterprise that probably could be logically modeled, but aren't, due to cost or some other limit – perhaps legal, perhaps extreme dynamism. In spite of the elusive nature of these factors, enterprise components have to reason about them using incomplete information (Goranson, 1998).

There are also *inherently* soft areas, that probably could not be logically modeled regardless of cost. The best examples come from the automobile industry, where the consumer is as concerned about a lifestyle statement as servicing a specific practical need. Nearly all of the fashion industry, much of the restaurant industry, mobile telephony, and so on also deal with these soft issues. When these industries advertise their products, some of these soft elements are involved.

Most of the important activity that goes on in an enterprise – and nearly all the elements and phenomenon that cause problems with it – are in this veiled, soft area. This includes essential planning for the unexpected, which is necessarily soft.

Determining the nature of soft elements is a matter of controversy, and any stance taken can itself be termed soft. Yet humans reason about these things all the time, just not by means that can be reduced to logic. This is a well known problem among logicians (Devlin, 1998; Barwise & Perry, 1983).

The third grand research challenge, therefore, is to create a science base that can devise practical models to support this soft reasoning. Further, they must be incorporated into enterprise engineering.

Each of these three grand challenges are known, hard problems. Intuition suggests that as difficult as each may be, considering them together is impossible. However, initial work indicates that working on all together mitigates difficulties in each. For example, when soft reasoning is applied to ontological assumptions, it might simplify description logic federation. Value features can be seen as higher level federated systems, in terms of product and process description languages. When modeling features are determined at that higher level, a means of accommodating ontological heterogeneity can be part of the method of reasoning.

Focusing the domain on enterprises, and perhaps advanced enterprises (rather than general knowledge representation), may make these challenges more tenable at the level of the science base.

## SOME PROMISING APPROACHES

A good research roadmap will present the challenges without favoring solutions. But we also have to have some confidence that previously intractable challenges are now tenable. In the case of our three grand challenges, there is reason to anticipate success.

### Category Theory

Category theory is the formal, mathematical exploration of the structure of other mathematical objects and theories (Pierce, 1991). It is a sort of metamathematics, and it has exploded in recent years. With this surge, many new tools have become available to both scientists and engineers.

Category theory has always been applied to logic, but the use is now widespread, as a second generation of trained mathematical logicians has entered professional life. We now have a robust ability to characterize the universe of logics. For instance, we can propose newly complex modes of well-known logics; an example is non-monotonic reasoning. We can reason over completeness, as well as closure dynamics over ontological structures that have been generated using different description logics (Krötzsch, Simančik, & Horrocks, 2012).

We can also formally specify and study wholly new logics, like the class of geometric logics separately noted below. All models, including desired value features and ontological federation, depend on logical foundations. It is therefore possible to use category theoretic tools to characterize them. All of these developments have occurred within the past few years. Due to this exciting area of mathematics, we are now poised for similar advances in the science base for modeling and model interaction.

Category theory has also, by a parallel but different path, become the formal basis for a real computer science (Pierce, 1991). This began a few decades ago, but category theory was not applied to practical programming methods, because the languages and frameworks in use were ad hoc. Now, formally based languages have emerged that have practical use (Bell, 2012). Conventional languages are adopting category-theory friendly programming styles, for example functional reactive programming (Amsden, 2011).

Additionally, better tools have been developed to analyze algorithms regardless of their host code.

These two trends, in which category theory is applied to both logic and computer science, are intersecting in ways that can underlie new foundations for enterprise modeling. These include how data is represented and shared; how code and agents are validated; and how ontologies are generated and related. The very definition of interoperability is expected to change. Coincident with this will be new metrics, management techniques and visualizations, all formally based.

## Situation Theory

Logic does not easily model either the real world or how we reason about it. This is a well known problem in the logic community (Heuer, 2001). Examples of this shortfall in the enterprise abound, ranging from psychological factors of collaboration to cultural issues. Much is unknown in an enterprise, either because it is unknowable or because maintaining an explicit model is too costly. Some great percentage of knowledge is tacit and much communication is implicit.

The general approach to these problems is to ignore them, or to collapse soft elements to a quantitative surrogate. More careful work is rare because of the immense cost, but it usually involves model logics for small tasks and domains. This increases the interoperability problem.

The cleanest solution from a formal perspective was developed three decades ago at Stanford's Center for the Study of Logic and Information, in the form of *situation theory* (Devlin, 1995). For decades this remained a largely philosophical proposal with a mathematical basis. More recently, we have been given the tools to implement workable systems of situation theory.

Situation theory provides a way to formally reason over soft elements and dynamics. (Note, the use of the term 'soft' here does not mean 'fuzzy' as in fuzzy logic. That community has a concept of 'soft computing' which is simply the introduction of probability into ordinary logic.)

Situation theory uses two integrated reasoning systems. One system uses logic (in fact, this system can employ any logic, to any degree of sophistication, as presented by the target domain). This system is simply ordinary reasoning via logic, the sort of logic that can be supported without situation theory. The second, new system enables reasoning over contexts (or 'situations and attitudes'). It can be based in logic as well, but not necessarily so. The power of that system is in the way it tracks the relationship between a (logical) instance and the way it can be recontextualized in multiple ways. Thus, category theory provides a larger foundation.

This second sort of reasoning is similar to the way humans comprehend. We easily understand how a new context can alter the interpretation of an event, or the formation of an artifact. In explaining, we rely on the logic within a situation to convey our ideas, yet the structure of the explanation itself carries more information than those nouns and verbs. Studies on the difference between logic and narrative have described this phenomenon, whilst noting that the later lacks formal structure (Bruner, 1985). We are at the cusp of a breakthrough in this area. Many of the challenges of interoperability involve soft qualities, so we may see some corresponding new foundations in the science base.

## Geometric Logics

John von Neumann is known as one of the founders of modern computing, and indeed all the computers in an enterprise are von Neumann machines. He is less known by the public for some subsequent work. He observed that while logic attempts to comment on the world objectively, it is also of the world. Neglecting this philosophical stance has made it possible to omit important soft behaviors. For example, logic – and here we mean Aristotelian (or *first order*) Logic – sits well enough with most of physics. But it doesn't work with the spookiness of quantum physics, which itself has parallels in some narrative behavior (Goranson & Cardier, 2007)

Von Neumann took this as an existence proof that there are at least two formal logics in the world. One is used in communication and computation. He characterized the other, the 'quantum logic', and supposed that these two were special cases of a collection of logics (Birkhoff & von Neumann, 1936). He challenged future mathematicians and physicists to explore this area. The class of supposed logics are so-called 'geometric logics'. These also offer formal tools to capture softness that are not currently employed in enterprise abstractions.

Work until recently (65 years!) has been disappointing, but some surprising progress has been made in the last decade (Bruza, Sofge, & Lawless, 2009). The promise is strong enough to believe that some useful science base for interoperability will emerge with some focused effort.

## ADOPTION

Managers of engineering projects often ask about how to transfer the results of this kind of research to vendors or users. Often, the question will be framed in terms of how to *convince* users to adopt the results. This betrays a misunderstanding of what science is.

Our experience has been that *good science* finds a way to be used, because it solves problems. 'Convincing' is not needed; in its place is relief. The problem is therefore simpler: how to expose the results, the logic behind those results, and the methods used. This transforms the task into one of exposure. But for a set of challenges this radical, even that is significant.

Work towards a new science base for enterprises will cross several disciplines. It will take risks and be designed to be disruptive, so pushback and denial would be expected. It will likely use exotic, difficult mathematics. The work would be performed at a pure science level, but be rationalized in an applied science context, so different target audiences would be involved. No single journal paper – or even a small collection – would be able to adequately expose it.

This is one reason why we believe it makes sense to conduct the work via some sort of open collaboration, possibly via Web tools that have yet to be created. Scientific work – especially of a radical nature – is usually best conducted in a small, tight, focused group. The new science base might therefore bear a relationship to traditional research methods that is similar to the way future forms of enterprise will relate to current practice. In both cases, we can expect them to be destabilizing, and yet at the same time, able to describe and predict such dynamism.

# REFERENCES

Amsden, E. (2011). *A survey of functional reactive programming*. Rochester Institute of Technology. Retrieved December 29, 2013, from http://www.cs.rit.edu/~eca7215/frp-independent-study/Survey.pdf

Barwise, J., & Perry, J. (1983). *Situations and attitudes*. Cambridge, MA: MIT Press.

Bell, J. L. (2012). The development of categorical logic. In D. M. Gabbay, & F. Guenther (Eds.), *Handbook of philosophical logic* (Vol. 12, pp. 279–361). Berlin, Germany: Springer.

Birkhoff, G., & von Neumann, J. (1936). The logic of quantum mechanics. *The Annals of Mathematics, 37*(4), 823. doi:10.2307/1968621

Bruner, J. (1985). *Actual minds, possible worlds*. Cambridge, MA: Harvard University Press.

Bruza, P., Sofge, D., & Lawless, W. (2009). Quantum interaction. In *Proceedings from AAAI Spring Series: Quantum Interaction*. Palo Alto, CA: AAAI Press. doi:10.1007/978-3-642-00834-4

Camarinha-Matos, L. M., & Afsarmanesh, H. (Eds.). (2004). *Collaborative networked organizations: A research agenda for emerging business models*. Berlin, Germany: Springer. doi:10.1007/b116613

Cheikes, B. A. (2006). *MITRE support to IKRIS (Final report)*. Washington, DC: Mitre Corporation.

Devlin, K. (2000). *The language of mathematics: Making the invisible visible*. New York, NY: Holt Paperbacks.

Devlin, K. J. (1995). *Logic and information*. Cambridge, UK: Cambridge University Press.

Devlin, K. J. (1998). *Goodbye, Descartes: The end of logic and the search for a new cosmology of the mind*. Hoboken, NJ: Wiley.

Goranson, H. T. (1998). Soft mathematics and information dynamics. *Bio Systems, 46*(1-2), 163–167. doi:10.1016/S0303-2647(97)00094-4 PMID:9648688

Goranson, H. T. (1999). *The agile virtual enterprise: Cases, metrics, tools*. Westport, CT: Greenwood Publishing Group.

Goranson, H. T., & Cardier, B. (2007). Scheherazade's will: Quantum narrative agency. In *Proceedings from AAAI Spring Series Workshop on Quantum Interaction*. Palo Alto, CA: AAAI Press.

Heuer, R. J. (2001). *Psychology of intelligence analysis. Center for the Study of Intelligence, Central Intelligence Agency*. Washington, DC: CIA.

Krötzsch, M., Simančik, F., & Horrocks, I. (2012). *A description logic primer*. Retrieved December 29, 2013, from http://arxiv.org/pdf/1201.4089

Pierce, B. C. (1991). *Basic category theory for computer scientists*. Cambridge, MA: MIT Press.

Walker, L. E., & Wickam, S. E. (1986). *From Huffman Prairie to the moon: The history of Wright-Patterson Air Force Base*. Washington, DC: United States Government Printing Office.

Winner, R. I., Pennell, J. P., Bertrand, H. E., & Slusarczuk, M. M. (1988). *The role of concurrent engineering in weapons system acquisition*. Arlington, VA: Institute for Defense Analysis.

# KEY TERMS AND DEFINITIONS

**Advanced Virtual Enterprise:** A virtual enterprise comprised of organizations that has some of these characteristics: are widely dispersed; not known to each other; being asked to perform work they have not done before; they are not prearranged for interoperability; they have radically heterogeneous processes.

**Agile Enterprises:** Enterprises that are structured and managed in such a way that they can robustly be re-engineered in response to competitive opportunities and existential threats. Flexibility is in contrast, being engineered within a known spectrum. Speed response is often irrelevant.

**Basic Science:** As opposed to applied science, the early phases of investigation where basic abstractions are devised, upon which, theories and models are built.

**Category Theory:** A mathematical approach to understanding the form of mathematics by positing abstractions that capture structure and influence. A means of implementing situation theoretic logics.

**Enterprise:** A collective activity necessarily involving disparate components to satisfy a common goal.

**Feature Abstractions:** A set of abstractions resulting from basic scientific work that wholly characterizes the space of interest.

**Geometric Logics:** A class of expanded logics first proposed by John von Neumann in 1936, a class that includes quantum logic, first order logic and a large class of others, largely unknown. A means of implementing situation theoretic logics.

**Interoperability Engineering:** A component of Enterprise Integration within Enterprise Engineering based on a notion of adequately shared information.

**Ontology Federation:** The ability to suitably deal with the case where essential representation systems were built using different ontologies, and when those ontologies cannot be mapped to one another.

**Ontology:** Here we use it in its more formal definition as a formal representation of the basic elements and behavior of a world of interest, used as reference for a modeling and reasoning system. All computing systems have at least one ontology.

**Radical Improvements:** An improvement that by standard measure produces from an order of magnitude improvement (nominally of productivity) but at least double.

**Situation Theory:** A mathematical foundation for a logical approach for reasoning about facts in the context of situations and attitudes that changes the interpretation of those facts. An approach to dealing with soft reasoning.

**Soft Reasoning:** The ability to reason confidently over situations which are not fully modeled in terms of first order logic.

**Value Feature Abstractions:** A set of abstractions that characterizes all the elements, separately and composed, of the nature and work of the enterprise. By definition, these have a lossless mapping to product, process and financial features.

**Virtual Enterprise:** A collection of small organizations that are integrated, and operate so as to accomplish what is expected of a traditional enterprise.

**Virtual Organization:** A term used in some communities to denote simple virtual enterprises that are: known to each other, will be performing work they have done before, have pre-arranged interoperability and use homogenous processes.

# Chapter 14
# On the Scientific Foundations of Enterprise Interoperability:
## The ENSEMBLE Project and Beyond

**Yannis Charalabidis**
*University of the Aegean, Greece*

**Fenareti Lampathaki**
*National Technical University of Athens, Greece*

**Ricardo Jardim-Goncalves**
*Centre of Technology and Systems (CTS) – UNINOVA, Portugal*

## ABSTRACT

*In a rapidly evolving landscape, enterprises face unprecedented challenges and opportunities to become more innovative, competitive, and efficient. Despite the technological readiness and the abundance of solutions, the interoperability issues still afflict enterprises as they remain untackled at design time and without a systemic approach. To this end, the scientific foundations of enterprise interoperability shall structure the knowledge gained through pragmatic research in the domain over the last decades and more in order to avoid repeating research and missing opportunities for application. This chapter aims at outlining the objectives of the Enterprise Interoperability Science Base at its various evolution phases and documenting the key achievements made by the ENSEMBLE project. An overview of the actions to be implemented in this quest for scientific rigour is provided and the perspectives opened up through such an initiative are discussed.*

## INTRODUCTION

Today with the advent of the Future Internet, entrepreneurship has taken new impetus (EC, 2013) and contributes to formulating new societal and business realities. However, enterprises are still faced with unprecedented challenges at technological and business level, with interoperability among organizations and information systems remaining an insurmountable barrier. Despite the plethora of solutions available to tackle interoperability issues from a research and application perspective, the lack of scientific foundations in the domain seems to hinder unlocking its real value and full

DOI: 10.4018/978-1-4666-5142-5.ch014

potential to all its stakeholders, from researchers to industry and SMEs.

In general, science is an activity of extending perception into new contexts and into new forms, and is viewed as a means of obtaining what may be called reliable knowledge (Bohm, 1977). Typically, an underlying scientific discipline evolves along several decades in incremental stages before being established as a science. Over the 20th century, though, links between science and technology have indeed grown increasingly strong. As Martin Rees (2010) argues, progress in scientific understanding and technology has been synergistic and vital to one another.

In this context, establishing an Enterprise Interoperability Science Base (EISB) has been a long-sought challenge that was originally documented back in 2006 in the 4th version of the EI Research Roadmap (as mentioned in (Charalabidis et al, 2008)). According to the European Commission, such a Science Base comprises a new set of concepts, theories and principles derived from established and emerging sciences, with a view to long-term problem solving as opposed to short-term solution provisioning. The overall objective in establishing an EISB is to formulate and structure the knowledge gained through pragmatic research in the domain over the last decades and more in order to avoid repeating research and missing opportunities for application. Indicatively, the following open research questions have been identified as a priority among those to be answered with the establishment of the EI scientific foundations:

- Why is there so much effort wasted in the development of dedicated technical solutions for interoperability problems? How can it be reduced?
- How can we predict and guarantee the long-term knowledge and behavior of interoperability in engineering systems? In this vein, can the principles of complexity science, namely systems self-organi-

zation, be applied on dynamic business networks, to contribute to a sustainable interoperability?

- Why do certain interoperability problems appear to be very complex at first, but are actually not complex at all once we find a dedicated solution for them? How can these solutions be generalized and formalized to guarantee reusability and repeatability?
- How do we reduce complexity in EI? Can interoperability services be used as "plug-and-play" mechanisms independently of the EI level for which they are designed (higher levels such as business, or lower ones such as technical applications)?

During the past years, an EU-based initiative entitled ENSEMBLE ("Envisioning, Supporting and Promoting Future Internet Enterprise Systems Research through Scientific Collaboration") was kicked-off in order to contribute towards the establishment of an Enterprise Interoperability Science Base, through defining the concepts, analysing the best practices, synthesising scientific methods and tools from neighbouring domains, defining problem and solution patterns, affecting standardisation, so that enterprises can be systematically assisted in exploiting the benefits of interoperability at strategic, organisational, semantic and technical levels, yielding products and services of unprecedented quality, return on investment and sustainability. Working with expert researchers and practitioners from across Europe, ENSEMBLE has investigated in a systematic manner the scientific foundations of the Enterprise Interoperability (EI) domain and structured its underlying knowledge. To this end, the state of the art has been meticulously analyzed, an action plan calling for coordinated action by diverse stakeholders has been created and the activities towards 3 Waves of evolution have been initiated. Particular care has been taken in order to ensure that the design of the prospective EISB is inclusive and neutral, not biased toward or against any existing discipline or approach.

The present paper is structured as follows: In Section 2, upon studying the fundamentals in creating a science as depicted in the history of science and epistemology, the action plan of related scientific disciplines is analyzed and designates the perspectives and lessons learnt from their paradigm. In Section 4, the Enterprise Interoperability Science Base Action Plan is presented in detail. Section 5 outlines the fundamentals and theoretic foundations of Enterprise Interoperability giving way to Section 6 that summarizes the achievements accomplished so far. Section 7 elaborates on future perspectives through a set of supporting tools and Section 8 concludes this chapter.

## FUNDAMENTALS IN SCIENCE

A theory or discipline which purports to be scientific needs to present the following characteristics (adapted by (Curd & Cover, 1998)): (a) it has been more progressive than alternative theories over a long period of time, and faces many unsolved problems, and (b) the community of practitioners makes great attempts to develop the theory towards solutions of the problems, shows concern for attempts to evaluate the theory in relation to others, and is considering confirmations and disconfirmations.

Science aims at finding models that will account for as many observations as possible within a coherent framework. In learning a paradigm, a scientist acquires theory, methods and standards together, usually in an inextricable mixture (Kuhn, 1996). Knowledge in science is gained by a gradual synthesis of information from different experiments, by various researchers, across different domains of science; it is more like a climb than a leap (Stanovich, 2007). According to Curd & Cover (1998), what we call science today is a reasonably striking and distinctive set of claims, which have a number of characteristic features:

- **Laws – Natural Regularities:** Science looks for unbroken, blind, natural regularities (laws). Bodies of science, known as theories or paradigms or sets of models, are collections of laws.

- **Explanation and Prediction:** The use of law to effect explanation since a scientific explanation must appeal to law and must show that what is being explained had to occur. The explanation excludes those things that did not happen. The laws indicate what is going to happen.

- **Testability, Confirmation and Falsifiability:** A genuine scientific theory lays itself open to check against the real world: the scientist can see if the inferences made in explanation and prediction actually obtain in nature.

- **Tentativeness, Simplicity and Unification:** A scientist must be prepared to reject his theory.

- **Integrity:** as science depends on the honesty in the realm of data.

Chronologically, Kuhn (1996) distinguishes between three phases during a scientific discipline creation:

- **Pre-Paradigm Phase:** In which there is no consensus on any particular theory, though the research being carried out can be considered scientific in nature. This phase is characterized by several incompatible and incomplete theories.

- **Normal Science:** Begins when the actors in the pre-paradigm community eventually gravitate to one of these conceptual frameworks and ultimately to a widespread consensus on the appropriate choice of methods, terminology and on the kinds of experiment that are likely to contribute to increased insights. In this phase, puzzles are solved within the context of the dominant paradigm. As long as there is consensus within the discipline, normal science continues. Over time, progress in normal science may reveal anomalies, facts that are difficult to explain within the context of the existing paradigm. While usually these anomalies are resolved, in some cases they may accumulate to the point where normal science becomes difficult and where weaknesses in the old paradigm are revealed.

- **Revolutionary Science:** In which the underlying assumptions of the field are re-examined and a new paradigm is established since the significant efforts of normal science within a paradigm have already failed.

In conclusion, the Enterprise Interoperability domain could be classified to the Pre-paradigm phase due to its several incompatible and incomplete application theories which are accompanied with the growing recognition that many aspects of interoperability cannot be completely understood from current disciplinary perspectives in the information society.

## ENTERPRISE INTEROPERABILITY SCIENCE BASE ACTION PLAN

An Action Plan for establishing the scientific foundations of a domain defines a concrete set of activities that need to be collectively undertaken by stakeholders with different backgrounds in a logical time frame in order to eventually lead to the general recognition of its scientific rigorousness. In particular, the Action Plan of the Enterprise Interoperability Science Base aims at reaching consensus on a broad set of actions that will eventually lead to the creation of a reusable Science Base for Enterprise Interoperability, at proposing the stages of development, the so-called EISB waves, for the Enterprise Interoperability Science Base, and at deciding on the actions that

can be undertaken by all stakeholders in order to contribute to the EISB development.

In order to pave the way towards structuring the EISB (Enterprise Interoperability Science Base) and eventually taking up some of the initial steps of the EISB building process by conducting focused research in specific areas, the action plans that resulted in established science based domains such as Computer Science (Denning et al., 1989) and Software Engineering (Perry & Wolf, 1992; Redwine & Riddle, 1985) were meticulously studied. It was deduced that the EISB will evolve in three (3) different but logically connected "waves" of activities (Charalabidis et al, 2010; Lampathaki et al., 2012):

- **EISB Wave 1 – Basic Elements:** With regard to the "Infancy" and "Childhood" stages.
- **EISB Wave 2 – Hypothesis and Experimentation:** Which corresponds to the "Adolescence" and "Young Adulthood" stages.
- **EISB Wave 3 – Empowerment:** Matching to the "Maturity" stage.

## EISB Wave 1: Basic Elements

The EISB first wave aims at providing the ability to identify and describe problems and solutions in the field of EI, and establishing the research community, towards a sound convergence on the concepts in use. It sorts out the fundamental aspects of the Interoperability scientific foundations towards the formation of inclusive and solid definitions of the main issues of the domain, while it deals with the identification and description of open scientific problems. In more detail, this wave includes the actions described in Table 1.

Table 2 summarizes the objectives of the EISB Wave 1, together with the anticipated results that accompany them.

*Table 1. EISB wave 1 rationale*

| Core Direction | Description |
|---|---|
| **Foundational Principles** | Investigation of basic ideas and concepts, initial formal methods to describe problems and solutions, patterns identification, critical research questions. Formal approaches in this area include a collection of methods stemming from mathematical formulation, such as First Order Logic, Category Theory, Pattern Theory. Another set of formalization attempts includes management and information technology systemic approaches, such as Model Driven Architecture (MDA), Business Process Management (BPM) or even Service Oriented Architecture (SOA) elements. It has to be noted that specific methodologies are probably needed for each interoperability facet, that generates the need for diversified formal methods for technical, semantic, organisational, legal and policy issues. |
| **Concept Formulation** | Circulation of solution ideas, development of a research community, convergence on a compatible set of ideas, solutions on specific sub-problems, refinement of fundamental problems structure. This step will now have to work extensively on the definition of solution ideas for various interoperability problems, as they are defined in the previous step, while also developing and stimulating the research community – possibly through the use of on-line, Web 2.0 or similar infrastructures. |

*Table 2. EISB wave 1 objectives outline*

| No | Objective | Anticipated Result |
|---|---|---|
| W1.O.1 | To consolidate the EISB structure and terminology | A unanimously accepted terminology and a taxonomy structuring the contents for the domain in a concise way |
| W1.O.2 | To identify evidence of interoperability in neighbouring domains | • A taxonomy of neighbouring domains indicating their relation to the EI scientific areas <br> • Shared sources of content, scientific communities and approaches among EI and neighbouring domains. |
| W1.O.3 | To set up the theoretical foundations of enterprise interoperability | An EISB problem and solution description framework |
| W1.O.4 | To define the enterprise interoperability problems and solutions space | • Initial identification of the core issues that constitute the fundamental aspects of EI <br> • Outline of the solution space, through documentation of solutions to key problems |
| W1.O.5 | To curate existing approaches to key problems | Sorting out of existing solutions to fundamental problems |
| W1.O.6 | To synthesize the EI community | Setup of a community for each major scientific area for focused research |
| W1.O.7 | To consolidate and validate the fundamental elements | • Mobilisation and validation by the key domain's stakeholders (industry, SMEs) and interest attraction from neighbouring domains <br> • 1 populated wiki platform for constant sharing and updating results |
| W1.O.8 | To monitor progress of the EISB establishment and further plan the waves | Creation of an updated Action Plan taking into consideration the advancements during the EISB Wave 1 |
| W1.O.9 | To identify research priorities and provide a set of concrete future research recommendations | • Identification of key research priorities, based on the FInES requirements and current trends <br> • Identification of problems open for research by academia and industry |

## EISB Wave 2: Hypothesis and Experimentation

The EISB second wave builds upon the initial EISB foundations defined in Wave 1, i.e. the identification and description of EI scientific problems and EI foundation principles, with a view to stabilizing research products, methods and tools in a reusable, extendable and sustainable manner as well to constructing application scenarios that will prepare for the popularization of EI in the third wave. Impact assessment and simulation, together with the development of a training curriculum, is a requirement for the accomplishment of this stage. Furthermore, targeting a broader community, this wave focuses on identifying hypothesis and nurtures discussions and experiments in order to reach consensus on the challenges or to improve the basic elements defined in the first Wave.

In more detail, this wave includes the actions described in Table 3.

Table 4 summarizes the objectives of the EISB Wave 2, together with the anticipated results that accompany them.

## EISB Wave 3: Empowerement

The EISB third wave aims at empowering the scientific foundations for Enterprise Interoperability through proper liaisons with the scientific, research and stakeholders communities, highlighting the quality of the industrial solutions and the substantiation of value. It focuses on the External Enhancement, Exploration and Popularisation of the EI as a science base as described in Table 5.

Table 6 summarizes the objectives of the EISB Wave 3, together with the anticipated results that accompany them.

## ENTERPRISE INTEROPERABILITY FUNDAMENTALS

In every scientific discipline, laws are defined as analytic statements, usually with an empirically determined constant. Such scientific laws must always apply under the same conditions, and imply a causal relationship between the elements which they contain. Laws are generally applicable observations or guidelines ("do's and don'ts"), which are grounded in observation and rationalisation from cases. Since a law is a distillation of the results of repeated observation, its applicability is generally to circumstances either resembling or extrapolating those already observed. Scientific laws must be confirmed and broadly agreed upon through the process of inductive reasoning.

In the domain of Enterprise Interoperability, a lot of debates have taken place with experts from the EI domain and neighbouring scientific disciplines and it was concluded that:

- The interoperability domain has not yet reached the required maturity level to establish laws. Interoperability like Software

*Table 3. EISB wave 2 rationale*

| Core Direction | Description |
|---|---|
| **Development and Extension** | Exploration of preliminary applications of the technological and scientific principles, populations of formal descriptions and generalization of the various approaches. This step will have to bring in extensive experimental applications, where several of the developed approaches can now be instantiated, thus formulating a more complete set of complete scenarios, including limitations in specific contexts. This exploration is most likely to bring a differentiated set of practices, followed in result-oriented approaches and real-life projects, to further enhance the available, populated exemplary patterns. It is also likely that such population approaches will soon result in the definition and maintenance of one or more, syndicated, Knowledge Bases with interoperability research methods and their results, in various contexts and domains. |
| **Internal Enhancement and Exploration** | Extension of the approaches to vertical domains, application of the technology in real problems, stabilization of technological means, initial assessment of impact, development of training curricula and material. This step constitutes a further, full width exploration of various interoperability problem solving methods and tools, now in real-life situations of specific industrial sectors. Specific approaches are bound to appear for sectors like manufacturing, process industry, health, government, small and medium enterprises, supply chain integration, telecommunications and so on. Also, the well-known issue of interoperability impact assessment is to be tackled in this step, most probably in a sector-specific way. The availability of formal methods, solution tools, real-life application examples and impact assessment will also form the core for the interoperability training curriculum, to be brought in a more systematic framework. |

*Table 4. EISB wave 2 objectives outline*

| No | Objective | Anticipated Result |
|---|---|---|
| W2.O.1 | To formalize the hypothesis for enterprise interoperability | Core set of hypothesis related to the EISB |
| W2.O.2 | To bridge the enterprise interoperability problems and solutions space | A matrix/graph matching solutions to problems and denoting solution paths |
| W2.O.3 | To assess the impact of the EI solution space | An EISB Assessment Framework |
| W2.O.4 | To enable real-life experiments on problem-solution paths | • A set of cases for experimentation purposes<br>• Availability of application data to be used during the testing of other solutions |
| W2.O.5 | To generalize models and tools | A set of calibrated, stabilized, reusable, generalized and extendable EI solutions |
| W2.O.6 | To enrich the solution space with result-oriented practices | • A set of verified hypotheses<br>• A wider solution space including field-tested solutions, as well as generalized solutions<br>• An extended, open and more collaborative EI science base |
| W2.O.7 | To lay the groundwork for a young generation of researchers that will advance research in enterprise interoperability | Training curricula based on the EISB contents |
| W2.O.8 | To consolidate and validate the fundamental elements | • Mobilisation and validation by the key domain's stakeholders (industry, SMEs) and interest attraction from neighbouring domains<br>• 1 populated wiki platform for constant sharing and updating results |
| W2.O.9 | To monitor progress of the EISB establishment and further plan the waves | Creation of an updated Action Plan taking into consideration the advancements during the EISB Wave 2 |
| W2.O.10 | To identify research priorities and provide a set of concrete future research recommendations | • Identification of key research priorities, based on the FInES requirements and current trends<br>• Identification of problems open for research by the academia and industry |

*Table 5. EISB wave 3 rationale*

| Core Direction | Description |
|---|---|
| **External Enhancement and Exploration** | Communication towards a broader community, substantiation of value and applicability, detailing towards complete system solutions, embodiment within training programmes. This is a rather progressed step, "announcing" the findings to a broader scientific community, while also continuing on the embodiment of the scientific approaches to university and vocational training programmes. Substantiation of applicability refers to convincing, detailed, sector-specific solution examples that are to be available. An important element will also be related to the completeness of the approach, realising end-to-end interoperability solutions, covering technical, semantic, organizational and enterprise issues in a sustainable way. |
| **Popularization** | Standardisation and methodologies for production quality, systematic assistance in commercialisation and marketing of scientific offerings. This last stream of activities is aimed at bringing an overall enhanced quality to the interoperability scientific offerings, elevating them, if possible, to industrial-strength level. If this level is reached, commercialisation of the various offerings will be made possible, for methods, tools and services to be provided towards administrations or enterprises of various sizes. |

*Table 6. EISB wave 3 objectives outline*

| No | Objective | Anticipated Result |
|---|---|---|
| W3.O.1 | To inspire a new generation of scientists that will advance research on enterprise interoperability | • Focused training seminars for industry, SMEs and broader academic programmes<br>• Syllabus for academic EI post-graduate programmes |
| W3.O.2 | To communicate results towards a broader community | • Key industrial players, SMEs and researchers from multiple disciplines and backgrounds are informed about the EISB and provide their valuable input and enhancements<br>• Sustainability of the EISB |
| W3.O.3 | To create EI business plans | Business plans for the exploitation of the research solutions promoted in the EISB problems/solutions paths |
| W3.O.4 | To commercialize the EI solutions | Groundwork and ideas for the development of industrial solutions based on research results |
| W3.O.5 | To define EI standards | A map of international standards for EI |
| W3.O.6 | To design the EI cookbook | A comprehensible manuscript documenting the engineered problem/solution paths |
| W3.O.7 | To identify research priorities and provide a set of concrete future research recommendations | • Identification of key research priorities, based on the FInES requirements and current trends<br>• Identification of problems open for research by the academia and industry |
| W3.O.8 | To monitor progress of the EISB establishment and further plan the waves | Creation of an updated Action Plan taking into consideration the advancements during the EISB Waves |

Engineering has not actually been overly concerned with its core theory up to date (Johnson et al, 2012).

- Laws in mathematical format are not applicable, yet we may observe regularities and patterns. Strict regularities, such as laws, can only be found in a very high and abstract level.
- However, it is a good approach to try to introduce some initial observations based on empirical data.

In summary, the thoughts on the guiding principles of interoperability expressed during a number of face-to-face and online brainstorming sessions are categorized in universal truths that are commonly accepted and methodological principles with regard to how interoperability should be addressed (see Table 7).

The high-ranked interoperability guidelines that have emerged from the online voting conducted and may eventually be the first interoperability laws are:

1. Design for interoperability early, in the life cycle; if left for the end, it will be too costly.
2. Don't solve interoperability between systems as a "one-to-one" problem; go for standards-based, generic, reusable and adaptive services instead.
3. The more systems appear, the more interoperability needs arise.
4. Understand your enterprise.
5. Define the boundaries of interoperability in an enterprise – define your core.

## ENTERPRISE INTEROPERABILITY SCIENCE BASE ACHIEVEMENTS

During the ENSEMBLE project implementation, the focus of the EISB activities has been on laying the groundwork for the scientific foundations of Enterprise Interoperability through the analysis of the State of Play, the elaboration on the Action Plan and the initiation of three evolution waves. It was acknowledged that an initiative like EN-

*Table 7. Interoperability guiding principles*

| Interoperability Guiding Principles | Type |
|---|---|
| Design for interoperability early, in the life cycle; if left for the end, it will be too costly. | Methodological Principles |
| Don't solve interoperability between systems as a "one-to-one" problem; go for standards-based, generic, reusable services instead. | Methodological Principles |
| Go after interoperability solving organizational, data, technical and policy issues. | Methodological Principles |
| Go for big impact on users; solving interoperability permits very high targeting. | Methodological Principles |
| The more systems appear, the more interoperability needs arise. | Universal Truths |
| Interoperability is a state of mind and not a state of things. | Universal Truths |
| Combine legal interoperability with technical interoperability | Methodological Principles |
| Don't leave assumptions unverified. | Methodological Principles |
| Define the boundaries of interoperability – define your core. | Methodological Principles |
| Go to the root of Interoperability (investigate incentive/strategy) | Methodological Principles |
| Don't try to achieve commercial dominance in a thorough technical segmentation, define the needs of your chosen market and build a (product) offering/solutions that build on the combined strengths of interoperable technology. | Methodological Principles |
| State how you want to interoperate. | Methodological Principles |
| You can't interoperate with everything. | Universal Truths |
| Complete lossless interoperability is not achievable in most of the cases – forget the optimum! | Universal Truths |
| Build interoperability solutions bottom-up; Top-down approaches could bring to standards, but most interoperability approaches are solved bottom-up. Talk with people. Exploit the wisdom of the network. | Methodological Principles |
| Understand your enterprise | Methodological Principles |
| There is nothing more practical than good theory. | Universal Truths |
| Whenever there is heterogeneity between two systems, there is a risk of non-interoperability. | Universal Truths |
| Connect to theory people. | Methodological Principles |
| Provide more formal background (hard science). Interoperability is about mapping, simulation and how to bridge. | Methodological Principles |
| Interoperability needs to be supported by top management. The higher you go in Io layers, the more top management support you need. | Universal Truths |
| Self realization is important towards Interoperability. | Methodological Principles |
| Abandon the illusion of control. | Methodological Principles |
| Shift from thinking as a single entity. | Methodological Principles |
| Whenever there is heterogeneity between two entities, there is a risk for Interoperability. | Universal Truths |
| Enterprises are always heterogeneous | Universal Truths |
| Wherever there is a lack of interoperability, there is always heterogeneity. | Universal Truths |

SEMBLE could not cover the full extension of the activities defined in the EISB Action Plan, yet it managed to kick-off all the Waves, taking into account that they will need to be completed with post-project activities. In summary, ENSEMBLE achieved a large percentage of the activities included under Wave 1; less under Wave 2; and the activities under Wave 3 have just begun since these are related with the exploitation of the EISB work. Essentially, all results require extensibility, follow-up and sustainability activities to ensure they remain up-to-date.

In this context, the results depicted at high-level in Figure 1 and described in the following paragraphs can be recognized among the key achievements during the past years. It needs to be noted that part of these achievements are discussed in detail in other chapters of this book (authored by Keith Popplewell, Sotiris Koussouris et al., Carlos Agostihno et al.).

With regard to Objective W1.O1 - To consolidate the EISB structure and terminology:

- **Definition of the EISB purpose:** To formulate and structure the knowledge gained through pragmatic research in the Enterprise Interoperability domain; to support application of EI knowledge by clearly documenting the route from domain problems to domain solution approaches and providing access to such solution methodologies; to identify domain-related problems which are currently not resolved or addressed effectively; and to recognize related problems addressed in other sciences that also apply in EI and to approach their communities for sharing knowledge, content and experiences.

- **Scoping of the EISB developments:** At a very high level 5 major assets have been identified:
  - **EISB Knowledge Base:** Enclosing all EISB- and EI- related knowledge using precise and semantically meaningful definitions and specifying the hidden internal relationships;
  - **EISB "Fluid" Knowledge:** That includes all borderline knowledge to the EISB brought by the neighbouring domains with corresponding methods, systemic approaches and also neighbouring communities that

*Figure 1. EISB achievements*

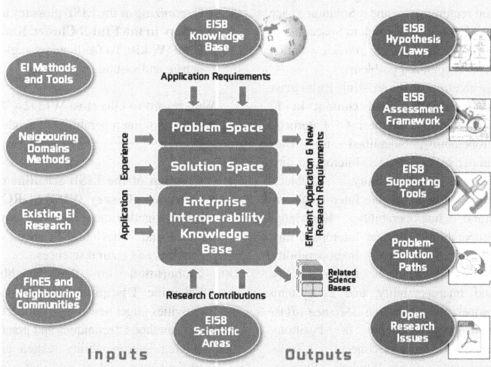

345

can contribute, validate and use EISB and EI research;

- ○ **EISB Concept:** Which lies the theoretical foundation of the science base developments, i.e. by defining the hypotheses/laws, the problem space, the solution space and also the EISB tools;
- ○ **EISB Community:** As the body of experts from the FInES and neighbouring domains that participate in this initiative; and the
- ○ **FInES Wiki:** That promotes and sustains the EISB advancements.

- **Structure of the Enterprise Interoperability Science Base:** With an EI Knowledge Base (EIKB), embracing methodological knowledge of how to do things, structural knowledge to enable ready access to required content, viable business models and value scenarios and links to relevant knowledge available in the neighbouring domains; a Problem Space which can be used to categorize EI application requirements; and a Solution Space referenced from the Problem Space and to the Knowledge Base, to provide solution paths to recognized problems.

- **Classification of the existing Enterprise Interoperability-related content in 12 main Scientific Themes:** Of Enterprise Interoperability, identified as: Data Interoperability, Process Interoperability, Rules Interoperability, Objects Interoperability, Software Interoperability, Cultural Interoperability, Knowledge Interoperability, Services Interoperability, Social Networks Interoperability, Electronic Identity Interoperability, Cloud Interoperability, and Ecosystems Interoperability; and *8 Science Base Dimensions*: Concepts & Positions, Methods, Proof-of-concept, Tools, Experiments, Case Studies, Surveys-

Empirical Data, Standards. Such a set of scientific areas emerged by focusing on the real object of observation, which is the "Enterprise", and by analysing it in its core components to identify the interoperability needs and repercussions within them.

- **Identifying the semantic relationships of the EISB taxonomy:** (containing more than 60 nodes) by clarifying the dependencies between the scientific areas. *Defining a more holistic approach* for the Scientific Areas that drove the EISB ontology building.

- **Defining the EISB Foundational Principles and the EISB Knowledge Space and Ontology:** In order to start generating a common understanding amongst the various EI terms and concepts. A draft EISB glossary with key terms and definitions (containing more than 50 terms) and an EISB taxonomy (with more than 60 nodes) have been defined, along with a 4-step Methodology for EISB Ontology Building.

- **Organizing of the EISB glossary and taxonomy in the FInES Cluster Knowledge Base (Wiki):** To facilitate its exploitation, debate and sustainability.

With regard to Objective W1.O2 - To identify evidence of interoperability in neighbouring domains:

- **Creation of the EISB scientific domain reference glossary (EISB-SDRG):** That brings together more than 180 terms from social and behavioural sciences, applied sciences and natural sciences.

- **Elaboration on the Neighbouring Scientific Disciplines:** Whose research activities target new sets of concepts, theories, methods, techniques and practices for solving interoperability related problems in their own context, and that can somehow contribute to answering the formulated EI open research questions on a scientific basis. Such an analysis contributed to investigating the boundaries between application fields, identifying shared methodologies, techniques and tools which may be applicable to problems in more than one domain, as well as conflicts in different approaches addressing the same problems.

- **Selecting and analysing in depth 5 Neighbouring Scientific Domains:** (Complexity Science, Software Engineering, Design Science, Services Science, and Music Composition) in terms of shared issues/values, in the form of methods and systemic tools contributing to the EISB and with regard to the Enterprise Interoperability assets that may contribute to each corresponding domain.

- **Approaching the neighbouring scientific domains:** For sharing ideas and thoughts on their relation with Enterprise Interoperability. In order to structure and initiate dialogues with key experts in the neighbouring domains, an online and offline questionnaire has been disseminated to more than 100 authors of papers in the most relevant scientific journals, indexed in the Web of Science with Impact Factor.

With regard to Objectives W1.O.3 - To set up the theoretical foundations of enterprise interoperability, W1.O.4 - To define the enterprise interoperability problems and solutions space, W1.O.5 - To curate existing approaches to key problems and W2.O.2 - To bridge the enterprise interoperability problems and solutions space:

- **Defining a bottom-up vision for the problem/solution space of the EISB:** As a space where known cases and issues regarding interoperability are stored, presenting a "before-after" situation for any of those issues, alongside with the solution paths, mainly referring to the utilisation of methods and tools, that have been employed in such cases in order to reach the optimised situation.

- **Analysis of the current state of research and application in each of the scientific themes:** Based on more than 650 published results. A further examination of the contributions made to each of these themes by European Framework Programme funded projects, specific scientific events, and research or application initiatives, was also conducted.

- **Formulating the EISB Core Concepts in the Problem and Solution Space:** For circulation of ideas within the EISB community. More than 50 research issues and 36 problems and problem domains have been identified to the EISB problem space (average of 4 issues and 3 problems per EI scientific area) and an initial solution elements matrix cross-matching the EI scientific areas and problem spaces with solution elements (methods, tools, proof-of-concept, case studies) has been elaborated.

- **Identifying an initial set of formal and other descriptive methods defining EI problems and solutions:** As well as critical research questions, amongst which is also the questioning of the EI community for the need of developing from scratch EI specific formal methods. More than 150 methods, coming from both the EI domain and from neighbouring domains, were initially matched with the 12 Scientific Areas, as they will help to identify the needs of the domain and support the transfer of knowledge from other domains that may actively contribute to the ever-standing problems.

- **Illustrating how the theoretical foundations of a neighbouring discipline, like Operations Research (OR), can be used for the specification of problems/solutions:** Specific examples how schema analysis and graph isomorphism can be applied in relation to Data Interoperability/ Schema matching, how game theory and equilibrium can be applied in relation to Process Interoperability/Automated process execution, and how OR models for project management can be applied in relation to Process Interoperability/Process re-engineering, have been provided.

With regard to Objective W2.O.1 - To formalize the hypothesis for enterprise interoperability:

- **Debating the interoperability laws or guiding principles of interoperability:** From an initial set of 27 thoughts gathered in online and face-to-face brainstorming sessions, 5 high-ranked Interoperability guidelines that have emerged from the online voting may eventually shape the first interoperability laws.
- **Drawing a set of EISB generic and specific hypotheses:** As examples of existing, yet unproven and unexplained phenomena to be further investigated by researchers in the domain.

With regard to Objective W2.O.3 - To assess the impact of the EI solution space

- **Elaborating on the EISB Assessment Framework:** That enables the identification of the status quo of an organisation, and the measurement of the interoperability level of enterprise systems and applications based on their performance on the different EI Scientific Areas' indicators.
- **Specifying the EISB supporting Tools:** Which implement and complement the assessment framework, form a toolbox that should be developed and deployed in order

to showcase how the EISB assets can influence any enterprise in its quest to achieve higher degrees of interoperability. Starting from analysing and evaluating the current status of an enterprise, and through simulating the benefits and analysing the complexity, a set of recommendations and problem solution-paths shall be provided for reaching the desired level of interoperation with other organisations.

With regard to Objective W2.O.4- To enable real-life experiments on problem-solution paths:

- **Demonstrating the EI assessment framework's capabilities through 3 indicative cases:** A small technological SME providing services for the IT sector, a large manufacturing industry, and a Large IT Integrator active in one country. In order to showcase how the EI assessment framework would work, a special simple online questionnaire was created addressed mainly to business users to help them self-assess the EI status of their organisations.

With regard to Objectives W2.O.7 - To lay the groundwork for a young generation of researchers that will advance research in enterprise interoperability, W3.O.1 - To inspire a new generation of scientists that will advance research on enterprise interoperability:

- **Outlining a syllabus for an EI Post-Graduate Programme in universities and organizing the resources for retrieving the EI-related Training Material, while developing the EISB fundamentals training material:** In order to nurture next generations of researchers.

## A GLIMPSE BEYOND ENSEMBLE: ENTERPRISE INTEROPERABILITY TOOLS

An initial set of EISB tools should be developed and deployed in order to facilitate the verification, the applicability and the expansion of the EISB developments. These tools, which can be also regarded as modules of a bigger infrastructure as depicted in Figure 2, will be based on the developments of the EISB and will be used in order to showcase how the EISB establishments can influence any enterprise in its quest to achieve higher degrees of interoperability. The EISB tools that are described in high level at the next paragraphs, will need to be able to interact and take advantage of the knowledge regarding the tools, the methods and the models that will be recorded in the EISB body of knowledge, as many of the assumptions and the recommendations to be issued by these tools will be based on the capabilities, the features and recorded operational evidence regarding the use of such EI methods, tools and models.

Starting from analysing and evaluating the current status of an enterprise in terms of Enterprise Interoperability, and through simulating the benefits and analysing the complexity, recommendations and problem solution paths will be recommended for reaching the desired level of interoperation with other organisations.

### EI Evaluator

The EI Evaluator is mostly based on the proposed Interoperability Assessment Framework with the addition of some automation mechanisms such as conformance testing to complement the assessment matrix. The main purpose of this specific tool is the evaluation whether a specific system is interoperable with another, or following a pre-defined data exchange standard.

The evaluation process envisages the maturity assessment of any of the 12 EISB Scientific Areas (SA) across same 3 EI levels/barriers defined for the EISB assessment framework:

1. The fist EI level to be addressed is the organizational one. Since it is a human-intensive level, this step can be performed using manual mechanisms such as questionnaires, interviews, etc., to calculate the assessment matrix. It allows to determine the interoperability maturity at the management levels of the enterprise, and when not sufficiently

*Figure 2. EISB tools*

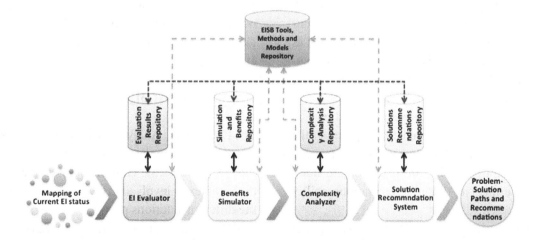

mature impedes interoperability at any of the other levels;

2. Then, the evaluation of conceptual interoperability follows, and besides the manual mechanisms, depending on the SA, in is possible to apply some automation and determine the effective interoperability as well as the maximum potential in term of the syntactic and semantic interoperation. As in the organizational level, if interoperability at the conceptual level is not sufficient it impedes technical interoperation;

3. The final evaluation is at the technological level to assess ICT mismatches and implementation mistakes. Here a number of frameworks are already defined and can be reused in the EISB scope, e.g. conformance testing and interoperability checking.

## Benefits Simulator

The main purpose of the Benefits Simulator (BS) tool will be the simulation of the various offerings/benefits of an enterprise if the latter decides to invest in the improvement of its status in any of the 12 Scientific Areas.

In order to operate, this tool will need to be aware of the following:

- The overall Interoperability Assessment of an enterprise under investigation, which will perform as the starting point for simulation. This kind of input is quite crucial as it is necessary to have a complete perception of the "as-is" status in order to be able to measure the distance between the current and the desired situation. For this reason, the benefits simulator will utilise the results of the EI Evaluator that will provide a thorough evaluation of an organisation regarding its Enterprise Interoperability capacity.
- The desired point of Interoperability degree that an enterprise is willing to achieve

(arrival point), which will be used to calculate and demonstrate the benefits that an enterprise might enjoy if it is able to reach to that point.

- A number of simulation methods and already performed simulations or documented real life experiences, which will populate a repository of knowledge in order for the benefits simulator to be able to retrieve knowledge from pre-existing situations/simulations, which will reinforce the reality check that needs to be conducted when planning and delivering a simulated version. This repository of knowledge will contain cases which will clearly provide a number of benefits, related to each one of the 12 EISB Scientific areas and based on conditions such as the degree of interoperability in each area, the type of the organisation, the tools/methods employed, etc. The repository that will be used for this purpose will also be populated with all simulated versions in order to expand constantly and cover many different alternatives.

In this context, as depicted in Figure 3, the Benefits Simulator will be able to support enterprises to comprehend the benefits that a more sophisticated degree of Enterprise Interoperability can offer them (at any given EI Scientific Area), pushing them in such a way towards investing the necessary resources to improve their operation, due to the presentation of scientific and pragmatic evidence.

## Complexity Analyzer

The Complexity Analyzer (CA) is a support system that based on the different problem/solution models provides the enterprise an estimation of the complexity involved in the implementation of the different solutions proposed.

CA works very closely to the EI Evaluator and the Recommendation System since it needs to be

*Figure 3. Benefits simulator*

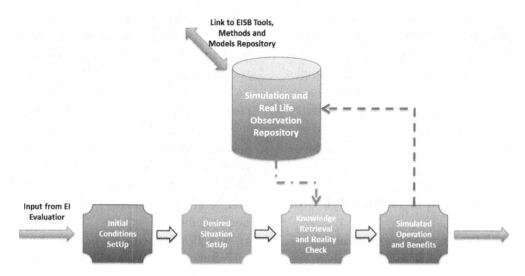

aware of parameters that are used or provided by them, i.e., the overall Interoperability Assessment of an enterprise under investigation or system under test (SUT) and the corresponding problem/solution model. As illustrated in Figure 4, besides those, the CA needs to look at the enterprise as a white box to analyse the micro-level relation-

ships among concepts, people, processes, that will need to be rearranged with the proposed developments. Therefore, complete enterprise models are required as input to the Complexity Analyzer.

Nevertheless, a complete complexity analysis cannot be constricted to the enterprise as a single system. In fact, the CA needs to analyze also the

*Figure 4. Complexity analyzer*

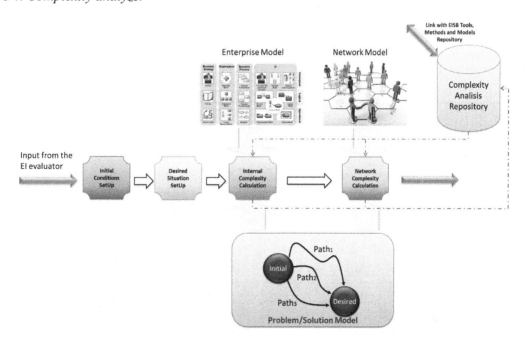

transient periods that the proposed changes will cause in the collaboration networks the enterprise under investigation belongs to, i.e. if changes are implemented, how will they impact its business relationships?. As a conclusion, the CA complements the results of the Benefits Simulator by providing an overview of how complex will it be to put in practice the proposed solutions and how it will affect the external relationships of the organization.

## Solutions Recommendation System

The Solution Recommendation System (SRS) is the last part of the initial EISB tools chain (see Figure 5), and it is intended to provide recommendations regarding the possible solutions that may be employed by the different organisations in their effort to improve their EI capacity. As it is obvious, this tool/module will need to be fed with data regarding the actual EI status of an organisation and the desired arrival point, quite similar to the input required also by the (BS).

In turn, the SRS will analyse the patterns of the enterprise under investigation (the "as-is" Enterprise Interoperability Assessment pattern and the "to-be" pattern) and will retrieve data

regarding similar patterns from its repository which is filled in with relevant data produced during previous executions of this module. Once a pattern is recognised to be similar (or even the same) with another pattern, the module communicates with the EISB Tools, Methods and Models repository to identify elements that are able to support the process of reaching the desired solution. As a result, an analysis of the required solutions and paths is provided to the enterprise, alongside with a set of tools and methods that are able to assist in achieving the desired level of interoperability.

The SRS Repository, which will have the format of the matrix of the Assessment Framework, will be filled with information indicating the way to improve the degree of interoperation (not only on the different Scientific Areas level, but also in the underlying layers/levels defined), associating these with the EISB repository content. On a conceptual level, a vector indicating a possible solution path will be constructed which will be able to connect the various endpoints of the "as-is" and the "to-be" situation.

This operation will in turn not only help to build an inclusive and constantly evolving map of the available tools and methods, but is expected

*Figure 5. Solutions recommendation system*

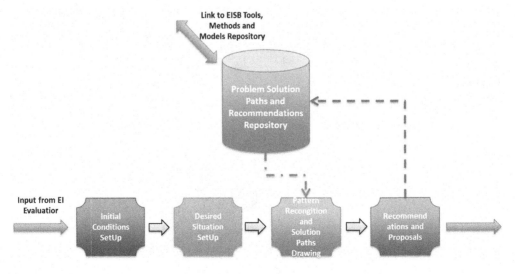

also to shed light on the empty solution spaces, contributing in such a way to future research and development activities.

## CONCLUSION

During its implementation, the ENSEMBLE project whose results are reported in this chapter has gained significant momentum in structuring the underlying knowledge of the Enterprise Interoperability (EI) domain by reinforcing an already vibrant and coherent community that has devoted more than a decade to such research and application. A Science Base for Enterprise Interoperability making explicit the knowledge and skills, which industry and academia have empirically observed, had been successfully initiated under the auspices of the FInES (Future Internet Enterprise Systems) community.

ENSEMBLE has achieved to study and, to an extent, bring together different scientific worlds: the formal background of neighbouring sciences, like Complexity Science and Software Engineering, with the practical needs of enterprises and organizations to tackle interoperability problems in a more systematic way. By nurturing conversations between researchers and with neighbouring scientific disciplines, it is highlighted how many assets and problems Enterprise Interoperability actually shares with its neighbours, despite their diverse cultures, and has eventually created a sense of shared boundaries among them.

Reaching consensus in definitions, analyzing state-of-the art solutions and problem patterns, and mapping a concrete action plan for the stakeholders can be listed as significant contributions eventually towards the establishment of an Enterprise Interoperability Science, so that enterprises can be systematically assisted in exploiting the benefits of interoperability at strategic, organisational, semantic and technical levels, yielding innovative products and services of unprecedented quality, return on investment and sustainability.

Taking into account that new scientific knowledge may lead to new applications, that new technological advances may lead to new scientific discoveries, and that potential applications actually motivate new scientific investigations, Enterprise Interoperability has the credentials to gradually evolve into a more rigorous scientific discipline (or sub-discipline). It is well acknowledged that an underlying scientific discipline typically evolves over several decades in incremental stages before being established as a science and there is actually no role model for showing that there is a successful way to initiate a new scientific discipline using a linear "push approach". Time will thus eventually prove the EI actual positioning and real perspective in relation to its neighbouring scientific disciplines.

In its quest for recognition, the key challenges that Enterprise Interoperability will have to face include, without being restricted to: substantiation of value, strong engagement and support by industry, sustainable research in the domain through appropriate curricula, and coordination of efforts undertaken by many stakeholders and neighbouring disciplines. In order to become sustainable, the EISB thus must clearly demonstrate its impact towards a vibrant and cohesive community consisting of different stakeholders such as:

- Researchers, since they are the owners of EI's body of knowledge and as much commitment as possible is necessary to reduce research duplication, allowing focus of effort on new areas; to identify areas requiring further research; to encourage collaborative work amongst researchers through the need to maintain consensus on EISB content.
- Standardization bodies, as they may initiate the standardization efforts required to gain international attention and recognition and further promote the EISB results.
- Software houses, as they can gain from a scientific method for developing interop-

erability through reduced tendency to re-invent technology, reduced tendency to focus on limited subset of solution approaches and development of generalised software solutions based on comprehensive domain knowledge and application of standards. In fact software might even suffer a paradigm shift from object-oriented, service-oriented or event-oriented towards interoperability-oriented;

- Industry, Enterprises and SMEs in general. They are the main beneficiaries of this effort since it could reduce significantly their business costs, enabling a seamless data exchange with their partners. However, this connection might not always be clear and the EISB needs their support and pull to become successful.
- Governance and policy makers, since the systemization and the knowledge reuse promoted by the EISB will facilitate their everyday operations and transactions, especially when taking into account that interoperability remains a key pillar in the Digital Agenda 2020.

## ACKNOWLEDGMENT

This work has been created closely to the activities of the EU-funded Support Action ENSEMBLE (Envisioning, Supporting and Promoting Future Internet Enterprise Systems Research through Scientific Collaboration), Contract No: FP7-ICT-257548.

## REFERENCES

Bohm, D. (1977). Science as perception-communication. In F. Suppe (Ed.), *The structure of scientific theories* (2nd ed.). Chicago: University of Illinois Press.

Charalabidis, Y., Gionis, G., Moritz Hermann, K., & Martinez, C. (2008). *Enterprise interoperability research roadmap, draft version 5.0*. Brussels: European Commission.

Charalabidis, Y., Jardim Gonçalves, R., & Popplewell, K. (2010). Towards a scientific foundation for interoperability. In Y. Charalabidis (Ed.), *Interoperability in digital public services and administration: Bridging e-government and e-business* (pp. 355–373). Hershey, PA: IGI Global. doi:10.4018/978-1-61520-887-6.ch019

COM. (2012) 795 final. Retrieved on September 12, 2013 from http://eur-lex.europa.eu/LexUriServ/LexUriServ.do?uri=COM:2012:0795:FIN:en:PDF

Curd, M., & Cover, J. A. (1998). *Philosophy of science: The central issues*. W. W. Norton & Company.

Denning, P., Comer, D. E., Gries, D., Mulder, M. C., Tucker, A., Turner, A. J., & Young, P. R. (1989). Computing as a discipline. *ACM Communications*, *32*(1), 9–23. doi:10.1145/63238.63239

EC. (2013). *Entrepreneurship 2020 action plan*.

ENSEMBLE Project. (2013). *Public results*. Retrieved on September 12, 2013, from http://www.fines-cluster.eu/fines/jm/ENSEMBLE-Public-Category/ensemble-deliverables.html

Jardim-Goncalves, R., Grilo, A., Agostinho, C., Lampathaki, F., & Charalabidis, Y. (2013). Systematisation of interoperability body of knowledge: The foundation for EI as a science. *Enterprise Information Systems*, *7*(1), 7–32. doi:10.1080/17517575.2012.684401

Johnson, P., Ekstedt, M., & Jacobson, I. (2012). Where's the theory for software engineering? *IEEE Software*, 94-96. Retrieved on September 12, 2013, from: http://semat.org/wp-content/uploads/2012/02/IEEESoftware_SepOct_2012.pdf

Kuhn, T. (1996). *The structure of scientific revolutions* (3rd ed.). Chicago: The University of Chicago Press. doi:10.7208/chicago/9780226458106.001.0001

Lampathaki, F., Koussouris, S., Agostinho, C., Jardim-Goncalves, R., Charalabidis, Y., & Psarras, J. (2012). Infusing scientific foundations into enterprise interoperability. *Computers in Industry*, *63*(8), 858–866. doi:10.1016/j.compind.2012.08.004

Perry, D.E., & Wolf, A.L. (1992). Foundations for the study of software architecture. *ACM SIGSOFT Software Eng. Notes*, 40–52.

Redwine, S., & Riddle, W. (1985). Software technology maturation. In *Proceedings of 8th Int'l Conf. Software Eng*. IEEE.

Rees, M. (2010). *Scientific horizons: The Reith lectures*. Retrieved on February 28th, 2011 from http://www.bbc.co.uk/iplayer/episode/b00sp194/The_Reith_Lectures_Martin_Rees_Scientific_Horizons_2010_What_Well_Never_Know/

Stanovich, K. E. (2007). *How to think straight about psychology*. Boston: Pearson Education.

## KEY TERMS AND DEFINITIONS

**Action Plan for Establishing the Scientific Foundations of a Domain:** A concrete set of activities that need to be collectively undertaken by stakeholders with different backgrounds in a logical time frame in order to eventually lead to the general recognition of its scientific rigorousness.

**Assessment Framework:** An assessment matrix to identify the status quo of an organisation, and classify it based on its performance on the different EI Scientific Areas.

**Enterprise Interoperability (EI):** The capacity of two or more enterprises, including all the systems within their boundaries and the external systems that they utilize or are affected by, in order to cooperate seamlessly in depth of time for a common objective.

**Enterprise Interoperability Science Base (EISB):** A rigorous formulation and structure of the knowledge gained through pragmatic research in the Enterprise Interoperability domain over the last decades and more. Through the EISB, it is established that there is indeed a coherent and specific body of scientific knowledge and understanding attributable to that research, and is rendered accessible to both future researchers aiming to build on existing knowledge, and to those wishing to use in industrial applications.

**Neighbouring Scientific Domains:** Scientific disciplines whose research activities target new sets of concepts, theories, methods, techniques and practices for solving interoperability related problems in their own context, and that can somehow contribute to answering the formulated EI open research questions on a scientific basis.

**Problem Space:** The range of application and theoretical problems addressed by the Enterprise Interoperability domain.

**Science:** A body of reliable knowledge that can be logically and rationally explained.

**Scientific Area:** A high level specific domain of knowledge of an Enterprise Interoperability related issue reflecting a core element of an Enterprise or a combination of those.

**Scientific Discipline:** A branch of scientific knowledge that is taught and researched at the college or university level. Disciplines are defined (in part), and recognized by the academic journals in which research is published, and the learned societies and academic departments or faculties to which their practitioners belong.

**Solution Space:** The range of application and theoretical solutions that are capable of addressing the issues included in the Problem Space.

**Wave:** A stage of the science base development that includes a coherent set of actions to achieve concrete objectives.

# Compilation of References

Aalst, W. M. P. d., Weske, M., & Grünbauer, D. (2005). Case handling: A new paradigm for business process support. *Data & Knowledge Engineering, 53*(2), 129–162. doi:10.1016/j.datak.2004.07.003

Abel, F., De Coi, J., Henze, N., & Koesling, A. (2007). Enabling advanced and context-dependent access control in RDF stores. In *Proceedings of the 6th Int. Semantic Web Conf. (ISWC-2007)* (LNCS), (vol. 4825). Berlin: Springer.

ABPMP. (2009). *Guide to business process management common body of knowledge (BPM CBOK)* (2nd ed.). New York: Association of Business Process Management Professionals.

ACM. (2006). *Computing degrees & careers*. Retrieved March 22, 2013, from http://computingcareers.acm.org/?page_id=12

*ADOLog - Supply Chain-Management mit ADOlog.* (2013). Retrieved February 25, 2013, from http://www.boc-group.com/products/adolog/

*ADONIS – Community Ed.* (2013). Retrieved February 25, 2013, from http://www.adonis-community.com/

*ADOxx.org.* (2013). Retrieved, June 24, 2013 from http://www.adoxx.org

Adriansyah, A., van Dongen, B., & van der Aalst, W. (2010). Towards robust conformance checking. In *Proceedings of Business Process Management Workshops* (pp. 122–133). Berlin: Springer.

Aduna Software. (2012). openRDF.org - Home of Sesame. *Aduna Software.* Retrieved February 25, 2013, from http://www.openrdf.org/

Agostinho, C., Jardim-Goncalves, R., & Steiger-Garcao, A. (2011). Using neighboring domains towards setting the foundations for enterprise interoperability science. In *Proceedings of International Symposium on Collaborative Enterprises (CENT 2011) in the Context of the 15th World-Multi-Conference on Systemics, Cybernetics and Informatics: WMSCI 2011.* Orlando, FL: CENT.

Agostinho, C., Goncalves, R., Sarraipa, J., Koussouris, S., Mouzakitis, S., Lampathaki, F., & Assogna, P. (2012). *EISB basic elements report.* Brussels: European Commission.

Agostinho, C., Sarraipa, J., Goncalves, D., & Jardim-Goncalves, R. (2011). Tuple-based semantic and structural mapping for a sustainable interoperability. In *Technological innovation for sustainability - IFIP advances in information and communication technology* (Vol. 349, pp. 45–56). Berlin: Springer. doi:10.1007/978-3-642-19170-1_5

*Airbus.* (2013). Retrieved 03 27, 2013, from http://en.wikipedia.org/wiki/Airbus

Allee, V. (2002). A value network approach for modelling and measuring intangibles. In *Proceedings of Transparent Enterprise Conference.* Madrid, Spain: TEC.

Allee, V. (2008). Value network analysis and value conversion of tangible and intangible assets. *Journal of Intellectual Capital, 9*(1), 5–24. doi:10.1108/14691930810845777

Allemang, D., & Hendler, J. (2011). *Semantic web for the working ontologist: Effective modeling in RDFS and OWL* (2nd ed.). Waltham, MA: Morgan Kaufmann.

Allen, S., Deragon, J. T., Orem, M. G., & Smith, C. F. (2008). *The emerge of the relationship economy.* Cupertino, CA: HappyAbout.

America Mathematical Society (AMS). (2010). *Mathematics subject classification.* Retrieved on March 15, 2013 from http://www.ams.org/mathscinet/msc/msc2010.html

American Health Information Management Association (AHIMA) & American Medical Informatics Association. (AMIA). (2007). *The value of personal health records: A joint position statement for consumers of health care.* Retrieved from http://www.amia.org/sites/amia.org/files/ahima-amia-phr-statement.pdf

Amsden, E. (2011). *A survey of functional reactive programming.* Rochester Institute of Technology. Retrieved December 29, 2013, from http://www.cs.rit.edu/~eca7215/frp-independent-study/Survey.pdf

Anderson, C. (2006). *The long tail: Why the future of business is selling less of more.* New York: Hyperion.

Anderson, P. W., Arrow, K., & Pines, D. (1988). *The economy as an evolving complex system.* Reading, MA: Addison-Wesley Longman.

Ang, C. L., Gu, Y., Sourina, O., & Gay, R. K. L. (2005). An ARIS-based transformation approach to semantic web service development. In *Proceedings of Cyberworlds Conference* (pp. 8-16). IEEE Computer Society Press.

Angelov, S., & Grefen, P. (2008). An e-contracting reference architecture. *Journal of Systems and Software, 81*(11), 1816–1844. doi:10.1016/j.jss.2008.02.023

Apache Any23. (2012). *Apache software foundation.* Retrieved February 25, 2013, from http://any23.apache.org/

Apache Jena. (2012). *Apache software foundation.* Retrieved February 25, 2013, from http://jena.apache.org/

ARIS. (2013). *ARIS community Ed. official product page.* Retrieved February 25, 2013, from http://www.ariscommunity.com/aris-express

Armstrong, D. J. (2006). The quarks of object-oriented development. *Communications of the ACM, 49*(2), 123–128. doi:10.1145/1113034.1113040

Arvanitis, S., & Loukis, E. (2009). Information and communication technologies, human capital, workplace organization and labour productivity in Greece and Switzerland: A comparative study based on firm-level data. *Information Economics and Policy, 21*, 43–61. doi:10.1016/j.infoecopol.2008.09.002

Ashburne, M., & Lewis, S. (2002). On ontologies for biologists: The gene ontology-untangling the web. In *Proceedings of the Novartis Found Symposium* (pp. 66-80). Novartis Found.

ASTM International. (2005). *E2369 - 05e1 standard specification for continuity of care record (CCR).* Retrieved from http://www.astm.org/Standards/E2369.htm

ASTM. (2003). *Standard specification for continuity of care record (CCR).* Retrieved from www.astm.org/Standards/E2369.htm

Athena, I. P. (2007). *Advanced technologies for interoperability of heterogeneous enterprise networks and their application* (FP6 IST-507849). Retrieved May 30, 2011, from http://interop-vlab.eu/ei_public_deliverables/athena-deliverables/list-of-public-deliverables-submitted-during-the-athena-project

ATHENA. (2003, April). *Advanced technologies for interoperability of heterogeneous enterprise networks and their applications.* FP6-2002-IST-1, Integrated Project Proposal.

Athena. (2005). *Deliverable D.A5.1: Perspectives in service-oriented architectures and their application in environments that require solutions to be planned and customisable.* Athena IP Project (FP6 IST-507849). Retrieved from http://interop-vlab.eu/ei_public_deliverables/athena-deliverables/A5/d-a5.1/

Axelrod, R. (1997). *The complexity of cooperation: Agent-based models of competition and collaboration.* Princeton, NJ: Princeton University Press.

Baader, F., McGuinness, D., Nardi, D., & Patel-Schneider, P. (2007). *The description logic handbook: Theory, implementation and applications.* New York, NY: Cambridge University Press. doi:10.1017/CBO9780511711787

Baida, Z., Gordijn, J., Akkermans, H., Sæle, H., & Morch, A. (2007). How e-services satisfy customer needs: A software-aided reasoning. In I. Lee (Ed.), *E-business innovation and process management* (pp. 198–233). Hershey, PA: IGI Global. doi:10.4018/978-1-59904-277-0.ch009

Bak, P., Tang, C., & Wiesenfeld, K. (1988). Self-organized criticality. *Physical Review A., 38*(1), 364–374. doi:10.1103/PhysRevA.38.364 PMID:9900174

Banks, J., Carson, J. S., & Nelson, B. L. (1996). *Discrete-event system simulation* (2nd ed.). Upper Saddle River, NJ: Prentice Hall.

Baraldi, E., & Nadin, G. (2006). The challenges in digitalising business relationships: The construction of an IT infrastructure for a textile-related business network. *Technovation, 26*, 1111–1126. doi:10.1016/j.technovation.2005.09.016

Barnett, W., Presley, A., Johnson, M., & Liles, D. (1994). An architecture for the virtual enterprise. In *Proceedings of the IEEE International Conference on Systems, Man, and Cybernetics*. San Antonio, TX: IEEE.

Barwise, J., & Perry, J. (1983). *Situations and attitudes*. Cambridge, MA: MIT Press.

Bauer, M. (Ed.). (2012). *D3.1 glonet platform design specification*. Retrieved February 25, 2013, from https://sites.google.com/site/glonetproject/8-download/GloNet-D3.1.pdf?attredirects=0&d=1

Bayer, F., Junginger, S., & Kühn, H. (2000). A business process oriented methodology for developing e-business applications In *Proceedings of the 7th European Concurrent Engineering Conference (ECEC'2000)*. Leicester, UK: ECEC.

Beale, T., & Heard, S. (2007). *Archetype definitions and principles*. Retrieved from http://www.openehr.org/svn/specification/TRUNK/publishing/architecture/am/archetype_principles.pdf

Bechhofer, S., Gangemi, A., van Harmelen, N. G., Horrocks, I., Masolo, M. K., & Oberle, D. et al. (2004). Tackling the ontology acquisition bottleneck: An experiment in ontology re-engineering. *Journal of Web Semantics*.

Bellinger, G., Castro, D., & Mills, A. (2004). *Data, information, knowledge, and wisdom*. Retrieved 3 25, 2013, from http://www.systems-thinking.org/dikw/dikw.htm

Bell, J. L. (2012). The development of categorical logic. In D. M. Gabbay, & F. Guenther (Eds.), *Handbook of philosophical logic* (Vol. 12, pp. 279–361). Berlin, Germany: Springer.

Bell, M. (2008). *Service-oriented modeling: Service analysis, design, and architecture*. Hoboken, NJ: Wiley & Sons. doi:10.1109/EDOC.2008.51

Bermell-García, P., Verhagen, W., Astwood, S., Krishnamurthy, K., Johnson, J. L., & Ruiz, D. et al. (2012). A framework for management of knowledge-based engineering applications as software services: Enabling personalization and codification. *Advanced Engineering Informatics, 26*, 219–230. doi:10.1016/j.aei.2012.01.006

Berner, E. S. (2009). *Clinical decision support systems: State of the art*. Retrieved from http://healthit.portaldev.ahrq.gov/portal/server.pt/gateway/PTARGS_0_1248_874024_0_0_18/09-0069-EF.pdf

Berners-Lee, T., & Connolly, D. (2013). *Notation3 (N3), a readable RDF syntax*. Retrieved from http://www.w3.org/TeamSubmission/n3/

Berners-Lee, T., & Fischetti, M. (1999). *Weaving the web: The original design and ultimate destiny of the world wide web by its inventor*. San Francisco: HapperOne.

Berre, A. et al. (2007). The ATHENA interoperability framework. In *Enterprise interoperability II* (pp. 569–580). London, UK: Springer. doi:10.1007/978-1-84628-858-6_62

Berry, L. L. (1983). Relationship marketing. In L. L. Berry, G. L. Shostack, & G. Upah (Eds.), *Emerging perspectives on services marketing* (pp. 25–28). Chicago, IL: American Marketing Association.

Bettahar, F., Moulin, C., & Barthes, J. (2009). Towards a semantic interoperability in an e-government applications. *Electronic. Journal of E-Government, 7*(3), 209–226.

Birkhoff, G., & von Neumann, J. (1936). The logic of quantum mechanics. *The Annals of Mathematics, 37*(4), 823. doi:10.2307/1968621

*BIVEE Project*. (n.d.). Retrieved 24, June, 2013 from http://www.bivee.eu

Bizer, C., Heath, T., & Berners-Lee, T. (2009). Linked data - The story so far. *International Journal on Semantic Web and Information Systems, 5*(3), 1–22. doi:10.4018/jswis.2009081901

Bizer, C., Lehmann, J., Kobilarov, G., Auer, S., Becker, C., Cyganiak, R., & Hellmann, S. (2009). DBpedia – A crystallization point for the web of data. *Journal of Web Semantics: Science. Services and Agents on the World Wide Web, 7*, 154–165. doi:10.1016/j.websem.2009.07.002

Blanc, S. (2005). Interoperability problems: Management of evolution of collaborative enterprises. In *Proceedings of Interoperability for Enterprise Software and Applications Conference, I-ESA* (Vol. 5). I-ESA.

Blechner, M., Saripalle, R., & Demurjian, S. (2012). Proposed star schema and extraction process to enhance the collection of contextual & semantic information for clinical research data warehouses. In *Proceedings of the 2012 International Workshop on Biomedical and Health Informatics*. Philadelphia: Academic Press.

Blokdijk, G. (2008). *Service level agreement 100 success secrets: SLA, service level agreements, service level management and much more*. New York: Emereo Publishing.

*BOC Research Projects*. (n.d.). Retrieved 24, June, 2013 from http://www.boc-group.com

Bodenreider, O. (2004). The unified medical language system (UMLS), integrating biomedical terminology. *Journal Nucleic Acids Research*, *32*(1), 267–270. doi:10.1093/nar/gkh061

Bodenreider, O., Smith, B., Kumar, A., & Burgun, A. (2007). Investigating subsumption in SNOMED CT: An exploration into large description logic-based biomedical terminologies. *Artificial Intelligence in Medicine*, *39*(3), 183–195. doi:10.1016/j.artmed.2006.12.003 PMID:17241777

Boh, W. F., Xu, Y., & Soh, C. (2008). VIS standards deployment and integration: A study of antecedents and benefits. In *Proceedings of the International Conference on Information Systems (ICIS) 2008*. ICIS.

Bohm, D. (1977). Science as perception-communication. In F. Suppe (Ed.), *The structure of scientific theories* (2nd ed.). Chicago: University of Illinois Press.

Booch, G. (1994). *Object oriented analysis and design with applications* (Vol. 2, p. 720). The Benjamin Cummings Publishing Co. Inc.

Bowers, S., & Delcambre, L. (2006). Using the unilevel description (ULD) to support data-model interoperability. *Data & Knowledge Engineering*, 59.

Branke, J., Deb, K., Miettinen, K., & Slowinski, R. (2008). Multiobjective optimization, interactive and evolutionary approaches, multiobjective optimization. *Lecture Notes in Computer Science*, 5252.

Brauer, M., & Schubert, S. (2013). *The OpenOffice.org XML project*. Retrieved from http://www.openoffice.org/xml/

Bravetti, M., & Zavattaro, G. (2009). A theory of contracts for strong service compliance. *Journal of Mathematical Structures in Computer Science*, *19*(3), 601–638. doi:10.1017/S0960129509007658

Breiter, A., & Light, D. (2004). Decision support systems in schools – From data collection to decision making. In *Proceedings of AMCIS 2004 - Tenth Americas Conference on Information Systems*. New York: AMCIS.

Brews, P., & Tucci, C. (2004). Exploring the structural effects of internetworking. *Strategic Management Journal*, *25*, 429–451. doi:10.1002/smj.386

Brinkkemper, S., Saeki, M., & Harmsen, F. (1999). Meta-modelling based assembly techniques for situational method engineering. *Information Systems*, *24*(3), 209–228. doi:10.1016/S0306-4379(99)00016-2

Britsch, J., & Kölmel, B. (2012). Anything relationship management as basis for global process management in networked enterprises. In M. Zelm, R. Sanchis, R. Poler, & G. Doumeingts (Eds.), *Enterprise interoperability I-ESA'12 proceedings* (pp. 227–234). London, UK: Wiley. doi:10.1002/9781118561942.ch33

Britsch, J., Schacht, S., & Mädche, A. (2012). Anything relationship management. *Business & Information Systems Engineering*, *4*(2), 85–87. doi:10.1007/s12599-012-0208-6

Brodie, R. J., Coviello, N. E., & Winklhofer, H. (2008). Contemporary marketing practices research program: A review of the first decade. *Journal of Business and Industrial Marketing*, *23*(2), 84–94. doi:10.1108/08858620810850191

Browne, E. (2008). *openEHR archetypes and terminology*. Retrieved from http://www.openehr.org/wiki/display/healthmod/Archetypes+and+Terminology

Bruner, J. (1985). *Actual minds, possible worlds*. Cambridge, MA: Harvard University Press.

Bruza, P., Sofge, D., & Lawless, W. (2009). Quantum interaction. In *Proceedings from AAAI Spring Series: Quantum Interaction*. Palo Alto, CA: AAAI Press. doi:10.1007/978-3-642-00834-4

Brynjolfsson, E., & Hitt, L. M. (2000). Beyond computation: Information technology, organizational transformation and business performance. *The Journal of Economic Perspectives, 14*(4), 23–48. doi:10.1257/jep.14.4.23

Brynjolfsson, E., & Saunders, A. (2010). *Wired for innovation – How information technology is reshaping the economy.* Cambridge, MA: The MIT Press.

Budinsky, F., Steinberg, D., Merks, E., Ellersick, R., & Grose, T. J. (2004). *Eclipse modeling framework.* Reading, MA: Addison Wesley.

Bughin, J., Doogan, J., & Vetvik, O. J. (2010). *A new way to measure word-of-mouth marketing.* New York, NY: McKinsey Quarterly.

Burstein, H. M., & McDermott, V. D. (2005). Ontology translation for interoperability among semantic web services. *AI Magazine, 26*(1), 71–82.

Busquets, J. (2010). Orchestrating smart business network dynamics for innovation. *European Journal of Information Systems, 19*(4), 481–493. doi:10.1057/ejis.2010.19

Butler, R. W. (2001). NASA langley formal methods. In *What is formal methods?* Retrieved June 03, 2013, from http://shemesh.larc.nasa.gov/fm/fm-what.html

C4ISR. (1998). *Levels of information systems interoperability (LISI).* C4ISR Architecture Working Group (AWG), Department of Defense. Retrieved February 25, 2013, from http://www.eng.auburn.edu/~hamilton/security/DODAF/LISI.pdf

Camacho, R., Guerra, D., Galeano, N., & Molina, A. (2005). An integrative approach for VO planning and launching. In *Proceedings of Sixth IFIP Working Conference on Virtual Enterprises (PRO-VE 2005)* (Vol. 186, pp. 81–88). Valencia, Spain: IFIP. doi:10.1007/0-387-29360-4_8

Camarinha-Matos, L. M., & Afsarmanesh, H. (2008). Collaborative networks: Reference modelling. Berlin: Springer Science+Business Media, LLC.

Camarinha-Matos, L. M., & Afsarmanesh, H. (2007). A framework for virtual organization creation in a breeding environment. *Annual Reviews in Control, 31*(1), 119–135. doi:10.1016/j.arcontrol.2007.03.006

Camarinha-Matos, L. M., & Afsarmanesh, H. (Eds.). (2004). *Collaborative networked organizations: A research agenda for emerging business models.* Berlin, Germany: Springer. doi:10.1007/b116613

Campelo, E., & Stucky, W. (2007). The supplier relationship management market trends. *Proceedings of the World Academy of Science, Engineering and Technology, 22,* 105-110.

Carroll, R., Cnossen, R., Schnell, M., & Simons, D. (2007). Continua: An interoperable personal healthcare ecosystem. *IEEE Pervasive Computing/IEEE Computer Society [and] IEEE Communications Society, 6*(4), 90–94. doi:10.1109/MPRV.2007.72

Castellacci, F. (2008). Technological paradigms, regimes and trajectories: Manufacturing and service industries in a new taxonomy of sectoral patterns of innovation. *Research Policy, 37,* 978–994. doi:10.1016/j.respol.2008.03.011

Caswell, N. S., Nikolaou, C., Sairamesh, J., Bitsaki, M., Koutras, G. D., & Iacovidis, G. (2008). Estimating value in service systems: A case study of a repair service system. *IBM Systems Journal, 47*(1), 87–100. doi:10.1147/sj.471.0087

Charalabidis, Y. (2007). *From people to systems interoperability: The interoperability service utility concept.* eChallenges 2007 Conference. Retrieved December, 2011 from ftp://ftp.cordis.europa.eu/pub/ist/docs/ict-ent-net/echallenges2-yc_en.pdf

Charalabidis, Y., Gionis, G., Moritz Hermann, K., & Martinez, C. (2008). *Enterprise interoperability research roadmap, draft version 5.0.* Brussels: European Commission.

Charalabidis, Y., Jardim Gonçalves, R., & Popplewell, K. (2010). Towards a scientific foundation for interoperability. In Y. Charalabidis (Ed.), *Interoperability in digital public services and administration: Bridging e- government and e-business.* Hershey, PA: Information Science Reference. doi:10.4018/978-1-61520-887-6.ch019

Charalabidis, Y., Jardim-Gonçalves, R., & Popplewell, K. (2010). Developing a science base for enterprise interoperability. In *Enterprise interoperability IV: Making the internet of the future for the future of enterprise* (pp. 245–254). Berlin: Springer. doi:10.1007/978-1-84996-257-5_23

Charalabidis, Y., Lampathaki, F., Kavalaki, A., & Askounis, D. (2010). A review of electronic government interoperability frameworks: Patterns and challenges. *International Journal of Electronic Governance*, 3(2), 189. doi:10.1504/IJEG.2010.034095

Cheikes, B. A. (2006). *MITRE support to IKRIS (Final report)*. Washington, DC: Mitre Corporation.

Chen, D. (2006). Enterprise interoperability framework. In *Proceedings of Open Interop Workshop on Enterprise Modelling and Ontologies for Interoperability*. Academic Press.

Chen, D., & Vernadat, F. (2002). Enterprise interoperability: A standardisation view. In *Proceedings of IFIP TC5/WG5.12 International Conference on Enterprise Integration and Modeling Technique: Enterprise Inter- and Intra-Organizational Integration: Building International Consensus*. IFIP.

Chen, L., & Li, S. (2004). Analysis of decomposability and complexity for sedign problems in the context of decomposition. In *Proceedings of DETC'04 ASME 2004 Design Engineering Technical Conferences and Computers and Information in Engineering Conference*. Salt Lake City, UT: ASME.

Chen, D., & Daclin, N. (2007). Barriers driven methodology for enterprise interoperability. In *Establishing the foundation of collaborative networks* (pp. 453–460). New York: Springer. doi:10.1007/978-0-387-73798-0_48

Chen, D., Doumeingts, G., & Vernadat, F. (2008). Architectures for enterprise integration and interoperability: Past, present and future. *Computers in Industry*, 59(7), 647–659. doi:10.1016/j.compind.2007.12.016

Chen, P. (1976). The entity-relationship model: Toward a unified view of data. *ACM Transactions on Database Systems*, 1(1), 9–36. doi:10.1145/320434.320440

Cheung, W., & Hsu, C. (1996). The model-assisted global query system for multiple databases in distributed enterprises. *ACM Transactions on Information Systems*, 14(4), 421–470. doi:10.1145/237496.237499

Chiang, M. F., Hwang, J. C., Yu, A. C., Casper, D. S., Cimino, J. J., & Starren, J. (2006). Reliability of SNOMED-CT coding by three physicians using two terminology browsers. In *Proceedings of the 2006 AMIA Annual Symposium* (pp. 131-135). AMIA.

Chiu, D. K. W., Li, Q., & Karlapalem, K. (1999). A meta modeling approach to workflow management systems supporting exception handling. *Information Systems*, 24(2), 159–184. doi:10.1016/S0306-4379(99)00010-1

Choi, S., & Whinston, A. (2000). Benefits and requirements for interoperability in the electronic marketplace. *Technology in Society*, 22, 33–44. doi:10.1016/S0160-791X(99)00034-2

Choi, T., Dooley, K. J., & Rungtusanatham, M. (2001). Supply networks and complex adaptive systems: Control versus emergence. *Journal of Operations Management*, 19(3), 351–366. doi:10.1016/S0272-6963(00)00068-1

Chong, G. (2002). *Smoothing spline ANOVA models*. New York: Springer-Verlag.

Clark, P., Thompson, J., & Porter, B. (2004). Knowledge patterns. In S. Staab, & R. Struder (Eds.), *Handbook on ontologies* (pp. 191–207). Berlin: Springer. doi:10.1007/978-3-540-24750-0_10

COM. (2012) 795 final. Retrieved on September 12, 2013 from http://eur-lex.europa.eu/LexUriServ/LexUriServ.do?uri=COM:2012:0795:FIN:en:PDF

Commission, E. (2010). *Interoperability solutions for European public administrations*. Retrieved on March 15, 2013 from http://ec.europa.eu/isa/documents/isa_annex_ii_eif_en.pdf

Commius Consortium. (2009). *Commius architecture (final version, deliverable D3.1.2)*. Retrieved from web http://www.commius.eu/index.php?option=com_remository&Itemid=2&func=startdown&id=84

ComVantage EU Project Page. (2012). *Deliverable D3.1.1 – Specification of modelling method including conceptualization outline*. Retrieved February 25, 2013, http://www.comvantage.eu/

COMVANTAGE FP7 Project Consortium. (2012). *D3.1.1 specification of modelling method including conceptualization outline*. Retrieved June 4, 2013, from http://www.comvantage.eu/

*ComVantage Project*. (n.d.). Retrieved 24, June, 2013 from http://www.comvantage.eu

Cook, S., Jones, G., Kent, S., & Wills, A. C. (2007). *Domain specific development with visual studio DSL tools (Microsoft.Net Development)*. Reading, MA: Addison-Weseley Longman.

Cooperstock, F. (2009). *General relativistic dynamics: Extending Einstein's legacy throughout the universe*. Singapore: World Scientific. doi:10.1142/7243

Corradi, A., Montanari, R., & Tibaldi, D. (2004). Context-based access control management in ubiquitous environments. In *Proceedings of the 3rd IEEE Int. Symposium on Network Computing and Applications (NCA-2004)*, (pp. 253-260). IEEE.

Costabello, L., Villata, S., Delaforge, N., & Gandon, F. (2012). Linked data access goes mobile: Context-aware authorization for graph stores. In *Proceedings of the 5th Workshop about Linked Data on the Web (LDOW2012)*. LDOW.

Courtney, J., Merali, Y., Paradice, D., & Wynn, E. (2008). On the study of complexity in information systems. *International Journal of Information Technologies and Systems Approach*, *1*(1), 37–48. doi:10.4018/jitsa.2008010103

Coviello, N. E., Brodie, E., Roderick, J., & Munro, H. J. (1997). Understanding contemporary marketing: Development of a classification scheme. *Journal of Marketing Management*, *13*(6), 501–522. doi:10.1080/0267257X.1997.9964490

Cox, T. F., & Cox, M. A. A. (2003). Multidimensional scaling. *Technometrics*, *45*(2).

Cumbers, A., Mackinnon, D., & Chapman, K. (2003). Innovation, collaboration, and learning in regional clusters: A study of SMEs in the Aberdeen oil complex. *Environment & Planning A*, *35*(9), 1689–1706. doi:10.1068/a35259

Cuppens, F., & Cuppens-Boulahia, N. (2008). Modeling contextual security policies. *International Journal of Information Security*, *7*(4), 285–305. doi:10.1007/s10207-007-0051-9

Curd, M., & Cover, J. A. (1998). *Philosophy of science: The central issues*. W. W. Norton & Company.

Cutting-Decelle, A.-F., Barraud, J. L., Veenendaal, B., & Young, R. I. M. (2012). Production information interoperability over the internet: A standardised data acquisition tool developed for industrial enterprises. *Computers in Industry*, *63*(8), 824–834. doi:10.1016/j.compind.2012.08.010

Cyganiak, R., & Bizer, C. (2012). *D2RQ - Accessing relational databases as virtual RDF graphs*. Retrieved from http://d2rq.org/

Daniel, F., Soi, S., Tranquillini, S., Casati, F., Heng, C., & Yan, L. (2010). From people to services to UI: Distributed orchestration of user interfaces. In R. Hull, J. Mendling, & S. Tai (Eds.), *Business process management* (pp. 310–326). Berlin: Springer. doi:10.1007/978-3-642-15618-2_22

Dassisti, M., & Chen, D. (2011). Interoperability analysis: General concepts for an axiomatic approach. In *OTM 2011 Workshops (LNCS)* (Vol. 7046, pp. 49–60). Berlin: Springer-Verlag. doi:10.1007/978-3-642-25126-9_13

Davis, J., Harris, S., Crichton, C., Shukla, A., & Gibbons, J. (2008). Metadata standards for semantic interoperability in electronic government. In *Proceedings of the 2nd International Conference on Theory and Practice of Electronic Governance* (pp. 67-75). Academic Press.

Deb, K. (2001). *Multi-objective optimization using evolutionary algorithms*. Hoboken, NJ: Wiley-Interscience Series in Systems and Optimization, John Wiley & Sons.

Delgado, J. (2012). Structural interoperability as a basis for service adaptability. In *Adaptive web services for modular and reusable software development: Tactics and solutions* (pp. 33–59). Hershey, PA: IGI Global. doi:10.4018/978-1-4666-2089-6.ch002

Demurjian, S., Saripalle, R., & Behre, S. (2009). An integrated ontology framework for health information exchange. In *Proceedings of the 21st International Conference on Software Engineering and Knowledge Engineering* (pp. 575-580). Boston: Academic Press.

Denning, P., Comer, D. E., Gries, D., Mulder, M. C., Tucker, A., Turner, A. J., & Young, P. R. (1989). Computing as a discipline. *ACM Communications*, *32*(1), 9–23. doi:10.1145/63238.63239

Devlin, K. (2000). *The language of mathematics: Making the invisible visible*. New York, NY: Holt Paperbacks.

Devlin, K. J. (1995). *Logic and information*. Cambridge, UK: Cambridge University Press.

Devlin, K. J. (1998). *Goodbye, Descartes: The end of logic and the search for a new cosmology of the mind*. Hoboken, NJ: Wiley.

Dewick, P., & Miozzo, M. (2004). Networks and innovation: Sustainable technologies in Scottish social housing. *R & D Management, 34*(4), 323–333. doi:10.1111/j.1467-9310.2004.00342.x

Diaz, G., & Rodriguez, I. (2009). Automatically deriving choreography-conforming systems of services. In *Proceedings of IEEE International Conference on Services Computing* (pp. 9-16). IEEE Computer Society Press.

Dietz, J. (2006). *Enterprise ontology: Theory and methodology*. Berlin: Springer-Verlag. doi:10.1007/3-540-33149-2

Dietz, J., & Hoogervorst, J. (2011). A critical investigation of TOGAF - Based on the enterprise engineering theory and practice. In *Advances in Enterprise Engineering V* (pp. 76–90). Berlin: Springer-Verlag. doi:10.1007/978-3-642-21058-7_6

DODD. (1977). *Standardization and interoperability of weapon systems and equipment within the north Atlantic treaty organization*. DODD.

Dodig-Crnkovic, C. (2002). Scientific methods in computer science. In *Proceedings of the Conference for the Promotion of Research in IT at New Universities and at University Colleges in Sweden* (pp. 126–130). Retrieved from http://www.mrt

Dogac, A., Laleci, G., Kennedy, J., Drissi, S., Sesana, M., Gonçalves, R., & Canepa, A. (2009). iSURF: RFID enabled collaborative supply chain planning environment. In *Proceedings of the 4th Mediterranean Conference on Information Systems, MCIS 2009*. Athens, Greece: Athens University of Economics and Business.

Donini, F. M., Lenzerini, M., Nardi, D., & Schaerf, A. (1991). A hybrid system with datalog and concept languages. In *Trends in Artificial Intelligence (LNCS)* (Vol. 549, pp. 88–97). Berlin: Springer Verlag. doi:10.1007/3-540-54712-6_221

Doumeingts, G., & Chen, D. (2013). Interoperability development for enterprise applications and software. In P. Cunningham, M. Cunningham, & P. Fatelnig (Eds.), *Building the knowledge economy: Issues, applications, case studies*. Amsterdam: IOS Press.

Dragoicea, M., & Borangiu, T. (2013). A service science knowledge environment in the cloud. In T. Borangiu, A. Thomas, & D. Trentesaux (Eds.), *Service orientation in holonic and multi agent manufacturing and robotics* (Vol. 472, pp. 229–246). Berlin, Germany: Springer. doi:10.1007/978-3-642-35852-4_15

DSM. (2012). *DSM-5 implementation and support*. Retrieved from http://www.dsm5.org/

Dudek, G., & Stadtler, H. (2007). Negotiation-based collaborative planning in divergent two tier supply chains. *International Journal of Production Economics, 45*, 465–484. doi:10.1080/00207540600584821

Dyba, T., & Dingsoyr, T. (2008). Empirical studies of agile software development: A systematic review. *Information and Software Technology, 50*(9-10), 833–859. doi:10.1016/j.infsof.2008.01.006

EC. (2013). *Entrepreneurship 2020 action plan*.

Edgington, T., Choi, B., Henson, K., Raghu, T. S., & Vinze, A. (2004). Adopting ontology to facilitate knowledge sharing. *Communictions of the Association for Computing Machinery, 47*, 85–90. doi:10.1145/1029496.1029499

Ehrlinger, E. (1979). Kundengruppenmangement. *Die Betriebswirtschaft, 39*(2), 261–273.

Eichelberg, M., Aden, T., Riesmeier, J., Dogac, A., & Laleci, G. B. (2005). A survey and analysis of electronic healthcare record standards. *ACM Computing Surveys, 37*, 277–315. doi:10.1145/1118890.1118891

EIF. (2010). *European interoperability framework (EIF) for European public services, annex 2 to the communication from the commission to the European parliament, the council, the European economic and social committee and the committee of regions 'towards interoperability for European public services'*. Retrieved June 22, 2013, from http://ec.europa.eu/isa/documents/isa_annex_ii_eif_en.pdf

El Raheb, K. et al. (2011). Paving the way for interoperability in digital libraries: The DL.org project. In *New trends in qualitive and quantitative methods in libraries* (pp. 345–352). Singapore: World Scientific Publishing Company.

EN 13606 Association. (2010). *Unofficial ISO/CEN 13606 XML schema*. Retrieved from http://www.en13606.org/resources/files/cat_view/53-xml-schemas

ENSEMBLE CSA. (2011). *Envisioning, supporting and promoting future internet enterprise systems research through scientific collaboration* (FP7-ICT-257548). Retrieved May 31, 2011, from http://www.fines-cluster.eu/fines/jm/ENSEMBLE-Public-Category/ensemble-project.html

ENSEMBLE EU Project. (2012). *Deliverable D2.1 – Envisioning, supporting and promoting future internet enterprise systems research through scientific collaboration*. Retrieved February 25, 2013, from http://www.fines-cluster.eu/fines/jm/Publications/Download-document/339-ENSEMBLE_D2.1_EISB_State_of_Play_Report-v2.00.html

*Ensemble EU-Project (concluded 2012.08)*. (n.d.). Retrieved, June 24, 2013 from http://www.fines-cluster.eu

ENSEMBLE FP7 Project Consortium. (2012). *D2.1 enterprise interoperability science base state of play report*. Retrieved March 18, 2013, from http://www.fines-cluster.eu

ENSEMBLE Partners. (2011). *Deliverable D2.3: EISB basic elements report*. Retrieved from http://www.fines-cluster.eu/fines/jm/Publications/ENSEMBLE-Deliverables/View-category.html

ENSEMBLE Partners. (2012a). *Deliverable D2.4: EISB models & tools report*. ENSEMBLE CSA Project (FP7-ICT-257548). Retrieved from http://www.fines-cluster.eu/fines/jm/Publications/ENSEMBLE-Deliverables/View-category.html

ENSEMBLE Partners.(2012b). *Deliverable D2.5: EISB empowerment actions report*. Retrieved from http://www.fines-cluster.eu/fines/jm/Publications/ENSEMBLE-Deliverables/View-category.html

ENSEMBLE Project. (2011). *EISB models and tools, deliverable 2.4*. Retrieved from http://www.fines-cluster.eu/fines/jm/Publications/Download-document/303-ENSEMBLE_D2.4_EISB-Models-and-Tools-Report-v1.00.html

ENSEMBLE Project. (2013). *Public results*. Retrieved on September 12, 2013, from http://www.fines-cluster.eu/fines/jm/ENSEMBLE-Public-Category/ensemble-deliverables.html

ENSEMBLE Support Action. (2010). *Description of work*.

*ENSEMBLE*. (2012). Retrieved 03 27, 2013, from http://www.fines-cluster.eu/fines/jm/FInES-Private-Information/ensemble.html

Enterprise Interoperability Cluster. (2008). *Enterprise interoperability research roadmap, version 5.0* (pp. 1–29). Brussels: European Commision. Retrieved from http://cordis.europa.eu/fp7/ict/enet/ei-research-roadmap_en.html

*EPCglobal Architecture Framework*. (2007). Retrieved on January 2013 from http://www.epcglobalinc.org/standards/architecture/architecture_1_2-framework-20070910.pdf

EPES FP7 Project Consortium. (2012). *D100.3 EPES concept* (FP7-FoF-ICT-2011.7.3-285093). Retrieved March 18, 2013, from http://www.epes-project.eu

Erl, T. (2005). *Service-oriented architecture: Concepts, technology, and design*. Upper Saddle River, NJ: Prentice Hall PTR.

European Commission. (2004). *European interoperability framework for pan-European egovernment services*. Retrieved from http://ec.europa.eu/idabc/servlets/Docd552.pdf?id=19529

European Commission. (2010). *FP7 ICT work programme 2011 - Objective ICT-2011.5.3 patient guidance services (PGS)*. Retrieved from ftp://ftp.cordis.europa.eu/pub/fp7/docs/wp/cooperation/ict/c-wp-201101_en.pdf

*European CPFR Insights*. (2002). Retrieved from web http://www.ecr-institute.org/publications/best-practices/european-cpfr-insights/files/pub_2002_cpfr_european_insights.pdf

Euzenat, J., & Shvaiko, P. (2007). *Ontology matching*. Berlin: Springer.

Fernandez Lopez, M., Gomez Perez, A., & Juristo, N. (1997). METHONTOLOGY: From ontological art towards ontological engineering. In *Proceedings of the AAAI97 Spring Symposium*. AAAI.

Fewell, S., & Clark, T. (2003). *Organisational interoperability: Evaluation and further development of the OIM model*. Defence Science and Technology Organisation. Retrieved February 25, 2013, from http://www.dtic.mil/dtic/tr/fulltext/u2/a466378.pdf

FIBO. (2013). *Financial report ontology*. Retrived from http://financialreportontology.wikispaces.com/home

Figay, N., Steiger-Garcao, A., & Jardim-Goncalves, R. (2006). Enabling interoperability of STEP application protocols at meta-data and knowledge level. *International Journal of Technology Management*, 402–421.

FInES Cluster Task Force. (2013). *FInES research roadmap 2025*. Retrieved February 25, 2013, from http://www.fines-cluster.eu/fines/jm/Deliverables/Download-document/323-FInES-Research-Roadmap-2025-v3.0.html

FInES Cluster. (2010). *FInES research roadmap*. Retrieved, June, 24, 2013 from http://cordis.europa.eu/fp7/ict/enet/documents/fines-researchroadmap-final-report.pdf

FInES Cluster. (2013). *FInES wiki main page*. Retrieved 03 26, 2013, from http://www.fines-cluster.eu/fines/mw/index.php/Main_Page

*FInES Cluster*. (2013). Retrieved 03 27, 2013, from http://www.fines-cluster.eu

FInES. (2010). *Research roadmap* (version 3.0). Retrieved on March 15, 2013 from http://www.fines-cluster.eu/fines/jm/Download-document/2-FInES-Cluster-2010-Research-Roadmap.html

Finin, T., Joshi, A., Kagal, L., Niu, J., Sandhu, R., Winsborough, W., et al. (2008). ROWLBAC: Representing role based access control in OWL. In *Proceedings of 13th ACM Symposium on Access Control Models and Technologies (SACMAT-2008)*, (pp. 73-82). ACM.

Fischer, C., Winter, R., & Wortmann, F. (2010). Design theory. *Business Information Systems Engineering*, *2*(6), 387–390. doi:10.1007/s12599-010-0128-2

Fleck, A. C. (2006). *22C/55:181 formal methods in software engineering*. University of Iowa. Retrieved from http://homepage.cs.uiowa.edu/~fleck/181.html

Fletcher, R., Leyffer, S., & Toint, P. L. (2006). A brief history of filter methods (Preprint ANL/MCS-P1372-0906). Argonne National Laboratory, Mathematics and Computer Science Division.

Folmer, E., & Bosch, J. (2004). Architecting for usability: A survey. *Journal of Systems and Software*, *70*(1-2), 61–78. doi:10.1016/S0164-1212(02)00159-0

Fonou-Dombeu, J. V., & Huisman, M. (2011). Semantic-driven e-government: Application of uschold and king ontology building methodology for semantic ontology models developments. *International Journal of Web & Semantic Technology*, *2*(4), 1–20. doi:10.5121/ijwest.2011.2401

Ford, T., Colombi, J., Graham, S., & Jacques, D. (2007). The interoperability score. In *Proceedings of the Fifth Annual Conference on Systems Engineering Research*. Hoboken, NJ: IEEE.

Fowler, M. (2002). Patterns of enterprise application architecture. In M. Fowler (Ed.), *Source* (Vol. 48, p. 560). Reading, MA: Addison-Wesley Professional.

Fraunhofer, I. A. O. (n.d.). *Industrie 4.0*. Retrieved, June, 24, 2013 from http://www.iao.fraunhofer.de/lang-de/geschaeftsfelder/unternehmensentwicklung-und-arbeitsgestaltung/1009-industrie-40.html

Freeman, E., Robson, E., Bates, B., & Sierra, K. (2004). *Head first design patterns*. Sebastopol, CA: O'Reilly Media.

Freund, J., Rücker, B., & Hitpass, B. (2011). *BPMN 2.0 manual de referencia y guía práctica*. Santiago de Chile: RPI Chile.

Friedman, A. L., & Peters, T. (2006). Make me a perfect match: Understanding transplant compatibility. *RENAL-IFE*, *21*(5).

Friedman, B. (1997). *Human values and the design of computer technology*. Chicago: Chicago University Press.

Fuentes-Fernández, L., & Vallecillo-Moreno, A. (2004). An introduction to UML profiles. *European Journal for the Informatics Professional, 5*(2).

Fuggetta, A. (1993). A classification of CASE technology. *Computer, 26*(12), 25–38. doi:10.1109/2.247645

Gadatsch, A. (2010). Grundkurs geschäftsprozess-Management. Wiesbaden, Germany: Vieweg+Teubner.

Gali, A., Chen, C. X., Claypool, K. T., & Uceda-Sosa, R. (2004). From ontology to relational databases. In S. Wang (Ed.), *ER workshops (LNCS)* (Vol. 3289, pp. 278–289). Berlin: Springer-Verlag.

Galtuno, J. (1967). *Theory and methods of social research*. New York: Allen and Unwin.

Gamma, E., Helm, R., Johnson, R., & Vlissides, J. (1995). Design patterns: Elements of reusable object-oriented software. In *Design* (Vol. 206, p. 395). Reading, MA: Addison-Wesley.

Gangemi, A. (2005). Ontology patterns for semantic web content. In *Proceedings of the 4th International Semantic Web Conference* (pp. 262-276). Academic Press.

Gangemi, A., & Presutti, V. (2009). Ontology design patterns. In S. Staab, & R. Struder (Eds.), *Handbook on ontologies: International handbooks on information systems* (pp. 221–243). IOS Press. doi:10.1007/978-3-540-92673-3_10

Garschhammer, M., Hauck, R., Hegering, H.-G., Kempter, B., Radisic, I., & Rolle, H. … Nerb, M. (2001). Towards generic service management concepts a service model based approach. In *Proceedings of 2001 IEEE/IFIP International Symposium on Integrated Network Management Proceedings* (pp. 719–732). IEEE. doi:10.1109/INM.2001.918076

Gartner Inc. (2011). *Gartner says consumerization of BI drives greater adoption*. Stamford, CT: Gartner. Retrieved February 22, 2013, from http://www.gartner.com/it/page.jsp?id=1748214

*Generic Model Environment (GME)*. (n.d.). Retrieved 20, February, 2013 from http://www.isis.vanderbilt.edu/Projects/gme

Genesereth, M. (1991). Knowledge interchange format. In *Proceedings of the 2nd International Conference on Priciples of Knowledge Representation and Reasoning* (pp. 238-249). Morgan Kaufman.

Gharajedaghi, J. (2005). *Systems thinking: Managing chaos and complexity: A platform for designing business architecture*. London: Butterworth-Heinemann.

Gilbert, N. (2007). Agent-based models. In *Environment and planning A* (Vol. 32). Thousand Oaks, CA: Sage Publications, Inc.

Gilchrist, A. (2003). Thesauri, taxonomies and ontologies - An etymological note. *The Journal of Documentation, 59*, 7–18. doi:10.1108/00220410310457984

Giunchiglia, F., Zhang, R., & Crispo, B. (2009). Ontology driven community access control. In *Proceedings of the 1st Workshop on Trust and Privacy on the Social and Semantic Web (SPOT-2009)*. SPOT.

Gold, N., Mohan, A., Knight, C., & Munro, M. (2004). Understanding service-oriented software. *IEEE Software, 21*(2), 71–77. doi:10.1109/MS.2004.1270766

Goranson, H. T., & Cardier, B. (2007). Scheherazade's will: Quantum narrative agency. In *Proceedings from AAAI Spring Series Workshop on Quantum Interaction*. Palo Alto, CA: AAAI Press.

Goranson, H. T. (1998). Soft mathematics and information dynamics. *Bio Systems, 46*(1-2), 163–167. doi:10.1016/S0303-2647(97)00094-4 PMID:9648688

Goranson, H. T. (1999). *The agile virtual enterprise: Cases, metrics, tools*. Westport, CT: Greenwood Publishing Group.

Gordijn, J., & Wieringa, R. (2003). A value-oriented approach to e-business process design. In *Proceedings of the 15th International Conference, CAiSE 2003*. CAiSE.

Gordijn, J., & Akkermans, H. (2001). E3-value: Design and evaluation of e-Business model. *IEEE Intelligent Systems, 16*(4), 11–17. doi:10.1109/5254.941353

Gordon, J. (2002). *Can sociologists study society in the same way that scientists study the natural world?* Retrieved 03 27, 2013, from http://www.jakeg.co.uk/essays/science.htm

Gorton, I. (2006). *Essential software architecture*. Berlin: Springer-Verlag.

Gottschalk, P., & Solli-Sæther, H. (2008). Stages of e-government interoperability. *Electronic Government: An International Journal, 5*(3), 310–320. doi:10.1504/EG.2008.018877

Greefhorst, D., & Proper, E. (2011). *Architecture principles: The cornerstones of enterprise architecture*. Berlin: Springer-Verlag. doi:10.1007/978-3-642-20279-7

Greenbaum, J. (2011, June). *Is CRM + xRM the new ERP?* Paper presented at the Decisions Spring Virtual Conference. New York, NY.

Grilo, A., Jardim-Goncalves, R., & Cruz-Machado, V. (2007). A framework for measuring value in business interoperability. In *Proceedings of the IEEE International Conference on Industrial Engineering and Engineering Management*, (pp. 520-524). IEEE.

Grilo, A., Jardim-Goncalves, R., & Cruz-Machado, V. (2009). Analysis of interoperability value proposition in the architectural, engineering and construction sector. In *Proceedings of the IEEE International Conference on Industrial Engineering and Engineering Management 2009*, (pp. 2217 – 2221). IEEE.

Grilo, A., & Jardim-Goncalves, R. (2010). Value proposition on interoperability of BIM and collaborative working environments. *Automation in Construction, 19*, 522–530. doi:10.1016/j.autcon.2009.11.003

Grönroos, C. (2008). Service logic revisited: Who creates value? And who co-creates? *European Business Review, 20*(4), 298–314. doi:10.1108/09555340810886585

Gruber, T. R. (1993). A translation approach to portable ontology specifications. *Journal of Knowledge Acquisition, 5*(2), 199–220. doi:10.1006/knac.1993.1008

Gruber, T. R. (1995). Toward principles for the design of ontologies used for knowledge sharing. *International Journal of Human-Computer Studies, 43*(5-6), 907–928. doi:10.1006/ijhc.1995.1081

Grüninger, M., & Fox, M. S. (1995). Methodology for the design and evaluation of ontologies. In *Proceedings of Workshop on Basic Ontological Issues in Knowledge Sharing, IJCAI-95*. Montreal, Canada: IJCAI.

Guarino, N., & D., O. (2009). What is an ontology?. In S. Staab & R. Studer (Eds.), *Handbook on ontologies*. International Handbooks on Information Systems.

Guarino, N., & Schneider, L. (2002). Ontology-driven conceptual modeling. In CAiSE 2002 (LNCS), (vol. 2348). Heidelberg, Gemany: Springer.

Guédria, W., Chen, D., & Naudet, Y. (2009). A maturity model for enterprise interoperability. In *On the move to meaningful internet systems workshops* (pp. 216–225). Berlin: Springer.

Gummesson, E. (2004). From one-to-one to many-to-many marketing. In B. Edvardsson et al. (Eds.), *Proceedings from QUIS 9 Symposium* (pp. 16-25). Karlstad, Sweden: Karlstad University. Retrieved February 20, 2013, from http://ipam5ever.com.sapo.pt/profile/QUISeg2004.pdf

Gummesson, E. (2008). Extending the service-dominant logic: From customer centricity to balanced centricity. *Journal of the Academy of Marketing Science, 36*(1), 15–17. doi:10.1007/s11747-007-0065-x

Gusmeroli, S. (2012). From enterprise interoperability to service innovation: European research activities in future internet enterprise systems. In *Enterprise Interoperability: 4th International IFIP Working Conference on Enterprise Interoperability* (LNBIP), (vol. 122). Berlin: Springer Verlag.

Hakansson, H., & Johanson, J. (1992). A model of industrial networks. In *Industrial networks—A new view of reality*. London: Routledge.

Hakansson, H., & Snehota, I. (Eds.). (1995). *Developing relationships in business networks*. London: Routledge.

Halamka, J. D., Mandl, K. D., & Tang, P. C. (2008). Early experiences with personal health records. *Journal of the American Medical Informatics Association, 15*(1), 1–7. doi:10.1197/jamia.M2562 PMID:17947615

Harald, K. (2004). *Methodenintegration im business engineering*. PhD Thesis.

Harmon, P. (2010). *The scope and evolution of business process management*. Berlin: Springer-Verlag. doi:10.1007/978-3-642-00416-2_3

Hasheminejad, S. M. H., & Jalili, S. (2012). Design patterns selection: An automatic two-phase method. *Journal of Systems and Software*, *85*(2), 408–424. doi:10.1016/j.jss.2011.08.031

Hashim, N., Murphy, J., & Law, R. (2007). A review of hospitality website design frameworks. In M. Sigala, L. Mich, & J. Murphy (Eds.), *Information and communication technologies in tourism* (pp. 219–230). New York: Springer Wien. doi:10.1007/978-3-211-69566-1_21

Haslhofer, B., & Klas, W. (2010). A survey of techniques for achieving metadata interoperability. *ACM Computing Surveys*, *42*(2), 7:1-37.

Hayek, F. (1945). The use of knowledge in society. *The American Economic Review*, *35*(4), 519–530.

Health Level Seven & ASTM International. (2008). *Continuity of care document (CCD) release 1*. Retrieved from http://wiki.hl7.org/index.php?title=Product_CCD

Health Level Seven. (2005). *Clinical document architecture (CDA), release 2*. Retrieved from http://www.hl7.org/implement/standards/cda.cfm

Health Level Seven. (2006). *TermInfo: Using SNOMED CT in HL7 version 3*. Retrieved from http://www.hl7.org/library/committees/terminfo/TermInfo_Ballot_DRAFT.30Jan2006.doc

Health Level Seven. (2008). *Personal healthcare monitoring report (PHMR)*. Retrieved from http://www.hl7.org/documentcenter/ballots/2008SEP/support/CDAR2_PHMRPTS_R1_DSTU_2008NOV.zip

Health Level Seven. (2010a). *Context-aware retrieval application (infobutton), knowledge request, release 1*. Retrieved from http://www.hl7.org/v3ballot/html/domains/uvds/uvds_Context-awareKnowledgeRetrieval(Infobutton).html

Health Level Seven. (2010b). *HL7 version 3 standard: Transport specification - Web services profile, release 2*. Retrieved from http://www.hl7.org/v3ballot/html/infrastructure/transport/transport-wsprofiles.html

Health Level Seven. (2010c). *Reference information model (RIM) release 3*. Retrieved from http://www.hl7.org/v3ballot/html/infrastructure/rim/rim.html

Health Level Seven. (2011a). *greenCDA project*. Retrieved from http://wiki.hl7.org/index.php?title=GreenCDA_Project

Health Level Seven. (2011b). *HL7 version 3 standard: Decision support service, release 1*. Retrieved from http://www.hl7.org/v3ballot/html/infrastructure/dss/HL7_Decision_Support_Service_%20Normative_Specification_Release_1.pdf

Healthcare Information Technology Standards Panel. (2009). *HITSP C32 - Summary documents using HL7 continuity of care document (CCD) component*. Retrieved from http://www.hitsp.org/ConstructSet_Details.aspx?&PrefixAlpha=4&PrefixNumeric=32

Healthcare Information Technology Standards Panel. (2010). *HITSP C83 - CDA content modules component*. Retrieved from http://www.hitsp.org/Handlers/HitspFileServer.aspx?FileGuid=717d69a5-6bc4-4f8b-a22c-197130b50567

Heath, T., & Bizer, C. (2011). *Linked data: Evolving the web into a global data space*. San Francisco: Morgan & Claypool. doi:10.1007/978-1-4614-1767-5_4

Heja, G., Surjan, G., & Varga, P. (2008). Ontological analysis of SNOMED CT. *BMC Medical Informatics and Decision Making*, *8*(S1), S8. doi:10.1186/1472-6947-8-S1-S8 PMID:19007445

Helmer, A., Lipprandt, M., Frenken, T., Eichelberg, M., & Hein, A. (2011). Empowering patients through personal health records: A survey of existing third-party web-based PHR products. *Electronic Journal of Health Informatics*, *6*(3), 1–19.

Herbst, H. (1996). Business rules in systems analysis: A meta-model and repository system. *Information Systems*, *21*(2), 147–166. doi:10.1016/0306-4379(96)00009-9

Heuer, R. J. (2001). *Psychology of intelligence analysis. Center for the Study of Intelligence, Central Intelligence Agency*. Washington, DC: CIA.

Hevner, A. R. (2007). A three cycle view of design science research. *Scandinavian Journal of Information Systems*, *19*(2), 87–92.

Hevner, A. R., March, S. T., Park, J., & Ram, S. (2004). Design science in information systems research. *Management Information Systems Quarterly, 28*(1), 75–105. doi:doi:10.2307/249422

Highsmith, J., & Cockburn, A. (2001). Agile software development: The business of innovation. *IEEE Computer, 34*, 120–127. doi:10.1109/2.947100

Hillegersberg, J. V., & Kumar, K. (1999). Using metamodeling to integrate object-oriented analysis, design and programming concepts. *Information Systems, 24*(2), 113–129. doi:10.1016/S0306-4379(99)00008-3

HL7 CDA R2. (2008). *HL7/ASTM implementation guide for CDA® R2 -Continuity of care document (CCD®) release 1*. Retrieved from http://www.hl7.org/implement/standards/product_brief.cfm?product_id=6

Hoffman, D. L., & Novak, T. P. (1996). Marketing in hypermedia computer-mediated environments: Conceptual foundations. *Journal of Marketing, 60*(3), 50–68. doi:10.2307/1251841

Holland, J. H. (1998). Emergence: From chaos to order. In *Complexity* (pp. XIII, 258). Perseus Books. Retrieved from http://video.yahoo.com/watch/111582/992708

Holland, J. H. (1992). Complex adaptive systems. *Daedalus, 121*(1), 17–30.

Holland, J. H. (1996). *Hidden order: How adaptation builds complexity*. Perseus Books.

Hollenbach, J., Presbrey, J., & Berners-Lee, T. (2009). Using RDF metadata to enable access control on the social semantic web. In *Proceedings of the Workshop on Collaborative Construction, Management and Linking of Structured Knowledge (CK-2009)*. CK.

Honour, E. (2008). Systems engineering and complexity. *INCOSE Insight, 11*(1), 20.

Horrocks, I. (2002). DAML+OIL: A description logic for the semantic web. *IEEE Computer Society on Data Engineering, 25*, 4–9.

HR-XML. (2013). *HR-XML consortium*. Retrieved from http://www.hr-xml.org/

Hsu, C. (2009). Editorial column--Service science and network science. *Service Science, 1*(2), i–ii. doi:10.1287/serv.1.2.i

Hu, B. (2010). Semantic interoperability for financial information: A component-based approach. In *Proceedings of 3rd IEEE International Conference on Computer Science and Information Technology* (pp. 228-232). IEEE.

Hughes, B., Schmidt, D., & Smith, A. (2006). Towards interoperable secondary annotations in the e-social science domain. In *Proceedings of 2nd International Conference on E-Social Science*. Manchester, UK: E-Social Science.

Hughes, J. (1980). *The philosophy of social research*. London: Longman.

Huizingh, E. (2011). Open innovation: State of the art and future perspectives. *Technovation, 31*, 2–9. doi:10.1016/j.technovation.2010.10.002

Hyvonen, J. (2007). Strategy, performance measurement techniques and information technology of the firm and their links to organizational performance. *Management Accounting Research, 18*, 343–366. doi:10.1016/j.mar.2007.02.001

Iakovidis, I. (1998). Towards personal health records: Current situation, obstacles and trends in implementation of electronic healthcare. *International Journal of Medical Informatics, 52*(1-3), 105–115. doi:10.1016/S1386-5056(98)00129-4 PMID:9848407

IBM Service Sciences. Management and Engineering. (n.d.). *Services definition*. Retrieved December, 2011 from http://www.research.ibm.com/ssme/services.shtml

ICD. (2013). *ICD-10*. Retrieved from http://www.cms.gov/Medicare/Coding/ICD10/index.html?redirect=/icd10

IDABC. (2008). *European interoperability framework draft version 2.0*. IDABC.

IEEE. Computer Society. (2005). *Guide to the software engineering body of knowledge 2004 version*. IEEE Computer Society. Retrieved from http://www.computer.org/portal/web/swebok/htmlformat

INCOSE, & OMG DSIG. (2011). Model based systems engineering. *MBSE Wiki*. Retrieved February 26, 2012, from http://www.omgwiki.org/MBSE/doku.php

Informal Study Group on Value Proposition for Enterprise Interoperability. (2008). *Unleashing the potential of the european knowledge economy value proposition for enterprise interoperability*. Brussels: European Comission. Retrieved from http://cordis.europa.eu/documents/documentlibrary/100123101EN6.pdf

*Informal Study Group on Value Proposition*. (2008). Retrieved 03 27, 2013, from http://cordis.europa.eu/fp7/ict/enet/ei-isg_en.html

Institute of Electrical and Electronics Engineers (IEEE). (1990). *IEEE standard computer dictionary: A compilation of IEEE standard computer glossaries*. IEEE.

Integrating the Healthcare Enterprise. (2008a). *Care management (CM) integration profile*. Retrieved from http://www.ihe.net/Technical_Framework/upload/IHE_PCC_Care_Management_CM_Supplement_TI_2008-08-22.pdf

Integrating the Healthcare Enterprise. (2008b). *Query for existing data (QED) integration profile*. Retrieved from http://www.ihe.net/Technical_Framework/upload/IHE_PCC_Query_for_Existing_Data_QED_SupplSuppl_TI_2008-08-22.pdf

Integrating the Healthcare Enterprise. (2009a). *Immunization content (IC) integration profile*. Retrieved from http://www.ihe.net/Technical_Framework/upload/IHE_PCC_Immunization_Content_IC_Supplement_TI_-2009-08-10.pdf

Integrating the Healthcare Enterprise. (2009b). *Request for clinical guidance (RCG) integration profile*. Retrieved from http://www.ihe.net/Technical_Framework/upload/IHE_PCC_Request_for_Clinical_Guidance_RCG_TI_-2009-08-10.pdf

Integrating the Healthcare Enterprise. (2010a). *Cross-enterprise document media interchange (XDM) integration profile*. Retrieved from http://www.ihe.net/Technical_Framework/upload/IHE_ITI_TF_Rev7-0_Vol1_FT_2010-08-10.pdf

Integrating the Healthcare Enterprise. (2010b). *Cross-enterprise document reliable interchange (XDR) integration profile*. Retrieved from http://www.ihe.net/Technical_Framework/upload/IHE_ITI_TF_Rev7-0_Vol1_FT_2010-08-10.pdf

Integrating the Healthcare Enterprise. (2010c). *Cross-enterprise document sharing (XDS) integration profile*. Retrieved from http://www.ihe.net/Technical_Framework/upload/IHE_ITI_TF_Rev7-0_Vol1_FT_2010-08-10.pdf

Integrating the Healthcare Enterprise. (2010d). *Exchange of personal health record content (XPHR) integration profile*. Retrieved from http://www.ihe.net/Technical_Framework/upload/IHE_PCC_TF_Rev6-0_Vol_1_2010-08-30.pdf

Integrating the Healthcare Enterprise. (2010e). *Patient care device (PCD) technical framework, volume 1, revision 1.2*. Retrieved from http://www.ihe.net/Technical_Framework/upload/IHE_PCD_TF_Rev1-2_Vol1_TI_2010-09-30.pdf

Integrating the Healthcare Enterprise. (2010f). *Web services for IHE transactions*. Retrieved from http://www.ihe.net/Technical_Framework/upload/IHE_ITI_TF_Rev7-0_Vol2x_FT_2010-08-10.pdf

International Organization for Standardization & Comité Européen de Normalisation. (2008). *EN 13606-1, health informatics – Electronic health record communication – Part 1: Reference model*.

International Organization for Standardization & The Institute of Electrical and Electronics Engineers. (2004a). *ISO/IEEE 11073 family of standards*.

International Organization for Standardization & The Institute of Electrical and Electronics Engineers. (2004b). *ISO/IEEE 11073-10201:2004(E) health informatics – Point-of-care medical device communication – Part 10201: Domain information model*.

International Organization for Standardization & The Institute of Electrical and Electronics Engineers. (2004c). *ISO/IEEE 11073-10101:2004(E) health informatics – Point-of-care medical device communication – Part 10101: Nomenclature*.

INTEROP NoE. (2007). *Interoperability research for networked enterprises applications and software* (FP6 IST-1-508011). Retrieved May 30, 2011, from http://interop-vlab.eu/ei_public_deliverables/interop-noe-deliverables

INTEROP Partners. (2005). *Deliverable DTG3.1 (MoMo.2), MoMo roadmap*. INTEROP NoE Project (FP6 IST-1-508011). Retrieved from http://interop-vlab.eu/ei_public_deliverables/interop-noe-deliverables/tg3-model-morphisms/DTG3.1/

INTEROP Partners. (2007). *Deliverable DTG2.3: Report on model driven interoperability*. INTEROP NoE Project (FP6 IST-1-508011). Retrieved from http://interop-vlab.eu/ei_public_deliverables/interop-noe-deliverables/tg2-model-driven-interoperability/dtg2-3-report-on-model-driven-interoperability/

INTEROP. (2007). *Enterprise interoperability-framework and knowledge corpus - Final report, INTEROP NoE, FP6 – contract n° 508011, deliverable DI.3 (May 21, 2007)*. Author.

Introna, L. D., & Nissenbaum, H. (2000). Shaping the web: Why the politics of search engines matters. *The Information Society*, *16*(3), 169–185. doi:10.1080/01972240050133634

Isele, R., Jentzsch, A., Bizer, C., & Volz, J. (2012). *Silk - A link discovery framework for the web of data*. Retrieved from http://wifo5-03.informatik.uni-mannheim.de/bizer/silk/

ISO. (2011). *CEN EN/ISO 11354-1, advanced automation technologies and their applications, part 1: Framework for enterprise interoperability*. Geneva: International Standards Office.

ISO/IEC. (1994). *ISO/IEC 7498-1, information technology – Open systems interconnection – Basic reference model: The basic model* (2nd Ed.). Geneva: International Standards Office. Retrieved February 25, 2013, from http://standards.iso.org/ittf/PubliclyAvailableStandards/index.html

ISO/IEC. (2008). *Systems and software engineering -- Software life cycle processes (ISO/IEC 12207:2008)*. ISO/IEC.

ISO/IEC/IEEE. (2010). *Systems and software engineering – Vocabulary*. Geneva: International Standard ISO/IEC/IEEE 24765:2010(E).

Jain, S., & Kibira, D. (2010). A framework for multi-resolution modeling of sustainable manufacturing. In *Proceedings of the 2010 Winter Simulation Conference* (pp. 3423–3434). Retrieved from http://www.informs-sim.org/wsc10papers/316.pdf

Jain, A. K., Murty, M. N., & Flynn, P. J. (1999). Data clustering: A review. *ACM Computing Surveys*, *31*(3). doi:10.1145/331499.331504

Janowicz, K., Scheider, S., Pehle, T., & Hart, G. (2012). Geospatial semantics and linked spatiotemporal data – Past, present, and future. *Semantic Web – Interoperability, Usability. Applicability*, *3*(4), 321–332.

Jardim-Goncalves, R., & Steiger-Garcao, A. (2009). *Rowards EI as a science: Considerations and points of view*. Unpublished.

Jardim-Goncalves, R., Agostinho, C., & Steiger-Garcao, A. (2010). Sustainable systems' interoperability: A reference model for seamless networked business. In *Proceedings of 2010 IEEE International Conference on Systems Man and Cybernetics (SMC)*. Istanbul, Turkey: IEEE.

Jardim-Goncalves, R., Agostinho, C., & Steiger-Garcao, A. (2012). A reference model for sustainable interoperability in networked enterprises: Towards the foundation of EI science base. *International Journal of Computer Integrated Manufacturing*, *25*(10), 855–873. doi:10.1080/0951192X.2011.653831

Jardim-Goncalves, R., Grilo, A., Agostinho, C., Lampathaki, F., & Charalabidis, Y. (2013). Systematisation of interoperability body of knowledge: The foundation for enterprise interoperability as a science. *Enterprise Information Systems*, *7*(1), 7–32. doi:10.1080/17517575.2012.684401

Jardim-Goncalves, R., Grilo, A., & Steiger-Garcao, A. (2006). Challenging the interoperability industry with MDA between computers in and SOA. *Computers in Industry*, *57*(8-9), 679–689. doi:10.1016/j.compind.2006.04.013

Jardim-Goncalves, R., Popplewell, K., & Grilo, A. (2012). Sustainable interoperability: The future of internet based industrial enterprises. *Computers in Industry*, *63*, 731–738. doi:10.1016/j.compind.2012.08.016

Jardim-Goncalves, R., Sarraipa, J., Agostinho, C., & Panetto, H. (2009). Knowledge framework for intelligent manufacturing systems. *Journal of Intelligent Manufacturing*. doi: doi:10.1007/s10845-009-0332-4

Jardim-Goncalves, R., Silva, J. P. M. A., Steiger-Garcao, A., & Monteiro, A. (2007). Framework for enhanced interoperability through ontological harmonization of enterprise product models. In *Ontologies: A handbook of principles, concepts and applications, information systems* (Vol. 14, p. 915). Secaucus, NJ: Springer.

Jardim-Goncalves, R., & Steiger-Garcao, A. (2002). Implicit multilevel modelling in flexible business environments. *Communications of the ACM*, 53–57.

Java Ontology Editor. (1998, May 19). *Java ontology editor (JOE)*. Retrieved from http://cit.cse.sc.edu/demos/java/joe/joeBeta-jar.html

Jeong, B., Lee, D., Cho, H., & Lee, J. (2008). A novel method for measuring semantic similarity for XML schema matching. *Expert Systems with Applications*, *34*, 1651–1658. doi:10.1016/j.eswa.2007.01.025

Jimenez-Martinez, J., & Polo-Redondo, Y. (2004). The influence of EDI adoption over its perceived benefits. *Technovation*, *24*, 73–79. doi:10.1016/S0166-4972(02)00047-0

Johnson, P., Ekstedt, M., & Jacobson, I. (2012). Where's the theory for software engineering? *IEEE Software*, 94-96. Retrieved on September 12, 2013, from: http://semat.org/wp-content/uploads/2012/02/IEEESoftware_Sep-Oct_2012.pdf

Kaelber, D. C., Shah, S., Vincent, A., Pan, E., Hook, J. M., Johnston, D., et al. (2008). *The value of personal health records*. Retrieved from http://www.citl.org/publications/_pdf/CITL_PHR_Report.pdf

Kajikawa, Y., Takeda, Y., Sakata, I., & Matsushima, K. (2010). Multiscale analysis of interfirm networks in regional clusters. *Technovation*, *30*, 168–180. doi:10.1016/j.technovation.2009.12.004

Kang, K., Cohen, S., Hess, J., Novak, W., & Peterson, A. (1990). *Feature-oriented domain analysis (FODA) feasibility study* (Technical Report CMU/SEI-90-TR-021). Pittsburgh, PA: Software Engineering Institute.

Kano, N., Nobuhiku, S., Fumio, T., & Shinichi, T. (1984). Attractive quality and must-be quality. *Journal of the Japanese Society for Quality Control*, *14*(2), 39–48.

Karagiannis, D. (2012). *Presentation at FInES workshop in Aalborg*. Retrieved, June 24, 2013 from http://www.fines-cluster.eu/fines/jm/news-section/past-news/fines-workshop-in-aalborg-may-9th-2012-presentations-videos-available.html

Karagiannis, D., & Höfferer, P. (2006). Metamodels in action: An overview. In *Proceedings of ICSOFT 2006 – First International Conference on Software and Data Technologies*. Insticc Press.

Karagiannis, D., & Kühn, H. (2002). Metamodelling platforms In *Proceedings of the Third International Conference EC-Web 2002 – Dexa 2002* (LNCS), (vol. 2455). Berlin: Springer.

Karagiannis, D., Grossmann, W., & Höfferer, P. (2008). *Open model initiative: A feasibility study*. Retrieved June 24, 2013, from http://cms.dke.univie.ac.at/uploads/media/Open_Models_Feasibility_Study_SEPT_2008.pdf

Kauffman, S. (1996). *At home in the universe: The search for laws of self-organization and complexity*. Oxford, UK: Oxford University Press.

Kauffman, S., & Clayton, P. (2006). On emergence, agency, and organization. *Biology and Philosophy*, *21*(4), 501–521. doi:10.1007/s10539-005-9003-9

Kawamoto, K., & Esler, B. (2006). *Service functional model specification - Decision support service (DSS)*. Retrieved from http://archive.hl7.org/v3ballotarchive/v3ballot2009jan/html/infrastructure/dss/Decision%20Support%20Service%20v1_0.pdf

Kawamoto, K., & Lobach, D. (2007). Proposal for fulfilling strategic objectives of the U.S. roadmap for national action on clinical decision support through a service-oriented architecture leveraging HL7 services. *Journal of the American Medical Informatics Association*, *14*(2), 146–155. doi:10.1197/jamia.M2298 PMID:17213489

Kearns, G. S., & Sabherwal, R. (2007). Strategic alignment between business and information technology: A knowledge-based view of behaviors, outcome and consequences. *Journal of Management Information Systems*, *23*(3), 129–162. doi:10.2753/MIS0742-1222230306

Kellogg, D. L., & Nie, W. (1995). A framework for strategic service management. *Journal of Operations Management*, *13*(4), 323–337. doi:10.1016/0272-6963(95)00036-4

Kelly, S., & Tolvanen, J.-P. (2008). *Doamin-specific modelling: Enabling full code generation*. Hoboken, NJ: John Wiley & Son, Inc. doi:10.1002/9780470249260

Kern, H., Hummel, A., & Kühne, S. (2011). Towards a comparative analysis of meta-metamodels. In *Proceedings of the 11th Workshop on Domain-Specific Modeling*. Retrieved, 01. January, 2011 from http://www.dsmforum. org/events/DSM11/Papers/kern.pdf

Key, J. J., Boyle, M., & Francis, G. (1999). An ecosystem approach for sustainability: Addressing the challenge of complexity. *Futures*, *31*(721).

Kim, D., & Shen, W. (2007). An approach to evaluating structural pattern conformance of UML models. In *Proceedings of ACM Symposium on Applied Computing* (pp. 1404-1408). ACM Press.

Kim, D. H., & Park, S. J. (1997). FORM: A flexible data model for integrated CASE environments. *Data & Knowledge Engineering*, *22*(2), 133–158. doi:10.1016/ S0169-023X(96)00042-0

Kim, T. Y., Lee, S., Kim, K., & Kim, C. H. (2006). A modeling framework for agile and interoperable virtual enterprises. *Computers in Industry*, *57*(3), 204–217. doi:10.1016/j.compind.2005.12.003

Kim, W., & Mauborgne, R. (2005). *Blue ocean strategy – How to create uncontested market space and make competition irrelevant*. Boston: Harvard Business School Press.

Kingston, G., Fewell, S., & Richer, W. (2005). *An organisational interoperability agility model*. Defence Science and Technology Organisation. Retrieved February 25, 2013, from http://www.dtic.mil/dtic/tr/fulltext/u2/a463924.pdf

Kitamura, Y., Kashiwase, M., Fuse, M., & Mizoguchi, R. (2004). Deployment of an ontological framework of functional design knowledge. *Ontology and It's Applications to Knowledge-Intensive Engineering*, *18*, 115–127.

Kodama, M. (2005). Knowledge creation through networked strategic communities: Case studies on new product development in Japanese companies. *Long Range Planning*, *38*, 27–49. doi:10.1016/j.lrp.2004.11.011

Koellinger, P. (2008). The relationship between technology, innovation, and firm performance: Empirical evidence from e-business in Europe. *Research Policy*, *37*, 1317–1328. doi:10.1016/j.respol.2008.04.024

Kohlborn, T., Korthaus, A., & Rosemann, M. (2009). Business and software lifecycle management. In *Proceedings of 2009 Enterprise Distributed Object Computing Conference (EDOC '09)*. EDOC.

Kohler, M. (2007). *UMLS for information extraction*. (Mater's Thesis). Vienna University of Technology, Vienna, Austria.

Kohonen, T. (1982). Self-organized formation of topologically correct feature maps. *Biological Cybernetics*, *43*(1), 59–69. doi:10.1007/BF00337288

Kokash, N., & Arbab, F. (2009). Formal behavioral modeling and compliance analysis for service-oriented systems. In *Formal methods for components and objects (LNCS)* (Vol. 5751, pp. 21–41). Berlin: Springer-Verlag. doi:10.1007/978-3-642-04167-9_2

Kokol, P. (1993). Metamodeling: How, why and what? *SIGSOFT Softw. Eng. Notes*, *18*, 2. doi:10.1145/159420.155834

Koussouris, S., Lampathaki, F., Mouzakitis, S., Charalabidis, Y., & Psarras, J. (2011). Digging into the real-life enterprise interoperability areas definition and overview of the main research areas. In *Proceedings of International Symposium on Collaborative Enterprises (CENT 2011) in the Context of the 15th World-Multi-Conference on Systemics, Cybernetics and Informatics: WMSCI 2011*. Orlando, FL: CENT. Retrieved from http://www.iiis. org/CDs2011/CD2011SCI/CENT_2011/PapersPdf/ ZB589UA.pdf

Krauthammer, M. (2002). *Brief review of clinical vocabularies*. Retrieved from http://www.cbil.upenn.edu/ Ontology/MKreview.html

Krötzsch, M., Simančik, F., & Horrocks, I. (2012). *A description logic primer*. Retrieved December 29, 2013, from http://arxiv.org/pdf/1201.4089

Kruchten, P. (2004). *The rational unified process: An introduction*. Boston: Pearson Education Inc.

Kuhn, M. (2010). Modeling vs encoding for semantic web. *Journal of Semantic Web-Interoperability, Usability. Applicability*, *1*(1), 11–15.

Kuhn, T. (1996). *The structure of scientific revolutions* (3rd ed.). Chicago: The University of Chicago Press. doi:10.7208/chicago/9780226458106.001.0001

Kuk, G. (2004). Effectiveness of vendor-managed inventory in the electronics industry: Determinants and outcomes. *Information & Management*, *41*, 645–654. doi:10.1016/j.im.2003.08.002

Laclavik, M. (2007). *COMMIUS: ISU via email*. eChallenges e-2007. Retrieved on March 2013 from ftp://ftp.cordis.europa.eu/pub/ist/docs/ict-ent-net/echallenges2-ml_en.pdf

Lacy, L. (2005). *OWL: Representing information using the web ontology language*. Victoria, Canada: Trafford Publishing.

Lampathaki, F., Koussouris, S., Agostinho, C., Jardim-Goncalves, R., Charalabidis, Y., & Psarras, J. (2011). Towards an interoperability science: Cultivating the scientific foundations for enterprise interoperability. In *Proceedings of International Symposium on Collaborative Enterprises (CENT 2011) in the Context of the 15th World-Multi-Conference on Systemics, Cybernetics and Informatics: WMSCI 2011*. Orlando, FL: CENT.

Lampathaki, F., Koussouris, S., Mouzakitis, S., Charalabidis, Y., & Psarras, J. (2011). Digging into the real-life enterprise interoperability areas – Definition and overview of the main research areas. In *Proceedings of CENT 2011: Collaborative Enterprises 2011 – Platforms, Processes, and Practices Advancing the Enterprise 2.0 Science Base for Enterprise Interoperability in the advent of the Future of Internet*. Orlando, FL: CENT.

Lampathaki, F., Koussouris, S., Agostinho, C., Jardim-Goncalves, R., Charalabidis, Y., & Psarras, J. (2012). Infusing scientific foundations into enterprise interoperability. *Computers in Industry*, *63*(8), 858–866. doi:10.1016/j.compind.2012.08.004

Lampathaki, F., Mouzakitis, S., Gionis, G., Charalabidis, Y., & Askounis, D. (2009). Business to business interoperability: A current review of XML data integration standards. *Computer Standards & Interfaces*, *31*, 1045–1055. doi:10.1016/j.csi.2008.12.006

Langegger, A. (2013). *XLWrap – Spreadsheet-to-RDF wrapper*. Retrieved from http://xlwrap.sourceforge.net/

Larman, C. (2004). *Applying UML and patterns: An introduction to object-oriented analysis and design and iterative development* (3rd ed.). Upper Saddle River, NJ: Prentice Hall.

Legal, X. M. L. (2008). *Overview of the OASIS LegalXML*. Retrieved from http://www.legalxml.org/

Legner, R., & Lebreton, B. (2007). Preface to the focus theme section: Business interoperability research: Present achievements and upcoming challenges. *Electronic Markets*, *17*(3), 176–186. doi:10.1080/10196780701503054

Lenzerini, M. (2002). Data integration: A theoretical perspective. In *Proceedings of the 21st ACM SIGACT-SIGMOD-SIGART Symposium on Principles of Database Systems* (pp. 233-246). ACM.

Lessig, L. (1999). *Code and other laws of cyberspace*. New York: Basic Books.

Lewin, D. L. (1999). Application of complexity theory to organization science. *Organization Science*, *10*(3), 215. doi:10.1287/orsc.10.3.215

Lewis, G., Morris, E., Simanta, S., & Wrage, L. (2008). Why standards are not enough to guarantee end-to-end interoperability. In *Proceedings of Seventh International Conference on Composition-Based Software Systems* (pp. 164-173). IEEE Computer Society Press.

Li, M. S. (2011). Utility service infrastructure in the future internet: PPP models and policy impact. *Samos Summit 2011*. Retrieved on December 2011 from https://pithos.grnet.gr/pithos/rest/irematz@ntua.gr/files/SamosSummit2011/Presentations/Session+I/ManSzeLi.pdf

Li, M. S., Crave, S., Grilo, A., & Van den Berg, R. (Eds.). (2008). *Unleashing the potential of the European knowledge economy – Value proposition for enterprise interoperability*. Brussels: European Commission, Information Society and Media.

Li, M.-S., Cabral, R., Doumeingts, G., & Popplewell, K. (2006). *Enterprise interoperability: A concerted research roadmap for shaping business networking in the knowledge-based economy*. Brussels: Commission for the European Communities.

Lind, S., Johansson, B., Stahre, J., Berlin, C., Fasth, Å., Heilala, J., et al. (2009). *SIMTER – A joint simulation tool for production development*. Retrieved from http://www.vtt.fi/inf/pdf/workingpapers/2009/W125.pdf

LOC. (2012). *Standards in the library of congress*. Retrieved from http://www.loc.gov/standards/

LOINC. (2013). *Logical observation identifiers names and codes (LOINC®)*. Retrieved from http://loinc.org/

Loutas, N., Kamateri, E., Bosi, F., & Tarabanis, K. (2011). Cloud computing interoperability: The state of play. In *Proceedings of International Conference on Cloud Computing Technology and Science* (pp. 752-757). IEEE Computer Society Press.

Lusk, E., Desai, N., Bradshaw, R., Lusk, A., & Butler, R. (2006). An interoperability approach to system software, tools, and libraries for clusters. *International Journal of High Performance Computing Applications*, *20*(3), 401–407. doi:10.1177/1094342006067473

Lutowski, R. (2005). *Software requirements: Encapsulation, quality, and reuse*. Boca Raton, FL: CRC Press. doi:10.1201/9781420031317

Maedche, A., Motik, B., Silva, N., & Volz, R. (2002). MAFRA - A mapping framework for distributed ontologies. In *Knowledge engineering and knowledge management: Ontologies and the semantic web (LNCS)* (Vol. 2473, pp. 235–250). Berlin: Springer. doi:10.1007/3-540-45810-7_23

Maglio, P. P., & Spohrer, J. (2008). Fundamentals of service science. *Journal of the Academy of Marketing Science*, *36*(1), 18–20. doi:10.1007/s11747-007-0058-9

Mainzer, K. (1996). *Thinking in complexity: The complex dynamics of matter, mind, and mankind*. Berlin: Springer-Verlag. doi:10.1007/978-3-662-03305-0

Makela, T., Rommel, K., Uskonem, J., & Wan, T. (2007). *Towards a financial ontology – A comparison of e- business process standards*. Retrived from http://www.soberit.hut.fi/T-86/T-86.5161/2007/FinancialOntology_final.pdf

Malik, N. (2009). Toward an enterprise business motivation model. *The Architecture Journal*, *19*, 10–16.

Malone, J. (1988). *The science of linguistics in the art of translation: Some tools from linguistics for the analysis and practice of translation*. Unpublished.

Mancinelli, S., & Mazzanti, M. (2009). Innovation, networking and complementarity: Evidence on SME performances for a local economic system in North-Eastern Italy. *The Annals of Regional Science*, *43*(3), 567–597. doi:10.1007/s00168-008-0255-6

Manson, S. M. (2001). Simplifying complexity: A review of complexity theory. *Geoforum*, *32*(3), 405–414. doi:10.1016/S0016-7185(00)00035-X

Martinez-Lorente, A. R., Sanchez-Rogriguez, C., & Dewhurst, F. W. (2004). The effect of information technologies on TQM: An initial analysis. *International Journal of Production Economics*, *89*, 77–93. doi:10.1016/j.ijpe.2003.06.001

Maturana, H., & Varela, F. (1980). Autopoiesis and cognition. *The Review of Metaphysics*, *42*, 141.

Maynard, D., Yankova, M., Kourakis, R., & Kokossis, A. (2005). Ontology-based information extraction for market monitoring and technology watch. In *Proceedings of the Workshop Of ESWC, End User Apects of Semantic Web*. Heraklion.

McCarthy, J. E. (1960). *Basic marketing – A managerial approach*. Homewood, IL: Richard D. Irwin.

McElroy, M. W. (2000). Integrating complexity theory, knowledge management and organizational learning. *Journal of Knowledge Management*, *4*(3), 195–203. doi:10.1108/13673270010377652

Mckelvey, B. (1999). Complexity theory in organization science: Seizing the promise or becoming a fad? Bottom-up organization science. *Emergence*, *1*(1), 5–32. doi:10.1207/s15327000em0101_2

Merali, Y., & McKelvey, B. (2006). Using complexity science to effect a paradigm shift in information systems for the 21st century. *Journal of Information Technology*, *21*(4), 211–215. doi:10.1057/palgrave.jit.2000082

Microsoft. (2012). Defining a many-to-many relationship. *Microsoft SQL Server*. Retrieved February 20, 2013, from http://technet.microsoft.com/en-us/library/ms170463.aspx

Mika, P. (2005). Ontologies are us: A unified model of social networks and semantics. *International Semantic Web Conference, 3729*, 552-536.

Minoli, D. (2008). *Enterprise architecture A to Z.* Boca Raton, FL: Auerbach Publications. doi:10.1201/9781420013702

Mirovsky, D. (2013). *Relationship marketing of start-ups – An empirical analysis of commercial and social startups' management of stakeholder relationships.* (Unpublished master thesis). University of Mannheim, Mannheim, Germany.

Missikoff, M., Charabilidis, Y., Goncalves, R., & Popplewell, K. (2012). *FInES research roadmap 2025-v3.0.* Retrieved 3 22, 2013, from http://www.fines-cluster.eu/fines/jm/Publications/Download-document/323-FInES-Research-Roadmap-2025-v3.0.html

Monfelt, Y., Pilemalm, S., Hallberg, J., & Yngström, L. (2011). The 14-layered framework for including social and organizational aspects in security management. *Information Management & Computer Security, 19*(2), 124–133. doi:10.1108/09685221111143060

Monin, J.-F. (2003). *Understanding formal methods.* Berlin: Springer. doi:10.1007/978-1-4471-0043-0

Moore, J. F. (1996). *The death of competition: Leadership & strategy in the age of business ecosystems.* New York, NY: HarperBusiness.

Morris, E., et al. (2004). *System of systems interoperability (SOSI), final report* (Report No. CMU/SEI-2004-TR-004). Carnegie Mellon Software Engineering Institute. Retrieved February 25, 2013, from http://www.sei.cmu.edu/reports/04tr004.pdf

Morris, C. G. (1992). *Academic press dictionary of science and technology.* New York: Academic Press.

Mosterman, P. J., & Vangheluwe, H. (2004). Computer automated multi-paradigm modeling: An introduction. *Simulation, 80*(9), 433–450. doi:10.1177/0037549704050532

Mouzakitis, S., Sourouni, A. M., & Askounis, D. (2009). Effects of enterprise interoperability on integration efforts in supply chains. *International Journal of Electronic Commerce, 14*(2), 127–155. doi:10.2753/JEC1086-4415140205

Mylopoulos, J., Borgida, A., Jarke, M., & Koubarakis, M. (1990). Telos: Representing knowledge about information systems. *ACM Transactions on Information Systems, 8*(4), 325–362. doi:10.1145/102675.102676

Nagarajan, M., Verma, K., Sheth, A., Miller, J., & Lathem, J. (2006). Semantic interoperability of web services – Challenges and experiences. In *Proceedings of the 4th IEEE International Conference on Web Services* (pp. 373-382). IEEE.

Nichols, G., & Prigogine, I. (1989). *Exploring complexity: An introduction.* New York: W.H. Freeman & Company.

Nikolaidou, M., & Anagnostopoulos, D. (2005). A systematic approach for configuring web-based information systems. *Distributed and Parallel Databases, 17*(3), 267–290. doi:10.1007/s10619-005-6832-0

Nissenbaum, H. (1998). Values in the design of computer systems. *Computers & Society*, 38–39. doi:10.1145/277351.277359

Nissen, H. W., & Jarke, M. (1999). Repository support for multi-perspective requirements engineering. *Information Systems, 24*(2), 131–158. doi:10.1016/S0306-4379(99)00009-5

Nonaka, I., Konno, N., & Toyama, R. (2001). Emergence of Ba. In I. Nonaka, & T. Nishiguchi (Eds.), *Knowledge emergence: Social, technical, and evolutionary dimensions of knowledge creation* (pp. 13–29). Oxford, UK: Oxford University Press.

Nurmilaakso, J. M. (2008a). Adoption of e-business functions and migration from EDI-based to XML-based e-business frameworks in supply chain integration. *International Journal of Production Economics, 113*, 721–733. doi:10.1016/j.ijpe.2007.11.001

Nurmilaakso, J. M. (2008b). EDI, XML and e-business frameworks: A survey. *Computers in Industry, 59*, 370–379. doi:10.1016/j.compind.2007.09.004

OASIS. (2013). *Standards.* Retrieved from https://www.oasis-open.org/standards#samlv2.0

*Obeo Designer.* (n.d.). Retrieved 20, February, 2013 from http://www.obeo.fr/pages/obeo-designer/en

Oberle, D. (2010). *Report on landscapes of existing service description efforts*. Retrieved from http://www.w3.org/2005/Incubator/usdl/wiki/D1

Object Management Group (OMG). (2003). *MDA guide version 1.0.1, 2007-01-22*. OMG.

Object Management Group (OMG). (2011). *Business process model and notation (BPMN) version 2.0*. Retrieved March 18, 2013, from http://www.omg.org/spec/BPMN/2.0/

Object Management Group. (2011). *OMG clinical decision support service (CDSS), version 1.0*. Retrieved from http://www.omg.org/spec/CDSS/1.0/PDF

Obrst, L. (2003). Ontologies for semantically interoperable systems. In *Proceedings of the Twelfth International Conference on Information and Knowledge Management (CIKM '03)* (pp. 366-369). New York, NY: ACM.

Oguz, F., & Sengün, A. (2011). Mystery of the unknown: Revisiting tacit knowledge in the organizational literature. *Journal of Knowledge Management, 15*(3), 445–461. doi:10.1108/13673271111137420

OMG. (2003). *MDA guide version 1.0.1 (omg/2003-06-01)*. Object Management Group. Retrieved from http://www.omg.org/cgi-bin/doc?omg/03-06-01.pdf

OMG. (2013). *MOF 2 XMI mapping*. Retrieved February 25, 2013, http://www.omg.org/spec/XMI/

OMG. (n.d.). *Meta object facility*. Retrieved at 24, June 2013 from http://www.omg.org/mof/

OMiLAB. (n.d.). *Open models initiative laboratory*. Retrieved 24, June, 2013 from http://www.omilab.org

Open Group. (2009). *TOGAF version 9 – The open group architecture framework (TOGAF)*. The Open Group.

Open, I. D. Foundation. (2012). *The OpenID foundation*. Retrieved February 24, 2013, from http://openid.net/foundation

OpenLink Software. (2013). *Virtuoso universal server*. Retrieved from http://virtuoso.openlinksw.com/

OpenText. (2013). *OpenText business process management*. Retrieved February 25, 2013, from http://bps.opentext.com/bpm-and-case-basics/

Ostadzadeh, S., & Fereidoon, S. (2011). An architectural framework for the improvement of the ultra-large-scale systems interoperability. In *Proceedings of International Conference on Software Engineering Research and Practice*. Las Vegas, NV: Academic Press.

OWL-S. (2004). *OWL-S: Semantic markup for web service*. Retrieved February 25, 2013, from http://www.w3.org/Submission/OWL-S/

OWL-S. (2004, November). *OWL-S: Semantic markup for web services*. Retrieved from http://www.w3.org/Submission/OWL-S/

Papadimitriou, C. H. (1994). *Computational complexity*. Reading, MA: Addison-Wesley.

Papazoglou, M. P. (2003). Service-oriented computing: Concepts, characteristics and directions. In *Proceedings of the Fourth International Conference on Web Information Systems Engineering (WISE'03)*. Roma, Italy: IEEE.

Peristeras, V., & Tarabanis, K. (2006). The connection, communication, consolidation, collaboration interoperability framework (C4IF) for information systems interoperability. *International Journal of Interoperability in Business Information Systems, 1*(1), 61–72.

Perry, D.E., & Wolf, A. L. (1992). Foundations for the study of software architecture. *ACM SIGSOFT Software Eng. Notes*, 40–52.

Peters, R. J., & Ozsu, M. T. (1993). Reflection in a uniform behavioral object model. In *Proceedings of the 12th International Conference on Entity-Relationship Approach*. Academic Press.

Pfeffer, J., Graube, M., Ziegler, J., & Urbas, L. (2012). Browsing reversible neighborhood relations in linked data on mobile devices. In *Proceedings of 2nd International Conference on Pervasive Embedded Computing and Communication Systems* (PECCS). PECCS.

Phelan, S. E. (2001). What is complexity science, really? *Emergence, 3*(1), 120–136. doi:10.1207/S15327000EM0301_08

Pierce, B. C. (1991). *Basic category theory for computer scientists*. Cambridge, MA: MIT Press.

*plugIT*. (n.d.). Retrieved 24, June, 2013, from http://plug-it.org/plugITwiki/

Popper, K. (1992). *Conjectures and refutations: The growth of scientific knowledge* (5th ed.). London: Routledge and Keagan Paul.

Popplewell, K., Lampathaki, F., Koussouris, S., Mouzakitis, S., Charalabidis, Y., Goncalves, R., & Agostinho, C. (2012). *ENSEMBLE deliverable D2.1 - EISB state of play report*. Retrieved from http://www.fines-cluster.eu/fines/jm/Publications/Download-document/339-ENSEMBLE_D2.1_EISB_State_of_Play_Report-v2.00.html

Popplewell, K., Lampathaki, F., Koussouris, S., Mouzakitis, S., Charalabidis, Y., Goncalves, R., & Agostinho, C. (2012). *ENSEMBLE: Promoting future internet enterprise systems research*. Retrieved from http://www.fines-cluster.eu/fines/jm/Publications/Download-document/339-ENSEMBLE_D2.1_EISB_State_of_Play_Report-v2.00.html

Popplewell, K., Stojanovic, N., Abecker, A., Apostolou, D., Mentzas, G., & Harding, J. (2008). Supporting adaptive enterprise collaboration through semantic knowledge services. In *Proceedings of IESA, Enterprise Interoperability III* (pp. 381–393). Berlin, Germany: Springer.

Popplewell, K. (2011). Towards the definition of a science base for enterprise interoperability: A European perspective. *Journal of Systemics, Cybernetics, and Informatics*, *9*(5), 6–11.

Popplewell, K., Lampathaki, F., Koussiris, S., Mouzakitis, S., Charalabidis, Y., Goncalves, R., & Agostino, C. (2012). *EISB state of play report*. Brussels: European Commission.

Powers, S. (2003). Practical RDF. Sebastopol, CA: O' Reilly Media.

*Proof of Concept*. (n.d.). Retrieved from http://en.wikipedia.org/wiki/Proof_of_concept

Protege. (2012). *Protege ontology editor*. Retrieved from http://www.protege.stanford.edu

Radjou, N., Orlov, L. M., & Child, M. (2001). *The Forrester report – Apps for dynamic collaboration*. Cambridge, MA: Forrester Research.

Ramaprasad, A., & Prakash, A. (2009). Fostering knowledge sharing in project management. In *Proceedings of the 42nd Hawaii International Conference on System Sciences (HICSS-42)*. IEEE.

RDF Working Group. (2004). *Resource description framework (RDF)*. Retrieved from http://www.w3.org/RDF/

Redwine, S., & Riddle, W. (1985). Software technology maturation. In *Proceedings of 8th Int'l Conf. Software Eng*. IEEE.

Rees, M. (2010). *Scientific horizons: The Reith lectures*. Retrieved on February 28th, 2011 from http://www.bbc.co.uk/iplayer/episode/b00sp194/The_Reith_Lectures_Martin_Rees_Scientific_Horizons_2010_What_Well_Never_Know/

*Research Areas*. (n.d.). Retrieved 03 27, 2013, from http://www.esf.org/research-areas.html

Rolland, C., Souveyet, C., & Moreno, M. (1995). An approach for defining ways-of-working. *Information Systems*, *20*(4), 337–359. doi:10.1016/0306-4379(95)00018-Y

Rycroft, R. W. (2007). Does cooperation absorb complexity? Innovation networks and the speed and spread of complex technological innovation. *Technological Forecasting and Social Change*, *74*, 565–578. doi:10.1016/j.techfore.2006.10.005

Sacco, O., & Passant, A. (2011). A privacy preference ontology (PPO) for linked data. In *Proceedings of the 4th Workshop about Linked Data on the Web (LDOW-2011)*. LDOW.

Saggion, H., Funk, A., Maynard, D., & Bontcheva, K. (2007). Ontology-based information extraction for business intelligence. In *Proceedings of the 6th International Conference on Semantic Web*. IEEE.

Salavisa, I., Sousa, C., & Fontes, M. (2012). Topologies of innovation networks in knowledge-intensive sectors: Sectoral differences in the access to knowledge and complementary assets through formal and informal ties. *Technovation*, *32*, 380–399. doi:10.1016/j.technovation.2012.02.003

Salesforce Inc. (2011). *Salesforce appexchange*. Retrieved February 23, 2013, from http://appexchange.salesforce.com/browse?type=Apps

Sanders, N. R. (2007). An empirical study of the impact of e-business technologies on organizational collaboration and performance. *Journal of Operations Management*, *25*(6), 1332–1347. doi:10.1016/j.jom.2007.01.008

Santner, T. J., Williams, B., & Notz, W. (2003). *The design and analysis of computer experiments*. Berlin: Springer Verlag. doi:10.1007/978-1-4757-3799-8

Saripalle, R., & Demurjian, S. (2012a). Towards a hybrid ontology design and development life cycle. In *Proceedings of the 11th International Conference on Semantic Web and Web Services*. IEEE.

Saripalle, R., & Demurjian, S. (2012b). Semantic patterns using the OWL domain profile. In *Proceedings of the 2012 International Knowledge Engineering Conference* (pp. 3-9). IEEE.

Saripalle, R., Demurjian, S., & Behre, S. (2011). Towards software design process for ontologies. In *Proceedings of the 1st International Conference on Software and Intelligent Information*. IEEE.

Sarraipa, J., Jardim-Goncalves, R., Gaspar, T., & Steiger-Garcao, A. (2010). Collaborative ontology building using qualitative information collection methods. In *Proceedings of Intelligent Systems (IS), 2010 5th IEEE International Conference Proceedings* (pp.61-66). IEEE.

Sarraipa, J., Silva, J. P., Jardim-Goncalves, R., & Monteiro, A. (2008). MENTOR – Methodology for enterprise reference ontology development. In *Proceedings of Intelligent Systems, 2008 (IS '08), 4th International IEEE Conference* (vol. 1, pp. 6-32, 6-40). IEEE.

Sarraipa, J., Jardim-Goncalves, R., & Steiger-Garcao, A. (2010). MENTOR: An enabler for interoperable intelligent systems. *International Journal of General Systems, 39*(5), 557–573. doi:10.1080/03081079.2010.484278

Schach, S. (2006). *Object-oriented and classical software engineering* (7th ed.). New York: McGraw-Hill.

Schacht, S., Botzenhardt, A., & Maedche, A. (2012). AskEris – A many-to-one communication platform for higher education. In Proceedings of System Science (HICSS), 2012 45th Hawaii International Confherence, (pp. 21-30). IEEE.

Schatten, M., & Žugaj, M. (2007). Organizing a fishnet structure. In *Proceedings of the ITI 2007 29th International Conference on Information Technology*. Zagreb: SRCE University Computing Centre.

Schmidt, D., Stal, M., Rohnert, H., & Buschmann, F. (2000). Pattern-oriented software architecture volume 2: Patterns for concurrent and networked objects. In Event London (Vol. 2, pp. 1–482). Hoboken, NJ: Wiley.

Scholl, H. J., & Klischewsky, R. (2007). E-government integration and interoperability: Framing the research agenda. *International Journal of Public Administration, 30*(8), 889–920. doi:10.1080/01900690701402668

Schrage, M. (2009, February 6). Interoperability: The great enabler. *Financial Times*.

Schubert, V. A. (2005). *XRM: Integrated customer relationship management for pharmaceutical innovation*. (Doctoral Dissertation). University of Berlin, Berlin, Germany.

Schulz, S., Suntisrivaraporn, B., Baader, F., & Boeker, M. (2009). SNOMED reaching its adolescence: Ontologists' and logicians' health check. *International Journal of Medical Informatics, 78*(S1), 86–94. doi:10.1016/j.ijmedinf.2008.06.004 PMID:18789754

*Scientific Method*. (2010). Retrieved 03 27, 2013, from www.merriam-webster.com/dictionary/scientific%20method

*Scientific Method*. (2013). Retrieved 2013, from http://en.wikipedia.org/wiki/Scientific_method

Séguin, N., Abran, A., & Dupuis, R. (2010). Software engineering principles. In *Proceedings of the Third C\* Conference on Computer Science and Software Engineering - C3S2E '10* (pp. 59–65). New York: ACM Press. doi:10.1145/1822327.1822335

Senn, J. A. (1992). *Análisis y diseño de sistemas de información* (2nd ed.). Mexico City, Mexico: McGraw Hill.

Seven, H. L. Integrating the Healthcare Enterprise, The Office of the National Coordinator for Health Information Technology & Health Story Project. (2011). *Implementation guide for CDA release 2.0 - Consolidated CDA templates (US realm)*. Retrieved from http://wiki.hl7.org/images/b/be/CDAConsolidationR12011.zip

Shaw, M., & Clements, P. (2006). The golden age of software architecure. *IEEE Software*. doi:10.1109/MS.2006.58

Shen, H., & Cheng, Y. (2001). A semantic context-based model for mobile web services access control. *International Journal on Computer Network and Information Security*.

Sheth, J. N., & Parvatiyar, A. (1995). The evolution of relationship marketing. *International Business Review*, *4*(4), 397–418. doi:10.1016/0969-5931(95)00018-6

Shuman, J., & Twombly, J. (2010). Collaborative networks are the organization: An innovation in organization design and management. *Vikalpa*, *35*(1), 1–14.

Silva, J., Cavaco, F., Sarraipa, J., & Jardim-Goncalves, R. (2011). Knowledge based methodology supporting interoperability increase in manufacture domain. In the *Proceedings of the ASME Congress 2011 - ASME International Mechanical Engineering Congress and Exposition IMECE 2011* (pp. 837-843). Denver, CO: ASME.

Simon, K. (2010). *SIPOC diagram*. Retrieved February 25, 2013, from http://www.isixsigma.com/tools-templates/sipoc-copis/sipoc-diagram

Simon, H. A. (1962). The architecture of complexity. *Proceedings of the American Philosophical Society*, *106*(6), 467–482. Retrieved from http://www.jstor.org/stable/985254

Simon, H. A. (1995). Near decomposability and complexity: How a mind resides in a brain. In H. J. Morowitz, & J. L. Singer (Eds.), *The mind the brain and complex adaptive systems* (pp. 25–44). Reading, MA: Addison-Wesley.

Simon, H. A. (1996). *The sciences of the artificial*. Cambridge, MA: MIT Press.

Simulation Interoperability Standards Organization (SISO). (2012). *Standard for core manufacturing simulation data – XML representation*. Retrieved March 20, 2013, from http://www.sisostds.org

Sitek, P., Gusmeroli, S., Conte, M., Jansson, K., & Karvonen, I. (2011). *The COIN book - Enterprise collaboration and interoperability*. Aachen, Germany: Druck und Verlagshaus Mainz.

Smith, B. A., & Ceusters, W. B. (2006). Ontology as the core discipline of biomedical informatics: Legacies of the past and recommendations for the future direction of research. In G. D. Crnkovic, & S. Stuart (Eds.), *Computing, philosophy, and cognitive science*. Cambridge, UK: Cambridge Scholars Press.

SNOMED CT. (2013). *SNOMED CT® technical implementation guide*. Retrieved from http://ihtsdo.org/fileadmin/user_upload/doc/

SOAP. (2007, April). *Simple object access protocol*. Retrieved from http://www.w3.org/TR/soap/

Sommerville, I. (2007). *Software engineering* (8th ed.). Harlow, UK: Pearson Education.

Soto-Acosta, P., & Meroño-Cerdan, A. L. (2008). Analyzing e-business value creation from a resource-based perspective. *International Journal of Information Management*, *28*, 49–60. doi:10.1016/j.ijinfomgt.2007.05.001

Sowa, J., & Zachman, J. (1992). Extending and formalizing the framework for information systems. *IBM Systems Journal*, *31*(3), 590–616. doi:10.1147/sj.313.0590

Spohrer, J. (2009). Editorial column--Welcome to our declaration of interdependence. *Service Science*, *1*(1), i–ii. doi:10.1287/serv.1.1.i

Spohrer, J., Maglio, P., Bailey, J., & Gruhl, D. (2007). Steps toward a science of service systems. *Computer*, *40*(1), 71–77. doi:10.1109/MC.2007.33

Sriram, R. D., & Fenves, S. J. (2009). A life-saving role: Health care information systems are essential medicine. *Industrial Engineer Magazine*, 34-39.

Stadtler, H. (2009). A framework for collaborative planning and state-of-the-art. *OR-Spektrum*, *31*, 5–30. doi:10.1007/s00291-007-0104-5

Stamper, R. (1996). Signs, information, norms and systems. In Signs of work (pp. 349–397). Berlin, Germany: de Gruyter.

Stanford Center for Biomedical Informatics Research. (2013). *Protege*. Retrieved from http://protege.stanford.edu/

Stanovich, K. E. (2007). *How to think straight about psychology*. Boston: Pearson Education.

Steiger-Garcao, A., Jardim-Goncalves, R., & Farinha, F. (2007). An open platform for interoperability of civil engineering enterprises. *Advances in Engineering Software*.

Strahringer, S. (1996). *Metamodellierung als instrument des methodenvergleichs: Eine evaluierung am beispiel objektorientierter analysemethoden*. Aachen, Germany: Shaker.

Strosnider, J. K., Nandi, P., Kumaran, S., Ghosh, S., & Arsnajani, A. (2008). Model-driven synthesis of SOA solutions. *IBM Systems Journal, 47*(3), 415–432. doi:10.1147/sj.473.0415

Sugihara, G., & May, R. M. (1990). (n.d.). Nonlinear forecasting as a way of distinguishing chaos from measurement error in time series. *Nature, 344*(734). PMID:2330029

Suh, N. P. (1990). *The principles of design.* Oxford, UK: Oxford University Press.

Sullivan, A., & Sheffrin, S. (2003). *Economics: Principles in action.* Upper Saddle River, NJ: Pearson Prentice Hall.

SUPER. (2012). *Integrated project SUPER.* Retrieved February 25, 2013, from http://www.ip-super.org/

Supply Chain Council. (2013). *Supply chain operations reference.* Retrieved February 25, 2013, from http://supply-chain.org/scor

Surajbali, B., Bauer, M., Bär, H., & Alexakis, S. (2013). A cloud–based approach for collaborative networks supporting serviced-enhanced products. In *Proceedings of PRO-VE 2013 Conference 2013.* PRO-VE.

Syed, A., & Shah, A. (n.d.). Data, information, knowledge, wisdom: A doubly linked chain? In *Proceedings of the 101st International Conference on Information and Knowledge Engineering.* IEEE.

Tamburaj, V., Camarinha-Matos, L. M., & Maltesen, T. (2013). *D6.1 detailed specification of the pilot demonstrator.* Retrieved June 24, 2013, from https://sites.google.com/site/glonetproject/8-download

Taylor, S. F. E. (2011). Challenges for web simulation science. In *Proceedings of the 2011 Winter Simulation Conference.* Retrieved from http://www.informs-sim.org/wsc11papers/259.pdf

*Technical Standard.* (n.d.). Retrieved from http://en.wikipedia.org/wiki/Technical_standard

The openEHR Foundation. (2006). *Introducing openEHR.* Retrieved from http://www.openehr.org/releases/1.0.2/openEHR/introducing_openEHR.pdf

Toninelli, A., Montanari, R., Kagal, L., & Lassi, O. (2006). A semantic context-aware access control framework for secure collaborations in pervasive computing environments. In *Proceedings of the 5th Int. Semantic Web Conf. (ISWC-2006)* (LNCS), (vol. 4273, pp. 473-486). Berlin: Springer.

Tsai, W. T. (2005). Service-oriented system engineering: A new paradigm. In *Proceedings of IEEE International Workshop on Service-Oriented System Engineering (SOSE'05)* (pp. 3–8). IEEE. doi:10.1109/SOSE.2005.34

Urbas, L., Pfeffer, J., & Ziegler, J. (2011). iLD-apps: Usable mobile access to linked data clouds at the shop floor. In *Proceedings of Workshop on Visual Interfaces to the Social and the Semantic Web* (VISSW). VISSW.

Uschold, M., & King, M. (1995). Towards a methodology for building ontologies. In *Proceedings of Workshop on Basic Ontological Issues in Knowledge Sharing, held in conjunction with IJCAI-95.* IJCAI.

van Aken, J. E. (2004). Management research based on the paradigm of the design sciences: The quest for field-tested and grounded technological rules. *Journal of Management Studies, 41*(2), 219–246. doi:10.1111/j.1467-6486.2004.00430.x

Van Langenhove, P., Dirkx, M., & Decreus, K. (2011). *European interoperability architecture (EIA), phase 2 - Final report: Common vision for an EIA.* Retrieved from http://ec.europa.eu/isa/documents/isa_2.1_eia-finalreport-commonvisionforaneia.pdf

Vargo, S. L., & Akaka, M. A. (2009). Service-dominant logic as a foundation for service science: Clarifications. *Service Science, 1*(1), 32–41. doi:10.1287/serv.1.1.32

Vargo, S. L., & Lusch, R. F. (2008). Service-dominant logic: continuing the evolution. *Journal of the Academy of Marketing Science, 36*(1), 1–10. doi:10.1007/s11747-007-0069-6

Vassiliadis, P., Simitsis, A., Georgantas, P., Terrovitis, M., & Skiadopoulos, S. (2005). A generic and customizable framework for the design of ETL scenarios. *Information Systems, 30*(7), 492–525. doi:10.1016/j.is.2004.11.002

Vijayasarathy, L., & Turk, D. (2012). Drivers of agile software development use: Dialectic interplay between benefits and hindrances. *Information and Software Technology, 54*(2), 137–148. doi:10.1016/j.infsof.2011.08.003

W3C. (2013). *SPARQL 1.1 query language*. Retrieved February 25, 2013, from http://www.w3.org/TR/sparql11-query/

Wagner, G. (2003). The agent-object-relationship metamodel: Towards a unified view of state and behavior. *Information Systems, 28*(5), 475–504. doi:10.1016/S0306-4379(02)00027-3

Waldrop, M. M. (1992). *Complexity: The emerging science at the edge of order and chaos*. New York: Simon & Schuster.

Walker, L. E., & Wickam, S. E. (1986). *From Huffman Prairie to the moon: The history of Wright-Patterson Air Force Base*. Washington, DC: United States Government Printing Office.

Walls, J. G., Widermeyer, G. R., & el Sawy, O. A. (2006). Assessing information system design theory in perspective: How useful was our 1992 initial rendition? *Journal of Information Technology Theory and Application, 6*(2). Retrieved from http://aisel.aisnet.org/jitta/vol6/iss2/6/

Wang, W., Tolk, A., & Wang, W. (2009). The levels of conceptual interoperability model: Applying systems engineering principles to M&S. In *Proceedings of Spring Simulation Multiconference*. San Diego, CA: Society for Computer Simulation International.

Wasserman, A. I. (1996). *Toward a discipline of software engineering*. Reading, MA: Addison Wesley Longman, Inc.

Weber-Jahnke, J., Peyton, L., & Topaloglou, T. (2012). eHealth system interoperability. *Information Systems Frontiers, 14*(1), 1–3. doi:10.1007/s10796-011-9319-8

West, D. M. (2011). *Enabling personalized medicine through health information technology: Advancing the integration of information*. Washington, DC: The Brookings Institution. Retrieved from www.brookings.edu/governance.aspx

Whitman, L., Huff, B., & Palaniswamy, S. (1998). Commercial simulation over the web. In *Proceedings of the 1998 Winter Simulation Conference* (pp. 335–339). Retrieved from http://www.informs-sim.org/wsc98papers/046.PDF

Whitman, L., Huff, B., & Presley, A. (1997). Structured models and dynamic systems analysis: The integration of the IDEF0/IDEF3 modeling methods and discrete event simulation. In *Proceedings of the 29th Conference on Winter Simulation*. IEEE Computer Society. http://doi.acm.org/10.1145/268437.268559

Whitten, J. L., Bentley, L. D., & Dittman, K. C. (2004). *System analysis and design methods* (6th ed.). Boston: McGraw-Hill Irwin.

Wieringa, R. (2009). Design science as nested problem solving. In *Proceedings of the 4th International Conference on Design Science Research in Information Systems and Technology DESRIST 09* (pp. 1). ACM Press. doi:10.1145/1555619.1555630

Williams, L. (2010). Agile software development methodologies and practices. *Advances in Computers, 80*(10), 1–44. doi:10.1016/S0065-2458(10)80001-4

Wilson, E. (1999). *Consilience: The unity of knowledge*. New York: Vintage.

Wimalasuriya, D. C., & Dou, D. (2010). Ontology-based information extraction: An introduction and a survey of current approaches. *Journal of Information Science, 36*(6), 306–323. doi:10.1177/0165551509360123

Winner, R. I., Pennell, J. P., Bertrand, H. E., & Slusarczuk, M. M. (1988). *The role of concurrent engineering in weapons system acquisition*. Arlington, VA: Institute for Defense Analysis.

Winter, R., & Aier, S. (2011). How are enterprise architecture design principles used? In *Proceedings of International Enterprise Distributed Object Computing Conference Workshops* (pp. 314-321). IEEE Computer Society Press.

Winter, R., & Fischer, R. (2007). Essential layers, artifacts, and dependencies of enterprise architecture. *Journal of Enterprise Architecture, 3*(2), 7–18.

Witten, I. H., Frank, E., & Hall, M. A. (2011). *Data mining: Practical machine learning tools and techniques* (3rd ed.). Burlington, MA: Morgan Kaufmann.

Wolfs, S. (2010). *Introduction to the scientific method.* Retrieved 05 2010, from http://teacher.pas.rochester.edu/phy_labs/appendixe/appendixe.html

WSDL. (2001, March). *Web services description language.* Retrieved from http://www.w3.org/TR/2001/NOTE-wsdl-20010315

Wu, I., & Chang, C. (2011). Using the balanced scorecard in assessing the performance of e-SCM diffusion: A multi-stage perspective. *Decision Support Systems.*

Wyatt, E., Griendling, K., & Mavris, D. (2012). Addressing interoperability in military systems-of-systems architectures. In *Proceedings of International Systems Conference* (pp. 1-8). IEEE Computer Society Press.

Wycisk, C., McKelvey, B., & Hulsmann, M. (2008). Smart parts: Supply networks as complex adaptive systems: Analysis and implications. *International Journal of Physical Distribution & Logistics Management, 38*(2), 108–125. doi:10.1108/09600030810861198

XPDL. (2013). *XML process definition language.* Retrieved February 25, 2013, http://www.xpdl.org/

Yamamoto, H., Sameshima, S., Sekiguchi, T., Kato, H., Yura, J., & Takashio, K. (2011). Interoperability of middleware for context-aware services. *Electronics and Communications in Japan, 94*(2), 67–74. doi:10.1002/ecj.10260

Yuksel, M., & Dogac, A. (2011). Interoperability of medical device information and the clinical applications: An HL7 RMIM based on the ISO/IEEE 11073 DIM. *IEEE Transactions on Information Technology in Biomedicine, 15*(4), 557–566. doi:10.1109/TITB.2011.2151868 PMID:21558061

Zaniolo, C., & Melkanoff, M. A. (1982). A formal approach to the definition and the design of conceptual schemata for database systems. *ACM Transactions on Database Systems, 7*(1), 24–59. doi:10.1145/319682.319695

Zbib, N., Archimede, B., & Charbonnaud, P. (2012). Interoperability service utility model and its simulation for improving the business process collaboration. []. London, UK: Springer.]. *Proceedings of Enterprise Interoperability, 5,* 403–413.

Zeng, S. X., Xie, X. M., & Tam, C. M. (2010). Relationship between cooperation networks and innovation performance of SMEs. *Technovation, 30,* 181–194. doi:10.1016/j.technovation.2009.08.003

Ziegler, J., Graube, M., Pfeffer, J., & Urbas, L. (2012). Beyond app-chaining: Mobile app. orchestration for efficient model driven software generation. In *Proceedings of 17th International IEEE Conference on Emerging Technologies & Factory Automation* (ETFA). IEEE.

Zweben, S. H., Edwards, S. H., Weide, B. W., & Hollingsworth, J. E. (1995). The effects of layering and encapsulation on software development cost and quality. *IEEE Transactions on Software Engineering, 21,* 200–208. doi:10.1109/32.372147

Zwegers, A., Wubben, H., & Hartel, I. (2002). Relationship management in enterprise networks. In V. Marik, H. Afsarmanesh, & L. M. Camarinha-Matos (Eds.), *Knowledge and technology integration in production and services* (pp. 157–164). Norwell, MA: Kluwer Academic Publishers. doi:10.1007/978-0-387-35613-6_17

# About the Contributors

**Yannis Charalabidis** is Assistant Professor in the University of the Aegean, in the areas of e-Governance Information Systems, coordinating policy making, and research and pilot application projects for governments and enterprises worldwide. A computer engineer with a PhD in complex information systems, he has been employed for several years as an executive director in Singular IT Group, leading software development and company expansion in Europe, India, and the US. He also serves as the scientific manager at the Greek Interoperability Centre, hosted at Decision Support Systems Laboratory, of the National Technical University of Athens, delivering high quality research in the area of interoperability. He has also been the coordinator or technical leader in numerous FP6, FP7, and National research projects in the areas of e-Business and e-Governance. He is a contributing member in several standardization and technology policy committees. He writes and teaches on Government Service Systems, Enterprise Interoperability, Government Transformation, and Citizen Participation.

**Fenareti Lampathaki** holds a Ph.D. Degree and a Diploma – M.Eng. Degree in Electrical and Computer Engineering (Specialization: Computer Science) from the School of Electrical and Computer Engineering of the National Technical University of Athens (NTUA) and an M.Sc. Degree in Techno-Economics (M.B.A.) from NTUA, University of Athens and University of Piraeus. She is currently working as a R&D Project Manager at the Decision Support Systems Laboratory (DSSLab) of the National Technical University of Athens (NTUA). During the last eight years, she has been involved in the research and management activities of several EU-funded and national R&D projects. Her research interests lie on e-Government and e-Business Interoperability, Semantics, Services and Data Engineering, Electronic Governance and Policy Modelling, Future Internet and Enterprise Systems, Social Computing, and Social Media. Her research results have been published in several international journals, edited books, and conference proceedings (e.g. EGOV Conference 2008 – best paper award, HICCS 2009 – best paper nominee).

**Ricardo Jardim-Goncalves** holds a PhD degree in Industrial Information Systems from the NOVA University of Lisbon. He is Assistant Professor at the NOVA University of Lisbon, Faculty of Sciences and Technology, and Senior Researcher at UNINOVA institute. He graduated in Computer Science, with an MSc in Operational Research and Systems Engineering. His research activities have focused on Standard-Based Intelligent Integration Frameworks for Interoperability, covering architectures, methodologies, and toolkits to support improved development, harmonisation, and implementation of systems and applications for data exchange in industry, from design to e-business. He has been a technical international project leader for more than 15 years, with more than 70 papers published in conferences, journals, and books. He is a project leader in ISO TC184/SC4.

\* \* \*

**Carlos Agostinho** is a Senior Researcher at UNINOVA center. He has an MsC in Computer Science and holds a PhD in the area of industrial information systems by the Faculty of Science and Technology of the NOVA University of Lisbon (FCT/UNL). He is deeply involved in the areas of Product and Process Meta-modeling, Interoperability and Harmonization using Standards since his participation in projects like CEN/AIDIMA/2002/004 funSTEP AP-DIS and IST-2001-52224 SMART-fm. He is quite experienced in research and coordination activities due to his work in several national and international research and development projects in UNINOVA since 2001, where he developed skills in the areas of model-based and semantic interoperability applying MDA/MDI technologies.

**Spiros Alexakis** studied Computer Science at the University of Karlsruhe and visited a post graduate course in Economics. After two years at SIEMENS, he joined CAS Software in 1992 as a software engineer. In the following, he became System Engineer and Project Manager. Since 1996, he has served in the position of Director Innovation and Business Design. In 2009, Spiros was appointed as Member of the Board. Spiros Alexakis has significant experience in leading large, international projects. He has represented CAS in more than 40 research projects and has coordinated numerous national and European research activities. Spiros now serves as expert for the European Commission and is an active member of the FINES cluster.

**Werner Altmann** finished his studies and his PhD in Computer Science at the Technical Faculty of the University Erlangen-Nürnberg in 1974 and 1978, respectively. He founded Kölsch and Altmann Software and Management Consulting GmbH in München with Dr. Raimund T. Kölsch in autumn of 1985. Since this time, he has served as managing director at K&A GmbH. Since January 1, 2007, he has served as single director and, with his wife Dorit, 100% single owner of K&A GmbH. In the time before K&A, he was a consultant at softlab GmbH and sd&m GmbH in München. His main functional emphasis is: Information Systems, Software Engineering and Software-Project-Management. His managerial emphasis at K&A GmbH is: Project Acquisition, Personnel and Public Relations. Since 1974, he has been a member of Gesellschaft für Informatik. Since the beginning of 2009, he has engaged in the Cluster BICC-NET as well as in the task group BESEC. Since the beginning of 2010, he has been engaged in the corporate association Embedded4You, where he is currently member and spokesman of the managing board. In 2011, he joined the ComVantage project to contribute his knowledge in the area of Testing Systems.

**Alberto Armijo** completed his MSc degree in Industrial Engineering (2002), Electrical Engineering intensification, at the ETSII of Bilbao (University of the Basque Country, Spain). He is Quality Management Technician and has experience in Quality Methodologies and Tools, such as Continuous Improvement, EFQM model and Business Process Management. He has been working as a scientific staff member at TECNALIA R&I since 2004, involved in methodologies and software development in the Knowledge Management area for the Virtual Factory. He is currently researching on new architecture solutions for the implementation and deployment of Business Process Management Systems within the industry. He has been involved in AmI-MoSES and DEMI projects on energy efficiency optimisation in the discrete manufacturing industry (SMEs), and in H-KNOW project on provision of knowledge based services for the construction industry. He is currently involved in NewBEE project and is also the scientific & technical coordinator of EPES FP7 project.

**Dimitris Askounis** is an Assistant Professor of Management Information & Decision Support Systems in the School of Electrical and Computer Engineering at the National Technical University of Athens (NTUA). Dr. Askounis has been involved in numerous IT research projects funded by the EU since 1988 (ESPRIT, BRITE-EURAM, FP5, FP6, FP7, CIP) in the thematic areas of eGovernance (CROSSROAD, COCKPIT, PADGETS, LEX-IS, FEED), eBusiness interoperability (e.g. IMAGINE, GIC, GENESIS), decision support, knowledge management, quality management, computer integrated manufacturing, enterprise resource planning, etc. Dr. Askounis has published over 100 papers in scientific journals and international conference proceedings.

**Markus Bauer** started his career 1998 as researcher at the research group Programmstrukturen at Forschungszentrum Informatik (FZI) in Karlsruhe. In 2003, he became manager of the research group Programmstrukturen, leading nine full-time researchers. In 2005, he joined CAS Software AG, where he is now leading the development of the company's next generation software platform. In his career, Markus Bauer gained vast experience in leading large national and international research and development projects. Examples include the ESPRIT project FAMOOS, where he developed a tool set to support the reengineering of object oriented software systems, and the IST project FUSION, which introduced interoperability among different software systems in order to implement complex business processes using semantic Web services.

**Etxahun Sanchez Bazterretxea** received his advanced Telecommunication Engineering bachelor's degree in 2006. Accompanying his studies, he gained experience as R&D researcher and joined Nextel's R&D team where he has been participating in several European research & innovation projects such as Multipol from ITEA2. His main research interests regard the identity and access control management technologies. In 2011, he joined the ComVantage project to contribute his knowledge in the area of identity and access control management for multi-domain/federated environments.

**Johannes Britsch** is an external PhD student at ifm Mannheim (Center for Small and Medium Sized Business Research), University of Mannheim. His research interests include Anything Relationship Management (xRM), software usabilty and user experience (UX), and the diffusion of IT concepts. Johannes Britsch holds a Diploma in Business Administration with Intercultural Qualification Japanese (University of Mannheim and University of Heidelberg). Next to his current PhD studies, he works at CAS Software AG as Assistant of the CEO.

**Robert Buchmann** received his doctoral degree in the field of E-commerce application models from Babeş Bolyai University of Cluj Napoca, Romania, in 2005. Since then, he has occupied a lecturer position in the same university, specializing in E-business and Semantic Web and managing several national research projects related to semantic aspects of e-commerce. In 2012, he joined University of Vienna on a temporary research position in order to extend his knowledge of the fields of meta-modelling and conceptual modelling and to identify ways of bridging these paradigms. This gave him the opportunity to work on the ComVantage research project, mainly in the tasks related to modelling method engineering.

**Beth Cardier**, PhD., is an expert on the use of narrative structures in the development of artificial intelligence. She is currently a researcher at the University of Melbourne, where she is developing a formal theory of cognitive structure based on the abstractions and dynamics inherent in shared story. Her work with colleague Ted Goranson has resulted in the invention of a "2-Sorted" Logic that may revolutionize research in the biological sciences. Beth is also an award winning writer and media analyst who understands narrative structure from poetry to news media. She won the Eisner Prize for fiction while at UC Berkeley and her prose has been published in numerous literary journals. As an accomplished media analyst, Beth worked for Australia's leading analysis company, Media Monitors (now iSentia), where she was responsible for many of the firm's most difficult cases. Her work for the Australian Federal Government won first place in the international AMEC Awards in 2003, and at the free-press syndicate, Project Syndicate, she worked closely with local Ethiopian media during the collapse of democratic elections there in 2005.

**José C. Delgado** is an Associate Professor at the Computer Science and Engineering Department of the Instituto Superior Técnico (Lisbon University), in Lisbon, Portugal, where he earned the Ph.D. degree in 1988. He lectures courses in the areas of Computer Architecture, Information Technology, and Service Engineering. He has performed several management roles in his faculty, namely Director of the Taguspark campus, near Lisbon, and Coordinator of the B.Sc. and M.Sc. in Computer Science and Engineering at that campus. He has been the coordinator of, and researcher in, several research projects, both national and European. As an author, his publications include 1 book, several book chapters, and more than 50 papers in international refereed conferences and journals.

**Steven A. Demurjian** is a Full Professor and Director of Graduate Studies in Computer Science and Engineering at the University of Connecticut and co-Director of Research Informatics for the Biomedical Informatics Division, with research interests of: collaborative security and access control models for role-based, mandatory, and discretionary approaches with security assurance for UML, XML, and cloud computing; biomedical informatics and software architectures for health information exchange; secure software engineering with UML; and, ontology design and development models and methodologies. Dr. Steven A. Demurjian has 150 archival publications, in the following categories: 1 book, 2 edited collections, 50 journal articles and book chapters, and 98 refereed conference/workshop articles.

**Vasiliki Diamantopoulou** is a PhD Candidate and Research Assistant in the Department of Information and Communication Systems Engineering, University of the Aegean, Greece. She is also a Teaching Assistant in undergraduate and postgraduate courses in the area of business information systems. She holds a BSc in Product and Systems Design Engineering and a Master of Science in 'Technologies and Management of Information and Communication Systems' in the area of IT Management from the University. Also, she has a good experience of participation in national and international research projects.

**Asuman Dogac** received her Ph.D. degree from the Department of Computer Engineering, Middle East Technical University (METU), Ankara, Turkey, in 1981. She is the founding president of Software Research Development and Consultancy (SRDC) Ltd. She has coordinated several European Commission-supported research and development projects; Artemis, RIDE, SAPHIRE, iSURF, and iCARDEA to name a few. She has provided consultancy services on detailed analysis and assessment of national eHealth systems to the Turkish Ministry of Health. She has published more than 100 papers in refereed international conferences and journals, and she is the recipient of several international and national awards, including the IBM (USA) Faculty Award 2004 and Mustafa Parlar Science Award 2000. Her research interests include healthcare informatics, semantic interoperability, Internet computing, e-business, and service-oriented architectures.

**Kostas Ergazakis** is an Electrical and Computer Engineer of the NTUA and also holds a PhD in Knowledge Management and Decision Support Systems (NTUA). Dr. Ergazakis has long professional experience as project manager of technical assistance and R&D projects funded by EU and Greek National Bodies in different fields: formulation of digital/knowledge Cities strategies, e-participation, interoperability, monitoring and evaluation, management information systems, etc. Dr. Ergazakis has more than 35 publications in Scientific Journals and presentations in International conferences.

**Adolfo Sanches Steiger Garção** is Emeritus professor at the Department of Electrical and Electronic Engineering of the Faculty of Science and Technology of the NOVA University of Lisbon (DEE/FCT/UNL). He is member of the board of UNINOVA, member of the senate of the NOVA University of Lisbon, and director of the CTS (Centre of Technology and Systems) of UNINOVA. He has more than 200 scientific publications, many of them in the area of computer science and interoperable systems, and responsible for more than 50 industrial and research international and national projects.

**Ted Goranson** has been the senior research scientist on a range of government projects where he worked with abstraction, advanced logics, and novel user paradigms. He has played several key research roles in the intelligence community, primarily focused on self-organizing agent systems and causal models. Ted also played a long time leadership role in a lab associated with NSA. Ted also spent a significant period working on organizational dynamics at ARPA: on SEMATECH, concurrent engineering, enterprise integration, agile industrial infrastructure and virtual enterprises. Ted wrote the classic book on Enterprise Agility, which among other effects was influential in the design of the modern Chinese manufacturing infrastructure. He has multiple degrees from MIT in computer science, philosophy, and architecture.

**Frank Haferkorn** (1968) is a Senior Software Engineer and is working for the RST Industrie Automation GmbH. In 1995, he earned a diploma degree in physics from the Technical University of Munich. His diploma thesis was about Psychoacoustics (Spatial Hearing). After two years at the university as scientific member of the institute for electroacoustics (TUM), he changed to the industry. He is at home in C/C++ and Python. His long term issues besides physics, signal- & image processing and system-theory are human computer interaction and algorithmic programming. His current issues at RST are C/C++, Python and ontology design the wide field of Linked Data and Semantic Web technology within the EU-Project ComVantage. In his spare time he likes programming, doing modern physics and is making music. He is a fan of legacy computers from the 1980s.

**Jan Hladik** obtained his diploma degree in computer science from RWTH Aachen in 2001. Subsequently, he started working as a researcher in the group of Franz Baader at TU Dresden. He completed his PhD thesis in the area of reasoning algorithms for expressive description logics in 2007. In the following year he joined the SAP Research Center in Dresden in order to gain experience with the application of semantic technologies in practice. At SAP, he worked in several publicly funded research projects in related areas. Within the ComVantage project, he is leading the efforts concerned with semantics and Linked Data.

**Dimitris Karagiannis** is head of the Knowledge Engineering research group in the Faculty of Computer Science at the University of Vienna. He is a member of IEEE and ACM and serves both on the executive board of GI as well as on the steering committee of the Austrian Computer Society. His research interests include meta-modelling, business process management, and knowledge management. Prof. Karagiannis has published several books and scientific papers in journals and conferences. In 1995, he established the Business Process Management Systems Approach (BPMS), which has been successfully implemented in several industrial and service companies, and is the founder of the European company BOC (http://www.boc-group.com). In 2011, he launched the Open Models Initiative Laboratory (http://omilab.org).

**Bernhard Kölmel** holds a Professorship for Global Process Management at Hochschule Pforzheim University. Until 2012, Bernhard Kölmel worked as Director of Innovation and Strategy Management at CAS Software AG. Before he joined CAS, he was head of technology transfer at FZI, Forschungszentrum Informatik Karlsruhe and gained international experience in Silicon Valley and entrepreneurial knowledge in own companies. Bernhard Kölmel received his PhD with honours from the University of Karlsruhe. Bernhard Kölmel is active as expert (evaluator, reviewer, rapporteur) for various organisations like the European Commission (since FP IV), the Ministry of Science in Germany and various international bodies and has coordinated some 25 large international R&D projects.

**Sotirios Koussouris** holds a PhD Degree in Information Systems and Business Process Management, a Dipl. Eng. in Computer and Electrical Engineering, and an MBA in Techno-Economic systems. He has more than five years' experience in information systems and telecommunication technologies, with special skills in areas like eBussiness Interoperability, eGovernment technologies and applications, eParticipation, Social media Business Process Re-Engineering, and Business Process Modelling for organizations seeking at installing and operating high-end IT systems, IT Consulting in private and public sector, Telecommunications Management, Management, and Monitoring of domestic EC co-founded Projects mainly for the public sector. Over the last years, he has worked on numerous EC- and Domestic- funded projects including the Greek eGif, GENESIS, the Greek Interoperability Centre, IMAGINE project but also in various private sector projects. He has various publications in journals such as CII, IJPR, IJEG, and eJETA and major conferences such as ASME, AIS, ICE, WETICE, I-ESA, eChallenges, and eGOV.

**Oscar Lazaro** is a Visiting Professor at the University of Strathclyde and Managing Director of Innovalia Association. He is leading research activities of Innovalia in the fields of ICT and Manufacturing and holds numerous publications and patents in the area of wireless communications, security, and software services. He is from 2013 chairman of the Future Internet Networked Enterprise System (FInES) Cluster and a permanent representative of Innovalia in EFFRA and Future Internet Steering Board. Innovalia is actively researching on real-time information management systems, mobile visual data analytics and trustful collaboration technologies in the domain of the factories of the future (smart, digital, and virtual factories).

**Euripidis Loukis** is Associate Professor of Information and Decision Support Systems at the University of the Aegean, Greece. Formerly he has been Information Systems Advisor at the Ministry to the Presidency of Government, Technical Director of the 'Program for the Modernization of Greek Public Administration' of the Second European Union Support Framework, and Representative of Greece at the Management Committees of the Programs IDA ('Interchange of Data between Administrations') and 'Telematics for Administration' of the European Union. He has participated in many international research programs and has authored numerous journal and conference papers.

**Ourania Markaki** was born in Athens, Greece, on June 15, 1983. She received the Diploma in Electrical and Computer Engineering from the National Technical University of Athens (NTUA), Greece in 2006 and an MBA in Techno-economic Systems in 2008. She is currently a PhD Candidate in the School of Electrical and Computer Engineering, NTUA, specializing in the field of Enterprise Interoperability. Since 2008, she has been working as a Research Assistant for the Decision Support Systems Laboratory of the National Technical University of Athens, where she has been involved in the preparation and implementation of several EU-funded and national R&D projects. Her research interests include eBusiness and eGovernment Interoperability and multi-criteria decision-making. Ourania Markaki has published more than 20 papers in international journals, conferences and scientific books.

**Irene Matzakou** holds a Diploma – M.Eng. Degree in Electrical and Computer Engineering from the National Technical University of Athens (NTUA) and she is currently finalizing her studies to obtain a M.Sc. Degree in Engineering-Economic Systems (MBA) from NTUA and University of Piraeus. She is also a PhD candidate in the field of Enterprise Interoperability at the Decision Support Systems Laboratory (DSSLab) of NTUA. She has been involved in several EU-funded (FP7) and national R&D projects, including the Greek Interoperability Centre (GIC), PLUG-IN, OURSPACE, and others. Her research interests lie on e-Government and e-Business Interoperability, e-Participation, Social Media, and Web 2.0, and her work has been published in International Conferences and Scientific Journals.

**Spiros Mouzakitis** is a research analyst for National Technical University of Athens (NTUA). He holds a diploma of Electrical and Computer Engineering from the National Technical University of Athens. In 2009, he successfully defended his Ph.D. dissertation, entitled "A Supportive Framework for the Capability and Interoperability Assessment of SMEs for the Adoption of B2B Integration Systems." He has nine years of industry experience in the conception, analysis, and implementation of information technology systems. His current research is focused on decision analysis in the field of eBusiness, enterprise interoperability, and eGovernment. He has published in *Computer Standards & Interfaces, Information Systems Management, Journal of Theoretical and Applied Electronic Commerce Research, Electronic Journal for eCommerce Tools and Applications*, and *Lecture Notes in Computer Science*, and has presented his research at international conferences.

**Tobias Münch** is a Senior Researcher at SAP Research in Karlsruhe. He has received his diploma degree from TU Dresden in Media and IT in 2008. Accompanying his studies, he gained experiences as researcher and software developer for the Comarch Software AG in Poland and Germany. After his studies, he joined the team of SAP Research in Dresden in 2008. His main research interest is located in the application of semantic technologies and the development of mobile applications. In 2011, he joined the ComVantage project to contribute his knowledge in the area of virtual enterprises. In 2012, he moved to Karlsruhe in order to join the Human Computer Interaction team of SAP Research.

**Patricia Ortiz** is an Electrical and Electronic Engineer from the University of the Basque Country. Patricia Ortiz got her degree in 2009 and soon after she joined Management Solutions as Senior Consultant, where she dealt with banking information systems and solutions. In 2011, she joined Innovalia to perform research in the area of semantic and Linked Data for manufacturing. Since 2011, she has worked in the ComVantage project dealing with security solutions and design of access control solutions for linked data in multi-domain (collaborative) environments.

**Oscar López Pérez** received his Technical Telecommunication Engineering degree from Catalonia Polytechnic University. After finishing his studies, he worked as a teacher on IT Technologies, and in 2000, he joined Nextel covering different stages as a technical and consultancy in ICT and Security, mainly regarding personal data protection regulations and standards regarding information security management systems. Since 2008 has been working as a R&D researcher, participating in European research projects as SECRICOM, BUGYO-BEYOND, and others.

**Johannes Pfeffer** is a research scientist and PhD-student at Faculty of Electrical and Computer Engineering at the Technische Universität Dresden. In 2010, he received his Master degree in Mechatronics. His research focuses on model driven app orchestration for industrial use. Other research topics related to this subject are model transformation, usability on mobile devices, mobile solutions for supervisory control, and industrial maintenance support.

**Keith Popplewell** started his career in operational research, and specialised in computer-aided engineering and production planning systems design with Raleigh Industries and Boots Company plc. During this time, he took a doctorate in production engineering and production management at the University of Nottingham. Subsequently, he became technical director in a software house specialising in the design, development, and implementation of CAE systems, before joining the Department of Manufacturing Engineering at Loughborough University in 1985. In 2000, he became Jaguar Cars Professor of Engineering Manufacture and Management and Head of Department at Coventry University, before, in 2006, he accepted the post of Director of Coventry University's Future Manufacturing Applied Research Centre (FMARC). His research interests centre on design, modelling and operation of global and network manufacturing enterprises, and in particular on providing intelligent knowledge oriented support for virtual organisations. In this context, he is General Secretary of the INTEROP-VLab AISBL.

**Angelika Salmen** is the local Research Manager of Human Computer Interaction at SAP Karlsruhe, Germany. She joined SAP in 2009 and initiated, amongst other activities, the project ComVantage, which she is coordinating. Angelika Salmen was engaged in the Dept. of Information Science, U Regensburg at Assisting Professor and was working in research projects, primarily in co-operation with the automotive industries focusing on multi-modal infotainment systems. She was co-founder and Managing Director of the spin-off SpeechExperts offering research for third parties and speech applications for SMEs. Then she joined VoiceObjects providing large-scale IVR telephony applications, where she was Manager User Interface Services. Additionally she was invited for lectures and seminars at the U Regensburg and U Hildesheim for several times. Angelika Salmen holds a PhD in Information Science, a Master in Linguistics, and a Diploma in Social Science.

**Rishi Kanth Saripalle** is a final year Ph.D. student in the Department of Computer Science & Engineering at the University of Connecticut, under the supervision of Dr. Steven A. Demurjian. His research interests include software engineering and modeling using various domain modeling standards and frameworks, ontology design and development, knowledge engineering and modeling, biomedical informatics, clinical data engineering, and secure software engineering applied to the domain of health care. His research focuses on imposing software engineering, modeling, and life cycle model concepts on the domain ontologies, with the end purpose of defining a software engineering-based approach to design and development of ontologies irrespective of the applicable domain. He received his Masters, with a major in Computer Engineering, from the University of Massachusetts, where he had research experiences in developing ontologies for aiding medical decision support system.

**João Sarraipa** is an experienced researcher at UNINOVA Research Centre. He holds a PhD degree in Electrical Engineering and Computers in the Industrial Information Systems area, from the Faculty of Science and Technology of the New University of Lisbon (FCT/UNL). He graduated in Electrical Engineering and has an MSc in Informatics Engineering from the same university. His area of expertise is Semantic Interoperability, Knowledge Management, Ontologies, and E-Training. He has been participated in European research projects (e.g. IDEAS; SMART-FM; INTEROP; ATHENA-IP; IN-NOVAFUN; CoSpaces; CRESCENDO) for more than 10 years, with more than 30 papers published in conferences, journals and books.

**Mikel Sorli**, Ph.D. Industrial Engineer, is currently manager of the Design Engineering Area in TECNALIA R&I. He is working with industrial companies promoting the use, and integrating, developing, and implementing tools in the fields of knowledge-based engineering, PDM systems, and advanced design methodologies. He has good expertise on European research projects and has been the Project Manager of many RTD projects. He is author and co-author of many papers and communications presented at different national and international Conferences and author of books: "Innovating in Product/Process Development" ISBN = 978-1-84882-544-4, "QFD. Una Herramienta de Futuro" (QFD. A Tool for the Future) ISBN 84-88734-02-6, as well as the Chapter "Supporting Innovation through Knowledge Management in the Extended Enterprise" in book "Information Technology: Entrepreneurship and Innovation" edited by Fang Zhao (2008), RMIT University Australia. He is currently the Project Coordinator of NewBEE and EPES FP7 projects.

**Cebrail Taskin** received the Doctoral Degree in Department of Electronic Engineering of the University of Sakarya, Turkey, in 2006. He received his MBA degree from Department of Economic and Business Administration, Middle East Technical University (METU), Ankara, Turkey, in 2013. He has a great deal of experience working within the Informatics and Telecommunication sector since 1995. Prior to joining Turk Telekom, he worked at Sakarya University as a manager of IT Systems. Dr. Taskin has been working in Turk Telekom Group since 1999. He has worked at Informatics Network Department, Strategy and Business Development Department and R&D Department. His main research areas are 'Telecommunication Networks' and 'Next Generation Internet Networks'. He regularly wrote articles related to telecommunications at *Telecom World Magazine* between 2003 and 2010. He is the author of *Network Technologies and Telecommunication* book that is published by Pusula in 2009 and 2012.

**Leon Urbas** is the chair of Process Control Systems Engineering at Technische Universität Dresden. His research interests include formal information models in automation, their application in model driven methods for engineering support systems and integrated workflows for automation engineering applied user modelling. These technology oriented topics are supported by research in human-centred automation, in particular process visualisation in control rooms and the shop floor, usability engineering in supervisory control and human performance modelling. Prof. Urbas is spokesman of the task force GMA FA 5.16 "Middleware in industrial automation," member of the board of the processNet working group PAAT and Editor-in-Chief of the renowned scientific journal atp edition – Automatisierungstechnische Praxis.

**Robert Woitsch** holds a PhD in business informatics and is currently responsible for European and National research projects within the consulting company BOC (www.boc-group.com) in Vienna, in the domain of networked enterprises and knowledge management. He deals with KM-projects since 2000 starting with the EU-funded projects ADVISOR, PROMOTE, and EKMF and has recently been working within the EU-projects like Akogrimo, LD-Cast, Brein, AsIsKnown, MATURE, and coordinated plugIT. Currently, he deals with the EU-projects BIVEE, ComVantage, and e-Save in the domain of networked enterprises. Mr. Woitsch is involved in commercial KM projects for skill management and knowledge balances and is a member of the Austrian Standardization Institute. Beside his engagement at BOC, he teaches at the Department of Knowledge and Business Engineering at the Faculty of Computer Science at the University of Vienna. He published about 40 papers and is involved as reviewer and member of programme committees in KM-conferences.

**Anil Yalcinkaya** received his BS and MS in Computer Engineering from Baskent University, Ankara, Turkey, in 2005 and 2008, respectively. Before joining Argela, he worked for Havelsan Corporation, Ankara, in Simulation Systems Directorate as a Software Engineer. Then he joined Ministry of Transport and Telecommunications, EU Coordination Department, Ankara where, he worked as an Assistant Specialist focusing on GIS and corresponding support and management. He also represented the Ministry in European Union information technologies adaptation projects. Then he joined Turk Telekom, Ankara where, he worked as network planning engineer, business development specialist, R&D specialist and R&D acting manager for 6 years. He has a strong technical background in IT and server administration, Web technologies, geographic information systems, artificial intelligence, android OS, network optimization and planning. In 2013, he joined Argela in Ankara, where he currently works as an R&D Team Leader in SME and R&D Collaboration Directorate.

**Mustafa Yuksel** received his Ph.D. degree from the Department of Computer Engineering, Middle East Technical University (METU), Ankara, Turkey, in 2013. He is a full-time senior researcher and software engineer at Software Research Development and Consultancy (SRDC) Ltd. He has actively participated to and led work packages in many European Commission supported research projects: epSOS, SALUS, and iSURF to name a few. He is also a contributor of some open source projects such as OpenNCP, the infrastructure for cross-border healthcare data exchange among European countries. He has provided consultancy services on the management of National Health Information System to the Turkish Ministry of Health as a part of SRDC consultancy team. His research interests include interoperability standards, healthcare informatics, Semantic Web, e-business, and service-oriented architectures.

**Jens Ziegler** is a research scientist and PhD-student at the Faculty of Electrical and Computer Engineering at the Technische Universität Dresden. He received his Diploma degree in Electrical Engineering in 2008. In 2010, he became the head of the Mobile Information Systems research group at the Chair for Process Control Systems Engineering. His research focuses on requirements engineering including task and context analysis and customer inquiry techniques, mobile interaction design for industrial environments, and the design and evaluation of mobile solutions for supervisory control and industrial maintenance support.

# Index

## A

advanced virtual enterprise 325, 327, 334
agile enterprises 323, 334
anything Relationship Management (xRM) 119-120, 122, 136
app orchestration 137, 151, 155-158, 160, 165
assessment framework 24-25, 32, 35-36, 349, 352, 355

## B

basic science 325, 335
Blue Ocean strategies 80, 94
business networks 5, 78, 80-83, 90, 94, 126
Business Process Management (BPM) 66, 166-167, 184, 186, 191

## C

category theory 66, 331-332, 335
clinical decision support service 193, 205, 208-210, 215
collaborative space 172, 181, 185, 191
conceptual models 97-98, 100-103, 110, 114, 117, 151
Continuity of Care Record (CCR) 196, 219, 250

## D

domain specific modelling language 117

## E

eco-constraint 182, 191
eco-service 179-181, 184, 191
EISB fluid knowledge 54, 76
Electronic Health Record (EHR) 7, 194, 196, 215, 250
ENSEMBLE project 4, 42-43, 54, 68, 126, 155, 168, 195, 308, 315, 336, 343, 353

enterprise architecture 280, 282, 285-286, 288, 295, 298-299, 305-306, 313, 321
    framework 280, 282, 286, 295, 298-299, 321
Enterprise Interoperability (EI) 2, 41, 76, 220, 224, 245, 250, 279, 337, 353, 355
    knowledge base 10, 22, 39
    Science Base (EISB) 8, 42, 76, 216, 257, 337, 355
eXtensible Markup Language (XML) 225, 250
    horizontal standards 84-86, 88, 94

## F

feature abstractions 328-329, 335
formal methods 44, 66, 76

## G

geometric logics 332-333, 335

## H

Health Information Exchange (HIE) 218, 250
Health Language Seven Clinical Document Architecture (HL7 CDA) 250
hybrid modelling 102, 117

## I

industry-specific standards 84-85, 87-90, 94
Information Systems (IS) interoperability 78, 89, 94
information value 97-98, 117
intelligent system 256, 272, 275, 279
interoperability engineering 322, 335
interoperability framework 26, 39, 195, 280-282, 284-285, 295, 298-299, 302, 308-309, 314-315, 321
interoperability method 321
interoperability service utility 253, 256, 258-259, 261, 271, 279